Monsters and the poetic imagination in *The Faerie Queene*

MANCHESTER
1824
Manchester University Press

The
Manchester
Spenser

The Manchester Spenser is a monograph and text series devoted to historical and textual approaches to Edmund Spenser – to his life, times, places, works and contemporaries.

A growing body of work in Spenser and Renaissance studies, fresh with confidence and curiosity and based on solid historical research, is being written in response to a general sense that our ability to interpret texts is becoming limited without the excavation of further knowledge. So the importance of research in nearby disciplines is quickly being recognised, and interest renewed: history, archaeology, religious or theological history, book history, translation, lexicography, commentary and glossary – these require treatment for and by students of Spenser.

The Manchester Spenser, to feed, foster and build on these refreshed attitudes, aims to publish reference tools, critical, historical, biographical and archaeological monographs on or related to Spenser, from several disciplines, and to publish editions of primary sources and classroom texts of a more wide-ranging scope.

The Manchester Spenser consists of work with stamina, high standards of scholarship and research, adroit handling of evidence, rigour of argument, exposition and documentation.

The series will encourage and assist research into, and develop the readership of, one of the richest and most complex writers of the early modern period.

Also available

Celebrating Mutabilitie: Essays on Edmund Spenser's Mutabilitie Cantos Jane Grogan (ed.)

Castles and Colonists: An archaeology of Elizabethan Ireland Eric Klingelhofer

Shakespeare and Spenser: Attractive opposites J.B. Lethbridge (ed.)

Renaissance erotic romance: Philhellene Protestantism, Renaissance translation and English literary politics Victor Skretkowicz

Literary Ralegh and visual Ralegh Christopher M. Armitage (ed.)

God's only daughter: Spenser's Una as the invisible Church Kathryn Walls

A Concordance to the Rhymes of The Faerie Queene Richard Danson Brown & J. B. Lethbridge

A Supplement of The Faerie Queene: *By Ralph Knevet* Christopher Burlinson & Andrew Zurcher (eds)

Monsters and the poetic imagination in *The Faerie Queene*

'Most ugly shapes, and horrible aspects'

MAIK GOTH

Manchester University Press

Published by Manchester University Press
Altrincham Street, Manchester M1 7JA, UK
www.manchesteruniversitypress.co.uk

British Library Cataloguing-in-Publication Data is available

ISBN 978 0 7190 9571 9 *hardback*
ISBN 978 1 5261 3949 8 *paperback*

First published by Manchester University Press in hardback 2015

This edition first published 2019

Contents

Figures

Acknowledgements

This study marks the end of a long scholarly engagement with Edmund Spenser's *The Faerie Queene*, which began as a PhD project under the supervision of Luuk Houwen, who was later joined by Uwe Klawitter. I would like to thank them both. Like Spenser's narrator, I frequently marvelled at the 'endlesse worke' I had untertaken. That I did not 'tread an endlesse trace, withouten guyde, / Or good direction' has to be specifically credited to two Spenserians. Åke Bergvall became an indispensable mentor over the years, providing generous advice and criticism, and guiding me through many a difficult monster battle. Julian B. Lethbridge, general editor of The Manchester Spenser, offered many astute critical comments, and steered me through all the stages of publication with relentless enthusiasm.

Thanks are also due to a host of colleagues and friends: John Banks, Matthias Bauer, Raphael Dammer, Stefan Erlei, Mechthild Fend, Reinhold F. Glei, Andrew Hadfield, Hartwig Heckel, Thomas Honegger, Maurice Hunt, Murat Kayı, Frank Kearful, Andreas Lenz, Lena Linne, Sandra Lowerre, Barbara and Wilfred Mueller, Torsten Müller, Burkhard Niederhoff, Thomas Paulsen, Jennifer Peters, John Poziemski, Newt Scamander, Sebastian Sobecki, Nina Tomaszewksi, Katie Walter, John Watkins, Roland Weidle, Matthew Woodcock and the anonymous reviewers of The Manchester Spenser. On more than one occasion, my friend Stefan Meier saved the day by performing his computer-wizardry. The staff at Manchester University Press, especially Matthew Frost, was always available for help. I gratefully acknowledge the research support provided by the Graduiertenförderung and the Research School of the Ruhr-Universität Bochum.

Most of all, I am indebted to my family: my parents Anna and Georg Goth, who passed on their curiosity to me, and my grandmothers Ilse Hirte and Božena Goth, who unfortunately died before the book was completed. My greatest thanks go to my wonderful wife Sandra Felix for

Note on texts and language

her unflagging love and support. This book is dedicated to her.

References to Edmund Spenser's *The Faerie Queene* are to *The Faerie Queene*, ed. by A. C. Hamilton; text ed. by Hiroshi Yamashita and Toshiyuki Suzuki, Longman Annotated English Poets (London: Longman, 2001). Upper-case roman numerals stand for books, and lower-case roman numerals for cantos; arabic numbers are used for stanzas and line references throughout. Spenser's minor poems and prose texts are quoted from the *Works of Edmund Spenser: A Variorum Edition*, ed. by Edwin Greenlaw, Charles Grosvenor Osgood and Frederick Morgan Padelford, 11 vols (Baltimore: Johns Hopkins Press, 1932–45), henceforth *Variorum*.

All citations from the Bible refer to the Vulgate, and all translations are taken from the Douay Rheims version. The following editions have been used: *Biblia Sacra iuxta vulgatam versionem*, ed. Robert Weber, 4th edition, revised by Roger Gryson (Stuttgart: Deutsche Bibelgesellschaft, 1994; originally published 1969) and *The Holy Bible – Douay Rheims Version*, revised by Richard Challoner (1749–52) (Rockford: Tan Books, 1971).

In accordance with general Renaissance usage, and wishing to avoid 'he or she', the use of the pronoun 'he' is gender-neutral in this book, referring to both the male and female genders.

Introduction

In Edmund Spenser's *The Faerie Queene*, an epic romance published in two parts in 1590 and 1596, monsters of all kinds hide in the caves, castles, mountains and woods of Faeryland and other regions. As soon as the poem starts, Redcrosse fights the monster Errour in her lair, and then overthrows the huge Dragon that terrorises the kingdom of Eden in a three-day fight; during their voyage to Acrasia's island, Sir Guyon and the Palmer encounter innumerable creatures from the bottom of the sea; a voracious monster reminiscent of a hyena is set on Florimell by a witch; and the Blatant Beast slanders its victims with a hundred tongues and bites them with teeth of rusty iron. Add to that the various giants, grotesque human–animal composites and monstrous humans that populate the stanzas of the text, and, I would argue, *The Faerie Queene* emerges as a poem in which monsters constitute a central theme that defines the world of the poem and informs its meaning.

This monograph is the first attempt at a comprehensive reading of monsters and monstrous beings in *The Faerie Queene*, and at positioning them in larger theoretical frames. It takes as its starting point Thomas Cooper's sixteenth-century definition of *monstrum* as something 'that exceedeth, lacketh, or is disordred in naturall forme. Any thing done against the course of nature. A token or shewing: a thing that signifieth', which appears in his influential *Thesaurus* (1565).[1] Cooper's dictionary entry covers the major areas of the Renaissance discourse on the monstrous: the notion of the physically deformed, the violation of the rules of nature (based on the Latin *in naturam*) and the idea of the sign that needs interpreting. These distinctions also represent the poet's use of monsters and monstrous beings in *The Faerie Queene*: Spenser fashions monsters and monstrous beings as physical deformities violating the rules of nature in

1 Thomas Cooper, *Thesaurus Linguae Romanae & Britannicae* (London, 1565), s.v. 'monstrum'.

order to establish them as meaningful ciphers in an '*extended Allegory*' designed to '*fashion a gentleman or noble person in vertuous and gentle discipline*'.[2] Following Cooper's definition and Spenser's poetic practice, the arc of the argument spans two interconnected areas, which elaborate on the poet's involvement in the monstrous discourse of the early modern period. This study first offers a taxonomic account of the monsters and monstrous beings in *The Faerie Queene*, which sets them in relation to the natural world of Faeryland and its geographical surroundings. It then analyses monsters and monstrous beings as signs interacting with the early modern discourse on the poet creating a secondary nature through the use of his transformative imagination, and as ciphers that need to be interpreted by the reader.

As teratology, i.e. the study of monsters and monstrous beings, has claimed a vast territory in critical inquiry over the last two decades, an introductory chapter acquaints the reader with the matter of the monstrous and its prevalent aspects. Part I first poses the question whether *The Faerie Queene* can be termed a poem of monsters (Chapter 1), before it traverses the terrain of the monster's cultural importance for the early modern period (Chapter 2). This discussion is then followed by a historico-cultural account of the word *monster* and the concept of the monstrous from the classical to the early modern period (Chapter 3). A survey of criticism on Spenserian monsters and an outline of the major trends in monster studies round off the first part (Chapter 4).

Parts II and III contain the actual critical analyses. Part II follows Cooper's definition of the monstrous as a physical deformity violating the rules of nature, and brings into relief the plenitude and diversity of monsters and monstrous beings in Spenser's poem by analysing them along systematic and anatomical parameters. Using Isidore's classification of monsters in *Etymologiae*, Book XI, the 'Taxonomic considerations' prefaced to this chapter (Chapter 5) focus on the monsters' bodies: as the monstrous manifests itself physically, this section proposes the concept of the 'monstrous signifier', i.e. the physical attribute that distinguishes the monstrous from the normative body. This concept is also applicable to those cases in which the monstrous reveals itself textually, i.e. when poetic language maps something 'other' on the normative body through similes and metaphors. The individual close readings which follow are embedded in a general taxonomical system that divides Spenser's monsters into 'Monstrous animals' (namely 'Dragons' and 'Four-footed

2 Spenser, 'Letter to Raleigh', 8. References to the 'Letter' are to the line numbers in Hamilton's edition of *The Faerie Queene*.

beasts'), 'Human–animal composites', 'Giants', 'Monstrous humans' and, finally, 'Automata' (Chapters 6–11). The description and interpretation of monsters through a necessarily artificial conceptual grid is designed to render insight into how Spenser creates permutations of the monstrous by reconfiguring normative bodies, and into how he integrates them into the unity of his work. Drawing on a vast number of classical, scriptural, medieval and contemporaneous traditions, Spenser fashions a plethora of monsters as opponents the heroes of his epic romance have to vanquish in battle, and additionally establishes the monstrous as a corrupting force that disfigures or even annihilates the normative body through transformation and metamorphosis. An intermediary conclusion summarises the major issues raised in this part (Chapter 12).

Taking up Cooper's definition of the monstrous as a sign requiring interpretation, Part III offers a theoretical discussion of the monstrosities and deformities in *The Faerie Queene*, and the insights they provide into Spenser's role as the maker of a poetic heterocosm. The chapters focus on the heavily contested status of the monster in the early modern period and relates it both to the contemporaneous idea of the poet as a secondary maker and to the discourse of the transformative imagination. Special attention is devoted to the work of the imagination as expounded in Renaissance medical and poetical treatises. These illustrate that the creation of monstrosities is intimately connected to the controversy over the malfunctioning imagination, and to the emergence of a more autonomous poet. I will demonstrate that Spenser, following the call for poetic autonomy, positions himself against the antipoetic sentiments of his age as a secondary maker who can deliberately create a secondary world that contains monsters and monstrous beings. Chapter 13 first surveys Renaissance views on the problem of the literary monster. Drawing on Sidney's *Defence of Poesy* (1595) and George Puttenham's *The Arte of English Poesie* (1589), it discusses the idea of the poet as maker, especially the role the imagination plays in the poet's creative process, and sets it in relation to Spenser's poem. Chapter 14 places Spenser's poem of monsters, new realms and characters in the emerging tradition of what M. H. Abrams terms the 'heterocosm', and establishes the entire poem as just such a textual realm, which seventeenth- and eighteenth-century critics significantly characterised as a place where the monster runs rampant. Spenser explicitly engages with the notion of the heterocosm at the beginning of the poem, where Redcrosse and Una enter the Wandering Wood and find Errour in her den. On one level, monster and wood define the poetic text as a labyrinth in which characters and readers have to orientate themselves through constant interpretation, and may encounter monsters and monstrous beings at any time. On another level, forest and monster also represent the notion of ὕλη, or *silva*, the major metaphor of primordial matter from which all things and beings were turned into form. The opening narrative of *The Faerie Queene* hence also allegorises the Wandering Wood and Errour as the material agencies from which the poem and its monstrosities are made. Chapter 15 examines Spenser's allegory of the imagination, Phantastes's chamber, which is situated in the brain turret of Alma's Castle, Spenser's representation of the human body and soul (*FQ*, II.ix). This section elaborates on Spenser's awareness of a monstrous discourse in epic romance and deals with the involvement of the imagination in the making of monstrous images. As Phantastes's chamber contains frescos that depict characters, animals, and monsters typical of romance, Spenser explicitly connects the images dwelling in the imagination to the creative work of the poet composing an epic romance. By likening the flies that buzz around Phantastes's head to honey-laden bees, Spenser consolidates the creative work of a transformative imagination that can turn confusing ideas and imaginings into the useful images of poetry. The remaining sections analyse Spenser's creation of monsters and monstrous beings in greater detail. Chapter 16 examines various kinds of malfunctions in the imagination as exemplified in Spenser's poem, namely excessive melancholy and uninhibited dream-work, the distortion and transformation of beings, as well as the spontaneous birth of monstrous images. These analyses press home that Spenser deliberately participates in the discourse of the monstrous imagination by turning the landscape of his poem into a breeding ground of the monster, and by creating characters that suffer from a hypertrophic imagination that transforms them into monstrous beings. Spenser's animating the monstrous imagination is a self-reflexive strategy indicative of a double imaginative act: it shows the source of the monstrous in the characters' overheated imaginations, and exemplifies the poet's deliberate depiction of such monstrous, or pathological situations to educate the reader. Chapter 17 more specifically draws on Spenser's version of the Prometheus myth in *The Antiquitee of Faery Lond* (*FQ*, II.x), which recounts how Prometheus created the first elf, to elaborate on the conflict inherent in the poet's creation of monsters. Spenser here contends that the poet, like Prometheus, has creative autonomy over his work. However, like the Greek god, he also has to act transgressively when creating something new and living from disparate parts, be it a new monster, or even a new poem. Chapter 18 consolidates Spenser's use of the monstrous for his didactic programme, namely '*to fashion a gentleman or noble person in vertuous and gentle discipline*',[3] by setting his literary practice in relation to George Puttenham's modes of poetic making and Sidney's notion of useful poetry. Spenser uses his poetic imagination to fashion monsters as viable rhetorical creations representing aberrations, corruption and vices in order to advance his readers' understanding of universal truths. Created in a textual milieu that gives them apprehensible form and poetic substance, the monsters and monstrous beings work on the readers' imagination and move them to lead a life according to the good and the virtuous. Finally, Chapter 19 elaborates on the problems posed by the interpretation of monsters as polyvalent, incongruent and unstable creatures in Spenser's multi-referential allegorical poem, and brings this discussion to bear on the Blatant Beast's escape from Faeryland. By setting his readers the task to make sense of the monsters in his poem, Spenser seeks to facilitate the readers' formation of identity, and educate them as gentlemen or noble persons. When the Blatant Beast escapes into contemporary England at the end of Book VI, Spenser makes his readers aware that the monsters in his allegorical poem are permutations of the monstrous forces in the real world, which they now have to trace and face on their own.

Finally, Part IV, 'Conclusions', reiterates the major findings of this study.

Parts of the monograph have appeared in different form in the following articles: '"Infinite Shapes of Things": Monsters and the Monstrous in Edmund Spenser's *The Faerie Queene*', in *Clerks, Wives and Historians: Essays on Medieval Language and Literature*, ed. by Winfried Rudolf, Thomas Honegger and Andrew James Johnston (Bern: Peter Lang, 2008), pp. 141–84; 'Spenser Dragons', in *Good Dragons are Rare. An Inquiry into Literary Dragons East and West*, ed. Fanfan Chen and Thomas Honegger (Frankfurt am Main: Peter Lang, 2009), pp. 97–118; and 'Spenser as Prometheus: The Monstrous and the Idea of Poetic Creation', *Connotations* 18.1–3 (2008/9), 183–207.

3 Spenser, 'Letter', 8.

PART I

'Complicated monsters head and tail':[1] A primer in Spenser, monsters and teratology

> … weete ye well,
> That yonder in that wastefull wildernesse
> Huge monsters haunt, and many dangers dwell;
> Dragons, and Minotaures, and feendes of hell,
> And many wilde woodmen, which robbe and rend
> All traueilers; therefore aduise ye well,
> Before ye enterprise that way to wend:
> One may his iourney bring too soone to euill end.
>
> Edmund Spenser, *The Faerie Queene*, III.x.40.2–9

1 The quotation is taken from John Milton, *Paradise Lost*, X.523; for the text, see John Milton, *A Critical Edition of His Major Works*, ed. by Stephen Orgel and Jonathan Goldberg, The Oxford Authors (Oxford: Oxford University Press, 1991).

1

The Faerie Queene – A poem of monsters?

In 1590, Edmund Spenser published the first instalment of his *Faerie Queene*, a mammoth project of twelve planned books, each consisting of twelve cantos, which in turn are made up of anything up to seventy nine-line stanzas. Essentially a heroic poem combining romance and epic traditions, the poem treats the adventures of chivalrous knights and beautiful damsels in Faeryland, an imaginary realm ruled by Gloriana, '*the Queene of Faeries*' ('Letter to Raleigh', 59). This first edition acquainted Elizabethan readers with Books I to III, and was followed by a painstakingly edited second one in 1596 that added Books IV to VI, and revised the earlier ones.[1]

The importance of the monstrous for *The Faerie Queene* is underscored by the poem's sole woodcut, which depicts St George fighting a dragon. The image appears on the verso side of the last page of Book I, and faces the beginning of Book II. By the time the readers in the 1590s turned the page to look at the illustration, they had made their way through the various trials and errors of the Knight of the Red Crosse, the titular hero of Book I, a St George of sorts who kills an enormous Dragon in a three-day fight to free the Kingdom of Eden.[2] Presumably, Spenser's printer, John Wolfe, added the woodcut, because he thought it an appropriate and attractive illustration for the final combat in the first book (see Figure 1). His choice bears witness to the cult centring on St George, the English Patron Saint, but also emphasises the popularity of

1 The 1609 folio edition added the so-called 'Two Cantos of Mutabilitie', allegedly Cantos vi and vii (with the first two stanzas of Canto viii) from Book VII.

2 For the fight, see I.xi. Before facing the Dragon in Eden, Redcrosse has already fought two other dragons or dragon-like creatures, namely Errour (I.i) and Orgoglio's beast (I.vii). Samantha J. E. Riches gives a good introduction to Spenser's use of the St George legend that draws attention to crucial similarities and differences (see *St George: Hero, Martyr and Myth* (Stroud: Sutton, 2005), pp. 182–5).

Figure 1 St George slaying the dragon; woodcut from Edmund Spenser, *The Faerie Queene*

the monstrous in early modern England.[3]

Monsters and monster battles had a long-standing tradition, which Renaissance artists and readers were acutely aware of. A brief analysis of the image's presentation of this topos can hence offer a first glance at early modern ideas of the monstrous, and may also hint at the thematic and conceptual implications of the monstrous for *The Faerie Queene*.[4] The proportions in the woodcut are especially striking: almost eighty per cent of the picture is taken up by an enormous knight sitting on a gigantic horse in full armour. Beneath them, submissive on its back, lies the dragon, which looks everything but terrifying: in size more like a larger dog with its paws up in the air, a folded short tail, a narrow maw, and modest fangs, it seems to shrink under the might of its opponent – so much that, by comparison, horse and rider appear to have gargantuan proportions.[5] The creature bears indeed little resemblance to the gigantic Dragon Spenser depicts in the poem, but is largely derived from smaller medieval specimens appearing in the bestiaries and traditional iconography. The dragon's neck is pierced by the knight's spear, which runs diagonally from left top to right bottom, and thus, at first sight, seems to divide the picture into a beastly half and a human half,[6] so that the weapon is not merely instrumental in defeating the beast[7] but also

3 On the popularity of the St George legend, see Michael Murrin, 'The Audience of *The Faerie Queene*', *Explorations in Renaissance Culture* 23 (1997), 1–21 (pp. 6–9); Paul J. Voss, '*The Faerie Queene* 1590–1596: The Case of Saint George', *Ben Jonson Journal* 3 (1996), 59–73; and, generally, John L. Flood, 'Sankt Georg', in *Herrscher, Helden, Heilige*, ed. by Ulrich Müller and Werner Wunderlich, Mittelalter Mythen, 1 (St Gallen: UVK, 1996), pp. 589–606.

4 On the role dragons play in the lives of saints, see Samantha J. E. Riches, 'Encountering the Monstrous: Saints and Dragons in Medieval Thought', in *The Monstrous Middle Ages*, ed. by Bettina Bildhauer and Robert Mills (Toronto and Buffalo: University of Toronto Press, 2003), pp. 196–218.

5 See also Alexander Judson, *The Life of Edmund Spenser* (Baltimore: Johns Hopkins University Press, 1945), pp. 140–1 (as *Variorum*, XI).

6 The pose of St George as well as the overall arrangement of the woodcut is similar to medieval and early modern renderings of the scene. See, among others, Vitale da Bologna, 'St. George's Battle with the Dragon' (fourteenth century), Andres Marsal de Saxe, 'Altarpiece of Saint George' (ca. 1400), Rogier van der Weyden, 'St. George' (fifteenth century) and Raphael, 'St. George and the Dragon' (ca. 1504–6). The images can be viewed at www.ucc.ie/archive/milmart/grgwstart.html.

7 Knight, horse and dragon as well as the nearly broken-off spearhead are kept in the frame of the woodcut. Unlike woodcuts in printed books, medieval manuscripts frequently feature monsters breaking the confines of the space allotted to them. Among others, the illustration depicting the Blemmyae, a race with their heads on their torso, in MS Cotton Tiberius B v, fol. 82r (British Library) and the impressive red dragon invading the text in Harley MS 3244, fol. 59r (British Library) show how the monstrous breaks the confinement of the frame.

seems to function as the artificial barrier between the human and the monstrous.

On closer inspection, however, St George's and the horse's lower bodies are placed in the beastly half of the woodcut in such close proximity with the dragon that they intersect with the monster's body. The composition of the woodcut makes the knight's position precarious, because it directs the viewer's attention to the saint's lower body, the traditional seat of lust.[8] The image enhances the physical connection between St George's body and the horse's rump, thus evoking iconographic depictions of the horse of the passions and concupiscence,[9] and additionally links both horse and rider with the dragon, which is traditionally associated with Satan.[10] Rather than visualise the saint's domination of and remoteness from the monstrous, the picture hence accentuates St George's innate beastliness. This makes the woodcut an example of a common motif in the medieval and early modern discourse of the monstrous: it depicts St George's temporal victory over the dragon and the monstrous forces, and at the same time highlights man's fallen and beastly nature.

From the perspective of this study, the woodcut, I propose, represents the function of the monsters and monstrous beings in Spenser's *The Faerie Queene*. As it appears on the verso side of the last page of Book I, and faces the beginning of Book II, the image is placed at an important juncture that joins the two books like the central part of a triptych. Placed between the Legends of Holiness and Temperance, it looks back on Redcrosse's monstrous encounters; at the same time, its theme anticipates the plot of Book II, where Guyon, the eponymous knight representing temperance, also faces a multitude of deformities. The monstrous thus poses a threat for both heroes. Although differing from the details in the poem itself, the woodcut hence underlines the role of the monstrous especially

8 See Michael Schoenfeldt, *Bodies and Selves in Early Modern England: Physiology and Inwardness in Spenser, Shakespeare, Herbert, and Milton*, Cambridge Studies in Renaissance Literature and Culture, 34 (Cambridge: Cambridge University Press, 1999), p. 9.

9 The *locus classicus* for this concept is Plato, *Phaedrus*, 246B–257B, a part of the dialogue that was well known in the early modern period, especially in Francesco di Piccolomini's interpretation (see John Erskine Hankins, *Source and Meaning in Spenser's Allegory: A Study of 'The Faerie Queene'* (Oxford: Oxford University Press, 1971), p. 130; for the Platonic source, see *Plato I: Euthyphro, Apology, Crito, Phaedo, Phaedrus*, trans. Harold North Fowler, Loeb Classical Library (Cambridge, MA: Harvard University Press, 1916; repr. 1960)). The topos of the Centaur's lustful lower body famously figures in Lear's mad railings against his daughters: 'Down from the waist they are centaurs, though women all above. But to the girdle do the gods inherit, beneath is all the fiend's' (*King Lear*, IV.6.121–3). For the text, see William Shakespeare, *King Lear*, ed. by R. A. Foakes, The Arden Shakespeare, 3rd Series (Walton-on-Thames: Thomas Nelson, 1997).

10 See Revelation 12.9: 'the great dragon, that olde serpent called the deuil and Satan'.

with regard to various psychological interpretations (the mastery over the monstrous) or political ones (England and St George); what is more, the exact position of the image also marks the monstrous as a cohesive force that joins the poem's different parts and segments together. In order to explore these and other contemporary implications of the monstrous in Spenser's England, Part I will first examine the role monstrous creatures played in the Renaissance, give a historical account of the word *monster* and then survey the ways in which monsters have been read by Spenserian and teratological critics.

2

The monstrous in the early modern period

A reader diagnosing the monstrous as a major principle at work in Spenser's poem may be tempted to explain it as a characteristic trait of early modern romances, and refer to the deformed beings figuring in Boiardo's *Orlando Innamorato*, and in Ariosto's *Orlando Furioso*.[1] But although these texts obviously embrace the narrative and poetic possibilities offered by the monstrous, this assumption misses the richness and complexity, the artistic and critical attention given to monsters for more than two millennia. From major exponents of classical 'monster literature', like the Bible, Homer's *Odyssey*, Ovid's *Metamorphoses*, Dante's *Divina Comoedia*,[2] and the medieval romances, such as the Old French *Lancelot–Grail* or *Vulgate Cycle* and Malory's *Le Morte Darthur*, monsters had generated a vast number of seminal texts at the heart of western culture. In addition to fiction, the monster had haunted the pages of zoological works. The *Physiologus* and, subsequently, the bestiaries, which spiced up the *Physiologus*'s terse entries with colourful descriptions and an extended moral,[3] frequently feature animals of doubtful existence, while even in the early modern period Conrad Gesner and his English translator Edward Topsell in their natural histories reflected many of the more exotic ideas associated with fabulous or not-so-fabulous animals.[4] Numerous

1 On monsters and magic in the Italian romance epics, see Julia M. Kisacky's *Magic in Boiardo and Ariosto*, Studies in Italian Culture: Literature in History, 25 (New York: Lang, 2000). Keala Jewell's collection of monster criticism, *Monsters in the Italian Literary Imagination* (Detroit: Wayne State University Press, 2001), completely disregards Boiardo's and Ariosto's poems.

2 Virginia Jewiss calls the *Inferno* 'an encyclopedia of the monstrous' ('Monstrous Movement and Metaphors in Dante's *Divine Comedy*', in *Monsters in the Italian Literary Imagination*, ed. by Jewell, pp. 179–90 (p. 181)).

3 See L. A. J. R. Houwen, 'Bestiarien', in *Dämonen, Monster, Fabelwesen*, ed. by Müller and Wunderlich, pp. 59–75.

4 See Conrad Gesner, *Historia animalium*, 5 vols (Zurich: Jacob Gesner, 1551–87), and Edward Topsell, *The Historie of Four-footed Beasts, Serpents, and Insects*, 3 vols (London: E. Cotes, 1607–8). References are to the reprint of the collected 1658 edition (New York: Da Capo, 1967).

biological, and philosophical treatises sought to explain the existence of 'real' monsters, such as deformed births, and theorised on the nature of imaginary ones.[5] Large-scale works like Sebastian Münster's *Cosmographia universalis* (1544) contained descriptions of monsters alongside more 'factual' entries.[6] Monsters also made their presence felt as grotesque ornaments in churches and architecture, as strange races and animals on the edges of *mappaemundi*,[7] and in the margins of medieval manuscripts.[8] Moreover, the Renaissance emblem book, that most influential joining of text and image, put the monstrous to good use for the moral instruction of its sixteenth-century readers. Such a confluence of texts and traditions inevitably blurs the dividing line between real and imaginary animals. An early modern writer like Spenser, grounded in scripture and the classics, and perceptive of recent trends, had this arsenal of monsters at his disposal, and would use it as inspiration for his own works.

The inherited early modern fascination with the monstrous was also in no small part fuelled by the presentation of monstrosities in all kinds of media. In the sixteenth century, physical abnormalities and oddities were exhibited as freaks in fairground attractions, took the stage in

5 See Hans Peter Broedel, '"Now I Will Believe That There Are Unicorns": The Existence of Fabulous Beasts in Renaissance *Historiae Naturales*', in *Renaissance Medievalisms*, ed. by Konrad Eisenbichler, Publications of the Centre for Reformation and Renaissance Studies, Essays and Studies 18 (Toronto: Centre for Reformation and Renaissance Studies, 2009), pp. 287–302. The article discusses the differing Renaissance assessments of fantastic animals in natural histories. These range from the appreciation of God's omnipotence in John Maplet's *A Green Forest* (1567) and the uncritical use of classical, scriptural and testimonial evidence for allegories and analogies in Wolfgang Franz's *Historia animalium sacra* (1612) to the critical assessment of textual, testimonial and empirical sources in Conrad Gesner's *Historia animalium* (1551–58).

6 The appeal of the strange and outlandish in the *Cosmographia* is testified by an abridged version of Münster's huge volume, which includes a large number of monstrosities and marvels: *A Briefe Collection and Compendium Extract of Straunge and Memorable Thinges, Gathered out of the Cosmographye of Sebastian Munster* (London: Thomas Marshe, 1572).

7 Major exponents are the Hebstorf, Hereford and Walsperger *mappaemundi*. The recent interest in the intersection between cartography and geography is well documented by a handful of articles in *Monsters, Marvels, and Miracles*, ed. by Leif Søndergaard and Rasmus Thorning Hansen (Odense: University of South Denmark Press, 2005): Evelyn Edson, 'Mapping the Middle Ages: The Imaginary and the Real Universe of the *Mappaemundi*', pp. 11–25; Naomi Reed Kline, 'The World of Strange Races', pp. 27–40; and John Block Friedman, 'Monsters at the Earth's Imagined Corners: Wonders and Discovery in the Late Middle Ages', pp. 41–64. See also Chat Van Duzer, '*Hic sunt dracones*: The Geography and Cartography of Monsters', in *The Ashgate Research Companion to Monsters and the Monstrous*, ed. by Asa Simon Mittman with Peter J. Dendle (Farnham: Ashgate, 2012), pp. 387–435.

8 See, for instance, Michael Camille, *The Margins of Medieval Art* (London: Reaktion, 1992).

many a dramatic performance,[9] figured in widely distributed broadsides and became the object of new scholarly investigations. Positioned at the intersection of the private and the public, *Wunderkammern* ('chambers of wonders') displayed anything from rare minerals to plants, strange animals and monsters, so that it became increasingly difficult to tell the authentic from the manufactured.[10] Add to that the Puritans' use of a language of the monstrous to tarnish the sinful and to warn against an impending apocalypse, and it becomes clear that the monster was an important aspect of early modern culture.[11]

When Spenser wrote *The Faerie Queene*, the collective mind of both educated and uneducated people was therefore well aware of the grotesque and the monstrous. The variety of monstrosities – ranging from strange races to human–animal composites like the manticore,[12] from unnatural births to humans with unnatural behaviour – poses the question of a common denominator for all these creatures. In order to make sense of and bring structure into the sheer complexity of different approaches to monstrosity and the meaning associated with them, this study begins with a simple question: what exactly was perceived as monstrous in Spenser's day and age?

9 The link between fairground attractions, monsters and actors is fully discussed in Mark Thornton Burnett's *Constructing 'Monsters' in Shakespearean Drama and Early Modern Culture*, Early Modern Literature in History (London: Palgrave Macmillan, 2002).

10 On *Wunderkammern*, see Lorraine Daston and Katharine Park, *Wonders and the Order of Nature 1150–1750* (New York: Zone Books, 1998), pp. 255–301.

11 Hence St John's Apocalypse becomes a monster book of sorts, where many-headed and deformed monsters play a decisive, if puzzlingly inconclusive, role.

12 A manticore is a lion with a human head; for an image consult Topsell, *Historie*, I, 344.

3

Historical perspectives on the monstrous

Although any study of monsters and deformities necessarily faces the problem of defining the monstrous, it is difficult to offer a universal explanation that covers the entire variety of monsters. Moreover, historical developments and an ever-changing cultural background with different approaches to education, society and religion rule out a straightforward assessment. In her influential monograph *The Monster in the Machine*, Zakiya Hanafi thus eschews particulars and resorts to generalisation when defining a monster as 'a set of characteristics constituted according to the cultural order of a particular time'.[1] Because of her over-generalisation, it is imperative to add that these characteristics have to deviate from norm and nature to make a being truly monstrous. As the monstrous is therefore firmly anchored in its historical reality, it is not an immutable concept, but develops over the centuries according to an ever-shifting cultural order: while the core, or central meaning of the monster, namely deviancy or otherness, remains the same, its secondary features or meanings are thus subject to change.[2]

A first means of approaching this question is that of Latin and Greek etymology. The term *monster* derives from the Latin *monstrum*, the conceptual relative of phenomena like *prodigia* ('prodigies') and *portenta* ('portents').[3] Hence, the monster did not begin its semantic career

1 Zakiya Hanafi, *The Monster in the Machine: Magic, Medicine, and the Marvelous in the Time of the Scientific Revolution* (Durham, NC, and London: Duke University Press, 2000), p. XII.

2 I follow Aristotle's notion of definition as expounded in *Metaphysics*, IV. Cf. Aristotle, *Metaphysics; Oeconomica; Magna moralia*, ed. and trans. by Hugh Tredennick and G. Cyril Armstrong, 2 vols, Aristotle: Works 17–18, Loeb Classical Library (Cambridge, MA: Harvard University Press; London: Heinemann, 1933; repr. 1960).

3 The fullest account of the etymology and history of the terms *monstrum* and *portentum* is given by John Block Friedman in *The Monstrous Races in Medieval Art and Thought* (Cambridge, MA: Harvard University Press, 1981), pp. 108–30; Beate Ochsner links etymology to a most comprehensive history of monsters in 'Monster: More than a Word.

as a strange beast or a specific monstrosity, but rather as a portent foreshadowing future events, mostly of an unpropitious nature, an influence traceable in Plutarch's and Suetonius's famous accounts of the strange signs preceding Caesar's assassination.[4] In the course of the classical period, the term underwent a semantic change, and was applied to specific monsters, as for instance in Virgil's *Aeneid*.[5] However, monsters and omens share the same conceptual space: they are strange phenomena which contradict nature, and they stir the gazer or beholder into admiration and wonder by suspending physical and biological laws. Subsequently filed under the same rubric as cosmological phenomena like meteors and haloes, which contradicted Aristotle's theory of an incorruptible translunary region,[6] monsters, no matter whether deformed births or strange animals, became the biological manifestations of a divine will. Writers like Pliny and Isidore of Seville would thus tackle the 'monstrous' from the vantage point of divination.

From Portent to Anomaly, the Extraordinary Career of Monsters', in *Monsters and Philosophy*, ed. by Charles T. Wolfe, Texts in Philosophy, 3 (London: College Publications, 2005), pp. 231–79. See also: David Williams, *Deformed Discourse: The Function of the Monster in Mediaeval Thought and Literature* (Montreal and Kingston: McGill-Queen's University Press, 1996), pp. 4–6 and pp. 12–13; J. J. Cohen, *Of Giants: Sex, Monsters, and the Middle Ages*, Medieval Cultures, 17 (Minneapolis and London: University of Minnesota Press, 1999), pp. XIV–XV; Hanafi, *The Monster in the Machine*, pp. 1–15; Timothy S. Jones and David A. Sprunger, 'Introduction: The Marvelous Imagination', in *Marvels, Monsters, and Miracles*, pp. XI–XXV (pp. XV–XVI and p. XX); Robert and Karin Olsen, 'Introduction: On the Embodiment of Monstrosity in Northwest Medieval Europe', in *Monsters and the Monstrous in Medieval Northwest Europe*, ed. by Karin Olsen and L. A. J. R. Houwen (Leuven: Peeters, 2001), pp. 1–22; and Jean Ceard, *La nature et les prodiges*, Travaux d'Humanisme et Renaissance, 158 (Geneva: Droz, 1977), pp. 3–30.

4 Plutarch and Suetonius mention that the animal sacrificed by Caesar the day before his death did not have a heart, that his horses broke free and wept, and that a king bird flew into the Hall of Pompey carrying a laurel sprig, where it was killed by other birds. See Plutarch, *Live of Caesar*, LXIII, and Suetonius, *Vita Divi Iulii*, LXXXI. References are to Plutarch, *Lives VII*, trans. by Bernadotte Perrin, Loeb Classical Library (Cambridge, MA: Harvard University Press; London: Heinemann, 1919; repr. 1970), and Suetonius, *Lives of the Caesars; Lives of Illustrious Men*, trans. by C. Rolfe, 2 vols (Cambridge, MA: Harvard University Press; London: Heinemann, 1914; repr. 1964), I.

5 Lewis and Short cite Ennius (239–169 BC) for *monster* in the sense of 'omen', Terence (195–159 BC) for *monster* in the sense of 'deformity', and Virgil for particular monstrous creatures (70–10 BC) in *A Latin Dictionary*, s.v. 'monstrum'. See also Friedman, *Monstrous Races*, pp. 108–30, and Ochsner, 'Monster', pp. 231–79.

6 The discussion figures in Aristotle, *On the Heavens*, I.2–3. For the text, see Aristotle, *On the Heavens*, ed. and trans. by W. K. C. Guthrie, Loeb Classical Library (London: Heinemann, 1939; repr. 1962). The controversy about the alleged perfection of the universe rekindled when Galileo published his research on the imperfections in the sun in his *Letters on Sunspots* in 1613. On Aristotle's and Galileo's views on the incorruptibility of the celestial regions, see Edward Grant, *Planets, Stars, and Orbs: The Medieval Cosmos, 1200–1687* (Cambridge: Cambridge University Press, 1996), pp. 455–66.

The source for the semantic confusion between omens and fantastic animals lies partly in the Greek noun τέρας, which exerted a formative influence on the semantic development of the Latin *monstrum*.[7] Originally applied mainly to strange and ominous signs, it expanded its semantic field, and could also refer to signs, portents and wonders, or to specific terrifying images, magic incidents and monsters, especially monstrous births.[8] Its appearance in other compounds bears out the semantic duplicity of the term. Most significantly, it appears in the verb τερατολογέω, which means 'to tell of wonders', and in the noun τερα(το)-σκόπος, which signifies 'a reader of signs and portents'. Matters become decisively vague when Plato in the *Phaedrus* (380–360 BC) assigns a fantastic animal the epithet τερατόλογος; contrary to common usage, where the word usually means 'portentous', it here defines the noun φύσις ('body'). Hence, Plato uses the term to describe mythological monsters.[9]

Etymologists in the classical and medieval ages, however, disagreed over the exact origin of *monstrum*. Some writers derived it from the verb *monstrare*, which means 'to show' or 'to point to'.[10] Broadly speaking,

7 On the indebtedness of Latin *monstrum* to Greek τέρας, see Friedman, *Monstrous Races*, pp. 108–11 (with reference to Latin–Greek lexica of the Early Middle Ages; cf. *Monstrous Races*, p. 239, n. 10).

8 See the entries on 'τέρας' in *Lexikon des frühgriechischen Epos*, ed. by Thesaurus Linguae Graecae, 4 vols (Göttingen: Vandenhoeck & Ruprecht, 1979–2010), IV, 398–9 (the entry cites the description of the Gorgon's head in *Iliad*, V.742; the majority of uses are, however, for divine signs, such as celestial bodies, as well as omens and portents, like thunder, rainbows or animal miracles); Henry George Liddell and Robert Scott, *A Greek English Lexicon*, 9th edn (Oxford: Clarendon, 1940), p. 1776, especially the entries on Aeschylus, Sophocles and Euripides; and Hjalmar Frisk, *Griechisches etymologisches Wörterbuch*, 3 vols (Heidelberg: Winter, 1960–70), II, 878. Ochsner correctly calls τέρας 'undefined … and semantically broad' ('Monster', p. 232).

9 See Plato, *Phaedrus*, 229D–E. In the context of the passage, Socrates also mentions Centaurs, the Chimera 'and a whole crowd of such creatures, Gorgons and Pegas, and multitudes of strange, inconceivable and portentous natures' ('καὶ ἐπιρρεῖ δὲ ὄχλος τοιούτων Γοργόνων καὶ Πηγάσων καὶ ἄλλων ἀμηχάνων πλήθη τε καὶ ἀτοπίαι τερατολόγων τινῶν φύσεων'). The passage occurs in Socrates's humorous answer to Phaedrus's query whether they are having their conversation in the same spot at the Ilissos where Boreas abducted Oreithyia.

10 The definition Cicero placed in the mouth of his brother Quintus runs as follows: 'Quia enim ostendunt, portendunt, monstrant, praedicunt, ostenta, portenta, monstra, prodigia dicuntur' ('Because they "make manifest" (*ostendunt*), "portend" (*portendunt*), "intimate" (*monstrant*), "predict" (*praedicunt*), they are called "manifestations", "portents", "intimations" and "prodigies"'; *De divinatione*, I.xlii.93). Augustine, *De civitate Dei*, XXI.8, and Isidore, *Etymologiae*, XI.iii.2–3, elaborate on this passage. See Augustinus, *De civitate Dei*, ed. by B. Dombart and A. Kalb, 2 vols, Opera, Pars XIV, Corpus Christianorum, Seria Latina, 47–8 (Turnhout: Brepols, 1955); English translations are taken from *The City of God against the Pagans*, ed. and trans. by R. W. Dyson, Cambridge Texts in the History of Political Thought (Cambridge: Cambridge University Press, 1998), p. 1063. See also Isidore, *Etymologiae*, XI.iii.2–3; for the Latin text,

a *monster* is therefore an uncanny, extraordinary object or signifier requiring interpretation, a puzzling sign that points to a truth. While this was the version with the highest currency, it was certainly not the only one. The influential Roman grammarian Varro in *De lingua Latina* (47–45 BC) traced *monstrum* back to *monere*, 'to warn', which turned a *monstrum* into a medium through which the gods communicated their warnings to man.[11] In the early seventh century, this supposition was taken up by Isidore of Seville in the *Etymologiae*. Isidore, however, was cautious enough to link references to *monere*, and *(de)monstrare* in such a way that he implicitly endorsed both explanations.[12] Although these etymologies pertain to the puzzling core of the monstrous, modern Latin etymologists argue that *monere* is the exact origin of *monstrum* – and stem-wise also of *monstrare*.[13] One might therefore see a relation between the term *monster* and its physical and literary embodiments in that both elude simple classifications.

Monsters as such might be a cultural constant, but there was never a time in which they were treated in a single way. Even in the classical period, opinions of the monster's secondary meaning differed much.[14] As *monstra* were exploited in pagan religion as signs of the future, or as the signs of divine will, they inevitably attracted the attention of rationalists. Aristotle (384–322 BC) criticised such superstition by assessing monsters from a distinctly biological point of view. Focusing on the physical features and reproductive processes of animals, he explained

see Isidore, *Etymologiae*, Scriptorum Classicorum Bibliotheca Oxoniensis (Oxford: Clarendon, 1911), and for the English translation *The Etymologies of Isidore of Seville*, trans. by Stephen A. Barney, W. J. Lewis, J. A. Beach and Oliver Berghof (Cambridge: Cambridge University Press, 2006), pp. 243–4. For Cicero's text, see p. 21, n. 17.

11 The exact quotation from Marcus Terentius Varro's *De lingua Latina* is not extant, but references to it are made in Isidore's *Etymologiae*, XI.3, and Augustine's *De civitate Dei*, XXI.8.

12 See Isidore of Seville, *Etymologiae*, XI.iii.3: '*Monstra* vero *a monitu* dicta, quod aliquid significando *demonstrent*, sive quod statim *monstrent* quid appareat' (emphases added) ('But omens (*monstrum*) derive their name from admonition (*monitus*), because in giving a sign they indicate (*demonstrare*) something, or else because they instantly show (*monstrare*) what may appear' (*Etymologies*, p. 244)).

13 See A. Ernout and A. Meillet, *Dictionnaire etymologique de la langue Latine: histoire de mots*, 4th edn (Paris: Librairie C. Klincksieck, 1967), p. 413, as well as L. T. Lewis and L. Short, *A Latin Dictionary* (Oxford: Oxford University Press, 1962), s.v. 'monstrum'. Cf. also Hanafi, *The Monster in the Machine*, p. 3, and p. 219, n. 7, as well as Burnett, *Constructing 'Monsters'*, p. 2.

14 For a good introduction to monsters from the classical age, see Felton, 'Rejecting and Embracing the Monstrous in Ancient Greece and Rome', in *The Ashgate Research Companion to Monsters and the Monstrous*, ed. by Mittman and Dendle, pp. 103–31.

deformed beings mainly as defective offspring.[15] As they are the outcome of a biological defect or malfunction, they merely stray beyond the mean of nature, and are thus not the manifest sign of divine will: falling short of perfection, monsters do not signify anything at all.[16] In his treatise *De divinatione*, Cicero (106–43 BC) discusses *monstra* at some length, devoting particular attention to their use as omens disclosing divine will, and their deployment in magic. While the preface to Book I contains an overview of divination, Cicero, however, refutes any possibility of divining the future through the contemplation and interpretation of god-sent signs.[17] Other kinds of monsters, especially those appearing in myth and literature, were even argued out of existence. Lucretius, e.g., negates the biological possibility of fantastic creatures in his *De rerum natura*.[18] On the other end of the spectrum, Pliny the Elder would welcome just about any unusual life form and celebrate it as an object of wonder testifying to nature's infinite liberality and inventiveness.[19]

15 To Aristotle, monstrous births are the outcome of an excess or splitting of semen (*Generation of Animals*, IV.3–4). In his conceptual grid, even the female is considered a deviation from the norm (*Generation*, IV.2). See Aristotle, *Generation of Animals*, ed. and trans. by Arthur Lee Peck, Loeb Classical Library (London: Heinemann, 1943; repr. 1961).

16 Aristotle's lengthy discussion of biological monstrosity and its cause never assigns monsters any 'higher' meaning. See *Generation*, IV.iii and iv, and *Physics*, II.8 (199b), where Aristotle explains that monsters simply fail their purpose in nature; references are made to Aristotle, *Physics*, ed. and trans. by P. H. Wicksteed and F. M. Cornford, 2 vols, Loeb Classical Library (London: Heinemann, 1929; repr. 1960), I.

17 See Cicero, *De divinatione*, I.i, and II. References are to Cicero, *De senectute, De amicitia, De divinatione*, ed. and trans. by William Armistead Falconer, Loeb Classical Library (London: Heinemann, 1923; repr. 1964). Hanafi summarises that Cicero discards 'the rigorously semiotic and scientific character of classical divinatory arts' (*Monster in the Machine*, p. 9).

18 Lucretius explains the existence of monsters in the minds of men through the theory of ideas, to wit, e.g., the images of human being and horse collide and unite to create a centaur (see *De rerum natura*, IV.722–48). He denies the existence of hybrid species, explicitly referring to the Centaurs and the Chimera (see *De rerum natura*, V.878–924); for the text, see Lucretius, *On the Nature of Things*, ed. and trans. by W. H. D. Rouse, rev. by Martin F. Smith, Loeb Classical Library (London: Heinemann, 1975). See Morgan Meis, 'Science as a Cure for Fear: The Status of Monsters in Lucretius', in *Monsters and Philosophy*, ed. by Wolfe, pp. 21–35 (p. 29).

19 Pliny sums up his treatise on the strange races with a eulogy on the inventive varieties of nature's creations (*Naturalis historia*, VII.32): 'Haec atque talia ex hominum genere ludibria sibi, nobis miracula, ingeniosa fecit natura. ex singula quidem quae facit in dies ac prope horas quis enumerare valeat? ad detegendam eius potentiam satis sit inter prodigia posuisse gentes' ('These and similar varieties of the human race have been made by the ingenuity of Nature as toys for herself and marvels for us. And indeed who could possibly recount the various things she does every day and almost every hour? Let it suffice for the disclosure of her power to have included whole races of mankind among her marvels'). For the Latin text and the English translation, see Pliny, *Natural History*,

With the advent of Christianity, monsters and deformities needed to be reassessed as part of God's creation, and were placed within a decisively theological framework. This led to a redefinition of the monsters' secondary features, partly to account for their existence in the Bible, which contains both hideous, evil monsters, such as the dragons of the Apocalypse, and benevolent, divine ones. Among the latter are the winged cherubim and seraphim, as well as Ezekiel's living many-eyed chariot, which is carried by glowing creatures that have the faces of man, lion, bullock and eagle, as well as wings and human hands.[20] The writer who contributed to Christian teratology most significantly is Augustine. In his *De civitate Dei*, written in the early fifth century, he attributes to God the freedom to suspend physical laws, so that monsters exist through His will alone, thereby figuring as demonstrations of His supreme power.[21] In consequence, Augustine sees monsters as embodiments of God's will,[22] employed as a means to instil into man a sense of wonder about His creation.[23] Such beings transcend the grasp of man's reason,[24] urging him into the contemplation of God's bountiful creation where nothing exists without a reason. One could thus argue that Augustine casts Pliny's views into a Christian mould. Some two centuries after Augustine, Isidore of Seville assessed monsters from an encyclopaedic point of view, and set up a highly influential typology of *portenta* that was based on the various kinds of physical features that distinguished monsters from regular

ed. and trans. by H. Rackham, 10 vols, Loeb Classical Library (London: Heinemann, 1938–62), II, 526–7.

20 For the description of Ezekiel's chariot, see Ezekiel, 1.4–29. The Geneva Bible offers an elaborate woodcut of the scene. Angels were inherently problematic, because they sired the giants and monsters on the daughters of men in Genesis 6 (cf. Williams, *Deformed Discourse*, pp. 117 and 150). Cf. also the tradition of the tricephalic Jesus as the representation of the trinity, discussed in Williams, *Deformed Discourse*, pp. 131–4.

21 See the extended discussion in *De civitate Dei*, X.16, where Augustine assigns the monstrous births of animals and the occurrence of cosmological signs to Divine Providence. Insight into Augustine's view on monsters is provided by Hanafi, *The Monster in the Machine*, pp. 12–14, and by Park and Daston, *Wonders and the Order of Nature*, pp. 39–41.

22 See Augustine, *De civitate Dei*, XXI.4–8. Thomas Aquinas explicitly follows Augustine: 'Quod ea quae Deus facit praeter naturae ordinem non sunt contra naturam' ('What God creates outside the order of nature does not exist against nature'); *Summa contra gentiles*, III.100 (cited from Thomas Aquinas, *Summa contra gentiles*, trans. by Karl Allgeier, 2nd edn, 4 vols (Darmstadt: Wissenschaftliche Buchgesellschaft, 2005), IV, 2). Augustine however adds that wonders can also be made by humans and magic, and additionally might be the work of demons (*De civitate Dei*, XXI.6).

23 For a synopsis of the Augustinian view, see Urban Tigner Holmes, 'The Monster in Mediaeval Literature', in *Studies in Honor of Alfred G. Engstrom*, ed. by R. T. Cargo and E. J. Mickel, Jr (Chapel Hill: North Carolina University Press, 1972), pp. 53–62.

24 See Augustine, *De civitate Dei*, XXI.5.

beings.[25] Like other writers interested in teratology, Isidore saw the monstrous as a cipher that, if interpreted properly, would disclose God's intentions. Again, the monstrous becomes the pathway to God's will.[26] As texts like Conrad Lycosthenes's *Prodigiorum ac ostentorum chronicon* (1552) show,[27] Augustine's and Isidore's treatises remained the authoritative guidelines to the explanation of the monstrous right up to the early modern period.

The Renaissance therefore inherited the divinatory, theological and taxonomic traditions of the monstrous from previous centuries, but did not leave untouched the secondary meanings they had given rise to.[28] For many authors in the vernacular literature of the Middle Ages, the monster had already lost much of its portentous quality: among others, travel literature like *Mandeville's Travels* from the mid-fourteenth century catered for the readers' fascination for the strange, exotic and marvellous,[29] while the verse romances presented terrifying monsters like dragons and giants that challenged the chivalric heroes.[30] In sixteenth-century

25 See Chapter 5 for an extensive treatment of Isidore's taxonomy.

26 The *locus classicus* is Isidore, *Etymologiae*, XI.iii.3. Park and Daston mark Isidore's statements as Augustinian reasoning (see *Wonders and the Order of Nature*, pp. 50–1). Augustine, however, expresses strong doubt about the reliability of divination (see *De civitate Dei*, XXI.8).

27 See Conrad Lycosthenes, *Prodigiorum ac ostentorum chronicon, quae praeter naturae ordinem, et in superioribus et his inferioribus mundi regionibus, ab exordio mundi usque ad haec nostra tempora acciderunt* (Basle: H. Petri, 1557).

28 Surekha Davies explains that the monstrous in the Renaissance referred to (1) occasional errors in nature, (2) omens and prodigies and (3) wonders of nature; see 'The Unlucky, the Bad and the Ugly: Categories of Monstrosity from the Renaissance to the Enlightenment', in *The Ashgate Research Companion to Monsters and the Monstrous*, ed. by Mittman and Dendle, pp. 49–75 (p. 50).

29 Mandeville defines monsters thus: 'A monstre is a thing disformed ayen kynde bothe of man or of best or of ony thing elles, and that is cleped a monstre' (*Mandeville's Travels (Cotton Version)*, ed. by M. C. Seymour (Oxford: Clarendon, 1967), p. 33). See also Sarah Salih, 'Idols and Simulacra: Paganity, Hybridity and Representation in *Mandeville's Travels*', in *The Monstrous Middle Ages*, ed. by Bildhauer and Mills, pp. 113–33. The tradition of travel literature goes back to Herodotus's *Histories* (*ca.* 485–425 BC). Among other things, Herodotus relates, although with scepticism, that in Asia there are gold-digging ants the size of small dogs (*The Persian Wars*, III.102); for the text, see Herodotus, *The Persian Wars*, trans. by A. D. Godley, 4 vols, Loeb Classical Library (Cambridge, MA: Harvard University Press; London: Heinemann, 1920–25; repr. 1961), I. On classical travel literature, see Felton, 'Rejecting and Embracing the Monstrous', pp. 122–6.

30 For the romances, see *Bevis of Hampton*, 2735–885, where the eponymous hero is confronted by a dragon, and Malory's *Le Morte Darthur*, which is teeming with giants and other monsters. References are made to *Four Romances of England*, ed. by Ronald B. Herzman, Graham Drake and Eve Salisbury (Kalamazoo: Medieval Institute Publications, 1999), and Sir Thomas Malory, *Le Morte Darthur: The Hoole Book of Kyng Arthur and of His Noble Knyghtes of the Rounde Table*, ed. by Stephen H. A. Shepherd, Norton Critical Editions (New York and London: W. W. Norton, 2004).

England, the monster had hence superseded the more general notion of the portent and referred predominantly to the deformed. Thomas Cooper's dictionary entry, for example, explains *monstrum* as something 'that exceedeth, lacketh, or is disordred in natural forme. Any thing done against the course of nature. A token or shewing: a thing that signifieth.'[31] The monstrous is therefore defined by (1) the notion of the physically deformed, (2) the violation of the rules of nature (the Latin *in naturam*), and (3) the idea of the sign that needs interpreting.[32]

William Fulwood's folio broadside *The Shape of ii. Monsters*, a print that consists of a double image at the top, a descriptive and explicative prose text in the middle and an 'Admonition unto the Reader' in verse at the bottom, confirms Cooper's definition.[33] The text describes a pig born on Ascension Day, with a head like a dolphin's, forefeet like hands with long fingers and outside thumbs, and hind legs growing backwards. Compared to a normal specimen, this piglet's body is disfigured, its monstrosity consisting in a composite corporeality that violates the rules of nature, which the writer stresses when pointing out that it is '*otherwise* then the *common* form' (emphases added). The animal's anatomical attributes are therefore perceived as deviations from its normal physical shape. Such comparative anatomy, an early modern vogue best represented by Giovanni Battista della Porta's *De humana physiognomia* (1586), translated into Italian as *Della fisionomia dell' huomo*, therefore sharpened man's mind to spot the differences and similarities between correlating body parts – and thus brought into focus possible monstrosity.[34]

In the striking violation of normality exhibited by the piglet, Fulwood perceives the manifestation of God's power, and draws the conclusion that such 'straunge monstrous sightes doe *premonstrate* vnto vs that his heauy indignacion wyl shortly come vpon vs for our monstrous lyuinge'

31 Cooper, *Thesaurus*, s.v. 'monstrum'.

32 Burnett narrows down Cooper's definition to the concept of disproportion, thus disregarding the full entry in the *Thesaurus* (see *Constructing 'Monsters'*, pp. 24–6). Ambroise Paré distinguishes between monsters and prodigies at the outset of his *Of Monsters and Prodigies*: while the former 'are brought forth contrary to the common decree and order of nature' like an infant born with two heads, the latter 'happen contrary to the whole course of nature' like a woman giving birth to a snake; see *The Workes of that Famous Chirurgion Ambrose Parey*, trans. out of Latin and compared with the French by Thomas Johnson (London: Th. Cotes and R. Young, 1634), pp. 961–1026 (p. 961). Paré's treatise was highly influential during the Renaissance.

33 See William Fulwood, *The Shape of ii. Monsters M.D. Lxii* (London: J. Alde, 1562).

34 See Giovanni Battista della Porta, *Della fisionomia dell' huomo et la celeste* … (Venice: Presso Sebastian Combi and Giovanni La Noù, Alla Minerva, 1652; facsimile Castel Negrino: Gruppo Editoriale, 2006). The work is discussed in Hanafi, *The Monster in the Machine*, pp. 100–13.

(emphasis added). Hence, the monster is read as a warning and a sign pointing to a possible apocalypse if man does not mend his ways.[35] This assessment is pressed home in the appellative 'Admonition vnto the Reader', which again explains these monsters as God's creations to shock man into the realisation of his wrongdoings. In addition, it creates a significant connection between the animal's deformity and man's corrupt minds:

> And loke what great deformitie,
> when that we doe them see:
> Much more is in our mindes, truly
> an hundreth thousand folde.[36]

Monstrous beings are therefore visualisations of man's fallen inner state. They figure as an other that points to man's tainted self, drawing in its wake God's anger and punishment.[37]

This text is representative of the early modern approach to the monstrous, in that the main feature of the Renaissance monster was its deviation from the norm of a divinely organised nature. While early modern authors base their perception of the monster's deformed façade on its difference from the proper form, this kind of monstrosity simultaneously pointed to the ideal physical body as the vessel of an incorrupt, and hence virtuous, soul.[38] This leads directly to *The Faerie Queene*, where Spenser explains the disfiguring chain reaction set off by a malfunctioning psyche. Book II, Canto ix of *The Faerie Queene* opens with a eulogy on the divine perfection of a well-governed body, culminating in an emphatic call for temperance that warns its readers of vicious overindulgence:

35 On the Renaissance obsession with the apocalypse, see *The Apocalypse in English Renaissance Thought and Literature: Patterns, Antecedents, and Repercussions*, ed. by C. A. Patrides and Joseph Wittreich (Ithaca: Cornell University Press, 1984), and Paul Christianson, *Reformers and Babylon: English Apocalyptic Visions from the Reformation to the Eve of the Civil War* (Toronto: University of Toronto Press, 1978).

36 See Fulwood, *The Shape of ii. Monsters*.

37 Broadsides of this kind were very popular in the late sixteenth century. Similar examples, which also moralised man's fallen nature and threatened with God's imminent punishment, are J. P[h]illips, *A mervaylous straunge deformed swyne* (London: W. How, 1570), *The description of a monstrous Pig* (London: A. Lacey, 1562) and John Barker, *The true description of a monsterous Chylde borne in the Ile of Wight* (London: W. Gryffith, 1564). Brammall notes the verbal identity between these folios, and concludes that these texts stem from the same historical sentiments (see Kathryn M. Brammall, 'Monstrous Metamorphosis: Nature, Morality, and the Rhetoric of Monstrosity in Tudor England', *Sixteenth Century Journal* 27 (1996), 3–21 (p. 13, n. 33)).

38 This notion harks back to medieval treatises on physiognomy. The 'Ashmole' version of the *Secretum secretorum* explains that physiognomy deduces 'out of þe fourme and makyng of man, the qualitees and the nature[s] of his soule' (*Secretum secretorum: Nine English Versions*, ed. by M. A. Manzalaoui, EETS, 276 (Oxford: Oxford University Press, 1977), p. 90).

Of all Gods workes, which doe this world adorne,
There is no one more faire and excellent,
Then is mans body both for powre and forme,
Whiles it is kept in sober gouernment;
But none then it, more fowle and indecent,
Distempred through misrule and passions bace:
It growes a Monster, and incontinent
Doth loose his dignity and natiue grace.

(II.ix.1.1–8)

Spenser uses the language of the monstrous so densely in the second half of this passage in order to emphasise the bond between body and soul, and the interdependency of physical shape and spiritual habit.[39] As spiritual corruption ('misrule', 'passions') is identified as the main cause for deterioration into the monstrous, monstrous images in literature and the visual arts serve as important assets in establishing the moral allegory underlying *The Faerie Queene*, and moralise the fallen nature of contemporary Elizabethan reality.

The use of a monstrous language stressing the precarious link between man's body and soul is a notable finding for the development of the monstrous in the late sixteenth century. In an article charting developments in the depiction of the monstrous in the Renaissance, Kathryn M. Brammall argues that the monstrous becomes progressively less of a *visible* trait after the 1550s, and develops into a metaphor for an *inward* monstrosity that lacks a visible referent.[40] Fulwood's emphasis on the interrelation between the pig's hideousness and man's moral deprivation thus bears witness to a crucial cultural change, which eventually establishes the monstrous as a language that can transform any historical or religious personality, and even the entire state into a disfigured monster.[41] This change in the secondary features of the monstrous paves the way for the literary monster, which, formed in the mind of the poet, illustrates

39 The *locus classicus* for the notion that man's loss of reason results in his loss of humanity, which ultimately turns him into an animal, is Boethius, *Consolatio philosophiae*, Pr. IV.3; for the text, see Anicius Manlius Severinus Boethius, *Theological Tractates; The Consolation of Philosophy*, ed. and trans. by H. F. Stewart, E. K. Rand and S. J. Tester, Loeb Classical Library (Cambridge, MA: Harvard University Press; London: Heinemann, 1918; repr. 1962).

40 See Brammall, 'Monstrous Metamorphosis', pp. 3–21, a genuine thesaurus of sources, which establishes the period between 1550 and 1570 as the transition towards such a development.

41 Brammall discusses political monsters, monsters as representations of sin, and monsters as political personalities, among them Mary Tudor; from her point of view, '[p]hysical deformity was only a shadow of the real monstrosity' ('Monstrous Metamorphosis', p. 17).

man's fallen state. Even *The Faerie Queene* is to some extent influenced by such a change, because, as we shall see in Part II, Spenser visualises the state of inner monstrosity and projects it on to the site of monstrous and human bodies by way of rhetorical deformation, and even maps something monstrous on to an intact human body by way of metaphor. Against the backdrop of Fulwood's folio and the early modern philosophy of man, it does not come as a surprise that Spenser draws on the contemporaneous discourse on man's 'swinish' self when composing the Grill episode at the end of Book II in the 1580s.[42] As Spenser by and large subscribes to the Renaissance emphasis on evil and corruption as the predominant secondary meanings of the monstrous,[43] the taxonomy of monsters in Part II focuses on evil or corrupt monstrosities; mere wonders, like Belphoebe, are largely excluded from the ensuing discussions.

42 The Grill passage in II.xii.86–7 is discussed in Chapter 10, 'Monstrous humans', below.

43 Spenser uses the term *monster* and its cognates almost always to describe evil monsters (e.g. the Dragon in I.xi.20.9), their attributes (Duessa's feet in I.viii.48.5) and their strength (Cymochles hitting Arthur in II.viii.38.2). For an exception, cf. II.iii.18.9, where *monster* is synonymous with 'marvel'.

4

How to read monsters: A survey of Spenser criticism and teratology

Spenser lived in a time of monsters; yet one quickly realises that there is no overt discourse of the monstrous among Spenserians. Rather, Spenser criticism seems to have developed independently from the larger, more recent trends in monster studies, and has only occasionally made forays into explicitly teratological matters. This circumstance makes it necessary to offer a discussion that combines a survey of Spenserian interpretations with an introduction to different theories of the monstrous. However, owing to the sheer abundance of scholarship in both categories, this chapter is not designed as a definitive account of these complex scholarly traditions, and gives only an exemplary overview.

When Spenser in the 'Letter to Raleigh' called his poem a '*continued Allegory, or darke conceit*' with the aim '*to fashion a gentleman or noble person in vertuous and gentle discipline*',[1] he basically self-fashioned the interpretative discourse of his own poem: thanks to this 'giveaway' comment, the amount of allegorical criticism accumulating from the 1590s to the early twenty-first century has grown into vast proportions – so vast in fact that it has eclipsed any other reading of *The Faerie Queene*. Naturally, this critical approach has exerted a formative influence on the perception, and reception of the monsters figuring in the poem. Ben Jonson is an early example of such 'direct' allegory. The terse explanations he gives for two of the most famous Spenserian monstrosities, namely the Blatant Beast, and Duessa, in the *Conversations with William Drummond of Hawthornden* are characteristic for such an attitude: 'by the Blating Beast the Puritans were understood, by the false Duessa the Q. of Scots'.[2]

1 Spenser, 'Letter to Raleigh', 4 and 8.

2 For Jonson's text, see R. M. Cummings, ed., *Spenser: The Critical Heritage* (London: Routledge and Kegan Paul, 1971), p. 136. Ben Jonson's marginalia to *The Faerie Queene* reveal the care and astuteness with which he read Spenser's poem; the text is reprinted in J. A. Riddell and S. Stewart, *Jonson's Spenser: Evidence and Historical Criticism* (Pittsburgh: Duquesne University Press, 1995).

Yet allegory need not be as easy to interpret as Jonson's comment suggests. The great Dragon that Redcrosse fights in Canto xi of Book I, for instance, has cued a host of complex allegorical readings based on the four senses of scripture,[3] namely the literal or historical, the allegorical or mystical, the moral or tropological and the anagogical or spiritual.[4] On the literary or historical level, literary characters were linked with legendary or real ones; Redcrosse's fighting the Dragon was therefore associated with St George's legendary vanquishing a similar monster. In medieval and still in early modern thought, the signs of the surrounding world were not only thought to relate to its positivist material reality but were also comprehended as signifiers relating metaphysical truths. In turn, the realm of language and words likewise consisted of signs that pointed beyond the physical object to the figurative, and eventually to the realm of the hereafter;[5] whence arises the desire to venture for higher levels of meaning. History therefore does not only disclose the identity of the hero but suggests an allegorical dimension: not too long ago, Elizabeth See Watson scanned the Dragon's description for allusions to Pope Gregory XIII, thus subjecting the Dragon to historico-theological allegory and to anti-Catholic sentiments.[6] Taken on its own, the Dragon's corporeal similarities with the red dragon of the Apocalypse likewise hint

3 See, e.g., Mark Rose's running commentary on I.xi in *Spenser's Art: A Companion to Book One of 'The Faerie Queene'* (Cambridge, MA: Harvard University Press, 1975), pp. 133–45, and Carol V. Kaske, 'The Dragon's Spark and Sting and the Structure of Red-Cross's Dragon-Fight: *The Faerie Queene*, I.xi–xii', *Studies in Philology* 66 (1969), 609–38.

4 The famous formula, with frequent variations, reads 'Littera gesta docet, quid credas allegoria, / Moralis quid agas, quo tendas anagogia' (quoted in Phillip Rollinson, *Classical Theories of Allegory and Christian Culture* (Oxford: Oxford University Press, 1989), p. xi). Although it would seem that the four senses of scripture were *passé* in the wake of the Reformation (but already starting before it), they nevertheless remained inherent in secular literature. John Harington explicitly advocated fourfold interpretation and applied short interpretations as guidelines for the individual cantos in his translation of Ariosto's *Orlando Furioso* (*Ludovico Ariosto's Orlando Furioso translated into English Heroical Verse by Sir John Harington (1591)*, ed. by Robert McNulty (Oxford: Oxford University Press, 1972)). See John N. King, *Spenser's Poetry and the Reformation Tradition* (Princeton: Princeton University Press, 1990), pp. 76–7, and Karol V. Kaske, 'Bible', in *Spenser Encyclopedia*, ed. by Hamilton, pp. 87–90 (p. 89), as well as her excellent monograph, *Spenser and Biblical Poetics* (Ithaca: Cornell University Press, 1999), pp. 15–17.

5 See Jan M. Ziolkowski, 'Literary Genre and Animal Symbolism', in *Animals and the Symbolic in Medieval Art and Literature*, ed. by L. A. J. R. Houwen, Mediaevalia Groningana, 20 (Groningen: Egbert Forsten, 1997), pp. 1–23 (pp. 5–6).

6 See Elizabeth See Watson, 'Spenser's Flying Dragon and Pope Gregory XIII', *Spenser Studies* 14 (1994), 293–301. As Gregory was *Pontifex Maximus* from 1572 to 1585, part of his pontificate coincided with the beginning of Spenser's work on *The Faerie Queene*. For the Dragon as a figuration of the Spanish Armada, see Rose, *Spenser's Art*, p. 135.

at a possible anagogical dimension, so that Redcrosse's fiendish opponent becomes a figuration of the End of Days.[7] But there is also a tropological, or moral, undercurrent discernible in the text. As the representative of evil, the Dragon becomes the touchstone for Redcrosse's *imitatio Christi*: the climactic fight between the monster and the knight becomes the representation of Christ's battle against Sin to redeem Mankind, which is stressed by the topos of the three-day fight.[8] Beyond these meanings, Spenser's Dragon could be subjected to an additional interpretation: as it scourges Eden, and combines references to its devilish as well as to its monstrous nature, the Dragon refers simultaneously to the serpent in Genesis, Leviathan in the Book of Job and the red dragon in the Book of Revelation, which makes it an example of typology. The traditional readings advanced here raise two suspicions. On the one hand, the dragon, when thus subjected to allegorical readings, is not perceived as a monstrous creature any more, but is aestheticised as an abstract cipher in an allegorical master text. In the process of deferring the monstrous to an allegorical meaning, the monster as creature is, as it were, tamed and ceases to exist.[9] On the other hand, such an interpretative strategy also constantly defers any finite meaning of the Dragon and marks the monster as an ultimately puzzling literary creation, which, just like allegory, rests on polysemy.[10]

Similar interpretations of Spenser's monsters, especially of the more notorious creatures like Errour, and the Blatant Beast, abound. Yet, even

7 See Florence Sandler, '*The Faerie Queene*: An Elizabethan Apocalypse', in *The Apocalypse in English Renaissance Thought*, ed. by Patrides and Wittreich, pp. 148–74; John Watkins, 'Apocalypse Deferred: Seventeenth-Century Appropriations of Spenser', in *Worldmaking Spenser: Explorations in the Early Modern Age*, ed. by Patrick Cheney and Lauren Silberman (Lexington: University Press of Kentucky, 2000), pp. 156–73; and Rose, *Spenser's Art*, p. 134.

8 This is essentially argued by A. C. Hamilton in 'The Visions of *Piers Plowman* and *The Faerie Queene*', in *Form and Convention in the Poetry of Edmund Spenser*, ed. by William Nelson, English Institute Essays, 35 (New York and London: Columbia University Press, 1961), pp. 1–34. Kaske's reading in 'The Dragon's Spark and Sting' is an advanced revision of Hamilton's argument. On Redcrosse as a Mankind figure, see Rose, *Spenser's Art*, p. 143.

9 In his involved Lutherian reading of Book I, Patrick Perkins argues that the Dragon represents the Law of God (see 'Spenser's Dragon and the Law', *Spenser Studies* 21 (2006), 51–81; 'When the Law attempts to do more than its office it becomes a dragon that keeps us imprisoned in despair', p. 68).

10 On polysemy as an essential quality of allegory, see Gordon Teskey, *Allegory and Violence* (Ithaca and London: Cornell University Press, 1996), pp. 30–1; on the importance of polysemy and indeterminacy for monsters, see Bettina Bildhauer and Robert Mills, 'Introduction', in *Monstrous Middle Ages*, ed. by Bildhauer and Mills, pp. 1–27 (p. 6).

in those cases, Spenserians normally focus on one of these beings, and approach it from a vantage point other than the monstrous. There are, of course, exceptions that emphasise the role and function of animals and monsters in *The Faerie Queene*. In the 1960s, *Studies in English Literature 1500–1900* printed two articles that investigated Spenser's animal world, and thus also offered a few glances on monsters: Madeleine Pelner Cosman presents the first full treatment of animal imagery in *The Faerie Queene*,[11] whereas Arthur F. Marotti directly responds to it, and addresses the shortcomings of her essay.[12] Although these companion pieces focus on animals and animal attributes, and are not explicitly interested in the monstrous, they also cast some light on monstrous creatures. By and large, both critics stress Spenser's functional use of animal imagery: in Cosman's view, the main function of the animals and hence also of the monsters is that of illustrating the battle between the vices and the virtues, while Marotti, who stresses the dual use of animals as participants in the plot of the allegory and as images to characterise the poem's *personae*,[13] argues that animal images serve the purpose of vivifying human phenomena and accentuating the meaning of the poem. Such an observation can be applied equally well to Spenser's use of the monstrous.

Neither Marotti nor Cosman could have known that their articles would anticipate the (post)modern interest in the animal–human divide during the medieval and early modern periods. A few decades later, Joyce E. Salisbury and Erica Fudge, taking advantage of such conceptual possibilities,[14] concentrate on the natural, and cultural, concepts underlying the notions of man and animal, and argue that the dividing line that tells man from beast does not work properly, because the human and the animal transgress into one another's territories, e.g. through hybrid combinations. Both Salisbury and Fudge hence elaborate on the medieval and early modern commonplace that man occupied a precarious middle position on the so-called ladder of creation between celestial beings like angels and earthly creatures like animals: like the former, human beings possess reason; like the latter, they are driven by bodily passions and

11 See Madeleine Pelner Cosman, 'Spenser's Ark of Animals: Animal Imagery in *The Faery Queene*', *Studies in English Literature 1500–1900* 3 (1963), 85–107. Among other things, she mentions the hyena (p. 98).

12 See Arthur F. Marotti, 'Animal Symbolism in *The Faerie Queene*: Tradition and Poetic Context', *Studies in English Literature 1500–1900* 5 (1965), 69–86.

13 Marotti explains that '[a]nimals are found in *The Faerie Queene* both as visual figures in the allegory and in illustrative similes and metaphors' ('Animal Symbolism', p. 69).

14 See Joyce E. Salisbury, *The Beast Within: Animals in the Middle Ages* (New York and London: Routledge, 1994), and Erica Fudge, *Perceiving Animals: Humans and Beasts in Early Modern English Culture* (Urbana and Chicago: University of Illinois Press, 2002).

instincts. Fudge engages especially with Pico della Mirandola's *Oratio de hominis dignitate*, a humanist manifesto which stresses that moving up this vertical axis towards to the divine and spiritual or moving down towards the beastly and brutish depends on man's choice alone.[15]

A first foray into overtly teratological criticism was made by the French critic Bernard Tannier. His article 'Un bestiaire maniériste' is the first to offer a more or less comprehensive reading of monsters and fantastic animals in Spenser's poem solely from the focal point of the monstrous.[16] By contextualising these deformities into the tradition of the bestiary and mannerist literature, Tannier accentuates the predominance of the deformed in *The Faerie Queene*, which Spenser, according to Tannier, describes with the rhetorical verve and sense of detail so characteristic of his age, and so markedly different from the dry descriptions of the bestiaries. Although the article is too brief, and too loosely argued, it is still a helpful and at times inspiring introduction to Spenser's use of monsters, as it offers interpretations of the more important creatures like the Dragon and the Blatant Beast, and classifies how Spenser uses the monstrous.[17] It is especially valuable because it also links the many monsters in the poem with the infinity of shapes figuring both in Phantastes's chamber and in the Garden of Adonis. That Tannier thematises the poet's role as a creator of monsters and that he sees similarities between Phantastes and the poet opens important interpretative possibilities,[18] also because he connects the monstrous with the imagination, and the '*darke conceit*' used by Spenser to describe his work in his 'Letter to Raleigh', with the monsters of the poem. Most importantly, however, Tannier advocates a polysemous essence for the monstrous, and stresses that there is never a single and easy way to deal with Spenser's monsters.[19]

15 See Fudge, *Perceiving Animals*, pp. 35–7, 75–6 and 80–1. On Pico's philosophy of man, see also Chapter 9.

16 See Bernard Tannier, 'Un bestiaire maniériste: monstres et animaux fantastiques dans *La Reine des Fées* d'Edmund Spenser', in *Monstres et prodiges au temps de la Renaissance*, ed. by M. T. Jones-Davies, Université de Paris-Sorbonne IV, Institut de Recherches sur les Civilisations de l'occident Moderne, Centre de Recherches sur la Renaissance, 5 (Paris: Université de Paris-Sorbonne, 1980), pp. 55–65. Tannier has also contributed the article 'Animals, fabulous' to the *Spenser Encyclopedia*, ed. by Hamilton, pp. 41–2.

17 Tannier argues that Spenser uses the monstrous as 'allegoria in actis', as emblems and 'tableaux vivants', and as symbols within complex allegory ('Bestiaire maniériste', p. 57). Monsters can illustrate nature's abundant creation of questionable life forms as well as highlighting the characters' fears and obsessions.

18 'Phantastes, l'imagination du poète, est mis en équation avec la Nature' ('Phantastes, the poet's imagination, is equated with nature'; Tannier, 'Bestiaire maniériste', p. 59).

19 Tannier defines the Blatant Beast and the three dragons in Book I (Errour, Orgoglio's

Of all Spenserian critics, Elizabeth Porges Watson shows the greatest sustained interest in Spenser's depiction of the natural world in readings that accentuate the various roles and functions assigned to animals and monsters. In two articles she argues that *The Faerie Queene* utilises strategies familiar from chivalric bestiaries,[20] but that it also exhibits strikingly anti-chivalric tendencies.[21] Other articles centre on particular kinds of beings, such as the sea-creatures,[22] the insects appearing at the various stages in Spenser's poems,[23] and the wolves and foxes figuring in the *Shepheardes Calender*.[24] Inevitably, these articles either touch or focus on the monstrous. Watson's remarks on Spenserian deformities are especially valuable because she does not solely follow the vestiges of allegorical criticism, although she does, of course, keep track of them in her readings,[25] but because she also displays a distinct interest in the physical or 'creational' aspects of the monstrous.

So the monsters in *The Faerie Queene* have been predominantly assessed through allegory. However, outside the field of Spenser scholarship, monster studies that emphasise the role of the monster *as* monster have been thriving for the past two to three decades.[26] Modern literary teratology begins with J. R. R. Tolkien's '*Beowulf*: The Monsters and the Critics', where he brings to the centre what had been marginalised in earlier philological inquiry: the monstrous, which Tolkien sees pertinent to the 'structure and conduct' of the poem.[27] Maintaining that the literary

---

dragon and the Dragon of Eden) as polysemic creatures (see Tannier, 'Bestiaire maniériste', pp. 62–3).

20 See Elizabeth Porges Watson, '*The Faerie Queene*: Spenser's Chivalric Bestiary', *Reinardus* 11 (1998), 161–74.

21 See Elizabeth Porges Watson, 'Forreine and Monstrous Beasts: Spenser's Anti-Bestiary', *Reinardus* 13 (2000), 169–80. Although this article shares the same interest as Tannier's, which also relates Spenser's creatures to the bestiary tradition and seeks to explain their existence, she either did not find it very valuable or is unaware of it. Compare, for instance, Watson's introductory remarks to *Mother Hubberds Tale* ('Forreine and Monstrous Beasts', pp. 170–2) with Tannier's ('Bestiaire maniériste', p. 55).

22 See Elizabeth Porges Watson, 'Spenser's Submarine Creation', *Reinardus* 9 (1996), 121–34.

23 See Elizabeth Porges Watson, 'Emblem and Experience: Spenser's Use of Insect Imagery', *Reinardus* 1 (1988), 113–20.

24 See Elizabeth Porges Watson, 'Shepherds, Wolves, Foxes and Others in Spenser's *Shepheardes Calender*', *Reinardus* 7 (1994), 113–26.

25 See, among other things, her remarks at the outset of her article on insect imagery ('Emblem and Experience', p. 113). In 'Shepherds, Wolves, Foxes', she interprets the foxes and wolves traditionally as 'spiritual predators' (p. 126).

26 For full overviews of monster criticism, see 'Further Reading', in *The Monstrous Middle Ages*, ed. by Bildhauer and Mills, pp. 219–26, and Olsen and Olsen, 'Introduction'.

27 J. R. R. Tolkien, '*Beowulf*: The Monsters and the Critics', in *An Anthology of 'Beowulf' Criticism*, ed. by Lewis E. Nicholson (Notre Dame: University of Notre Dame Press,

power of the poem is inextricably linked to the depiction of the dragon and the Grendelkin, Tolkien stresses that *Beowulf* 's monsters are 'not an inexplicable blunder of taste; they are essential, fundamentally allied to the underlying ideas of the poem',[28] and play an important part as touchstones of the hero's prowess in both halves of the poem.[29] Tolkien's study establishes the monsters as beings fashioned by the poet's imagination for specific purposes;[30] it illustrates the scope of what monsters can mean, especially with regard to their corporeality, and places special emphasis on the actual encounter with the monstrous. Tolkien also interprets the monsters as transitional or liminal creatures, because they are positioned on the threshold between older Norse mythology and the growing influence of Christianity, which turned monstrous beings into evil spirits adverse to man.[31] By stressing the monster's role as man's eternal enemy, Tolkien emphasises its underlying universality: the battle between man and monster represents the archetypal struggle between Good and Evil.

The mass of articles and book-length studies following the wake of Tolkien's address is enormous. Mainly interested in source studies and utilising a host of different texts and illustrations, John Block Friedman's *Monstrous Races in Medieval Art and Thought* showcases the history of the Plinian races, bringing into view their geographical and ethnic aspects.[32] Another highly influential addition to medieval teratology is Andy Orchard's monograph *Pride and Prodigies*, which offers an in-depth study of the monsters in the *Beowulf* manuscript.[33] Studies like these approach the monstrous from the vantage point of history, looking at texts to see whether a particular type of monster has antecedents in works available to artists and poets in order to establish the artistic and cultural

1963), pp. 51–103 (the article originally appeared in *Proceedings of the British Academy* 22 (1936), 245–95). For a brief critical assessment of Tolkien's article, see Bildhauer and Mills, 'Introduction', pp. 2–3. In 1904, W. P. Ker had famously criticised the *Beowulf* poet for placing the 'irrelevancies [i.e. the monsters] in the centre and the serious things at the outer edges' (*The Dark Ages* (London: Nelson, 1904), p. 253). For Tolkien's retort to Ker's claim, see '*Beowulf*', pp. 57–8; for structural remarks, see pp. 52–3.

28 Tolkien, '*Beowulf*', p. 68.

29 See Tolkien, '*Beowulf*', p. 81 and p. 86.

30 The dragon, for example, is 'a thing made by imagination' for the purpose of enhancing the hero's fortune (Tolkien, '*Beowulf*', pp. 85–6). Cf. also Tolkien's wry comment that the poet 'liked [dragons] – as a poet, not as a sober zoologist' (p. 60).

31 See Tolkien, '*Beowulf*', pp. 72–3.

32 See John Block Friedman, *The Monstrous Races in Medieval Art and Thought* (Cambridge, MA: Harvard University Press, 1981).

33 See Andy Orchard, *Pride and Prodigies: Studies in the Monsters of the 'Beowulf' Manuscript* (Cambridge: Brewer, 1995), which also contains editions of *The Wonders of the East*, *The Letter of Alexander to Aristotle* and the *Liber monstrorum* in Latin, Old English and Modern English.

traditions that informed the depiction of monsters and monstrous beings in literary works, manuscripts and *mappaemundi*.

Another more traditional approach to the monstrous that has yielded important recent scholarship is taxonomy. Deriving from the Greek nouns τάξις ('order, arrangement'), and νόμος ('law'), taxonomy denotes a referential system that organises life forms within groups and hierarchies. Classifications of this kind date back to Aristotle via Isidore, but were also prominent in the early modern period. As the nature of the monster is largely determined by its extraordinariness, an organised presentation of monstrous beings seems to be a contradiction in terms.[34] Despite this inhibition, recent scholars, especially David Williams, Claude Lecouteux and Claude Kappler,[35] have resorted to typology to advance our systematic knowledge of medieval monstrosities.[36] But while Lecouteux and Kappler set themselves the task to find decisive features of monsters by looking at specimens, their habitats, and the genre they appear in, Williams, in his *Deformed Discourse*, uses taxonomy as the starting point for a highly theoretical inquiry into the nature of the medieval monster, which he also brings to bear on perceptive interpretations of heroes' and saints' lives. Resorting to the Neo-Platonism of Pseudo-Dionysius and Eriugena, he establishes the monstrous as the manifestation of God's greatness, which offers to man a gateway to a fuller comprehension of His nature. In simple terms, the monstrous constitutes an alternative mode of thinking that goes beyond the two seminal medieval schools of thought: while rationalism, which stressed the capabilities of human reason, sought to access divine truth through logical thought processes, negative mysticism attempted to map God's truth through the byroad of the *via negativa* – i.e. through comprehending what God is not. The monstrous, however, by definition the embodiment of paradox, teases man into making sense of its grotesque multiformity, which reifies the unspeakable; in the

34 David Williams adroitly calls it 'an ordering of disorder' (*Deformed Discourse*, p. 14).

35 See Williams, *Deformed Discourse*; Claude Lecouteux, *Les Monstres dans la littérature allemande du moyen âge: Contribution à l'étude du merveilleux médiévale*, 3 vols (Göppingen: Kummerle, 1982), and *Les monstres dans la pensée médiévale européenne essai de presentation*, Cultures et civilisations médiévales, 10 (Paris: Presses Universitaires de Paris-Sorbonne, 1993); and Claude Kappler, *Monstres, démons et merveilles à la fin du Moyen Age* (Paris: Payot, 1980).

36 For other taxonomic works, ranging from beginner's to advanced scholarship, see *Dictionary of Deities and Demons in the Bible*, ed. by Karel van der Toorn, Bob Becking and Pieter W. van der Horst, 2nd rev. edn (Leiden: Brill, 1998); *Mythical Beasts*, ed. by John Cherry (London: British Museum, 1995); and *Mythic and Fabulous Creatures: A Source Book and Reference Guide*, ed. by Malcolm South (Westport: Greenwood Press, 1987).

process of contemplation, the human being undergoes an advancement of knowledge, and rises on to a higher level of understanding. Williams's assessment of Pseudo-Dionysian theses is notable because it allocates a high significance to the monstrous as a tool for elevating the human mind to the divine, an exercise of the intellectual faculties reserved for man,[37] and thus testifies to Balthasar Gracian's (1601–55) *bon mot* that '[p]aradoxes are the monsters of truth'.[38]

On the other end of the spectrum, the monster has lent itself well to postmodernist notions. I would like to single out two representative scholars, who draw on a different, and highly specialised vocabulary to make sense of the monstrous, namely Jeffrey Jerome Cohen and Mary Campbell.

In 1996, Jeffrey Jerome Cohen published his seven-part essay 'Monster Culture (Seven Theses)',[39] where he addresses important cultural and psychological issues of the monstrous.[40] This manifesto leads to one of the most important single studies of monsters: *Of Giants* (1999),[41] in which Cohen approaches the monstrous from a pronounced psycho-analytical angle. To be more precise, he resorts to the Lacanian principle of *extimité*, i.e. 'external intimacy' or 'familiar alterity', to investigate the process of identity formation that the protagonists in medieval English texts undergo during their encounters with giants. Mainly discussing medieval romances,[42] Cohen conceptualises giants as intimate strangers that make manifest and produce the masculine body, because this type of monster, defined by an exaggerated physicality, is the *agens* that inscribes identity on the body of the hero, and helps form his gender through the desire for and repulsion of the monstrous. The giant, as a being both alien and close to home, thus occupies a position at the limits of the self and the

37 See Williams, *Deformed Discourse*, p. 6.

38 Quoted from Williams, *Deformed Discourse*, p. 47.

39 Cohen aims at 'reading cultures from the monsters they engender'. See Jeffrey Jerome Cohen, 'Monster Culture (Seven Theses)', in *Monster Theory: Reading Culture*, ed. by Jeffrey Jerome Cohen (Minneapolis: University of Minnesota Press, 1996), pp. 3–25 (p. 3).

40 The theses are: 'The Monster's Body Is a Cultural Body'; 'The Monster Always Escapes'; 'The Monster Is the Harbinger of Category Crisis'; 'The Monster Dwells at the Gates of Difference'; 'The Monster Polices the Borders of the Possible'; 'Fear of the Monster Is Really a Kind of Desire'; and 'The Monster Stands at the Threshold … of Becoming' (Cohen, 'Monster Culture (Seven Theses)', pp. 3–25).

41 See J. J. Cohen, *Of Giants: Sex, Monsters, and the Middle Ages*, Medieval Cultures, 17 (Minneapolis and London: University of Minnesota Press, 1999).

42 The main texts discussed by Cohen are *Beowulf*, Chrétien de Troyes's *The Knight and the Lion*, Geoffrey of Monmouth's *History of the Kings of Britain*, *Sir Gowther*, Chaucer's *Sir Thopas* and *Sir Gawain and the Green Knight*.

Other.[43] Giants, representing the 'dangerous excesses of the flesh' are in themselves the products of masculine embodiment, which both forbids and indulges in the pleasures of the body.[44] Such a reading drives home that the monstrous has not changed in significance from the premodern to the postmodern age. As the monster's objectionable physicality still stirs its beholder into pleasurable contemplation and disgust at the same time, it continues its life as a transhistorical phenomenon of unfaltering ambiguity that scares and fascinates, triggering desire and repulsion.[45]

In a vein different from Cohen's, Mary Campbell scans 1200 years of travel writing to penetrate the nature of exotic monsters in her monograph *The Witness and the Other World*.[46] Focusing her study on the so-called 'matter of the east', the geographical region inhabited by strange races and animals, and its subversive grotesquery,[47] she examines the universal ideas immanent in the monstrous from a colonial background of monsters and monstrous races whose monstrosity is constituted by 'hyperbolic dimensions, multiplication of body parts, and fusion of species'.[48] With such a cultural point of view, the monstrous again emerges as a transhistorical phenomenon, so that there is no difference between teratology in the fifth century, say Ctesias's *Indika*, and the Renaissance.[49]

Campbell's enterprise is therefore strongly informed by post-colonialism, a branch of New Historicism that was inaugurated by Edward Said's *Orientalism*.[50] It brings into view the power-relationship set up by the coloniser, who encounters the colonised Other through the overpowering feeling of ontological difference. In order to come to terms with the uncanny creatures of the east, colonisers define themselves through what

43 See Cohen, *Of Giants*, p. xv: 'The giant reveals the limits of selfhood, reveals that identity is intersubjective, ex-centric, suspended across temporalities, as historically contingent as it is monstrously incomplete. If the giant is Other, then he is the Other as something "strange to me, although … at the heart of me".'

44 Cohen, *Of Giants*, p. xiii.

45 See Cohen, *Of Giants*, p. 66. Throughout his study, Cohen underlines the historical continuity of the monstrous by starting his chapters with brief analyses of (post)modern literature and film, which he then brings to bear on his interpretations of medieval monstrosities.

46 Mary Campbell, *The Witness and the Other World: Exotic Travel Writing 400–1600* (Ithaca and London: Cornell University Press, 1988), especially pp. 47–86.

47 Campbell argues that the *Wonders of the East* is largely informed by the grotesque through a 'hybridized approach to the categories of natural history and … the rhetorical techniques of its *descriptio*' (*Witness*, p. 62). She defines the grotesque mode as 'expressive, symbolic, shocking, but never mimetic' (*Witness*, p. 80).

48 Campbell, *Witness*, p. 71.

49 See Campbell, *Witness*, p. 47.

50 See Edward Said, *Orientalism: Western Conceptions of the Orient* (New York: Random House, 1978).

the Other is not. Urged into interpreting the Other's puzzling bodies and rites, discoverers made sense of the Indians by identifying them with the monsters they knew. Culture and societal identity are therefore defined through the marginalisation of the monstrous.[51] Thanks to the plethora of strange races in travel literature, illustrated maps and artworks of the medieval and early modern periods, an impressive number of teratological investigations with similar unified theories exploiting this particular brand of (post-)colonial discourses has followed in the wake of Said's and Campbell's works.[52]

While testifying to the enduring fascination monsters and monstrous beings have exerted on the scholarly community, the sheer diversity of approaches to these creatures surveyed in this section stresses their multifarious and puzzling nature: monsters do indeed *point to* something – just *what* they point to is open to interpretation. These theories also bring into relief the main difference between Spenser criticism and teratological studies: whereas the former has always been essentially allegorical, the latter has been at the forefront of recent theoretical trends in literary and cultural criticism. In other words, there is a tension between the monster *as allegorical cipher* and the monster *as monster*. A way out of this cul-de-sac is an approach that allows for the interaction between both critical paradigms and occasionally makes room for ideas pertaining to the Other as a psychological or cultural category alongside taxonomic criticism. Such interplay is especially important, because the monsters in *The Faerie Queene* are in every sense as complex as other textual and artistic monstrosities and as such elude simple approaches.

51 Paul Freedman examines whether the concept of the Other is applicable in this context, and whether the *medium aevum* could in itself be seen as an Other in his insightful article 'The Medieval Other: The Middle Ages as Other', in *Marvels, Monsters, and Miracles*, ed. by Jones and Sprunger, pp. 1–24.

52 Olsen and Olsen offer a detailed introduction to the monstrous in northwest Europe, claiming that monsters are 'the tangible representations of … otherness', while simultaneously arguing that the monstrous is multiform (Olsen and Olsen, 'Introduction', p. 6). See also J. J. Cohen, 'The Limits of Knowing: Monsters and the Regulation of Popular Culture', *Medieval Folklore* 3 (1994), 1–37.

PART II

Reading the monster: Taxonomy

5

Taxonomic considerations

> The Lion looked at Alice wearily. 'Are you animal – or vegetable – or mineral?' he said, yawning at every other word.
>
> 'It's a fabulous monster!' the Unicorn cried out, before Alice could reply.
>
> Lewis Carroll, *Through the Looking-Glass*, Ch. VII[1]

In Chapter VII of Lewis Carroll's *Through the Looking-Glass*, Alice, the novel's famous heroine, has a singular encounter with anthropomorphised animals, which perceive her as a talking, walking creature that thwarts any biological category known to them. Of all creatures, it is the unicorn – the fantastic animal *par excellence* – that finally assigns her the label of 'fabulous monster'. To the reader, the scene evokes amusement, because the incident, set in the topsy-turvy world on the other side of the looking-glass where flowers talk and beings change their shapes, shows the monster staring back. But the short scene also makes clear that the perception of what is monstrous and what is not depends entirely on the beholders and the historico-cultural system that defines their sensibilities: if the unicorn is a fabulous animal for Alice, why should Alice not be a monster for the unicorn? In *The Faerie Queene*, however, there is no such reversal of perspective: the normative system that permeates the poem is that of late sixteenth-century England, where, as Cooper explains in his *Thesaurus*, the monster is a physical or moral deformity that violates the rules of nature.

Spenser takes great care to emphasise the otherness of the monsters and monstrous beings he creates by employing a language riddled with monstrous terms. This shorthand of the monstrous signposts deviancy through standard epithets like *hideous*, *monstrous* and *deformed*, as well

1 Lewis Carroll, *Alice's Adventures in Wonderland and Through the Looking-Glass*, ed. by Roger Lancelyn Green, Oxford World's Classics (Oxford: Oxford University Press, 1998), p. 206.

as through attributes like *blood*, *filth*, *gore* and *poison*.[2] These are deployed as a referential frame on which Spenser bases his monstrous creations.[3]

But these are mere preliminaries. How we perceive monsters is informed by an inherited system of norm-giving parameters into which any given 'normal' or 'normative' life form can be placed.[4] If one wants to determine the nature of the monster in Spenser's *The Faerie Queene*, one needs to focus on the anatomical aspects of monsters and monstrous beings. This approach takes into account the sixteenth-century interest in anatomical curiosities, as well as the influential taxonomic views that began to take shape in the classical period. As the extraordinary monstrous body upsets known biological categories, the scrutiny of physical signifiers becomes a method that can point to the exact attribute that transcends, or transgresses, natural conventions in creatures that are not as openly monstrous as dragons. While the historical survey in Chapter 3 identified the monster as a creature that 'points to' something, be it as a sign of man's tainted self or a warning of God's impending vengeance, the task of setting up a taxonomy means finding attributes that 'point to' the monstrous. In order to answer this query I will briefly turn to Isidore's influential typology of monsters and prodigies in the *Etymologiae*.

Beginning from the vantage point that monstrosity manifests itself through physical deformity, Isidore bases his investigation on analytical readings of monstrous bodies, and develops them into a system of categories into which any monstrous being can be placed.[5] After an extended chapter in which he describes the human body and its organs, Isidore adds a concise account of different kinds of monsters. Although Isidore's

2 For black blood, see I.i.24.9 (Errour), I.xi.22.4 (the 'gushing riuer of blacke gory blood' issuing from the Dragon in Eden), IV.vii.27.8 (Lust) and V.xi.14.6 (Geryoneo; cf. also Spenser's description of Cocytus in II.vii.56.7). Blood is likewise linked to poison and ink in I.i.20.2 and 22.7. For gory blood, see I.ii.30.9 (Fradubio), and for blood infected with poison, see I.xi.8.9, II.ii.4.7, II.iv.38.8–9, III.x.59.3–4 and V.xii.I.30.9. See III.xii.20 (Amoret) for a depiction of normative red blood. For poison, see, among other places, I.xi.8.9 (the Dragon Redcrosse fights has a body 'swoln with wrath, and poyson, and with bloody gore'), and V.xii.30 (the disfigured mouth of the hag Enuie is foaming with poison).

3 See also Watson, 'Forreine and Monstrous Beasts', p. 170.

4 From the perspective of the early modern period such a normative system would be the Great Chain of Being. Classic accounts are E. M. W. Tillyard's *The Elizabethan World Picture* (Harmondsworth: Penguin, 1943; repr. 1973), C. S. Lewis's *The Discarded Image: An Introduction to Medieval and Renaissance Literature* (Cambridge: Cambridge University Press, 1964) and Arthur O. Lovejoy's *The Great Chain of Being: A Study of the History of an Idea. The William James Lectures Delivered at Harvard University, 1933* (Cambridge, MA, and London: Harvard University Press, 1936).

5 Isidore gives an overview of deformities in the section *De portentis*, in *Etymologiae*, XI.iii.7–12.

Latin original leaves room for different subdivisions of his list, I will here follow the twelve-part structure Williams offers in *Deformed Discourse*.[6]

Isidore's first entries concern the size of creatures. According to his definition, some beings, like Tityon, are monstrous, because their bodies exceed the mean of human growth,[7] a phenomenon that Williams calls 'hypertrophy of the body'. Others, like the pygmies, are notable through the smallness of their bodies,[8] which Williams dubs the 'atrophy of the body'. However, monstrosity is determined not only through body size but also through body parts. Some beings are monstrous by dint of an 'excrescence of bodily parts',[9] a 'superfluity of parts',[10] or, quite differently, by dint of a 'deprivation of parts'.[11] But the sheer number of possible monstrous mutations is increased through human–animal composites, i.e. creatures that sport a 'mixture of human and animal parts'. Isidore explains this phenomenon as incomplete metamorphosis, for these beings are only 'partly transformed'.[12] The border between man and animal is further crossed when human women give birth to animals, as for example the woman who gave birth to a calf.[13] Isidore also sees monstrosity in the 'mislocation of organs or parts in the body', pointing out that some creatures carry their eyes on their chests.[14] A rarer phenomenon is 'disturbed growth', which, for instance, manifests itself in offspring that is born old.[15] In addition to these classes, monsters can also be 'composite beings',[16] 'hermaphrodites'[17] and, more generally, 'monstrous races', like giants, Cynocephali (i.e. dog-headed men) and Cyclops.[18]

6 See Williams, *Deformed Discourse*, p. 107, for the entire catalogue, from which I will also take over the headings for the different categories. Olsen and Olsen distinguish between ten types of monstrosities (see 'Introduction', p. 7).

7 'magnitudine totius corporis ultra communem hominum modum' (Isidore, *Etymologiae*, XI.iii.7).

8 'parvitate totius corporis' (Isidore, *Etymologiae*, XI.iii.7).

9 'a magnitudine partium' (Isidore, *Etymologiae*, XI.iii.7).

10 'superfluis membrorum partibus' (Isidore, *Etymologiae*, XI.iii.7).

11 'a defectu partium … [aut] a decisione' (Isidore, *Etymologiae*, XI.iii.8).

12 'in parte transfigurantur' (Isidore, *Etymologiae*, XI.iii.9).

13 'ex omni parte transfigurantur in alienae creationis portentum, ut ex muliere vitulum dicit historia generatum' (Isidore, *Etymologiae*, XI.iii.9).

14 'quae sine transfiguratione mutationem habent locorum' ('which have a change in the position of features without any transformation'; Isidore, *Etymologiae*, XI.iii.9).

15 'secundum connaturationem … secundum inmaturam et intemperatam creationem' ('because of a joined begetting … because of a premature or untimely creation'; Isidore, *Etymologiae*, XI.iii.10).

16 'multiforme portentum' (Isidore, *Etymologiae*, XI.iii.10).

17 'conmixtione generis', i.e. creatures of mixed gender (Isidore, *Etymologiae*, XI.iii.11).

18 'in universo generum humano quaedam monstra sunt gentium' ('in the whole of humankind there are certain monstrous races'; Isidore, *Etymologiae*, XI.iii.12).

At first sight, Isidore's system of descriptive physical markers appears to be fairly comprehensive. A second glance, however, reveals that the catalogue is rather erratic, moving from the detailed to the cursory, and from aspects of the body to biological matters like gender and procreation. Such an arrangement leaves open a number of crucial points. Among other things, it is not entirely clear where to draw the dividing line between proper composites, or humans with animal parts. The lack of precision in Isidore's categories points to two central problems inherent in taxonomies: one of these lies in establishing unambiguous and distinctive, because mutually exclusive, categories based on differentiating properties; the other in dealing with cases of transgression that test the viability of the proposed classificatory system. Matters become even more complicated when monsters are concerned. As the monster is of an ever-shifting, indefinable nature, any systematic arrangement of the monstrous is a contradiction in terms. Thus, Isidore's guide to the monstrous testifies to the difficulty of classifying something that ultimately resists classification: Isidore here encounters essentially the same problem as the Lion in *Through the Looking-Glass*, who cannot find a proper label for Alice, because she upsets all categories known to him.[19] There is, however, a common denominator for the monstrosities Isidore mentions. Although he does not make it explicit, his idea of the monstrous is based on the concept of the normative body, and normative behavioural parameters. It does not come as a surprise that the discussion of the monsters is preceded by a treatise on normative human anatomy, which implicitly becomes the yardstick by which strange creatures can be measured. This notion is suggestive of the sentiments expressed in Fulwood's broadside treated above, where the monstrous is that which violates an imagined, perfect form. Moreover, this precept is also linked to anatomical treatises of the sixteenth and seventeenth centuries that displayed comparative anatomical illustrations aimed at foregrounding similarities and differences between correlating body parts.[20] Among others, Porta's *De humana physiognomia* (1616; 1668) features an array of such figures, presenting its readers with illustrations juxtaposing, for instance, a monkey's paw with the imbricated, hard nails of a man (see Figure 2). It is between these two adjacent anatomical details that the

19 The monster's breach of taxonomic boundaries opens a link to Mary Douglas's theory that the categorically interstitial, anomalous, and ambiguous is epistemologically unclean (see *Purity and Danger: An Analysis of the Concepts of Pollution and Taboo* (London: Routledge and Kegan Paul, 1966)).

20 See Hanafi, *The Monster in the Machine*, pp. 97–134.

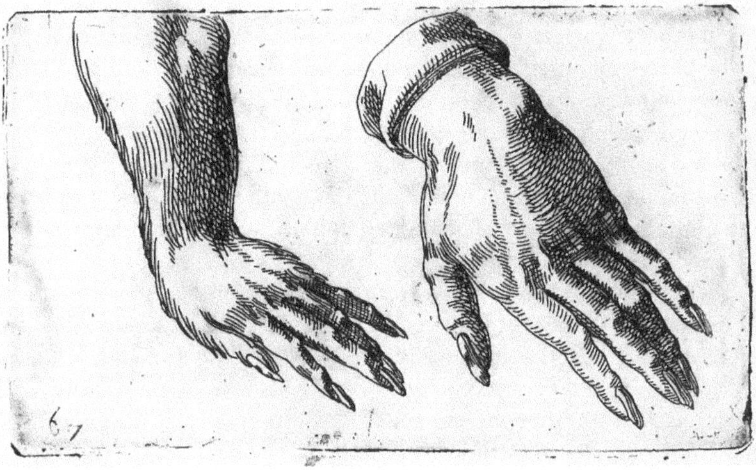

Figure 2 Monkey's paw conferred to human hand; from Gio. Battista della Porta, *De humana physiognomia*

spark of difference within sameness is struck. Likewise, Spenser's readers unwittingly read the monstrous against a received norm.

Hence, behind these taxonomic categories lurks a simple and pervasive concept: that of the monstrous signifier, the decisive physical attribute that distinguishes the normative from the deviant body. It may consist in size, as e.g. the giant's excessively large body; in an animal part attached to a human body, as e.g. the goat legs of the satyr; or even in a misallocated organ or body part, as e.g. the face on the chest of the Blemmyae, or the piglet's hind legs growing backwards on Fulwood's broadside. These examples underline that the monstrous signifier is never autonomous or independent, but exists only in relation to the normative body and its inherent idea of wholeness or perfection that Fulwood, Cooper and Spenser assume. The monstrous signifier is, however, also the attribute that gives the monster meaning, because it is the deviant attribute that turns the monster in what Cooper calls 'the thing that signifieth': the giant's oversize body into a figure of physical excess, the Satyr's goat legs into a cipher for lustfulness, the Blemmyae's misallocated face into the manifestation of the monstrosity dwelling on the edges of the world, or the piglet's mislocated hind feet into a sign of man's moral corruption. As will be seen in the following sections, the idea of the monstrous signifier lends itself easily to more intricate instances of monstrosity in Spenser's text, because *The Faerie Queene* generally conceives of the body as the manifestation of the soul. The monstrous signifier can hence also point beyond the downright physical, and become a 'spiritual' signifier, for, just as the lack of symmetry points to a monstrous body, so does vice point to a deviation from a behavioural norm. More abstractly, this illustrates a less tangible kind of monstrosity, which may consist in body movement or in a deviant spirit. Ultimately the monstrous may reveal itself textually when poetic language maps something 'other' on to the normative human body through similes, and metaphors, which function as substitutes for corporeal monstrous signifiers.

The following sections bring into relief the plenitude and diversity of monsters and the monstrous in *The Faerie Queene* by analysing them along systematic and anatomical parameters. Placing monsters within a necessarily artificial conceptual grid highlights how Spenser constructs the monstrous and how he integrates it into the unity of his poem. The first two categories treat monstrous animals (namely dragons and four-footed beasts),[21] while the third puts the spotlight on human–animal composites that cross the dividing line between monsters and humans. The fourth class brings into focus giants as another set of monstrosities. In a fifth chapter, the study inquires as to how the human characters in *The Faerie Queene* relate to or embody the monstrous. Finally, these chapters discuss automata as specimens of mechanical monstrosity, a category that was on the rise by the late sixteenth and early seventeenth centuries.

21 Like Topsell in *The History of Four-footed Beasts and Serpents*, I will file four-footed dragons under dragons, and not under four-footed beasts.

6

Monstrous animals (1): Dragons

Of all the monsters appearing in the margins of medieval manuscripts and in the text of many tales ancient and modern, the dragon has proved especially mesmerising.[1] Maintaining its position at the heart of the human imagination, the dragon defies any attempt at categorisation: it is a composite monstrosity to whose rump are sutured mutually exclusive monstrous signifiers, such as a powerful serpentine tail, wings and multiple heads; in size, the creature ranges from a small crocodile to a giant serpent.[2] The name itself derives from the Greek δράκων (Latin *draco*), which derives from the verb δέρκεσθαι, 'to see' or 'to look at', a circumstance that hints at the creature's proverbial vigilance. As the Greek verb is used in collocations like '*flashing* fire from his eyes' or describes light in the sense of to '*flash, gleam*, like the eye', it also refers to the dragon's fiery eyes.[3]

As the formidable, and eminently formable, monster of the cultural and artistic imagination (see Figure 3),[4] the dragon is a ubiquitous phenomenon that figures in virtually all literary and artistic genres, where it embodies all that is 'other' than human. Dragons, for instance, appear in scripture, most significantly in the Book of Revelation, where

1 A good general introduction with instructive illustrations figures is Sheila R. Canby, 'Dragons', in *Mythical Beasts*, ed. by Cherry, pp. 14–43; see also Winder McConnell, 'Mythos Drache', in *Dämonen, Monster, Fabelwesen*, ed. by Müller and Wunderlich, pp. 171–83, and Jonathan D. Evans, 'The Dragon', in *Mythical and Fabulous Creatures*, ed. by South, pp. 27–59.

2 This is also noted by McConnell, 'Mythos Drache', pp. 174–5; Riches, 'Encountering the Monstrous', p. 200; and Lecouteux, *Monstres*, II, 183.

3 For the full entry, see Liddell and Scott's Greek Lexicon, s.v. 'δέρκωμαι', p. 379. Etymological issues are discussed with varying degrees of depth by McConnell, who merely refers to the Latin term (see 'Mythos Drache', pp. 172–3), Marijane Osborne, who refers δράκων back to Indogermanic *drk* (see 'Die Monster in *Beowulf*, in *Dämonen, Monster, Fabelwesen*, ed. by Müller and Wunderlich, pp. 161–9 (p. 166)), and Evans, 'The Dragon', p. 29.

4 Evans rightly remarks on the 'free variation' possible in dragon morphology ('The Dragon', p. 28).

Figure 3 Variety of dragons; from Jan Jonston, *Historiae naturalis*

the red seven-headed dragon fights against Michael and the Angels.[5] As stock ingredients of romance literature, they make major appearances in the *Arthurian Vulgate*,[6] in Middle English romances like *Sir Degaré* and *Bevis of Hampton*,[7] and in Italian Renaissance romances like Boiardo's *Orlando Innamorato* and Ariosto's *Orlando Furioso*.[8] It is therefore hardly surprising that dragons also haunt the pages of *The Faerie Queene*. In fact, it can be argued that the entire first book is structured around dragons: Errour, a kind of 'hybrid dragonette', is slain by Redcrosse already in Canto i,[9] while Orgoglio's seven-headed dragon makes its gruesome appearance half-way through the book (I.vii–viii). It is only then that the most terrifying specimen appears at the climax of Book I, namely the Great Dragon that terrorises Eden (I.xi). After this upsurge of serpentine life forms, dragons almost necessarily recede into the background, making room for other monstrous creatures; yet, they are not extinct in Spenser's poem, for in Book V Arthur fights a lethal battle with Geryoneo's Sphinx-like dragon (V.x–xi). In addition to these major specimens, Spenser uses minor dragons as iconographic details,[10] as in the House of Pride episode,

5 See Revelation 12.3–17. Even Leviathan, the chaos monster from the Old Testament, is described as a dragon. In turn, the dragon in Revelation 12, 3–13 and 18 is generally referred back to Leviathan (see Wallace, 'Leviathan and the Beast in the Revelation', *Biblical Archaeologist* 11 (1948), pp. 61–8).

6 See, among others, the episode of Voltigern's tower in *The Story of Merlin*, 2, where a white dragon defeats a red dragon in battle, but dies three days later, and the Valley of No Return section in *Lancelot, Part III*, 94–5, where first the Duke of Clarence and then Lancelot encounter two dragons (see *Lancelot-Grail: The Old French Arthurian Vulgate and Post-Vulgate in Translation*, ed. by Norris J. Lacy, 5 vols, Garland Reference Library to the Humanities (New York and London: Garland, 1993–96), I, 183–5, as well as II, 306 and 308).

7 For *Sir Degaré*, see *The Middle English Breton Lays*, ed. by Anna Laskaya and Eve Salisbury (Kalamazoo, MI: Western Michigan University for TEAMS, 1995); for a medieval version of *Bevis of Hampton*, see *Four Romances of England*, ed. Ronald B. Herzman, Graham Drake and Eve Salisbury (Kalamazoo: Medieval Institute Publications, 1999). Andrew King discusses Spenser's indebtedness to *Bevis of Hampton* in astute and perceptive detail, mainly using the late sixteenth-century print *Syr Bevis of Hampton* (London: T. East, 1585; see *'The Faerie Queene' and Middle English Romance: The Matter of Just Memory*, Oxford English Monographs (Oxford: Clarendon Press, 2000), pp. 129–45).

8 In Boiardo's *Orlando Innamorato*, Orlando vanquishes a fire-breathing dragon in the first book (I.xxiv.42–52). In Ariosto's *Orlando Furioso*, Ruggiero rescues Angelica from a serpentine sea monster, and Orlando saves Olimpia from a land dragon (X.100–10, and XI.34–45). For the texts, see Matteo Maria Boiardo, *Opere*, ed. by Ferruccio Olivi, I classici italiani (Milan: Mursia, 1986), and Ariosto, *Orlando Furioso*, ed. by Lanfranco Caretti, La Letteratura Italiana: Storia e testi, 19 (Milan: Ricciardi, 1963).

9 See Belinda Humfrey, 'Dragons', in *Spenser Encyclopedia*, ed. by Hamilton, pp. 223–4. The monster Errour is discussed in the section on human–animal composites, below.

10 See *Spenser Encyclopedia*, 'Cupid's Dragon', Fig 1. C. S. Lewis interprets the dragon in the House of Busirane as the guardian of chastity (see *Spenser's Images of Life*, ed. by Alastair Fowler (Cambridge: Cambridge University Press, 1967), p. 50).

where '[a] dreadfull Dragon with an hideous trayne' lies under Lucifera's feet (I.iv.10.5), and in the House of Busirane, where a blinded dragon is placed beneath the God of Love on Cupid's altar (III.xi.48.6–9).

The Dragon in Eden

The overall methodology underlying Spenser's creation of monsters can be seen in his protracted description of the 'Dragon horrible and stearne' (I.i.3.9) over seven stanzas in Canto xi of Book I (I.xi.8–14).[11] This descriptive strategy emphasises the enormous magnitude of the beast, which literally spreads its entire body through the poem. The number seven is ambiguous, because it refers not only to the number of perfection but also to the Seven Deadly Sins, and explicitly links the Dragon to the seven-headed beast in the Apocalypse.[12] Although the size of the Spenserian Dragon can never be determined exactly,[13] Spenser is careful to give a systematic rendering of the monster by breaking down the description into individual segments. Every single stanza is devoted to one or two of the Dragon's anatomical aspects: after giving a general depiction (8), Spenser first zooms in on significant parts of its body, i.e. its scales (9), wings (10),[14] tail and stings (11) and claws (12); he then proceeds to the beast's head, describing its jaw (12), teeth and the smoke emitted from its mouth (13), as well as its eyes (14). In visualising the Dragon's physique, Spenser relies heavily on imagery, a circumstance that enhances the idea that the beast surpasses every other specimen of its species in size and ferocity. Its indestructible scales, which it rustles like an eagle when seeing prey (9.5–7), emphasise its proximity to the beasts of the air, but also render the monster less organic: since they are likened to a 'plated cote of steele' (9.2)[15] and since the noise they make is reminis-

11 Hamilton identifies the following scriptural monstrosities as possible influences: Leviathan in Job 40.25–41.26, the red dragon in Revelation 12, the harlot's beast in Revelation 17 and the beast in Daniel 7 (note to I.xi.9.2–4). The biblico-cultural connection between Leviathan and the serpent was traditional, as U. Cassuto points out, and is also inherent in the word Leviathan, which derives from the Semitic root *lwy*, 'to writhe' (see *A Commentary on the Book of Genesis. I: From Adam to Noah*, trans. by I. Abraham (Jerusalem: Magnes Press, 1961), pp. 140–2). See also the respective entries in *Variorum*, I, 166–75.

12 The dragon in the Apocalypse thus also links the dragon with Orgoglio's seven-headed beast; see the discussion, below.

13 See Watson, 'Forreine and Monstrous Beasts', p. 178.

14 For a historico-political interpretation of the wings, cf. Watson, 'Spenser's Flying Dragon'.

15 The Dragon 'all with brasen scales was armd, / Like plated cote of steele' (I.xi.9.1–2). King rightly observes that Spenser's description recalls *Syr Bevis*, where the dragon's scales are 'harder … then any brasse' (East, f. 121.v.26, quoted in *Middle English Romance*, p. 134).

cent of 'the clashing of an Armor bright' (9.8), the Dragon is turned into a male warrior who fuses with his iron armour.[16] Such a hunt for imagery – there are no fewer than three similes in a single stanza – is evidence for the difficulty of naming the true nature of the Dragon, or realising it as a unified being. It therefore does not come as a surprise that Spenser introduces a different lexical set when he likens the wings and their ribs to sails and 'mayne-yardes' (10.5), and then extends the simile by associating the Dragon's body with a naval vessel.[17]

Spenser changes gear again when describing the creature's mouth, for he now resorts to medieval iconography when conceiving of the monster's jaws, set with three sets of iron teeth with which it destroys its victims, as 'the griesly mouth of hell' and as a 'darke abysse' (12.8–9).[18] Spenser elaborates on this image further when referring to the 'smoke and sulphure' that is emitted from the 'stinking gorge' (13.7–8) of its maw.[19] This calls to mind the 'tristo fiato', the 'evil smell' that numbs Dante's and Virgil's senses in the *Inferno*, XI.12,[20] and additionally points to the stench with which hell mouth was traditionally associated.[21] In medieval and Renaissance art, the mouth of hell was frequently depicted as a monstrous, disembodied orifice devouring the souls of the sinful, as for instance in Bruegel's *The Last Judgement*, the final engraving in the

16 Paul J. Alpers remarks that the Dragon is compared to 'something heroic' (*The Poetry of 'The Faerie Queene'* (Princeton: Princeton University Press, 1967), p. 363).

17 In Ariosto's *Orlando Furioso*, the fight between Rinaldo and Gradasso is interrupted when Baiardo is attacked by a bat-like bird whose wings are also likened to sails (see *Orlando Furioso*, XXXIII.84.8; the entire episode covers stanzas 84–8). The comparison also refers the Dragon to Satan in Dante's *Inferno*, because the wings beneath Satan's three heads are described as sails (XXXIV.46–8).

18 The references to the primeval abyss and the Dragon's maw evoke associations of the Leviathan's mouth (cf. also the Dragon's 'darksom hollow maw' in I.xi.53.8). That the Leviathan is a sea-creature representing the forces of chaos, as Cassuto argues, is therefore also pertinent to the interpretation of Spenser's Dragon (see *Commentary*, pp. 140–2). By referring explicitly to a dragon and implicitly to a whale, Spenser combines two scriptural devourer traditions that informed the idea of hell mouth; for these traditions, see Gary D. Schmidt, *The Iconography of the Mouth of Hell: Eighth Century Britain to the Fifteenth Century* (London: Associated University Presses, 1995), pp. 35–60.

19 Spenser picks up this detail again in V.xi.32 (the death of Geryoneo's monster).

20 See Dante Alighieri, *The Divine Comedy of Dante Alighieri. Volume 1: Inferno*, ed. and trans. by Robert M. Durling; introduction and notes by Ronald M. Martinez and Robert M. Durling (New York and Oxford: Oxford University Press, 1996).

21 See Thomas H. Seiler, 'Filth and Stench as Aspects of the Iconography of Hell', in *The Iconography of Hell*, ed. by Clifford Davidson and Thomas H. Seiler, Early Drama, Art, and Music Monograph Series, 17 (Kalamazoo: Medieval Institute Publications, Western Michigan University, 1992), pp. 132–40. Cf. also the stench of the harpies in Virgil, *Aeneid*, III.228. See *Virgil*, trans. by H. Rushton Fairclough, revised by G. P. Goold, new and rev. edn, 2 vols, Loeb Classical Library (Cambridge, MA: Harvard University Press, 2000).

Seven Deadly Sins series, which depicts hell as the gigantic mouth of a whale (see Figure 4).[22] Spenser thus deploys a monstrous maw to present a traditionally monstrous locus.[23] He enhances this link when he refers to the Dragon's 'infernall fournace' (44.2), whose smoke and brimstone darken the heavens during the long battle between the two contestants. By combining the idea of hell mouth with the concept of the dragon as a fire-breather,[24] Spenser stresses the beast's size and satanic dimension.[25] Significantly, the Dragon's wide mouth and sharp teeth differ from the bestiary specimens,[26] while such attributes are characteristic of the dragons in romances.[27]

The terrifying nature of the Dragon is also accentuated by the beast's glaring eyes, an instance of extramissive sight that directly refers to the etymology of the word *dragon*, the Greek verb δέρκεσθαι, which means

22 Klein notes that 'hell-head itself looms like a monstrous Leviathan or whale' (H. Arthur Klein, *The Graphic Worlds of Pieter Bruegel the Elder* (Toronto: Dover, 1963), p. 287).

23 Among others, the margin of the Hereford Map and the Winchester Psalter depict hell mouth as a dragon's maw. On the mouth of hell as a monstrous orifice, see Williams, *Deformed Discourse*, pp. 143–5; the passage also offers an illustration from the Winchester Psalter (BL, Cotton MS Nero C.IV, fol. 39r). For a detailed description and interpretation of the Psalter, see Aleks Pluskowski, 'Apocalyptic Monsters: Animal Inspirations for the Iconography of Medieval North European Devourers', in *The Monstrous Middle Ages*, ed. by Bildhauer and Mills, pp. 155–76. On hell mouth, see also Malcolm Andrew, '*Patience*: The *Munster Dor*', *English Language Notes* 14 (1977), 164–7, and Ernst Guldon, 'Das Monster-Portal am Palazzo Zuccari in Rom', *Zeitschrift für Kunstgeschichte* 32 (1969), 229–61, and Schmidt, *The Iconography of the Mouth of Hell*.

24 *Batman vppon Bartholome*, when explaining that the dragon has a high concentration of venom in his tongue and gall, cites Pliny's theory that it is the heat of the poison in the dragon's tongue that sets the air on fire (in Bartholomaeus Anglicus, *Batman vppon Bartholome, his Booke De proprietatibus rerum* (London: Thomas East, 1582), XVIII.38).

25 Watson calls the Dragon 'Hell on earth, Everyman's ultimate enemy' ('Forreine and Monstrous Beasts', p. 178). The interpretation of the dragon as a figuration of the Devil or Satan originates from St Michael's combat with the dragon in Revelation 12.7–9; from there it made its way into many a saint's legend (Riches, 'Encountering the Monstrous', p. 211).

26 Solinus in his *Collectanae*, for example, refers to their 'ora parva' ('small mouths') and 'artae fistulae' ('narrow gullets'); the same notion can be found in the *Ashmole Bestiary*. See Julius Solinus Caius, *C. J. Solini Collectanea Rerum Memorabilium*, revised by Theodor Mommsen (Berolini: Weidmann, 1864), p. 132 (30. 15); and *Bestiarium: Die Texte der Handschrift MS. Ashmole 1511 der Bodleian Library Oxford in lateinischer und deutscher Sprache*, ed. by Franz Unterkircher, Codices Selecti, 76 (Graz: Akademische Druck- und Verlags-Anstalt, 1986), pp. 172–5, henceforth *Ashmole Bestiary*; for an early modern perspective, see Topsell, *Historie*, III, 701–16.

27 See, e.g., *Guy of Warwick*, 3859–64, and *Sir Degaré*, 347–54; references are to *The Romance of Guy of Warwick*, ed. from the Paper MS. Ff. 2.38 in University Library by Julius Zupitza, EETS, ES, 25/26 (London: Trübner, 1875), and *The Middle English Breton Lays*, ed. by Anna Laskaya and Eve Salisbury (Kalamazoo: Western Michigan University for TEAMS, 1995). Spenser also draws heavily on the description of the dragon and the dragon fight in *Bevis of Hampton*, Episode 4; see King, *Middle English Romance*, pp. 129–45.

Figure 4 Pieter Bruegel, *The Last Judgement*

'to see, to look at', but is also used to describe glowing eyes. Since the Dragon's eyes are likened to 'shining shieldes' and 'broad Beacons' set in a 'hollow glade' (14.1, 3 and 8), Spenser once again combines natural imagery (glade) with artificial elements (beacon) to emphasise the beast's contradictory nature.

The high density of disparate imagery marks the Dragon as a variation on the traditional motif of the dragon as compound animal.[28] As legendary and unknown creatures of vast proportions, dragons transcend human knowledge and understanding, and cannot be contained in simple, direct descriptions; whence arises the necessity to describe the unknown and indescribable by resorting to familiar concepts, a strategy that results in a creature made of inchoate referents that defy the notion of physical unity. Spenser's specimen is a sophisticated literary emulation of this topos, a monster at once animal, quasi-rational creature and animated machine. Such breaking of classification is consonant with the

28 For the notion of the dragon as a compound monster, see Stith Thompson, *Motif-Index of Folk-Literature. A Classification of Narrative Elements in Folktales, Ballads, Myths, Fables, Mediaeval Romances, Exempla, Fabliaux, Jest-Books, and Local Legends*, 6 vols, FF Communications, 106 (Helsinki: Suomalainen Tiedeakatemia, 1932), I, 274–5, motif B.11.2.1 ('*Dragon as compound animal*').

poet's attempts to come to terms with the beast's length. With a 'huge long tayle' that is 'wownd vp in hundred foldes' (11.1) and almost three furlongs long, the beast transcends what one can actually describe, let alone visualise:[29] paradoxically, measuring the beast emphasises its immeasurableness.[30]

There is, however, more to this than size. By comparing its body and shadow to a mountain, Spenser does not only associate the Dragon with formless magnitude, but also identifies it as a creature of the earth, a chthonic monster embodying a larger-than-life animality.[31] The image of the eagle additionally establishes its connection with the air, while the ship simile and the fish-like scales link the beast with the sea. Thus associated with mutually exclusive habitats, the Dragon upsets the traditional division between the animals of water, earth and air and in itself combines properties of all these classes.[32] Since the Dragon additionally breathes fire, it could also be argued that it embodies all four elements. While this finding harks back to the general notion that all creatures, including humans, are made up of the four elements, it also points to the beast's difference from ordinary animals. The Dragon is not a harmonious combination of the elements; rather, its massive body contains the four elements at their most chaotic, destructive and unruly, so that the monster

29 The whole stanza enhances the gargantuan proportion of the Dragon's tail, winding down from line to line (I.xi.11): 'His huge long tayle wownd vp in hundred foldes, / Does ouerspred his long bras-scaly back, / Whose wreathed boughtes when euer he vnfoldes, / And thick entangled knots adown does slacke / Bespotted as with shieldes of red and blacke, / It sweepeth all the land behind him farre, / And of three furlongs does but litle lacke; / And at the point two stinges in-fixed arre, / Both deadly sharp, that sharpest steele exceeden farr.' Spenser here is influenced by the traditional notion that the dragon's power lies in its tail, which derives from Isidore, *Etymologiae*, XII.2.4 ('vim … in cauda habet').

30 Cf. Bordman for traditional attempts at measuring a dragon's limbs (motif B11.2.4.4 ('Dragon's paw a "span" long'; ref. to *Arthur and Merlin*, 1491); motif *B11.2.8.03 ('Dragon's tail 5 fathoms long'; ref. to *King Alisaunder*, 547); motif *B11.2.8.3.1 ('Dragon's tail 7 yards long'; ref. to *Torrent of Portyngale*, 544)); Gerald Martin Bordman, *Motif-Index of the English Metrical Romances*, FF Communications, 190 (Vol. 79, 2) (Helsinki: Suomalainen Tiedeakatemia, 1963), p. 19.

31 In I.xi.4.5–6 the Dragon lies on 'the sunny side, / Of a great hill, himselfe like a great hill', and in 8. 5 it makes a shadow '[a]s mountaine doth the valley ouercaste'. The description in xi.4.5–6 resembles Ovid's depiction of the giant Python slain by Apollo in *Metamorphoses*, I.438–40; see Ovid, *Metamorphoses*, ed. and trans. by Frank Justus Miller, 2 vols, Loeb Classical Library (Cambridge, MA: Harvard University Press; London, Heinemann, 1921; repr. 1961). King notices that the first appearance of the Great Dragon in I.xi.4 is closely modelled on the dragon's appearance in *Syr Bevis* (East, f. 121.v.11–13, 22–5), particularly because 'the thundering roar[,] … the sighting of the beast, the dragon's exposure to the sun, and its prodigious size all occur in the same order' (*Middle English Romance*, pp. 135–6).

32 See Williams, *Deformed Discourse*, pp. 177–8.

images forth universal disorder.[33] Moreover, the Dragon's combining hell (*qua* the image of hell mouth) with heaven (*qua* wings) stresses that the monster is a powerful combination of opposites.[34] Hence, Spenser's description of the dragon's body, which underlines the monster's disproportion and formlessness through the use of inchoate imagery and the rhetoric of the immeasurable, undercuts the poet's attempt at confining the creature in seven neatly organised stanzas: this combination between rhetorical form and the Dragon's vast, indescribable and transgressive body makes the monster a paradox.[35]

The Dragon's size and disparate imagery also emphasise the discontinuity with the dragon in the woodcut placed between Books I and II of the Ponsonby editions: while the woodcut harks back to the dragon's – and St George's – iconographic tradition, Spenser sutures a large number of sources and images into a gigantic creature that ultimately dwarfs its conceptual ancestors. The discord struck between the two specimens therefore brings into sharp relief the inventiveness with which Spenser revised and elaborated on traditional notions of the dragon in *The Faerie Queene*.

Orgoglio's beast

Whereas Spenser's Great Dragon is both the scourge of Eden and apocalyptic monster, Orgoglio's beast predominantly images forth the beast of the Apocalypse,[36] since it is a dragon with seven heads,[37] which later becomes the mount of evil Duessa, who represents the Whore of Babylon

33 See Williams, *Deformed Discourse*, p. 202. Williams's account of the monstrous is generally based on the notion of the four elements (see *Deformed Discourse*, pp. 177–215, especially pp. 177–9).

34 This interpretation is congruent with Williams's theoretical discussion of dragons (see *Deformed Discourse*, pp. 202–7). For full analyses of the dragon fight, see Kaske, 'The Dragon's Spark and Sting', Isabel G. MacCaffrey, *Spenser's Allegory: The Anatomy of Imagination* (Princeton: Princeton University Press, 1976), pp. 188–207, and Michael Leslie, *Spenser's 'Fierce Warres and Faithfull Loves': Martial and Chivalric Symbolism in 'The Faerie Queene'* (Woodbridge: Brewer, 1983), pp. 105–18.

35 Cf., e.g., I.xi.8.7 and 9, where Spenser describes the Dragon's body as 'monstrous, horrible, and vaste … swoln with wrath, and poyson, and with bloody gore'.

36 See I.vii.16.6–18.

37 This is in keeping with medieval iconography, since dragons were sometimes depicted with seven heads. Whereas Aptekar notes that seven heads frequently stand for the Seven Deadly Sins, the *Fasciculus Morum* more specifically associates them with the seven heads of *avaritia*; see Jane Aptekar, *Icons of Justice: Iconography and Thematic Imagery in Book V of 'The Faerie Queene'* (New York: Columbia University Press, 1969), p. 208, and *Fasciculus Morum: A Fourteenth-Century Preacher's Handbook*, ed. by Siegfried Wenzel (University Park and London: Pennsylvania State University Press, 1989), pp. 372–3.

Figure 5 Albrecht Dürer, *The Whore of Babylon*

(see Figure 5).[38] Hence, Orgoglio's many-headed monster is the permutation of a scriptural deformity whose monstrosity is constituted by the multiplicity of body parts.[39] It exhibits the same anatomical attributes as the Dragon in Eden: its 'yron brest' (I.vii.17.8) is reminiscent of the Dragon's scales, its 'back of scaly bras' (17. 8) directly connecting with the 'bras-scaly back' in I.xi.11.2.[40] Orgoglio's dragon also shares the Dragon's filthy mixture of blood, poison and gore.[41]

The tail of the monster is of enormous, hyperbolic proportions, since it reaches the 'hous of heuenly gods' (I.vii.18.2), and is able to cast down the stars from the firmament as if they were nothing.[42] The beast thus threatens God's cosmological order like the red dragon in the Apocalypse. This aspect of the dragon's monstrosity also suggests that the creature perverts the Renaissance image of Dame Nature as God's servant, whose head touches the heavens and stars:[43] as the embodiment of everything that is *in naturam*, i.e. against nature, Orgoglio's dragon figures as the infernal instrument threatening heaven, God's creation and divine order. Accordingly, size and transgression define the monstrosity of Orgoglio's beast just as much as they determine the Dragon's unnaturalness in Canto xi. Even more than Redcrosse's foe, Orgoglio's monster seems impossible to visualise, having a tail of 'wondrous length' (18.1), which it puts to good use in combat (viii.17.3).[44] As the creature's tail seems to exceed the bulk of its body and heads, such lack of symmetry enhances its deformity.[45]

There is a further significant difference: Orgoglio's beast is likened to a popular mythological creature, namely the Lernean Hydra that Hercules vanquished in his second labour.[46] Yet, by claiming that this dragon

38 John E. Hankins makes reference to Isaiah 47 (see *Source and Meaning*, p. 101). On Duessa, see Daryl J. Gless, *Interpretation and Theology in Spenser* (Cambridge: Cambridge University Press, 1994), pp. 124–5, who also treats the anti-Catholic satire in the episode critically.

39 Cf. Revelation, 13.1. This scriptural link is underlined by the reference to 'her purple beast' in I.viii.13.3.

40 See Hamilton, note to I.vii.17.8.

41 Cf. I.vii.17.9 with I.xi.14.1 (see Hamilton, note to I.vii.17.9). As the monster's blood-defiled eyes 'shine as glas' (17.9), its physical attributes hark back to the etymology of the dragon (δέρκεσθαι), like the Dragon's eyes at I.xi.14.

42 Cf. Revelation 13.13.

43 See *Integrae Naturae Speculum Artisque imago* in *The Spenser Encyclopedia*, Nature and Art, Fig. 1. Cf. also Spenser's introducing Nature in the 'Mutabilitie Cantos' as '(great goddesse) great Dame *Nature*', who is 'far greater and more tall of stature / Then any of the gods or Powers on hie' (VII.vii.5.1, 3–4).

44 This is another item that underlines the connection between Orgoglio's monster and the Great Dragon.

45 See also I.viii.16.5, where the poet calls the beast a 'misformed shape'.

46 Henry Gibbons Lotspeich cites Ovid, *Metamorphoses*, IX.68–74, and Virgil, *Aeneid*,

surpasses the legendary serpent in hideousness, Spenser identifies classical monsters as inferior prefigurations of allegorico-Christian beasts.[47] The simile is also pertinent to the beast's perversion of ordered nature, for the comparison combines two aspects that constitute the dragon's deformity: like the Hydra it is 'fruitfull-headed' (I.viii.20.1) and, like the mythological monster, it was reared in amphibious surroundings crossing the threshold between earth and water.[48] However, the dragon's ontology is not limited to these two elements: the monster's shining eyes and 'heades like flaming brandes' (12.6) emphasise its fiery nature, while the tail's reaching the sky associates the beast with the air. Again, Spenser sees the beast's monstrosity in a contaminated combination of the four elements, so the creature contains within its body the highest form of disorder. The monster's size and chaos additionally identify it as an infernal agent that, after abiding in the filth of a fen and 'in darksom den' (I.vii.16.9), poses a universal threat to the heavens.

Geryoneo's dragon

Almost four books pass before another great dragon appears in *The Faerie Queene*: Geryoneo's beast. In Book V, Arthur is asked by Mercilla to rescue Belge and her offspring from the clutches of Geryoneo, an evil, triple-bodied tyrant, who forces her to sacrifice her children and people to a 'dreadfull Monster' (V.x.13.7), which completely devours their carcasses, both 'flesh and bone' (29.7).[49] The female dragon with the face of a maiden dwells in a temple under an edifice of Geryoneo's legendary father Geryon, a triple-bodied giant who first appeared in Hesiod's *Theogony*.[50] The

VIII.300, and VI.576–7, in his good introduction to Spenser's use of the Hydra in *Classical Mythology in the Poetry of Edmund Spenser* (Princeton: Princeton University Press, 1932; repr. New York: Gordian Press, 1965), p. 71.

47 Gless attributes the dragon's supreme ugliness to its seven heads, which represent 'sin's infinite variety' (*Interpretation and Theology*, p. 126).

48 Whereas the Hydra was fostered in '*Lerna* lake' (I.vii.17. 3), Orgoglio's monster was bred 'in filthy fen' (I.vii.16.8). – On Spenser's view of 'amphibians', see Watson, 'Forreine and Monstrous Beasts', p. 173, and 'Spenser's Submarine Creation', p. 122.

49 Geryoneo and his monster are first mentioned in V.x.6–13; Arthur's encounter with the dragon covers stanzas xi.21–32.

50 See *Theogony*, 287–94 and 979–83, where Hesiod draws Geryon's lineage from Chryasor and Kallirhoe (for the text, see *Hesiod*, ed. and trans. by Glenn W. Most, new and rev. edn, 2 vols, Loeb Classical Library (London: Heinemann, 1936; repr. 1964)). Spenser remarks that Geryoneo has set up 'an Idole of his owne, / The image of his monstrous parent *Geryone*' (V.x.13.8–9), and recounts that Geryon's cowherd Eurytion owned a bicephalic dog called Orthrus, who was likewise sired by Typhon on Echidna. As Chryasor was begot on Medusa, who was the offspring of Typhon and Echidna, Geryon is in fact obliquely related to Orthrus. Arthur's vanquishing Geryon's triple-bodied son, as well

dragon's name and physique also suggest Dante's Gerïon, the serpentine image of Fraud on whose back Dante and Virgil descend to the eighth circle of hell.[51] Dante's transferring the giant's name to a dragon, and Spenser's creation of a monster serving Geryoneo, seem to be suggested by Natale Conti's remark that Geryon owned a dragon born of the two notorious monstrous and dragon-like parents, Typhon and Echidna.[52]

Although Geryoneo's monster harks back to the Dragon of Eden in some important particulars and recalls the beast of the Whore of Babylon, which Orgoglio's dragon was modelled on,[53] this terrifying creature is explicitly a composite deformity. Coming alive to defend the idol under which it hides,[54] it exceeds any other monstrosity seen by those who lived to tell.[55] What sets this dragon apart is its capacity for blasphemous speech,[56] which it shares with another major monster in the poem, the Blatant Beast.[57] But although speech is the traditional marker of an animal or monster trespassing into the human realm, Spenser points to a more thoroughgoing intersection between human speech and monstrous physique: as the dragon does 'bray [her blasphemous words] / Out of her poysnous entrails' (20.8–9), the narrator does not only emphasise the voice's monstrous quality ('bray').[58] He also relocates the source of the she-dragon's language to her noxious viscera rather than to her head, the seat of the rational faculty, thereby emphasising the monster's irra-

as his defeating the tyrant's three knights suggest the feats of Hercules. On Herculean patterns in *The Faerie Queene*, see Patrick J. Cook, *Milton, Spenser, and the Epic Tradition* (Aldershot and Brookfield: Scolar, 1996), pp. 100–14.

51 Dante names the beast 'quella sozza imagine di froda' ('that filthy image of Fraud') in *Inferno*, XVII.7. Aptekar's discussion of Geryoneo's dragon is entirely based on the concept of guile and its pictorial renderings, especially Ripa's Fraude in the *Iconologia* (see *Icons of Justice*, pp. 142–7).

52 See Conti, *Mythologiae*, VI.1 (p. 205.a.47–8); noted in Lotspeich, *Classical Mythology*, p. 63, and Evans, 'The Dragon', p. 33.

53 Kenneth Borris argues for continuity between Spenser's monster and the dragon in Revelation 17.3–8 (see *Spenser's Poetics of Prophecy in 'The Faerie Queene' V* (Victoria: English Literary Studies, 1990), p. 12).

54 Geryoneo's dragon therefore suggests the dragon in the House of Pride (I.iv.10.4–5).

55 Belge's underlining the baseness and fierceness of the dragon, '[w]hose vgly shape none euer saw, nor kend, / That euer scap'd' (V.xi.20.5–6), accentuates Arthur's chivalric courage and 'great desire' (21.2) to battle the creature.

56 See V.xi.20.6–9: 'for of a man they say / It has the voice, that speaches forth doth send, / Euen blasphemous words, which she doth bray / Out of her poysnous entrails, fraught with dire decay.'

57 See VI.xii.27–8. This monster is discussed in the section on four-footed beasts, below.

58 The verb *to bray* is a defining feature of Geryoneo's dragon, as it is used three times for the monster (V.xi.20.9, 26.2, and 28.1), and once for its owner (V.xi.8.2). The verb occurs mostly with monsters, namely Errour (I.i.17.5), Corflambo (IV.viii.62.2), Orgoglio (I.viii.11.3), Grantorto (V.xii.20.9) and the Blatant Beast (V.xii.41.7).

tionality. The monster's violation is inherent in the Greek word λόγος itself, which means both reason and speech.[59] Since, in the context of the textual monster, language is disconnected from reason, speech transgresses linguistic boundaries to become a part of the monster's body.

Just like her language, the monster's body also violates creational boundaries. After Arthur has struck the idol three times – an action that emphasises the creature's magic quality[60] – it rises from beneath the altar to fill the church, thus threatening to reach beyond its confining space like the monsters in medieval manuscripts. Although she has the face of a maiden to hide her terrifying features and to beguile her victims,[61] her body is a disfeatured combination of animal parts:

> Thereto [i.e. her face] the body of a dog she had,
> Full of fell rauin and fierce greedinesse;
> A Lions clawes, with powre and rigour clad,
> To rend and teare, what so she can oppresse;
> A Dragons taile, whose sting without redresse
> Full deadly wounds, where so it is empight;
> And Eagles wings, for scope and speedinesse,
> That nothing may escape her reaching might,
> Whereto she euer list to make her hardy flight.
>
> (V.xi.24)

Spenser's catalogue of attributes is more than a mere enumeration of body parts, as he meticulously anatomises, and explains the significance of the she-monster's canine torso, leonine claws,[62] dragon's tail and sting,

59 See the entry on λόγος in Liddell and Scott, *Greek Lexicon*, pp. 1057–9. Cicero underscores this proximity by the Latin word-play on *ratio* and *oratio* in *De officiis*, I.16 (cf. also Quintillian, *Institutio oratoria*, 2.16.11–15). For the texts, see Cicero, *De officiis*, trans. Walter Miller, Loeb Classical Library (Cambridge, MA: Harvard University Press; London: Heinemann, 1913; repr. 1961), and Quintillian, *Institutio oratoria*, ed. and trans. by H. E. Butler, 4 vols, Loeb Classical Library (London: Heinemann; Cambridge, MA: Harvard University Press, 1920–21; repr. 1960), I. See S. K. Heninger, Jr, *Sidney and Spenser: The Poet as Maker* (University Park, London: Pennsylvania State University Press, 1989), pp. 123–4, and pp. 534–7.

60 It also marks a notable reappearance of the number three that informs much of Cantos x and xi.

61 'For of a Mayd she had the outward face, / To hide the horrour, which did lurke behinde, / The better to beguile, whom she so fond did finde' (V.xi.23.7–9). The image calls to mind representations of the maiden-faced satanic serpent in medieval and early modern art; see N. C. Flores, '"Effigies amicitiae ... veritas inimicitiae": Antifeminism in the Iconography of the Woman-Headed Serpent in Medieval and Renaissance Art and Literature', in *Animals in the Middle Ages: A Book of Essays*, ed. by N. C. Flores (New York: Garland, 1996), pp. 167–95.

62 The dragon in *Sir Degaré*, 35, also sports lion's feet. In *The Faerie Queene*, the monster's physical attributes also suggest Duessa, and Errour (cf. Aptekar, *Icons of Justice*, pp. 142–3).

and eagle's wings.[63] Since Spenser resorts to a rhetorical description-*cum*-explication to bring the monster and its defining monstrous signifiers in full view, the extended syntactical parallelism contains the monster in tight structures, and enacts his creation of the monster's body on the stylistic level of the text as well. As Spenser's 'formalist' stance adds shape to the deformed monster, Geryoneo's dragon is as much a paradoxical product as the Dragon slain by Redcrosse.[64]

Geryoneo's beast is also a combination of scriptural and mythological sources. Spenser bases the monster's physique on the locusts in the Book of Revelation, which have the faces of men, wings and scorpion-like tails with stings,[65] as well as on Natale Conti's portmanteau description of the Sphinx, which Conti assigns the head and hands of a maiden, the body of a dog, the voice of a human, the tail of a dragon, the nails of a lion and the wings of a bird.[66] Spenser makes the mythological link explicit when likening Geryoneo's dragon to the Sphinx:

> Much like in foulnesse and deformity
> Vnto that Monster, whom the Theban Knight,
> The father of that fatall progeny,
> Made kill her selfe for very hearts despight,
> That he had red her Riddle, which no wight
> Could euer loose, but suffred deadly doole.
> So also did this Monster vse like slight
> To many a one, which came vnto her schoole,
> Whom she did put to death, deceiued like a foole.
>
> (V.xi.25)

The incompatible physical features of the Sphinx correspond to those of Geryoneo's monster in such a way that they form the basic design, or pattern on which Spenser bases his own, physically horrific creation. The comparison of Spenser's monster to the Sphinx is notable in another respect. Not only does it provide an important mythic backdrop

63 The tail and sting of Geryoneo's beast recall those of the Dragon in I.xi. Geryoneo's dragon shares some of its physical attributes with Dante's Gerïon, namely a human face, paws, and a tail with a poisonous, forked sting like that of a scorpion; moreover, the dragon's serpentine tail suggests Gerïon's serpentine body. For the full description, see *Inferno*, XVII.10–27.

64 Neither Gerïon in Dante, *Inferno*, XVI–XVII, nor the Sphinx in Boiardo, *Orlando Innamorato*, I.v.69–75, is created along such formalistic parameters.

65 See Revelation, 9.7–10. The combination of a beguiling face and a poisonous sting recalls Bartholomaeus Anglicus's etymological explanation of the word *scorpion*, which derives from *scorpius*, 'sting', and *poio*, 'to feign' (see *Batman vppon Bartholome*, XVIII, 98).

66 See Natale Conti (Natalis Comes), *Mythologiae* (Venice: n. pub., 1568), IX.18 (p. 286.b.18–19). Cooper uses the same definition of the Sphinx in his *Thesaurus*.

against which one can read Spenser's dragon, but, more importantly, it offers insight into the nature of the monstrous in general, and into the monsters of *The Faerie Queene* in particular. The key word in the stanza quoted above, significantly capitalised, is the term 'Riddle'. Positioned in the exact middle of the stanza, it calls to mind the Sphinx's emblematic and hieroglyphic traditions.[67] This term is central, because the simile does more than simply enhance the physical hideousness of Geryoneo's dragon: it draws particular attention to the use of puzzling language. But while the Sphinx speaks a riddle that should be deciphered verbally through logical thinking (Spenser uses the term 'loose'), the language used by Geryoneo's dragon is, as has already been shown, of a more thoroughgoing monstrosity, because the monster speaks 'from her entrails', uttering riddles in an illogical language that are, as it were, her bodily effluvia.[68] Through such monstrous rhetoric, Spenser links her blasphemies and false riddles to her body, a connection which renders her entire corporeality as inexplicable to the reader as her verbal quibbles to Arthur. Geryoneo's dragon is hence a fully realised verbal deformity whose riddles, like the Sphinx's, can only confuse and deceive; but unlike the Sphinx's riddle, which was solved by Oedipus, the dragon's riddles directly emanate from her body, which makes them irrational, impenetrable and physically abject. In that respect, the dragon transcends the Sphinx in her monstrosity.

The notion of reading the riddle thus thematises the monstrous sign and the effect it has on the readers of *The Faerie Queene*, since it marks the interpretation of monsters as one of their most substantial tasks. It also has its bearing on the knights encountering them. While Oedipus was allegedly able to overcome the Sphinx through exercising his superior intellect, and hence figures as a mythic reader of monsters and the puzzles they pose,[69] romance knights, Spenser's heroes included, solve the puzzle posed by monsters either by literally taking them apart[70] or by wounding their bodies. Arthur hence does not only sever the monster's claws and tail to struggle free from Geryeoneo's dragon;[71] in order to

67 On the Sphinx, see Frank A. Scafella, 'The Sphinx', in *Mythical and Fabulous Creatures*, ed. by South, pp. 179–91 (pp. 182–3).

68 Cf. Errour spewing out 'written language' in the form of books (I.i.20); the passage is discussed in the section on human-animal composites, below.

69 Boiardo parodies the myth of the Sphinx in *Orlando Innamorato*, I.v.69–75, where Orlando slays the monster brutally rather than answering its question. It seems that Spenser sees the more serious implications of such behaviour, and thus makes Boiardo's joke relevant for his poem.

70 Spenser's giants are also dismembered in battle; see Chapter 9, below.

71 See V.xi.27 and 29.

annihilate the unsolvable riddle she poses, he also destroys the seat of her language by piercing her 'wombe' (31.2), causing her entrails to spill out.[72] The linguistic dimension of the monster battle makes Geryoneo's serpentine dragon more than a mere 'emblem of fraud', as Jane Aptekar would have it.[73] This monster is the very embodiment of irrational monstrous language, which perverts meaning and challenges interpretation.

The dragon fights

Defeat becomes any dragon's ultimate fate. Like its romance precursors, Geryoneo's dragon thus meets its fate at the hands of an outstanding hero, whose helmet is crested with an awe-inspiring couchant dragon,[74] while the dragons of Book I are likewise destined to be vanquished by the prowess of Redcrosse and Arthur. Or are they? The end Orgoglio's monster meets at the hand of Arthur remains strangely uncertain. Although Arthur splits one of the creature's heads in twain (I.viii.16),[75] as well as dazing its sense and making it blind with his magic shield (20), the formulation that the monster only '*seemd* himselfe as conquered to yield' (20.5; emphasis added) casts serious doubt on Arthur's success.

72 As with other monsters, Spenser describes her lower body as a stinking 'infernall sinke', filled with 'vgly filth' and 'poyson' that numb the senses (V.xi.31.6–8). He enhances the connection between source and phenomenon by rhyming 'sinke' with 'stinke'.

73 Aptekar, *Icons of Justice*, p. 144.

74 The dragon helmet not only marks Arthur as a potent leader, but also as a dragon slayer: 'His haughtie Helmet, horrid all with gold, / Both glorious brightnesse, and great terrour bredd; / For all the crest a Dragon did enfold / With greedie pawes, and ouer all did spredd / His golden winges: his dreadfull hideous hedd / Close couched on the beuer, seemd to throw / From flaming mouth bright sparkles fiery redd, / That suddeine horrour to faint harts did show; / And scaly tayle was stretcht adowne his back full low' (I.vii.31). Arthur's helmet, which may also serve an apotropaic function, is inspired by Turnus's helmet in *Aeneid*, VII.785–88, and the Soldan's helmet in *Gerusalemme Liberata*, I.25 Tasso, *Poesie*, ed. by Francesco Flora, La Letteratura Italiana: Storia e testi, 22 (Milan: Ricciardi, 1952). Kaske discusses the dragon on Arthur's helmet as the only instance of a Spenserian dragon used *in bono*, paying particular attention to Arthur's lineage and destiny (see Kaske, *Spenser and Biblical Poetics*, pp. 37–8; she also mentions Psalms 148.7, and Isaiah 43.20 as the only two examples of 'good' biblical dragons). In the *Old French Arthurian Vulgate*, Arthur is frequently related to dragons, be it in the miraculous dragon standard brought by Merlin and carried mostly by Kay the Seneschal (see *The Story of Merlin*, 5; in *Lancelot–Grail*, I, 218); in Arthur's prophetic dream at the beginning of the giant of Mont Saint Michel episode, in which Merlin identifies the dragon with Arthur and the bear with the giant (see *Merlin*, 53 in *Lancelot–Grail*, I, 403); or in the Palace of Adventures at Corbenic, where Bors sees a dragon symbolising Arthur fight a leopard (see *Lancelot*, Part VI, in *Lancelot–Grail*, III, 270).

75 When pointing out that Arthur makes 'that misformed shape misshaped more' (I.viii.16.5), Spenser underlines the monster's deformity by recombining the key terms *shape* and *form* with the suffix *mis-* in a tautological repetition.

Since the modality of the verb seems to imply that the beast continues to exist despite its demise, critics are challenged to redress this narrative fissure. Hamilton, among others, notes that Orgoglio's beast is really vanquished only when it reappears in the shape of the Dragon in Eden,[76] a hypothesis that takes into account the thematic unity of Book I, in which holiness is variously assaulted by satanic powers (like Archimago), and dragons drawn from scripture. While such a hypothesis is indeed attractive, it suggests interpretative closure where there is none: both dragons are distinctly different specimens challenged and vanquished by two different champions. The similarities and differences between the two dragons testify to Spenser's method of creating permutations of the dragon on the basis of an underlying model, which forces the reader of the poem to find overarching textual and physical patterns. Spenser defers the end of Orgoglio's hell-beast in order to imply that any victory over the monstrous is temporal: there will always be another monster to challenge the hero.[77]

In Book I, this ultimate challenge is of course posed by the Dragon of Eden, Redcrosse's final and most powerful opponent. Both in textual and in temporal terms, this is the longest and hardest of the dragon fights in *The Faerie Queene*. While its three-day duration, its Edenic setting and the Well of Life in which the knight is reanimated have cued a host of responses from theologically oriented Spenserians,[78] the combat also has a more immediately monstrous theme. With a fight of three rounds,[79] and a Dragon that becomes the epitome of its kind during the battle, Spenser is on the familiar teratological ground of medieval dragon lore, also because he explicitly uses the battle in *Bevis of Hampton* to rewrite the most famous event in the legend of St George.[80] In the context of his monstrous discourse, the battle gains significance by bringing both

76 See Hamilton, note to I.viii.20.5.

77 Julian B. Lethbridge similarly notices the constant resurgence of evil in all its manifestations (as human characters and monsters) throughout *The Faerie Queene*: vice simply cannot be permanently quelled by virtue. See 'Spenser's Last Days: Ireland, Career, Mutability, Allegory', in *Edmund Spenser: New and Renewed Directions*, ed. by Julian B. Lethbridge (Madison: Fairleigh Dickinson University Press, 2006), pp. 302–36 (pp. 334–5).

78 See also the discussion of criticism on Spenserian monsters in Chapter 4, above. Kaske interprets the three-day battle as an allegory of the battle against concupiscence (see 'Dragon's Spark and Sting').

79 This is also the structure underlying the famous dragon fight in *Beowulf*, 2554–2723 (see *Klaeber's Beowulf*, ed. by R. D. Fulk, Robert E. Bjork and John D. Niles, 4th edn, Toronto Old English, 21 (Toronto: University of Toronto Press, 2008)).

80 King offers an exhaustive comparison between the dragon fights in *Syr Bevis of Hampton*, and *The Faerie Queene* (see *Middle English Romance*, pp. 129–45).

participants exceedingly close to one another, an intimacy with the other that proves as painful for the hero as it does for the Dragon. The battle is therefore largely dominated by the contestants' aiming at invading each other's spaces, which characterises the liminal zone where confrontations between the monstrous and the human take place as a dangerous and lethal locus of crisis. While chivalric fights also depend on the knights' mutual and violent attempts at invading each other's spaces with lance or sword to wound their bodies lethally, monster battles, like Redcrosse's against the Dragon, are more critical, because here the champions encounter creatures whose fire and venom, superhuman ferocity and hellish nature mark them as more dangerous and corrupting opponents, the very embodiment of otherness. Accordingly, battles between man and monster are of a different category from those between humans, and exceed theirs in mayhem and carnage, as I shall show in the ensuing discussion of the Dragon fight that closes off Book I.[81]

The mutual transgression of the opponents, further instigated by their joint inclination to wrath and anger that marks their temporal sameness,[82] becomes immediately apparent in the Dragon's attempt at catching Redcrosse and his horse like a hawk, and in his coiling his tail around them. More importantly, the Dragon's sting penetrates the knight's armour and shoulder so deeply that it cannot be removed and begins to infect Redcrosse's body (I.xi.38–9). But while the monster's piercing the knight with its mortal sting as well as its burning his beard, face and skin[83] are attempts at physically marring the knight's humanity by letting him partake of its infernal and monstrous nature, Redcrosse's analogous attempts at crossing the boundary are indicative of his desire to de-anatomise the monster. This is noticeable in Redcrosse's striking the Dragon's head with his blade (35), and in piercing the monster's left

81 In chivalric combat knights are wounded or die by being stabbed or beheaded, as, e.g., in Cambell's battle with the brothers Priamond, Diamond and Triamond in IV.iii.3–35. Decapitations often figure with evil characters; cf., e.g., Arthur vanquishing Cymochles at II.viii.45, and Arthegall beheading Pollente in V.ii.18.1–5. Spenser frequently underlines the ferocity of chivalric battles by using animal similes; among others, he compares Arthegall and Pollente's combat in the river to a battle between a dolphin and a seal (V.ii.15). Numerous other examples can be found throughout the poem, but during the tournament that Satyrane holds for Florimell's girdle in Book IV, Canto iv, they occur in an especially condensed form: here, bulls, boars, wolves and lions turn the chivalric contest almost into a battle of the beasts (for the bull, see IV.iv.18, for the boar IV.iv.29, for the wolves IV.iv.35 and for the lions IV.iv.32 and 41).

82 See I.xi.38–9. See also 35.1–4, where the Dragon experiences wonder at Redcrosse's revivification in the Well of Life.

83 See I.xi.26. The comparison to the shirt of Nessus in I.xi.27 associates Redcrosse with Hercules.

wing and open jaws with his spear (20; 53), the latter killing the beast.[84] By severing five joints from the monster's enormous tail half-way through the fight, which reduces it to a mere 'stump' (39.9),[85] and by cutting off the dragon's claw-like paw (43), Redcrosse literally deprives the monster of its defining characteristics, i.e. its monstrous signifiers, and, hence, of its monstrosity: the knight attacks sites where the monstrous signifier is sutured to the main body of the dragon, namely wings, claws, tail and monstrous orifice.[86] What remains is a monster progressively dispossessed of its defining attributes.

Spenser's heroes therefore vanquish the dragons by wounding those organs and body parts that constitute their monstrosity: the wings, tail and infernal jaw of the Great Dragon; the heads and eyes of Orgoglio's beast; and the claws, tail and monstrous entrails of Geryoneo's monster. It is no coincidence that the reader's attention, just like the hero's, is also directed at the dragons' generic body parts. It thus stands to reason that both the reader and the hero engage in a discourse with the monstrous, but, while the hero's reading of the dragon is expressed through physical dismemberment, the reader analyses and anatomises these beings textually, distinguishing the monstrous signifier from the entire body.

Spenser's major dragons thus bear witness to the author reconfiguring the creatures he knew from visual representations and textual sources into new specimens. As beings that suggest religious and moral implications, these untameable fantastic animals do not only dwell in a remote romance wilderness, but invade and occupy human and cultural spaces, be it the Kingdom of Eden or Geryoneo's temple. Penetrating their victims' bodies with their stings and teeth, they transgress violently into the human realm. Such trespassing is also evident in the boundary-breaking ontology that underlies their creation, and which combines a large variety of textual sources and disparate animal material. The Great Dragon of Eden, and the monsters of Orgoglio and Geryoneo, are thus

84 King argues that the blow under the wing derives from *Bevis*, where the eponymous hero hits the dragon 'vnder the wing, as he was flying' (East, f. 122.r.38 in King, *Middle English Romance*, p. 135).

85 Spenser's description recalls the text of *Bevis* in Caius College Cambridge MS 175: 'Aboue þe tayl ffyue ffoot & more / He hew ffrom þe body þore' (*Bevis*, 99–100; quoted from the Köbing edition in King, *Middle English Romance*, p. 135).

86 In its fight with Arthur, Geryoneo's monster replays many of the Dragon's manoeuvres when battling Redcrosse, such as the attack with her tail (V.xi.28), the flying movement (30) and her assaulting Arthur's head and beard (30); see also Spenser's recourse on naval imagery (29). Most powerfully, the description of the monster's downfall recalls the Great Dragon's demise almost *verbatim* ('Then downe to ground fell that deformed Masse', 32.1).

instrumental in destabilising ontological categories in the poem. This is best exemplified by Geryoneo's dragon, whose maidenly face disturbs the reader in his appraisal of beauty, and whose subverted use of language is taken up by the Blatant Beast just one canto later (*FQ*, V.xii).

7

Monstrous animals (2): Four-footed beasts

Monsters in *The Faerie Queene* do not necessarily belong to traditional monstrous species like the dragons discussed in the previous section, but may also belong to inconspicuous biological categories, such as, for example, that of the four-footed beasts. This chapter focuses on two specimens that violate the norm of this class of animals, namely the monstrous hyena in Book III and the Blatant Beast, which enters the narrative in the final canto of Book V, and is hunted by Calidore at the end of Book VI.

The hyena

When creating dragons, Spenser resorts to elaborate imagery and sweeping descriptions to render them as vividly as possible. However, when introducing a beast conjured up by a witch in Book III, Canto vii, he pursues a method that underlines the monster's indescribability. Like so many other monsters in *The Faerie Queene*, it emerges from a cave,[1] a circumstance that emphasises its hellish nature:[2]

> Eftesoones out of her hidden caue [the witch] cald
> An hideous beast, of horrible aspect,
> That could the stoutest corage haue appald;
> Monstrous, mishapt, and all his backe was spect
> With thousand spots of colours queint elect,

1 The hyena's cave calls to mind Jeremiah, 12.9, which tells of the *spelunca hyaenae*. Caves occur in *The Faerie Queene* as the dens of monsters, such as Errour (I.i), the monstrous hyena (III.vii) and Malengin (V.ix), or as places of temptation occupied by evil men, namely the caves of Despayre (I.ix), Mammon (II.vii), Lust (IV.vii) and the Brigands (VI.x–xi; see Hankins, *Source and Meaning*, pp. 74–80). Caves may, however, also figure as dungeons (Proteus keeps Florimell in a submarine cave at III.viii), or have positive connotations as the rocky cave in the Garden of Adonis where the boar is kept (III.vi; see Blissett, 'Caves', in *Spenser Encyclopedia*, ed. by Hamilton, pp. 138–9).

2 In III.vii.32.2 the beast is called a 'wicked feend'; it is further characterised through its 'diuelishe despight' (28.7) and 'hellish gorge' (29.2).

> Thereto so swifte, that it all beasts did pas:
> Like neuer yet did liuing eie detect;
> But likest it to an *Hyena* was,
> That feeds on wemens flesh, as others feede on gras.
>
> (III.vii.22)

It is worth noting that Spenser structures his nine-line stanza almost like a sonnet: keeping the beast's form deliberately vague for the first seven lines, he becomes specific only in the final couplet.[3] Up to that point, he basically heaps adjective upon adjective in a series of synonyms ('hideous', 'horrible', 'appaling', 'Monstrous', 'mishapt') that characterise the beast as a terrifying deformity, and emphasise the immediate threat it poses to Florimell. As none of these terms, however, specifies the beast's exact looks, this monster evades visualisation, a vagueness that makes it all the more horrifying. The one attribute that describes the monster's anatomy is the spots on its back, a monstrous signifier that can traditionally refer to sinfulness (especially concupiscence),[4] corruption[5] and evil.[6] In consequence, Spenser evokes visual horror through indeterminacy and evasion. The only additional information he gives is the hyena's supernatural speed – the narrator later calls the animal 'swifte as word' (23.6) – which underlines the beast's strangeness and associates it with mythological creatures noted for their velocity.[7] It additionally makes the monster the embodiment of the witch's vicious orders, and as such a parody of God's word made flesh.[8]

3 Watson offers a concise analysis of Spenser's use of the hyena in 'Forreine and Monstrous Beasts', p. 177.

4 See Hamilton, note to III.vii.22.5: 'The spots signify spots of sin or its "corrupted flesh" (32.6), specifically concupiscence'. Topsell explains that the hyena is 'bespeckled on the sides with blew spots, which make him look more terrible, as if it had so many eies' (*Historie*, I, 340). Spenser uses spots and speckles mostly to describe the bodies and tails of monsters (see Errour in I.i.17.6; the Dragon in I.xi.11.5, 15.2; and the hyena in III.vii.22.4 and 5). Accordingly, the lack of spots encodes virtue; Una, e.g. is 'All lilly white, withoutten spot, or pride' (I.xii.22.7).

5 Cf. also III.vii.32.6, which refers to the hyena's 'corrupted flesh'.

6 On the notion that the spots of animals may indicate the beast's evil nature, see Rowland's entry on the leopard in *Animals with Human Faces: A Guide to Animal Symbolism* (London: George Allen and Unwin, 1974), pp. 116–18, which cites St Ambrose, Garnerus, St Jerome and Rabanus Maurus.

7 Speed allies the hyena with mythical creatures like the swift harpies (cf. Hesiod, *Theogony*, 265–9), and Achilles's fast horses Balios and Xanthos, sired by parents noted for their swiftness: Zephyrus (the west wind) and the harpy Podargo (see Homer, *Iliad*, XVI.150–1). For the *Iliad*, see Homer, *The Iliad*, ed. and trans. by A. T. Murray, 2 vols, Loeb Classical Library (Cambridge, MA: Harvard University Press: London: William Heinemann, 1924; repr. 1960).

8 The notion of Christ as the divine word originates from John 1.1–3 (cf. also the marginalia in the Geneva Bible).

Only after Spenser has raised the suspense of his readers by constantly stressing the beast's hideousness and evading clear description does he offer a comparison for the monster, namely the indeterminate hyena (see Figure 6).[9] This designation is well chosen, for the hyena contains a rich subtext that Spenser readily draws on: from the Middle Ages to the early modern period the animal is considered a hybrid monstrosity frequently associated with witches;[10] as a voracious man-eater, it violates the norm of expected animal behaviour, just like Diomedes's man-eating horses, which Hercules captured during his eighth labour.[11] That the monstrous hyena in *The Faerie Queene* feeds on women alone underscores its masculine animality,[12] while its slaughtering and cruelly disembowelling Florimell's palfrey to vent its anger at the lady's escape drives home its abnormal atrocity.[13] While these ideas derive from the traditional image of the hyena, Spenser also endows this creature with a new trait, namely invulnerability: when defending Florimell against the hyena, Satyrane is able to wound, but not kill the monster. What is more, the monster grows stronger with every injury,[14] and can be overcome and tamed only temporarily.[15]

The hyena additionally exhibits signs of an ability to use language, for it initially intends to 'tell the idle tidings [of Florimell's escape] to his Dame' (28.6).[16] The monster's use of language breaches the traditional distinction between man and the animals, for God granted both reason

9 Topsell notes the hyena's indiscriminate number and subspecies, and records that this beast cross-breeds with other four-footed beasts, which increases the sheer number of physical possibilities. Hence, the hyena emerges as a rather undefined animal, a hypothesis that is also borne out by Topsell's many comparative references to other animals (see *Historie*, I, 339–42). In his *History of the World*, Sir Walter Raleigh claims that hyenas did not have to be included in Noah's ark because of their mixed nature; see Sir Walter Raleigh, *The Works of Sir Walther Raleigh, Now First Collected. To which are prefixed the Lives of the Author, by Oldys and Birch*, 8 vols, Burt Franklin Research and Works Series, 73 (Oxford: Oxford University Press, 1829; facsimile New York: Burt Franklin, 1966), II, 214.

10 See Topsell, *Historie*, I, 341.

11 The incident is recounted in Apollodorus, *Library*, II.v.8. Spenser uses the topos in *FQ*, V.viii.28, where the narrator explains that the Souldan's chariot is drawn by horses fed on the flesh of men. Cf. also the flesh-eating harpies in Virgil, *Aeneid*, III.210–58.

12 Cosman notes that Spenser invents the hyena's taste for the flesh of women (see 'Spenser's Ark of Animals', p. 98).

13 See III.vii.28.7–9. Drawing on Renaissance iconography, Hamilton suggests that the milk-white palfrey the hyena feeds on is a figuration of Florimell's body (see Hamilton, *Structure*, p. 150).

14 See III.vii.32–3. The hyena's immortality harks back to Maleger, who may also signify concupiscence (see Hamilton, *Structure*, p. 150).

15 On the battle between the hyena and Satyrane, see the passage on Satyrane in Chapter 10, 'Monstrous humans'.

16 Topsell records Solinus, who maintains that the hyena is able to imitate human language as a means of luring humans out of their houses (see *Historie*, I, 341); cf. also the *Ashmole Bestiary*, pp. 36–9.

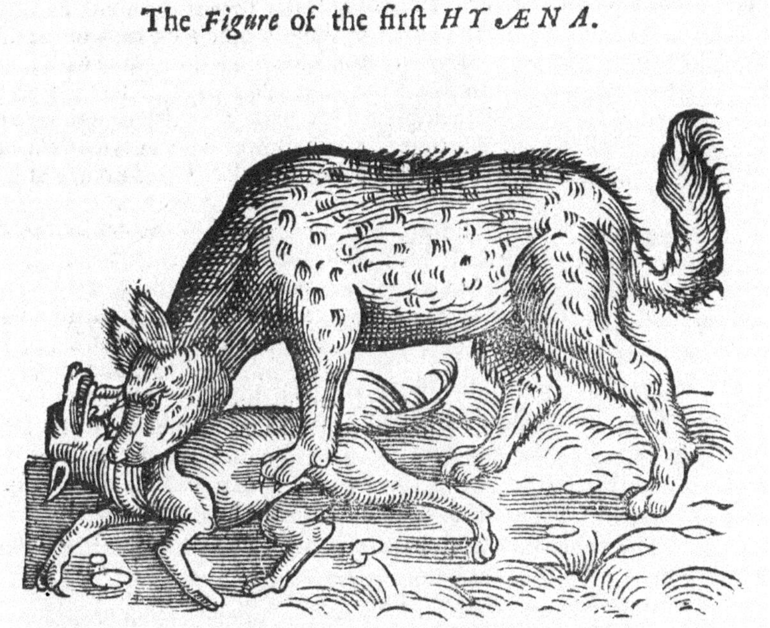

Figure 6 Hyena; from Edward Topsell, *The History of Four-footed Beasts and Serpents*

and speech only to human beings. La Primaudaye, for example, explains that God has not given speech to the animals,

> & by that he hath put a difference betweene him & the beasts, as also by reason and vnderstaning, wherof he hath made him partaker, & in respect whereof he hath giuen him speech, which is as naturall vnto him as reason, which is the spring head thereof, and from whence it proceedeth, as a riuer from his fountaine.[17]

La Primaudaye's explication of the causal link between reason and speech can be used as a gloss on the hyena's use of language: while speech is 'naturall' for human beings, it is unnatural, i.e. *in naturam*, for animals, which have no reason. The beast's trespassing into the human realm hence violates the norm of language,[18] and furnishes it with a more profound monstrosity. The label Spenser attaches to the witch's beast is therefore

17 Pierre de La Primaudaye, *The Second Part of the French Academie*, trans. by T. B. (London: G.B., R.N., R.B., 1594), p. 87.

18 Topsell groups the manticore (a lion with a human head), with the hyena in *Historie*, I, 344).

insufficient. The creature might resemble a hyena and share some of its traits,[19] but, as the phrase 'Like neuer yet did liuing eie detect' (22.7) explains, it is a creature without precedent, and hence without a name that could sufficiently describe its nature. Instead, the monster's combination of the beastly, human and infernal renders any attempt at visualising, describing and containing it through language impossible.

The Blatant Beast

By likening the monster to a hyena, Spenser calls upon the shared knowledge of his readers to create and describe new phenomena that transcend the limitations of common experience and known linguistic signs. Spenser goes one step further with the ubiquitous Blatant Beast, a monster with a thousand tongues of beasts and men that bites its victims with teeth of rusty iron. It is traditionally interpreted as slander, and, like its conceptual relative, the hag Sclaunder (IV.viii), the physicalisation of abusive, aberrant speech.[20] In addition to multiple mythological predecessors,[21] the Blatant Beast at first glance evokes Malory's Questing Beast, and the French Yelping Beast, or Beste Glatissant.[22] Like its romance predecessors, the Blatant Beast barks and brays, and, like Malory's Questing Beast, is the goal of a quest.[23] Hence, the monster's phrasal name (consisting of

19 Spenser uses a similar method when likening Orgoglio's beast to the Lernean Hydra.

20 For a full account, see Merrit Y. Hughes's time-honoured article 'Spenser's Blatant Beast', *Modern Language Review* 13 (1918), 266–75. James Nohrnberg interprets it as 'Rancorous speech' and notes its relation to Envy and Discord (see *The Analogy of 'The Faerie Queene'* (Princeton: Princeton University Press, 1977), pp. 688–97). On slander in *The Faerie Queene*, see M. Lindsay Kaplan, *The Culture of Slander in Early Modern England* (Cambridge: Cambridge University Press, 1997), pp. 34–51, and Kenneth Gross, 'Reflections on the Blatant Beast', *Spenser Studies* 13 (1999), 101–23 (pp. 102–4).

21 Nohrnberg relates the Blatant Beast to classical monsters like Python, Hydra, Scylla, Fama (especially its description in Virgil, *Aeneid*, IV), and Cerberus, and links it with Spenserian monsters like Errour, Orgoglio's dragon, and the Dragon of Eden (see *Analogy*, pp. 688–96).

22 For the beast's names, see also W. A. Nitze, 'The Beste Glatissant in Arthurian Romance', *Zeitschrift für Romanische Philologie* 56 (1936), 409–18 (p. 409). On the difficulty to determine the Beste's name and function, see Catherine Batt, 'Malory's Questing Beast and the Implication of Author as Translator', in *The Medieval Translator: Theory and Practice in the Middle Ages*, ed. by Roger Ellis (Cambridge: Cambridge University Press, 1989), pp. 143–66 (pp. 152–3), as well as *Variorum*, VI, 268–71 and 382–4. Leslie argues for a link between the Blatant Beast and the wolf in Canto I of Dante's *Inferno*, because the wolf, like the Blatant Beast, is set loose by Envy, and has to be pursued through every city (see *Spenser's 'Fierce Warres'*, pp. 60–1; compare *Inferno*, I.109–11 with *FQ*, VI.xii.22.6–9 and 31.1).

23 Gloriana has assigned Calidore the quest to catch the Blatant Beast, which is related in Book VI.

article, adjective and noun)[24] and its cacophonic ring join crucial aspects of the role and function the Beast performs in the poem.[25]

However, this first assessment explains only part of the Beast's nature, for the epithet 'blatant', inviting polysemy and multilingual punning, challenges interpretation without satisfying it. Suggested etymologies are Latin *blaterare*, 'to prattle', 'to babble', and *blateratus* 'barking';[26] English *to blatter*, 'to speak or prate volubly'; and Greek βλάπτειν, 'to hurt'.[27] Inconsistent spelling further complicates matters, as the monster is referred to both as '*Blatant*' (V.xii.37.7) and 'Blattant' (e.g. in VI.i.7.1). These conjectural etymologies confirm the trend observed in the previous discussions of the dragons and the hyena: attempts to circumscribe the monster's nature rationally through language and naming are rendered impossible. This is especially puzzling for a being whose name ('Blatant') ostensibly denotes both its action and its significance in an allegorical context. The indeterminate, multilingual etymology of the word *blatant* is striking, even in a work as abundant in polysemous names as *The Faerie Queene*.[28] This is especially so, as the monster's bewildering *nomen*, a composite of various languages and etymologies, is animated in its likewise bewildering array of tongues and voices. The close bond between the monster's name and its physical appearance directly relates the creature to the Renaissance notion of the name as the essence of a thing or being.[29] Paradoxically, the multiple meanings and etymologies of the monster's name show that the Beast does, indeed, harbour a single, univocal significance: as the monster of defamation and slander, the creature's quiddity lies in generating conflicting and misleading interpretations.

24 See Horstmann, *Namen*, p. 89.

25 Shepherd notes that Malory chooses a multivalent and cacophonic name to increase the enigma posed by the beast (see *Morte Darthur*, p. 31, n. 9). The similarities between these creatures have been noted by various commentators; see, e.g., Nohrnberg, *Analogy*, p. 693, and Hamilton, note to V.xii.37.7.

26 In his *Thesaurus*, Cooper defines *blatterare* as '[t]o bable in vayne. to clatter out of measure. to make a noise like a cammel'. Ben Jonson confuses suffixes when calling the Blatant Beast 'Blating' (see also Chapter 4, above).

27 For an excellent introduction to the Blatant Beast, see Ronald B. Bond, 'Blatant Beast', in *Spenser Encyclopedia*, ed. by Hamilton, pp. 96–8. See also the extensive entry in Hamilton's commentary (Hamilton, note to V.xii.37.7), and, for an advanced account, Kenneth Gross, *Spenserian Poetics: Idolatry, Iconoclasm, and Magic* (Ithaca: Cornell University Press, 1985), p. 230, n. 22; see also Gross, 'Reflections', pp. 101–23.

28 Cf. Herbert Marks, and Kenneth Gross, 'Names, Naming', in *Spenser Encyclopedia*, ed. by Hamilton, pp. 494–6. See also Horstmann's monograph *Spensers Namen* for an exhaustive study on Spenser's rationale of naming.

29 The notion that words have an intrinsic meaning and essence is argued by *Cratylus* in Plato's eponymous dialogue, which, according to Heninger, is 'the basic document in any philosophical discussion of language' (*Sidney and Spenser*, p. 115).

Thus, the mark of the Beast is linguistic. But monstrosity also informs the Blatant Beast's origin, since it boasts two lineages that establish not only genetic connections but also elemental implications. According to the first genealogy the monster is related to Cerberus, the infernal dog, and Chimera, a composite creature with three heads that spits fire;[30] according to the second, it was '[b]egot of foule *Echidna*' (VI.vi.9.9), a monster from classical mythology that is half nymph and half snake,[31] and the wind god Typhon, a hundred-headed dragon.[32] Spenser explicitly corroborates the first mythological origin when likening the Beast to Cerberus (VI.xii.35); he implicitly elaborates on the second mythological origin when comparing the Beast to 'hell-born Hydra' (32.1), like Orgoglio's dragon before,[33] because they were all sired by Typhon on Echidna, and reared in marsh-like surroundings.[34] Such a rich mythological context, which emphasises the Blatant Beast's proximity to dragon-like beings, is evidence for Spenser's creating new species by emulating known creatures: since each of its four parents is a terrifying deformity, the Blatant Beast emerges as a monster surpassing its multiple precursors, who can all be assigned to one of the four elements.[35] If one bears in mind the previous discussion on dragons, it seems to be Spenser's standard method to create monstrosities on the basis of a chaotic mingling of the elements.[36] The circumstance that Cerberus is Echidna's

30 See VI.i.7–8. Homer depicts the Chimera (Gr. Χίμαιρα) as a tripartite monster with the body of a goat, the hind parts of a δράκων (i.e. either dragon or serpent) and the front part of a lion (*Iliad*, VI.179–82); Hesiod describes it as a polycephalic creature that sports the three heads of goat, lion, and serpent (*Theogony*, 319–36).

31 The *locus classicus* is Hesiod, *Theogony*, 295–305. Spenser devotes two stanzas to her description (VI.vi.10–11); the passage is discussed by J. D. Pheifer in 'Errour and Echidna in *The Faerie Queene*: A Study in Literary Tradition', in *Literature and Learning in Medieval and Renaissance England. Essays Presented to Fitzroy Pyle*, ed. by John Scattergood (Dublin: Irish Academy Press, 1984), pp. 127–74 (pp. 128–9). On the Blatant Beast's link to Errour, see also Nohrnberg, *Analogy*, p. 694.

32 The passage covers VI.vi.9–12. For the mythological context, see Lotspeich, *Classical Mythology*, p. 56.

33 See I.vii.17.

34 Aptekar reads the Blatant Beast as a permutation of the Hydra, also because it was considered to be the embodiment of evil speech by early modern mythographers (see *Icons of Justice*, pp. 201–4). Humphrey Tonkin goes so far as to interpret the creature as a 'Cerberus-Hydra', a notion that, however, does not conform to the Beast's physical features (*Spenser's Courteous Pastoral: Book Six of 'The Faerie Queene'* (Oxford: Clarendon, 1972), pp. 265–6).

35 A suggested classification of her mythological parents would run thus: Cerberus stands for earth, Chimera for fire, Echidna for water and Typhon for air.

36 Nohrnberg points out the relation between Typhon and the Blatant Beast. When labelling the beast a 'wind-monster' (and thus a conceptual relative of Orgoglio) he does not recognise its association with the other three elements (see *Analogy*, p. 694).

and Typhon's offspring connects the two evil pedigrees with one another and marks the Beast as the embodiment of incestuous deformity. The monster's erratic and unspecified background hence fits its name: just like its etymology, the Beast's lineage combines mutually exclusive properties. Breaking the confines of language and lineage, the monster resists taxonomy, and transcends the boundary of any category.

On the narrative level, the Blatant Beast is just as elusive, since it appears suddenly and sporadically:[37] it roams freely through the poem and attacks its victims at random. This elusiveness makes problematic any attempt to divine the Beast's nature, so the reader is in search of the Blatant Beast just as much as Calidore himself is. Against this background, Spenser conceives the Blatant Beast as a fierce 'hellish Dog' (VI.vi.12.2), a 'dreadfull feend of gods and men ydrad' (V.xii.37.8).[38] Anatomical details of this infernal creature are rare: they basically supply necessary additions to endow the Beast with a familiar shape, a strategy Spenser also uses for the monstrous hyena. Accordingly, when Spenser describes how the Beast 'rampt vpon' Calidore 'with his rauenous pawes, / As if he would haue rent him with his cruell clawes' (VI.xii.29.8–9), he presents the monster as a four-footed beast perverting a heraldic posture and action.[39] The two instances of hypallage in the description of the attack add deliberate ferocity to the monster's assault.[40]

The Blatant Beast's physical shape is eclipsed by its mouth, a 'wide great' orifice (VI.iii.24.4)[41] containing one hundred or one thousand tongues that utter the voices of beasts and men.[42] When Spenser compares the

37 The Beast, which links the end of Book V with Book VI, appears in V.xii.37–41, VI.i.7–10, iii.24–6, and v.14–21; it is talked about in VI.vi.9–16 and is seen again ix.2–6, before it makes a more enduring appearance in the final canto of Book VI. Its reappearances suggest that it is on its own quest to bring evil to the worlds depicted in the poem.

38 When the three brothers Despetto, Decetto and Defetto attack Calidore after using the Blatant Beast as a lure, they are likened to three aggressive dogs, a comparison that induces Nohrnberg to see them as Cerberus's three heads (see *Analogy*, p. 688). On a simpler level, this evil trinity serves to underline the allegorical affinity between the three brethren and the slanderous dog. On the dog's relation to Envy, see Aptekar, *Icons of Justice*, pp. 205–6.

39 Remarked by Hamilton, note to VI.xii.29.7–9. The same holds true for Orgoglio's dragon in I.viii.12, as Nohrnberg observes (see *Analogy*, p. 695).

40 Here the hypallage lies in the transference of the epithets 'rauenous' and 'cruell' from the beast to its body parts.

41 The Blatant Beast's maw is big enough to hold Serena (see VI.iii.23–5).

42 For one hundred tongues, see V.xii.41.7, for one thousand, VI.i.9.3 and VI.xii.27.1. The combination of human and animal tongues suggests the Virgilian Fama in *Aeneid*, IV.173–97 (see Nohrnberg, *Analogy*, p. 688). Virgil's personification of rumour is a fully realised monstosity: Fama is a swift, winged monster, covered in a multitude of features, eyes, mouths, tongues, and ears.

Figure 7 Hell mouth; Winchester Psalter

Blatant Beast's maw to 'the mouth of *Orcus* griesly grim' (VI.xii.26.9), he harks back to earlier figurations of hell mouth, especially the description of Errour's maw and den at the beginning of Book I, and the Dragon's open jaws in I.xi.12.2–7.[43] Calling to mind the Beast's infernal heritage, this simile magnifies the creature's mouth and brings it out of proportion, so the monster appears just as disfigured and gigantic as Redcrosse's final opponent. Indeed, iconographic depictions of hell mouth frequently magnify the maw to such an extent that legs and body become insignificant, as e.g. in the Winchester Psalter, which could be seen as the Blatant Beast's conceptual predecessor (see Figure 7).[44] Given such magnitude, it does not come as a surprise that the Blatant Beast barks and brays with so much rage that nature trembles and the air bellows in return.[45] Such behaviour does more than accentuate the Beast's canine fierceness: it marks the creature as a gargantuan monstrosity that figures forth elemental chaos, and hence establishes a close mythological link to one of its alleged parents, among them the wind god Typhon.

The monstrosity of the Beast's mouth, its major monstrous signifier, lies in the combination of mutually exclusive tongues, as well as in their large and indeterminate number:

> And therein were a thousand tongs empight,
> Of sundry kindes, and sundry quality,
> Some were of dogs, that barked day and night,
> And some of cats, that wrawling still did cry;
> And some of Beares, that groynd continually,
> And some of Tygres, that did seeme to gren,
> And snar at all, that euer passed by:
> But most of them were tongues of mortall men,
> Which spake reprochfully, not caring where nor when.
>
> (VI.xii.27)

43 See also Watson, 'Forreine and Monstrous Beasts', p. 180.

44 Iconographic depictions of hell mouth frequently magnify the maw to such an extent that legs and body become insignificant (see Pluskowski, 'Apocalyptic Monsters', p. 161).

45 See, for instance, V.xii.41.2, and VI.i.9.5. As noted in the discussion of Geryoneo's dragon, the verb *to bray* is mainly used for monsters. The Blatant Beast almost animates the woods and rocks in parody of Orphean song, for they 'nigh to that way / Began to quake and tremble with dismay; / And all the aire rebellowed againe' (V.xii.41.4–6). Orgoglio's first appearance, preceded by a noise and an earthquake, is described in almost the same terms: the giant makes a sound '[w]hich through the wood loud bellowing, did rebownd, / That all the earth for terror seemd to shake, / And trees did tremble' (I.vii.7.5–7). As these passages show, the verb *to bellow* is often used by Spenser to describe the gigantic noise of monsters (see VI.v.19.8 for the Blatant Beast, and II.xii.39.1 for the beastly men in the Bower of Bliss). The verb *to echo*, on the other hand, is mainly used either in positive contexts or describes the actions of virtuous characters (see, e.g., II.iii.20.8 on Belphoebe sounding her horn, and I.iii.8.2 on the wood echoing Una's crying bitter tears).

Spenser stresses that the Beast's mouth is in itself a compound by linking the tongues of four-footed beasts (dogs, cats, bears and tigers) through an extensive parallelism-*cum*-anaphora (27.3–6) and by enumerating onomatopoeic verbs to echo the cacophony the tongues create.[46] That human tongues are embedded into such a monstrous orifice drives home the point that monstrosity is frequently constituted by conjoining body parts from creatures belonging to mutually exclusive categories.

Matters turn more complex when the poet adds that the mouth is also filled with serpents' tongues and stings:

> … them amongst were mingled here and there,
> The tongues of Serpents with three forked stings,
> That spat out poyson and gore bloudy gere
> At all, that came within his rauenings,
> And spake licentious words, and hatefull things
> Of good and bad alike, of low and hie;
> Ne Kesars spared he a whit, nor Kings,
> But either blotted them with infamie,
> Or bit them with his banefull teeth of iniury.
>
> (VI.xii.28)

This passage, which thematises the injury the Blatant Beast can inflict on every person regardless of rank, is a rich find for the critic who makes allegorical sense of the monster by stressing the traditional association of serpent tongues with slander.[47] The stings on the Blatant Beast's split tongues also connect it with the Dragon's twofold sting at the end of Book I, an association which foregrounds the Beast's devilish quality and its relation to concupiscence. A closer look at the properties of the Blatant Beast's gigantic maw, however, shows that the exact relation between the

46 Nohrnberg comments that this description 'develops from Cerberus into a bestiary' (*Analogy*, p. 691). On another note, the combination of a single beast with many canine tongues conjures up the Questing Beast in Malory's *Le Morte Darthur*, X.13. Typhon, one of the Blatant Beast's suspected fathers, also makes the noise of lions, bulls, dogs and snakes (in Hesiod, *Theogony*, 825–35; cf. Nohrnberg, *Analogy*, p. 694).

47 The association of serpent tongues with slander is traditional. See, e.g. Psalms 13.3: 'Their throat is an open sepulchre; with their tongues they acted deceitfully: the poison of asps is under their lips. Their mouth is full of cursing and bitterness'. Cf. also St James's homily on the tongue as a sinful and poisonous organ (James 3.5–8). Serpents and forked tongues form a significant image cluster in *The Faerie Queene*: Sclaunder's words are compared to the stings of asps ('For like the stings of Aspes, that kill with smart, / Her spightfull words did pricke, and wound the inner part'; IV.viii.26.8–9); Detraction has a tongue 'like Aspis sting' (V.xii.36.4; cf. also 42.7); her companion Enuie chews a poisonous snake (30.5–9); and Ate, who represents Discord, also has a split tongue (IV.i.27.6–8). Kenneth Borris relates the Beast's tongues to the volatile and erratic nature of speech (see 'Fortune, Occasion, and the Allegory of the Quest in Book Six of *The Faerie Queene*', *Spenser Studies* 7 (1987), 123–45 (p. 127)).

tongues and the stings remains unclear. The preposition 'with' (28.2) could refer back to 'mingled here and there', which indicates that the Beast has three sets of stings in its entire mouth. It is, however, also possible to maintain that they are on the tips of each split tongue, a circumstance that multiplies these venomous organs and enhances the Beast's deformity. Large numbers and disproportion are decisive features of the monstrous, which Spenser here exploits to render the description of the monster so ambivalent that it becomes impossible to visualise it.

The Beast's advanced monstrosity is also echoed in its language: just as the ambiguous suturing of animal tongues and stings precludes a definite anatomical form, the multitude of disparate tongues and voices in the Beast's gigantic maw renders the Beast's language unexplainable. The Beast is a terrifying monster of language, partly because it is devoid of a rational faculty controlling its actions,[48] and partly because it utters a paradoxical language mixing 'inhuman, non-signifying'[49] voices and human speech, which may contain potentially meaningful words.[50] The deviousness and ferocity of the Beast's language is enhanced by its two ranks of teeth '[m]ade all of rusty yron' (VI.vi.9.3), which hark back to the Dragon's three sets of teeth and brings to mind connotations of the rotten and the infectious.[51] Since they are sharp and venomous, causing wounds that lead to internal putrefaction,[52] the Beast's teeth are as much of a weapon as the tongues and stings.[53] In effect, Spenser equates the actions of speaking and biting, in that the biting of the teeth, like the stinging of the tongues, becomes the physical form of a speech act that perverts communication, because it transmits the Beast's irrational and abject language to its victims.

There is an important scriptural subtext inherent in the Beast's anti-language, its cacophony of voices, polyglot name, and double lineage: all these suggest the scriptural confusion of the tongues, the *confusio linguarum*, which ensued when God, in reaction to man's building the Tower of Babel, divided one language into many different ones.[54] In the

48 Gross notes that the beast is 'not only loose in the world; it is loose in the word' (*Spenserian Poetics*, p. 229).

49 Gross, 'Reflections', 112.

50 The combination of the Beast's tongues also reflects its multilingual name and indeterminate lineage.

51 See I.xi.13.1–2, and Hamilton's note to VI.vi.9.1–3.

52 See VI.vi.5.

53 See VI.vi.9.1–6.

54 See Genesis 11.1–9. The Renaissance quest to regain the original, adamic proto-language resulted in a host of cabbalistic, hermetic and Neo-Platonic treatises, as well as the invention of entirely new languages. See Wolf Peter Klein, *Am Anfang war das Wort:*

wake of God's punishment, the original adamic words, which denoted the essence of things, were irretrievably lost; the new languages consist of arbitrary words.[55] Read against this scriptural backdrop, the language of the Blatant Beast figures as the monstrous embodiment of speech in a fallen world,[56] the tool of arbitrary backbiting and slander, marring everyone, regardless of rank or merit.[57]

The Blatant Beast's poisonous speech resembles similar instances of monstrous language, which Spenser frequently allegorises as a physically revolting substance emanating from the monsters' poisonous intestines that injures the bodies of their victims. A brief look at Spenser's personification of Sclaunder, a loathly hag replete with poison, malice and gall (IV.viii),[58] helps explain the Beast's perversion of language. Such a comparative assessment of Sclaunder and the Blatant Beast is reminiscent of what Kaske calls a 'concordantial reading': like the reader of the Bible, the reader of *The Faerie Queene* is required to compose a mental concordance of images, words and concepts, which may complement or contradict each other.[59] The Beast and the hag illustrate different, yet corresponding aspects of slanderous language and monstrosity: while the Blatant Beast reifies slander as a multi-vocal monster of defamation, Sclaunder exemplifies the intricate workings of irrational language as malcommunication. Taken together, the monsters proffer a comprehensive view of aberrant utterance, and reveal how closely Spenser's notion of monstrous language is pitted against the idea of the λόγος as rationality producing language.[60]

Theorie- und wissenschaftsgeschichtliche Elemente frühneuzeitlichen Sprachbewußtseins (Berlin: Akademie-Verlag, 1992), pp. 62–79, and 145–60, as well as Umberto Eco, *The Search for the Perfect Language* [*La ricerca della lingua perfetta nella cultura Europea*], trans. by James Fentress, The Making of Europe (Oxford: Blackwell, 1995), pp. 7–20.

55 Cf. the Geneva Bible, gloss to Genesis 10.7: 'By this great plague of the confusion of the tongues, appeareth God's horrible iudgment against mans pride and vaine glorie'.

56 Nohrnberg underscores the link between the Tower of Babel and the Blatant Beast by dubbing the monster 'a veritable confusion of tongues' (*Analogy*, p. 666).

57 See VI.vi.12.7–9: 'Ne euer Knight, that bore so lofty creast, / Ne euer Lady of so honest name, / But he them spotted with reproch, or secret shame'.

58 See *FQ*, IV.viii.23–6. As Gross explains correctly, Sclaunder derives from Old Greek σκάνδαλον, 'trap' or 'stumbling block', and hence 'something that gives offence'; in the 1570s, *sclaunder* could mean both 'slander' and 'scandal' (see 'Reflections', 118–19, note 12). See also the entries on σκάνδαλον and σκανδαλίζω in Liddell and Scott's *Greek Lexicon*, p. 1604.

59 See Kaske, *Spenser and Biblical Poetics*, pp. 18–24.

60 Bond refers to the Beast as the embodiment of the *antilogos* (see 'Blatant Beast', p. 98), a hypothesis that tallies well with the analysis put forward in this section (see also Peter Bayley, *Edmund Spenser: Prince of Poets*, English Literature (London: Hutchinson, 1971), pp. 142–3).

A representative description of the λόγος is offered by Philippe Duplessis-Mornay's *A Woorke Concerning the Trewnesse of the Christian Religion*, which serves as the foil against which Sclaunder's and the Blatant Beast's abuse of language can be read.[61] Duplessis-Mornay contends that communication in accordance with the λόγος happens in three stages. It begins with the 'spéech of the mynd', i.e. the immaterial realm of reason, and proceeds to the 'Spéech of the mouth', turning immaterial language into physical speech.[62] Thence, language, as the 'Spéech of the understa*n*ding', reaches the psyche of the addressee, thus completing the communicative process. In his account of Sclaunder, Spenser explicitly characterises slander as the perversion of the λόγος. Like the Blatant Beast, she violates language by exploiting it to abuse goodness, accuse the guiltless, and rob them of their good name (25):

> Here words were not, as common words are ment,
> T'expresse the meaning of the inward mind,
> But noysome breath, and poysnous spirit sent
> From inward parts, with cancred malice lind,
> And breathed forth with blast of bitter wind[.]
>
> (IV.viii.26.1–5)

When Kaplan claims that Sclaunder's language works 'less like discourse and more like a physical assault',[63] she ignores the hag's subversion of the three stages of communication outlined by Duplessis-Mornay. Sclaunder's words are critically disconnected from her 'inward mind' (24.2) in that her words are not the physical realisation of her internal language (the 'spéech of the mind'). As they, instead, originate from her 'inward parts' (26.4),[64] they are devoid of true meaning, which makes her language the very embodiment of irrationality. Accordingly, her 'Spéech of the mouth' is not the communicative instrument of virtue and truth, but an abject physicality, consisting of a stream of poison and gall that brings Sclaunder's victims into disrepute.[65] When her words finally enter through the addressee's ears, they pierce the heart and wound the soul

61 Philippe Duplessis-Mornay, *A Woorke concerning the Trewnesse of the Christian Religion* (1578), trans. Philip Sidney and Arthur Golding, *The Prose Works of Sir Philip Sidney*, ed. Albert Feuillerat, 2nd edn, 4 vols (Cambridge: Cambridge University Press, 1962), III, 267 (247–367). The text is discussed by Heninger in *Sidney and Spenser*, pp. 123–4.

62 Heninger, *Sidney and Spenser*, p. 124.

63 Kaplan, *Culture of Slander*, p. 38.

64 Since Sclaunder's words are disconnected from a rational agency (her 'inward mind'), she violates Duplessis-Mornay's notion of 'dubble Spéech', according to which the speech of the mouth is linked to the speech of the mind (Duplessis-Mornay, *Woorke*, III, 267).

65 Cf. Geryoneo's dragon spilling forth words out of her noxious viscera.

(26.6–7), thus perverting the function of the 'Spéech of understanding', and the normative communication of the λόγος. Sclaunder hence turns speech into an instrument of miscommunication and spiritual corruption, which ultimately affects the addressee's body.[66]

The Blatant Beast's abusive language is a more fully realised corporeal monstrosity than Sclaunder's: while the hag's verbal malice is illustrated by an asp simile,[67] the Beast literally bites its victims with a mouth containing the tongues and stings of serpents, the tongues of men and four-footed beasts, as well as two ranks of iron teeth. Spenser here embodies monstrous language in order to stress its guile and brutality and to elaborate on its corrupting and debilitating effect on the body. The monster's venom represents the essence of its language, which functions as the interface connecting mind and body, a circumstance that Spenser allegorises by using the language of physical interiority: the wounds have 'festred priuily' and are now 'ranckling inward' (VI.vi.5.2–3). This phenomenon, which emphasises the interdependency of interior body and inward soul so characteristic of *The Faerie Queene*, also marks the Blatant Beast as a transgressive monster that can affect the spirit through its corrupt, irrational language. As the Hermit, a healer of the body who also knows the art of good words and counsel,[68] tells Timias and Serena, there is no direct cure for the damage inflicted by the teeth, a circumstance which he explains by referring to the Beast's infernal heritage (9–13).[69] Such poisonous potency exceeds the natural, which tallies well with the one possible source of the cure: solely through cleansing themselves spiritually, by disciplining themselves through serious counsel,[70] can victims overcome these wounds[71] – unless they learn to prevent the outward senses from succumbing to a flare-up of the passions instigated by provocative objects (7.6–7), and thus 'auoide the occasion of the ill'

66 Gross astutely notices that the poison 'emerges from and to attack the "inner parts" of human beings' ('Reflections', 103).

67 'For like the stings of Aspes, that kill with smart, / Her spightfull words did pricke, and wound the inner part' (IV.viii.26.8–9).

68 See VI.vi.6.1–3. Hamilton identifes the Hermit's dual role in the note on VI.vi.3; cf. also 5.9: 'Giue salues to euery sore, but counsell to the minde'.

69 The passage on infamy covers VI.vi.1–15. The Beast's untreatable poison recalls Deuteronomy 32.33: 'Their wine is the gall of dragons, and the venom of asps, which is incurable'. Cf. also the reference to the Beast's 'poysnous gall' in *FQ*, VI.vi.12.4. Nohrnberg draws a parallel between the Blatant Beast wounding Serena, and Archimago slandering Una (see *Analogy*, p. 695).

70 See VI.vi.5.6–8; cf. also 13.3 ('wise read and discipline').

71 'For in your selfe your onely helpe doth lie, / To heale your selues, and must proceed alone / From your own will, to cure your maladie' (VI.vi.7.1–3).

(14.2).[72] That the Hermit's counsel depends on Timias's and Serena's souls becomes apparent in the repeated use of the word *self*: 'in your selfe your onely helpe doth lie, / To heale your selues' (7.1–2). In these lines, *self* is used in its two interconnected senses: in the reflexive sense as one's willingness to take measures of self-healing; and in the sense of *anima*, or soul, from which such self-healing proceeds and to which it returns. Both the retroactive and the preventive measures propagated by the Hermit depend on intercepting the Beast's, and hence language's, attempts at transgressing into the physical. Spiritual healing through self-discipline proves effective, resulting in the patient's physical regeneration, because it obviates the venom's passage through the body. The preventive measure, on the other hand, depends on the individual's immunity to sensory input: as the monster's poisonous language cannot be transmitted to the bodies of its victims, it cannot contaminate their souls. It needs to be added, however, that there is no complete safety from the Beast's attacks, because man depends on the five senses and, tainted with original sin, is fallible by nature.

The Beast's link to language and slander points to a major difference between the dragons and the Blatant Beast. The section on dragons has identified the Great Dragon and Orgoglio's monster with universal disorder, because they had access to the high heavens and to hell. With the Beast, danger is horizontal rather than vertical, since the Beast, donning the robe of the great leveller, wreaks havoc on the human plane, affecting all estates and all human beings regardless whether they are 'worthy blame, or clear of crime' (VI.xii.40.6). Its wind-like speed does not only mark it as Typhon's son, but also links the Beast to the witch's monstrous hyena, which is 'swifte as word' (III.vii.23.6).[73] Similarities also include the beasts' fates in the plot of the poem: both endure a period of diminishing when taken captive by Satyrane and Calidore,[74] but can finally break free, so that their existence in Faeryland (and beyond) continues.[75] But while

72 The whole passage covers VI.vi.13–14.

73 Gross connects the Blatant Beast's wind-like speed with Agrippa's 'aeromancy', a kind of magic in which the air is used as the carrier medium of communication, transmitting human language and actions to the addressee's mind and senses even without their knowledge (see 'Reflections', 117, note 7).

74 Berger observes that the Beast, when made obedient by Calidore, turns into an 'unsymbolical animal' and even into 'a muzzled cur' (Harry Berger, Jr, 'A Secret Discipline: *The Faerie Queene*, Book VI', in *Form and Convention*, ed. by Nelson, pp. 35–75 (p. 43)). Calidore's leading the Blatant Beast into town draws on a topos familiar from dragon narratives, which Spenser subverts by letting the monster escape (the topos is discussed in Riches, 'Encountering the Monstrous', p. 208).

75 Borris relates the details of the Blatant Beast's escape to the old serpent in Revelation

the hyena merely returns to its master, the Blatant Beast unleashes its supernatural power at the end of Book VI and encroaches upon the world of Arthurian romance. It then enters contemporary, late sixteenth-century England and attacks the poet, with the phrase 'of late' (in VI.xii.40.4) emphasising the Beast's proximity to the poet and his times.[76] By letting the monster escape out of the poem Spenser thematises not only the physicalisation of allegory but also the impact of monstrous forces on his own day and age. The act of breaking free has a decisive effect on the monster: with a new supply of victims and no one to catch it, it grows both in size and strength.[77] Such growth renders explicit a phenomenon that has been observed in other monsters: just like their composition and proportions, their size may change. As the bulk of the monster grows in its progressive transformation, so does its monstrosity.

From there, the Blatant Beast makes its way through time and space, a movement that raises important issues with regard to Spenser's poem and the fictional cosmos he creates. Spenser transfers the never-ending hunt for the Questing Beast into Faeryland, and from there into contemporary society, thereby establishing a connection between the individual realms of his poem.[78] On a more theoretical level, one could argue that the Blatant Beast surpasses every other monster by transcending the boundaries of fiction, Faeryland and reality at the end of Book VI, where it figures as a border crosser with the potency to destroy Faeryland's pastoral idyll as well as the poem itself. As the Beast's tongues and voices are agents of destruction ultimately even of the poem itself, the monster perverts the notion of the λόγος as a creative force, and becomes a figuration of the antilogos.[79] The Blatant Beast is also significant in another

20–2 (see 'Allegory of the Quest', p. 135).

76 See VI.xii.38.6–9. The Blatant Beast escaped either through 'wicked fate' or 'fault of men'. The repeated use of the term *wicked* for the Beast implies a morally reprehensible incident (cf. VI.i.9.9, vi.12.3 and ix.6.2). McCabe refers 'wicked fate' back to Arthegall's observation that flawed men like to 'attribute their folly vnto fate' (V.iv.28.2; see *Pillars of Eternity*, p. 78).

77 See VI.xii.40.3–6: 'Ne any is, that may him now restraine, / He growen is so great and strong of late, / Barking and biting all that him doe bate, / Albe they worthy blame, or cleare of crime'.

78 That the hunt for the Questing Beast is significantly non-finite is observed by Corinne J. Saunders, 'Malory's *Book of Hunting*: The Tristram Section of the Morte Darthur', *Medium Aevum* 62 (1993), 270–84 (p. 281).

79 See Lotspeich, who purports that such a circumstance identifies the Beast as Cerberus's true descendant (*Classical Mythology*, p. 43). Balachandra Rajan similarly maintains that the Beast 'embod[ies] the extraordinary destructive force of language misused' (*The Form of the Unfinished: English Poetics from Spenser to Pound* (Princeton: Princeton University Press, 1985), pp. 68–9).

respect: its flight not only transgresses the boundary between fiction and reality, it also establishes it as an (almost) autonomous monstrosity that has the ability to act independently from its creator, Spenser the poet.

8

Human–animal composites

As monstrosity is usually associated with creatures that combine human with animal elements,[1] composite creatures like Errour, the mermaids Guyon encounters in II.xii and Duessa, perforce best illustrate the encroachment of the monstrous upon *The Faerie Queene*. In this section, I subdivide these monsters tentatively into two categories, namely into theriomorphic and anthropomorphic beings. Whereas the former category labels creatures that sport corrupt human features and do not exhibit traits of human behaviour, the latter contains beings that hide their monstrosity under a seemingly normative human body.

The monster ERROUR, whom Redcrosse fights in her lair in the Wandering Wood,[2] falls into the first category. Although she is sometimes grouped together with Orgoglio's seven-headed monster and the Dragon,[3] her physique significantly bridges the gap between man and beast, since she is '[h]alfe like a serpent horribly displaide', while 'th'other halfe [does] womans shape retaine' (I.i.14.7–8). She therefore crosses the border to the human much more than Geryoneo's monster, which had a female face, but did not 'retaine' any human features. Her name, from Latin *errare*, 'to err', and her physical ugliness identify her as the very opposite of verity, which in Boethius's *Consolatio philosophiae* is figured as beautiful Dame Philosophy, and in *The Faerie Queene* as the likewise beautiful and pure Una, whose name refers to the uniqueness and singularity of truth.[4]

Redcrosse, when confronting the monster in her den, first looks down at her tail and then directs his gaze upwards:

1 See Isidore, *Etymologiae*, XI.iii.9. Caroline Walker Bynum defines the human–animal composite, which she calls a 'hybrid', as 'a double being, an entity of parts, two or more' (*Metamorphosis and Identity* (New York: Zone Books, 2001), p. 29).

2 The encounter covers I.i.14–26.

3 See Humfrey, 'Dragons', pp. 223–4.

4 Una is identified as Truth in the argument to *FQ*, I.ii.

And as she lay vpon the durtie ground,
Her huge long taile her den all ouerspred,
Yet was in knots and many boughtes vpwound,
Pointed with mortall sting. Of her there bred,
A thousand yong ones, which she dayly fed,
Sucking vpon her poisnous dugs, eachone
Of sundrie shapes, yet all ill fauored:
Soone as that vncouth light vpon them shone,
Into her mouth they crept, and suddain all were gone.

(I.i.15)

Since she sports a long tail with a sting, her nether parts are those of a serpentine dragon, and foreshadow the tails sported by Orgoglio's dragon (I.vii–viii), the Dragon in Eden (I.xi) and Geryoneo's beast (V.xi).[5] This observation is in keeping with the strategy Errour pursues when fighting Redcrosse, since she winds her tail around the knight, trying to suffocate him like a boa constrictor. The tail's speckled colour (a detail the narrator adds in 17.6) links the monster not only to the Dragon and the monstrous hyena,[6] but also to Errour's ultimate model, Hesiod's Echidna:

… θείην κατερόφρον Ἔχιδναν,
ἥμισυ μὲν νύμφην ἑλικώπιδα καλλιπάρηον,
ἥμισυ δ' αὖτε πέλωρον ὄφιν δεινόν τε μέγαν τε
αἰόλον ὠμηστὴν ζαθέης ὑπὸ κεύθεσι γαίης.

… the goddess fierce Echidna who is half nymph with glancing eyes and fair cheeks, and half again a huge snake, great and awful, with speckled skin, eating raw flesh beneath the secret parts of the holy earth.

(Hesiod, *Theogony*, 297–300)[7]

Yet Errour is a more thoroughgoing monstrosity than her mythological model, because the properties of her upper, human half, which Redcrosse

5 See I.xi.11, and V.xi.24.5–6.

6 See I.xi.11 and 15 for the Dragon, and III.vii.22.4–5 for the hyena.

7 On Echidna and Errour, see Douglas Brooks-Davies, *Spenser's 'Faerie Queene': A Critical Commentary on Books I and II* (Manchester: Manchester University Press, 1977), p. 19, note to I.i.13–16. For a detailed account of the literary tradition informing Spenser's monster, see J. D. Pheifer, 'Errour and Echidna'. Errour shares Echidna as her conceptual mythological relative with Geryoneo's dragon, which connects the class of dragons with the class of human–animal composites. For Spenser's description of Echidna, see VI.vi.10–11. In Greek the term *echidna* can refer to the monster from the *Theogony* as well as to the viper (noted by Pheifer, 'Errour and Echidna', p. 131). Steadman argues that Spenser invests 'the legendary woman-serpent with characteristics of the female viper', thus 'merging Echidna with *echidna*' (John M. Steadman, *Nature Into Myth: Medieval and Renaissance Moral Symbols* (Pittsburgh: Duquesne University Press, 1979), p. 169).

now looks at, pervert the human form:[8] her breasts, here referred to as animal 'dugs', give poisonous milk to a likewise deformed offspring.[9] Her spawn's indeterminate shape and uncountable number mark them as monstrous offspring, which Errour seems to breed herself without the need of a male.[10] When she lets them enter her mouth – an action that makes for an internal climax in the tripartite description of tail, teats and mouth – Errour's action is in perfect keeping with animal lore, according to which adders and vipers hide their young in their maws when disturbed.[11] However, such behaviour perverts the mouth's function as a human orifice designed for the reception of food and drink.[12] Hence, what Spenser introduces as a binary opposition in the introductory remarks on the monster is rendered null and void. Errour might look like a combination of serpent and woman in which both natures are equally mixed; her behaviour, however, subverts such associations.[13]

Spenser stages a sequence of three incidents to demonstrate how monstrousness obliterates and distorts Errour's human features. As each of these three events presents a specific aspect of her maternity and perverts a particular site of her body, Errour emerges as a loathsome and wholly monstrous female. The first occurs when Redcrosse tries to strangle the

8 The dichotomy between maiden's face and serpent's tail is also reminiscent of Melusine. For a description of the legendary fairy, see *The Romans of Partenay, or of Lusignen, Otherwise Known as the Tale of Melusine*, ed. by W. W. Skeat, EETS, OS 22 (London: K. Paul, Trench, Trübner & Co., 1866), ll. 2801–10. Melusine was associated with both the Avignon and the Lusignan dynasties. On the influence of the Melusine legends on Spenser's conceptualisation of Faerie, see Matthew Woodcock, *Fairy in 'The Faerie Queene': Renaissance Elf-Fashioning and Elizabethan Myth-Making* (Aldershot and Burlington: Ashgate, 2004), pp. 33–7.

9 Caroline McManus reads Errour's poisonous nurture as the allegorical representation of a corrupt moral education; see 'The "carefull Nurse": Female Piety in Spenser's Legend of Holiness', *Huntington Library Quarterly* 60 (1997), 381–407 (p. 394).

10 This is one of many similarities to Sin in Milton's *Paradise Lost*, II.629–984. See also Pheifer, 'Errour and Echidna', pp. 161–2.

11 See Thomas Warton, *Observations on 'The Faerie Queene' by Spenser*, 2 vols (London: Dodsley, 1762; facsimile Farnborough: Gregg, 1969), ii, 122, and Pheifer, who refers to Sir Thomas Browne, *Pseudodoxia epidemica*, III.xvi: 'upon any fright … the old one receives [her young] in at her mouth, which way their fright being past, they will return again, which is a peculiar way of refuge' (see 'Errour and Echidna', pp. 131–2, and Sir Thomas Browne, *Pseudodoxia epidemica* (London: Edward Dod, 1646)).

12 See Williams, *Deformed Discourse*, pp. 141–9, for further background. McManus argues that the corruption of Errour's mouth and speech 'connotes verbal transgression' ('The "carefull Nurse"', p. 394).

13 The transgression of the beastly into the human half is a distinctive difference between Errour and her mythological model Echidna. Whereas Hesiod merely contrasts Echidna's two halves with one another, Spenser mixes the serpentine with the human in order to make the woman-half 'more revolting than the serpent-half' (Pheifer, 'Errour and Echidna', p. 130).

monster in order to break free from her 'endlesse traine' (18.9): Errour first spews out a mass of poison, flesh and gore, which is also 'full of bookes and papers …, / With loathly frogs and toades, which eyes did lacke, / And creeping sought way in the weedy gras' (20.6–8).[14] In these lines, Spenser elaborates on the concept of the mouth as a monstrous orifice to stress Errour's disgusting monstrosity. Her giving life to blind amphibians, which are in themselves monstrous and poisonous,[15] can be interpreted as a crude form of abiogenesis.[16] As her effluvia mingle living beings with inanimate matter and the dead remains of her spoils,[17] Errour's stinking vomit is in itself a paradoxical image that joins the monstrous with the textual,[18] thus teasing the reader into allegorical inter-

14 Brooks-Davies identifies the vomit of books and papers as Catholic doctrine (see *Critical Commentary*, p. 22, note to I.i.20, with reference to the Geneva gloss to Revelation 16.13).

15 See Revelation 16.13, and Topsell, who brings the toad into close connection with avarice (in *Historie*, III, 727–8). Jacques Berlioz identifies the toad as the medieval embodiment of evil, and Doris Adler interprets it more specifically as a signifier embodying envy; see Berlioz, 'Le crapaud, animal diabolique: une exemplaire construction médiévale', in *L'animal exemplaire au Moyen Âge Ve–XVe siècles*, ed. by Jacques Berlioz and Marie Anne Polo de Beaulieu (Rennes: Presses Universitaires de Rennes, 1999), pp. 267–88, and Adler, 'Imaginary Toads in Real Gardens', *English Literary Renaissance* 11 (1981), 235–60. Shakespeare uses toad imagery as a leitmotif in *Richard III* to characterise the play's eponymous villain (see e.g. I.ii.151, and I.iii.246). References are to William Shakespeare, *King Richard III*, ed. by Antony Hammond, The Arden Edition of the Works of William Shakespeare, 2nd series (London: Methuen, 1981).

16 This is also reminiscent of the second plague of Egypt (Exodus 7.25–8.11), where the Nile was teeming with frogs (see Nohnberg, *Analogy*, p. 101 and p. 147). Horapollo records that frogs are born from the mud of rivers in entry I.25 of his *Hieroglyphics*; for the text, see Horapollo, *Des Niloten Apollon Hieroglyphenbuch*, Vol. 1, Text und Übersetzung, ed. and trans. from the Latin by Heinz Josef Thissen, Archiv für Papyrusforschung und verwandte Gebiete, Beiheft 6 (Munich, Leipzig: K. G. Saur, 2001), pp. 20–1. Topsell maintains that frogs and toads are engendered either 'by carnal copulation' or 'of the slime and rottenesse of the earth'; more specifically, toads can be born of the 'putrefaction and corruption of the earth'; out of the ashes of a burnt frog; and out of water and air (*Historie*, III, 718 and 728).

17 The books illustrate the monster's theological implications, as Helen Cooper points out in *The English Romance in Time: Transforming Motifs from Geoffrey of Monmouth to the Death of Shakespeare* (Oxford: Oxford University Press, 2004), p. 97.

18 In an epic simile, the narrator compares the amphibians in Errour's vomit to the '[t]en thousand kindes of creatures' (I.i.21.7) that were thought to have been spawned by the river Nile's mud during the season in which the water leaves the riverbed. On the Nile as a breeding-ground of the monstrous, see *Liber monstrorum*, II.21 (in Orchard, *Pride and Prodigies*, pp. 298–9). Cf. also *FQ*, V.xi.32, where the effluvia of Geryoneo's dragon are described as a 'puddle of contagion' (V.xi.32.3). Surprisingly, Spenser uses the Nile simile in a positive sense (i.e. *in bono*) when relating how Chrysogone conceived Belphoebe and Amoret by a ray of light (III.vi.8). As Kaske explains, this is an instant of tapinosis, i.e. 'the choice of undignified symbols … for divine subjects' (see Kaske, *Spenser and Biblical Poetics*, pp. 176–7, and 181).

pretations.[19] In the context of the poem's deformed discourse, Spenser moreover stresses the monster's inherent unnaturalness: Errour's mouth is so monstrous because it constantly violates its natural function.[20] As the entrance and exit of creatures and matter, Errour's maw is also associated with the mouth of the cave she hides in. Spenser's describing the den's entrance as a 'gate' (I.i.13.4) leading into a 'hollowe caue' (11.6) strongly suggests the mouth of hell, so that, by analogy, Errour's maw, the orifice of a serpentine, satanic monster, becomes an animated figuration of hell mouth.[21] As early as Canto i, Spenser hence introduces the monstrous orifice as an important theme for his poem on which he will subsequently elaborate.

In the second incident, the monstrous inversion of anatomical sites is rendered even more poignant when Errour pours 'out of her hellish sinke / Her fruitfull cursed spawne of serpents small' (22.5–6).[22] This spontaneous release of innumerable '[d]eformed monsters' (22.7), either from her womb or from her bowels,[23] functions as a mirror image of the abiogenesis of frogs and toads as creatures of the same category. Additionally, the circumstance that these deformed creatures issue from both mouth and 'sinke' connects the mouth to the vagina or the anus *qua* anatomical homology and inverts the function of the mouth as a place of ingress. Such a perversion of orifices turns Errour into a deformity that violates normative femininity, and additionally embodies contradiction and monstrous paradox.[24]

The contradictory nature of the woman-serpent culminates in the third incident, which occurs after Redcrosse has defeated the monster by

19 Cf. Brooks-Davies, *Critical Commentary*, p. 22, note to I.i.20, with reference to the Geneva gloss to Revelation 16.13.

20 For an interpretation, see Lawrence F. Rhu, 'Romancing the Word: Pre-Texts and Contexts for the Errour Episode', in *Spenser Studies* 11 (1994), 101–9.

21 Cf. also the discussions of the Dragon's and the Blatant Beast's mouths in Chapters 6 and 7.

22 This links Errour to Geryoneo's female dragon, whose abdomen is an 'infernall sinke' (V.xi.31.6).

23 The term 'sinke', which turns Errour's body into an inanimate object, does not denote one specific orifice, as Hamilton correctly observes in his commentary (note to I.i.22.5–6). James W. Broaddus argues that Errour's spawn is the product of the middle and upper level of the monster's digestive system and mouth, and conjectures that such spawning is 'analogous to the generation of worms in the stomach and guts out of "a putrid and rotten humour"' (*Spenser's Allegory of Love: Social Vision in Books III, IV, and V of 'The Faerie Queene'* (London: Associated University Press, 1995), pp. 65–6, with reference to Helkiah Crooke, *Mikrokosmographia: A Description of the Body of Man* (London: William Iaggard, 1615), p. 297).

24 The possible reference to Errour's anus again links her to Satan, down whose bottom Dante and Virgil pass in *Inferno*, XXXIV.91–3.

decapitating her: Errour's spawn seeks shelter in her mouth again, but, finding her headless, starts feeding on her blood.[25] The result of their action is just as abominable as the action itself: once they have satisfied their hunger, Redcrosse witnesses how '[t]heir bellies swolne … with fulnesse burst, / And bowels gushing forth' (26.5–6). True, their action is recognisably unnatural, but their living and dying through their mother's blood enhances the supposition that Errour images forth the monstrous inversion of the causality between life and death.[26] Unlike other deformities, Errour's monstrosity is thus largely based on the breaking down of natural physiological signifiers and, especially, the violent mingling of the external and the internal, which images forth from the triad of vomiting, spontaneous birth and bursting bowels. As Spenser takes great care to anatomise Errour's distinctly female features and bodily functions as aberrations, she is realised as a heavily gendered monstrosity whose contaminated physique may mark her as an image of 'sexual pollution'.[27] However, her sexual foulness is in turn only an image accentuating Errour's complete pollution, which affects nature, language, written texts (the books and papers she vomits) and truth in equal measure.[28]

With Errour figuring prominently at the outset of the poem, the distinction between man and monster is already permanently questioned. Similar combinations between animal and human reappear at important stages of the poem. Among others, composite creatures surface during Guyon and the Palmer's voyage to Acrasia's island in the form of strange sea beasts,[29] as, e.g, the 'griesly Wasserman',[30] and the 'horrible Sea-satyre'

25 On Errour's abominable and corrupt bodily fluids, see McManus, 'The "Carefull nurse"', p. 393. Cf. also Ate's taste for blood in IV.i.25–6.

26 Steadman (*Nature into Myth*, pp. 168–73) and Pheifer ('Errour and Echidna', pp. 133–40) argue that the incident is based on the notion that young vipers are born by eating through their mother's belly. Pheifer, who quotes a host of source material, draws the conclusion that 'Errour's fate combines that of the male and female viper, and her brood are not guilty of matricide, but only of sucking up her mother's blood' ('Errour and Echidna', p. 163). See also Matthew Fike's thesis that Errour embodies both *eros* and *thanatos* (see '"Not without Theseus": The Mythic Weave of *The Faerie Queene*, Book 1', *Classical and Modern Literature* 17 (1997), 231–49 (p. 239)).

27 Fike, '"Not without Theseus"', p. 237.

28 On Errour's books and papers, see Debora Shuger, *Censorship and Cultural Sensibility: The Regulation of Language in Tudor–Stuart England* (Philadelphia: University of Pennsylvania Press, 2006), pp. 43–4, 47.

29 For a standard interpretation, see Martha Craig 'The Secret of Wit of Spenser's Language', in *Elizabethan Poetry: Modern Essays in Criticism*, ed. by Paul J. Alpers (New York: Oxford University Press, 1967), pp. 447–72 (pp. 466–7).

30 On Spenser's conceptualisation of the 'Wasserman', see *The Book of Beasts, Being a Translation from a Latin Bestiary of the Twelfth Century*, trans. and ed. by T. H. White (New York: G. P. Putnam, 1954), pp. 251–2.

(II.xii.24.3 and 5). The most famous composite species in this passage is that of the alluring MERMAIDS, who look like beautiful women, but are fish from the waist down. They are given one of the few relatively unadulterated appearances of classical monsters in Spenser's poem. That they sing to tempt Guyon,[31] and that they are explicitly related to Greek mythology,[32] is evidence for Spenser's identifying mermaids with sirens,[33] just as Chaucer does in the *Nun's Priest's Tale*.[34] The mermaids were once humans who challenged the muses to a singing contest, lost and were subsequently turned into fish-women:

> They were faire Ladies, till they fondly striu'd
> With th'*Heliconian* maides for maystery;
> Of whom they ouer-comen, were depriu'd
> Of their proud beautie, and th'one moyity
> Transformd to fish, for their bold surquedry,
> But th'vpper halfe their hew retayned still,
> And their sweet skill in wonted melody;
> Which euer after they abusd to ill,
> T'allure weake traueillers, whom gotten they did kill.
>
> (II.xii.31)

Spenser's aetiological explanation differs significantly from its precedents, where, as a consequence of the contest, the bird-like sirens are deprived of their wings.[35] Although Spenser's rendering likewise culminates in punishment for hubris (their 'bold surquedry'), it explicitly foregrounds their metamorphosis into devouring hybrids ('th'one moyity / Transformd to fish'; xii.31.4–5), an element that differs radically from other versions, where they are human–animal composites already before the contest

31 See II.xii.32.7–9. Like their medieval predecessors they indulge in flattery, an element L. A. J. R. Houwen discusses in his article 'Flattery and the Mermaid', in *Animals and the Symbolic*, ed. by Houwen, pp. 77–92 (pp. 91–2). For a similar temptation, cf. Tasso, *Gerusalemme Liberata*, XIV.60–75.

32 See II.xii.30–1.

33 See Lotspeich, *Classical Mythology*, p. 81.

34 See Geoffrey Chaucer, *The Canterbury Tales*, VII.3270–2 (in *The Riverside Chaucer*, gen. ed. by Larry D. Benson, 3rd edn (Oxford: Oxford University Press, 1987)). For a thorough investigation into Chaucer's view of mermaids, cf. Houwen, 'Flattery and the Mermaid', pp. 77–92.

35 Brooks-Davies identifies Pausanias, *Descriptions of Greece*, IX.xxxiv.3 as the ultimate source (see *Critical Commentary*, p. 185, note to II.xii.30–2). In classical mythology and the bestiaries, sirens are usually depicted as half woman, half bird. For a detailed account of how images of sirens and mermaids changed throughout the Middle Ages, see L. A. J. R. Houwen, 'Sex, Songs and Sirens: A New Score for an Old Song', *The Profane Arts / les arts profanes* 6 (1996), 103–21. For classical sources, Houwen refers to Homer, *Odyssey*, XII, and Ovid, *Metamorphoses*, V.551–63.

commences.[36] Spenser thus deliberately alters the older version in order to highlight the threat of metamorphosis, and to accentuate the dysfunctioning dichotomy between man and animal. Such poetic revision is evidence for the poet's adaptation of mythological material to the overall teratological context of *The Faerie Queene*. Hence, the physical hybridity of the mermaids is meaningful in that it illustrates the lasting spiritual corruption brought about by their transgressive actions of pride and concupiscence.[37]

The fact that Errour and the mermaids are obvious monstrosities should not suggest that compound creatures can be recognised instantly, since the poem also features characters that hide deformity underneath a feasible human semblance. Duessa, Una's evil counterpart in Book I, appears to be a ravishing beauty when deceiving Fradubio and Redcrosse.[38] However, when she is stripped bare her ugly body is revealed under her richly ornamented 'roiall robes' (I.viii.46.2).[39] Her upper half is that of a 'loathly, wrinckled hag' (46.8):[40] her bald head is covered in scabs and scall, her 'rotten gummes' (47.4) lack teeth, and her breath is odoriferous. Her breasts are described as 'dried dugs' that hang down 'lyke bladders lacking wind', emanating filthy matter (47.6–7), while her skin, full of scabs, is wrinkled 'as maple rind' (47.8). Spenser is, of course, eager to evoke his readers' abominations through the graphic depiction of disease and deformity.[41] But the passage is also rich in intratextual references. The anatomy of Duessa's mouth, for instance, is reminiscent of other orifices, namely those of the Blatant Beast, Orgoglio's dragon and Lust,[42] a circumstance that brings Duessa into close company with these monsters. Even her sagging breasts emphasise monstrous associations. On one level, they

36 Although Ovid's *Metamorphoses* contain an account of their transformation into birds, it is not related to a singing contest with the muses (see *Metamorphoses*, V.551–63).

37 See Lotspeich for a brief characterisation of mermaids and sirens (*Classical Mythology*, p. 81). The association between mermaids and lust is traditional, as Geoffrey Whitney, *A Choice of Emblemes, and other Deuises* (Leyden: Christopher Plantyn, 1586), p. 10, shows.

38 See I.ii and Chapter 10, 'Monstrous humans'.

39 The entire passage covers I.viii.46–8. Cf. also the end of Fradubio's tale for a first rendering of Duessa's ugliness, however *sans* lower body parts, which are hidden under water (I.ii.38–41).

40 For a similar case of hidden ugliness, see Alcina in Ariosto, *Orlando Furioso*, VII.72–4.

41 Nohrnberg interprets Duessa's dugs as the 'parody of a nursing mother'; they thus stand in marked contrast to Charissa's breasts in I.x.30 (*Analogy*, p. 714; see also Gail Kern Paster, *The Body Embarrassed: Drama and Disciplines of Shame in Early Modern England* (Ithaca: Cornell University Press, 1993), pp. 206–7). Pendent dugs are a notorious topos in misogynist images and literature; see Malcolm Jones, 'Monsters of Misogyny: Bigorne and Chicheface – Suite et Fin?', in *Marvels, Monsters, and Miracles*, ed. by Jones and Sprunger, pp. 203–21 (p. 206).

42 For Lust, see Chapter 9, 'Giants', below.

are described as the teats of a female mammal, a periphrasis that turns Duessa into a grotesque figure with overt animal traits and harks back to Errour's dugs from the beginning of the poem (see I.i.15.6).[43] On another, her pendant dugs also echo the 'empty windbag' into which the body of the giant Orgoglio is reduced after he is killed by Arthur.[44] Such associations are especially relevant because these events take place in close textual proximity: Orgoglio's death, his monster's defeat and the stripping of Duessa occur within some twenty stanzas. Hence, they form a monstrous trinity driven by the same infernal and monstrous impulses.[45]

Duessa's bottom half, which is structurally cut off from her upper half through stanzaic arrangement, is even more repulsive:

> Her neather parts, the shame of all her kind,
> My chaster Muse for shame doth blush to write;
> But at her rompe she growing had behind
> A foxes taile, with dong all fowly dight;
> And eke her feete most monstrous were in sight;
> For one of them was like an Eagles claw,
> With griping talaunts armd to greedy fight,
> The other like a beares vneuen paw:
> More vgly shape yet neuer liuing creature saw.
>
> (I.viii.48)

That Duessa's stunning beauty drew attention away from this kind of corruption suggests that Spenser conceives of her as the 'embodiment of falsehood'.[46] Her name, which is traditionally interpreted as a reference to her double-dealing deception or 'duplicity',[47] might also encode her bi-natural appearance as half woman, half animal: Duessa is a compound whose physical features make manifest her sinful nature, a circumstance stressed by Spenser's use of scatological detail.[48] Her deformed physique is

43 Paster goes one step further when purporting that 'metonomy transforms [Duessa's] breasts into the lower parts, an oozing excretory bladder-womb' (*The Body Embarrassed*, p. 206). For Errour's dugs, see I.i.15.6.

44 See I.viii.24.7–9.

45 Alpers analyses Duessa's close relation to Orgoglio's dragon (see *Poetry*, pp. 86–7).

46 Graham Hough, *A Preface to 'The Faerie Queene'* (New York: Norton, 1963), p. 132. Mihoko Suzuki points out that Duessa is a composite of Una and Errour (see *Metamorphoses of Helen: Authority, Difference, and the Epic* (Ithaca: Cornell University Press, 1989), p. 198). See also Alpers, *Poetry*, p. 147.

47 Martha Craig identifies her thus (see 'Secret Wit', pp. 454–5).

48 See Hankins, *Source and Meaning*, pp. 101–2, for a discussion of possible influences. Matthew Woodcock claims with some justification that Duessa is reminiscent of Melusine, who is half woman, half serpent (see 'Elf-Fashioning Revisited: A Response to Maik Goth', *Connotations* 20 (2010/11), 210–20 (pp. 213–14), with reference to *The Romans of Partenay*, 2801–10). Both women are associated with the watery regions: as

determined by the complete absence of symmetry, as the epithet 'vneuen' suggests, which originally defines the bear's paw but which also comments on Duessa's wholly disproportionate body. In this context, the term 'rompe' takes on special significance, for it indicates that Duessa is created by uniting various disparate parts of predatory animals into an unspecified body. Such anatomical compounding is already prefigured when her breasts are likened to mammal teats in the previous stanza. In other words, the poet's penchant for new combinations, which has also been traceable in the creation of the dragons, is reflected in his fashioning grotesque novelties from existing animal parts. Fox's tail,[49] eagle's claw and bear's paw are, of course, mutually exclusive limbs belonging to animals populating different habitats: the eagle is associated with the air, while bear and fox belong to wood and open plain. In order to connect these disparate *membra*, Spenser utilises rhyme as rhetorical glue, thus combining the 'Eagles claw' (fully anatomised with talons) with the 'beares ... paw'. The grotesquery of Duessa's torso and members evokes the deformed physique of Melanchthon's 'Popish Asse', which circulated widely in print both on the European continent and in Britain (see Figure 8). The 'Popish Asse' is a scaly humanoid monster that has the head of an ass, the front torso of a woman, the left hand of a man, the right hand of an elephant, a cloven left foot and a griffin's gigantic claw for a right foot. Additionally, the heads of a dragon and an old man issue from its bottom. That Melanchthon moralises every physical feature of the monster in anti-papal terms associates Duessa closely with anti-Catholic satire, and points to important visual analogies between Melanchthon's and Spenser's monsters.[50]

Within the extended allegory of *The Faerie Queene*, the traditional animal images used for Duessa are monstrous signifiers that help differentiate between the various aspects of her deviousness: the fox signifies deceit, the eagle stands for predatory greedliness (an interpretation that the poet adds himself) and the bear symbolises cruelty.[51] With Duessa,

Nohrnberg points out, the scene in which Fradubio sees Duessa bathe and catches a glimpse of her true monstrosity ('Her neather partes misshapen, monstruous, / Were hidd in water, that I could not see'; I.ii.41.1–2) recalls the incident in which Raymond spies on the bathing Melusine and sees her serpentine tail (see *The Romans of Partenay*, 2787–821, and Nohrnberg, *Analogy*, pp. 243–4).

49 Aptekar notes that Spenser's use of a fox's tail, rather than a dragon's or serpent's, is 'relevantly original', because it emphasises Duessa's fraudulence (*Icons of Justice*, p. 143).

50 See Philipp Melanchthon, *Of two VVonderfull Popish Monsters* (London: Thomas East, 1579). On the theological implications of Duessa, see especially D. Douglas Waters, *Duessa As Theological Satire* (St Louis: University of Missouri Press, 1970).

51 For extended commentary, see Brooks-Davies, *Commentary*, pp. 85–6, note to I.viii.46–8.

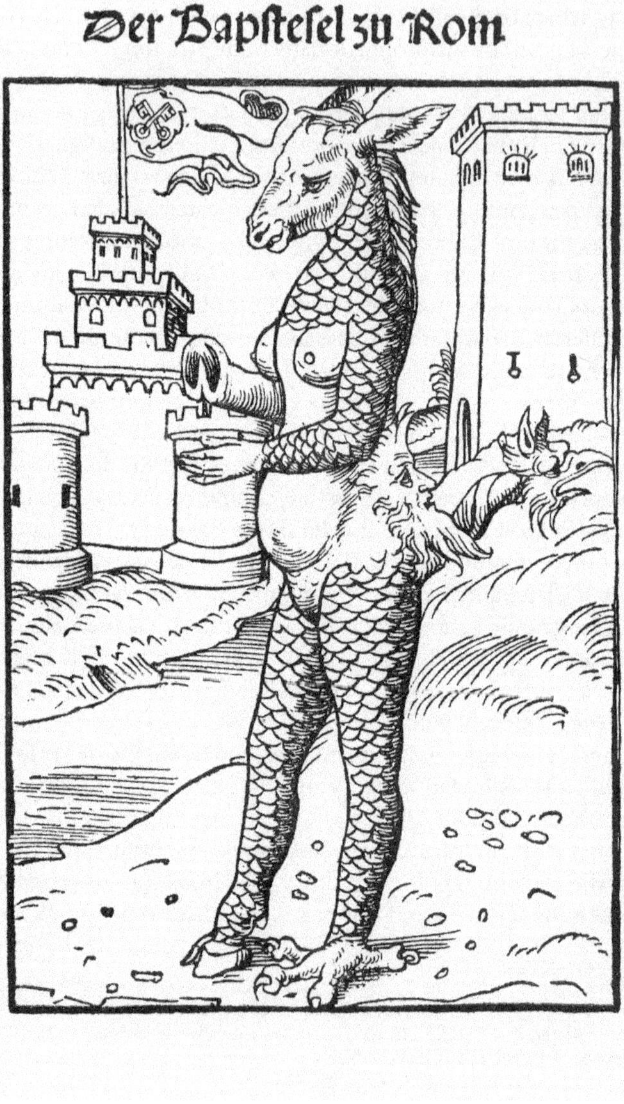

Figure 8 The Popish Ass; from Martin Luther and Philipp Melanchthon, *Deuttung der czwo grewlichen Figuren, Bapstsesels czu Rom und Munchkalbs zu Freijberg ijnn Meijsszen funden*

composite monstrosity openly displays the truth behind the semblance. Ironically, the moment of revelation marks Duessa as more than duplicity; Spenser clearly envisions her as the image of multiplicity that transcends simplified interpretation, for she is a completely fragmented being that lacks wholeness and unity. Her heinousness is created by a well-organised web of physical references. As in the seven-stanza depiction of the Dragon, Spenser contains the deformed in tight structures: he works his way directly from the upper to the lower half of her face before turning to her breasts and skin, her tail and, finally, her feet. Thus, the entire passage parodies the arrangement of the Petrarchan beauty catalogue, which, as the figuration of the voyeuristic gaze, is deployed as the rhetorical representation of the actual stripping.[52] This strategy, which relies heavily on the composition of fragmented and re-membered body parts, brings her ugliness and her lack of human nature into clear focus.[53] Truly 'abhominable', she is – in the etymological sense – *ab homine*,[54] more monster than beast, blending animal deformity with human heinousness.

Duessa shares with Errour the dichotomy of upper and lower parts; but, unlike Errour, she is still recognisable as a human corruption. Thus, within the suggested typology, Errour is a distinctly theriomorphic monster, since she does not have the slightest trace of human behaviour: Spenser creates her monstrosity by combining a partly human physique with the absence of any human characteristic.[55] Duessa, on the other hand, is anthropomorphic, because she combines traces of a woman's shape with seemingly genuine human behaviour. Hence, both monsters are conceived as inversed types, which is also suggested by the differing movements of the counter-blazons, the one up, the other one down. Between these two, the mermaids take a firm middle position as metamorphosed beings whose two body segments are sutured so convincingly that they do not seem to interact physically.

52 Theresa M. Krier makes a similar observation; see *Gazing on Secret Sights: Spenser, Classical Imitation, and the Decorums of Vision* (Ithaca: Cornell University Press, 1990), p. 134. Cf. also Woodcock's critical note in 'Elf-Fashioning Revisited', p. 210, note 10.

53 On the blazon's fragmentariness, as well as the processes of seeing and bodily disintegration, see Nancy J. Vickers, 'Diana Described: Scattered Woman and Scattered Rhyme', *Critical Inquiry* 8 (1981), 265–79.

54 The etymology is pointed out by Hamilton, note to I.viii.47.5.

55 This is, of course, different with the mermaids Guyon and the Palmer encounter on their voyage in II.xii.

9

Giants

Just like dragons and strange animals, giants belong to the repertory of the epic romance. In his chapter on portents, Isidore of Seville identifies hypertrophy of the body, i.e. extreme size, as their defining monstrous signifier.[1] Unlike the monstrous creatures treated above, giants hence mark physical excess as an innate human possibility, which mostly sallies forth from their indulging in the sinful triad of gluttony, lust and homicide.[2] Isidore famously draws an analogy between the monstrous men contained in individual races and the monstrous races contained in the human species, asserting that 'in universo genere humano quaedam monstra sunt gentium, ut Gigantes, Cynocephali, Cyclopes, et cetera'.[3] As the preposition in the phrase 'in universo genere humanum' makes clear, giants are not merely in contiguity with man, but a monstrous subspecies existing within the human realm. Their name, Isidore explains, derives from γηγένεις, a compound of the nouns Γῆ, 'Earth', and γένος, 'birth', which characterises giants literally as tellurean creatures brought into the world by mother Earth, who 'begot them as like itself, with their immense mass'.[4] These *terrae filii*, whose true origin remains unknown,[5] are placed among the monstrous races. Spenser's resorting to the etymological spelling 'Geaunt' connects giants to the earth, and Spenser's own views on the giant to that of his literary predecessors.

As Spenser creates an impressive phalanx of giants, the gigantic rears its ugly head throughout *The Faerie Queene*. There is at least one major giant in every book of the poem: in Book I, Orgoglio first defeats

1 See Isidore, *Etymologiae*, XI.iii.7.

2 This is observed by Cohen (see *Of Giants*, p. 162).

3 'in the whole of humankind there are certain monstrous races, like the Giants, Cynocephali, Cyclops and others'. The full reference features in Isidore, *Etymologiae*, XI.iii.12–14; see also Chapter 5, above.

4 'parens terra immensa mole et similes sibi genuerit' (Isidore, *Etymologiae*, XI.iii.13).

5 'quorum genus incertum est' (Isidore, *Etymologiae*, XI.iii.13).

Redcrosse and casts him into his dungeons, but is then cut down to size by Arthur; in Book II, Disdayne, who guards the court of Philotime, threatens Guyon in the House of Mammon; in Book III, the incestuous twins Argante and Ollyphant wreak carnal havoc; in Book IV, Lust abducts, rapes and eats hapless virgins; in Book V, Arthegall discusses the politics of equality with a giant holding scales; and in Book VI, Matilde tells of Cormoraunt, who was vanquished by her husband Sir Bruin in three battles;[6] moreover, the two cantos from Book VII that have come down to us centre on the titanic giantess Mutabilitie.[7] Apart from a few exceptions, such as Awe, the guard of Mercilla's palace, and Mutabilitie,[8] most giants figure as embodiments of evil and otherness, thus challenging the prowess of the knights seeking adventure in Faeryland and beyond.[9] Spenser incorporates various kinds of giants in his poem: some of them are steeped in the allegorical tradition, while others can be traced back to scripture and to Britain's pre-Roman history.[10] As embodiments of excess, they are elemental forces that lend themselves to Spenser's didactic poetry rather well.

The names of the giants give a first hint at Spenser's overall design of the gigantic. Two of them refer to animals noted either for their enormous size, like Ollyphant,[11] or for their potential monstrosity, like Cormoraunt, whose name derives from the sea-raven that Spenser groups with the

6 For Orgoglio see I.vii and viii; for Disdayne II.vii and VI.vi; for Argante III.vii; for Ollyphant III.vii and ix; for Lust IV.vii; for the Giant with the Scales, who is also known as the Egalitarian Giant, V.ii.29–54; and for Cormoraunt VI.iv.28–33.

7 Robert Lanier Reid notes that giants usually occur in Canto vii of Books I–VI, where they signify 'ambitious bodily pride', and are defeated in Canto viii. He argues that these *titanomachiae* lead to a reversal, and generate new figurations of pride in the final cantos of each book. In his analysis of the 'Two Cantos of Mutabilitie', he conjectures that Mutabilitie represents a new kind of giant, as she is of cosmic significance, and is not vanquished but 'redeemed': '[b]eginning with Book VII, the titan is reconceived, reformed, and preserved alive' ('Spenser's Mutability Song: Conclusion or Transition?', in *Celebrating Mutabilitie: Essays on Edmund Spenser's Mutabilitie Cantos*, ed. by Jane Grogan (Manchester: Manchester University Press, 2010), pp. 61–84 (pp. 71–2, and p. 82, note 39)).

8 For Awe, see V.ix.22–3, and for Mutabilitie, the so-called 'Cantos of Mutabilitie' from Book VII.

9 Although usually Arthur receives the title of giant-slayer (see Nohrnberg, *Analogy*, p. 264), his fellow Britons Britomart and Arthegall also vanquish giants to underscore their chivalric superiority.

10 In the *Chronicle of Britain Kings* (II.x.7–9), giants and beastly men are identified as Britain's original inhabitants. See Anne Lake Prescott, 'Giants', in *Spenser Encyclopedia*, ed. by Hamilton, pp. 332–3.

11 For Ollyphant, Spenser draws on the giant fighting the absurd hero in Chaucer's *Sir Thopas* (*CT*, VII.712–918); for an extended treatment of the Chaucerian specimen, see Cohen, *Of Giants*, pp. 96–118.

'birds of rauenous race' (II.xii.8.5) populating Acrasia's island.[12] On a figurative level, Spenser frequently accentuates the monstrous quality of the giants by using similes that map a particular monster or animal on to the giants' bodies. Corflambo, the tall and hideous son of a giantesse, is an especially good example of this strategy. In a striking epic simile, Spenser likens the shining eyes of the giant, a notion that may derive from the Judaeo-Christian tradition,[13] to the eyes of the legendary basilisk, a monster that kills its victims with its looks:

> For from his fearefull eyes two fierie beames,
> More sharpe then points of needles did proceede,
> Shooting forth farre away two flaming streames,
> Full of sad powre, that poysonous bale did breede
> To all, that on him lookt without good heed,
> And secretly his enemies did slay:
> Like as the Basiliske of serpents seede,
> From powrefull eyes close venim doth conuay
> Into the lookers hart, and killeth farre away.
>
> (IV.viii.39)

The passage shows how the use of a simile can accentuate the monstrosity of a humanoid creature: alluding to a vast teratological tradition,[14] Spenser turns the eyes of the giant into monstrous signifiers that stress the giant's deviousness, and his ability to infect his victims.[15] Such interaction between text and tradition, which plays to the readers' knowledge and

12 Spenser chooses the name Cormoraunt because cormorants have a rich moral and theological subtext: as Hamilton explains (note to II.xii.8.5), they feature in the episode of fallen Edom (Isaiah 34.11), and represent gluttony and usury in medieval iconography (see Chaucer, *The Parliament of Fowles*, 362). Tonkin's explanation that Cormoraunt 'belong[s] with the monsters at fords who so frequently appear in Arthurian romance' (*Courteous Pastoral*, p. 68) also relates the giant to the notorious amphibious habitats of infernal monsters.

13 According to the Judaeo-Christian tradition, these monsters were sired by angels on Cain's daughters: as the angels were associated with fire, the monsters inherited the fiery, glowing eyes from them (see Genesis 6.1–6, and Williams, *Deformed Discourse*, pp. 149–50).

14 For the basilisk, see Pliny, *Naturalis historia*, VIII.32–3; Isidore, *Etymologiae*, XII.4.6–9; *Ashmole Bestiary*, p. 114; *Batman vppon Bartholome* XVIII.16; and Topsell, *Historie*, III, 677–81. The vast history of the basilisk is surveyed in: Marianne Sammer, 'Basilisk – regulus', in *Dämonen, Monster, Fabelwesen*, ed. by Müller and Wunderlich, pp. 135–60, and R. McN. Alexander, 'The Evolution of the Basilisk', *Greece and Rome*, 2nd Series, 10 (1963), 170–81. Williams relates the concept of the lethal look to Pliny, *Naturalis Historia*, VII.2.6–17 (see *Deformed Discourse*, pp. 150–1).

15 The giant has the power to cast 'secret flakes of lustfull fire / From his false eyes, into their [i.e. his victims'] harts and parts entire. // 49 // Therefore *Corflambo* he was cald aright' (IV.viii.48.8–49.1). See Watson, 'Forreine and Monstrous Beasts', p. 176.

education, realises giants as humanoid creatures constantly bordering on the beastly and the monstrous.

Other means of adding to the giant's otherness is the multiplication of body parts already discussed with regard to Orgoglio's dragon and the Blatant Beast.[16] This monstrous signifier appears in various specimens. While Doubt, the Porter of the Temple of Venus, resembles Janus in that he has 'a double face, / Th'one forward looking, th'other backeward bent' (IV.x.12.3–4), Geryoneo is Spenser's new version of the triple-bodied giant Geryon, as the suffix *-neo* suggests.[17] Geryoneo, who evokes the King of Spain through his mythological father Geryon,[18] does not only sport the excessive strength and size usually associated with the giants; he also has an excess of body parts that goes beyond what the reader can actually visualise: he has three bodies joined at the waist (V.x.8.8), 'armes and legs of three' (x.8.9) and 'three double hands thrise multiplyde' (xi.6.2), which give him such subtleness in combat that he is as good as invincible.[19] Geryoneo is therefore a deviant variation on the human body, positioned at the very limit of what can be described through language.[20]

As almost all the giants in *The Faerie Queene* have allegorical names, they seem to be vessels for Spenser's allegory, even more so than the dragons and four-footed monsters discussed above. However, Spenserians from various generations have sensed that allegory alone cannot comprehend their nature. S. K. Heninger, Jr, in his valuable article on the Orgoglio episode, suggests that Orgoglio, whose name signifies pride,[21] should not be interpreted allegorically *before* Spenser assigns him

16 On the superfluity of body parts, see Isidore, *Etymologiae*, XI.iii.7.

17 In classical mythology, Geryon is a monstrous giant who draws his lineage from Chryasor and Kallirhoe. Hesiod explains that Hercules killed the giant and captured his herd of enormous red oxen, thus accomplishing one of the labours that eventually won him the hand of Deianeira (see Hesiod, *Theogony*, 287–94 and 979–83).

18 See Conti's abstract of Geryon in *Mythologiae*, VI.1 (p. 205.a.44–8). This correlation in *The Faerie Queene* is observed by Richard F. Hardin in *Civil Idolatry: Desacralizing and Monarchy in Spenser, Sidney, and Milton* (Newark: University of Delaware Press, 1992), pp. 112–13. Geryoneo and his monster are explicitly related to the Spanish Inquisition in *FQ*, V.x.27–8.

19 Spenser's versification here makes it sound as if Geryoneo had eighteen hands. Along similar lines, Nohrnberg compares Geryoneo to Shiva the Destroyer (see *Analogy*, p. 420).

20 By contrast, Alciato's emblem of Geryon lacks such monstrosity, as it illustrates harmony. For the image, see Andrea Alciato, *Emblematum liber* (Padua: Tozzi, 1621), emblem 40 (accessed via www.mun.ca/alciato/).

21 Orgoglio is Italian for 'pride, disdaine, haughtines', as John Florio explains in *A Worlde of Wordes, or Most copious, and exact Dictionarie in Italian and English* (London: Arnold Hatfield, 1598), p. 248. Cf. Book of Wisdom 14.6, which interprets giants as symbols of overbearing pride.

a name.[22] More recently, Hamilton, when commenting on Disdayne, a giant made of metal, hypothesises that Spenser endows him with 'both life and sence' (II.vii.40.8), because '[t]he allegorist insists that his most allegorical figure is not merely allegorical'.[23] Following the lead that the giants in *The Faerie Queene* are more than just allegorical ciphers, the following analyses approach these creatures through their corporeality.

The Albion giants

Spenser's familiarity with giant lore is perhaps best attested by his treatment of the Albion giants, one of the rare cases where he draws extensively on an already existing monstrous race. The giants of Britain appear most notably in the *Chronicle of Briton Kings* (II.x), where they are described as the isle's original inhabitants:

> But far in land a saluage nation dwelt,
> Of hideous Giaunts, and halfe beastly men,
> That neuer tasted grace, nor goodnes felt,
> But like wild beastes lurking in loathsome den,
> And flying fast as Roebucke through the fen,
> All naked without shame, or care of cold,
> By hunting and by spoiling liueden;
> Of stature huge, and eke of corage bold,
> That sonnes of men amazd their sternesse to behold.
>
> (II.x.7)

Spenser here uses a repertoire of stock epithets and stock characteristics to mark the wild giants as a race of huge and bold creatures inhabiting caves in the heart of Albion,[24] and living as a pre-civilised nation of wild men that seem to resemble animals more than humans.[25] However, they are

22 S. K. Heninger, Jr, 'The Orgoglio Episode in *The Faerie Queene*', *English Literary History* 26 (1959), 171–87.

23 Hamilton, note to II.vii.40.8. Disdayne is discussed in the section on automata, below.

24 In Geoffrey's *Historia*, 21, the giants are driven *to* the caves ('gigantes ad cauernas montium fugant' ('they drove the giants into the caves of the mountains')). For the text, see Geoffrey of Monmouth, *The Historia Regum Britannie of Geoffrey of Monmouth. I: Bern, Burgerbibliothek, MS. 568*, ed. by Neil Wright (Cambridge: Brewer, 1985), pp. 13–14. Waswo rightly points out that they 'aren't identified with the land at the outset; they are literally driven *into* it, scattered into its nonarable parts, by the invaders' (Richard Waswo, 'The History That Literature Makes', *New Literary History* 19 (1987/88), 541–64 (p. 554); emphasis added).

25 According to Harper, Spenser's Albion giants – both fierce and terrifying, as the term 'sternesse' suggests – are modelled on a passage in Holinshed's *Chronicles*, where they are described as beings that 'seemed little or nothing to differ from brute beasts' (*Variorum*, II, 305–6). The Albion giants' 'flying fast as Roebucke' (*FQ*, II.x.7.5) suggests I

not only beastly in the corporeal sense, for their living outside the realm of grace, goodness and shame also places them outside moral and theological categories. Spenser additionally maligns the giants as a godless, monstrous perversion of pre-lapsarian man by stressing that they are '[a]ll naked'. These giants may resemble humans, but negate human norms and principles: like the strange races, they are creatures of exile, dwelling on the edge of the world, and outside divine order.[26]

As Spenser develops his version of the Albion giants by resorting to a vast tradition, he refrains from in-depth anatomisation, focusing instead on the unclear origin of these monstrosities, which he partly explains with the myth of Dioclesian's fifty daughters, who were stranded on the British Islands through a 'monstrous error' (8.3).[27] Once there, they copulated with 'feends and filthy Sprights' (8.6), excited with the 'vaine illusion of their lust vnclene' (8.7), and gave birth to the giants that consecutively populated and polluted the island (8.8–9.2). This story, which Spenser does not take over in unadulterated form,[28] marks the women as physically and morally contaminated humans that willingly indulge in a gross transgression, in which the human becomes one with the devilish, and in which the physical (i.e. the women's bodies) joins the immaterial (i.e. the evil spirits). As the offspring of this union, the giant is the embodiment of a monstrous transgression, and, in turn, becomes a physically and morally transgressive monster. In effect, the giants, created in an act of wantonness reminiscent of Genesis 6.1–2, where 'the sons of God went in to the daughters of man' to create giants, cannot help but be creatures with insatiable basic instincts and a downright appetite for destruction:[29]

Chronicles 12.8, where the Gadites, fierce warriors that ally themselves with David, have faces like lions, and the swiftness 'of the roes upon the mountains'. Spenser also likens the giant Ollyphant's swiftness to that of the roe (III.xi.5.8).

26 The Albion giants thus also conform to the three distinctive features of monstrous races identified by Debra Higgs Strickland: '(1) remote location, (2) unusual physical form, and (3) bizarre behaviour' ('Monstrosity and Race in the Late Middle Ages', in *The Ashgate Research Companion to Monsters and the Monstrous*, ed. by Mittman and Dendle, pp. 365–86 (p. 370)).

27 Lotspeich claims that this is 'material on the borderland between classic myth and English chronicle history' (*Classical Mythology*, p. 54). Spenser here seems to hint at one of the possible etymologies of the word *Albion*, for legend has it that the eldest of Dioclesian's (or Daunus's) daughters went by the name of Albine (see also Hugh MacLachlan, 'Britains, Britons', in *Spenser Encyclopedia*, ed. by Hamilton, p. 113; for an extended discussion, see Cohen, *Of Giants*, p. 33 and pp. 44–60).

28 In the chronicles, 'all but one of Dioclesian's fifty daughters killed their husbands on their wedding night, the exception being Albine who gave birth to Albion' (Hamilton, note to II.x.8.4).

29 Against such a backdrop, the account of the giants and their origin reads like a 'heathen' version of Genesis 6.1–2.

in her version of the fall of Troy, Britomart adds the grisly detail that the 'huge nation of Geaunts … fed on liuing flesh, and dronck mens vitall blood' (III.ix.49.8–9).[30] That the giants here figure as a race of cannibals underscores their monstrous and immoral nature, especially since the collocation 'liuing flesh' implies that they eat their victims alive, and that they gain their own life force through the ingestion of their blood.[31] Such unnatural behaviour is employed as a monstrous signifier supplementing their physical monstrosity.[32]

While these daughters are therefore presented as the (conjectural) parents of the giants of Albion, Spenser undercuts this account with a verbal quibble: after relating the giants' parentage, he switches to the etymological spelling 'Geaunts' to indicate their inherent connection to the earth they inhabit. The change in spelling creates confusion as to the giants' genuine origin, because it relates them to the Mother Earth of Albion.[33] As the chronicler explains, these giants so violate and pollute the 'gentle soyle' (II.x. 9.2) of Albion 'That their owne mother loathd their beastlinesse, / And gan abhorre her broods vnkindly crime, / All were they borne of her owne natiue slime' (9.3–5). This passage identifies them as the sons of Albion, a circumstance underlined by the possessive phrases informing this short passage ('their owne mother', 'her broods …'). That they are made of the 'slime' of Albion additionally marks them as earth-born creatures, who share their corporeality with the soil they live on. It thus seems rather likely that Spenser here resorts to Holinshed's theory that these giants 'tooke their name of the soile where they were borne',[34] and turns it into a more thoroughgoing familial relation. He stresses this bond by investing Albion with the traits of a mother, and by assigning her human emotions and the sense to tell the natural from the unnatural ('vnkindly').

The giants, appearing as wild men, can only be overcome by the forces of civilisation. Brutus and his men, landing on the island by error just like Dioclesian's daughters before him, vanquish the Albion giants in a series of 'great batteils' (10.3). Spenser's account of the fights stresses the kinship between the soil of Albion and the giants because he points out

30 See III.ix.49–60 for the full passage.

31 Cf. also Cohen, *Of Giants*, p. 38.

32 On the notion of behavorial deformity, see also Davies, 'The Unlucky, the Bad and the Ugly', p. 71.

33 This confusion tallies well with the *caveat* expressed by Spenser's chronicler in II.x.8.1–3: 'But whence they sprong, or how they were begott, / Vneath is to assure, vneath to wene / That monstrous error'.

34 Raphael Holinshed, *Chronicles: England, Scotland, Ireland*, ed. by Henry Ellis and others, 6 vols (London: J. Johson, 1807–8; repr. New York: AMS Press, 1965), I, 432. The reference is Hamilton's (see note to II.x.9.2–4).

that 'many Giaunts [were] left on groning flore' (10.5). The phrase at the end of this line suggests two interpretations: it could be an instance of prosopopeia, that is it describes the pain felt by the earth of Albion when the giants fall. If, however, Spenser here uses an *enallage*, 'groning' could obliquely refer to the giants, who experience pain when being beaten and killed by the invaders. Such a deliberately ambivalent rhetorical strategy establishes a bond between the giants and the earth they live on. Hence, the monstrous fights have left their traces on Albion's soil: the destruction of the giant inevitably leads to the violation of their mother earth. Again, Britomart's rendering of the fall of Troy in Book III, Canto ix, makes such a connection more profound, for she recounts that the earth even 'quaked vnder [the giants'] so hideous masse' (50.6). The falling giant thus creates an earthquake, which stresses the elemental forces at work in these monstrosities.

The interdependence between the giants and the earth of Albion is further elaborated in the short depictions of the battles, which Spenser takes over in condensed form from Geoffrey of Monmouth's *Historia*.[35] In these battles, both Gogmagog, whom Spenser calls Goëmot, and Coulin appear briefly: Spenser records that the former was beaten and slain by Corineus (10.8–9), and that the latter, after Debon forces him to perform a leap over 'eight lugs of grownd' (11.3), falls back and crash-lands into the 'ample Pitt' (11.1) he has just jumped over. This feat, Spenser's chronicler writes, is second only to Godmer's throwing 'three monstrous stones' at 'bold *Carnutus*' (11.9).[36] To this roll-call, Spenser adds geographical details when explaining that, to this day, one can see '[t]he westerne Hogh, besprincled with the gore / Of mighty *Goëmot*' (10.7–8). Although the bloody details of the giant's death point firmly to Geoffrey, the location is at odds with both Geoffrey and Holinshed, who locate the event at Totnesse (Geoffrey) and Dover (Holinshed).[37] As scholars have noted, Spenser's source is a local legend recorded by William Camden in his *Britannia*,[38] which refers it to Plymouth Hoe, where the giants' 'effigies were cut into the chalk of the hillside and preserved'.[39] In his chronicle,

35 See Geoffrey of Monmouth, *Historia*, 21.

36 Whether Carnutus, who eventually kills Godmer, is a giant himself, or whether he is one of Brutus's army, is left unexplained. This part of the chronicle is supposed to be Spenser's own invention (Hamilton, note to II.x.11.5–9). Godmer is the son of 'hideous *Albion*' (11.6–7) who was defeated by Hercules in France. Spenser elaborates on Albion in IV.xi.16.

37 See Harper in *Variorum*, II, 307–8.

38 See Harper in *Variorum*, II, 307–8.

39 Hamilton, note to II.x.10.7–9. For the local tradition, see Harper, *Variorum*, II, 307–8.

Spenser hence does not only use a description that relates how the gigantic is literally inscribed into Britain's landscape but also resorts to a local tradition that again foregrounds the union between the earth and the giant, and emphasises the physicality of the monster. As the syntax makes clear, Spenser also summons the 'ample Pitt', where Coulin perished, as a geographical witness to Britain's history of giants, thus again stressing that the monstrous is visible on England's soil.[40] With such gigantism even Albion's rocks become susceptible to the enormous: that Godmer hurls 'three *monstrous* stones' (emphasis added) at Carnutus identifies the entire country as a potentially monstrous habitat. Spenser's take on the Albion giants hence focuses on the giant as the representation of pre-cultural forces: omitting to describe the giants' corporeality in greater detail (something he clearly reserves for his own gigantic creatures, to which we now turn), Spenser shows that the giant's transgressive body, and his disfigured entrails are writ large across Britain's landscape and history at the very moment civilisation begins.[41]

Spenser's major giants

Spenser mainly inscribes the gigantic into *The Faerie Queene* to force his heroes into proving their manliness. At first sight, Orgoglio, who is the first of his kind to appear in the epic, seems to be the blueprint of a romance giant: he is a club-wielding monster, tall as three of the tallest men and an almost invincible opponent who defeats Redcrosse and is vanquished only by Arthur.[42] Spenser elaborates on these traditional features to turn the standard giant into a monstrosity that outmeasures all natural creations. Orgoglio is furnished with a distinctly titanic lineage: as is expounded in I.vii.9, he was sired by Æolus, the wind god, who filled the womb of Mother Earth with air. She then gave birth to her son in an earthquake, bringing 'forth this monstrous masse of earthly slyme, / Puft vp with emptie wynd, and fild with sinfull cryme' (9.8–9): this description identifies the giant as a combination of the elements of earth and water ('slyme') with air, that is Orgoglio embodies three of the four elements.[43]

40 Whereas Harper (*Variorum*, II, 308) und subsequent critics note that no source has been found for Coulin and his leap, Sheryl L. Forste-Grupp purports that Spenser bases his account on traditional Irish lore ('A Possible Irish Source for the Giant Coulin in Spenser's *Faerie Queene*', *Studies in Philology* 96 (1999), 42–50).

41 Britomart notes that the quelling of the giants is a 'famous history to bee enrold / In euerlasting moniments of brasse' (III.ix.50.7–8).

42 See I.vii–viii.

43 Hamilton, note to I.vii.9.8, makes a similar observation. Spenser's text evokes Isidore's

Spenser's use of rhetoric underlines Orgoglio's grotesque nature, since the giant consists of shapeless matter filled with insubstantial wind: this joining of the material with the immaterial is reminiscent of Spenser's take on Genesis in his history of the Albion giants, where women copulate with evil spirits. In ontological terms, such a conception is parodic of human creation and birth,[44] and renders the giant's corporeality, whose inflated body suggests the phallus,[45] a striking paradox.[46]

Spenser elaborates on another decisive feature of giants and wild men, namely the 'snaggy Oke' (10.7) on which Orgoglio leans. Since he ripped the tree '[o]ut of his mothers bowelles' (10.8) in an act of mutilation, the club is not merely used as a sign of the giant's proverbial strength, but rather corroborates his monstrous character.[47] When his oaken club later misses Arthur in single combat,[48] he unwittingly inflicts further violence on his mother, causing a wound that runs three yards deep:[49]

> The sad earth wounded with so sore assay,
> Did grone full grieuous vnderneath the blow,
> And trembling with strange feare, did like an erthquake show.
> (I.viii.8.7–9)

description of the birth of the giants in *Etymologiae*, XI.iii.13: 'eo quod fabulose parens terra immensa mole et similes sibi genuerit' ('because in their fable the parent Earth begot them as like itself, with their immense mass'; *Etymologies*, p. 244). Heninger reads Orgoglio as the 'mythical embodiment of an earthquake' ('Orgoglio', pp. 172–3).

44 Interpretations of this stanza are numerous; see Hamilton's commentary for a good overview of possible hypotheses (Hamilton, note to I.vii.9). Seznec points out that William of Conches, in his commentary on Boethius's *Consolatio Philosophiae*, identifies giants as images of human bodies (see Jean Seznec, *The Survival of the Pagan Gods: The Mythological Tradition and Its Place in Renaissance Humanism and Art*, trans. from the French by Barbara F. Sessions, Bollingen Series, 38 (Princeton: Princeton University Press, 1972), p. 91; remarked by Hamilton, p. 93, note to I.vii.9.8). This observation suggests that Orgoglio is a parody of the human body.

45 Orgoglio's phallic nature is discussed at length in John W. Schroeder, 'Spenser's Erotic Drama: The Orgoglio Episode', *English Literary History* 29 (1962), 140–59. Marks and Gross refer to Greek ὀργάω, 'to swell with moisture or lust', and ὄργη, 'passion, ire' ('Names', p. 494).

46 Spenser's building the final two lines on the rhyme 'slyme/cryme' links the giant's corporeal matter to his immoral nature (see I.vii.9.8–9).

47 For the detail, see also Geoffrey of Monmouth's *Historia*, 21, which records that Gogmagog could tear up an oak tree 'uelut uirgulam corili' ('like a hazel twig').

48 Nohrnberg states that Arthur is *the* giant-slayer in *The Faerie Queene* (see *Analogy*, p. 264). Other giant slayers are the virgin Palladine, who pursues Argante (III.vii.37–44; 52), and Belphoebe, who kills Lust (IV.vii.29–32). Reid also includes Britomart's victory over Radigund (V.vii.9–10) in his list, although she is an Amazon and not a giant (see 'Spenser's Mutability Song', p. 72).

49 In *Sir Eglamour of Artois*, the giant misses the eponymous hero, ramming his club so deep that he cannot immediately dislodge it (see *Sir Eglamour of Artois*, 307–12; in *The Thornton Romances*, ed. by James Orchard Halliwell (London: Camden Society, 1844)).

In Spenserian criticism, this description has been taken to indicate that the fight becomes progressively more elemental.[50] In conjunction with the earlier section, however, this detail is expressive of a more thoroughgoing monstrosity. Since Spenser anatomises Earth by referring to her intestines and wounds, and since he animates her through prosopopeia, i.e. through furnishing her with voice, movement and emotion, he defames Orgoglio as the violator of his own mother. The giant's act of deformation hence puts the spotlight firmly on his own moral deformity. Even more critically, these acts of atrocity are also moments of self-violence, as Orgoglio consists of earth himself.

Thus, Spenser's depiction of Orgoglio's heinousness works along different parameters than that of other monsters, because the poet largely disregards visible physiology. Instead, he focuses on the giant's internal processes in a notable simile that likens the force of his blows directed at Redcrosse to cannon fire:

> As when that diuelish yron Engin wrought
> In deepest Hell, and framd by *Furies* skill,
> With windy Nitre and quick Sulphur fraught,
> And ramd with bollet rownd, ordaind to kill,
> Conceiueth fyre, the heauens it doth fill
> With thundring noyse[.]
>
> (I.vii.13.1–6)

This simile, which calls to mind the invention of the cannon in Ariosto's *Orlando Furioso*,[51] associates the workings of Orgoglio's body with those of a cannon, emphasising the ogre's quasi-mechanical quality, which, in turn, undermines his organic basis. The references to warfare also associate the giant with hell, the classical underworld and the element of fire: as the term 'windy', which harks back to his Æolian heritage,[52] is linked with the fiery quality of the 'quick Sulphur' to image forth Orgoglio's violent rage, he becomes as infernal as the machine itself. The reference to fire is especially significant, for it adds the last of the four elements to Orgoglio, so that he finally emerges as the embodiment of the four elements at their most chaotic and unruly. Both the machine and the giant, infernal and earthy as they may be, pose a threat to heaven: as Orgoglio's vertex almost touches the sky,[53] and the cannon's noise resounds in heaven, both are

50 See Hamilton, note to I.viii.9.

51 See Ariosto, *Orlando Furioso*, IX–XI. John Milton drew on Ariosto's idea in the episode where Satan invents cannon warfare in *Paradise Lost*, VI.469–523.

52 The epithet 'windy' refers back to the wind caused by Orgoglio's blow (cf. I.vii.12.7–9).

53 See I.vii.8.4–5. This monstrous topos can be found, e.g., in the Aloidae's attempt at touching and destroying the sky with their hands. See the *Liber Monstrorum*, I.55:

realised as vertical forces that endanger nature and the universe. As this simile turns Orgoglio into an igniting and exploding cannon that works through chemistry, his ontology transcends the natural and marks him as a 'machina infernal'.[54]

So far, external anatomy has not played a major part in constituting Orgoglio's monstrosity. This changes in the giant's fatal fight with Arthur. Orgoglio's strokes now resemble Jupiter's 'threeforked engin' (I.viii.9.6), an image that reads like an Olympian sublimation of the cannon simile. Such imagery, which enhances the giant's strength, makes Arthur's victory all the more heroic. The knight's first blow, which cuts off Orgoglio's left arm (10),[55] induces the giant to cry in pain. Here, Spenser resorts to animal imagery to depict how the monster experiences dismemberment: since he 'lowdly brayd with beastly yelling sownd' (11.3) like a herd of bulls in want of their dams' milk, Orgoglio is labelled as a subhuman creature whose reactions and ways of experience mirror those of animals rather than those of rational beings.[56] In the subsequent combat, Arthur cuts off the giant's right leg below the knee (22) before he finally decapitates him (24), thereby cutting Orgoglio down to size.[57] The minutiae of Orgoglio's death tie in with the former depictions of the giant: when falling, he is first likened to 'an aged tree' (22.5) that is cut down and tumbling down a cliff, then to a castle whose foundation is destroyed by mechanical warfare (23). The first of these two similes harks back to the giant's lineage: like the aged tree, whose roots reached into the soil, his origin is the earth, and like the oak he tore out of Mother Earth's entrails, he is finally uprooted.[58] That Spenser extends the lexical set when referring to the tree's 'mightie trunck' (22.8) emphasises the bearing of this image on the giant's nature; the phrase also relates obliquely to the giant's dismem-

'Scribunt et geminos Aloidas tam immensae corporum magnitudinis fuisse ut ter caelum manibus adgressi essent destruere, ut Iovem, pro flammae regnandi cupidine, summo detruderunt Olympo' ('They also write that the twin Aloidae were of such immense bodily size that that they tried three times to destroy the sky with their hands, because of a burning desire to rule, so that they could hurl down Jupiter from high Olympus'; the translation is taken from Orchard, *Pride and Prodigies*, p. 287). It is also reminiscent of Dame Nature as a gigantic deity; see the discussion of Orgoglio's dragon, above.

54 The quotation is from *Orlando Furioso*, XI.23.1.

55 Spenser likens the severed member to an inanimate block in I.viii.10.6.

56 Compare Hesiod, *Theogony*, 831–2.

57 Arthur's action is reminiscent of the alliterative *Morte Arthure*, 2126–9, where Arthur slices a giant through above the knees before beheading him (references are to *King Arthur's Death: The Middle English Stanzaic Morte Arthur and Alliterative Morte Arthure*, ed. by Larry D. Benson (Kalamazoo, : Western Michigan University for TEAMS, 1994)).

58 In his notes to I.viii.22, Hamilton interprets the tree simile as a reversal of I.viii.18, where the epic narrator claims that Orgoglio could have overthrown 'the strongest Oake'.

bered body, which now consists only of the torso without head, arm and leg. Thus mutilated and deprived of his superhuman size and strength, the giant is bereft of his monstrosity.[59] Orgoglio's death is ultimately depicted as an act of reversed creation: when the giant is beheaded by Arthur, his demise is accompanied by an earthquake, a natural disorder that had already turned his birth into a prodigy. This is consonant with his return to the slime and air he is made of:

> That huge great body, which the Gyaunt bore,
> Was vanisht quite, and of that monstrous mas
> Was nothing left, but like an emptie blader was.
>
> (24.7–9)

Spenser's thematic *repetitio* brings into view the monstrous nature of the giant, but adds an even more grotesque note to it, as 'monstrous mas' and 'emptie bladder' are incongruent terms. In consequence, Orgoglio's physical diminishment rounds off the life of a being whose existence parodied humanity.[60]

Another significant variation on the gigantic is LUST, who appears in Canto vii of Book IV, a section of the poem narrating the abduction and escape of courtly Amoret. Although never named in the main text of the poem, the argument of IV.vii identifies the creature as 'greedie lust'.[61] Like the Blatant Beast, this being unexpectedly rushes out of the wood,[62] but in stark contrast to the doggish fiend he seizes women to hold them as captives in his cave to rape and eat them. Unlike other monsters discussed so far, Lust is not defined through a pedigree; it is not even clear whether he was born of beasts or of the earth.[63] Negative description additionally defines him as a subhuman entity: as he is neither man (IV.vii.5.2) nor beast (7.7–8), his nature is more difficult to determine than that of most other creatures in the poem. He resembles the Wild Man in that his

59 Similarly, Redcrosse dismembers the Great Dragon to deprive the monster of its monstrosity; see the discussion in Chapter 6, above.

60 Hankins confers Orgoglio to de Guilleville's Pride, Satan's puffed-up daughter, in *The Pilgrimage of the Life of Man*, 14162–7 (see Hankins, *Source and Meaning*, pp. 126–7; cf. also Cohen, *Of Giants*, p. 51).

61 James W. Broaddus explains that Spenser uses the term *lust* to signify 'the corruption of sexual desire caused by the complex of idleness, lewdness, inconstancy, and the like' ('Renaissance Psychology ane Britomart's Adventures in *Faerie Queene* III', *English Literary Renaissance* 17 (1987), 186–206 (p. 193)).

62 The topos of the giant's sudden and inexplicable appearance also surfaces in Mannyng's *Chronicle*, 11965–70; see Robert Mannyng of Brunne, *The Chronicle*, ed. by Idelle Sullens, Medieval and Renaissance Texts and Studies, 153 (Binghamton: State University of New York at Binghamton University, 1996).

63 See IV.vii.7.7–9.

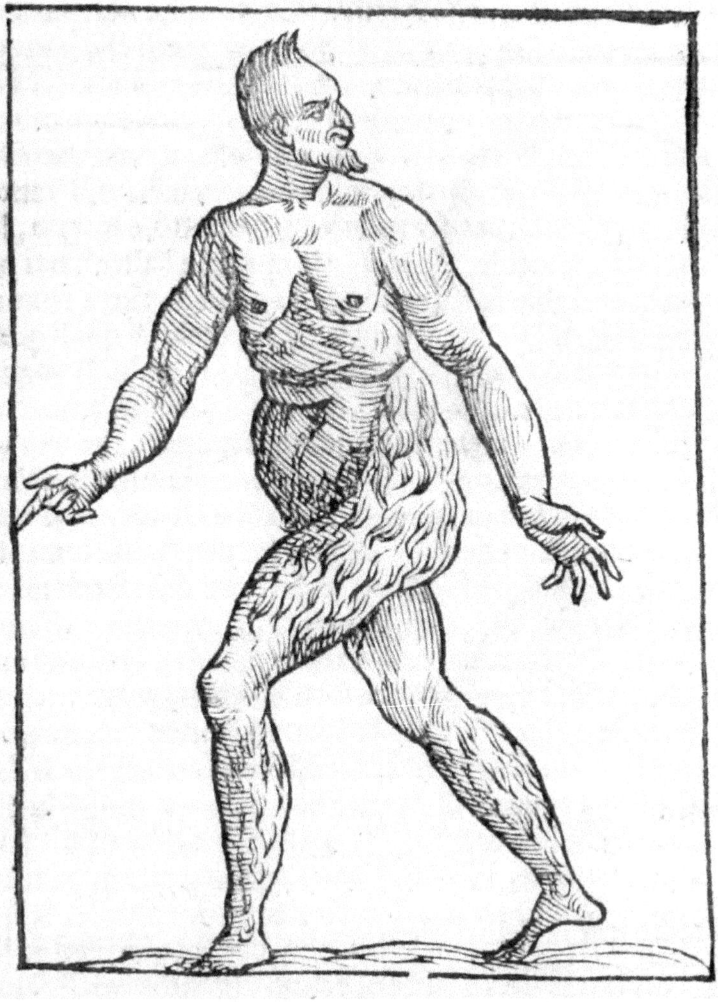

Figure 9 Lustful man; from Gio. Battista della Porta, *Della fisionomia dell'huomo*

entire body is covered with hair (5.4–5 and 7.3) and his waist with ivy; like Orgoglio, he carries 'a tall young oake' with 'knottie sags' (7.4–5). Although he has human attributes, his height marks his excessive size, exceeding that of a human being by a span (5.3). Into such a sketchy outline of his body Spenser embeds signifiers that characterise the creature as extremely lustful: the giant's carrying an oak suggests phallus-like virility,[64] and ivy encodes sexual appetite.[65] His excess of hair further underscores his covetousness. The woodcut of the lustful man in della Porta's *Della fisionomia dell'huomo* illustrates the currency of this notion: the image depicts a naked man covered in hair, and displaying large limbs, especially legs. His torso segues from the lower belly straight into the rest of his nether body parts, which illustrates the degree to which his beastliness infects his upper body (see Figure 9).[66] In the giant Lust, Spenser exaggerates this traditional image into the downright monstrous.

Lust's most impressive physical feature, however, is his head, which Spenser anatomises *ad nauseam* (5.5–6.9):

> … his wide mouth did gape
> With huge great teeth, like to a tusked Bore:
> For he liu'd all on rauin and on rape
> Of men and beasts; and fed on fleshly gore,
> The signe whereof yet stain'd his bloudy lips afore.
>
> His neather lip was not like man nor beast,
> But like a wide deepe poke, downe hanging low,
> In which he wont the relickes of his feast,
> And cruell spoyle, which he had spard, to stow:
> And ouer it his huge great nose did grow,
> Full dreadfully empurpled all with bloud;
> And downe both sides two wide long eares did glow,
> And raught downe to his waste, when vp he stood,
> More great then th'eares of Elephants by *Indus* flood.

The size and the shape of his teeth, lower lip, nose and ears mark Lust's head as a giant deformity.[67] Stock tautologies such as 'huge great' (which

64 Orgoglio also carries such an implement; Leslie notes that 'clubs and maces are primarily the attributes of figures either representative of or strongly associated with lust' (*Spenser's 'Fierce Warres'*, p. 77).

65 See Hamilton, note to IV.vii.7.1–4.

66 In the Middle Ages, Huguccio of Pisa derived the word *monster* from *mastruca*, 'hairy garment' (Rome, Vat. Bib. Reg. Lat. 1627, fol. 144; quoted in Friedman, 'Monsters at the World's Imagined Corners', p. 56).

67 In Chrétien de Troyes's *Le chevalier au lion*, Calogrenant encounters a churl whose facial features also resemble those of animals; among others, 'oroilles mossues et granz / autiex com a uns olifanz' ('his ears were as hairy and as huge as an elephant's'; *Le chevalier*, 297–8). The English *Yvain and Gawain*, 257, renders this passage as 'He had eres als ane olyfant'; see *Sir Perceval of Galles and Ywain and Gawain*, ed. by Mary Flowers Braswell (Kalamazoo: Medieval Institute Publications, 1995). The description of the giant covers *Le chevalier au lion*, 288–326; for text and translation of Chrétien's romance, see Chrétien de Troyes, *The Knight with the Lion, or Yvain (Le chevalier au lion)*, ed. and trans. by William W. Kibler, Garland Library of Medieval Literature, Series A, 48 (New York and London: Garland Publishing, 1985).

Spenser uses twice) and 'wide long' are one stylistic means of emphasising size; similes are another: the image of the boar's tusks,[68] an animal that encodes lust, illustrates the fierceness of these oversized teeth. His gigantic ears, which dwarf those of an elephant, reach down to his waist,[69] a circumstance that suggests the likewise hairy and lustful Cyclops in medieval art,[70] but also the *panotii*, a monstrous race with extremely large ears.[71] But Spenser does not only represent the giant's beastly nature by a set of animal similes; he also accentuates Lust's monstrosity by characterising his maw as a monstrous orifice, whose lips are tainted by blood and gore.[72] Spenser here establishes a significant link to other monstrous mouths, especially those of the Blatant Beast and Orgoglio's dragon.

What makes Lust's face especially repulsive is the graphic depiction of nose and lower lip ('poke'), which resemble phallus and scrotum.[73] By relocating the sexual to the face, thus combining unrelated organs through 'iconographic inversion',[74] Spenser does not only disclose what is usually concealed; he also creates, as MacCaffrey rightly points out, 'an animated version of the male genitalia'.[75] But as in a picture puzzle, a shift in focus adds a new dimension to Lust's anatomy. His mouth, gaping wide with huge teeth, suggests another deformity, namely the *vagina dentata*.[76] If this hypothesis is correct, Lust emerges as a most grotesque

68 In *Yvain and Gawain*, 262, the giant also has 'tethe like bare-tuskes'.

69 On Lust's elephantine physiognomy, which links him to Ollyphant, see Nohrnberg, *Analogy*, p. 637.

70 See, e.g., the illustration of the Cyclops in Ovid, *Metamorphose d'Ovide figurée*, 81; and, for a discussion of this creature, Mary Baine Campbell, 'The Nude Cyclops in the Custome Book', in *Marvels, Monsters, and Miracles*, ed. by Jones and Sprunger, pp. 285–301.

71 See among others Pomponius Mela, *De chorographia*, III.56 (for the Latin text, see Pomponius Mela, *Kreuzfahrt durch die Alte Welt*, ed. and trans. by Kai Brodersen (Darmstadt: Wissenschaftliche Buchgesellschaft, 1994)), and *Mandeville's Travels*, p. 148.

72 The association with beasts tallies well with Spenser's referring to Lust's animal nurture, since the poet conjectures that he 'was with milke of Wolues and Tygres fed' (IV.vii.7.9).

73 See Hamilton, note to IV.vii.6.2. Nohrnberg, on the other hand, purports that the ears signify the scrotum (see *Analogy*, p. 637, n. 543). Like Lust, the cannibals depicted on the Hereford Map also have big noses.

74 The term is Williams's (*Deformed Discourse*, p. 165). It also corresponds to item eight on Isidore's list of monstrosities, the 'mislocation of organs or parts in the body' (see Chapter 5, above).

75 MacCaffrey, *Spenser's Allegory*, p. 288; see also Silberman, *Transforming Desire*, p. 121. In medieval iconography, genitalia and face are sometimes inverted (see Williams, *Deformed Discourse*, pp. 161–8).

76 William C. Oram maintains that the 'poke' evokes female associations, so that Lust is a bisexual creature diametrically opposed to the likewise bisexual Venus in IV.x (see 'Elizabethan Fact and Spenserian Fiction', *Spenser Studies* 4 (1983), 33–47 (p. 42)). Hence Lust and Venus are conceived as *in malo* and *in bono* figurations of sexual desire.

and horrifying being that conjoins mutually exclusive opposites. Spenser's strategy brings to mind combinatory representations of these organs in medieval art,[77] and finally marks the giant as the embodiment of both Amoret's and Timias's sexual desires.[78] A look at the monster's indulging in the (alliterative) actions of ravin and rape offers further evidence for the claim that the giant is created through conjoining opposites.[79] Aemilia tells the abducted Amoret that Lust lives 'on the spoile of women', whom he 'with his shamefull lust doth first deflowre, / And afterwards themselues doth cruelly deuoure' (12.5; 12.8–9).[80] Hence, Spenser utilises rhyme to combine two interdependent, yet disparate ideas:[81] whereas the former is in keeping with the performance of an obscene beastly masculinity (robbing maidens of their virginity), the latter is reminiscent of the all-swallowing female orifice that represents the union of sex and eating, so his entire face represents the horrors of sexual invasion and dietary ingestion.[82] Thus, the rhyming couplet, which on a simple level encodes the link between lechery and gluttony,[83] is as grotesque as the figure it characterises.

In effect, Lust perverts the concept of the head as the seat of reason and language,[84] and turns it into a 'sexed' body signifying irrationality and beastliness.[85] Such a verdict is confirmed when Spenser brings into focus Lust's bestial habits: he abducts women and keeps them in a cave

77 Williams points out that pictorial renderings of this deformity were frequently found in medieval iconography (see *Deformed Discourse*, pp. 161–4). Oram suggests a parallel to Bruegel's *Allegory of Lust* (1557), which depicts a demon with a large nose and an open mouth (see 'Elizabethan Fact', p. 47, n. 21).

78 See Oram, 'Elizabethan Fact', p. 43. On the interchangeability of vagina and mouth, cf. Cohen, *Of Giants*, p. 68.

79 Although uttered in a different context, Michael W. Twomey's statement that 'among the giants love is merely appetite' brings into relief the universal perverseness of Spenser's carnal giants ('Falling Giants and Floating Lead: Scholastic History in the Middle English *Cleanness*', in *Marvels, Monsters, and Miracles*, ed. by Jones and Sprunger, pp. 141–65 (p. 156)).

80 Lust's dedication to rape and cannibalism suggests the Giant of Mont St Michel's horrific practices in the alliterative *Morte Arthure*, 840–1151. The source of this version is *The Story of Merlin*, 53, in *Lancelot-Grail*, I, 403–5.

81 Susumu Kawanishi diagnoses that the 'connection between eating and sexual activity is made emphatic by the rhyme *deflower/devoure*' but does not draw further conclusions from this observation ('Lust', in *Spenser Encyclopaedia*, ed. by Hamilton, pp. 442–3 (p. 442)).

82 For further background, cf. Williams, *Deformed Discourse*, p. 165.

83 Cf. Cohen, *Of Giants*, p. 48 (on the giant of Mont Saint Michel).

84 For theoretical background, cf. Williams, *Deformed Discourse*, p. 156.

85 On the general nexus between the male and the monstrous, see Liz Herbert McAvoy, 'Monstrous Masculinities in Julian of Norwich's *A Revelation of Love* and *The Book of Margery Kempe*', in *Monstrous Middle Ages*, ed. by Bildhauer and Mills, pp. 55–74. See also the use of speech by Geryoneo's dragon, the hyena and the Blatant Beast.

he covers with a stone, a method reminiscent of Polyphemus in the *Odyssey*.[86] His self-centred sexual appetite is rendered in a covert description of masturbation:[87] after entering the cave, Lust, 'spredding ouer all the floor alone, / Gan dight him selfe vnto his wonted sinne; / Which ended, then his bloudy banket should beginne' (20.7–9). Spenser here implies that Lust commits what Thomas Aquinas calls the *vitium contra naturam* ('the unnatural vice') by stressing that the giant performs the act 'alone', and by using reflexive pronouns ('him selfe' and 'his').[88] That Lust's action is habitual ('his wonted sinne') adds to the impression that this is lechery at its most monstrous. But Lust, like Orgoglio, has to pay for his vicious nature and sinful, non-normative behaviour by meeting his deserved end at the hands of Belphoebe, whose arrow pierces his throat. Although she here acts as the executrix of poetic justice, her attitude towards Lust's corpse, however, is rather ambiguous: 'Yet ouer him she long there gazing stood, / And oft admir'd his monstrous shape, and oft / His mighty limbs' (32.6–8). True, the verb *to admire* covers a broad spectrum of meaning, such as 'to regard with wonder'; 'gaze at passionately'; 'desire';[89] but Belphoebe's female gaze at the giant's body and, suggestively, at his legs implies that she admires his virility despite her immunity to lust.[90] She thus experiences a momentary paralysis which usually befalls male gazers when catching sight of a woman.[91] This implies her obscene enjoyment when eying a sexual grotesquery. By leaving her reaction deliberately ambivalent, Spenser seems to suggest that lust continues to pose a threat to mankind, because it is a quality innate in every human being.[92]

86 The passage covers Homer, *Odyssey*, IX.105–567. Reference is made to Homer, *The Odyssey*, trans. by A. T. Murray, 2 vols, Loeb Classical Library (Cambridge, MA: Harvard University Press: London: Heinemann, 1919; repr. 1960). Cf. also the sea-orc in Ariosto's *Orlando Furioso*, VIII–XI.

87 See Hankins, *Source and Allegory*, p. 160, Hamilton, note to IV.vii.20.7–9, and James Nohrnberg, '*The Faerie Queene*, Book IV', *Spenser Encyclopedia*, ed. Hamilton, pp. 273–80 (p. 277).

88 According to Thomas Aquinas, masturbation is the worst form of sexual aberration; see *Summa theologiae* IIaIIae, question 154, article 12, in Thomas Aquinas, *Summa theologiae*, ed. by P. Caramello (Turin and Rome: Marietti, 1952), II, 674–6.

89 See *OED*, s.v. 'admire, *v.*'.

90 Broaddus underestimates the relevance of the monstrous for Belphoebe's gaze when pointing out that the scene 'continues her characterization as a personage whose commitment to the virgin life governs a potentiality for the sexual' (*Spenser's Allegory of Love*, p. 103). Belphoebe's admiration of Lust's corpse suggests not only the spectators staring at the dragon at I.xii.10–11 and the Blatant Beast at VI.xii.37.7–9, but also Leda ogling the swan's 'pryde' at III.xi.32.9.

91 On male paralysis, see Krier, *Gazing on Secret Sights*, pp. 113–14.

92 Nohrnberg lists some parallels between Lust and the monstrous hyena (see *Analogy*, pp. 636–7).

Although Orgoglio and Lust are creatures representing monstrous excess, Spenser creates them along very different parameters. Part of Orgoglio's monstrosity is conveyed through lineage, while his materiality is characterised by a formless mixture of elements. Hence, he is much more of an internal monstrosity whose gigantism parodies human nature. Lust, on the other hand, is depicted as an external anatomical deformity that exists without a traceable pedigree; his physical appearance, unlike Orgoglio's, is clearly delineated and does not hinge on the anatomy of the shapeless. In effect, Spenser creates one giant as a monstrous nothing and the other as a deformed blending of disparate, wrongly relocated body parts, thus showing the variety possible within one single teratological category.

Lust's urge to eat and rape marks him as a creature that constantly transgresses the boundaries of his own body. In *The Faerie Queene*, such gigantic transgression is most fully realised in the twins who were conceived in an act of incest committed by the Titan Typhon on his mother Earth when he was 'drunke with [the] blood of men' he had just slain (III.I.vii.I.47.7): [93] Argante,[94] a man-snatching giantess wielding an iron mace,[95] and her brother Ollyphant.[96] The circumstance that Typhon is not only known as a Titan but also called 'a great puissant wynde: a whirlwynde' by Thomas Cooper[97] connects him to the wind god Æolus, who sired Orgoglio on Earth. Spenser thus does not simply assign these gigantic beings similar parents; since these parents also represent different elements, he creates his giants from similar ingredients, and thus points to common teratological ground.

In order to accentuate both the moral and the sexual depravity of the

93 Lotspeich notes that Spenser was inspired by Conti's account in *Mythologiae*, VI.22, which makes Typhon the sire of all serpents and dragons (see *Classical Mythology*, p. 114).

94 Argante is one of only three female giants in *The Faerie Queene*. While one remains nameless (the gentle Squire relates that Corflambo was born of a [nameless] 'huge Geauntesse'; IV.viii.47.2), the other, Mutabilitie, features prominently in the 'Cantos of Mutabilitie'.

95 That Argante abducts young men and brings them to a secret island where she can consume them, reminds the reader of Acrasia and her captives in the Bower of Bliss (II. xii), as well as of Lust's carrying off maidens into his secret cave (see III.vii.50).

96 Possible sources for Spenser's giantess are Argante from Tasso's *Gerusalemme Liberata*, and Argante, the Faerie Queen of Avalon, in Laȝamon's *Brut* (see Anderson, 'Arthur, Argante, and the Ideal Vision', in *The Passing of Arthur*, ed. by Baswell and Sharpe, pp. 193–206 (pp. 195–6)). Spenser's source for her brother Ollyphant is Chaucer's *Sir Thopas* (*CT*, VII.807–9).

97 See Cooper's *Thesaurus*, s.v. 'Typhoeus', to which Hamilton also refers (see note to VI.vi.10–12).

siblings, Spenser has the Squire of Dames give a quasi-legendary account of their birth:

> These twinnes, men say, (a thing far passing thought)
> Whiles in their mothers wombe enclosd they were,
> Ere they into the lightsome world were brought,
> In fleshly lust were mingled both yfere,
> And in that monstrous wise did to the world appere.
> (III.vii.48.5–9)

The twins, created in an act of incest, re-enact the sexual transgression committed by their parents.[98] Their monstrosity thus does not lie primarily in their size, but in their indulging in pre-natal intercourse. This aberrant behaviour is a monstrous signifier that drives home the extreme unchastity of their attachment,[99] and marks their birth as unnatural ('that monstrous wise', 48.9). Monstrous births are frequently treated in medieval and early modern writing, and it seems that Spenser here draws on accounts of abnormal humanoid forms, such as conjoined twins.[100]

He arguably turns this biological phenomenon (see Figure 10) into an emblematic image of gigantic carnal transgression: as Argante and Ollyphant play the beast with two backs, they create a unified being with four hands and four legs, which is joined in the midst. Like Lust's exaggerated carnal appetite, Argante's and Ollyphant's shameful practices are grotesquely parodic:[101] their sexual intercourse in the womb may be generally read as a monstrous parody of mutual desire and sexual unity; or more specifically as a grotesque prefiguration of the love consummated by Amoret and Scudamour at the end of Book III, where they embrace to grow 'together quite' into Hermaphroditus (III.xii.46.5).[102]

98 Spenser might have been influenced by the myth of Isis and Osiris, who, as mythographers relate, also indulged in pre-natal copulation (see Nohnberg, *Analogy*, p. 432, and Hamilton, note to III.vii.48.5). Pliny the Elder, in his entry on monstrous births (*prodigiosi partus*), recounts that Alkippe gave birth to an elephant, and admits that this is more miracle than prodigy (see *Naturalis historia*, VII.31–7). This is notable in so far as Ollyphant's name suggests the animal's proportions. See the discussion below for further commentary on the giant's name and shape.

99 Their sexual transgression violates chastity, the governing virtue of Book III.

100 Park and Daston survey the history of conjoined twins from the Middle Ages to the Renaissance and beyond (see *Wonders and the Order of Nature*, p. 57, pp. 66–7, p. 145 and pp. 173–4).

101 Spenser's giants hence parody essential human experiences: whereas Orgoglio is a parody of human conception, physicality and death, Argante and Ollyphant are parodic of human desire and sexuality.

102 Spenser famously deleted the happy ending from the 1596 version of *The Faerie Queene*. Anderson suggests that Argante and Ollyphant are 'a nightmarish parody of the immaculate birth of the twins Amoret and Belphoebe two cantos earlier' ('Arthur,

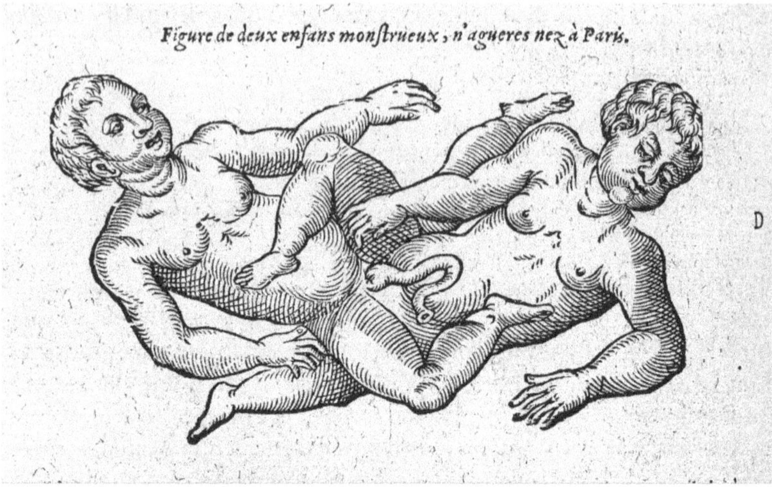

Figure 10 Conjoined twins; from Ambroise Paré, *Les Oeuvres d'Ambroise Pare*

Both interpretations relate the incestuous, ever-fornicating twins to the influential Platonic and Judaeo-Christian discourses on the hermaphrodite: whereas Plato in the *Symposium* explains how Zeus punished the race of human androgynes by separating their bodies into a male and a female half, Judaeo-Christian legends often depict pre-lapsarian man as a bisexual being that was divided into two sexes only after the Fall.[103] Spenser's tale of Argante and Ollyphant subverts the notion of the originary hermaphrodite as the image of idealised mutual love: their constant, undisciplined attempts at regaining their pre-natal sexual bond is a monstrous, and grotesque enactment of the prelapsarian genital union, which stresses that such a union is irretrievably lost after the Fall: 'So liu'd they euer after in like sin, / Gainst natures law, and good behaueoure' (49.1–2).

Argante, and the Ideal Vision', p. 193; see also Leonard Barkan, *Nature's Work of Art: The Human Body as the Image of the World* (New Haven and London: Yale University Press, 1975), pp. 238–9). Both couples, the lovers and the twins, are figurations of mutual desire: whereas the former stresses its positive aspects (and is an image used *in bono*), the latter elaborates on its aberrant sexual excess (and is hence an image used *in malo*). On Amoret's and Scudamour's union in III.xii.46 as an image of mutual love, see Broaddus, *Spenser's Allegory of Love*, pp. 95–6, and Silberman *Transforming Desire*, pp. 69–70.

103 See Plato, *Symposium*, 189D–93D, in *Lysis; Symposium; Gorgias*, trans. by W. R. M. Lamb, Plato: Works 3, Loeb Classical Library (Cambridge, MA: Harvard University Press; London: Heinemann, 1925; repr. 1961). On Platonic and Judaeo-Christian notions of the hermaphrodite, see Williams, *Deformed Discourse*, pp. 168–73.

Spenser generally uses parody as an important feature of the gigantic body. In Argante and Ollyphant's case, he more specifically elaborates on the unnaturalness of their sexual practices, and establishes their different types of abnormal behaviour as monstrous signifiers. Argante's sexual appetite is especially insatiable, and prefigures Spenser's depiction of Lust in Book IV:

> But greatest shame was to that maiden twin,
> Who not content so fowly to deuoure
> Her natiue flesh, and staine her brothers bowre,
> Did wallow in all other fleshly myre,
> And suffred beastes her body to deflowre[.]
>
> (III.vii.49.3–7)

As in his description of Lust's deflowering and eating women (IV.vii.12.8–9), Spenser elaborates on the nature of Argante's sexual transgression by rhyming on the verbs *to devoure* and *to deflower*. By choosing the verb *to devoure* to characterise Argante's incestuous desire, Spenser thus again describes sexual intercourse in terms of greedy consumption, but, as he additionally combines the verb with reflexive pronouns which blur distinctions between the giantess and her brother ('her' is used twice in 49.5), he also shows that such excess carnality amounts to an act of self-pleasuring that leads to self-violation ('fowly', 'staine').[104] Beyond incest, which fails to satisfy her appetite, lies bestiality: when pointing out that she allows her body to be 'deflowered' by wild beasts ('suffred beastes her body to deflowre'), Spenser not only accentuates the giants' subhuman, beastly nature but critically shows an even more corrupt stage of wilful mutilation. The correlation between devouring and deflowering accentuated by Spenser's choice of rhyme hence marks the full ambit of Argante's aggressive and transgressive sexual appetite, and enhances the link between endogamous lust and bestiality.

Argante is related to her kin through a number of decisive features that accentuate her 'masculine gendering'.[105] That her resistance to Satyrane's blows is likened to the resilience of an aged oak connects her with the giants of Albion and with Orgoglio,[106] who have either used oaks for battle

104 A more eroticised example of female self-pleasuring is featured at the end of Book II, where Acrasia is 'her selfe now solacing' (II.xii.72.2; cf. Marion D. Hollings, 'Fountains and Strange Women in the Bower of Bliss: Eastern Contexts for Acrasia and Her Community', in *Consuming Narratives: Gender and Monstrous Appetite in the Middle Ages and the Renaissance*, ed. by Liz Herbert McAvoy and Teresa Walters (Cardiff: University of Wales Press, 2002), pp. 140–56 (pp. 149–50)).

105 The phrase is culled froom Cohen, *Of Giants*, p. 187, n. 3.

106 See III.vii.41.1–3.

or who have been compared to them. More importantly, though, she also bears an iron mace. Hamilton comments that this is 'the weapon of choice for sexual predators',[107] but seems to overlook that the mace suggests the phallus, and is hence a male signifier, so that Argante may be seen as a figuration of the male–female body just as much as Lust's face. Such male attributes also explain her overtly 'male' predatory behaviour, when she abducts young men to her secret island, where she forces them into sexual intercourse.[108] As Argante embodies key aspects of sexual excess like incest, insatiability, aggression, self-pleasure and self-mutilation, she becomes the very epitome of gargantuan carnality.

As already mentioned at the beginning of this section, names often establish the giant's monstrosity. Argante's brother Ollyphant is a particularly good example of how a name may map something monstrous on to a humanoid body. As he is assigned a non-allegorical animal name, his humanoid physique blurs into the image of the elephant. The pachydermate background, while somewhat questioning the giant's alleged wantonness,[109] does, of course, emphasise Ollyphant's size, strength[110] and monstrousness, because it implicitly projects the animal's enormous attributes on to the giant. But anatomical projection is not the only corporeal foil against which the giant is envisioned, for his name can likewise connote the ivory tusks of the elephant,[111] so that the giant also bodies forth a phallic symbol, which is the equivalent to his sister's iron mace. This attribute additionally suggests Lust's oversized teeth, a supposition that becomes even more suggestive if one takes into account that Lust's ears have been likened to those of an elephant. The effect of such a strategy is strikingly ambivalent: on the one hand, Spenser creates a web of near-identical reference terms to unify his gigantic creations; on the other hand, he renders Ollyphant's physique less definite by generating friction between the three distinct shapes of the giant's human shape, the

107 See Hamilton, note to III.vii.40.1.

108 See III.vii.37 and 50.

109 The elephant was usually seen as an animal lacking in sexual appetite, as e.g. in the *Ashmole Bestiary*, where it is stated that 'in [elephante] non est concupiscencia coitus' ('there is no desire for intercourse in the elephant') (p. 34).

110 Sidney points to the animal's strength in his *New Arcadia* (see *Prose Works*, I, 300).

111 Topsell notes that its etymology derives 'from the *Hebrew* word *Dephil*; signifying the Ivory tooth of an Elephant' (*Historie*, I, 150). The name usually refers to the animal's tusks, as for instance in Orlando's horn Olifant; see, e.g., *Chanson de Roland*, 1070 (for the text, see *Das altfranzösische Rolandslied*, ed. by A. Hilka, rev. and emend. by Gerhard Rohlfs, Sammlung romanistischer Übungstexte (Tübingen: Max Niemeyer, 1960)).

elephant's body and the tusk.[112] Such polyvalent signification, which lets the reader actively re-create the monster in the act of reading, emphasises the giant's anatomical indefiniteness.

The gigantic human

The monstrous nature of Spenser's giants lies most obviously in their excessive size, in that they are refigurations of a gigantic phenotype; but Spenser additionally creates a web of other meaningful attributes to disfigure these beings into more thoroughgoing and terrifying monstrosities. At the same time, he establishes a much more complex discursive pattern, taking great pains to underline the humanoid corporeality of giants in such a way that they can figure as animations of human excess and sexual depravity. Such physical and creational kinship eventually makes any possible border separating the human from the gigantic permeable. Sansfoy, the brother of Sansjoy and Sansloy, is a case in point. The narrator's describing him as 'full large of limbe and euery ioint' (I.ii.12.8) already hints at his outstanding proportions. Spenser however adds another significant detail when depicting the manner of his death: Sansfoy, mortally wounded by Redcrosse, kisses 'his *mother* earth' (I.ii.19.6; emphasis added), thus enacting the demise of the giants. If Spenser's phrase is taken literally, it additionally identifies Earth as Sansfoy's mother, and thus marks the Saracen as a potential giant. This strategy helps Spenser to place his own Saracens silently in line with the enormous Saracens from the romance tradition,[113] as well as to suggest

112 That the elephant's anatomy was considered monstrous is confirmed by other sources. Jordanus, in his *Mirabilia descripta*, V.1, describes the elephant very much in monstrous terms: it 'hath a big head; small eyes, smaller than a horses; ears like the wings of owls or bats; a nose reaching quite to the ground, extending right down from the top of his head; and two tusks standing out of remarkable magnitude [in both] bulk and length, which are [in fact] teeth rooted in the upper jaw' (Friar Jordanus, *Mirabilia Descripta: The Wonders of the East*, trans. from the Latin original, as published at Paris 1839, in the Recueil de Voyages et Mémoires, of the Society of Geography (London: Printed for the Hakluyt Society, 1863; repr. New York: Burt Franklin, no year), p. 26). For an early modern account, see Topsell, *Historie*, I, 149–65.

113 The notion of the gigantic Saracen probably originated from the *chanson de geste*, in which they are identified as descendants of Cain. See Ruth Mellinkoff, 'Cain's Monstrous Progeny in *Beowulf*: Part II, Post-diluvian Survival', *Anglo Saxon England* 9 (1981), 183–97 (p. 192). Classic examples of such monstrous Saracens feature in *King Horn*, the alliterative *Morte Arthure*, and *Ywain and Gawain* (see also Cohen, *Of Giants*, pp. 78 and 103, and Friedman, *Monstrous Races*, pp. 34 and 67). The EETS edition of the *Ywain* notes that 'according to tradition monsters, elves, giants, and spirits of hell were descended from Cain, who was the father of all evil progeny' (*Ywain and Gawain*, ed. by Albert B. Friedman and Norman T. Harrington, EETS, OS, 254 (London: Oxford, 1964), pp. 116–17).

their proximity to unnatural creatures within the world of his own poem. While this interpretation seems unproblematic with evil or devious characters, these markers of transgression become all the more important once largeness of limb is established as a distinctive feature of genuinely heroic characters. Against the backdrop of the interpretation advanced in this section, the circumstance that Britomart's nurse Glauce takes note of her being 'tall, / And large of limbe' (III.iii.53.6–7) acquires a new dimension in that it accentuates the lack of any border between monstrous gigantism and the human: it inscribes the gigantic into the human physique, and sees bodily excess, which is one of Isidore's categories of monstrosity, as an innate human possibility.[114] Even St George, the alter ego of Redcrosse, sports such a proximity to the gigantic, as his name 'Ge-orgos' stems from the Greek word for earth (Γῆ), so that ultimately the raw material of man and giant is the same.[115] The many encounters with giants as well as the character's possible gigantism reveal man's continuing struggle against his innate proneness to excess and monstrosity. Defeating the giant therefore amounts to man's fashioning of the self, and results in the constitution of identity and culture. Hence, the combats with the giants provide the textual equivalent to Spenser's overall programme of *The Faerie Queene*, namely the fashioning of a gentleman.

114 Malgo is likened to a giant in Merlin's visionary chronicle (III.iii.32.3). See also the forester's description at III.i.17.8.

115 The name George has the same root as the name Orgoglio (see Hamilton, note to I.vii.14.5).

10

Monstrous humans

The interpretations in the previous sections of Geryoneo's maiden-faced dragon, of Errour's disfigured composite body and of the humanoid giants emphasise the role that familiar human attributes play in the creation of monstrous beings. But there is a more thoroughgoing monstrosity at work in *The Faerie Queene*, one that infects the human realm. Such monsterised humans do not only appear in every part of the poem but significantly display the greatest gamut of deformities in any category. As the variations on human monstrosities are so numerous and diverse, the ensuing chapter is broken down into four subdivisions: the first deals with characters who belong to the monstrous races and have a monstrous identity *sans* constituting physical attributes; the second deals with 'carles' and hags; the third with transformations and metamorphoses; and the fourth with monstrous humans of an 'ephemeral' kind. In these analyses, the 'human' is used in its most inclusive sense: as Spenser lets the human constantly interact with representations of abstract entities, he purposely blends the barriers between tendentiously 'human' and 'representational' characters. Both classes are hence treated under the same rubric.

Monstrous races

In many cases under survey so far, the monstrous is explicitly allied to the sinful and satanic. But the upsurge of hybrid life does not necessarily encode such overt monstrosity, even if the core of particular characters is undoubtedly monstrous, or if they belong to a monstrous race. Two races famous from classical literature appear in *The Faerie Queene*: the satyrs and the Amazons. Spenser endows the satyrs, a people of half-goats noted for their lustful and primitive nature,[1] with traditional attributes,

1 Satyrs appear twice in *The Faerie Queene*, namely in I.vi, and III.x–xi. These two groups differ from one another: while the former exhibits a naive belief in Una's divine

namely horns, knees bent backwards and horned feet.[2] The Amazons, on the other hand, are depicted as a race of fierce and warlike women who lack signs of visible monstrosity; it is their revolt against male rule that marks them as monstrous.[3] While Spenser's overall treatment hence appears to be largely traditional, his presentation of the two principal characters belonging to these races, namely SATYRANE, the son of a satyr and a human mother, and RADIGUND, the Queen of the Amazons, warrants closer analysis, because these characters, who exemplify man's innate animality and unruliness, hide their monstrosity under a normative human form.

Satyrane

When Satyrane enters the woods where Una is hosted by the satyrs,[4] he is introduced into the narrative as 'a noble warlike knight', and not immediately named.[5] However, it soon becomes apparent that he is not what he seems, since his coming '[t]o seeke his kindred' (I.vi.20.3) suggests that he, too, is a satyr, or at least part satyr.[6] At this point, the narrator seizes the opportunity to acquaint his audience with the story of Satyrane's conception and childhood, a section of Canto vi that elaborates on man's monstrous heritage.[7] It chances that Thyamis, daughter of Labryde, goes out to seek Therion, her spouse, who roams the woods for prey and game (21–2). There she is abducted by a satyr who rapes her and then imprisons her until she gives birth to a boy (22–3). Although the story appears to be largely traditional – monstrous intercourse of this kind was a popular topos in the Middle Ages and the Renaissance[8] – there is more to it than

---

teachings, the latter is merely licentious. For general treatments consult Lotspeich, *Classical Mythology*, pp. 105–6; Richard D. Jordan, 'Satyrs', in *Spenser Encyclopedia*, ed. by Hamilton, p. 628; and Nohrnberg, *Analogy*, pp. 218–22. See above all the entry on satyrs in Topsell, *Historie*, I, 10–13. Paul Grootkerk gives a detailed historical account of the satyr (see 'The Satyr', in *Mythical and Fabulous Creatures*, ed. by South, pp. 207–24). On goats, see Bloomfield, *The Seven Deadly Sins*, p. 248.

2 See I.vi.11–14.

3 See V.iv–vii. On the Amazons as a monstrous race, see Friedman, *Monstrous Races*, pp. 129–30 and pp. 134–5, as well as Salisbury, *The Beast Within*, p. 147. See also Carol Schreier Rupprecht, 'Radigund', in *Spenser Encyclopedia*, ed. by Hamilton, pp. 580–1.

4 See I.vi.20.

5 His name is mentioned for the first time in I.vi.28.6.

6 See I.vi. For a good introduction to Satyrane, see Watson, 'Spenser's Chivalric Bestiary', pp. 165–8.

7 The whole passage covers I.vi.21–9.

8 For the Middle Ages, see Salisbury, *The Beast Within*, pp. 77–101, and, for the Renaissance, see Fudge, *Perceiving Animals*, pp. 136–42. The fate of Satyrane's mother, who seeks her lecherous husband in the woods only to be sexually assaulted by a satyr, resembles especially that of Gowther's mother in the romance *Sir Gowther*, whose desires

the plot at first suggests, since each name carries significant meaning: '*Thyamis*' (I.vi.21.4) derives from Greek θυμός, 'passion', whilst '*Therion*' (vi.21.6) is a direct transcription of the Greek word for 'wild beast', θηρίον.[9] Thus, Thyamis's encounter with the satyr turns out to be a self-fulfilling prophecy: it is exactly because she seeks her beastly husband in the woods that she encounters the even beastlier satyr,[10] whose portrayal is in keeping with traditional depictions of satyrs that foreground their lustful nature, inherited from the proverbially lustful goats.[11]

Satyrane's lineage, which marks him as a *monstrum* in the sense of a strange birth, places him at the threshold between pure and bestial(ised) humanity: whereas his mother is the embodiment of mildness,[12] his father is reduced to his brutish nature.[13] In consequence, Satyrane's upbringing illustrates the tension between the opposite poles of humanity and animality. His ferocious taming of wild beasts illustrates his aspiring dominance over his feral drives, while the excessive amount of brutality he uses stigmatises him as a character still governed by his brutish origin.[14] It is only through exercising chivalry that Satyrane learns to maintain control over his parental lineage, a character development that finds expression in the potentially positive epithets assigned to the knight.[15] Among other things, he instantaneously recognises Una's holiness,[16] just as the lion and the satyrs did before him, but, as he naturally transcends their levels of understanding, the champions assisting Una in her flight thus clearly progress *up* the scale, from lion to satyr to half-satyr. This

likewise materialise when she seeks her husband in an orchard (see *Sir Gowther*, 70–4; the text is taken from *Sir Gowther*, in *Six Middle English Romances*, ed. by Maldwyn Mills, Everyman's Library, 190 (Rutland, VT: Charles E. Tuttle, 1988), pp. 148–68).

9 See Hamilton, note to I.vi.21.4–6; for the Old Greek terms, see Liddell and Scott, p. 810 (for θυμός) and p. 800 (for θηρίον).

10 Thyamis's role as mother is treated in McManus, 'The "carefull Nurse"', pp. 398–9.

11 Goat imagery features, e.g., in Shakespeare's *Othello*, where it is used by Iago to trigger Othello's jealousy (III.iii.406), and is later taken up by the tragic hero (IV.i.263; references are to William Shakespeare, *Othello*, ed. by E. A. J. Honigmann, The Arden Edition of the Works of William Shakespeare (Walton-on-Thames: Thomas Nelson, 1997)). For a discussion of Iago's use of animal imagery, see Maik Goth, *From Chaucer's Pardoner to Shakespeare's Iago: Aspects of Intermediality in the History of the Vice*, Studien zur englischen und amerikanischen Literatur, 22 (Frankfurt am Main: Lang, 2009), pp. 94–7.

12 In I.vi.21.3, the epic narrator calls her 'a Lady myld'.

13 The narrator refers to the satyr's 'beastly kind' (I.vi.22.9), and 'sensuall desyre' (23.2), thereby defining him as a 'saluage syre' (23.4).

14 Watson provides a detailed account of Satyrane's early years ('Chivalric Bestiary', pp. 166–9).

15 Stock phrases used for Satyrane include 'noble' (I.vi.20.1), and 'good Sir *Satyrane*' (III.vii.30.1, and 45.1).

16 Satyrane meets Una in I.vi.30–1.

is not to suggest that Satyrane reaches a stage beyond the reciprocity between man and animal. When he is reintroduced into the poem as a knight seeking 'aduentures wilde', he is equipped not with shining armour but with 'rugged steele vnfilde, / As in the smoky forge it was compilde' (III.vii.30.2 and 4–5). Such attributes display a fierceness of disposition reminiscent of his youthful wildness. This assumption is strengthened by the 'Satyres hedd' (vii.I.30.6) featuring on his shield, which functions as a powerful *memento* of his monstrous heritage. It is a heraldic emblem that reinscribes the monstrous signifier into a character who constantly tries to cast aside his bestial origins.

Satyrane's constant combat against his animal instincts is especially well exemplified in his fights against monsters and humans. In fact, the very details of his battle against the monstrous hyena bespeak his internal struggle: that he mounts the beast to overcome it and that he eventually leads it 'along the way' (III.viii.37.1) are instances that mark the passage as a textual projection of his internal struggle to maintain human dominance over his monstrous past and his bestial instincts. The monster's indestructibility – that is it can be wounded but not killed[17] – illustrates that he will never vanquish them completely. This supposition helps illustrate the frequent use of animal imagery during Satyrane's combats: whenever he faces an opponent, chances are that he unleashes the animal within.[18] To this effect, Satyrane, whose name forever denotes his animal heritage, represents the human potential to control one's instincts and thus to rise to humanity.[19] Satyrane is hence conceived as a sublimated version of monstrosity, seeking to transcend his monstrous nature and nurture in order to grow into a being that reaches for chivalric fulfilment,[20] to attain the ideal of the gentleman. Only during chivalric combat is his fiercer character allowed to break free.

17 See III.vii.32–3, and the discussion of the hyena, above.

18 See, e.g., Satyrane's combat against Bruncheval in IV.iv.18, which Spenser likens to a fierce fight between two bulls striving for dominance.

19 Rosamund Tuve acknowledges Satyrane's chivalric potential when pointing out that his narrative illustrates 'the reasons why he alone could learn, and be "plaine, faithfull, true"' (*Allegorical Imagery: Some Mediaeval Books and Their Posterity* (Princeton: Princeton University Press, 1966), p. 123).

20 This is especially the case in his tournament for false Florimell's girdle in IV.iv, a part of the poem that features a high density of animal similes. However, Satyrane is excluded from chivalric fulfilment, unlike Sir Gowther in his eponymous romance (cf. Cohen, *Of Giants*, pp. 136–7, citing *Gowther*, 623–30). When Satyrane takes 'in hand / An huge great speare, such as he want to wield' (IV.iv.17.1–2) at the beginning of the tournament, the phallic implications of this image mark Satyrane's heightened lustfulness, which he has inheritated from his father.

Radigund

Spenser's treatment of another strange race, namely the Amazons, is less conspicuously monstrous than one would expect, and consists in the loss of normative female behaviour. Radigund's otherness is established by a series of beast similes that function as monstrous signifiers: in the course of five stanzas, she is likened to a queen bee (V.iv.36), a 'fell [i.e. fierce, savage] Lionesse' (iv.39.6), and a she-bear (iv.40).[21] This visual onslaught of animals keeps her feral passions in the spotlight of attention, but her conduct, unlike Satyrane's, lies completely outside chivalric endorsements. A closer look at the passage reveals how Spenser organises imagery to create a web of animal references that foreground Radigund's boldness and ferocious beastliness. Her entrance when she is about to fight Arthegall marks her as a superior animal among animals:

> And like a sort of Bees [the Amazons] in clusters swarmed:
> Ere long the Queene her selfe, halfe like a man
> Came forth into the rout, and them t'array began.
>
> (iv.36.7–9)

Spenser's formulation that she is 'halfe like a man' is conspicuous, because he uses a phrase he employed to describe the hybrid nature of monsters like Errour, who is '[h]alfe like a serpent horribly displaid' (I.i.14.7) and the Mermaids, who also consist of two halves (II.xii.31).[22] As a human joining two disparate gender halves, Radigund is a performative gender hybrid, and as such a latent monstrosity like Satyrane.

Spenser further underlines Radigund's violation of the female norm by using a bee simile. The bee state, usually codifying the ideas of order and rank, is here used to parody the concept of a well-governed, male state, especially since bees were said to have a king.[23] By conjoining the animal image with the reversal of gender roles, Spenser inverts the idea of power and sovereignty, thus endowing the Amazon Queen with the

21 In V.iv.42 Radigund is likened to a goshawk attacked by the eagle Arthegall, an image that is reversed in V.v.15, where she is likened to a buzzard defeating a female falcon, which represents the now effeminate Arthegall.

22 The importance of the word *half* is also observed by Rupprecht, 'Radigund', p. 581.

23 See Watson, 'Emblem and Experience', pp. 118–19. The notion surfaces in many medieval texts, as e.g. in the *Fior di Virtu*, 57–8 (*The Florentine Fior di Virtu of 1491*, translated into English by Nicholas Fersin with facsimiles of all of the original woodcuts, ed. by L. J. Rosenwald (Washington: Library of Congress, 1953)). In Chapter I.ii of his *Book Named the Governor*, Sir Thomas Elyot also refers to the bee state as the ideal *regnum* (see Sir Thomas Elyot, *The Book Named the Governor*, ed. by S. E. Lehmberg, new edn, Everyman's Library (London: Dent; New York: Dutton, 1967)). This assumption might be partly influenced by classical concepts, since in Virgil's *locus classicus* of the bee state, *Georgics*, IV.149–218, the bees are also ruled by a *rex*.

strength and determination of a fierce ruler readying himself for battle. Radigund's description, as Hadfield points out, relates to 'the problem of women's rule'.[24] Her transgression of gender roles suggests especially John Knox's mid-sixteenth-century view that a female ruler is a 'monster in nature: so I call a woman clad in the habit of a man, yea, a woman against nature reigning above man'.[25] These terms are directly applicable to Radigund, because she emerges as such a female 'monster' ruling over men 'against nature'. The ensuing similes in Radigund's portrayal supplement the idea of deviance with traditional animal concepts: both the savage lioness and the cruel she-bear illustrate her bent towards brutality. But while the image of the lioness mainly portrays her strength in battle,[26] the image of the she-bear brings into relief a more thoroughgoing savagery, for Radigund does not stop short once she has subdued Sir Terpine, but rather continues to torture him:

> Soone as she saw him on the ground to grouell,
> She lightly to him leapt, and in his necke
> Her proud foote setting, at his head did leuell,
> Weening at once her wrath on him to wreake,
> And his contempt, that did her iudg'ment breake.
> As when a Beare hath seiz'd her cruell clawes
> Vppon the carkasse of some beast too weake,
> Proudly stands ouer, and a while doth pause,
> To heare the piteous beast pleading her plaintiffe cause.
>
> (V.iv.40)

This beast image actualises both the internal and the external aspects of the fight, a circumstance that becomes apparent in Spenser's close-up of the bear's 'cruell clawes'. In stylistic terms, the alliterative phrase is a hypallage that transposes moral judgement ('cruell') from the doer ('Beare') to its

24 See Andrew Hadfield, '*The Faerie Queene* IV–VI', in *The Cambridge Companion to Spenser*, ed. by Andrew Hadfield (Cambridge: Cambridge University Press, 2001), pp. 124–42 (p. 132). For a full treatment of Radigund's gender implications, cf. Lillian S. Robinson, *Monstrous Regiment: The Lady Knight in Sixteenth-Century Epic*, Garland Publications in Comparative Literature (New York: Garland, 1985), pp. 331–41. Cf. also Rupprecht, who argues that Radigund is a variation on the topos of the martial maid (in 'Radigund', p. 580).

25 John Knox, *The First Blast of the Trumpet Against the Monstrous Regiment of Women* (Whitefish: Kessinger Publishing, 2004), p. 39. The passage is discussed and related to the Amazons in Dana Oswald, 'Monstrous Gender: Geographies of Ambiguity', in *The Ashgate Research Companion to Monsters and the Monstrous*, ed. by Mittman and Dendle, pp. 343–63 (p. 356).

26 For a general overview of lions in *The Faerie Queene*, see Cosman, 'Spenser's Ark of Animals', pp. 85–6, and, for a more detailed account, Marotti, 'Animal Symbolism', pp. 69–77.

executive agent ('claw').[27] Such pronounced anthropomorphism shifts focus to Radigund's moral turpitude.[28] This is especially so, since, in the course of the combat, she vents her pride and the desire for mastery to such an extent that she eventually loses her claim to humanity just as much as Satyrane in his battles. The simile thus anthropomorphises the animal while simultaneously bestialising Radigund, a joint strategy that successfully damages the dividing line between man and beast. In her case, the repetitive use of animal similes makes visible the full ambit of her beastliness, which is stressed when Clarin points out to Arthegall that Britomart 'yet forgets, that she of men was kinded' (V.v.40.8). On a more abstract level, such imagery also has its bearing on the larger pattern of Book V: since her ferocity endows her with enough power to vanquish Arthegall, the paragon of Justice, her intemperate behaviour violates the norm, and poses a physical and spiritual threat to the virtue governing this part of *The Faerie Queene*.

Both Radigund and Satyrane are characters battling their beastly unruliness under a perfect human exterior. But while Satyrane, the offspring of a human mother and a satyr, quells his instincts in the regulating framework of chivalry and hence undergoes the constant process of claiming his humanity against his monstrous heritage, Radigund's revolt against hierarchy and sanctioned order is accentuated by Spenser's heavy use of animal imagery, which marks her as irredeemably lost to her innate monstrosity. Their counter-movements on a vertical axis between the human and the brutish are informed by the Renaissance notion that man, as Giovanni Pico della Mirandola explains in his *Oratio de hominis dignitate* (1486/87), occupies a middle position on the divine ladder of creation between the heaven and the earth, between the spiritual and the beastly. Endowed with free will, man becomes an 'arbitrarius honorariusque plastes et fictor', a free and proud shaper and maker, who can fashion himself in the form he prefers. Through such self-fashioning man can either ascend to higher, divine orders or descend to lower, brutish forms of life.[29] Satyrane and

27 Spenser uses the same device when referring to Radigund's 'proud foote' (V.iv.40.3).

28 Ziolkowski raises awareness of the vagueness and the many levels of the term *anthropomorphism* (see 'Literary Genre', p. 22).

29 'Poteris in inferiora, quae sunt bruta, degenerare; poteris in superiora, quae sunt divina, ex tui animi sententia regenerari' ('It will be in your power to degenerate into the lower forms of life, which are brutish. Alternatively, you shall have the power, in accordance with the judgment of your soul, to be reborn into the higher orders, those that are divine'). Text and translation are from Pico Della Mirandola, *Oration on the Dignity of Man: A New Translation and Commentary*, ed. and trans. by Francesco Borghesi, Michael Papio and Massimo Riva (Cambridge: Cambridge University Press, 2012), pp. 116–17. See also Fudge, *Perceiving Animals*, pp. 35–7.

Radigund exercise their free will differently: while the former aspires to ascend the ladder of creation despite being burdened by his animal heritage, the latter descends it because she has forgotten her human origin and has turned into a 'monster in nature'.

'Carles' and hags

With Radigund and Satyrane, Spenser introduces two humans that keep their monstrosity under physical cover. Usually, however, Spenser's monstrous humans feature a distorted physique that combines a host of monstrous signifiers. Two types of this category, which Spenser uses throughout *The Faerie Queene*, are the 'carle', and his female counterpart, the hag. Specimens of these categories occur in *The Faerie Queene* so frequently that they form their own, if loosely connected, sub-species.

'Carles'

That the plethora of 'carles' is made up of characters like Mammon, Care, Lust, Turpine, the witch's brutish son, Despayre, Maleger, Malbecco, Malengin, Maleffort and Disdayne[30] shows that these figures are always of a questionable, morally deviant nature. Mostly dwelling in caves, dens and amphibious habitats that are connected to the underworld,[31] the 'carle' is a hellish being whose basic shape is recognisably human, but whose physical features are so distorted that they point to the monstrous. The frequent use of negative suffixes like *de-*, *mal-* or *dis-*additionally corroborates the impression that they represent the disfiguration, or malformation of a concept or form.[32] Spenser's lexical compounding hence inscribes their deformity into their names. The carle's uncouth nature sallies forth from his shaggy hair,[33] his hollow, burning or blind eyes,[34] hollow cheeks,[35] a frequently blackened face,[36] and his filthy clothing, which is made from

30 See, in order of appearance, I.ix for Despayre, II.vii for Mammon, II.xi for Maleger, III.vii–viii for the witch's son, III.ix for Malbecco, IV.v for Care, IV.vii for Lust, V.ix for Malengin, VI.i for Maleffort, VI.iii for Turpine and VI.vii–viii for Disdayne.

31 Despayre, Mammon, Care and Malengin are cave-dwellers. While Despayre's dwelling place evokes the deathly otherworld, full with ghosts and owls (I.ix.33–4), Care's abode is strikingly amphibious (IV.v.33).

32 See Horstmann, *Namen*, p. 82, p. 88 and pp. 172–3 (on the prefixes *mal-*, and *dis-*).

33 For the shaggy hair, see Despayre (I.ix.35), Care (IV.v.34) and Malengin (V.ix.10); Lust's body is entirely covered in hair (IV.vii.5 and 7).

34 Despayre's, Care's and Malengin's eyes are hollow (I.ix.35; IV.v.34; V.ix.10.5), Mammon's are 'inflamed' (II.vii.3), and Malbecco has one blinking or blind eye (III.ix.5.5 and 27.6).

35 Such is the case with Despayre (I.ix) and Care (IV.v.34).

36 See Mammon and Care (II.vii.3.6–9; IV.vii.34).

bushes or unspecified abject material, and which is also highly reminiscent of the Wild Man.[37] These physical features are frequently arranged to exhibit signs of excessive melancholy.[38] In addition to this unwholesome humorous disposition, 'carles' are characterised by an aggressive, predatory nature with particular emphasis on the lustful. Spenser visualises their bent to the basic instincts of concupiscence and destruction by endowing them with iron clubs. The most prominent example of such monstrosity, which is determined not only by a horribly 'sexed' physique but also by the performance of an exaggerated masculinity, is the giant Lust.[39]

The carles' behaviour and movement enhance their monstrous nature and nurture, because they are used as supplementary monstrous signifiers. While Despayre's combining an ugly physique with a smooth, deceptive tongue is strongly suggestive of Duessa's double-dealing deception, his movement is of a clearly monstrous kind: 'creeping close' to his victims like a snake (I.ix.28.8), and presiding over a cave that evokes hell mouth and the netherworld, Despayre is a truly infernal creature.[40] In addition to his hellish connections, the 'carle' is also largely determined by his lack of the gentlemanly ideals propagated by Spenser. This uncivil nature is exceptionally well exemplified by Care (whose name is just one letter short of the carle), because he crudely rends the food he holds in blistered, filthy hands with uncut nails.[41] Similar descriptions additionally undermine the humanity of the carle's physique to such an extent that Sir Guyon cannot help but wonder whether Mammon, in whose cave he is about to stand his trial of temperance, is human at all: 'What art thou man, (if man at all thou art)' (II.vii.7.1). Although Guyon's remark also hints at Mammon's representational character which divests him of proper human qualities, his query relates more immediately to the carle's anatomy, for which Spenser assembles a number of disfiguring monstrous signifiers, both anatomical and behavioural, to create a human devoid of human qualities. This ontological rift is mirrored in the dichotomy between the abject responses of the characters that resist admitting the human core of these beings, while their impact depends largely on the inherent ability to acknowledge their

37 Despayre is clad in rugs (I.ix.36), and Mammon in shrubs (II.vii.3), whereas Malengin's back is covered with 'an vncouth vestiment / Made of straunge stuffe' (V.ix.10.7–8).

38 Physical traits indicating melancholy can be traced in Despayre, Mammon, Malbecco, Care and Malengin. As Brooks-Davies explains, even caves may signify excess melancholy (see *Critical Commentary*, p. 89, note to I.ix.33–4).

39 Similarly, Care has gigantic proportions (see IV.v.37).

40 See I.ix.28.

41 See IV.v.35.

human origin. The 'carle' therefore remains a recognisable humanoid that paradoxically evokes the absence of the truly human and civil.[42]

The 'carle' forms a flexible category, which includes the discourteous knight Sir Turpine, who is defeated by the wild yet courteous Salvage Man, as well as monstrous humans like the witch's son, and allegorical characters like Lust and Disdayne. The underlying method that Spenser employs here is that of variation, for which he sets up a cluster of recurrent images and monstrous signifiers that allow him to create permutations of a common type whose core is recognisable for his readers.

The most puzzling 'carle' is undoubtedly MALEGER, the tiger-riding captain of the monstrous troop besieging the Castle of Alma. His name suggests a host of multilingual etymologies, and characterises him as an evil, deformed and sick being.[43] Although sharing the Saturnian, melancholy quality with other 'carles',[44] Maleger, who is frequently associated with the theology of sin,[45] but could also represent the misrule of the passions,[46] is a much more radical paradox: his body, though appearing to be solid and bordering on the gigantic,[47] is 'of such subtile substance and vnsound' (II.xi.20.8) that he seems to be more ghost or demon than human. The corporeality of this monstrous being thus generally combines the mutually exclusive principles of materiality and immateriality. Yet the alliterating phrase 'subtile substance and vnsound' deserves closer scrutiny. Hamilton interprets the adjective 'subtile' as a reference

42 Spenser's 'carles' hence conform to some of the criteria Friedman sets up for the monstrous races, namely: clothing, abode, speech (because perverted), and diet (as visible in their unwholesome appearances; see *Monstrous Races*, pp. 26–36).

43 He appears chiefly in II.xi.20–46, accompanied by the hags Impatience and Impotence, and is named at II.xi.23.1. Etymologies suggested by Brooks-Davies are *malaugurio*, 'ill omen'; *malus*, 'evil', 'deformed', or *male*, 'badly', connected to *aeger*, 'sick' (Brooks-Davies, *Critical Commentary*, pp. 176–7, note to II.xi.20–3); following Osgood, Hamilton translates the name into 'desperately diseased' (Hamilton, note to II.xi.23; and Charles G. Osgood, 'Comments on the Moral Allegory of *The Faerie Queene*', *Modern Language Notes* 46 (1931), 502–7).

44 Brooks-Davies associates Maleger with Mammon and Despayre, and connects him with Saturn, the god of old age, death and graveyards (see *Critical Commentary*, pp. 176–7, note to II.xi.20–3).

45 The seminal contribution is A. S. P. Woodhouse's article 'Nature and Grace in *The Faerie Queene*', *English Literary History* 16 (1949), 194–228. Woodhouse interprets Maleger as 'original sin or human depravity, the result of the fall' (p. 221).

46 See II.ix.i.6, and Rollinson, 'Arthur, Maleger', pp. 107–8. In his entry on Maleger in the *Spenser Encyclopedia*, ed. by Hamilton, p. 450, Rollinson accordingly explains that Maleger's name can also derive from Latin *male* and *regere*, 'to rule badly or wrongly'. James W. Broaddus reads him as the curse of mortality; see 'Renaissance Psychology and the Defense of Alma's Castle', *Spenser Studies* 19 (2004), 135–57 (p. 135). Endnote 1, which covers pp. 150–1 of Broaddus's article, contains an instructive survey of critical literature on Maleger.

47 'Full large he was of limbe, and shoulders brode' (II.xi.20.7).

to the delicacy of Maleger's body.[48] While this is undoubtedly correct,[49] it needs to be stressed that the word covers a much broader semantic spectrum that eventually distinguishes three major aspects of Maleger's nature: the adjective *subtle* can also refer to something 'difficult to grasp'; to something that is intelligently fashioned; and to something exposing a devious cleverness.[50] All three additional usages, which are well documented for the late sixteenth century, obliquely relate to Maleger: he is a paradox eliding easy interpretation; his complexity points to the clever poetic design underlying his creation; and during his fight with Arthur he exhibits wicked cunning. In addition to describing the texture of his body, the adjective therefore telescopes the full ambit of Maleger's deviousness by defining him as a poeticised, and textually manufactured, monstrosity.[51] The same revealing interplay of concurring senses can be traced in the adjective 'vnsound': although it is usually explained as 'lacking in solidity and firmness' (the *OED* quotes this passage from *The Faerie Queene*),[52] it also encodes the diseased and morally vitiated, hence: evil.[53] The different aspects of these adjectives, which are just as suggestive as Maleger's name, produce a semantic polyvalence that creates a complex allegorical monstrosity.

Although Maleger's body mainly conjoins materiality with immateriality, this is not the only dichotomy he embodies. As Spenser describes Maleger's corporeality through references to dead wood and grass,[54] and as he endows him with attributes of death itself – he is dressed in rags resembling 'graue-clothes' (20.9),[55] and wears a human skull for a helmet (22.9) – Maleger is also a figuration of the living dead, an animate being made up of seemingly inanimate matter that poses an insuperable threat to any of his victims.[56] Arthur, his ultimate opponent, is thus faced not only with an invincible enemy, but also with a 'supreme paradox'[57] that

48 See Hamilton, note to II.xi.20.8–9.

49 Delicacy is indeed the first definition given in the *OED*, s.v. 'subtle, *a.*', 1.

50 This conforms with *OED*, s.v. 'subtle, *a.*', 5–6, 8 and 10.

51 Spenser uses the term *subtle* predominantly in negative contexts such as deception, and magic (see, e.g., I.ii.9.1, I.vii.51.1, III.iv.28.7 and IV.vii.27.1). Occasionally, the adjective and its corresponding adverb are used *in bono*, especially in the context of sophisticated craftsmanship (II.ix.46.5, IV.vi.20.6 and V.v.2.2).

52 *OED*, s.v. 'unsound, *a.*', 6.

53 See *OED*, s.v. 'unsound, *a.*', 1 and 2.

54 His complexion is reminiscent of 'ashes', his skin 'all withered like a dryed rooke' (II.xi.22.1 and 3).

55 See also the 'canuas' in II.xi.22.6.

56 See also the terms 'dead corse' (used twice in II.xi.37.8–9), 'carcas' (38.3), and 'carrion corse' (46.2); cf. Harold L. Weatherby, 'Two Images of Mortalitie: Spenser and Original Sin', *Studies in Philology* 85 (1988), 321–52 (p. 347).

57 The phrase is Rollinson's ('Arthur, Maleger', p. 449).

defies logical categories. As for ethnicity, most critics aver that Maleger represents the Irish.[58] Although David Read's recent view that he belongs with the Americas convincingly refutes such a limited point of view, Maleger's ethnic traits defy any attempt at situating him in a single location.[59] In fact, Maleger is made up of characteristics that label him as a geographical anomaly: while his mount, the tiger,[60] links him to the Persian abode of the animal, especially Hyrcania,[61] his arrows, which he can fire at his pursuers by looking back like the Tartars (26.6–9),[62] are poisoned and feathered like those of 'the *Indians*' (21.5).[63] He thus combines ethnic traits of the wondrous races living in opposite geographical directions near the edges of the known world.[64]

Set against the backdrop of Maleger's paradoxical monstrosity, the grotesque and horrid fight between the two characters, in which Spenser uses the rhetoric of wonder to great effect, validates and even surpasses the reader's expectations. Surprisingly, Maleger can be vanquished neither by Arthur's iron mace (34–5) nor by his sword (36–8). Wrestling and suffocation are of no use, either, because Maleger, despite experiencing the pains of each death, revives every time he touches the earth (42–3):[65] as the figuration of the living death,[66] Maleger is himself immortal. When Arthur even cuts through Maleger's chest with his blade, he thinks the

58 This traditional view is mainly inspired by Spenser's reference to the 'fennes of Allen' in the gnat simile defining Maleger's monstrous rabblement (II.ix.16). For classical discussions, see Pauline Henley, *Spenser in Ireland* (Dublin: Cork University Press, 1928), pp. 114–19, and M. M. Gray, 'The Influence of Spenser's Irish Experiences on *The Faerie Queene*', *Review of English Studies* 6 (1930), 413–28 (pp. 415–16). *David Read levels judicious criticism against these traditional notions in Temperate Conquests: Spenser and the Spanish New World* (Detroit: Wayne State University Press, 2000), pp. 83–92.

59 See Read, *Temperate Conquests*, pp. 83–92.

60 Marotti stresses the moral deprivation associated with the tiger (see 'Animal Symbolism', p. 77).

61 See *Ashmole Bestiary*, pp. 26–7. Topsell assigns the tiger a much larger territory (see *Historie*, I, 548). He also explains that the tiger is so called because of the swiftness of an arrow (see *Historie*, I, 547; see also *Batman vppon Bartholome*, XVIII.104).

62 In the Renaissance, the Tartars were ranked among the monstrous races. Donald Lupton purported in 1636 that '[t]he Tartarians are [the] most deformed of all men' in terms of body and behaviour (quoted in Burnett, *Constructing 'Monsters'*, p. 43).

63 See William M. Hamlin, *The Image of America in Montaigne, Spenser and Shakespeare: Renaissance Ethnography and Literary Reflection* (New York: St Martin's Press, 1995), pp. 69–96 (pp. 72–3).

64 While Read's argument that Spenser refers to a New-World tiger is not implausible, he seems to bend sources and probability for the sake of his colonial argument (see *Temperate Conquests*, pp. 85–6). Spenser is more interested in establishing Maleger's monstrosity by geographical indeterminacy than by assigning him a definite locale.

65 This echoes and parodies Redcrosse's revivification in the Well of Life in I.xi (also noted by Weatherby, 'Two Images', p. 348).

66 See the term 'carcas' in II.xi.38.3.

creature's death imminent, and expects the usual emission of blood and gore. Neither is the case:

> Ne drop of blood appeared shed to bee,
> All were the wownd so wide and wonderous,
> That through his carcas one might playnly see[.]
>
> (II.xi.38.1–3)

Unlike other monstrous beings in the poem, whose hideousness is defined through the spilling of blood – the Dragon's blood, for instance, breaks from his body with such force that it could even run a water-mill –[67] Maleger's monstrosity is determined by the very absence of any vital bodily fluid. The most perplexing image of such anatomical lack, which in itself becomes a monstrous signifier, is the wound that forms a channel through Maleger's chest: Arthur might be able to see through his opponent literally, but not figuratively, because he still does not understand Maleger's quiddity. The display of anatomical wonder, which is the key to Spenser's conception of the monstrous sign, is here carried to the extreme. Arthur's reaction to such monstrosity is, significantly, a mixture of horror and intellectual puzzlement, which also marks the monstrous as a phenomenon which causes stupefaction and bewilderment.

Assessed from this perspective, Maleger brings Spenser's readers to the conceptual core of the monstrous sign, a supposition borne out by the series of riddles he poses for Arthur, and which transcend his 'reasons reach' (40.1), and experience. Maleger is

> Flesh without blood, a person without spright,
> Wounds without hurt, a body without might,
> That could doe harme, yet could not harmed bee,
> That could not die, yet seemd a mortall wight,
> That was most strong in most infirmitee;
> Like did he neuer heare, like did he neuer see.
>
> (II.xi.40.4–9)

This catalogue, which makes up a nuanced synopsis of Maleger's characteristic traits, enumerates paradoxes created on a set of affirmative and negative statements. The sum total of these riddles is seven, an ambivalent number which encodes opposite meanings. While this is the sum of the Deadly Sins, which Maleger can be associated with,[68] it is also the number

67 On the Dragon's violent emission of blood, see I.xi.22.3–6.

68 See Woodhouse, 'Nature and Grace', pp. 220–2. Revisionist readings by Weatherby, who stresses the connection between lust and inherited guilt (see 'Two Images', pp. 345–8), and Rollinson, who opines that Maleger represents the passions (see 'Arthur, Maleger', pp. 103–21), have brought new perspectives to this question.

of perfection, which here refers to the excellence of the enigma he has been made to embody. The chain of these irreconcilable contradictions is most poignantly rendered in the phrase 'dead-liuing swayne' (44.7),[69] which contains an epithet yoking together mutually exclusive terms into a paradox. As Maleger is neither 'dead' nor 'liuing', his essence is positioned between these opposites. This is precisely the relevance of the riddles quoted above: they drive home that Maleger exists on the border between positive and negative statements, and is placed on the limit of what can be conceived, and, consequently, described.[70]

Arthur is only able to solve the logical problem that Maleger poses through a flash of inspiration. He recollects that Maleger must not be layed in a 'graue terrestriall' (45.8), because he is the offspring of Mother Earth, who restores him to life and endows him with greater powers as soon as he touches the ground: hence, Arthur suffocates Maleger, carries him '[a]boue three furlongs', and throws him in a 'standing lake', where he can never touch the ground again (46.5–6).[71] Yet Spenser withholds complete closure: Arthur might know enough to defeat his enemy, but he certainly has not answered the seven-part riddle in stanza 40. If one applies this finding to the discussion of the monstrous, then Maleger emerges as a monster whose every aspect cannot be sounded out successfully. Arthur's 'tak[ing] life' from 'dead-liuing' Maleger (44.7) therefore amounts to destroying or at least suspending the paradox through isolating its constituent linguistic segments, i.e. severing 'liuing' from 'dead', but does not offer any logical solution: Maleger is a complex literary monstrosity marring creational, geographical, ontological and logical categories.

Hags

Spenser creates the hag in analogy to her male counterpart, a kinship that is reified in the family relation between the haggish witch, in whose house Florimell seeks shelter, and her love-stricken son, a 'carle' with a bent towards the lustful.[72] The hags in *The Faerie Queene* combine

69 This is the only occurrence of the compound in *The Faerie Queene*. Compare the phrase 'lifeless shadow' in II.xi.44.3.

70 Broaddus also acknowledges the intricacies of Maleger's nature: his 'attributes and capacities represent a complex of forces – disease, decay, cold, the desiccation of age, and death itself – against which the postlapsarian body is inherently vulnerable no matter how we conduct ourselves' ('Renaissance Psychology and the Defense of Alma's Castle', pp. 147–8). Weatherby's proposed solution that Maleger is simply Death himself disregards the semantic and logical complexities of Maleger's description: 'when Arthur slays Maleger we witness the death (not of original sin but) of death' ('Two Images', p. 347).

71 The three furlongs suggest the length of the Dragon's tail in I.xi.11.7.

72 The witch's son experiences the thralls of 'brutish lust, that was so beastly tind' (III.vii.15.9).

various characteristics of the witch, the demonic agent and the loathly old woman.[73] The *OED* entry on 'hag' indeed suggests that these three aspects were competing in the late sixteenth and early seventeenth century.[74] This semantic breadth accordingly figures in Spenser's hags, as he realises them as witches and evil agents whose ugliness signals their inner corruption.[75] Like the names of the 'carles', the names of the hags – namely Duessa, Occasion, Ate, Sclaunder, Impatience and Impotence, Detraction and Envie, as well as an old woman and the witch who sets the hyena on Florimell – often point to the perversion of concepts as the key element in their poetic conception.[76] Spenser's most notable variation on this topos is Duessa, whose true anatomy shows that hags can trespass into the realm of composite monsters.[77] Of course, the hag can also be only mildly disfigured, especially in those cases where her deviancy is partly determined by practising witchcraft.[78] She may, moreover, invade allegorical spaces to challenge the readers' expectations. As Manning and Fowler argue, Spenser's Occasion stands in sharp discontinuity with the traditional iconography of *Occasio* featuring in the emblem books:[79] while the pictorial rendition is usually represented as a young, beautiful and naked woman, Spenser's textual version is old and ugly.

The hag's repulsiveness lies mainly in the link between old age and vicious deformity, in other words, in her lacking the traditional physical correlatives of virtue, namely youth and beauty. Duessa's dual physique emphasises this sharp discontinuity particularly well in the 'before and after' effect of the stripping. Other specimens of her kin are just as abom-

73 On the hag in Spenser's *The Faerie Queene*, see Sheila T. Cavanagh, *Wanton Eyes and Chaste Desires: Female Sexuality in 'The Faerie Queene'* (Bloomington: Indiana University Press, 1994), pp. 60–7.

74 See *OED*, s.v. 'hag, *n.*', 1a ('An evil spirit, dæmon, or infernal being, in female form'), 2 ('A woman supposed to have dealings with Satan and the infernal world; a witch') and 3a ('An ugly, repulsive old woman: often with implication of viciousness or maliciousness').

75 This is similarly noted by Cavanagh, *Wanton Eyes*, p. 63, with reference to the *OED* entry.

76 For hags see: Duessa (Bk I), Maleger's companions Impatience and Impotence (II.ix and xi), Occasion (II.iv), the witch that sets the hyena on Florimell (III.vii–viii), Ate (IV.i–ii and iv–vi; V.ix.47), an old woman (IV.vii.34), Sclaunder (III.viii), as well as Detraction and Envie, who lead the Blatant Beast (V.xii).

77 Duessa has been analysed in detail in the Chapter on human–animal composites, above.

78 See the witch in III.vii–viii, and D'Orsay W. Pearson, 'Witches', in *Spenser Encyclopedia*, ed. by Hamilton, p. 729–30 (p. 730).

79 See John Manning and Alastair Fowler, 'The Iconography of Spenser's Occasion', *Journal of the Warburg and Courtauld Institutes* 39 (1976), 263–6. David W. Burchmore argues that Occasion is given attributes reminiscent of iconographical and textual renderings of misfortune; see 'The Medieval Sources of Spenser's Occasion Episode', *Spenser Studies* 2 (1981), 93–120.

inable: with grim or wrinkled faces,[80] bald heads,[81] unkempt hair,[82] a lame leg[83] and loathly garments,[84] they appear as a diseased subhuman category that stirs abominations in both Spenser's characters and his readers. Spenser himself implies the importance of anatomy for an understanding of these deformed beings when he explains that Envie's cheeks are so lean that 'all her teeth arew, / And all her bones might through her cheeks be red' (V.xii.29.5–6). The circumstance that Calidore (and the readers with him) can see and analyse Envie's inner anatomy through a skin so thin that it becomes translucent reveals that her monstrous body lacks a recognisable biological boundary that separates inside from outside. This implies the dissolution of the monstrous body, which is in no small part underscored by a plethora of references to old age which accrue to become monstrous signifiers: the hag is a creature on the brink of 'unbecoming' or annihilation, the image of deception and death walking through *The Faerie Queene*. Like the 'carle', the hag is essentially an infernal being that brings, as it were, death and hell to the world of Spenser's poem.

The degree to which Spenser can transform individual physical attributes to create monstrosities within the human realm is perhaps best illustrated by Ate, who enters the scene with Duessa at the opening of Book IV, the Legend of Friendship. Ate, as 'mother of debate, / And all dissention' friendship's natural antagonist (IV.i.19.1–2), lives underground in an abode near the gates of hell (20).[85] While her subterranean cave, which Spenser calls a 'darksome delue' (20.4), is replete with the spoils of the discord she has sown in Thebes, Troy, and other legendary places (21–4),[86] her garden is a fascinating *locus horribilis* diametrically opposed to the Garden of Adonis in III.vi. In it, she grows the 'seedes of euill wordes, and factious deedes' (IV.i.25.5), which will develop into war and chaos.[87] That she feeds on the seeds 'for bread' (26.2), and sucks her victims' life and

80 See Occasion (II.iv.4), Impotence and Impatience (II.xi.23).

81 See Duessa (I.viii.46) and Occasion's bald back head (II.iv.4).

82 See Occasion (II.iv.4), Envie (II.xi.23) and the witch (III.vii.6).

83 See Occasion (II.iv.4) and Impotence (II.xi.23).

84 See Impatience and Impotence (II.xi.23), the witch (II.vii.6) and Occasion (II.iv.4).

85 Hamilton argues that Spenser drew on Homer's goddess of Discord in *Iliad*, XIX.91–94 and 126–31; Virgil's Alecto in *Aeneid*, VII.324–7; and Ariosto's Discordia in *Orlando Furioso*, XIV.83–4. While Discord does not share Ate's ugliness, Alecto and Discordia certainly do. In *The Faerie Queene*, Ate is lexically and conceptually related to Atin (II.iv.42).

86 See also Care's cave (IV.v.33).

87 Spenser establishes the causative nexus between 'wordes … trouble … bloudshed', and 'deedes … iarre … warre' through the use of stylistic *correlatio* (see Hamilton, note to IV.i.25.5–9).

blood,[88] is a clear deviation from normative human conduct, and hence renders her monstrosity more profound.[89] Ate's food of choice generally characterises the hag as a female devourer figure draining her victims of life and blood; more specifically, it violates Old Testament prohibitions,[90] and parodies the Eucharist which also conjoins the ingestion of bread and blood.[91] Spenser therefore combines the type of the hag with that of the bloodsucker to heighten Ate's vileness and infernal implications.

Ate, who seems to be as beautiful as rejuvenated Duessa, is a humanoid deformity that reifies the concept of the monstrous signifier in its most extreme form.[92] Her monstrosity, underscored by her ugliness, is the outcome of her hellish nature and nurture.[93] With eyes looking in opposite directions, a disfigured mouth replete with 'gall', 'venim', and 'wicked wordes' (27.4–5), a lying tongue divided into two parts that speak and contend at the same time and a 'doubly … guided' heart (27.9),[94] Ate is an *omnium gatherum* of monstrous signifiers.[95] Her distorted ears do not match one another, just as her 'odde' and 'much vnlike' feet (28.6–7) point in opposite directions, while her hands act in contradictory, literally opposite ways.[96] The Duessan concept of monstrosity as an uneven body made up of incompatible *membra* hence also surfaces in Ate, who figures not only as a thorough perversion of truthful sense perception but also as

88 'That she may sucke their life, and drinke their blood, / With which she from her childhood had bene fed' (IV.i.26.5–6). Cavanagh notes that witches and hags reportedly sucked the blood of their victims (see *Wanton Eyes*, p. 52, with reference to John Webster, *The Displaying of Supposed Witchcraft*).

89 On bloodsucking women, see Bettina Bildhauer, 'Bloodsuckers: the Construction of Female Sexuality in Medieval Science and Fiction', in *Consuming Narratives*, ed. by McAvoy and Walters, pp. 104–15. She particularly focuses on the bloodsucking woman as 'other' and object of fear.

90 Ate violates the Old Testament prohibitions that 'you shall not eat the blood of any flesh at all' (Leviticus 17.14), and 'eat not the blood, for the blood is for the soul' (Deutoronomy 12.23). On the violation of dietary rules and its relation to monstrosity, see Douglas, *Purity*, pp. 54–72 ('The Abominations of Leviticus').

91 See John 6.51–2: 'I am the living bread which came down from heaven. If any man eat of this bread, he shall live for ever: and the bread that I will give is my flesh, for the life of the world' (Hamilton, note to IV.i.26.1–6).

92 See IV.i.27–29.

93 Spenser explains the connection between nature and nurture in IV.i.26.7–9: '… she at first was borne of hellish brood, / And by infernall furies nourished, / That by her monstrous shape might easily be red'.

94 Cf. Occasion's wagging tongue (II.iv.5), which is a stereotype in antifeminist writing (see Cavanagh, *Wanton Eyes*, pp. 65–6).

95 The phrase 'vnmeete a mouth to bee' (IV.i.27.3) underscores the deformity and perversion of this orifice.

96 Broaddus notes that Ate's description is 'a composite of unresolvable contrarities' (*Spenser's Allegory of Love*, p. 113).

an example of unnatural, hence monstrous, movement.

Spenser, however, does not merely coerce a substantial number of physical details into one distorted being, for his deployment of formal syntactical features, especially comparative connectives such as 'likewise' and 'as', readily joins these disparate parts into an anatomy that feigns unity.[97] At the same time, he accentuates Ate's monstrosity by deliberately deviating from the traditional arrangement of the beauty blazon, instead taking opposite directions in the presentation of individual items. Spenser's ability to translate the contradictory nature of the hag into a likewise inverted rhetoric emphasises that the monstrous, as a deviation from the norm, may also be represented in the poet's deviating from rhetorical rules.

In addition to their anatomical features, the filthy and uncouth nature of the hags is also manifest in disgusting effluvia, which particularly emphasise their gendered monstrosity: blood, gore, poison and filth combine into a horrible mix that serves as an important signifier to enhance the hags' monstrous nature. Spenser also assigns his hags attributes that corroborate their monstrosity in the context of the poem. As monstrous aberrations of the human, hags are frequently associated with other potentially monstrous beings. That Duessa rides Orgoglio's monster; that the witch commands the monstrous hyena; and that Enuie and Detraction set the Blatant Beast on Calidore – these examples show that monstrous humans are assigned higher rungs in the hierarchy of monsters. In some cases, these monstrous affinities can form recurrent patterns, or even new ontological units. Detraction, for instance, has a 'mouth distort' (V.xii.36.1), which foams with poison and holds a tongue that appears to have an asp's sting.[98] That this sting additionally grows 'out of her vile tongue' (42.7) makes manifest the conceptual continuity between the Blatant Beast and its part-time master, so the four-footed beast is a permutation of Detraction that exceeds its master in monstrosity. As Enuie and Detraction both reify distinct aspects of the Blatant Beast, their unity results in a conceptual overlay between these beings, which Lobsien interprets as a rhetor-

97 Compare the following passages: 'And as her tongue, so was her hart discided' (IV.i.27.8); 'Als as she double spake, so heard she double' (28.1); 'And as her eares so eke her feet were odde' (28.6); '*Likewise vnequall* were her handes twaine' (29.1; emphasis added).

98 The connection of serpentine tongues with slander is highly reminiscent of Psalms 140.3: 'They have sharpened their tongues like a serpent: adders poison *is* under their lippes.' The Geneva Bible gloss reads: 'He sheweth what weapons ye wicked vse, when power & force faile the*m*'. The scriptural parallel is also noted by Hamilton, note to V.xii.36.3–4.

ical space of allegorical surplus.[99] Such monstrous mutuality destabilises the individuality of the hags, and leads to the temporary creation of, as it were, 'dual hags'. Hence, doubles like Impatience and Impotence are more than just partners in vice and crime; especially Enuie and Detraction correlate in such a way that Spenser momentarily joins them into one unified monstrosity: 'These two now had themselues combynd in one, / And linckt together gainst Sir *Arthegall*' (V.xii.37.1–2). Spenser's choice of the synonymous verbs *to combine* and *to link* therefore leads to a temporal 'twinning' of these characters and their designs. Such links may also be books apart: although the hag Sclaunder (IV.viii) and the Blatant Beast never meet in the poem, both are clearly complementary physicalisations of slander, which reify different aspects of aberrant language. As one monstrous creature may thus join with another to form new units or relate to them, and, as one monstrous signifier may be shared by conceptually similar monstrosities to create new interrelating patterns, the monstrous emerges as an omnipresent and fluctuating category in Spenser's allegorical poem. Such correlations necessitate what Kaske calls a 'concordantial reading', an early modern exegetical practice used to interpret the Bible: according to Kaske, the reader of *The Faerie Queene*, like the reader of Scripture, is required to compose a mental concordance of images, words, and concepts, which may contradict or complement each other, and interpret their similarities and differences.[100] Accordingly, Spenser also sets his readers the task to compile references to monsters, their body parts and allegorical concepts to arrive at comprehensive interpretations of his poem.

Transformation and metamorphosis

Man's inherent monstrosity is perhaps best illustrated by the instability of the human shape. Significant instances of physical volatility feature in the multiple transformations and metamorphoses Spenser incorporates in his poem, which attest that the human body is constantly threatened to become something other than itself.[101] Transformation and metamor-

99 See Eckhard Lobsien, *Imaginationswelten: Modellierungen der Imagination und Textualisierungen der Welt in der englischen Literatur, 1580–1750*, Neues Forum für allgemeine und vergleichende Literaturwissenschaft, 15 (Heidelberg: Winter, 2003), pp. 103–4.

100 See Kaske, *Spenser and Biblical Poetics*, pp. 18–24.

101 Colin Burrow discusses Spenser's transformations from an Ovidian perspective in 'Original Fictions: Metamorphoses in *The Faerie Queene*', in *Ovid Renewed: Ovidian Influences on Literature and Art from the Middle Ages to the Twentieth Century*, ed. by Charles Martindale (Cambridge: Cambridge University Press, 1988), pp. 99–119.

phosis can be self-manipulated by characters with magical shape-shifting abilities, inflicted on human characters by a magical agent, or even self-inflicted by the characters' proneness to the vices. Thus subjected to the process of becoming monstrous, the human body can transgress into every realm of biological existence, be it monster, beast or even vegetation; in extreme cases, the human being can turn into a deformed representation of an abstract concept, or entirely lose his human form. Such transformations to the beastly hark back to Pico's philosophy of man, because they address man's precarious middle position between the spiritual and the beastly, and underline the difficulty of moving up the ladder of creation for proper self-fashioning. They particularly illustrate man's inherent liability to corruption and deterioration, and make man's fall to the beastly and monstrous his own responsibility. As we shall see in this section, Spenser follows Pico's ethics of proper choice, and employs transformations and metamorphoses to illustrate man's degeneration.

Wilful transformation

Evil characters like Archimago and Malengin are introduced as shape-shifters who show their deviousness and power through a series of boundary-crossing transformations.[102] Malengin's polymorphous flight, which takes place in V.ix, is an especially impressive instance of shape-shifting, also because it is fully integrated into the plot of the poem. Malengin, whose name suggests deceit,[103] and who is given attributes of the Wild Man,[104] is associated with the infernal regions, while his wild laughter connects him with other churlish characters, especially Lust.[105] With him, simile precedes metamorphosis,[106] for he first flees swiftly '[l]ike a wyld Gote' (V.ix.15.4), before literally transforming into fox,

102 Spenser relates that Archimago sometimes becomes 'a fowle, sometime a fish in lake, / Now like a foxe, now like a dragon fell' (I.ii.10.5–6; the latter connects the magician with the dragons in Book I). The classical deity Proteus tries to terrify Florimell, the damsel he saved from distress, by assuming various 'dreadfull shapes' (III.viii.41.1), among which there are the brute giant, and the centaur, two creatures that vividly depict the god's threatening brutality and sexual desire (41–2). For the classical depiction of Proteus's shape-shifting, see Homer, *Odyssey*, IV.456–9.

103 See Hamilton, note to V.ix.5.8. Fletcher goes so far as to dub him 'a monstrous chthonic embodiment of the principle of deceit itself' (*The Prophetic Moment: An Essay on Spenser* (Chicago and London: University of Chicago Press, 1971), p. 234). Richard Mallette suggests that he is modelled on Despair (see 'Book V of *The Faerie Queene:* An Elizabethan Apocalypse', *Spenser Studies* 11 (1994), 136–49 (p. 143)).

104 For the description, see V.ix.10–11.

105 See IV.vii.24.9 and 26.9 for Lust's inane grinning, which partly marks his monstrosity. For Geryoneo, see V.xi.9.6–9.

106 Spenser applies the same method to Adicia, who is first likened to an 'enraged cow' (V.viii.46.1), and a 'mad bytch' (V.viii.49.1), before turning into a tiger.

bush, bird, stone, hedgehog and serpent to deceive his pursuers.[107] Spenser hence prepares his readers for Malengin's continuous shape-shifting by employing a metaphorical transformation as a thematic preface to the physical transformations. As Malengin deliberately alters his shape to delude his pursuers, his bodily changes do not bring into relief his true character; rather, they accentuate his deviousness and wiliness. Malengin's powers of shape-shifting are especially accomplished, because he has access to all three subhuman planes in the Great Chain of Being, namely minerals, plants and animals.[108] Hence, man's physical boundaries, which usually determine and in the literal sense de-*fine* his human existence, are rendered null and void, which circumstance blurs the clear demarcation between human and subhuman categories. Spenser makes Malengin's aberration explicit when explaining that the carle 'leaue[s] his *proper* forme' to change into another (16.9; emphasis added). The wilful alteration of his 'proper', i.e. apt and sanctioned shape, results in the violation of the normative human body. His monstrosity is hence mainly constituted by his physical malleability. Despite his consummate shape-shifting, Malengin's life ends when Talus kills him after he has assumed the form of a snake, an animal that significantly encodes infernal deviousness and deception. Malengin is therefore squashed by Talus's thresh, which crushes his bones and disembowels him, the very moment his transformation represents his true nature (V.ix.19). Assuming a symbolically appropriate shape, Malengin is reduced to his mere corporeality.

Transformation inflicted by a magical agent

While shape-shifting of this kind is transient, metamorphoses into common or fabulous animals, and even vegetation, are often irreversible, unless the magically transformed humans are restored to their proper shape by a virtuous character or agent. Most frequently, the human is turned into an animal or a composite creature, but other transformations are even lower on the scale of being, as is the case with Fradubio and Fraelissa, who have been turned into trees by Duessa's powerful black magic.[109]

The episode relating Redcrosse's and Duessa's encounter with Fradubio and Fraelissa, Spenser's variation on the topos of the bleeding-speaking

107 See V.ix.17–19. Malengin's flight is a less exuberant version of the giant Balisardo's consecutive metamorphoses into serpent, monstrous boar (with burning eyes, serpent's tail, huge wings and horns), the knight Dudone, panther, hyena, giraffe, tiger, griffin, crocodile and many more in Boiardo's *Orlando Innamorato*, II.x.22–49.

108 See Tillyard, *Elizabethan World Picture*, pp. 87–90, for the classic account of this system.

109 For the magical transformation, see I.ii.42.

tree, shows how metamorphosis can turn the human being into a botanical monster.[110] Fradubio's story suggests moral implications in accord with Pico's *Oratio de hominis dignitate*, which explains that the man who gives in to his appetites moves down the divine ladder of creation and becomes a plant.[111] Against the backdrop of Pico's humanist manifesto, Fradubio's transformation into a tree by the temptress Duessa becomes the allegorical representation of his giving in to his sexual appetites.

When Redcrosse and Duessa, who now poses as Fidessa, seek shelter from the blazing sun under these two shady trees the magic transformation has long been completed.[112] However, the passage acquires a dynamic of its own, because Spenser effects a stylistic retransformation of the trees into human beings through largely anthropomorphic language and ambivalent anatomical terms. As the trees spread '[t]heir *armes* abroad, with gray *mosse* ouercast' (I.ii.28.4, emphases added), their leaves 'trembling with euery blast' (28.5),[113] the poet, right at the beginning of this episode, accentuates the trees' human origin through deploying a transformative language that offers surprising hints at their human nature. Ignorant of the tree's real identity, Redcrosse breaks off a bough, thereby unwittingly inflicting a quasi-human wound on Fradubio: 'out of the [tree's] rifte there came / Smal drops of gory bloud' (30.8–9).

110 The episode covers I.ii.28–45. Spenser's main sources are Virgil's story of Polydorus (*Aeneid*, III.22–48), Dante's Wood of the Suicides (*Inferno*, XIII) and Ariosto's tale of Astolfo (*Orlando Furioso*, VI.26–53). For extensive discussions of Spenser's major and minor sources, see Shirley Clay Scott, 'From Polydorus to Fradubio: The History of a Topos', *Spenser Studies* 7 (1986), 27–57; and Elizabeth Jane Bellamy, 'The Broken Branch and the "Living Well": Spenser's Fradubio and Romance Error in *The Faerie Queene*', *Renaissance Papers* 32 (1985), 1–12. Douglas Biow focuses on Spenser's evocation of wonder (see *Mirabile Dictu: Representations of the Marvelous in Medieval and Renaissance Epic* (Ann Arbor: University of Michigan Press, 1996), pp. 167–8).

111 'Si quem enim videris deditum ventri, humi serpentem hominem, frutex est, non homo, quem vides' ('If you see someone who is a slave to his belly, crawling along the ground, it is not a man you see, but a plant'). Pico, *Oration*, pp. 130–1.

112 As Fradubio explains, Duessa's evil spell can be broken only when he bathes 'in a liuing well' (I.ii.43.4). The living well has been explained as the grace of God; scriptural sources are John 4.10 and Jeremiah 2.13, as well as Revelation 21.6 and 22.1–2 (see Upton in *Variorum*, I, 205; see also Scott, 'From Polydorus to Fradubio', p. 51). Redcrosse revives during the fight against the Dragon when falling into a living well (I.xi.31.6). Cf. also Bellamy, 'Broken Branch', p. 6.

113 Anthropomorphism and arborisation move in opposite directions: the term *moss* is ambivalent, as it is frequently used interchangeably with 'hair' in the Renaissance. See *OED*, s.v. 'mossy, *adj.* and *n.*1', 5 ('for downy or velvety hair'), with reference to Arthur Golding, *Ovid's Metamorphoses*, XII.320, and E. K.'s gloss to 'May Eclogue', 187, 'young and mossy heares'. See also the *OED* entry on 'moss, *n.*', II.4, with reference to John Gerarde, *The Herball, or General Historie of Plants* (London: John Norton, 1597), p. 1374, which explains that goldilocks 'might also be termed Golden Mosse, or Hairie Mosse'.

The injury underscores that the tree is a deviation from biological norms. When Fradubio, who retains his ability to experience pain and to speak,[114] screams out in anguish with 'a piteous yelling voice' (31.1),[115] Spenser presents the tree as a *monstrum* in the process of becoming human, but simultaneously enhances the deviant, disgusting and monstrous quality of Fradubio's blood, which is 'gory', that is clotted and unwholesome.[116] Redcrosse hence experiences the tree as a manifest monster (although failing to interpret it correctly),[117] and approaches it with a sense of dread and wonder that is maintained throughout the entire episode.[118] With Fradubio's plaint 'O spare with guilty hands to teare / My tender sides in this roughe rynd embard' (31.2–3), the tree finally becomes more fully anthropomorphised.[119] The malleability of physical forms thus creates a truly 'liuing', i.e. feeling, talking, hence wholly animated tree (44.5). Simultaneously, however, Redcrosse regresses into an arboreal being when standing astonished and speechless at the sight: 'Astond he stood, and vp his heare did houe, / And with that suddein horror could no member moue' (31.8–9). At this critical moment, Redcrosse's and Fradubio's descriptions move into opposite directions to create a space of interaction between vegetable and human life, and suggest that Redcrosse may well suffer Fradubio's fate now that he is under the spell of Duessa.

These incidents are evidence for a double transformative development in the Fradubio episode. While, in the course of the canto, Fradubio's embedded narrative relates how the human has become the tree (exemplified by Redcrosse's astonishment), Spenser at the same time chooses a rhetorical presentation that emphasises the tree's becoming human. Both counter-movements, the one up the ladder of creation, the other down, are anchored in Spenser's literary sources and the transformative power of his poetic language. They generate a textual intersection of the human and the plant that ultimately violates the clear distinction between both realms. Fradubio's self-evaluation as 'once a man *Fradubio*, now a tree, / Wretched man, wretched tree' (33.3–4), and Redcrosse's bewil-

114 Cf. also I.ii.33.9.

115 Cf. also I.ii.33.1: 'groning deep'.

116 See *OED*, s.v. 'gore, *n.*1', and 'gory, *a.*'; etymologically, the word denotes filth and slimy matter. Fradubio's blood critically differs from Idalogos's (in Boccaccio's *Il filocolo*, V.6), which has a vermilion colour and no overt disgusting features (for a similar case, cf. Tasso, *Gerusalemme Liberata*, XIII.39). The passage is discussed in Scot, 'From Polydorus to Fradubio', p. 38.

117 Biow explains that Redcrosse 'cannot recognize a *monstrum* as a portentous warning' (*Mirabile dictu*, p. 161).

118 Cf. Redcrosse's reaction in I.ii.32. See also Biow, *Mirabile dictu*, p. 167.

119 Cf. I.ii.42.8.

dering address, 'Say on *Fradubio* then, or man, or tree' (34.1), additionally stress the profound interdependency between human and arboreal natures in this passage. The Fradubio episode, where the tree gradually receives human features without returning to his human shape, attests that transformation does not necessarily happen physically, but may also be realised textually through the deliberate deployment of an animating poetic language that maps the human body on to the site of the vegetative, and vice versa.

The singularly most potent agent of transformation in *The Faerie Queene* is Acrasia, the evil enchantress and 'monster fell' presiding over the Bower of Bliss, which Sir Guyon violently destroys in the final canto of Book II. On their voyage to her island, right after making their way past the 'quickesand of *Vnthriftyhed*' and the '*Whirlepoole of decay*' (II.xii.18.9 and 20.2), the Champion of Temperance and the Palmer encounter numerous marine creatures rising violently from the waters. This prompts Spenser into composing a catalogue of aquatic monsters that figures as a miniature encyclopaedia of deep sea life.[120] In this passage, Gesner's *Historia animalium* is an all-pervasive influence, traceable in creatures such as the walrus (or morse), the 'Wasserman' (24.3), and the 'Sea-saytre' (24.5), as well as the 'Huge *Ziffius*' (24.7; a sword-fish), and the 'greedy *Rosmarines* with visages deforme' (24.9; a sea horse).[121] Spenser additionally includes 'Spring-headed *Hydres*' (23.6),[122] whales, strange fishes,[123] the 'Mighty *Monoceros*' (23.9)[124] and the Scolopendraes, a species of his own invention.[125] These beings are endowed with attributes such as 'immeasured tayles' (23.9), horns[126] and sword-like protrusions at the head, which

120 See II.xii.23–5. The passage is heavily discussed; see *Variorum Spenser*, II, 359–64. Jonson glossed this passage as 'the Descr[iption] of certaine monstrous fishes' (see Riddell and Stewart, *Jonson's Spenser*, pp. 181–2).

121 On Spenser's indebtedness to Gesner's *Historia animalium*, see Watson's exhaustive article 'Spenser's Submarine Creation', pp. 121–34. John Boardman's article '"Very Like a Whale" – Classical Sea Monsters' traces the history of aquatic creatures in the arts of the classical age (in *Monsters and Demons*, ed. by Farkas, Harper and Harrison, pp. 73–84).

122 The hydres connect to Spenser's dragons, especially to Orgoglio's beast, which is likened to the Hydra slain by Hercules.

123 Among them 'sea-shouldring Whales' (II.xii.23.6), and 'Great whirlpooles' (23.7; a type of whale; see P. A. Robin, *Animal Lore in English Literature*, quoted in *Variorum*, II, 360).

124 Watson notes that Spenser's monoceros differs from Gesner's in that it has 'immeasured tayles' (II.xii.23.9).

125 Hamilton identifies it thus (note to II.xii.23.8) against Brooks-Davies's assumption that this is the sea-centipede (*Critical Commentary*, pp. 183–4, note to II.xii.23; see also *OED*, s.v. 'scolopendra', 1).

126 This is the case with the monoceros, which resembles the narwhal (II.xii.23.9).

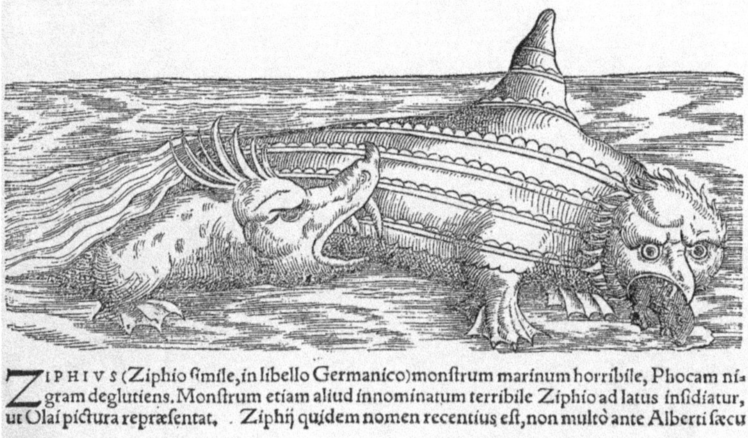

Figure 11 Ziphius; from *Nomenclator aquatilium animantium*

become monstrous signifiers illustrating the violation of the normative body (see Figure 11).[127]

Spenser also translates the monstrosity of the sea, a classical and scriptural tradition,[128] into monstrously long and exotic names,[129] and enhances them with fitting epithets.[130] Largely elaborating on Armida's ability to transform men into fish in Tasso's *Gerusalemme Liberata*,[131] Spenser demonstrates the varieties of shapes such transformations may take to lay bare how completely monstrous these humans have become. The submarine monsters, human victims who have been transformed into animal shapes by the sorceress Acrasia, represent 'fantastic disorder', and occupy 'levels some little way above original chaos itself'.[132]

Spenser contextualises these monstrous humans into natural history, which described the sea as a space of evil spawning countless horrible

127 Cf. Spenser's description of the Zifius (II.xii.24.7–8).

128 The depiction of marine life in II.xii suggests that the deviant anatomical attributes of sea creatures ultimately stem from the pictorial tradition of the classical period (for a discussion of that tradition, see Boardman, '"Very Like a Whale"', p. 74). See Psalm 104.25.

129 On the link between unfamiliar names and monstrosity, cf. Sidney's complaining about 'far-fet words that may seem monsters' (*Defence*, p. 117). For the text, see p. 200, n. 6.

130 Spenser employs monstrous terms such as 'dreadfull', 'griesly', 'horrible', 'huge' and 'greedy' (II.xii.24).

131 See Tasso, *Gerusalemme Liberata*, X.61–4. Cf. also Boiardo, *Orlando Innamorato*, II.xiii.57–66, for a less elaborated romance adventure involving fish, whales, a siren and an island.

132 See Watson, 'Spenser's Submarine Creation', pp. 121–34.

Figure 12 Sea devil; from Ulisse Aldrovandi, *Opera omnia*

and miraculous beings,[133] a tradition he acknowledges explicitly when reporting that 'thousand thousands many more, / And more deformed Monsters thousand fold' (25.1–2) come rushing to the surface. Spenser's heavy use of *geminatio* and line repetition accentuates the unrestrained plenitude and deformity of aquatic creation.[134] Contemporary broadsides and treatises, which also feature impressive pictorial representations of unknown marine creatures, indeed played on the horror and wonder these beings induced in the reading public, and so does Spenser when drawing attention to the 'ten thousand monsters foule abhor'd' in Proteus's submarine cave two books later (IV.xi.3.8).[135] Spenser's sea creatures in II.xii might thus obviously interact with the cultural stereotypes of the late sixteenth century; yet, in the context of the monstrous humans in *The Faerie Queene*, these creatures become exemplars of the deformation and complete annihilation of traceable human features, with the notable exceptions of the 'Wasserman' and the 'Sea-satyre', which figure as terrifying human–animal composites (see Figure 12).[136] Consequently, the loss of the normative body becomes not solely manifest in the usual addition of animal attributes as monstrous signifiers; more critically, it becomes visible in their excess size, which results in huge, shapeless bodies that terrify through their immeasurableness.[137] This development is critical because it underlines man's physical instability: the human frame can be obliterated, and enlarged to the gigantic proportions of aquatic creatures. Thus, all human beings can become 'dreadfull pourtraicts of deformitee' (II.xii.23.5).

The sea monsters are not the only creatures that have been transformed 'into these fearefull shapes' by Acrasia (xii.26.3), as the Palmer

133 See Daniel, 7.3, which concerns the emergence of the four beasts from the sea.

134 Spenser stresses that the monsters from the deep exceed the monsters of the land in horribleness: 'For all that here on earth we dreadfull hold, / Be but as bugs to fearen babes withall, / Compared to the creatures in the seas entrall' (II.xii.25.7–9).

135 See, for instance, the awe-inspiring woodcuts of Zifius, Rosmarus, Morsz and Monoceros in Gesner, *Historia animalium*, IV, 208–11 (reprinted in the *Spenser Encyclopedia*, 'natural history', fig. 1–3); for broadsides, see *The discription of a rare or rather most monstrous fishe taken on the East cost of Holland the xvii of Nouember, 1566* (London: Thomas Purfoote, 1566); Thomas Granger, *A Moste true and marueilous straunge wonder ... of. XVII. Monstrous fishes* (London: Thomas Colwell, 1568); Anon., *A Description of a strange (and miraculous) Fish, cast upon the sands in the meads* (London: Thomas Lambert, no year).

136 See the Palmer's explanation that these monsters are humans 'into these fearfull shapes disguiz'd' by Acrasia (II.xii.26.3).

137 See, e.g., the 'Great whirlpooles', the 'immeasured tayles' of the Monoceros (II.xii.23.7 and 9) and 'Huge Ziffius' (24.7). Boardman generally observes that marine life, especially whales, hardly have a shaped body at all ('"Very Like a Whale"', p. 73). Isidore also identifies excessive size as the mark of the monstrous (see Chapter 5, above).

and Guyon find out as soon as they arrive on the witch's island, where they are again attacked, first by birds and then by tellurian beasts.[138] It is only after Guyon has destroyed the Bower of Bliss that the Palmer fully explicates the nature of these hideous beings, who are, in fact, victims of the witch's pleasure garden, and have been turned into creatures that image forth their individual moral corruption:

> ... These seeming beasts are men indeed,
> Whom this Enchauntresse hath transformed thus,
> Whylome her louers, which her lustes did feed,
> Now turned into figures hideous,
> According to their mindes like monstruous.
> Sad end (quoth [Guyon]) of life intemperate,
> And mournefull meed of ioyes delicious[.]
>
> (xii.85.1–7)

Unlike the mermaids discussed in the chapter on human–animal composites, Acrasia's gullible victims have no traceable human features any more. This completeness of transformation, highlighted by deixis and *epimone*,[139] contains more than a mere exchange of physical shapes. To underline the complexity of this passage, it makes good sense to compare Acrasia in *The Faerie Queene* with Armida in *Gerusalemme Liberata*. Although Acrasia shares Armida's magic ability to transform human beings into animals, these animal shapes do not indicate their true nature. The transformed men in the Bower of Bliss, however, are given animal shapes befitting their spiritual conditions, for they are turned into 'figures hideous / According to their mindes like monstruous' (xii.85. 4–5).[140] The alliterative phrase at the end of the explanation adds force to the correlation between the beastly and the spiritual, thus didactically illustrating the outcome of over-indulgence in worldly, especially carnal, pleasures. The precarious link between physical form and spiritual corruption again suggests Pico's moralising man's susceptibility to the sinful, especially his propensity to the delusions of lust, which Pico likens to Calypso: 'si quem in fantasiae quasi Calipsus vanis praestigiis cecucientem et, subscalpenti delinitum illecebra, sensibus mancipatum, brutum est, non homo, quem vides' ('if you see someone who is enslaved by his own senses, blinded by the empty hallucinations brought on by fantasy

138 Rosemarie Freeman sees a connection between the beast-headed men besieging the Castle of Alma and those appearing in the Bower of Bliss (see '*The Faerie Queene*': *A Companion for Readers* (London: Chatto and Windus, 1970), pp. 49–50).

139 The repetition occurs in II.xii.85.2 and 4.

140 Spenser already refers to such interdependence when he remarks that in Maleger's beastly troop '[a]ll [are] shap't according their conditions' (II.xi.11.6).

(as if by Calypso herself) and entranced by their bedevelling spells, it is a brute animal you see, not a man').[141] In the context of Pico's notion of human frailty leading down the ladder of creation, Acrasia is a figuration of Calypso and her allurements, because she triggers innate beastliness and lust, and endows them with a fitting outward appearance that points to the monstrous quality of the soul.

Such a correlation between man's inner beastliness and its physical manifestation in a monstrous signifier is traceable even after the Palmer has restored Acrasia's victims to their human shape. The narrator's paradoxical observation that 'being men they did vnmanly looke' (xii.86.3) reveals the degree to which they remain spiritually and morally discredited especially if one takes the term 'vnmanly' to be a litotes for 'beastly' or 'monstrous'. Hence, Spenser leaves in doubt whether the restoration to human shape reactivates their rational powers. Moreover, when saying that they 'stared ghastly, some for inward shame, / And some for wrath to see their captiue Dame' (86.4–5), he deliberately leaves undecided the question whether they experience this upsurge of emotion because they realise how loathsome they have become,[142] or because they see their beloved Acrasia in captivity.

The next episode raises even stronger doubts as to whether moral progression can succeed beastly regression (xii.86.6–9):

> But one aboue the rest in speciall,
> That had an hog beene late, hight *Grylle* by name,
> Repyned greatly, and did him miscall,
> That had from hoggish forme him brought to naturall.

Grill, whose name marks his animal persuasion (Old Greek γρύλλος means 'pig'),[143] prefers beastly pleasures over his natural human inclinations. His unruly behaviour casts a quizzical light on the accomplishment of the transformation effected by the Palmer, who has changed their shapes, but who has certainly not altered their minds.[144] Here, Spenser draws on Plutarch's dialogue *Beasts Have the Use of Reason* as his ultimate

141 Pico, *Oration*, pp. 130–1.

142 In the Homeric Circe episode Ulysses's retransformed shipmates are younger and more handsome than before (see *Odyssey*, X.395–6).

143 See Liddell and Scott, *Greek Lexicon*, p. 361. The *OED* defines *grill* as 'a. Ill-will, vexation; harm, mischief. b.? Fierceness, violence'. See also Dietrich Schmidtke, *Geistliche Tierinterpretation in der deutschsprachigen Literatur des Mittelalters* (Berlin: Ernst-Reuter-Gesellschaft, 1968), pp. 405–6.

144 Whitney, *A Choice of Emblemes*, p. 82 ('*Homines voluptatibus transformantur*') similarly reads the reluctance of Circe's victims to become human again from the viewpoint of concupiscence.

model.[145] In this text, Ulysses asks Circe to retransform his shipmates, because, he argues, the shape of beasts is an unnatural guise[146] that lets them lead 'a pitiable and ignominious life'.[147] Circe endows one of these beasts with the power of speech, the hog Gryllos, who argues in favour of his beastly existence, pointing out that animals have better rational faculties than human beings. If one considers Gryllos's twisted logic, it does not come as a surprise that Ulysses asks him whether it was 'a pleasure towards herding together that bewitched [him] into this shape'.[148] Plutarch's text, albeit sporting crucial differences (his Gryllos is given speech, while Spenser's is retransformed), raises many issues that Spenser elaborates on. The motif of shame caused by a beastly life, for instance, crops up again in the shameful looks on the faces of the newly retransformed men of the Bower of Bliss. More importantly, the concept of an inner monstrosity translating into a deformed human shape, as voiced by Ulysses, is consonant with the assumption that Acrasia endows her victims with shapes befitting their spiritual condition.

Given the didacticism at work in *The Faerie Queene*, it is inevitable that Spenser darkens and moralises his source, especially if one contextualises the Grill episode in Pico's humanist philosophy of man. There are no mitigating circumstances for Grill, since he seeks to reclaim his non-human, 'swinish' life, an existence contaminated by the sins of gluttony, and lechery.[149] The commentary supplemented by Guyon and the Palmer drives home the moral and didactic implications of his 'obstinate bestiality':[150]

> Said *Guyon*, See the mind of beastly man,
> That hath so soone forgot the excellence
> Of his creation, when he life began,
> That now he chooseth, with vile difference,
> To be a beast, and lacke intelligence.
> To whom the Palmer thus, The donghill kinde
> Delightes in filth and fowle incontinence:

145 The text follows Plutarch, *Moralia*, Vol. VII, Fasc. 1, ed. by C. Hubert, Bibliotheca Scriptorum Graecorum et Romanorum Teubneriana (Leipzig: Teubner, 1959). Gelli's *Circe* is usually taken to be another source for this scene (see Supriya Chaudhuri, 'Grill', in *Spenser Encyclopedia*, ed. by Hamilton, p. 342).

146 It is 'παρὰ φύσιν', i.e. against nature (Plutarch, *Moralia*, 985E).

147 'οἰκτρὰν καὶ ἄτιμον οὕτω δίαιταν' (Plutarch, *Moralia*, 985E; my translation).

148 'ἦ σέ τις αὖ συνηθείας ἡδονὴ πρὸς τόδε τὸ σῶμα καταγεγοήτευκεν;' (Plutarch, *Moralia*, 986E; my translation).

149 Bloomfield identifies the pig as a marker of gluttony and lechery (see *The Seven Deadly Sins*, pp. 149–51 and pp. 248–9).

150 Donald Cheney, *Spenser's Image of Nature: Wild Man and Shepherd in 'The Faerie Queene'* (New Haven and London: Yale University Press, 1967), p. 180.

Let *Gryll* be *Gryll*, and haue his hoggish minde;
But let vs hence depart, whilest wether serues and winde.
(II.xii.87)

Here, Grill emerges as Satyrane's counter-image. Fashioning themselves according to very different preferences, both move into opposite directions on Pico's ladder of creation: while Satyrane rises to humanity, Grill degenerates to the beastly, because he willingly forfeits humanity and reason.[151] With such effrontery against divine creation, neither Guyon nor the Palmer can remain detached: their pulpiteering on the 'donghill kinde', which bears witness to their resignation, is heavily charged with moral terminology ('filth and fowle incontinence'). The Palmer's final verdict, 'Let *Gryll* be *Gryll*', then presses home Grill's fallen state with the power of tautology. However, it is far from clear how Book II ends exactly, for the phrase '[let him] haue his hoggish minde' is open to interpretation. It could of course refer to his sullied soul; but, if 'minde' stands for 'wish', it would imply another retransformation. Spenser's ambivalent moral wordplay deliberately reinforces the threat of metamorphosis posed by animal regression.[152]

In the light of the previous analysis, Grill's wish to remain a pig, and to abscond from humanity forever is clearly informed by classical sources and by Pico's notion of Renaissance man. However, Spenser's vision of human monstrosity also calls to mind a more immediate, Elizabethan influence. In the 1570s and the 1580s, exactly the time in which Spenser conceived the Bower of Bliss episode, man's inner monstrosity was addressed in pamphlets and broadsides whose authors sermonised just how monstrous man had become. The recurrent cipher for man's sinfulness was the deformed pig, which figured prominently in J. Phillips's *A mervaylous straunge deformed Swyne* (1570), and Fulwood's *The Shape of ii. Monsters* (1562). While Fulwood draws an elaborate comparison between the pig's abnormality and man's monstrous minds,[153] Phillips is very curt indeed: when he adds in his lengthy doggerel exhortation that the monster in the woodcut 'resembles some of those / as on the same do gape',[154] he commands his reader to find similarities between the pig's

151 In his late nineteenth-century edition of *The Faerie Queene*, Book I, G. W. Kitchin observes that Grill shows 'the degradation and loss of human qualities, of self-respect, of aims above sense' (quoted in *Variorum*, II, 395).

152 Schoenfeldt acknowledges Grill's universal relevance when purporting that 'he is the beast that all are capable of becoming in a moment of relaxation' (*Bodies and Selves*, p. 72).

153 See Fulwood, *The Shape of ii. Monsters*.

154 J. P[h]illips, *A Mervaylous Straunge Deformed Swyne*.

strange physical deformity and their own 'Swinish … lives'.

This kind of crude address, intended to insult readers and to shock them into recognition, is diametrically opposed to Spenser's elaborate and allusive style. In *The Faerie Queene*, severe moralisations of this kind are always directed at the characters committing sinful acts, as in the Palmer's reprehending Grill (II.xii.87), while general moral statements are placed at the beginning of a canto to direct the reader's attention to the allegorical core of the plot, as in the narrator's praising the excellence of the human form and his exhorting his readers to keep their temperance (II.ix.1). While Grill's tale is thus obliquely directed at the reader, the rhetoric of the Palmer's emphatic call against overindulgence mirrors the blatant exhortation of the broadsides. The conceptual and verbal resemblances between Spenser's text and the broadsides point to the same cultural agenda, and show that Spenser participates in the monstrous rhetoric of the late sixteenth century, albeit in a much more nuanced and layered way.[155] In this interplay of cultural testimonies, Grill and the monsters on the broadsides, as well as the aquatic creatures in the poem and on the contemporary folios, are the monstrous visualisation of man's fallen inner state, an other that points to man's tainted self.[156]

Self-inflicted metamorphosis

Grill's unruly wish mars the happy ending of Book II, and points to a baser nature at work in man, which absconds humanity and desires transformation into the beastly. *Ergo*, self-inflicted transformation must be the ultimate manifestation of a physical border-crossing that accentuates a character's deviant inclinations and may turn him completely into an animal, a grotesquely deformed human being, or even a demonic abstraction.

Cantos viii–ix in Book V offer a sequence of metamorphoses and transformations that bear witness to man's innate otherness,[157] as they stage not only Malengin's polymorphous escape but also Adicia's turning into a tiger. Adicia's flight into the woods takes place when she finds out that Arthur killed her husband, the Souldan,[158] and culminates in a transformation that visualises her being overcome by the forces of grief and wrath:[159]

155 On the verbal identity between the monster folios, see Brammall, 'Monstrous Metamorphosis', p. 13, n. 33.

156 See also Anon., *The description of a monstrous Pig*, and Barker, *The true description of a monsterous Chylde*.

157 See Cheney, *Spenser's Image of Nature*, pp. 164–5.

158 For the Souldan's demise at the hands of Arthur, see V.viii.39–45.

159 Marotti interprets Adicia as the 'lawlessness in a fallen world' (Marotti, 'Animal Symbolism', p. 78).

As a mad bytch, when as the franticke fit
Her burning tongue with rage inflamed hath,
Doth runne at randon, and with furious bit
Snatching at every thing, doth wreake her wrath
On man and beast, that commeth in her path.
There they doe say, that she transformed was
Into a Tygre, and that Tygres scath
In crueltie and outrage she did pas,
To proue her surname true, that she imposed has.

(V.viii.49)

Adicia's degradation into an animal takes place in two stages: Spenser first disfeatures her rhetorically through the imaginary evocation of a rabid dog that indiscriminatingly threatens all that come in her way. He stresses her abnormality further by describing that the bitch's tongue burns with rage ('burning', 'inflamed'), thus turning the organ into a monstrous signifier of wrath. Only after thus setting the scene does he relate her supposed metamorphosis into a tiger. In her interpretation of this stanza, Watson observes that Adicia's 'loss of humanity and human reason elides through simile into metamorphosis'.[160] More precisely, simile and offstage transformation are two interlinked strategies through which Spenser stages Adicia's crossing the species boundary. That Adicia out-tigers the tiger in cruelty and rage additionally tarnishes her behaviour as non-normative, and even marks her as a monster among proverbially fierce animals. Quite paradoxically, then, her metamorphosis does not annihilate the transformed subject, but rather emphasises a decisive part of her personality: at the end of the transformation, Adicia bodies forth her inherent nature, and becomes true to her name, which translates into Injustice.[161] Accordingly, she finally becomes an exile to human society, biding her days in a den 'farre from resort of men' (V.ix.2.1): as in so many medieval texts, human monstrosities in *The Faerie Queene* occupy the edges of the world.[162]

Transformations are effected not only by crossing the species boundary but also by permanent physical distortion.[163] This method is especially

160 Watson, 'Chivalric Bestiary', p. 169. Unlike Radigund, who was merely *likened* to a tiger, Adicia allows her beastly self to subsume her human self completely.

161 See, among others, Horstmann, *Namen*, p. 77.

162 Cf. also Duessa's flight into the wilderness in I.viii.50.

163 Distortion is an ongoing process, e.g., during Malbecco's metamorphosis into jealousy, and, in transient form, in similes and metaphors that stress his monstrous traits (see below). Also note Louise Gilbert Freeman's statement that '[a]llegory attempts to make its transformations irreversible' ('The Metamorphosis of Malbecco: Allegorical Violence and Ovidian Change', *Studies in Philology* 97 (2002), 308–30 (p. 329)).

well exemplified in the famous Procession of the Seven Deadly Sins in the House of Pride (I.iv), where the six personified sins Idlenesse, Gluttony, Lechery, Auarice, Enuy and Wrath draw the chariot of Lucifera, who represents Pride.[164] The extended description, in which the sins ride in three pairs and each of them is described in three stanzas, is informed by a sustained grotesquery heavily indebted to traditional iconography:[165] the personifications are endowed with dresses, symbolic objects, diseases and mounts that accentuate particular symptoms of the sins they represent.[166] As sins per se deviate from the norm of Christian behaviour, so do the bodies of Spenser's personifications. When Spenser thus moralises that Gluttony '[i]n shape and life' is 'more like a monster, then a man' (I.iv.22.9), this statement is equally applicable to his fellow sins (and, by analogy, every other human monstrosity), precisely because it critically stresses that every part and aspect of the human body can become a monstrous signifier under the transformative impact of the vices. As deformity pervades the sequence,[167] the human body becomes a site of disease and aberration, with limbs affected by a 'shaking feuer' (20.8; Idlenesse), belly and eyes swollen with fatness and luxury (21; Gluttony),[168] conditions rotting the marrow and the brain like dropsy and syphilis (26.7–8; Lechery), gout in foot and hand immobilising Auarice (29), Enuy spewing up poison from his 'leprous mouth on all, that euer writt' (32.8) and Wrath's eyes sparkling fire, 'swelling splene' and 'shaking Palsey' (35.7–8). These examples characterise the human body as a critically unstable and formable entity that readily transforms into a monstrosity by taking on features representing its inner corruption.

In consequence, it is not only the human–animal composites, strange races or demonic 'carles' and hags that qualify as monstrous humans but also every body transgressing from the realm of the licit into the realm of the vicious, thereby allowing the spiritual condition to mar the human

164 See I.iv.18–35. The passage is heavily glossed (see *Variorum*, I, 217–23).

165 See Brooks-Davies, *Critical Commentary*, pp. 47–51, notes to I.iv.18–36, as well as John M. Crossett and Donald V. Stump, 'Spenser's Inferno: The Order of the Seven Deadly Sins at the Palace of Pride', *Journal of Medieval and Renaissance Studies* 14 (1984), 203–18 (p. 215).

166 Spenser creates interdependency between the mount and its rider by letting their physical features and syntactical markers overlap (see, e.g., I.iv.18.1–4, and 24.1–4).

167 See I.iv.21.2 ('Deformed creature').

168 That Gluttony has a 'long and fyne' neck like a crane (I.iv.21.5) is an iconographical detail figuring in Alciato, *Emblematum liber*, emblem 91, and *Henry Peacham's Manuscript Emblem Books*, ed. by Alan R. Young, The English Emblem Tradition, 5 (Toronto: University of Toronto Press, 1998), p. 48 (Rawl., 3.5) and p. 115 (Harl, 3.2). Alciati's rendering is far less openly monstrous than Peacham's.

frame. The Procession of the Seven Deadly Sins hence freezes a final moment in the transformation towards complete disfigurement. As the personifications mark the ultimate state of man's falling to the sinful,[169] they are not merely allegorical, but exemplars of innate and recognisable human monstrosity, also with respect to appearance and behaviour. The Seven Deadly Sins hence figure as *monstra* in both etymological senses, 'pointing to' (Latin *monstrare*), and 'warning against' (Latin *monere*) the debilitating effects of the vices.

In contrast to the beastly men in the Bower of Bliss, and similar to Adicia and Malengin, Malbecco undergoes two very different transformations: one into a goat, and one into personified Jealousy. The first is performative. Malbecco, an old, impotent man who has a 'blinde eie' (III. ix.27.6),[170] loses his young wife Hellenore first to Paridell, who steals her from his castle,[171] and then to a group of satyrs, with whom she lives a life of carnal pleasures.[172] In order to win her back, he disguises himself as a goat among the satyrs' flock and creeps to her on all fours, but is unable to make her change her mind. The epic narrator gives a full description of Malbecco's performance in III.x.47:

> Which when *Malbecco* saw, out of his bush
> Vpon his hands and feete he crept full light,
> And like a Gote emongst the Gotes did rush,
> That through the helpe of his faire hornes on hight,
> And misty dampe of misconceyuing night,
> And eke through likenesse of his gotish beard,
> He did the better counterfeite aright:
> So home he marcht emongst the horned heard,
> That none of all the *Satyres* him espyde or heard.

The grotesquery of this passage is conveyed through the success of Malbecco's impersonation, who imitates both the physical features and the characteristic movement of the satyrs' goats. This involves his extremities (hands and feet) as well as his beard and false horns.[173] In effect, Malbecco turns himself into a four-footed beast, a transformation that

169 Cf. Spenser's use of the phrase 'carcas blew' to describe Gluttony's body (I.iv.23.6).

170 Malbecco is described in III.ix.5.

171 Spenser parodies the Menelaos–Helen–Paris triangle by turning it into a fabliau. See Leslie Brill, 'Paridell', in *Spenser Encyclopedia*, ed. by Hamilton, p. 529.

172 See III.x.

173 Even if the horns, the traditional attributes of the cuckold, are merely metaphorical, as Wood argues, Spenser's description momentarily maps the horns of a goat on to Malbecco's front. See Rufus Wood, *Metaphor and Belief in 'The Faerie Queene'* (London: Macmillan; New York: St Martin's, 1997), pp. 84–7.

reflects his state as horned husband, with artificially added monstrous signifiers.[174] If one adds to that the significance of his name, which translates into 'bad goat', his transformation seems to be more feasible than it at first appears. There is, however, a significant fissure in this interpretation: at second glance, Malbecco's disguise is strangely incomplete. A passage in Ariosto's *Orlando Furioso* helps flesh out this supposition. In Canto xvii.45–7, Norandino seeks access to Lucina, who is held captive by an orc; to make his disguise as perfect as possible, he covers his body in goat skin and oils himself to take on the smell of beasts. Since Malbecco does not have to take these measures to appear as a goat, the narrator questions his humanity right from the start. Malbecco's passing off as a goat is more serious than comic,[175] because it marks him as a partly deformed, grotesque creature with animal attributes: he is a goatish being among goats herded by half-goats,[176] and hence descends Pico's ladder of creation from the human to the beastly.

Malbecco's animal disguise, however, is just the first level of a complete transmutation. His second transformation, which evokes Ovidian metamorphosis but also the figure of Suspicion in Gascoigne's *The Adventures of Master F. J.*,[177] is the direct outcome of Hellenore's rejection. This incident work as a catalyst to bring out the full scope of his monstrosity.[178] Mad with fury, pricked forward by grief, despite and jealousy, Malbecco starts running. During his flight he shows the first significant traces of

174 Louis A. Marre recognises the irony of Malbecco's 'using the horns of a cuckold as literal disguise' (*Ironic Historian: The Narrator of Books III and IV of 'The Faerie Queene'*, Salzburg Studies in English Literature: Elizabethan and Renaissance Studies, 98 (Salzburg: Institut für Anglistik und Amerikanistik, Universität Salzburg, 1980), p. 57).

175 Rainer Lengeler makes a strong case for the serious quality of Malbecco's disguise; see *Tragische Wirklichkeit als groteske Verfremdung bei Shakespeare*, Anglistische Studien, 2 (Cologne: Bohlau, 1964), p. 29.

176 The convolution of goatish details brings into the relief various degrees of lustfulness and their performance; see, e.g., Carmen Brown, 'Bestiary Lessons on Pride and Lust', in *The Mark of the Beast: The Medieval Bestiary in Art, Life, and Literature*, ed. by Debra Hassig, Garland Medieval Casebooks (New York: Garland Publishing, 1999), pp. 53–70 (pp. 63–4).

177 On Gascoigne, see W. Nelson, 'A Source for Spenser's Malbecco', *Modern Language Notes* 68 (1953), 226–9. Burrow discusses both influences on the passage, maintaining that the passage develops from an Ovidian metamorphosis into Gascoigne's description, which ultimately derives from Ariosto ('Original Fictions', pp. 114–15). Quite differently, Louise Gilbert Freeman stresses Ovid's influence on Malbecco's transformation(s), especially with regard to Spenser's penchant for detail ('Metamorphosis', pp. 308–30). For George Gascoigne's description of Suspicion in *The Adventures of Master F. J.*, see *An Anthology of Elizabethan Prose Fiction*, ed. by Paul Salzman, The World's Classics (Oxford: Oxford University Press, 1987), pp. 48–9.

178 The metamorphosis figures in III.x.54–60.

monstrous transformation.[179] He is now 'straungely ... bestadd' with 'vpstart haire, and staring eyes' (III.x.54.7–8). As his vicious instincts take over control, Malbecco's animal and monstrous traits surface: his shaggy hair marks his subhuman status,[180] while the shining eyes recall those of giants and dragons.[181] By bringing into focus these anatomical changes, Spenser disintegrates physical features from the unity of Malbecco's body.

By now it has become clear that the *senex amans* has taken a course from which he cannot return, for people react to him as if he were an escapee '[f]rom Limbo lake' (54.9), a description that marks him as a lost soul,[182] but also as an other, a stranger to humans and himself.[183] This supposition is corroborated when he finally reaches a cliff by the sea after running over hills and dales. His swiftness appears to stem from his being borne on the wings of winds (55.2). Such speed connects him with the Blatant Beast and the hyena, whereas the wind links him to Orgoglio. On another note, however, this passage also makes Malbecco appear less physical. The tendency to dematerialise finds its most powerful expression in his jumping off the cliff, for Malbecco has wasted away so completely that he does not fall to his death.[184] Rather, his physical substance is consumed by 'anguish, and selfe-murdring thought',[185] so that he 'like an aery Spright' alights on a 'craggy cliff' (57): similar to Orgoglio, he changes into a monstrous, immaterial nought and nothing. After alighting on the cliff, he seeks shelter in a cave, crawling over the cliff with 'crooked claws' (57.8). The claws, both crooked and (arguably) long,[186] are disfiguring attributes representing the human being's degradation into the monstrous and the sinful,[187] even more so than the 'vpstart haire' and 'staring eyes'. This is the case especially because Spenser here combines the physical with the immaterial, thus fragmenting Malbecco

179 Hamilton suggests that the line 'And ran away, ran with him selfe away' (54.6) already points to his 'disintegration' (note to III.x.54.6).

180 Here Malbecco's hirsute look recalls Lust's hairy body, as well as Porta's 'Lustful Man'.

181 Cf. e.g. the eyes of the Dragon and Errour, and Watson's remarks on Corflambo's eyes, which are likened to those of the basilisk (IV.viii.39; see Watson, 'Forreine and Monstrous Beasts', p. 176). On eyes as monstrous signifiers, see Williams, *Deformed Discourse*, pp. 149–55.

182 See Hamilton, note to III.x.54.9.

183 See Nohrnberg, *Analogy*, p. 770, and Freeman, 'Metamorphosis', p. 324.

184 Cf. Lengeler's remarks on reader response in *Tragische Wirklichkeit*, p. 30.

185 In IV.vi.1, Spenser explicitly moralises the physical and psychological effects of anguish, arguing that it cannot be cured by physicians.

186 This interpretation is suggested by Spenser's choice of ambivalent syntax: since 'so long' is adjacent to both 'crooked clawes' and 'did crall', it is associated with both parts of the verse.

187 Alpers identifies claws as a 'common sign of monstrosity' (*Poetry*, p. 220).

even further. His deformity, however, goes beyond physiological signifiers: the old man does not walk erect any more, but rather crawls on his limbs.[188] This action echoes his impersonation of the goat earlier in the canto, and now presses home that Malbecco has forfeited humanity, and has become wholly monstrous.[189]

Such dehumanisation finds further expression in the habitat he chooses, the cave, a place filled with darkness and dread that connotes Hades, hell and death.[190] Here Malbecco experiences his own *inferno*; for, like Tantalus, he fears that the cliffs will topple down and crush him. His human self is now completely subsumed by the monstrous: like Argus, he sleeps with his eye open,[191] while his body undergoes significant dietary changes: he lives on toads and frogs,[192] which make up his 'pasture poysonous' (59.2), and which work on his blood and internal organs (namely heart, stomach and liver) to destroy them and to affect his psyche.[193] Here, Spenser turns Malbecco into a wholly demonic being who follows his base affections. But the final stage has not been reached, yet. In the end, Malbecco, feeding on his own immaterial sorrows and fears, embodies the death-in-life paradox ('Yet can he neuer dye, but dying liues'; 60.1). Hence, he has gradually grown into an abstraction,[194] or rather: has been abstracted into a monster. This change has its effect on Malbecco's experience of self: he is now 'so deform'd that he has quight / Forgot he was a man, and *Gelosy* is hight' (60.8–9).[195] The narrator chooses the term 'deform'd' to label Malbecco's complete loss of humanity and to enhance his 'ultimate degradation'[196]

188 The verb *to creep* in stanza 58 signifies monstrous movement.

189 Freeman stresses that such dehumanisation also defamiliarises Malbecco (see 'Metamorphosis', p. 324).

190 Malbecco's cave fits the comparison to Limbo lake in stanza 54.

191 On the relation between Argus's eyes and deformity, see Williams, *Deformed Discourse*, p. 151.

192 These animals were associated with Errour in I.i.20; see Hamilton, note to III.x.59.

193 See Alpers, *Poetry*, pp. 222–6, for a reading of the physiological inconsistencies in this passage.

194 See Harold Skulsky, *Metamorphosis: The Mind in Exile* (Cambridge, MA: Harvard University Press, 1981), pp. 319–26.

195 The punch-line that gives Malbecco his new name has a distinct Ovidian ring to it. – The connection between jealousy and gnawing might stem from Isidore, who explains that the canker worm (*eruca*) receives its name from his 'gnawing away' (*erodere*) bits from the green leaves they feed upon (*Etymologiae*, XII.v.9). The notion of jealous self-consummation becomes significant when Britomart's winning Florimell during Satyrane's tournament affects Scudamour to such an extent that he 'gnaw[s] his gealous hart' (IV.vi.7.5).

196 The phrase is Skulsky's (Harold Skulsky, 'Malbecco', in *Spenser Encyclopedia*, ed. by Hamilton, pp. 448–9 (p. 449)).

through grotesque, aetiological transformation.[197] Marre nicely observes that Malbecco can now '*become* what he only *represented* before'.[198] Moreover, Malbecco's movement is directed towards the edge of Faeryland,[199] and simultaneously also away from the thematic core of this part of the poem, love. When becoming marginalised like the strange races and monsters in *mappaemundi*, the reactions he stirs in himself and others are those of disgust and horror.[200] The driving force behind Malbecco's attempted suicide and final transformation, however, is his inclination to self-hatred and self-damage. Other humanoid deformities exhibit these non-human tendencies towards the self as well: Orgoglio's mutilating himself by hurting Mother Earth, and Lust's acts of self-gratification likewise reveal a lack of normative humanity.

Spenser structures the end of Malbecco's tale around two transformations. While the first of these could be termed an impersonation, the second is a clear case of dehumanisation and disembodiment poeticised first in a mobility of images, and then rendered into a final form.[201] By playing off one against the other, the narrator also makes clear that the distinction between human and monstrous categories is not as clear and comfortable as one would wish.[202] Rather, while Grill reveals man's bent towards the beastly through his animal instincts, Malbecco images forth the monstrous lurking in God's (and also the poet's) superior creation and the constant danger of trespassing into the realm of subhuman existence, where a character can become alien to himself while turning into the embodiment of his innermost anxieties. In consequence, both Grill and Malbecco are serious examples of the irreversibility of dehumanisation, and the powerful influence of the monstrous. The diverse instances of transformation and metamorphosis in *The Faerie Queene* reveal the category-defying fullness of Spenser's natural world, where the monstrous lurks behind every newly turned page.

197 Lengeler emphasises the grotesque quality of the transformation, and underlines the circumstance that the aetiology is to be seen in allegorico-Christian terms (see *Tragische Wirklichkeit*, p. 30). Quite differently, Alpers emphasises that the metamorphosis is incomplete, so that the human being remains visible in Malbecco's deformity (*Poetry*, p. 228).

198 Marre, *Ironic Historian*, p. 59. See also Nohrnberg, *Analogy*, p. 770.

199 This is similarly observed by Freeman, 'Metamorphosis', p. 324.

200 He is '[h]atefull both to him selfe, and euery wight' (III.x.60.6). Cf. also III.x.54.7–9 and 55.7.

201 See also Freeman on the tension between semantic flux and fixity ('Metamorphosis', p. 321 and p. 326).

202 Marre, when contrasting the two episodes as satire and horror, disregards the complex interplay between the two transformations (see *Ironic Historian*, p. 58).

Ephemeral monstrosity

Metamorphosis, as permanent transformation, unveils man's bent towards the monstrous. In addition to these lasting changes, Spenser incorporates various types of impermanent or momentary transformations on the narrative and on the figurative levels of the poem, which underline the threat of the monstrous and show the instability of the poem's natural world. These ephemeral monstrosities are not monsters in the strict sense of the word, but humans whose bodies or behaviour temporarily transgress beyond accepted norms. Including these instances in the present taxonomy may, at first glance, seem moot. However, Spenser is explicit about the danger the monstrous forces pose for every human being when explaining that the human body 'growes a Monster' under the influence of 'misrule and passions' (II.ix.1.6–7). I would argue that the notion of monstrosity in these lines extends to fleeting moments of monstrosity as well.[203] While some characters temporarily cross the border to monstrosity and bestiality when they give in to their baser nature, others change their physique under the impact of a simile. Spenser's descriptive method is hence informed by the sixteenth-century trend to conceive of the monstrous not only as a visible trait but also as imagery bringing to the surface an *inward* monstrosity that lacks a visible referent.[204] Such comparisons can liken an entire character to a monstrous or fantastic being, or compare an individual body part to that of an animal or monster, a distinction that recalls Isidore's division into fully transformed and partly transformed beings.[205] Even in those cases where monstrous bodies are not immediately involved, similes create an incongruous physique by mapping an unmatching image on the human body of Spenser's characters. Spenser accordingly transforms the character's human physique into that of the source image, thereby creating a momentary composite monster with the human frame still visible, that is the simile or metaphor functions as a monstrous signifier. Apart from

203 I am not suggesting that every character in *The Faerie Queene* is a monster; rather, every character is threatened by monstrous forces. The notion of the human being as a potential deformity had some currency in the early modern period. John Watkins cites John Calvin, who conceived of the human being after the Fall as a deformity corrupted by sin. See 'Spenser's Monsters: A Response to Maik Goth', *Connotations* 20 (2010/11), 201–9 (p. 204), with reference to John Calvin, *Calvin's Bible Commentaries: Genesis, Part I*, trans. by John King (London, 1847), p. 49, and *Institutes of the Christian Religion*, trans. by Henry Beverige (Peabody: Hendrickson, 2008), p. 107.

204 Brammall explains that the transition took place between 1550 and 1570 (see 'Monstrous Metamorphosis', pp. 3–21).

205 See Isidore, *Etymologiae*, XI.iii.9.

these immediately recognisable rhetorical ramifications, humans can also be turned into temporary monsters through animating an individual aspect of their character or anatomy through the use of deforming metaphors.

Some characters forfeit their humanity only temporarily under unwholesome influences that transform their human bodies into something 'other'. Redcrosse suffers such a change after Orgoglio has cast him into his dungeons, a place that Spenser describes as an infernal locus.[206] By the time the knight is freed by Arthur, his physique has become radically disfigured, making the Champion of Holinesse 'a ruefull spectacle of death and ghastly drere' (I.viii.40.9). The poet's anatomical description, which recalls the rhetorical blazon, marks Redcrosse as the living death: thin and emasculated, with 'sad dull' eyes sunk deep into their sockets, 'bare thin' cheeks, and empty sides,[207] the knight sets an example for the frailty of the human body and its susceptibility to monstrous transformation. As a being in the process of decay, Redcrosse is, at this point of his *aventure*, brought to the brink of physical disintegration and spiritual annihilation.[208] Spenser animates the champion's precarious state by combining the hag's body as the site of physical decomposition and disintegration with the carle's monstrous features,[209] thus turning Redcrosse, who earlier in the poem betrayed signs of melancholy and choler, into a temporary abjection. While Redcrosse's physical features become monstrous signifiers figuring forth the other at work within the human body, they more specifically violate the norm of chivalric masculinity and the hero's representation of holiness in the narrative context of Book I.

Similarly, Timias's transformation into a melancholy recluse after Belphoebe catches him caressing Amoret sets an example for man's inherent otherness, which in this case is caused by the transformative effect of love sickness.[210] Under the influence of love's 'sad melancholy' (IV.vii.38.9), Timias casts away his weapons, abjures speech, tears apart his clothing and lets his hair grow '[v]ncomb'd, vncurl'd, and carelesly vnshed' (40.6) until it covers his face and shoulders. He thus revokes his entire courtly identity, and, with it, his chivalric body, which wastes away

206 See I.viii.35–42.

207 See I.viii.41.

208 Spenser describes that Redcrosse's arms '[w]ere clene consum'd, and all his vital powres / Decayd, and al his flesh shronk vp like withered flowres' (I.viii.41.8–9).

209 Brooks-Davies similarly likens Redcrosse's 'physical debility' to Maleger's, especially because of the latter's bent to Saturnian melancholy and sin (see *Critical Commentary*, pp. 84–5, note to I.viii.38–41).

210 See IV.vii.38–47, and viii.2–18.

and becomes haggard.[211] Consequently, neither his champion Arthur nor his beloved Belphoebe can recognise him.[212] More significantly, both experience a powerful sense of alienation when meeting him in his self-imposed exile. Arthur sees Timias as a 'strange wight' (43.7), i.e. both as someone he fails to recognise and as a human who appears to be a freak of nature.[213] Belphoebe's reaction is more emphatic:

> … when she saw [Timias] in wretched weedes disguiz'd,
> With heary glib deform'd, and meiger face,
> Like ghost late risen from his graue agryz'd,
> She knew him not[.]
>
> (IV.viii.12.5–8)

As the density of evocative phrases in this passage shows, Belphoebe experiences her meeting with Timias much more intensely than Arthur, namely as the confrontation with a being that differs markedly from the human and for that reason induces alienation and horror in the spectator.[214] Terms like 'deform'd' and 'agryz'd',[215] as well as the hairy 'glib',[216] and the comparison to a ghost just risen from the grave mark Timias as a distorted being whose humanity has been obliterated by the physical symptoms of his melancholy condition. Belphoebe's reaction has to be taken seriously, for it points to Timias's unruly, uncouth features as attributes that make him more monster than man, a creature positioned between the savage and the ghostly.[217] Timias's chivalric aspirations hence do not make him immune to a debilitating transformation; at this point in his *vita*, he has regressed into a monstrous human.

Redcrosse's and Timias's temporary transformations into monstrous versions of their chivalric selves accentuate the human being's fallible and

211 'who he whilome was, vneath was to be red' (IV.vii.40.9).

212 See IV.vii.43–4, and viii.12.

213 The term *wight* can be applied to supernatural, preternatural and unearthly beings, and can additionally imply contempt or commiseration (see *OED*, s.v. 'wight, *n.*', 1b, and 2).

214 Cf. also IV.vii.41.4 ('That like a pined ghost he [i.e. Timias] soone appears'), and I.viii.40.9 (Redcrosse has become 'a ruefull spectacle of death and ghastly drere').

215 The *OED* explains that the verb *agrize* derives from French *grís*, 'horror'. In the present context 'agryz'd' can mean both 'horrified' and 'of horrible appearance' (Hamilton, note to IV.viii.12.6).

216 The term *glib* might carry ethnic connotations. The *OED* defines it as a 'thick mass of matted hair on the forehead and over the eyes, formerly used by the Irish' ('glib, *n.*'). Hamilton refers to Spenser's *A View of the Present State of Ireland* (note to V.ix.10.6–9), which explains that Irish rebels wore 'mantles and long glibs, which is a thick curled bush of hair hanging down over their eyes, and monstrously disguising them'; for the text, see Edmund Spenser, *A View of the Present State of Ireland*, ed. by W. L. Renwick (Oxford: Clarendon, 1970), p. 50.

217 Timias's condition resembles Malbecco's (compare IV.viii.12.7 with III.x.54.9).

fallen nature. While their respective careers show that such transformations need not be irrevocable, they are reversible only through external forces: in Redcrosse's case, his liberation at the hands of Prince Arthur in I.viii; in Timias's case, the intervention of the turtle dove that leads Belphoebe back to him in IV.viii. These two case studies show that, in *The Faerie Queene*, human bodies, under the impact of the passions, are subject to extreme transformations and deformations. Timias's and Redcrosse's important crises hence exemplify the body's potential to take on monstrous signifiers and to become something 'other', and stress the possible monstrosity even of the human and Elfin heroes.[218]

Less conspicuous examples of monstrous humanity appear in similes that liken human characters to animals or monsters. A rich example for a momentary rhetorical transformation into monsters figures during Redcrosse's battle with Sansjoy (I.v.6–13), which Spenser stages as the fierce combat between a griffin and a dragon:

> So th'one for wrong, the other striues for right:
> As when a Gryfon seized of his pray,
> A Dragon fiers encountreth in his flight,
> Through widest ayre making his ydle way,
> That would his rightfull rauine rend away:
> With hideous horrour both together smight,
> And souce so sore, that they the heauens affray:
> The wise Southsayer seeing so sad sight,
> Th'amazed vulgar telles of warres and mortall fight.
>
> (I.v.8)

The epic simile transforms Redcrosse and Sansjoy into notorious fabulous beasts of the air, whose extensive literary and cultural backgrounds furnish both combatants with a number of differentiating aspects – or so it seems. A first reading would thus note the satanic implications of the dragon, its irate temper and the important link to the main dragons of Book I, a host of references that characterise Sansjoy as a proverbially monstrous Saracen, who however lacks monstrous physical features. This largely negative picture is pitted against the more positive associations of the griffin, a compound monster half lion and half eagle. Partly owing to the regal associations of these animals, the griffin encodes a valorous and heroic nature.[219]

218 Cf. also Britomart's love sickness, which likewise emphasises the transformative power and monstrous aspects of love (III.ii.32–52).

219 On the griffin's valour and nobility, see Thomas Browne, *Pseudodoxia*, p. 131; a griffin appears in Dante's *Purgatorio*, XXIX.106–8 as an emblem of Christ (see Teskey, *Allegory*

However, distinctions are not as comfortable as they appear. Indeed, Spenser takes rhetorical precautions to mar the differences between the knight and the pagan by introducing their respective monsters in a disorienting chiasm,[220] which helps confuse beasts, pronouns and the monstrous aspects of both characters.[221] The griffin, in Thomas Browne's words a 'mixt and dubious animal',[222] also embodies unnatural fierceness, lust and covetousness, and is frequently depicted as a voracious man-eater.[223] The moment these monsters clash thus enhances the excess monstrosity of both animals, whose ferocity creates universal repercussions and casts doubt on the griffin's nobility. As the monsters clash, so do the human antagonists. At this point of Book I, Redcrosse collides with and partakes of Sansjoy's defining 'joylessness', which prefigures the knight's demise at the hands of Orgoglio, and his later encounter and temporal yielding to Despayre. The fight therefore deploys emblematic imagery in a more ambivalent sense than is usually acknowledged. Thus, the griffin simile does not trigger a single preconceived meaning; like most other animals, it can be interpreted both *in bonam partem* and *in malam partem*. Such openness, which is consonant with the *sensus spiritualis*,[224] makes the interpretation of an image dependent on a particular aspect of the animal's behaviour, and on the context in which it is embedded.[225] As Spenser, however, seeks to disorient the reader in this epic simile, he sets this principle entirely off course.

The ambiguity of the simile is accentuated in the concluding comparison which turns the monster fight into the meteorological phenomenon of the firedrake.[226] Spenser here reduces the battle of the monsters, and accordingly the epic *monomachia* of his characters, to a marvellous

and Violence, p. 52). For Dante's text, see *The Divine Comedy of Dante Alighieri. Volume 2: Purgatorio*, ed. and trans. by Robert M. Durling; introduction and notes by Ronald M. Martinez and Robert M. Durling (New York and Oxford: Oxford University Press, 2003). See also the *Ashmole Bestiary*, pp. 34–5.

220 He correlates 'wrong' with the 'Dragon', and 'right' with the 'Gryfon' (I.v.8.1–3).

221 See also Peter C. Herman, *Squitter-wits and Muse-haters: Sidney, Spenser, Milton and Renaissance Antipoetic Sentiment* (Detroit: Wayne State University Press, 1996), pp. 147–9.

222 Thomas Browne, *Pseudodoxia*, p. 129.

223 The *Ashmole Bestiary* records that the griffin tears apart humans (pp. 34–5).

224 For an elucidating discussion of the *sensus spiritualis* which takes into account the manifold meanings of the lion, see Friedrich Ohly, 'Vom geistigen Sinn des Wortes im Mittelalter', *Zeitschrift für deutsches Mittelalter und deutsche Literatur* 89 (1958/59), 1–23 (pp. 6–7). See also Kaske's *Spenser and Biblical Poetics* for a book-length study on Spenser's using images *in bono* and *in malo*.

225 See Ohly, 'Vom geistigen Sinn', p. 7.

226 See S. K. Heninger, Jr, *A Handbook of Renaissance Meteorology* (Durham, NC: Duke University Press, 1960), p. 95.

portent, a *monstrum* in the classical sense that has to be interpreted by the human witness.[227] The soothsayer Spenser introduces at the end of the simile thus points to the direction in which this sight needs to be read, namely as a 'sad' (8.8) omen of troubled times. As a portent it emphasises the critical moment of Redcrosse's career in Book I, and anticipates his fall – which eventually turns out to be a fortunate one, but only through the joint help of Arthur, Una and the House of Holiness.

The simile therefore does not simply set off the villainous Saracen from the virtuous Christian, and magnify Redcrosse's heroic qualities. It is a much more problematic image that creates a figurative space where two characters can play out their monstrosity and vent their unnatural, savage impulses of wrath and anger. In such a problematic context, the image becomes multifarious, and an interpretation *in bonam* or *in malam partem* impossible. If one extrapolates from this finding, the poem's metaphorical level establishes a monstrous world which does not only stand in close proximity with the human but which is constantly detected as its inherent quality. This assessment is equally applicable to other monstrous or beastly similes in the poem.[228] The momentary shifting of shapes they generate appears, for once, in covert form in the frequent animal similes, which could thus be interpreted as punctual transformations of humans into beasts and monsters.[229]

Every simile or descriptive phrase that defamiliarises a physical attribute maps something alien on to the human frame through rhetorical means, and thus turns an aspect of the human into a monstrous signifier. While Spenser's genuine monsters exhibit the poet's penchant for inventing new monstrosities, similes and metaphors resort to well-known images stored in the collective memory of his readership. If one acknowledges the power that Spenser's similes exert on the human characters to accentuate their monstrous traits, the effect of smaller textual and rhetorical units that morph human body parts into monstrous members becomes all the more lucid. When, for instance, Sansjoy's eye is 'flaming with wrathfull fyre' (I.v.10.2), Spenser exploits the topos of the monstrous, 'evil' eye, which is also used for the dragons and giants, to stress Sansjoy's monstrosity.[230]

227 For the development of the term *monstrum* and its close connection with *portentum*, see Chapter 3, above.

228 Spenser, for example, imagines the river battle between Arthegall and Pollente as the wild fight between a dolphin and a seal (V.ii.15).

229 This is consonant with Watson's verdict that these similes 'give exact definition to a particular moment in the career of a character' (see 'Spenser's Chivalric Bestiary', p. 163).

230 On the concept of the monstrous eye, see Williams, *Deformed Discourse*, pp. 149–55.

Similar phrases can accentuate the monstrous qualities of any given character and body part. For example, Redcrosse's 'flaming corage' (I.v.1.6) illustrates the knight's *virtus* through etymologically animating his *cor*, Latin for heart, as a burning organ. Additional instances feature in the topos of the furies setting the heart ablaze, which the reader maps on to the human body in the process of reading.[231]

Some characters even exhibit transitory conditions reminiscent of Spenser's monsters. One such phenomenon is the swelling of the body, which has been observed in Spenser's dragons and giants. Amoret's paramour Scudamour, for instance, exhibits these monstrous symptoms when meeting Britomart, whom he suspects of infidelity with Amoret: 'Tho gan he swell in euery inner part, / For fell despight, and gnaw his gealous hart' (IV.vi.7.4–5).[232] While his condition is reminiscent of Malbecco's excessive jealousy, the emphatic use of terms describing physical aberration marks Scudamour's attributes as momentary monstrous signifiers. Yet such transformations can also be implicit and unintended. During her escape from the witch's hyena in the fisherman's boat, Florimell is assaulted by a lascivious fisherman, who 'ne car'd to spill / Her garments gay with scales of fish, that all did fill' (III.viii.26.8–9). For a brief moment, the fish covering Florimell's dress suggest the scaly fishtail of a mermaid: surprisingly, the fisherman's defiling the damsel in the attempted rape turns her into a fabulous creature. Yet her near-transformation reveals that she is not a monster,[233] but a human who becomes alien and unfamiliar through the sexual violence exerted by a vicious character who stains her in a sudden lecherous frenzy. Here it is the obsession of the fisherman that turns Florimell into the object of desire, and thus into the traditionally alluring mermaid of the folktale.[234]

Eventually, Spenser's deformed discourse encroaches upon the micro-level of the text, where he resorts to an arsenal of terms working as

231 See, e.g., IV.i.54.3 and 7 (Scudamour wants to revenge himself on Britomart), and VI.iii.43.5 (Calepine is angered by Turpine). The idea of disfiguring fury is all the more relevant for *The Faerie Queene* because Spenser describes Furor as a monstrous human with iron teeth, burning eyes and hair like copper wires in II.iv.15. Furor is hence intratextually figured in moments of fury, especially in close proximity to the Furor episode (see II.ii.20.4, II.iv.30.2, II.iv.33.4 and II.v.8.3). As the personification of wrath, Furor cannot be wounded or vanquished (II.iv.10). On the etymological link between fury and the furies, see Susanne Lindgren Wofford, *The Choice of Achilles: The Ideology of Figure in Epic* (Stanford: Stanford University Press, 1992), p. 305.

232 Scudamour's jealousy is prompted by Ate's and Duessa's false accusations (IV.i.46–9).

233 Hamilton interprets this incident as 'the beginning of a metamorphosis' (*Structure*, p. 151).

234 On the bond between desire and the imagination, see Chapter 16, below.

monstrous signifiers that momentarily disfigure humans. In accord with Cooper's sense of the monstrous as the physically deformed, attributes like *transformed,*[235] *deformed,*[236] *defeatured*[237] and, maybe less conspicuously, *dismaid* [238] are small lexical units that hint at the malleability of the human frame and its propensity to the monstrous. In *The Faerie Queene*, the monstrous hence penetrates the various parts of the poem, ultimately operating on the micro-level of the text to be an ever-present threat for the human characters. In the larger frame of the text these details interplay with the fully developed textual monsters to create a web of references between the various levels of the poem. This method is especially effective because it is based on recurrent patterns of physical or rhetorical distortions that generate multiple links to other monsters with similar physical or rhetorical disfigurements.[239]

The monstrous humans constitute by far the most complex and pervasive teratological category in Spenser's poem. Permutations of monstrosity include characters belonging to strange races, like Satyrane and Radigund, and the devious and disgusting 'carles' and hags, who may even cross the boundary between life and death (Maleger). Apart from these examples, Spenser frequently uses transformation and metamorphosis to stress that the human frame is constantly threatened by monstrous forces. These processes devalue the human to various subhuman planes of biological existence, from the arboreal (Fradubio and Fraelissa) to the beasts of the land and the sea (the sea monsters in II.xii), and even to the demonic (Malbecco). Quite critically, monstrosity in the human realm may also be an ephemeral phenomenon that can become virulent even in the most heroic characters (Redcrosse, Timias). *The Faerie Queene* hence does not merely stage the dissolution of the species boundary; it, more significantly, emphasises the perpetual threat of losing the human to a

235 Among others, Amavia interprets Mordant's change under the spell of Acrasia as a transformation (he was 'so transformed of his former skill'; II.i.54.4; cf. II.v.27.6 and II.xii.85.2). See also II.xii.31.5 (the mermaids) and III.viii.41.1 (Proteus). In the Garden of Adonis passage, Spenser uses the term *in bono* (III.vi.47.7).

236 See e.g. V.iii.38.4, where Guizor's face is 'deform'd with infamie', and III.v.29.2, where Timias is '[w]ith blood deformed', as well as I.viii.16.2 (Orgoglio's dragon), II.vii.35.7 (the fiends in Mammon's Cave) and IV.i.28.2 (Ate's ears).

237 'Certes some hellish furie, or some feend / This mischiefe framd, for their first loues defeature' (IV.vi.17.6–7).

238 See I.vii.51.3, where Una tells Arthur about Redcrosse's 'dissolute, dismaid' condition after his defeat at the hands of Orgoglio (cf. I.vii.11.6). See also IV.v.45.9 (Scudamoure in the House of Care), I.ix.22.3 (Trevisan) and I.ix.30.5 (Trevisan on Despayre). In V.xi.26.4, Arthur is much 'dismayd with that dismayfull sight' of Geryoneo's dragon.

239 Wofford similarly notes allegory's power to represent human characters through deforming them (see *Choice of Achilles*, p. 305).

monstrosity that can at all times overcome man's rational control and thereby deform the normative human body. By making the human visible in the monster and by making the monster visible in the human, Spenser teaches his readers a powerful lesson on the mutability and frailty of humanity. The monstrous humans in *The Faerie Queene* hence serve as monsters in both etymological senses, demonstrating the weakness of humans, and warning of the result of letting loose the monster within.

11

Automata

In *The Faerie Queene*, monsters invade every form of animated nature. But Spenser's vision of the monstrous even includes inanimate matter, and brings to life metallic and mechanical beings that move, or seem to move, on their own.[1] Spenser's interest in such automata, a term for self-moving machines in the sixteenth century since Cornelius Agrippa used it in *De occulta philosophia* (1533),[2] partly reflects the contemporaneous fascination with technology. Machines were on the rise by the late sixteenth and early seventeenth centuries, which marked the beginning of the mechanical age. But for Spenser and his contemporaries, the appeal of the automaton lay predominantly in its paradoxical, and hence potentially monstrous, nature: as a category breaking the binary opposition between 'living/dead, animate/inanimate, creature/object',[3] the automaton was perceived as a violation of the norm, a creature of questionable origin, which existed only through the sacrilegious alliance between the mechanical and the magical.[4]

The Renaissance inherited a rich tradition of automata and machines from antiquity to the *medium aevum*: in the classical age, robots appear as early as the *Iliad*, where Hephaistos is assisted by maidens he

1 This is the basic definition of the monstrous automaton given by Hanafi: 'what makes an automaton monstrous is … the fact that matter formed by artificial means and moving of its own volition would seem to be endowed with a spirit' (*The Monster in the Machine*, p. 54). See also Minsoo Kang's recent cultural history of the automaton, *Sublime Dreams of Living Machines: The Automaton in the European Imagination* (Cambridge, MA: Harvard University Press, 2011).

2 Kang, *Sublime Dreams*, p. 7. Agrippa's work also contains an influential catalogue of automata, which includes, among other things, Daedalus's self-moving creations and Hermes Trismagistus's speaking statues (see Kang, *Sublime Dreams*, pp. 84–91).

3 Kang, *Sublime Dreams*, p. 36. On automata in the Middle Ages and the Renaissance, see Chapter 2 of her monograph.

4 The link between technology and demonology is treated exhaustively in Hanafi's *The Monster in the Machine* and Kang's *Sublime Dreams*.

manufactured out of gold to assist him.[5] In the early and high Middle Ages, automata appear as remnants from a legendary past in the romances: in Benoît de Sainte-Maure's *Roman de Troie*, for example, four man-sized robots are placed in Hector's chamber.[6] Automata are also associated with the miracles from the edge of the world, as for instance in *Mandeville's Travels*, where Mandeville describes the Great Khan's golden tables, which feature animated birds.[7] But not only legendary rulers owned automata: in the fifteenth century, Philip the Good of Burgundy allegedly presented automata in the shape of humans, and monsters in court entertainments.[8] By the late Renaissance, the dividing line between human being and machine was questioned: in the wake of medical investigations, even the human body was conceived as an automaton.[9] In a perceptive article, Jonathan Sawday investigates the nature of the Renaissance cyborg, concluding his study with a reading of Spenser's Talus and his literary ancestor, Talos, the mythical bronze man guarding Crete.[10] In another entry to Spenser criticism, 'Spenser's Robots', Lara Bovilsky deals with Snowy Florimell, an automaton created by a witch as a stand-in for the real Florimell, with whom her son is infatuated.[11] Interestingly,

5 See Homer, *Iliad*, XVIII.416–18. On classical automata, see J. Douglas Bruce, 'Human Automata in Classical Tradition and Mediaeval Romance', *Modern Philology* 4 (1913), 511–26 (pp. 512–15), and Kang, *Sublime Dreams*, pp. 14–22. Kang distinguishes four types of classical automata: of mythic and supernatural creation (Hephaistos's maids); of mythic and of human creation (Daedalus); of actual human creation (Hero of Alexandria); and speculative automata (Aristotle's fantasy of automata in the *Politics*).

6 For text and translation, see Penny Sullivan, 'Medieval Automata: The "Chambre de Beautés" in Benoît's *Roman de Troie*', *Romance Studies* 6 (1985), 1–20 (p. 13).

7 See *Mandeville's Travels*, Chapter 23 (p. 143).

8 See Park and Daston, *Wonders and the Order of Nature*, pp. 95 and 100.

9 When Hobbes wrote his *Leviathan* (1651), man's similarity to the automaton had become a commonplace: 'Nature (the Art whereby God hath made and governes the world) is by the *Art* of man, as in many other things, so in this also imitated, that it can make an Artificial Animal. For seeing life is but a motion of Limbs, the beginning whereof is in some principall part within; why may we not say, that all *Automata* (Engines that move themselves by springs and wheeles as doth a watch) have an artificiall life? For what is the *Heart*, but a *Spring*; and the *Nerves*, but so many *Strings*; and the *Joynts*, but so many *Wheeles*, giving motion to the whole Body, such as was intended by the Artificer? *Art* goes yet further, imitating that Rationall and most excellent worke of Nature, *Man*.' The text is taken from Thomas Hobbes, *Leviathan*, ed. C. B. Macpherson, Penguin Classics (Harmondsworth: Penguin, 1985), p. 81.

10 See Jonathan Sawday, '"Forms Such as Never Were in Nature": The Renaissance Cyborg', in *At the Borders of the Human: Beasts, Bodies and Natural Philosophy in the Early Modern Period*, ed. by Ruth Gilbert, Erica Fudge and Susan Wiseman (Basingstoke: Palgrave, 1999), pp. 171–95.

11 Sarah Bovilsky's paper 'Spenser's Robots', which was given at the 2006 MLA conference, pays particular attention to the 'human artificiality and the mechanics of erotic desire' (for the abstract, see *Spenser Review* 37.1 (2006), 29).

neither reader is aware of the full significance these creatures have for Spenser's conceptualisation of the monstrous. If one, however, adds the giant Disdayne, whose body is made of solid metal, to Talus and Snowy Florimell, Spenser's *The Faerie Queene* features a triad of singularly important mechanical creatures informing key episodes of the poem.[12]

Talus

The android Talus plays a major role in the Legend of Justice. It is at the very beginning of this book that Spenser relates how the goddess Astræa, when leaving Faeryland, grants Arthegall, the book's eponymous hero, an 'yron man' (V.i.12.2) to attend him and carry out his will:

> His name was Talus, made of yron mould,
> Immoueable, resistlesse, without end.
> Who in his hand an yron flale did hould,
> With which he thresht out falshood, and did truth vnfould.
> (V.i.12.6–9)

As Astræa's earthly representative, Talus is the chief executor of justice.[13] He is a mechanical creature with a vast literary background, ranging from jurisdiction (his name evokes the *lex talionis*)[14] to scripture and myth,[15] and to the copper men of the romances.[16] His name invites comparison

12 Kang distinguishes four types of medieval and Renaissance automata: those of fictional and of otherworldly origin; those of fictional and of human manufacture but involving some form of magic; those of actual human instruction or design; and speculative ones (see Kang, *Sublime Dreams*, p. 61). Spenser's cyborgs fall into the first two categories: Disdayne and Talus belong to category 1, Snowy Florimell fits in category 2.

13 Gough distinguishes between Talus's representing the power to execute decrees and the executive force serving a ruler (in *Variorum*, v, 167). For a good synopsis of Talus's deeds and their meaning, see Padelford in *Variorum*, v, 276–80, and, for a comprehensive interpretation of Talus's role in Book V, see Fletcher, *Prophetic Moment*, pp. 137–46.

14 As Hamilton notes, the name suggests Latin *talio*, retributive justice (note to V.i.12.1–6, with reference to Cooper, *Thesaurus*, s.v. 'talio'). The ample sources Nohrnberg cites for Talus (see *Analogy*, pp. 412–14) suggest that the giant is most probably the result of Spenser's contaminating two myths: one is that of Astræa absconding from the earth at the beginning of the chaotic Bronze Age, yet leaving behind a *testamentum* of laws (see Conti, *Mythologiae*, II.2 (pp. 37.a–b)); the other is that of Talos, the warden of Crete and guardian of the law, who carries with him the tablets on which the principle laws were inscribed (see pseudo-Plato's *Minos*, 320C, in Plato, *Charmides. Alcibiades I and II. Hipparchus. The Lovers. Theages. Minos. Epinomis*, ed. and trans. by W. R. M. Lamb, Plato: Works 12, Loeb Classical Library (Cambridge, MA: Harvard University Press; London: Heinemann, 1927; repr. 1999)).

15 Fletcher refers to Nebuchadnezzar's dream in Daniel, 2.32–3 (see *Prophetic Moment*, p. 141). Also compare Nohrnberg's notion of a 'triple' Talus: 'legalistic', 'martial' and 'technological' (*Analogy*, p. 410).

16 Nohrnberg follows C. G. Leland (*The Unpublished Legends of Virgil* (New York, 1900),

with his mythological near-namesake Talos, but Talus is more than Talos's clone transferred to Spenser's Iron Age,[17] for he is devoid of the very characteristics that define Talos as a living being. Talos, who according to Apollodor was either the descendent of the bronze race or manufactured by Hephaistos, was the mythic guardian of the isle of Crete.[18] A single vein, filled with divine blood (Old Greek ἰχώρ), ran from his neck to his ankles and was closed by a nail. During the encounter with the Argonauts, he bled to death either by accidentally cutting open his vein on a stone, or because Medea unblocked the vein.[19] Talos therefore emerges as an individual with a will of his own and a body whose functions depend on the soundness of divine organic material. Talus, on the other hand, is defined through what he is not: as he is '[i]mmoueable, resistlesse, without end' (12.7),[20] he is an absolute, invincible, spatially and temporally infinite agent undeterred by human emotions and affections. Spenser's asyndetic tricolon, which showcases a chain of various semantic negations – from prefix (*im-*) to suffix (*-less*), and to preposition (*without*) – stresses Talus's lifelessness and lack of organic material, and displays an exaggerated stability that diametrically opposes the constant threat of change displayed in other monstrous specimens.

As Spenser's rhetoric of the monstrous makes clear, Talus's monstrosity lies in his strength and indestructible powers, as well as in his awe-inspiring iron body and flail, which represent the violence with which he carries

p. 152) and John Steadman ('Spenser and the *Virgilius* Legend: Another Talus Parallel', *Modern Language Notes* 73 (1958), 412–13) in tracing the prose romance *Virgilius* as Spenser's major source. The text presents a copper or brass man holding an iron flail and riding a brass horse. The romance is included in *Early Prose Romances*, ed. by Henry Morley (London: George Routledge, 1889); see pp. 223–4 and p. 233. Copper knights also appear in the Dolorous Guard episode of the prose *Lancelot* in the *Old French Arthurian Vulgate* (see *Lancelot, Part I*, 40 in *Lancelot-Grail*, II, 102–3), and in the *Perlesvaus* during Percival's adventure at the Copper Castle (the texts are also reprinted and discussed in Bruce, 'Human Automata', pp. 520–1).

17 See specifically the proem to Book V for Spenser's critique of the contemporary world.

18 See Apollonius of Rhodes, *Argonautica*, IV.V.1638–88, and Apollodorus, *Library*, I.ix.29. For the texts, see Apollonius of Rhodes, *Argonautica*, ed. and trans. by William H. Race, Loeb Classical Library 1 (Cambridge, MA: Harvard University Press, 2008); and Apollodorus of Athens, *The Library*, ed. and trans. by J. G. Frazer, 2 vols, Loeb Classical Library (Cambridge, MA: Harvard University Press; London: Heinemann, 1921; repr. 1963).

19 'εἶχε δὲ φλέβα μίαν ἀπὸ αὐχένος κατατείνουσαν ἄχρι σφυρῶν· κατὰ δὲ τὸ τέρμα τῆς φλεβὸς ἧλος διήρειστο χαλκοῦς' ('He had a single vein extending from his neck to his ankles, and a bronze nail was rammed home at the end of the vein'; Apollodorus, *Library*, I.ix.29).

20 The tricolon supports the assumption that his name can also derive from the Greek adjectives ταλαός, and ταλᾶς, 'enduring steadfastly' (see the respective entries in Liddell and Scott, *Greek Lexicon*, p. 1754). Nohrnberg interprets this tricolon as a reference to the steadfastness of the law (*Analogy*, p. 413).

out his missions.[21] He is a depersonalised creature sporting a machine-like body moulded into human shape, and moved by an exterior agent.[22] His behaviour betrays his irate nature through a revealing homoeophonic pun on ire/iron.[23] Accordingly, his exploits in Book V, which he performs in lieu of Arthegall, the champion of justice,[24] develop an unprecedented series of brutal victories over minor violators and major enemies of justice, ranging from the dismemberment of Munera to the slaughter of the Amazons.[25] His marvellous corporeality adds to the horror of these scenes.[26] As a piece of insentient machinery, he is defined as an artificial being who performs the function of a powerful mechanism in the larger workings of justice.[27] On a meta-poetical level, he also works as an engine invented by the poet to serve the allegory of Book V.[28] He is a proto-robot who exterminates his and Arthegall's enemies,[29] while his identity is erased through the larger purpose of the text in which he is animated.

Talus's body hence suggests machine-like rigidity similar to, say, Coriolanus's gait, which Menenius likens to the moving of an engine of war in Shakespeare's eponymous Roman tragedy ('When he walks, he

21 Spenser's joining the threshing of the flail to the unfolding of truth stresses the incongruous nature of Talus's deeds through the combination of unmatching verbal concepts (see V.i.12.8–9).

22 Cf. also Sawday, 'Cyborg', p. 190. However, Talus casts the Giant with the Scales from his cliff without Arthegall's order (V.ii.49–54). Nohrnberg calls Talus '*animated* hardware' (*Analogy*, p. 416; the italics are Nohrnberg's).

23 This is similarly argued by Nathaniel Wallace, who draws attention to the rhyme on 'ire' in V.vii.37; see 'Talus: Spenser's Iron Man', *Spenser Studies* 10 (1989), 277–9.

24 See Stephen Greenblatt's observation that 'heroic actions' are 'now imputed to a mechanical monster' ('Murdering Peasants: Status, Genre, and the Representation of Rebellion', *Representations* 1 (1983), 1–29 (p. 23)).

25 For the Munera episode, see V.ii, and for the the slaughtering of the Amazons V.vii. Fletcher discusses the necessity of Talus's violence in *Prophetic Moment*, p. 206.

26 Talus's terrifying corporeality tallies well with Kang's notion that '*The more powerful (often but not always because it is bigger) a machine, the less amusing it is and the more sublime*' (Kang, *Sublime Dreams*, p. 43; the italics are Kang's).

27 Michael O'Connell argues that Talus becomes the manifestation of 'Superman-like wish-fulfilment' ('*The Faerie Queene* Book V', in *Spenser Encyclopedia*, ed. by Hamilton, pp. 280–3 (p. 280)). Kang notes Talus's progressively unrestrained violence (see *Sublime Dreams*, p. 65).

28 Also note Nohrnberg's perceptive claim that Talus 'represents the kind of automatic process that, once set in motion, cannot reverse or stop itself' (*Analogy*, p. 418). As automaton and destructive force of a potentially monstrous masculine law, Talus is also a highly problematic executive that has to be kept in check (see Nohrnberg, *Analogy*, pp. 417–18).

29 On the idea of the proto-robotic in the early modern period, see Roy Strong, *The Renaissance Garden in England* (London: Thames and Hudson, 1979), pp. 75–8. Nohrnberg interprets Talus as 'the resulting objectification of laborer into the class of a *thing*' (*Analogy*, p. 409).

moves like an engine'; *Coriolanus* V.iv.18–19).[30] Yet, despite the usual connotations of iron, Talus has the ability to move 'so light, / As that it seem'd aboue the ground he went: / For he was swift as swallow in her flight' (V.i.20.2–4). Such speed, which recalls Talos's traversing Crete thrice during one day, marks Talus as a gravity-defying monstrosity, a paradox that Spenser stresses through comparing the automaton's swiftness to that of a swallow, whose corporeality is diametrically opposed to Talus's. Spenser therefore animates the iron man's monstrosity by constructing him on a simple physical matrix, and by disrupting such simple and immutable continuity through the application of incoherent details.

Disdayne

Physical determinacy need not always be the case with Spenser's robots, as shown by his presentation of the giant Disdayne, whom Sir Guyon meets during his journey through the underworld. Disdayne is an exceptional creature not only because he is made from different metals in Spenser's two editions of the poem but also because he appears as a robot with a conscience.[31] Spenser first introduces the giant, who is reminiscent of the copper men in the romances, as the guard of the gate leading to the court of Philotime in the House of Mammon:

> He [i.e. Mammon] brought him through a darksom narrow strayt,
> To a broad gate, all built of beaten gold:
> The gate was open, but therein did wayt
> A sturdie villein, stryding stiffe and bold,
> As if that highest God defy he would;
> In his right hand an yron club he held,
> And he himselfe was all of yron mould,
> Yet had both life and sence, and well could weld
> That cursed weapon, when his cruell foes he queld.
>
> *Disdayne* he called was, and did disdayne
> To be so cald, and who so did him call:
> Sterne was his looke, and full of stomacke vayne,
> His portaunce terrible, and stature tall,

30 'When he walks, he moves like an engine and the ground shrinks before his treading. He is able to pierce a corslet with his eye, talks like a knell, and his hum is a battery. He sits in his state as a thing made for Alexander' (*Coriolanus*, V.iv.18–22). For the text, see William Shakespeare, *Coriolanus*, ed. by Philip Brockbank, The Arden Edition of the Works of William Shakespeare, 2nd series (London: Methuen, 1976).

31 Disdayne figures in II.vii.40–3 and in VI.vii–viii, where he is joined by the fool Scorn to punish Mirabella.

> Far passing th'hight of men terrestriall;
> Like an huge Gyant of the *Titans* race,
> That made him scorne all creatures great and small,
> And with his pride all others powre deface:
> More fitt emongst black fiendes, then men to haue his place.
> (II.vii.40–1; 1590 edition)

Disdayne, as his name explains, holds every creature and himself in disdain.[32] Since he is a club-wielding, villainous and terrifying monster out-measuring man, he fits the conceptual grid of the Spenserian giant set down in Chapter 9, above. Despite such generic similarities, however, the fiendish giant sports one surprising difference: he is not organic, but, like Talus, made of iron, so that he markedly differs from his 'airy' counterpart Orgoglio. On a simple level, Disdayne's body, as much as Talus's, first and foremost suggests the Iron Age, the very source of disdain and discord among people, as Ovid notes.[33] Spenser underscores Disdayne's metallic corporeality by endowing him with a gait fitting his nature. Seen from a teratological point of view, his 'stryding stiffe and bold' (40.4) does not merely emphasise his enormous proportions, and illustrate the transgressive amplitude and might witnessed in other monstrous beings; rather, the adjective *stiff* denotes a lack of suppleness, therefore giving his movement an unnatural, almost 'robotic' quality. Spenser's rough alliteration emphasises engine-like movement, and again suggests Shakespeare's description of Coriolanus's gait quoted above,[34] which makes Disdayne resemble Talus. However, Disdayne is not a mechanical contrivance, although he seems to fuse with the iron mace he carries. The circumstance that he is made of metal, yet has 'both life and sence' (40.8), identifies his essence as similar to that of animated creatures, and endows him with the ability of self-motion, which Talus lacks as he is merely obedient to Arthegall's commands.[35] Disdayne's feasibility as a living being equipped with sense is emphasised through the instances of extended animation, which elaborate on his looks and feelings. In rhetorical terms, Disdayne is a Spenserian golem made of 'miscreated mould' (42.9), and animated by means of extended prosopopoeia.

32 Teskey argues that Disdayne's disdaining self-awareness carries 'the sign to a remoter level of abstraction, where the contradiction [between being Disdayne *and* disdaining to be this personification] at this level is overcome' (*Allegory and Violence*, p. 22).

33 For the Ovidian ages, see *Metamorphoses*, I.89–150 (for the *aetas aurea*, see I.89–112, and for the *aetas ferrea*, see I.127–50). The iron and the gold out of which the giant is made hence allegorically represent Ovid's *aetates*.

34 See Shakespeare, *Coriolanus*, V.iv.14–26.

35 Spenser accentuates the creature's paradoxical, monstrous nature with the syntactical marker 'yet' (II.vii.40.8).

Matters become complicated with the addition of Part Two (Books IV–VI) and the second edition of Part One (Books I–III) of *The Faerie Queene* in 1596, because Spenser assigns Disdayne one of the major roles in Book VI, and retroactively changes the giant's appearance in the revised version of Book II. Critics have long since explained that Spenser changed Disdayne from iron into gold not only to give him a unified appearance but also to make him a more suitable part in the House of Mammon episode,[36] especially since his aureate nature now emphasises the link between gold, vanity and disdain.[37] But the upgrade Spenser gives Disdayne in the 1596 edition also points to a more thoroughgoing reconstruction, which is largely based on reinventing and recalibrating the giant's different features.

Picking up on Disdayne's terrifying outward appearance in Book II, Spenser now establishes the giant's lineage, and elaborates on his physique and looks. While Disdayne's pedigree remains rather vague – he is now the direct descendant of the 'old Gyants'[38] and 'sib to great *Orgoglio*' (VI.vii.41.6, and 41.8)[39] – his physical makeover causes friction with his former self, as Spenser uses a series of differing descriptions to present the giant. He first magnifies Disdayne's appearance by resorting to two similes that measure his body from top to bottom:

> His lookes were dreadfull, and his fiery eies
> Like two great Beacons, glared bright and wyde,
> Glauncing askew, as if his enemies
> He scorned in his ouerweening pryde;
> And stalking stately like a Crane, did stryde
> At euery step vppon the tiptoes hie,
> And all the way he went, on euery syde
> He gaz'd about, and stared horriblie,
> As if he with his lookes would all men terrifie.
>
> (VI.vii.42)

36 Spenser changed 'And he himselfe was all of yron mould' (II.vii.40.7; 1590 edition) into 'But he himselfe was all of golden mould' (II.vii.40.7; 1596 edition). Tonkin argues that Disdayne is 'an appropriate addition to [Philotime's] palace of the representative of worldly wealth', thus overlooking the revision of the passage he discusses (*Courteous Pastoral*, p. 90).

37 Ovid sees a direct link between the *aetas aurea* and the *aetas ferrea* in that the latter spawned the lust for gold; see *Metamorphoses*, I.137–43.

38 In Book II he was merely compared to the Titans (see II.vii.41.6).

39 The exact meaning of the term *sib* remains open to discussion, because it connotes both blood relation and kinship (see *OED*, s.v. 'sib, *n.*'). That there is a semantic bond between the two giants is shown in Florio's late sixteenth-century Italian–English dictionary, which translates *orgoglio* as 'pride, disdaine, haughtines' (*A Worlde of Wordes*, p. 248, s.v. 'orgoglio').

According to the narrator, Disdayne's fiery eyes, which look askew, shine like 'two great Beacons',[40] while the giant is 'stalking stately like a Crane' on 'tiptoes hie' (42.5–6).[41] These two images, one mechanical and one ornithological, are, as it were, the flint stones whose sparks bring the giant to life: by conjoining inchoate similes within one single stanza, Spenser reanimates the living automaton of Book II as a tower-like apparatus that moves horizontally and looks in every direction. Furthermore, Spenser implies conceptual continuity by using the same staccato-like alliteration to describe Disdayne's walk, changing 'stryding stiff' in Book II into 'stalking stately' in Book VI. Additionally, the poet invokes the reader's horror by combining the minute depiction of monstrous movement with the threat of the giant's extramissive sight.[42]

Spenser again defers determinacy in the next stanza, where Disdayne is portrayed as a giant who is dressed in costly golden cloth,[43] wearing a turban like 'the Mores of Malaber' (43.6) on his pitch-black locks, and carrying an iron club. Under the impact of this description, the giant, now racialised, shifts his appearance, and is closely associated with the orient, especially since he carries Muslim insignia.[44] By bringing into play the eastern region and its religion, Spenser invokes the marvellous realm of the monstrous races, unknown creatures and strange machines as the main textual material of his monster-making. It is against this backdrop of the marvellous that Spenser stages Disdayne's battle with Arthur. The depiction of single combat reads like a permutation of other giant battles elsewhere in the poem, for Disdayne's attacking Arthur with his 'dreadfull instrument of yre' (VI.viii.15.2),[45] threatening to pulverise Arthur or to 'embowel' him in the earth are basic components of giant narratives. However, the very moment Arthur strikes Disdayne at the knee, making him enact the giant's traditional fall, Spenser surprises his readers with Disdayne's creational difference: 'But all that leg, which did his body

40 Spenser uses the same image to describe the Dragon's eyes ('two broad Beacons, sett in open fieldes'; I.xi.14.3). Other creatures emitting dazzling rays are Acrasia (II.xii.78.7) and Corflambo, whose eyes have the power of the basilisk (IV.viii.39).

41 Spenser here departs from traditional crane imagery, which deploys the bird's neck as an image for human gluttony (as in I.iv.21.5).

42 For extramissive sight, see Krier, *Gazing on Secret Sights*, p. 30 and pp. 52–3.

43 Disdayne's guise is made of 'checklaton' (Spenser's spelling of ciclatoun, 'a stuff of silk or cloth of gold'), which relates the giant to the orient (see *OED*, s.v. 'ciclatoun, *n.*').

44 On evil muslims in the *Chanson de Roland*, see Paul Freedman, 'Medieval Other', pp. 6–7. Cohen rightly observes that racialised giants point not only to moral but also to ethnic alterity (see *Of Giants*, p. 158).

45 As Spenser here puns on the terms 'yre' and 'iron', he identifies the material from which the mace is made with its emotional significance.

beare, / It crack't throughout, yet did no bloud appeare' (VI.viii.16.4–5). Spenser here eschews the blood and gore that informs violent endgames, therefore heightening the giant's difference through the lack of blood.[46] This detail does not only render Disdayne dissimilar to other giants in Spenser's poem but also distinguishes him from metal monstrosities in other literary works, for even Talos bleeds to death after he accidentally cuts open a vein in his ankle.

Spenser stresses the feat of Arthur's victory over Disdayne by emphasising that the giant's leg was never bent before.[47] From the teratological vantage point, however, the cracking of the leg, which Spenser highlights through onomatopoeia,[48] underscores that the giant is made of inorganic material: whereas Disdayne's fall recalls that of other giants, the details of his fall accentuate his difference from his kin.[49] In the climactic battle of Canto viii, Arthur thus literally deconstructs the giant, which Spenser has just reconstructed after Book II to suit the purpose of his narrative in Book VI. Unlike the other giants, however, Disdayne survives Arthur's assault, but needs to be helped up and supported by Scorn (viii.25–6). The incident is especially striking, because the giant consciously tries to recreate his old self by striking a pose to appear as a tall, fierce and proud giant, a circumstance Spenser emphasises by a triple anaphora on *as if*:

> But being vp, he lookt againe aloft,
> As if he neuer had receiued fall;
> And with sterne eye-browes stared at him oft,
> As if he would haue daunted him withall:
> And standing on his tiptoes, to seeme tall,
> Downe on his golden feete he often gazed,
> As if such pride the other could apall[.]
>
> (VI.viii.26.1–7)

As his monstrosity becomes performative, Disdayne loses much of his terrifying impressiveness: his behaviour betrays his self-consciousness, and thus reveals the giant's sense and identity, as well as his ability to

46 Spenser uses the same method for Maleger; see the discussion of 'carles' and hags, above.

47 Spenser emphasises Disdayne's invincibility through the complex interplay of various kinds of *repetitio*: 'that [i.e. the knee] neuer yet was bent. // 16 // It neuer yet was bent, ne bent it now' (VI.viii.15.9–16.1). In Book II, Mammon warns Sir Guyon that Disdayne cannot be defeated (II.vii.42.8–9).

48 Spenser uses the verb *to crack* again when explaining that the leg '[w]as crackt in twaine' (VI.viii.25.8), thus unifying his account of the giant's fall.

49 As Disdayne has a golden body, his falling down like a lump of dirt is a suggestive image that downgrades him (see VI.viii.16.8–9).

reflect on his appearance. In Book VI, Spenser thus puts a thematic frame around the Disdayne episode, namely that of posture and movement, to finally undermine the giant's power.

Snowy Florimell

Although the physique of Talus and Disdayne suggests that the mechanical being consists of a solid single body animated through poetic means, the creation of Snowy Florimell in a magic ritual involving evil spirits suggests a more complex interplay of raw materials. Snowy Florimell is fashioned by the nameless witch in Book III as a walking, talking substitute for the real Florimell to please her lovesick son.[50] She appears as a female robot manufactured on the interacting yet self-exclusive concepts of love poetry, alchemy, magic and technology. Since her body is a combination of contradicting elements, Florimell's artificial *doppelgänger* and moral antitype emerges as a creature with an unprecedented ontology, a 'wondrous worke … / Whose like on earth was neuer framed yit' (III.viii.5.2–3).[51] Her body is a compound of 'purest snow in massie mould congeald' (6.2),[52] which is 'tempred with fine Mercury / And virgin wex' (6.6–7); to this, the witch adds vermilion to make the inanimate body look lively. On a simple level, this anatomical description shows an incompatible mixture of fusible material ranging from the elemental (snow), to the organic (wax), and the transgressive metal quicksilver, which oscillates between fluidity and solidity. This assortment not only stresses the artificiality of the witch's creation; it also underscores its logical unfeasibility: in addition to suspending the rudimentary laws of the physical world, the solidified snow, which is the main substance she is made of, marks her as a highly evanescent, even immaterial creature.

The creation of her body hinges on two principles: alchemy, and love poetry. While the topological praise of beauty is apparent in her snow-white body, its waxen softness and the vermilion-coloured skin of the

50 Spenser characterises the witch as the evil maker of Snowy Florimell through using terms like *make*, *fashion*, and *temper*; at III.viii.10.9, she is explicitly called a 'Creatresse'.

51 The full episode covers III.viii.1–10. Kaske points out that the double of Florimell and Snowy Florimell invites Spenser's readers to compare the woman with the automaton, and to explain the *distinctiones* between them; such *distinctiones* are originally part of biblical hermeneutics, 'a list of meanings … which purports to exhaust all the meanings of a given word, object, or concept in Scripture' (*Spenser and Biblical Poetics*, p. 24). Kaske formulates the basic distinction between Florimell and her manufactured counterpart thus: 'some apparent beauty is not true beauty, because it is purely material and not subtended by the soul' (p. 63).

52 The snow was gathered by spirits from the '*Riphœan* hils' (III.viii.6.4). Thomas Cooper explains that the Scythian mountains are forever wintry (see *Thesaurus*, s.v. 'Ripæi').

traditional Petrarchan lady,[53] these components also share an alchemical subtext: mercury is one of the most frequently used alchemical ingredients, noted for its 'volatility, fluidity, malleability',[54] and the 'virgin wex' is obliquely linked to the notorious *lac virginis*, the virgin's milk of the alchemists.[55] That alchemical lore assigned quicksilver the status of 'spirit', and not strictly 'matter' renders False Florimell's physique even more of a creational paradox.[56] Against this backdrop, she exemplifies the misrepresentation, and hence latent deformation, caused by inadequate similes that objectify women to suit them to male fantasies.[57]

A piece of plastic art, as the term *idol* suggests,[58] Snowy Florimell's body thus literalises the major topoi of Petrarchan love poetry, and points to their inherent grotesquery.[59] So does her face:

53 The snow-white body, its waxen softness and the vermilion-coloured skin of the traditional Petrarchan lady are all topological. See, among other things, Pyrocles's extended praise of Philocleas's beauty in Sir Philip Sidney's *Old Arcadia* (for the text, see Sir Philip Sidney, *The Countess of Pembroke's Arcadia (The Old Arcadia)*, ed. by Jean Robertson (Oxford: Clarendon, 1973), pp. 238–43). The entire poem, which marks the end of Book III, could well have served as a blueprint for the snowy lady, because almost all the details of Philoclea's description, albeit in themselves conventional, can be detected in Spenser's creation of Florimell's eidolon: Philoclea's skin is 'more white than snow' (p. 238, l. 12), and in the hand 'with strange compact doth lie / Warm snow, moist pearl, soft ivory' (p. 242, ll. 8–9); the blushing red of her skin is here conferred to 'kindly claret' (p. 238, l. 28). Additionally, the phrase 'strange compact' recalls the process of congealing and moulding snow.

54 See Robert M. Schuler, 'Alchemy', in *Spenser Encyclopedia*, ed. by Hamilton, pp. 12–14 (p. 13). Its concurring properties made mercury enigmatic matter, as Isidore's entry in *Etymologies*, XVI.19, suggests. Cf. also *Batman vppon Bartholome*, XVI.8. In his treatise *On the Soul*, 406b, Aristotle quotes Philippus's explanation that Daedalus may have poured quicksilver into his statues to give them the ability of self-motion. For the text, see *On the Soul; Parva naturalia; On Breath*, trans. W. S. Hett, Loeb Classical Library (Cambridge, MA: Harvard University Press; London: Heinemann, 1957).

55 Schuler cites an anonymous poem which expounds that 'Lac virgynen / [is] cauled virgins wax in englysh tonge' (reference is to MS Ashmole 1480, fol. 72a; see 'Alchemy', p. 13).

56 'Spirits' are volatile substances like sulphur or arsenic which could be combined with metals ('bodies'). Chaucer's Yeoman in *The Canterbury Tales* also exhibits confusion when listing quicksilver both as body and as spirit (*CT*, VIII.822 and 827). John Reidy observes that the Yeoman's confusion stems from Geber's classifying quicksilver as a spirit, and later describing its mundification, or cleansing (see explanatory notes to the *Canon's Yeoman's Prologue* and *Tale*, note to *CT*, III.820; cf. Geber, *The Works of Geber, the Most Famous Prince and Philosopher*, trans. by Richard Russell (London: Thomas James, 1678), p. 54, pp. 73–4, pp. 102–4 and p. 186).

57 Suzuki maintains that the snowy lady is the product of the male desire for beauty, and hence a possession fantasy (see Suzuki, *Metamorphoses*, pp. 176–7).

58 She is called an 'Idole' in III.viii.11.2, and IV.v.15.7, and hence evokes the scriptural refutation of idols expounded in Leviticus, 19.4. With view to her end – she melts and dissolves when placed next to the real Florimell – Spenser might pun on *idle* in the sense of 'vain, empty'.

59 See Rufus Wood's lucid analysis of Snowy Florimell in *Metaphor and Belief*, pp. 114–26.

In stead of eyes two burning lampes she set
In siluer sockets, shyning like the skyes,
And a quicke mouing Spirit did arret
To stirre and roll them, like to womens eyes;
In stead of yellow lockes she did deuyse,
With golden wyre to weaue her curled head;
Yet golden wyre was not so yellow thryse
As *Florimells* fayre heare: and in the stead
Of life, she put a Spright to rule the carcas dead.

(III.viii.7)

Silver sockets wherein lamps shine like the skies, and hair made of golden wire: Spenser again draws on the inventory of love poetry.[60] However, he turns its traditional images into monstrous signifiers by literalising them in the world of his poem, thus disclosing the beauty blazon's divesting human women of their natural physique through the substitution of artificial parts.[61] This strategy has obvious poetical implications in that it elaborates on the possible aberration of poetic language,[62] but also contains a technological dimension, because it describes the process of producing an automaton of human likeness through using inorganic raw material. In the description of her creation, Spenser utilises rhetoric to underline Snowy Florimell's artificial otherness from her female model,[63] and from humans in general. The label for such difference is the preposition *instead of*, which Spenser uses thrice in this stanza, and which characterises Snowy Florimell as a surrogate being whose prosthetics are monstrous signifiers contradicting the human organs they are substitutes for.[64] Her monstrosity lies exactly in attempting to conform to, and even mimic, the ideals of beauty, especially in the sharp discontinuity

60 For eyes, see Sidney, *Astrophel and Stella*, 6. 9; the gold wires do not necessarily represent choice blondness, but can also refer to the use of golden wires in hair ornamentation (for the text, see *The Poems of Sir Philip Sidney*, ed. by William A. Ringler, Jr (Oxford: Clarendon, 1962)). Again, Pyrocles's praise of Philocleas in the *Old Arcadia* comes to mind, as her hair is like 'threads of finest gold' (*Old Arcadia*, p. 238, l. 3).

61 Ferry sees a more specific resemblance to the description of Belphoebe, especially to her eyes, in which 'two liuing lamps did flame, / Kindled aboue at th'heuenely makers light' (II.iii.23.1–2), and her hair, which Spenser describes as 'yellow lockes crisped, like golden wyre' (30.1); see Anne Ferry, *The Art of Naming* (Chicago: University of Chicago Press, 1988), pp. 166–7. Although such reasoning is beyond a doubt, I would argue that the fashioning of Florimell points beyond the specific to a more general critique of the beauty blazon.

62 See also Wood, *Metaphor and Belief*, pp. 114–26.

63 See Wood, *Metaphor and Belief*, p. 119.

64 This assumption tallies well with Teskey's argument that '[s]he demonstrates art's potential to usurp the position of the real' (*Allegory and Violence*, p. 94).

between the materials and what they are supposed to represent.[65] On a more theoretical level, the creation of Snowy Florimell is indicative of the late sixteenth-century craze for machines and automata, which were manufactured to imitate humans and other natural beings.[66] Devices like animated hydraulic machines and clockwork creatures would likewise move their artificial limbs, and, to resort to the phrase Spenser uses for Snowy Florimell, stir and roll their eyes.[67] This suggests an important link between anatomy and technology, for anatomical knowledge becomes the prerequisite for attempting to recreate life. In the text of *The Faerie Queene*, Snowy Florimell henceforth proves a successful device, because she creates '*an effect the causes of which are concealed*'.[68] Spenser's poem thus interacts with central aspects of contemporary science.

The addition that makes Snowy Florimell's creation wholly illicit is the satanic spirit whose task is 'to rule the carcas dead' (7.9).[69] Spenser's exact phrasing triggers the reader's repugnance, because it gives the impression that Snowy Florimell is a decomposing corpse possessed by a demon.[70] Again, Snowy Florimell's creation evokes alchemy: the insertion of the

65 That the creation of such robots was sensitive matter is perhaps best attested in the anecdote of Albertus Magnus's fashioning an android, which was destroyed at the behest of St Thomas Aquinas (see Hanafi, *The Monster in the Machine*, p. 77, and Kang, *Sublime Dreams*, pp. 70–1).

66 Cf. Sawday, 'Cyborg', p. 181.

67 For descriptions and illustrations of such contrivances, see Klaus Maurice and Otto Mayr, eds, *The Clockwork Universe: German Clocks and Automata* (Washington: Smithsonian Institution, DC; New York: Neale Watson Academic Publications, 1980), 'Artificial Life: Automata and Figure Clocks', pp. 234–89, as well as p. 170 (automaton figure of a monk). Cf. also Kang, *Sublime Dreams*, p. 81. Snowy Florimell's ability to roll her eyes is reminiscent of Malacesta's: her 'wanton eyes, ill signes of womanhed, / Did roll too lightly, and too often glaunce' (III.i.41.7–8; the 1590 print reads 'highly' for 'lightly'); both suggest 'the light and wanton motions of their eyes' Thomas Wright adduces to harlots (*The Passions of the minde in generall* (London: Valentine Simmes, 1604), p. 29). For the link between harlots and Malacesta, see Broaddus, 'Britomart's Adventures', p. 192.

68 This is generally claimed for mechanical inventions by David Summers ('Pandora's Crown: On Wonder, Imitation, and Mechanism in Western Art', in *Wonders, Marvels, and Monsters in Early Modern Culture*, ed. by Peter G. Platt (Newark: University of Delaware Press, 1999), pp. 45–75 (p. 51); the emphasis is Summers's).

69 The phrase 'carcas dead' supports Wood's notion that Snowy Florimell is essentially a dead metaphor brought to life (see *Metaphor and Belief*, pp. 119–20). – The inserted agent is a spirit that fell with Satan (III.viii.8).

70 On another level, Spenser's description recalls a passus in Campanella's *De homine* which relates that a boy killed by Simon Magus transformed bodies according to the magician's orders, while the dead body was actually moved by an evil spirit. Campanella's phrase 'diabolus … fingens' adequately describes the works of the demon in Snowy Florimell's body, as he also performs to dissemble (see Tommaso Campanella, *De homine: Theologicorum liber IV*, ed. and trans. by Romano Amerio, Edizione nazionale dei classici del Pensiero Italiano, II, 13 and 14 (Rome: Centro Internazionale di Studi Umanistici, 1960), I, 158).

evil spirit recalls the alchemical practice of making gold, which usually consists of inserting a 'spirit' (also called 'seed') into 'prime matter' (or 'chaos'), a process which Spenser here parodies.[71] But alchemy is only one subtext with which the creative process interrelates. As Snowy Florimell is a mere contrivance she cannot move on her own accord, and needs an agent to control her movement and turn her into the performing doll the witch sought to create. She is hence rather like an apparatus depicted in the machine books of the late sixteenth century, in which complex machinery is worked by a human being or an animal.[72] Yet Snowy Florimell's monstrosity transcends the merely mechanical, because Spenser uses an evil spirit as her motive faculty: this draws more specifically on the connection between the mechanical and the demonic established in teratological and magical treatises of the sixteenth and seventeenth centuries.[73] The infernal agent as the operator of mechanical contrivances is indeed so well documented that it is possible that Spenser consciously places Snowy Florimell in a context that enhances her highly dubious nature. This contemporary background relates her to other monstrous beings discussed so far. In previous sections, beings were made monstrous through the process of 'monstrous relocation', as could be witnessed in Spenser's disfiguring Lust by transferring phallus and vagina to the giant's face. In Snowy Florimell's case, Spenser varies this principle through displacing an alien spirit into the automaton's body.[74]

With Snowy Florimell, the monstrous is closely linked to performance.[75] Since her agent is a male spirit, Snowy Florimell is also a gendered combination of the female and the male, and thus evades classification. While Gareth Roberts might have a strong case for specifically comparing the male spirit's acting like a female to the boy-actor impersonating a woman on the Elizabethan stage,[76] Snowy Florimell's nature suggests a far more

71 See Schuler, 'Alchemy', p. 13.

72 Sawday discusses such machines and presents valuable illustrations in 'Cyborg', pp. 179–82.

73 For a full account, see Hanafi, *The Monster in the Machine*, pp. 53–96. On the tradition of the demon in the machine, see Kang's survey of the *Asclepius* in *Sublime Dreams*, pp. 75–7.

74 Hanafi points to the potential danger that such a 'displacement of spirit into an inappropriate body' posed for the early modern mind. She states that 'whenever spirit is called into or forcibly inhabits formed matter, there is a danger of monstrosity arising' (*The Monster in the Machine*, p. 74 and p. 54).

75 III.viii.8 is replete with performative terms. While some of them are rather general, like 'fawning guyle', 'fayre resemblance', 'counterfesaunce', others read like a catalogue of performative codes ('to fashion', 'to speake', 'to vse his gest').

76 See Gareth Roberts, 'Women and Magic in English Renaissance Love Poetry', in *Representing Women in Renaissance England*, ed. by Claude J. Summers and Ted-Larry Pebworth (Columbia: University of Missouri Press, 1997), pp. 59–75 (p. 74).

comprehensive breaking of boundaries. Much more than the product of transsexual gender-crossing she is a monstrous imitation of life that defies just about every natural category, combining alchemical, magical and poetical principles with the mechanical into a discordant combination that identifies her as a wholly illicit creature. By making Snowy Florimell a complete compound, Spenser hammers home the incongruity of inside machine and outside humanoid by characterising her as a monstrous aberration.[77]

As creational deformity, the snowy lady misdirects any character she encounters, and becomes the touchstone of bestial discord during her existence. Her end, like Orgoglio's, recalls and annuls the major opposition on which her body is constructed, namely that of immateriality and solidity:

> Streight way so soone as both together met,
> Th'enchaunted Damzell vanisht into nought:
> Her snowy substance melted as with heat,
> Ne of that goodly hew remayned ought,
> But th'emptie girdle, which about her wast was wrought.
> (V.iii.24.5–9)

When literally juxtaposed with the real Florimell, the snowy lady's body is forced back into the normal parameters of the physical world, and melts. The false 'Idole' finally reveals her 'idle' nature, i.e. the emptiness behind a sign that was founded on an obsessive masculine fancy, like many idealised ladies in sixteenth-century love poetry.[78]

Whereas in the interpretations of dragons and four-footed beasts Spenser used metal either as imagery or as body parts to enhance their degree of monstrosity,[79] he creates Talus and Disdayne as fully realised golems by casting the characteristic features of man and giant into a full-metal *physis*, and manufactures the snowy lady as complex coagulation of different matters and subtexts. These robots upset ontological categories through different means. In the allegorical framework of Book V, Talus

77 On the disparity between inside and outside cf. also Sawday, 'Cyborg', p. 182.

78 Similarly in the *Old Arcadia*, Pyrocles's gaze turns Philoclea into a sustained fantasy (note his admitting that his 'tongue doth tell what fancy sees'; *Old Arcadia*, p. 241, l. 6). Spenser characterises Snowy Florimell as the male 'fancies wonderment' (V.iii.26.5); see Sheila T. Cavanagh, 'Nightmares of Desire: Evil Women in *The Faerie Queene*', *Studies in Philology* 91 (1994), 313–38. This makes her a close relative of Archimago's false Una, who was created to dissemble Redcrosse's fantasy.

79 See the cannon simile illustrating the explosiveness of Orgoglio's blows (I.vii.13.1–6), the windmill simile for the Dragon of Eden (I.xi.22) and Geryoneo's dragon (V.xi.31), as well as the teeth of the Blatant Beast (VI.vi.9.3).

figures as a mindless recipient of orders who points to the uncanny nature of an all-too-virile, inhuman police system. Disdayne, however, pushes beyond the allegorical to become a fully realised, even self-conscious being that challenges the robot's dependence on someone else's control.[80] When fashioning Disdayne, Spenser dons the robe of the metallurgist to bring a metallic giant into being, and to transform the corporeality of his creation at his own will through what resembles textual *mouvance*, a term coined by the French medievalist Paul Zumthor to conceptualise the frequent differences between various manuscripts of the same text in the vernacular of oral cultures.[81] This transformation by creating differing versions of the text is a strategy that makes it impossible to determine a unified original creature, and heightens the indeterminacy of both the monster and the text in which it appears. Quite differently, Snowy Florimell, an automaton 'made [by art] to move as though it were alive',[82] is a body with which male fantasy is obsessed, and therefore a being that exists in a textual environment governed by male desire. As her corporeality is created through the puzzling interaction of incompatible processes, she figures as an impossible creature manufactured by impossible means.

While Spenser's robots generally anticipate the rise of technology and mark man and monster as possible machines, they more specifically explore the possible monstrous aspects of technomorphic man. In the context of the poem, the interpretation of Talus, Disdayne and Snowy Florimell considerably broadens the scope of the Spenserian monster. The poet's imaginative creativity is the energising catalyst to set static images in motion and to reveal meaning through the creature's life and sense.[83] These three automata hence ultimately function as engines or mechanisms in the poem's many plots.[84]

80 Hamilton astutely observes that '[t]he allegorist insists that his most allegorical figure is not merely allegorical' (note to II.vii.40.8).

81 See *Essai de poétique médiévale*, Collection Poétique (Paris: Seuil, 1972), Ch. 1.

82 The definition is taken from Summers, 'Pandora's Crown', p. 54.

83 Cf. also Barkan's interpreting the Castle of Alma as a machine in *Nature's Work of Art*, pp. 168–9.

84 Even Malengin, one of Spenser's shape-shifting 'carles', bears witness to the robotic subtext of *The Faerie Queene*, because his name, which derives from Latin *malum* and *ingenium*, took on the meaning of 'evil machinery' from the late fourteenth century onwards; this is also observed by Skulsky (see 'Malengin', in *Spenser Encyclopedia*, ed. by Hamilton, p. 450).

12

Taxonomy reconsidered

The fantastic beasts, human–animal composites, giants, variously monsterised humans and mechanical creatures in *The Faerie Queene* demonstrate the continuous threat of monstrous forces in the epic romance, and warn Spenser's readers of the deforming effect the monstrous can exert on humans. Throughout the poem Spenser hence manifests his awareness of the etymological tradition which derived the term *monster* from the Latin verbs *monstrare* ('to point to') and *monere* ('to warn'). In addition to etymology, Spenser's monstrous beings predominantly conform to the contemporaneous idea of the monster exemplified by Cooper's dictionary definition of *monstrum*: they are physically deformed (or rhetorically disfeatured by metaphors and similes); they violate the rules of nature; and they are conceived as signs requiring interpretation.

As a poet, Spenser prefers creating new monstrosities to imitating familiar ones, a circumstance he stresses by pointing out that his creatures have never been seen or described before.[1] Within the context of the novel and the marvellous, Spenser's harking back to the monsters and monstrous beings of the scriptural, classical, medieval and contemporaneous traditions is a means of resorting to the readers' common knowledge. His major monsters are hence novel transmutations of famous creatures and individual monstrous elements. Known beings, such as famous fantastic beasts, are chiefly used as imagery, most significantly in similes and comparisons, as well as in lineages, which serve the dual function of establishing the 'biological' and textual heritage of the monsters in *The Faerie Queene*.[2] It is in these instances that Spenser resorts to famous

1 Cf. I.viii.48.9 and III.vii.22.7.

2 This is implicit in Watson's observation that fantastic animals are actually rare in *The Faerie Queene*: 'The strange or exotic seems in itself to have had no appeal for [Spenser]. There is one unicorn in Faerie land, one basilisk, and gryphons occur twice' (Watson, 'Submarine Creations', p. 121). However, these creatures do not at all occur in Faeryland, at least not strictly speaking; rather, they occur on the figurative level of the poem.

monstrosities like Echidna, Typhon, Cerberus and the Chimera, which make up a purely referential meta-bestiary that helps create Spenser's original specimens.[3]

Maleger's troops and the problem of taxonomy

The richness of these monstrous creatures bespeaks the inventiveness of the poet, and also makes rigid taxonomy futile. This claim is perhaps best exemplified in the passage figuring the densest and most sustained account of monstrous beings, namely the siege of Alma's Castle, during which '[a] thousand villeins' (II.ix.13.2) commanded by Maleger rise from the rocks and caves around the fortress.[4] This multitude of variously deformed creatures, which bear man-made arms such as clubs, spears, knives and staves, and have '[s]taring ... hollow eies, and stiffe vpstanding heares' (13.9), are the very epitome of the monstrous. They form twelve troops: seven of them represent the deadly sins, and assault the castle gate (xi.6); the other five are individual squads attacking each of the five senses, namely sight, hearing, smell, taste and touch (xi.7–13).[5] Rosemary Freeman calls these creatures, which advance in 'huge and infinite' numbers (xi.5.6), the 'Beast-headed men',[6] thereby disregarding the variety of animal parts they possess:

> The first troupe was a monstrous rablement
> Of fowle misshapen wightes, of which some were
> Headed like Owles, with beckes vncomely bent,
> Others like Dogs, others like Gryphons dreare,
> And some had wings, and some had clawes to teare,
> And euery one of them had Lynces eyes,
> And euery one did bow and arrowes beare:
> All those were lawlesse lustes, corrupt enuyes
> And couetous aspects, all cruel enimyes.
>
> (II.xi.8)

(There is however one reference to griffin-headed monsters in Maleger's army; see II.xi.8.4.) As important elements in Spenser's vast body of references, they are used to underline the monstrous traits of individual characters or beings, rather than become directly present in the poem.

3 Horstmann notes that whereas Spenser's monsters are the offspring of classical ones, Ariosto's evoke the world of classical mythology only in imagery (see *Namen*, p. 52).

4 See especially II.ix.13–17, and xi.5–14.

5 See Hamilton, notes to II.xi.6, and 8–13, Brooks-Davies, *Critical Commentary*, pp. 174–5, notes to II.xi.8–13, as well as *Variorum*, II, 281–5 and 339–41. Cf. also Alcina's troop of monsters in Ariosto's *Orlando Furioso*, VI.60–6.

6 Freeman, '*The Faerie Queene*': *A Companion for Readers*, p. 50.

True, the terrifying mob attacking the sense of sight contains creatures with the heads of owls, and dogs; but matters turn more complex with griffins, i.e. lions with wings, because they are more than merely beast-headed. Even in syntactical terms, Spenser is deliberately vague about them and forgoes linking the griffin explicitly with the wings (8.4–5). That he adds other attributes, namely the claws and the lynx's eyes, heightens the sense of a perverse creation that confuses sight and resists classification. The humanoid resemblance of these 'fowle misshapen wightes' helps Spenser make his didactic point, because physical hideousness is the yardstick that measures spiritual corruption, which Spenser emphasises by appending a moral explanation to their description.[7]

Correspondingly, Spenser also moralises the impending danger of the vices in the following stanzas, where different composite monsters threaten the four other wits, by resorting to traditional animal emblems.[8] There, creatures with the heads of harts, snakes and boars assail the sense of hearing (10); monsters with bodies shaped like hounds, apes and puttocks stupefy smell (11); composite creatures with an ostrich's mouth, a toad's face or a pig's waist assault taste (12); and strange creatures looking like snails, spiders and hedgehogs tickle sensual delight (13).[9] In order to make the rebel rout as physically revolting as possible, Spenser employs a pictorial technique that is rather reminiscent of Hieronymus Bosch's paintings, for these hellish creatures combine the beastly with the human, resting firmly in a textual habitat where all are 'shap't according their conditions' (xi.11.6).[10] This literary strategy renders any attempt at an Aristotelian, quasi-zoological classification impossible, and may even question the overall valence of teratological taxonomies. Freeman's critical blunder hence reflects the successful bewilderment of the readers' senses through the excessive diversity of monstrous forms.

Apart from figurations in Spenser's allegory of the body, Maleger's troops make manifest the inexhaustible combinatory possibilities of the

7 The stanza is broken down into three distinctive sense units, namely into a general introduction, a depiction of various monsters and an appended moralisation. This arrangement, which Spenser employs for every single troop, closely resembles the tripartite arrangement of the emblem books into heading, picture and explanatory verse. Broaddus explains that Maleger's troops 'resemble vices resulting from habitual exercise' ('Renaissance Psychology and the Defense of Alma's Castle', p. 144).

8 See II.xi.10–13.

9 The commentaries by Hamilton (notes to II.xi.9–13), and Brooks-Davies (*Critical Commentary*, pp. 174–5, notes to II.xi.9–13) stress the iconographic, and traditional implications of the animals Spenser uses in this passage.

10 For a comprehensive account of monstrous deformity, see Williams, *Deformed Discourse*, pp. 107–76.

monstrous, which circumstance accounts for the infinity of creatures attacking the Castle of Alma, and, consequentially, for the onslaught of the monstrous in the entire poem. In addition to making it a showcase of anatomical variation, Spenser stages this passage as an extended variation on the rhetoric of the monstrous, creating a cluster of terms, such as *monstrous*, *foul*, *misshaped*, *deformed*, *hideous* and *horrible*, that connects the stanzas with one another.[11] Hence, Maleger's rabblement is the *summa* of Spenserian teratology, the most condensed catalogue of monstrous creatures, monstrous signifiers and monstrous rhetoric in the poem, bringing to the fore the creativity, erudition and inventive ardour underlying Spenser's monster-making.

Making monsters

Spenser's poetic venture is informed by his penchant for fashioning elaborate monstrous beings. In her article on 'Forreine and Monstrous Beasts', Watson advances a threefold classification of Spenserian monster-making, which distinguishes between combining at least two known creatures into a new being, exaggerating size and disintegrating composite elements.[12] The textual and anatomical analyses have shown that Spenser employs much more elaborate strategies to fashion monsters. Many of these creatures sport a hypertrophy of the body (as is the case with the giants and the dragons), and/or contain novel combinations of disparate body parts, as is most notably the case in composite creatures joining elements from different animals into one body. In its most advanced form, the compound creature mingles human with animal components, thus creating a horrendous life form existing in the interstices between exclusive biological categories (cf. Geryoneo's dragon). In other cases, the monster is created through multiplying body parts (cf. Orgoglio's dragon, and Geryoneo), or through the anatomical displacement of body parts to inappropriate physical areas (cf. Lust's nose, and Errour's body). Quite differently, monstrous beings can also be made of disparate matter. Orgoglio is mainly created out of earth and wind, while Snowy Florimell, whose body amalgamates different inchoate ingredients into an artificial

11 See, for example, Spenser's use of rhetorical variation in the generalising introductions for each individual group: 'a monstrous rablement / Of fowle misshapen wightes' (II. xi.8.1–2; the monsters attacking sight); 'Deformed creatures, in straunge difference' (10.3; the monsters attacking hearing); 'Whose hideous shapes were like to feendes of hell' (11.3; the monsters attacking smell); 'a grysie rablement' (12.3; the monsters attacking taste); 'most horrible of hew' (13.1; the monsters attacking touch).

12 See Watson, 'Forreine and Monstrous Beasts', pp. 176–7.

contrivance, is part mechanical, part demonised marvel. In many cases, however, the monster contains in its body the chaotic mingling of the elements (cf. the Dragon in I.xi, and Orgoglio). Other monstrous beings, especially the monstrous humans, may appear physically whole, but either have a monstrous lineage or behave in such that way that their behaviour suggests their animal heritage (cf. Satyrane, and Radigund). Moreover, the normative human body can become the sight of permanent or ephemeral deformation, both physically and rhetorically, and thus deteriorate into the monstrous (cf. Malbecco's, Grill's and Timias's transformations). Hence, Spenser's encyclopaedic programme informs his creation of monsters and monstrous beings, which display types of deformation established by Isidore. On a poetical level, Spenser's plethora of monstrous permutations also bespeaks the poet's bountiful invention,[13] and penchant for variety,[14] two standard principles of early modern rhetoric that the skilful poet needed to master in order to compose a text that would catch and hold the attention of his readers.

From a Renaissance point of view, Spenser's strategies to create monsters frequently resemble the manipulations of the artisans who manufactured strange creatures for the chambers of wonder with such consummate skill that it was difficult to tell the fantastic from the real.[15] The poetical equivalent of the creationist's toolbox is the literary arsenal of rhetorical and stylistic devices. Throughout the previous interpretations and anatomical analyses, Spenser's descriptions of the monstrosities have claimed as much attention as his constant use of denigrating terms and epithets that underline the horrible deformity of these creatures. Against this backdrop, Spenser's monstrous discourse emerges as a *discordia concors* yoking together two disparate voices into a paradoxical unity: while his use of descriptive referents taints monsters as gross and

13 On the significance of *inventio*, see Pierre de Ronsard, *Abbregé de l'Art poétique françois* (in Pierre de Ronsard, *Œuvres complètes*, ed. by Jean Céard, Daniel Ménager and Michel Simonin, 2 vols (Paris: Gallimard, 1994), II, 1178), and Gascoigne, *Certayne Notes of Instruction Concerning the Making of Verse or Ryme in English* (in *Elizabethan Critical Essays*, ed. by G. Gregory Smith, 2 vols (Oxford: Oxford University Press, 1904; repr. London, 1959), I, 47–8).

14 On the significance of variety for Renaissance rhetoric, see Heinrich F. Plett, *Rhetorik der Affekte: Englische Wirkungsästhetik im Zeitalter der Renaissance*, Studien zur Englischen Philologie, New Series, 18 (Tübingen: Niemeyer, 1975), p. 71, pp. 77–8 and p. 125. Plett quotes the Latin proverb *delectat varietas* ('variety brings pleasure') to stress the currency of this principle (see *Rhetorik*, p. 71).

15 Hanafi explains that strange animals like the basilisks or dragons were frequently manufactured by inventive taxidermists, who severed the parts of animals, reassembled them and sutured them into a new creature (see *Monster in the Machine*, p. 47). On the impact of *Wunderkammern* on the collective mind of the Renaissance, see also Chapter 2, above.

abject deformities, his poetic practices belie such heinousness, because these monsters, created by adhering to the normative poetic language of the entire poem, are realised as perfect rhetorical forms.

Spenser also takes great pains to maintain the monsters' puzzling essence. As creations of polyvalent allegory, they challenge interpretation, because they have no single meaning and may even make language monstrous (as is the case with Geryoneo's dragon, and the Blatant Beast). Additionally, the use of disparate imagery and inconsistent details in the descriptions of monstrous beings makes it difficult to assign them a definite form, exactly because monsters transcend the notion of corporeal unity and definiteness. Accordingly, the exact anatomy of many a creature becomes inconclusive by ambivalent description (see, e.g., the Blatant Beast's tongues and stings). Under these influences, the visualisation and interpretation of monsters and monstrous beings becomes a major task for Spenser's readers.[16]

As monsters and monstrous beings in *The Faerie Queene* tend to have an indeterminate and fragmented nature,[17] measuring and fully dissecting such monstrosity inevitably leads into an interpretative cul-de-sac.[18] Hence, Spenserian monsters do not only exist for the sake of 'direct' allegory, since they frequently evade clear-cut interpretations and cannot be approached exclusively as signifiers ready for instant decoding. Such a hypothesis is borne out by their lack of homogeneous corporeality, and by their crossing the boundaries to other planes of being. Behind Spenser's strategy lies the aim to describe monsters so vividly that they can forcefully impact on the reader. This observation points to two important principles of early modern rhetoric that would allegedly ensure the aesthetic and emotional efficacy of a text, namely *enargeia* (or *evidentia*), which means 'lively presentation',[19] and *energeia*, which denotes the force that

16 On the interpretation of monsters, see especially Chapter 19, below.

17 Cf. also Watson's remarks on the difficulty of visualing Spenserian monsters in 'Forreine and Monstrous Beasts'.

18 See also Spenser's frequent references to indeterminate size, such as 'huge great' (I.vii.44.2, for Orgoglio's dragon; I.viii.24.7, for Orgoglio; III.vii.40.1, for Argante's iron mace; IV.vii.5.6, for Lust's tusk-like teeth, IV.vii.6.6, for his nose; V.ii.30.3, for the Egalitarian Giant's scales; V.xi.5.3, for Geryoneo's iron axe; V.xi.23.1, for Geryoneo's dragon), 'huge long' (I.i.15.2, for Errour's tail; V.ix.11.1 and V.xi.28.6, for the tail of Geryoneo's dragon), 'huge and tall' (I.vii.51.2, for Orgoglio), 'huge and horrible' (I.xi.55.2, for the Great Dragon), 'huge and hideous' (VI.vii.41.2, for Disdayne).

19 *Eliotes Dictionary* defines *enargeia* thus: 'Enargeia, ae, foem. gene. an euident and playne demonstracion when a thyng is so described, that it seemeth to the reader or hearer, that he beholdeth it as it were in dooyng, euidencie, perspicuitie' (Sir Thomas Elyot, *Bibliotheca Eliotae: Eliotes Dictionarie*, the third tyme corrected by Thomas Cooper (London: Th. Bertheleti, 1559)). For shorter definitions, see Cooper, *Thesaurus*, and

the thing described exerts on the reader or hearer.[20] It therefore seems likely that Spenser anatomises monsters to such a great extent because he wants them to work on the readers' imagination, rather than merely provide ready-made meaning.[21] How exactly Spenser manipulates his monstrous descriptions to involve his readers in complex and advanced allegorical interpretation is discussed in Chapter 19, below.

The use of taxonomy

The diversity of Maleger's monstrous rabblement, and consequently the plenitude of Spenserian monstrosities point to the difficulty of assigning monstrous beings definitive positions in a classificatory system. Every teratological taxonomy ultimately questions its applicability, for the monstrous remains a mixed category marring any attempt at strict classification, but inviting concordantial readings, which arrange different kinds of creatures in groups. The interpretative essays in these chapters have shown that no single category is hermetically separated from another. On the contrary, properties of one monstrous species resurface in another, rendering strict distinctions untenable. Taxonomy thus emerges as a means of imposing artificial boundaries on a category which resists conceptual restraints.[22] This verdict supports Cohen's postulation that the monstrous 'is a genus too large to be encapsulated in any conceptual system; the monster's very existence is a rebuke to boundary and enclosure'.[23] Similarly, David Williams utters a notable *caveat* when reflecting on the applicability of his own taxonomy in *Deformed Discourse*.[24] Against such critical views,

---

Florio, *Worlde of Wordes*, s.v. 'enargeia'. S. K. Heninger, Jr, surveys the development of *enargeia* from Aristotle to Quintilian, from Erasmus to Thomas Wilson (see 'Speaking Pictures: Sidney's Rapprochement between Poetry and Painting', in *Sir Philip Sidney and the Interpretation of Renaissance Culture*, ed. by Gary F. Waller and Michael D. Moore (London and Totawa: Croom Helm, 1984), pp. 3–16 (pp. 13–14)).

20 The *Bibliotheca Eliotae* defines *energeia* thus: 'Energeia, ae, foem. gene. an efficacie, or effectuall operation'. See also Florio, *Worlde of Wordes*, s.v. 'energeia'. For discussions that distinguish *enargeia* from *energeia*, see Plett, *Rhetorik der Affekte*, pp. 72–3, pp. 135–7 and pp. 182–3.

21 Tannier notes the elaboration Spenser puts into the making of his monsters, but does not explain what this observation may entail (see 'Bestiaire Maniériste', pp. 55–6).

22 Spenser addresses such resistance directly in the description of the giant Grantorto, who 'gaped like a gulfe, when he did gerne, / That whether man or monster one could scarse discerne' (V.xii.I.15.8–9). On the epistemological implications of breaking boundaries, see also Douglas, *Purity and Danger*.

23 Cohen, 'Seven Theses', p. 7; the entire argument is laid down on pp. 6–7 of his essay.

24 At the outset of his taxonomy, Williams admits to the arbitrariness of 'a taxonomy of monstrous forms', and the contradiction of structuring disorder (*Deformed Discourse*, p. 108).

Spenser's monsters become exemplars of the continuous breaking of boundaries observed in other texts and historical contexts. This does not make taxonomies invalid; a classificatory approach to monsters remains a necessary tool for a comprehensive understanding of the elements and attributes that constitute monstrosity, and of the *ratio* informing the poet's creation of monsters. This is especially so when monstrous beings appear continuously in a longer literary text, as in *The Faerie Queene*. The constraints of classification accentuate the illicit aspects of the hideous and ugly body, culminating in the interpretation of the monstrous signifier, an analytical process that establishes the monster as an eminently readable text *because* of its deformity.[25] Additionally, classification gives pressing evidence for the monster's tendency to work on all biological and ontological planes. As monsters are moving in and out of species categories, they threaten and in some cases entirely upset creational hierarchies by constantly advancing their territory, ultimately invading the realm of the human.

On the human plane, the monster's constant reflex to transgress species boundaries also stresses the overall susceptibility of organic, especially human forms to become monstrous. In a lecture on the relation between man and beast in Shakespeare's tragedies, Andreas Höfele argues that the essence of the human, which distinguishes God's supreme creation from other living beings, is unstable, and may be well-nigh eliminated in dramatic experiments that foreground a character's beastliness.[26] While drama, bound to the necessities of onstage representation, cannot fulfil such liquidations of the human entirely, an epic romance like *The Faerie Queene* surely can effect such changes because the poetic text can reify the permeability of physical boundaries, and hence depict, without inhibition, the change and obliteration of physical forms.

With monsters and monstrous beings leaving their indelible mark on the text and the plots of *The Faerie Queene*, the poem receives a precarious position in the anti-poetic discourse of the Renaissance, which stigmatised the imagination as a potentially monstrous agency. Elaborating on Cooper's notion of the monster as a sign requiring interpretation, Part III inquires, partly by elaborating on rhetorical issues raised on these pages, whether the analysis of the monstrosities and deformities can be brought

25 Cf., among others, Marjorie Garber's notes on Richard III's deformity in *Shakespeare's Ghost Writers: Literature as Uncanny Causality* (New York: Routledge, Chapman & Hall, 1988), p. 30.

26 See Andreas Höfele, *Zoologie der Tragödie: Von Menschen und Tieren bei Shakespeare. Vorgetragen am 26. Oktober 2002*, Schriften der Philosophisch-historischen Klasse der Heidelberger Akademie der Wissenschaften, 30 (Heidelberg: Winter, 2003), pp. 27–8.

to bear on a more theoretical discussion of the imaginative process generating the poem, and whether this offers insight into Spenser's role as the maker of Faeryland and the reader's task to interpret the poem.

PART III

Making monsters: The monstrous imagination and the poet's autonomy in *The Faerie Queene*

13

The problem of the literary monster in the discourse of the poetic imagination

In accord with Cooper's definition of *monstrum* as a deformity violating nature, the taxonomical discussion of Spenser's monsters carried out in Part II demonstrated how the plenitude of monstrous beings and deformities encroaches upon every level of animate and inanimate nature in *The Faerie Queene*. This raises the question why the monstrous figures so prominently in the poem, especially because monsters during the Renaissance often illustrated the faults of poetry, and were seen as symptoms of a diseased imagination. Taking up Cooper's definition of *monstrum* as a 'token or shewing: a thing that signifieth', the following chapters investigate the interaction between the monstrous text and these specific contemporary contexts, and brings into relief the self-reflexivity and autonomy with which the 'new Poete'[1] composes his prestigious work as a secondary nature or heterocosm defined by the presence of the monstrous. In order to establish the bearing of the monstrous on poetry and poetic theories, this chapter begins with an overview of critical Renaissance views that particularise the problem of the literary monster. The survey is followed by a discussion of the Renaissance concept of the poet as maker, especially as it is expounded in the works of Sidney and Puttenham.

The problem of the literary monster

A poet choosing monsters as a characteristic feature of his work engages with a major poetic controversy. The monstrous was so problematic that even poets were in two minds about its use in literary texts. On one end of the scale, Torquato Tasso, whose *Gerusalemme Liberata* was a major inspiration for *The Faerie Queene*, expresses strong reservations about the appearance of fantastic creatures in heroic poetry, pointing out that

1 Spenser is dubbed thus by E. K. in the letter to Gabriel Harvey, which is prefaced to the *Shepheardes Calender* (1579).

> Ma i Centauri, l'Arpie e i Ciclopi non sono adeguato principal subietto de la poesia, né i cavalli volanti e gli altri mostri de' quali son piene la favole de' romanzi.
>
> Centaurs, Harpies and Cyclopes are neither an adequate nor a principal subject for poetry, nor are flying horses and the other monsters that fill the fables of romance.[2]

Tasso's discussion of the 'fantastic imagination',[3] in which he mentions types of creatures that would also figure in *The Faerie Queene*, takes issue with Jacopo Mazzoni's defence of Dante's *Comoedia*,[4] and implicitly charges his romance predecessors like Boiardo and Ariosto with taking too much poetic licence, because good poetry is supposed to hold the mirror up to nature and not to stray beyond the paths of probability, or to annul the rules of physical nature altogether.[5] If this became the accepted view about monsters in poetry, it was by no means the only one. On the other end of the scale, Sir Philip Sidney, in his *The Defence of Poesy* (published in 1595, nine years after the poet's death), sees the excellence of the poet in his very fashioning 'quite anew, forms such as never were in nature, as the Heroes, Demigods, Cyclops, Chimeras, Furies, and such like'.[6] As the vast number of monsters appearing in literature, in printed books and manuscripts, in art and architecture shows, many creative artists did not necessarily share Tasso's misgivings about monsters, but

2 For the Italian text of Tasso's *Discorsi Dell' Arte Poetica E Del Poema Eroico*, see Torquato Tasso, *Prose*, ed. by Ettore Mazzali, La Letteratura Italiana: Storia e testi, 22 (Milan: Ricciardi, 1959), p. 527; the English translation is taken from: Torquato Tasso, *Discourses on the Heroic Poem*, trans. by Mariella Cavalchini and Irene Samuel (Oxford: Oxford University Press, 1973), p. 30. Tasso here directly refutes the concept of the imagination proposed by Mazzoni. Cf. also Syrithe Pugh, *Spenser and Ovid* (Aldershot: Ashgate, 2005), p. 52.

3 This also proves that Tasso, unlike the English writers, still distinguishes between *fantasia* and *imagination*. Hence, the phrase should not be read as pleonastic wordplay.

4 See Tasso, *Prose*, pp. 524–9, and, for the English translation, *Discourses*, pp. 28–32. Nohrnberg points out that Tasso bans monstrous creatures like the harpies, sphinxes and chimeras as well as strange and unknown monsters to the inferno in *Gerusalemme Liberata*, IV.5 (see *Analogy*, p. 761, note 55).

5 As early as 1572, Edward Dering branded the romances as 'childish follye' (*A briefe and necessary Instruction* (London: John Awdely, 1572), A.2v). Thomas Nashe labelled the romance *Bevis of Hampton*, Spenser's principal source for Book I and its final dragon fight, a textual absurdity (see Thomas Nashe, *Anatomie of Absurditie* in *The Works of Thomas Nashe*, ed. by R. B. McKerrow, 2nd edn, rev. by F. P. Wilson (Oxford: Oxford University Press, 1958), I, 26).

6 Sidney, *The Defence of Poesy*, p. 78. The quotation is taken from the definitive critical edition of Sidney's treatise in *Miscellaneous Prose of Sir Philip Sidney*, ed. by Katherine Duncan-Jones and Jan van Dorsten (Oxford: Clarendon Press, 1973), pp. 73–121.

exulted in the deviation from the norm to make their art more appealing.[7]

In early modern aesthetics, which depends very much on poetical formalism,[8] the discourse of the monstrous is used to criticise the contravention of poetical form, and to point to the precarious relation between poem, poet and audience. As monstrosity violates the governing force of harmony, it bodies forth the half-formed or misshaped text. This tenet originates from the preface of the *Ars poetica*, in which Horace asks his Pisonic readership whether a composite monster fashioned by a painter would not stir them into laughter:

> Humano capiti ceruicem pictor equinam
> iungere si uelit et uarias inducere plumas
> undique collatis membris, ut turpiter atrum
> desinat in piscem mulier formosa superne,
> spectatum admissi, risum teneatis, amici?

> If a painter wanted to join a horse's neck to a human head, and to spread different feathers on limbs collected from all over the place, so that a beautiful woman above ends as a foul black fish below, would you hold your laughter, if you were invited to view it, friends?[9]

Horace's monster, if read in anatomical terms, is a disproportionate compound made up of all classes of beings, ranging from human head and female torso to horse's neck, bird's feathers and fish's tail, which in turn refer to earth, fire, air and water. Horace additionally underlines the grotesque nature of this being by blending the rational with the irrational, and by combining the beautiful with the ugly. The 'miscarried' creature therefore sports the same chaotic mingling of elements, body parts and habitats that has already been observed in the Spenserian monsters.

7 Cf. Norman R. Smith's introductory remarks to his article 'Portentous Births and the Monstrous Imagination in Renaissance Culture' for a similar observation (in *Marvels, Monsters, and Miracles*, ed. by Jones and Sprunger, pp. 267–83 (pp. 267–9)).

8 For the early modern emphasis on poetical form, see George Puttenham's *The Arte of English Poesy* (1589), especially Books II and III, which contain long lists of devices and rhetorical 'colours'; see George Puttenham, *The Arte of English Poesy*, ed. by Gladys Doidge Willcock and Alice Walker (Cambridge: Cambridge University Press, 1936); the latest edition is *The Art of English Poesy: A Critical Edition*, ed. by Frank Whigham and Wayne A. Rebhorn (Ithaca and London: Cornell University Press, 2007).

9 Horace, *Ars poetica*, 1–5. The Latin text is taken from Horace, *Satires; Epistles; The Art of Poetry*, ed. and trans. by H. Rushton Fairclough, Loeb Classical Library (Cambridge, MA: Harvard University Press: London: Heinemann, 1929; repr. 1961); the translation is mine. In the late sixteenth and early seventeenth century, the Horatian creature was used by neo-classical critics to ridicule depictions of monsters in literature and painting (see Daston and Park, *Wonders and the Order of Nature*, p. 212).

Horace's half-jocose, half-serious refutation of the composite creature maligns grotesquery as something that cannot be taken seriously because it violates the norms of unity and credibility, and misdirects the viewers' responses.[10] In Horace's poetics, the creature therefore exemplifies the essence of the transgressive monstrous being.

Horace's grotesquely mismatched monster suggests an intertextual and conceptual link between transgressive monsters and the Renaissance emphasis on harmonious poetic form and beauty.[11] In her exhaustive monograph on Spenser's Ovidian origins and emulations, Syrithe Pugh has advanced such a connection between Horace's so-called 'Chimera' and, specifically, Spenser's Errour. While her argument rests on the unspecific, and hence disputable, observation that Errour's 'form resembles the opening image of Horace's *Ars Poetica*',[12] her claim that Errour 'disobeys the rules of unity', as well as her analogy between Errour's knotty winding tail and the entangled tales of heroic romance, indicates that Spenser's monstrous poem is diametrically opposed to the early modern paradigm of the unified artwork.[13] Indeed, the romance, Spenser's genre of choice, through its merging innumerable narrative strands and levels of diction, by definition violates the norms of poetry, so that it becomes a monster in itself.[14] The monstrous thus emerges as the marker of a 'miscarried' poem violating the unifying tenets of poetry.

Maybe the most telling evaluation of this tenet was uttered by Camillo Pellegrino, who, in his poetical treatise *Il carrafa* (published in 1586), critiques the romance as 'un mostro di più capi e di diverse membra non ordinate, che l'intelleto si stanca in considerarle'.[15] In order to under-

10 The beginning of the *Ars poetica* also prefigures Horace's important analogy between literature and the visual arts, which is most forcefully expressed in the dictum 'Ut pictura poesis' (Horace, *Ars*, 361).

11 See Hanafi, *Monster in the Machine*, p. 115: 'Monstrosity, like ugliness, is a lack of proper means and proportions between parts, the principles that define classical notions of beauty'.

12 Pugh, *Spenser and Ovid*, p. 51.

13 Pugh draws attention to the rich semantic breadth of the terms *knot* and *bought* in Spenser's description of Errour, with reference to the respective *OED* entries (see *Spenser and Ovid*, p. 51). Prime examples of interlaced narratives are Ovid's *Metamorphoses*, Boiardo's *Orlando Innamorato* and Ariosto's *Orlando Furioso*.

14 When discussing the logics of plot, Aristotle explains that the individual segments of an artefact need to correlate with one another (cf. *Poetics*, VIII, 1–4 (1451a)). As romance moves back and forth in time and space, and conjoins discordant sections, it does not consist of correlating elements. References are made to Aristotle, *The Poetics*, trans. by W. Hamilton Fyfe; 'Longinus', *On the Sublime*, trans. by W. Hamilton Fyfe; Demetrius, *On Style*, trans. by W. Rhys Roberts, Aristotle: Works 23, Loeb Classical Library, rev. edn (Cambridge, MA: Harvard University Press; London: Heinemann, 1932).

15 'a monster of many heads and various irregular limbs that tires the intellect considering

score the monstrosity of romance, Pellegrino yokes together two kinds of monsters into one powerful textual emblem, namely a polycephalic creature like the Hydra ('un mostro di più capi') with a composite being like the Chimera ('… di diverse membra non ordinate'). The romance is therefore even more monstrous than classical mythical creatures or Horace's own textual monster. The 'multiformity' of any work of literature points to the problem of invention in relation to the poet's obligation to imitate nature: if the poet does not narrow down his search for new matter, and if he uses too many sources and levels of diction injudiciously, his creative efforts result in a textual coagulation whose individual parts do not fit one another. Here the argument takes a decidedly generalising turn: any creature resembling Horace's 'Chimera' violates the precept of mimesis or imitation through its excess or licence, and is thus poetically undesirable.[16] On the meta-poetic level, the being sketched in the opening lines of Horace's *Ars* and the double monster described by Pellegrino both become emblems of the poem that is ill-conceived and badly put together, thereby making the defence of the imagination imperative.[17]

Another bone of contention in Renaissance poetic discourse was the influence that such miscarried poetry could exert on the reader. In a

---

them'; Camillo Pellegrino, *Il carrafa, o vero della epica poesia*, in *Trattati di poetica e retorica del cinquecento*, ed. by Bernard Weinberg, 4 vols (Bari: Laterza, 1983), III, 307–44 (p. 317). The sixteenth-century debate on (especially Ariosto's) heroic poetry, whose main exponents were Pellegrino and Salvati, is fully expounded in Daniel Javitch's *Proclaiming a Classic: The Canonisation of 'Orlando Furioso'* (Princeton: Princeton University Press, 1991), pp. 106–33. For the above translation of Pellegrino's original Italian, see p. 107 of Javitch's monograph. Matthew Woodcock makes a similar statement on the nature of the romances when explaining that the fifteenth-century French prose romance *Huon of Burdeux* (trans. into English in 1533) 'is something of a generic monster', because it 'brings together the feudal, homosocial world of Charlemagne and the *chanson de geste* with the fantastic commonplaces and amorous interactions of chivalric romance' ('Elf-Fashioning Revisited', p. 201).

16 While Plato uses μίμησις in the sense of imitation and treats it as a form of feigning (*Republic*, 598B–603A), Aristotle redefines it to mean any representation in words (*Poetics*, XXIII.1–7 (1459a)). He thus frees the poet from the necessity to depict what actually exists, and endows him with the freedom to describe what is probable and possible, a view which was adopted by early modern critics (see Claus Uhlig, 'Sidneys *Defence of Poesie* und die Poetik der Renaissance', in *Englische und amerikanische Literaturtheorie: Band I: Renaissance, Klassizismus und Romantik*, ed. by Rüdiger Ahrens and Erwin Wolff (Heidelberg: Winter, 1978), pp. 73–93 (pp. 77–82)). For Plato's text, see *Republic*, trans. by Paul Shorey, 2 vols, Plato: Works 5–6, Loeb Classical Library (Cambridge, MA: Harvard University Press; London: Heinemann, 1930 and 1935; repr. 2006).

17 On this connection, cf. James Biester, 'Fancy's Images: Wit, the Sublime, and the Rise of Aestheticism', in *Wonders, Marvels, and Monsters in Early Modern Culture*, ed. by Peter G. Platt (Newark: University of Delaware Press, 2000), pp. 294–327 (p. 297).

famous statement that may also refer to the Italian romances by Boiardo and Ariosto, Roger Ascham rants against the (especially Italian) siren song that transforms an English reader into a

> meruelous monster, which, for filthines of liuyng, for dulnes to learning him selfe, for wilinesse in dealing with others, for malice in hurting without cause, should carie at once in one bodie, the belie of a Swyne, the head of an Asse, the brayne of a Foxe, the womb of a wolfe.[18]

Ascham here moralises the transformative quality of 'luxurious' literature, and explains that Italian poetry exerts a power over the reader that is reminiscent of Circe's transforming her victims into pigs, foxes, asses and wolves.[19] The communicative act of reading is thus brought under the suspicion of 'othering' the readers through accessing their unrestrained imagination.[20] In such passages, early modern poetic theorists draw on a basic rhetoric of the deformed that was also used by medical writers like Timothy Bright and Robert Burton, who anatomised the effects of an imagination turning monstrous under the influence of melancholy.[21] Conceiving of the monstrous along similar parameters, both types of writers engage in a mutual dialogue that demonstrates how a hypertrophic imagination could affect the human being.

Ultimately, the problem of the monstrous text and image points directly to the poet. Stephen Gosson famously turned the poet into a monster who brings forth a horrible textual spawn: 'So grosse are the errours, so great the abuses, so horrible the blasphemies we finde in Poetes, that wee

18 Roger Ascham, *The Schoolmaster*; the text is taken from *English Works of Roger Ascham: Toxophilus, Report of the Affairs and State of Germany, The Schoolmaster*, ed. by William Aldis Wright (Cambridge: Cambridge University Press, 1904), p. 228. For the '*Siren* songes of *Italie*', see p. 226.

19 It is also reminiscent of the connection between sins and animals found throughout the Middle Ages. Cf. especially Boethius, *Consolatio Philosophiae* IV.Pr.3. Gosson draws on the same rhetoric when criticising fiction as 'the Cuppes of *Circe*, that turn reasonable Creatures into brute Beastes' (Stephen Gosson, *The School of Abuse and A Short Apologie for the Schoole of Abuse*, ed. by E. Arber, English Reprints (London: Murray, 1868), p. 77).

20 Spenser takes up the charge of feeding his youthful readers' fancy for love and folly in IV.Pr.1.6–9.

21 See Timothy Bright, *A Treatise of Melancholie*. Reproduced from the 1586 edition printed by Thomas Vautrollier, with an introduction by Hardin Craig, Publication No. 50 of the Facsimile Text Society (New York: Columbia University Press, 1940); Robert Burton, *The Anatomy of Melancholy*, ed. by Holbrook Jackson, 3 vols (London: J. M. Dent, 1932; repr. 1964). Cf. Günter Ahrends, 'Transformationen des Subjekts und der Realität: Konzepte der Imagination im medizinischen und poetologischen Diskurs der englischen Renaissance', in *Zum Begriff der Imagination in Dichtung und Dichtungstheorie: Festschrift für Rainer Lengeler zum 65. Geburtstag*, ed. by Manfred Beyer (Trier: Wissenschaftlicher Verlag Trier, 1998), pp. 1–15 (p. 4). The works by Bright and Burton are discussed in Chapter 16, 'Animating the monstrous imagination', below.

may rather judge them monsters of nature, then men of learning'.[22] In a discourse that attacks both the work of art and its addressees as potential monstrous others, even the author of such a work becomes suspect to the charges of deviation and otherness.

The poet and the literary monster

As a poem replete with monstrous beings and written in a genre suspected of monstrosity, *The Faerie Queene* lies at the very heart of early modern poetic controversy. Spenser, a poet whose work displays a high degree of self-consciousness,[23] was fully aware of the precarious reputation of poets and their fantastic works, and consequently of the monstrosity of his epic romance.[24] In a cultural milieu where each and every aspect of poetry could become a monstrosity, Spenser's use of the monstrous is all the more significant, even if it was not without precedents. A positive evaluation of the poet's creative powers that also includes monsters figures in the earliest comprehensive English poetics, namely Sidney's *The Defence of Poesy*, a text which S. K. Heninger, Jr, sees as a 'sophisticated apology for the human imagination'.[25] The poet, Sidney writes,

> lifted up with the vigour of his own invention, doth grow in effect another nature, in making things either better than nature bringeth forth, or, quite anew, forms such as never were in nature, as the Heroes, Demigods, Cyclops, Chimeras, Furies, and such like: so as he goeth hand in hand with nature, not enclosed within the narrow warrant of her gifts, but freely ranging only within the zodiac of his own wit. Nature never set forth the earth in so rich tapestry as diverse poets have done[.][26]

In this passage, Sidney fervently praises the poet as a creator bringing to life a second nature into which he also places hitherto unknown creatures and monsters. Sidney is deliberately tapping into the loaded early modern discourse on monstrosity outlined above, a circumstance which gives the passage more weight than its length would suggest. The monsters Sidney cites as examples form a deliberately composed triad. The 'Cyclops,

22 Stephen Gosson, *School of Abuse*, p. 67.

23 On Spenser's self-consciousness, see A. Bartlett Giamatti, *Play of Double Senses: Spenser's 'Faerie Queene'* (Englewood Cliffs, London: Prentice-Hall, 1975), pp. 106–17 (p. 106).

24 See, e.g., Spenser's self-reflexive remarks in the 'Letter', and the proems to the individual books of *The Faerie Queene*, esp. to Books II and VI.

25 S. K. Heninger, Jr, 'The Aesthetic Experience of Reading Spenser', in *Contemporary Thought on Edmund Spenser*, ed. by Richard C. Frushell and Bernard J. Vondersmith (Carbondale: Southern Illinois University Press, 1975), pp. 79–98 (p. 85).

26 Sidney, *Defence*, p. 78.

Chimeras, Furies' provide a miniature taxonomy of possible monstrous beings, with the one-eyed Cyclops representing giants and strange races, Chimeras epitomising composite monsters and Furies exemplifying human–animal composites. Sidney thus shows his awareness of the teratological possibilities informing the making of mythological creatures, as well as its usefulness for making exciting poetry. Quite surprisingly, Sidney does not only refrain from stigmatising fantastic creatures *a priori* but evaluates them as constituent parts in the poet's world-making. Monsters, not only the half-divine but also the significantly hideous, become, up to a point, the yardstick of poetic achievement.

Sidney indeed makes room for the existence of monsters as useful poetic images elsewhere in the *Defence*, although less explicitly than in the *natura altera* passage. When discussing the notion of *movere*, he cites Aristotle, who maintained that 'those things which in themselves are horrible, as cruel battles, unnatural monsters, are made in poetical imitation delightful'.[27] The source of Sidney's quotation is *Poetics*, IV.3, where Aristotle explains that the description of 'especially unsightly animals' can bring enjoyment, provided they are described in a feasible manner.[28] As Sidney mentions 'unnatural monsters' rather than the ugly animals of Aristotle's original, this passage supplements the note on 'Cyclops, Chimeras, Furies' appearing in the poet's golden world: the 'unnatural monsters' are claimed as elements of poetic imitation which can delight readers, and become essential ingredients in the poetic artwork. Sidney's positive revisionist assessment of the poet and his creative powers runs counter to received anti-poetic views that make the poet who creates a new world and populates it with monsters open to the charge of creative over-indulgence. His theory also suggests that poetry, by dint of the imagination, is a privileged art form that can disconnect itself from empirical reality to form new beings and to create a secondary world entirely on its own while drawing on perceived reality. This tension is made manifest in Sidney's conflicting statements that the poet goes 'hand in hand with nature' but is not 'enclosed within the narrow warrant of her gifts'.[29]

27 Sidney, *Defence*, p. 92.

28 See Aristotle, *Poetics*, IV.3 (1448b): 'οἷον θηρίων τε μορφὰς τῶν ἀτιμοτάτων'; my translation.

29 This is the classical history versus poetry argument. See Inge Leimberg, 'Die Dichtungstheorie der englischen Renaissance unter dem Gesichtspunkt von Kunst und Natur', in *Englische und amerikanische Literaturtheorie*, ed. by Ahrens and Wolff, pp. 94–120 (pp. 103–4). She points out that Sidney's argument bypasses the opposition between nature and art, and thus puts prime emphasis on the whole process of poetic creation (see p. 101). Lobsien characterises the transforming power of the imagination as a key quality of poetic making (see *Imaginationswelten*, pp. 22–6).

Sidney's remarks call to mind a slightly earlier statement by J. C. Scaliger, who observes in his *Poetices libri septem* (1562) that poets can create a *natura altera*, for they do not retell events like historians, but create new lives and matters like a second god:

> At poeta et naturam alteram et fortunas plures etiam ac demum sese istoc ipso perinde ac deum alterum efficit. Nam quae omnium opifex condidit, eorum reliquiae scientiae tamquam actores sunt. Poetica vero, cum et speciosius quae sunt et quae non sunt eorum speciem ponit, videtur sane res ipsas non ut aliae quasi histrio narrare, sed velut alter deus condere.

> But the poet creates both a second nature and even more fortunes, and thereby then turns himself, as it were, into a second god. For what the maker of all created, the remaining sciences merely act. But poetry, since it presents more beautifully both what exists and what does not exist at all, does indeed not seem to narrate these matters like the others, just as an actor does, but to create them like a second god.[30]

Scaliger grants the poet the title of *deus alter*, and thus endows him with the liberty to create a *natura altera* with new characters and stories. Such abilities assign him a higher status than scientists or historians. However, the phrase '*velut* alter deus', '*like* another god' (emphases added) shows that Scaliger still thinks in analogies and does not see the poet as a creator *sui generis*.[31] Nevertheless his poetical statement might contain the germ of Sidney's theory, which of course goes one decisive step further when emphasising the possibility of a more autonomous kind of poetry that can create its own poetical world and populate it with monstrous beings.[32]

Sidney's appreciation of the poet's creative abilities is directly related to the etymology of the word *poet*, which, Sidney explains, derives from Old Greek ποιεῖν, 'to make':

> The Greeks called him a 'poet', which name hath, as the most excellent, gone through other languages. It cometh of this word ποιεῖν, which is to

30 Julius Caesar Scaliger, *Poetices libri septem: Sieben Bücher über die Dichtkunst*, ed., trans. and intr. by Luc Deitz, 5 vols (Stuttgart–Bad Cannstadt: Frommann-Holzboog, 1994–2003), I (1994), 70–2 (Ch. 3); the translation is mine. Cf. also Baxter Hathaway, *Marvels and Commonplaces: Renaissance Literary Criticism*, Studies in Language and Literature, 23 (New York: Random House, 1968), p. 89.

31 Puttenham similarly maintains that poets are 'as creating gods' (*Arte*, p. 4).

32 For a similar interpretation, see Uhlig, who argues that Sidney's passage reads 'als sei der nachahmend schaffende "right poet" an die Stelle Gottes selbst getreten' ('as if the imitating "right poet" had taken God's place'; 'Sidney's *Defence*', p. 81). Lobsien does not acknowledge this distinction (see *Imaginationswelten*, p. 34, n. 67). Sidney however never likens the poet directly to God (see Volkhard Wels, 'Imaginatio oder Inventio: Das dichterische Schaffen und sein Gegenstand in Puttenham, Sidney und Temple', *Poetica* 37 (2005), 65–91 (pp. 81–2, and n. 30)).

make; wherein, I know not whether by luck or wisdom, we Englishmen have met with the Greeks in calling him a Maker[.][33]

This definition, which had a high currency in the Renaissance, characterises the poet as a maker of the manifest textual artwork through his own creative efforts.[34] Similar etymologies are given in William Webbe's *A Discourse of English Poetrie* (1586)[35] and George Puttenham's magisterial *The Arte of English Poesie* (1589).[36] Spenser himself must have been fully aware of the office he had to fulfil as a poet, since E. K., the elusive annotator of *The Shepheardes Calender* (1579), glosses the verb *to make* as 'to rime and versifye', and also explains the word *poet* etymologically.[37] Triangulated from these critical views, Spenser's *The Faerie Queene* emerges at a time when poetry was elevated to the work of an ambitious maker who sought to create a rich textual world.[38]

The fullness of this new poetic world, which Sidney describes as a 'rich tapestry', originates from the poet's power of 'invention' and 'wit',[39] two terms that are closely associated with the workings of the human imagination, the source of the poet's creative work.[40] Sidney explicitly establishes

33 Sidney, *Defence*, p. 77; for a full discussion of Sidney's view of the poet, see Shepherd, 'Introduction', pp. 75–9.

34 On the poet as maker, see generally Heninger, *Touches of Sweet Harmony: Pythagorean Cosmology and Renaissance Poetics* (San Marino: The Huntington Library, 1974), pp. 287–324.

35 In the *Discourse of English Poetrie*, William Webbe calls poetry 'the arte of making', and deems the term *poet* a title of honour; see Webbe, *A Discourse of English Poetrie. Together with the Authors Iudgment, Touching the Reformation of Our English Verse* (London, 1586), in *Elizabethan Critical Essays*, ed. by Smith, II, 230. On Sidney's definition, cf. also William Nelson, 'The Boundaries of Fiction in the Renaissance: A Treaty Between Truth and Falsehood', *English Literary History* 36 (1969), 30–58 (pp. 46–50).

36 See Puttenham, *Arte*, p. 3.

37 See E. K.'s note to Spenser's 'April Eclogue'. The late medieval Scots poets like Henryson and Dunbar were also known as *makars*, i.e. 'makers'.

38 Heninger argues that Spenser demonstrates Sidney's concept of ποιεῖν through his poetry (see *Touches of Sweet Harmony*, pp. 296–7).

39 Bundy argues that invention was progressively identified with imagination in the sixteenth century (see '"Invention" and "Imagination"', p. 542). In the *Naugerius*, Fracastoro emphasises the importance of *inventio*, whereby poets 'add sublimity and wonder to discourse' ('haec tum magnitudinem, tūum admirationēem affere sermoni solent'; see Girolamo Fracastoro, *Naugerius, sive de poetica dialogus*, trans. by Ruth Kelso, with an introduction by Murray W. Bundy, University of Illinois Studies in Language and Literature, Vol. IX, No. 3 (Urbana: University of Illinois, 1924), p. 128 and p. 41). See also de Ronsard, *Abbregé de l'Art poétique françois* (in *Œuvres complètes*, II, 1178), and Gascoigne, *Certayne Notes* (in *Elizabethan Critical Essays*, I, 47–8); these texts are treated in Wels, 'Imaginatio oder Inventio', pp. 66–7, and Heninger, *Touches of Sweet Harmony*, p. 294.

40 This view is stated in John Huarte's widely read *Examen de ingenios*: 'From a good imagination, spring all the Arts and Sciences, which consist in figure, correspondence, harmonie and proportion: such are Poetrie, Eloquence, and the skill of preaching: the

the imagination as an independent faculty where the idea is located.[41] The imagination furnishes the poet with the divine potency to effect a second creation out of the chaos of sounds and signs, and to turn ideas, i.e. ideal images, into fore-conceits, and finally into proper conceits.[42] The latter lend an idealness to the fictional world which surpasses factual reality:[43] in the writer's creative faculty, the ideal image becomes an image in his mind, which then is reified as an image or representation in his poem.[44] From there, the speaking picture is transmitted to the reader's imagination,[45] where it participates in elevating the human soul by the 'purifying of wit', which consists in the 'enriching of memory, enabling of judgement, and enlarging of conceit'. Sidney here explains that the poetic image is a powerful didactic tool because it activates and elevates the three major faculties of the soul: memory, judgement and the imagination, which he here calls 'conceit'. For Sidney, the imagination hence plays a decisive role in humanist education.

George Puttenham, in his *Arte of English Poesie*, additionally establishes an analogy between the imagination and the poet's divine nature when he explains that the poet resembles God in His making:

> Such as (by way of resemblance and reuerently) we may say of God: who without any trauell [i.e. study, labour] to his diuine imagination, made all the world of nought, nor also by any paterne or mould as the Platonicks with their Idees do phantastically suppose. Euen so the very Poet makes and contriues out of his owne braine, both the verse and matter of his poeme, and not by any foreine copie or example, as doth the translator, who therefore may well be sayd a versifier, but not a Poet.[46]

---

practise of Phisicke, the Mathematicals, Astrologie and the gouerning of a Commonwealth, the art of Warfare, Paynting, drawing, writing, reading, to be a man gratious, pleasant, neat, wittie in managing, and all the engins and devises which artificers make.' The text is taken from Juan Huarte, *The Examination of mans Wits* [*Examen de ingenios*], trans. out of the Spanish tongue by M. Camillo Camili, Englished out of his Italian, by R. C. Esquire (London: Adam Islip, 1594), p. 103.

41 Also noted by Herman, *Squitter-wits*, p. 67.

42 See Sidney, *Defence*, p. 79. Wood gives a good explanation of the three stages of poetic creation in Sidney's *Defence* (see *Metaphor and Belief*, p. 95). On idea and fore-conceit, cf. also Forrest G. Robinson, *The Shape of Things Known: Sidney's 'Apology' in Its Philosophical Tradition* (Cambridge, MA: Harvard University Press, 1972), pp. 108–22.

43 On the idealness of the poetic image, see Herman, *Squitter-wits*, pp. 66–7, and Wels, 'Imaginatio oder Inventio', p. 79.

44 Cf. Theseus's speech in Shakespeare's *Midsummer Night's Dream*, V.i.14–17: 'And as imagination bodies forth / The forms of things unknown, the poet's pen / Turns them to shapes, and gives to airy nothing / A local habitation and a name.'

45 On the poet's planting images in the reader's mind, see *Defence*, pp. 85 and 92, and the discussion of Sidney's poetics in Chapter 18.

46 Puttenham, *Arte*, p. 3. He differs from Sidney in considering verse as the central part of

In order to elevate the status of the poet and his imagination, Puttenham draws an extended simile between God, whose 'diuine imagination' effortlessly created the world out of nothing, and the poet, who 'makes and contriues out of his owne braine both the verse and matter of his poeme'.[47] On one level, Puttenham here introduces the argument of form ('verse') and content ('matter') into his discussion of the poet, and thereby stresses the necessity of an artistic pattern in which the poet can place his subject matter. In the wider context of the argument, the analogy also suggests the poet's producing his work almost *ex deo*, an observation that puts emphasis on the creative energy of the imagination.[48] Hence, to Puttenham, the poet is an agent invested with the power of making: God's effortless creation of the universe through the workings of His imagination resembles the poet's exercising his *fantasia* to bring forth new texts.[49] In marked unison with Sidney, Puttenham therefore sees the imagination as a divine gift, or, in other words, as a creative faculty that results from man's divine heritage.[50] Both perspectives establish the poet as a genuine creator figure with the ability to fashion a poem, both in form

---

literary works (cf. also Jürgen Schäfer, '"Twins by Birth": Literaturtheoretische Aspekte elisabethanischer Rhetorik', in *Englische und amerikanische Literaturtheorie*, ed. by Ahrens and Wolff, pp. 45–72 (p. 59)).

47 Patricia A. Parker refers the idea of God as maker to Boethius and Tasso in *Inescapable Romance: Studies in the Poetics of a Mode* (Princeton: Princeton University Press, 1979), pp. 60–1.

48 In 1574, Thomas Blundeville had expressed the relation between creation and poetic making thus: 'Of those that make anye thyng, some doe make much of nothing, as God dyd in creating the Worlde of naught, and as Poets in some respect also doe, whilest they fain fables and make thereof theyr poesies, and poeticall Hystories'; Thomas Blundeville, *The True Order and Methode of Wryting and Reading Hystories*, ed. by Hans Peter Heinrich, Bibliotheca Humanistica, 2 (Frankfurt am Main: Lang, 1986), pp. 39–40. Heninger quotes Landino's commentary on Dante's *Comoedia*: 'therefore the figment of the poet is not completely out of nothing, yet it departs from "making" and comes very close to "creating"' (*Touches of Sweet Harmony*, p. 289). For a discussion of the Renaissance analogy between physical procreation and artistic propagation, see Chapter 16, below.

49 See Puttenham, *Arte*, p. 4: 'It is therefore of Poets thus to be conceiued, that if they be able to deuise and make all these things of them selues, without any subiect of veritie, that they be (by a maner of speech) as creating gods'.

50 The entire passage in the *Arte* runs as follows (Puttenham, *Arte*, p. 3): 'And this science in his perfection, can not grow, but by some diuine instinct, the Platonicks call it furor: or by excellencie of nature and complexion: or by great subtiltie of the spirits & wit, or by much experience and obseruation of the world, and course of kinde, or/peraduenture by all or most part of them.' I underwrite Heninger's view that Puttenham seems to favour the combination of these individual elements (see Heninger, *Touches*, pp. 304–5). Dorothee Rölli-Alkemper, *Höfische Poetik in der englischen Renaissance: George Puttenhams 'The Arte of English Poesie' (1589)*, Figuren 4 (Munich: Fink, 1996), p. 47, also follows Heninger's argument.

and in content, through the God-given powers residing in his mind, thus heralding the poet's sovereignty over his own creations. Positioned in this poetical discourse, Spenser's *The Faerie Queene* becomes the textual manifestation of the poet in charge of his own invention. The degree of self-reflexivity traceable in Spenser's proems to the individual books of his epic romance,[51] and especially the deliberation expressed in his 'Letter to Raleigh', which is replete with synonyms of active poetic making, place the 'new Poete' in the poetic development marked by Sidney and Puttenham.[52] If contextualised into Sidney's poetics, the poet of Faeryland is a maker who consciously fashions and manufactures his poem as a textual entity, and, as Sidney had argued, in this entity there is also space for the monstrous. When inventing and composing *The Faerie Queene*, Spenser, like Sidney's ideal poet, 'doth grow … another nature', and creates a new poetic world constituted by a novel realm, infinite inhabitants and fantastic beings.

The problem of the fantastical imagination

Sidney's theory of the secondary world did not, however, make the imagination less problematic and the monster more desirable. Among other things, the imagination was deemed ambiguous, because it uneasily connected the lunatic with the deluded lover and the poet, as Theseus reminds us right before the craftsmen enact their version of Pyramus and Thisbe in Shakespeare's *A Midsummer Night's Dream*.[53] Pierre de LaPrimaudaye stresses the controversial nature of the imagination when he more specifically reprehends the imagination for the 'newe and monstrous things it forgeth and coyneth'.[54] Thus under suspicion, poetry needed to be defended on the grounds of the images it created. In order to exculpate the poets from these charges, Sidney and Puttenham both

51 The proem to Book II is discussed in Chapter 14, below.

52 See also Spenser's use of verbs like *to fashion* ('Letter', 7–9 and 36), *to labour* ('Letter', 9, 29 and 33), *to form* ('Letter', 16) and *to conceive* ('Letter', 18, 28; *conceit*: 'Letter', 2, and 83).

53 For the whole speech, see Shakespeare's *A Midsummer Night's Dream*, V.i.4–22. For an elucidating interpretation of this passage, which can also be brought to bear on Spenser's poem, see Heinrich F. Plett, '"…of imagination all compact": Ein metapoetischer Kommentar zu Shakespeares *Sommernachtstraum* V.i.4–22', in *Zum Begriff der Imagination*, ed. by Bayer, pp. 16–33.

54 Pierre de LaPrimaudaye, *The Second Part of the French Academie*, pp. 154–7 (p. 156). Excellent overviews of early modern theories of the imagination in faulty psychology are given by William Rossky, 'Imagination in the English Renaissance: Psychology and Poetic', *Studies in the Renaissance* 5 (1958), 49–73, and Ahrends, 'Transformationen', pp. 1–15.

offer insightful taxonomies that ultimately engage with Spenser's literary monsters and the secondary world that harbours them.

Sidney frees the poet from the traditional charges of vanity and madness by distinguishing between two kinds of poetic images brought forth by the imagination: namely *eikastike*, the 'figuring forth good things', and *phantastike*, which 'doth infect the fancy with unworthy objects'.[55] While the former is a speaking image, a meaningful manifestation of sense and beauty produced by a proper, deliberate imitation, the latter is a mere dream appearance, which afflicts the soul like a contagious disease.[56] In the larger discourse of the imagination, Sidney's definition is a notable attempt at unravelling the tangled discursive skein into which the imagination had developed: as the Platonic distinction between the two types of imagination – namely εἰκαστική, which created likeness through reproducing images, and φανταστική, which recombined perceived material – had by and large vanished,[57] the word 'imagination' had become synonymous with 'fancy' or 'fantasy'.[58] By distinguishing between *eikastike* and *phantastike*, i.e. between truthful and delusive images, Sidney hence seeks to re-establish a clear distinction between types of imagination that would ultimately exculpate the poet from the charges of uninhibited, miscarried making.[59]

55 Sidney, *Defence*, p. 104.

56 The evaluation of 'bad fancy' as a disease resembles the argumentation of the medical writers. Sidney's exact source for the distinction between *eikastike* and *phantastike* is still open to some discussion. Heninger argues that the classification originates from Jean de Serres's introduction to his translation of Plato's *Ion* ('Sidney and Serranus' *Plato*', in *Sidney in Retrospect: Selections from 'English Literary Renaissance'*, ed. by Arthur F. Kinney (Amherst, MA: University of Massachusetts Press, 1988), pp. 27–44), while Plett ('"… of imagination all compact"', pp. 26–7), Madsen (note to *Defence*, p. 104, ll. 19–20) and Herman (*Squitter-wits*, pp. 85–7 and pp. 235–6, note 42) refer it to Plato's *Sophist*, 235–36D (for the text, see Plato, *Theaetetus; Sophist*, trans. by Harold North Fowler, Plato: Works 7, Loeb Classical Library (Cambridge, MA: Harvard University Press; London: Heinemann, 1921; repr. 1999)).

57 See Plato, *Sophist*, 236B–C. Bundy refers this polarity back to the Stoic tradition; in this classification, the imagination serves the function of merely reproducing images, whereas fantasy has the power to recombine images and other sense perceptions; see *The Theory of Imagination in Classical and Mediaeval Thought*, University of Illinois Studies in Language and Literature 12, Nos 2–3 (Urbana: University of Illinois Press, 1927; facsimile Norwood: Norwood Editions, 1978), pp. 89–92 and pp. 278–9.

58 Conclusive evidence for the confusion between imagination and fantasy figures in John Davis of Hereford's *Mirum in Modum*, and Pierre de LaPrimaudaye's *French Academie* (see John Davies of Hereford, *Complete Works*, I, 6; and Pierre de LaPrimaudaye, *The Second Part of the French Academie*, p. 155 and p. 157). Cf. Rossky, 'Imagination', p. 50, n. 4, and Ahrends, 'Transformationen', p. 5, n. 17.

59 Such arguments aimed at the courtly and 'public' exculpation of the poet and his literary works. Cf. Rossky, 'Imagination', p. 64.

In a distinction that recalls Sidney's telling good images from misleading ones, Puttenham differentiates between two kinds of poets to define the differences between the various creations of the imagination:[60]

> Euen so is the phantasticall part of man (if it be not disordered) a representer of the best, most comely and bewtifull images or apparances of thinges to the soule and according to their very truth. If otherwise, then doth it breede Chimeres & monsters in mans imaginations, & not onely in his imaginations, but also in all his ordinarie actions and life which ensues. Wherefore such persons as be illuminated with the brightest irradiations of knowledge and of the veritie and due proportion of things, they are called by the learned men not phantastici but euphantasiote, and of this sorte of phantasie are all good Poets …, in whose exercises the inuentiue part is most employed and is to the sound & true iudgement of man most needful.[61]

Puttenham's argument rests on the ability to tell the beautiful from the ugly, the well-proportioned from the deformed; it also separates the uniform from the multiform, as the reference to the Chimera suggests.[62] With regard to teratology, this is a notable point of departure from Sidney's appraisal of the world-making poet: Puttenham conjures up the image of the Chimera as the prime example of the fantastic and malfunctioning imagination, while Sidney ranks this mythic monster as a potential marker of the poet's creating a secondary nature.[63] In addition, Puttenham's choice of the word 'breede' marks unrestrained poetic making as procreation and propagation in a most unwholesome sense. The argument culminates in a distinction between good and bad poets.[64] The

60 The exact relation between the Sidney's *Defence* and Puttenham's *Arte* can be gathered only by circumstantial evidence, as Puttenham never mentions Sidney's treatise explicitly. Since Puttenham quoted frequently from Sidney's poems at a time when they circulated only in manuscript form, and as John Harington commented on the excellence of the *Defence* in the 'Preface' for his translation of Ariosto's *Orlando Furioso* before Sidney's work had been published, Puttenham might in fact have had access to Sidney's poetics. Hathaway is not quite so cautious when he maintains that 'Puttenham obviously copied Sidney in many respects' (*Marvels and Commonplaces*, p. 97).

61 Puttenham, *Arte*, pp. 19–20; he illustrates the two kinds of imagination as two types of mirrors, one of which reflects an object truthfully, while the other distorts it (cf. also Rölli-Alkemper, *Höfische Poetik*, p. 53).

62 The conceptual link between the two paradigms becomes apparent when Burton's frequent references to deformed shapes (such as chimeras), and fantastic locales (as e.g. castles in the air) are taken into consideration. See, among others, Burton, *Anatomy*, I, 254.

63 See Sidney, *Defence*, p. 78. As infamous spawn and dam of monsters, the Chimera is the epitome of all that is monstrous and multiform: she is the offspring of Echidna and Typhon, and, in turn, mother to a host of other notorious creatures, among them the Hydra, the Sphinx, and Cerberus (cf. also Rossky, 'Imagination', p. 60).

64 Wels argues with some justification that Puttenham does not strictly differentiate between two types of poets, but more generally tells madmen from people whose reason

so-called '*phantastici*' are poets with an overactive, because overheated, imagination, whose infected brain hampers their 'sounde iudgment' with grotesque shapes.[65] The '*euphantasiotae*' have an imagination controlled by reason, which assists them in conceiving images useful for the poet's moral aim.[66] Unlike the 'monstrous imaginations or conceits', these images are characterised by poetic form; they are like a glass in which the reader can glance at beautiful visions,[67] and gather insight into a better *modus vivendi*. Whereas Sidney's argument allows for the existence of prodigious monsters if certain conditions be kept, Puttenham's more categorical approach stigmatises creative artists that overstep the boundaries of normative representation as 'phantastics'. [68] Puttenham thus does not advocate the concept of a second nature created by the poet,[69] but admits that the imagination can create wonderful images and bring them to the viewer's soul, provided that the poet's reason remains in charge. The imagination is therefore the handmaiden of invention,[70] and the *sine qua non* for human understanding.[71] If the imagination becomes hypertro-

is in charge of their imagination. I would contend that Puttenham implies the distinction between two kinds of poets when maintaining that 'all good poets' are '*euphantasiote*' (Puttenham, *Arte*, pp. 19–20).

65 Puttenham, *Arte*, pp. 18–19.

66 For the synthesis of the imagination and judgement, see Puttenham, *Arte*, p. 19. Puttenham defines 'the instruction of morall doctrines' as one of the major functions of the poet (*Arte*, p. 24). Cf. also Plett, '"… of imagination all compact"', pp. 26–7. Rölli-Alkemper derives Puttenham's '-ωτοι' ending from Quintilian's terminology in the *Institutio oratoria*, VI.ii.29–31, which defines an εὐφαντασίωτος as an especially gifted poet (see *Höfische Poetik*, p. 54; for the Latin text and English translation, see Quintilian, *Institutio oratoria*, trans. by H. E. Butler, 4 vols (London: Heinemann; Cambridge, MA: Harvard University Press, 1960), II, 432–5).

67 Patricia Springborg contextualises the glass image in early modern mirror theory, and emphasises its significance for the concept of the imagination (see 'Leviathan, Mythic History, and National Historiography', in *The Historical Imagination in Early Modern Britain: History, Rhetoric, and Fiction, 1500–1800*, ed. by Donald R. Kelley and David Harris Sacks (Cambridge: Cambridge University Press, 1997), pp. 267–97 (pp. 280–1)). Possibly the fullest account of the looking glass as metaphor is Herbert Grabes's *Speculum, mirror und looking-glass*, which relates Puttenham's passage to its contemporary discourse (see *Speculum, mirror und looking-glass: Kontinuität und Originalität der Spiegelmetapher in den Buchtiteln des Mittelalters und der englischen Literatur des 13. bis 17. Jahrhunderts*, Buchreihe der Anglia, 16 (Tübingen: Niemeyer, 1973), pp. 96–8).

68 Cf. Ahrends, 'Transformationen', pp. 13–14.

69 For a similar statement, cf. Ahrends, 'Transformationen', p. 12.

70 At the end of the *Arte*, Puttenham again stresses that poetic creation relies on 'an excellent sharpe and quick inuention, holpen by a cleare and bright phantasie and imagination' (*Arte*, p. 307). Hence, Puttenham sees invention as the close ally of an inspiring imagination.

71 See also Thomas Wright's verdict that 'whatsoever we vnderstand, passeth by the gates of our imagination' (*The Passions of the minde in generall* (London: Valentine Simmes, 1604), p. 51). Rossky, who also quotes this passage, gives an in-a-nutshell description of

phic, these newly fashioned images become distorted, lose their mimetic quality, and are merely fantastical, as the reference to the Chimeras suggests.[72] Like Sidney's telling *eikastike* from *phantastike*, Puttenham's distinguishing between *phantastici* and *euphantasiote* argues in favour of a 'good' imagination creating 'useful' images. Thus used, the imagination, according to Broaddus, can be 'deliberate and purposeful, moral and rational'.[73]

Spenser's interaction with contemporary poetics is rendered problematic by his liberal use of the monstrous, which usually suggests a malfunctioning imagination. In the following, I will address a number of important queries that bring light to Spenser's idea of the monster-creating poet: Chapter 14, 'The monstrous and the literary heterocosm', places Spenser's poem of monsters, new realms and characters in the emerging tradition of what M. H. Abrams terms the 'heterocosm', and establishes the entire poem as just such a textual realm, which seventeenth-century critics significantly characterised as a place where the monster runs rampant. Chapter 15, 'In Phantastes's chamber', presents Spenser's allegory of Alma's Castle with particular emphasis on its tripartite brain turret (II.ix), and discusses how the sequence elaborates on the power of transformation and the making of monstrous images. Chapter 16, 'Animating the monstrous imagination in *The Faerie Queene*', argues that Spenser conceives his text as a breeding ground for monsters and monstrous beings. Chapter 17, 'Poetic creation: Spenser as Prometheus', more specifically deals with the creation of monstrous beings on the basis of Spenser's version of the Prometheus myth in Book II, Canto x. Chapter 18, 'The poet's autonomy and the use of the monstrous' addresses the use of the transformative imagination by setting Spenser's poetical practice against tenets uttered in Puttenham's and Sidney's poetic treatises. Finally, Chapter 19, 'Interpreting the monstrous', elaborates on the problems the interpretation of monsters and monstrous beings poses for the reader of Spenser's allegorical poem and brings this discussion to bear on the Blatant Beast's escape from Faeryland.

---

the process of cognition in the internal faculties (see 'Imagination', p. 51).

72 Biester explains that the fantastic imagination according to Puttenham is 'not an autonomous imagination working miracles but simply disease' ('Fancy's Images', p. 297).

73 Broaddus, 'Britomart's Adventures', p. 190.

14

The monstrous and the literary heterocosm

Spenser's interaction with contemporary poetics is both complicated and determined by his use of the monstrous: complicated, because monsters in poetry usually suggest a malfunctioning imagination and are hence reprehensible; determined, because the monstrous was, according to Sidney, one manifestation of the maker creating 'another nature'. M. H. Abrams sees in the Renaissance notion of the secondary nature the origin of what he calls the poetic heterocosm.[1] According to Abrams, this concept of an independent, fantastical realm, literally an 'otherworld',[2] which gradually took shape in the eighteenth and nineteenth centuries,[3] was originally developed to liberate poems and, consequently, poetic worlds from the necessity to conform to everyday reality, and to escape the imperative of the strictly mimetic. Once untied from such rules, the poem could bypass the physical laws of this world to be 'envision[ed] as *its own* world'.[4] Through the positive reassessment of the poetic imagination, the poem as mere *imitation* of earlier poetry was superseded by the

1 See M. H. Abrams, *The Mirror and the Lamp: Romantic Theory and the Critical Tradition* (Oxford: Oxford University Press, 1971), pp. 272–85. Berger traces such a development even from the medieval to the Renaissance romance, marking 'art and play', as well as 'fantasy, tapestry, masque' as the decisive characteristics of the poems by Ariosto and Spenser ('Renaissance Imagination', pp. 47–8); for a general critique of Berger's somewhat simplifying theses, see Michael Murrin, 'The Varieties of Criticism', *Modern Philology* 70 (1973), 342–56. In a more recent discussion, Roland Greene engages with such criticism and offers a more conceptualised account of Spenser's heterocosm (see 'A Primer of Spenser's Worldmaking: Alterity in the Bower of Bliss', in *Worldmaking Spenser*, ed. by Cheney and Silberman, pp. 9–31).

2 The term *heterocosm* combines Greek ἕτερος ('other') with κόσμος (among other things: 'division, order'; 'the world'); see Liddell and Scott, *Greek Lexicon*. Hence, κόσμος implies something that has been organised, com-posed, given order by a maker.

3 Jeffrey Knapp rightly critiques that Abrams 'remains vague about its [i.e. the heterocosm's] sources', especially the insular ones (*An Empire Nowhere: England, America, and Literature from 'Utopia' to 'The Tempest'*, New Historicism: Studies in Cultural Poetics Series, 16 (Berkeley and Los Angeles: University of California Press, 1991), p. 258).

4 Abrams, *The Mirror and the Lamp*, p. 327; emphasis added.

poem as *second nature* that becomes 'an object in itself, a self-contained universe of discourse'.[5] This model also accounts for the supernatural elements riddling overtly fantastic works in an intellectual milieu that criticised medieval romances and the use of the fantastic in poetry.[6] Hence, Sidney's treatise and Spenser's poem are decisive markers of an important change taking place in poetic discourse.[7]

This chapter first sketches the historical development of the heterocosm by surveying early critical statements on *The Faerie Queene*. It then discusses two passages in which Spenser openly engages in the discourse on the poet's autonomous creation of a secondary nature: first, the proem to Book II, in which Spenser defends Faeryland against the charge of grotesquery as a possible secondary world whose true meaning can be unravelled by careful interpretation; then, the Wandering Wood episode, which defines the heterocosm as a labyrinthine *textus*, and additionally thematises the process of creating 'an other nature' from *prima materia*, or first matter, with Errour as the material agency from which the monstrosities in Spenser's textual world originate.

The monster in the heterocosm: Historical perspectives

The notion that the monster makes the heterocosm is already accentuated by Spenser's earliest critics, whose views confirm Abrams's advocating a paradigmatic change towards the eighteenth century.[8] In the mid-seventeenth century, for instance, Abraham Cowley implicitly devaluates Spenser's '*fantastique Fairy-land*' with its '*Gods, Devils, Nymphs, Witches, and Giants' race*'[9] as an inferior creation, while praising instead

5 Abrams, *The Mirror and the Lamp*, p. 272.

6 See Dering, *A briefe and necessary Catachiseme or Instruction*, A.iiiv, and Nashe, *Works*, I, 26. Both texts are cited in Chapter 13.

7 On Spenser's *The Faerie Queene* as a heterocosm, see the general statements by Hough, *Preface*, pp. 95–9; Kathleen Williams, *Spenser's 'Faerie Queene': The World of Glass* (London: Routledge, 1966), p. xviii; and MacCaffrey, *Spenser's Allegory*, p. 70.

8 The focus on the monster suggests a change from the other world in medieval romance, where the monster is merely one of many possible ingredients, to the early heterocosm of the Renaissance, where the monstrous acquires central significance. The other worlds in medieval romances are mainly defined by their idealness, as is exemplified in *Sir Orfeo*, 351–76 (in: *The Middle English Breton Lays*, ed. by Anne Laskaya and Eve Salisbury (Kalamazoo: Medieval Institute Publications, 1995)). See Jeff Rider, 'The Other Worlds of Romance', in *The Cambridge Companion to Medieval Romance*, ed. by Roberta L. Krueger, Cambridge Companions to Literature (Cambridge: Cambridge University Press, 2000), pp. 115–32.

9 Abraham Cowley, 'To Sir William D'Avenant Upon his First Two Books of *Gondibert*, Finished Before his Voyage to America', 2–3. The poem, which dates from 1651,

Davenant's now forgotten *Gondibert*, an unfinished epic poem which treats the fates of Lombardian knights and is set in an '*Empire*' that does '[*n*]*ot like some dreadfull ghost*' affright the reader's eyes.[10] The poem, which follows a straightforward colonialist agenda,[11] displays the author's poetical precepts: Cowley's criticism that '*all but Man, in Mans best Work had place*'[12] openly accuses Spenser of violating poetic decorum by driving man away from his poem rather than the monsters.[13] *The Faerie Queene* thus loses sight of poetry's proper subjects, '*Men* and *Manners*' (4). Cowley vents his misgivings about the otherness of Spenser's heterocosm at the end of the short poem, claiming that the Muses inspired Davenant to leave England for America, '*to seek new Worlds*' ('To Sir William D'Avenant', 38). Regressing into literalism, Cowley discards the creation of new mental or fictional worlds that could challenge the reader in favour of corporeal ones that strengthen the contemporary call for easy didacticism and English governance.[14] Faeryland, by comparison, is an otherworld occupied by elfish and human characters, but also a world of others inhabited by monstrous figures that embody what is alien to, yet innate in, man.[15] As such, it requires taming.

This negative assessment of the monstrous heterocosm, which is also expressed by Thomas Rymer,[16] changes in the eighteenth century,

immediately precedes Davenant's epic in the 1651 print: William Davenant, *Gondibert: An Heroick Poem* (London: J. Holden, 1651).

10 See Cowley, 'To Sir William D'Avenant', 15–16. Cowley maintains that the poet's task lies in elevating nature, not in altering it ('To Sir William D'Avenant', 21–2).

11 Knapp argues concisely that Cowley's categorical distinction between these two poems also stems from a colonialist reflex: 'the implication is that Spenser's Fairyland either failed to encourage colonization or revealed as mere fantasies those colonial ventures it supported' (Knapp, *An Empire Nowhere*, p. 244).

12 Cowley, 'To Sir William D'Avenant', 4.

13 Cowley, 'To Sir William D'Avenant', 7. In another dedicatory poem prefaced to *Gondibert*, Edmund Waller praises Davenant's eschewing to tell '*bold tales of* Gods *or* Monsters' in favour of relating human passions ('To Sir William D'Avenant Upon his First Two Books of *Gondibert*, Finished Before his Voyage to America', 29).

14 Cowley's distinction between the monstrous world of the imagination and the true new world of the Americas impairs Friedman's thesis that in the early modern period the monstrous was relocated from Asia and Africa to allegorical landscapes and the New World (see Friedman, 'Monsters', p. 58). Cf. also Søndergaard's tripartite classification of *terra incognita*: (1) 'the *Other World* (or in German: das *Jenseits*)'; (2) 'the *unexplored parts of the world* in Asia, Africa, and Northern Europe'; and (3) 'a *fictional world* that existed only in the imagination' ('Far West of Spain – The Land of Cockaigne', in *Monsters, Marvels, and Miracles*, ed. by Søndergaard and Hansen, pp. 173–208 (p. 173)).

15 On the influence of the monstrous on the other worlds in medieval romance, see Rider, 'The Other Worlds', pp. 126–9.

16 'All is fanciful and chimerical, without any uniformity, without any foundation in truth; his Poem is perfect *Fairy-land*'; in Thomas Rymer, *Preface to the Translation of Rapin's Reflections on Aristotle's Treatise of Poesie* (1674); the quotation is taken from *Critical*

when the idea of the heterocosm is developed into a fully fledged literary theory.[17] Abrams assigns Joseph Addison's essays on the 'fairy way of writing'[18] the key role in this development, because they contain a concise description of fantastic literature. Addison observes that

> There is a kind of writing wherein the poet quite loses sight of Nature, and entertains his reader's imagination with the characters and actions of such persons as have many of them no existence but what he bestows on them; such are fairies, witches, magicians, demons, and departed spirits.[19]

Addison argues that this type of composition, which brings into existence novel characters, exceeds in difficulty any other kind of writing, because the poet has no pattern on which he can model his creations, and therefore has to draw on his own invention.[20] The exciting force that animates these beings is description, which is informed by rhetoric. Accentuating horror as one essential quality of a poetry that embraces the monstrous,[21] Addison takes particular delight in the depiction of monsters like Hunger, Envy, Fame, Sin and Death in the poetry of Ovid, Virgil and Milton, claiming that '[w]e find a whole creation of the like shadowy persons in Spenser, who had an admirable talent in representations of this kind'.[22] In Addison's view, Spenser's poetry appeals to the imagination: it 'makes new worlds of its own, shows us persons who are not to be found in being, and represents even the faculties of the soul, with her several virtues and vices, in a sensible shape and character'.[23] The poet's new worlds are hence the superior realms created by the imagination. Although Addison's critical statements are worlds apart from Cowley's, whose new worlds are the

---

Essays of the Seventeenth Century, ed. by J. E. Spingarn, 3 vols (Bloomington: Indiana University Press, 1957), II, 167–8.

17 On the development of the second world from the fourteenth to the seventeenth century, see also Berger, 'Renaissance Imagination', pp. 44–7.

18 The famous phrase occurs in Dryden's dedication of *King Arthur* (1691) to the Marquis of Halifax, where he describes the 'fairy way of writing' as one that rests solely 'upon the force of the imagination'; for the text, see John Dryden, *The Dramatic Works*, ed. by Montague Summers, 6 vols (London: Nonesuch Press, 1932), VI, 242.

19 Essays Nos 411–21 in the *Spectator* originally constituted one continuous treatise on the pleasures of the imagination. For the text, see *The Spectator*, ed. by Donald F. Bond, 5 vols (Oxford: Clarendon, 1965), III, 535–82 (p. 570).

20 Addison maintains that the fantastic poet 'ought to be very well versed in legends and fables, antiquated romances, and the traditions of nurses and old women, that he may fall in with our natural prejudices, and humour those notions which we have imbibed in our infancy' (*Spectator*, III, 570).

21 Depictions of strange and novel characters, Addison states, excite 'a pleasing kind of horror in the mind of the reader' (*Spectator*, III, 570).

22 *Spectator*, III, 570.

23 *Spectator*, III, 570.

recently discovered parts of the real world, both assign monsters the major role in the creation of a heterocosm transforming common reality.[24]

While Addison and Cowley argue correctly that the monstrous is constitutive of the heterocosm, they are imprecise in one significant respect. Although the main site of Spenser's heterocosm is indeed Faeryland, monsters and monstrous beings are not confined to Faeryland alone, but appear in almost every realm of the poem. Eden, for instance, is a kingdom harrowed by the Great Dragon, which has features reminiscent of monstrous beings in Faeryland, and also recalls romance specimens; Belge's country is usurped by triple-bodied Geryoneo and his Sphinx-like dragon; and pre-Roman England is inhabited by a host of monstrous men and giants. As the borders between the realms of the poem, the quests and adventures it stages, are permeable and connected through the monstrous, the other is at large in every part of Spenser's work, not only in those parts set in Faeryland, so that a clear ontological distinction between the settings of the poem cannot be maintained throughout. In other words, *The Faerie Queene* is not coequal with Faeryland.[25] More precisely, Faeryland is the main setting of the poem, with other adjacent territories constituting a far wider poetic realm, including various locales that are entirely invented (Faeryland), legendary (Radigund's Kingdom of the Amazons), biblical (Eden), historical (England and Wales), mythic (Duessa's descent to Hades) and contemporary (Mount Acidale, among others).[26] Spenser's transformation of topographical spaces through the monstrous thus establishes an underlying continuity on which the poem's joint geography is based, a connection that marks every place in *The Faerie Queene* as a locale constituting the overarching 'otherworld' of the poem as such. In MacCaffrey's poignant words, the whole text thus becomes 'the universe of discourse in which the poem unfolds'.[27]

24 Addison and Cowley hence engage with the role of the monstrous more explicitly and at greater length than Sidney in his *Defence*, who interpreted the monstrous as one possible feature of a secondary nature created by the poet.

25 As Erickson shows in his perceptive study of the geography of *The Faerie Queene*, generations of Spenserians have handed down a rather unclear idea of the relationship between the poem and Faeryland, treating both as coextensive entities, and emphasising the idealness of this realm (see Erickson, *Mapping 'The Faerie Queene': Quest Structures and the World of the Poem*, Garland Studies in the Renaissance, 3 (New York and London: Garland Publishing, 1996), pp. 4–7). Gordon Teskey, for instance, limits the notion of the heterocosm to Faeryland (see *Delirious Milton: The Fate of the Poet in Modernity* (Cambridge, MA: Harvard University Press, 2006), p. 16).

26 Spenser's creation is therefore much less perspicacious than that of the Italian tradition, with Boiardo, Ariosto and Tasso setting the scenes of their respective poems in clearly identifiable geographical locales. Cf. also Erickson, *Mapping*, pp. 42–3.

27 MacCaffrey, *Spenser's Allegory*, p. 67. Although she does not acknowledge it, her formu-

Reading the heterocosm: The proem to Book II

Spenser predicted that his embracing the possibilities of the monstrous for the creation of a secondary world would not be met with unanimous approval. In the proem to Book II, which takes the form of an extended address to Queen Elizabeth, Spenser forestalls criticism that would censure his poem for its fictive setting, and deprecate it as the product 'of an ydle braine' and a 'painted forgery' that is not the 'matter of iust memory' (II.Pr.1.3–5).[28] These imagined negative responses condemn Spenser's poem for depicting an unreliable fantastic world that does not qualify as history proper.[29] Even Spenser's reference to the 'famous antique history' of Faeryland (II.Pr.1.2) discredits the poem as a place of grotesquery: the adjective 'antique' characterises Spenser's Faeryland not only as an 'ancient' or 'time-honoured' but also as a 'bizarre' or 'monstrous' place.[30] The epithet hence labels a poetic world that, up to that point, has confronted its readers with numerous monstrous beings and horrific monster fights.

Spenser meets these charges first by creating imaginative room for Faeryland, and then by elaborating on how to read this secondary world. Spenser here introduces a possible-world argument to disprove the accusation that the poem is the product of an unchecked imagination. Citing 'th'Indian *Peru*' (II.Pr.2.6), '[t]he *Amazons*' (2.8) and 'fruitfullest *Virginia*' (2.9) to represent the age's discovery of unknown realms, Spenser argues that hitherto unseen places cannot be ruled out of existence just because they remain as yet undiscovered.[31] Indeed, only very little is known of

lation closely echoes Abrams's claim that the heterocosm is 'a self-contained universe of discourse' (*The Mirror and the Lamp*, p. 272). Berger's call for a careful distinction between 'the second world *in* fiction, and the second world *as* fiction' is nowhere more justified than in *The Faerie Queene* ('Renaissance Imagination', p. 14). Cf. also Barkan's view that *The Faerie Queene* consists of many heterocosms (see *Nature's Work of Art*, p. 205).

28 In his dedicatory sonnet to Lord Burghley, Spenser similarly describes his poem as 'ydle rimes …, / The labor of lost time, and wit vnstayd' (Dedicatory Sonnet 2, 'To the Right Honourable the Lo. Burleigh Lo. High Threasurer of England', 7–8).

29 Such negative views on poetry are examined at length in Herman, *Squitter-wits*. The topos of the otherworld also figures in Ariosto's *Orlando Furioso*, VII.1–2 (also noted by Upton; see *Variorum*, II, 185–6).

30 On the development of the term *antique*, see Rainer Lengeler's authoritative and well-documented word history in *Tragische Wirklichkeit*, pp. 4–23.

31 In the proem, Spenser hence tricks the inquisitive reader into acknowledging the hypothetical validity of Faeryland. See Clarke Hulse, '"Painted Forgery": Visual Approaches to *The Faerie Queene*', in *Approaches to Teaching Spenser's 'Faerie Queene'*, ed. by David Lee Miller and Alexander Dunlop, Approaches to Teaching World Literature, 50 (New York: Modern Language Association of America, 1994), pp. 93–105 (pp. 95–6).

the world ('of the world least part to vs is red'; 2.2).[32] The same holds true for the universe: Spenser concedes the possibility of wondrous 'other worldes' (3.7) on the moon and beyond, a supposition that conjures up the contemporary vogue that deemed a plurality of worlds probable.[33]

These commonsensical manoeuvres, however, are mere preliminaries for the more important second part of Spenser's argument, which explains how the secondary world of *The Faerie Queene* is to be read and interpreted. The readers are invited to discover the novel world Spenser places before them much like explorers confronted with new-found lands, and may therefore partake in man's advancement of knowledge beyond known geography and the conceivable cosmos.[34] As Spenser here teases his readers into looking for 'certaine signes' (4.2) that might lead their imagination to disclose the true nature of Faeryland (4.1–5),[35] he stresses that the quest for Faeryland requires constant and accurate textual analysis.[36] The intellectual practice he propagates is closely tied to the interpretation of allegory: when Spenser finally reveals to his Queen that Faeryland and its ancestry are a 'fayre mirrhour' (4.7) of her own reign and ancestry, he lifts the veil off Faeryland, and explains to his readers

32 The stanza is riddled with the language of discovery, as terms like 'hardy enterprize', 'great Regions', 'discouered' and 'venturous vessell' illustrate (II.Pr.2.3–4 and 7). See also Erickson, *Mapping*, pp. 30–3.

33 Paul H. Kocher records the proem to Book II as one of the first documents to acknowledge such a plurality; see *Science and Religion in Elizabethan England* (San Marino: Huntington Library, 1956), p. 86. For an extensive historical account of the 'infinite worlds' paradigm (e.g. in Giordano Bruno's influential writings), see Lobsien, *Imaginationswelten*, pp. 8–23, and especially the outline of views and texts on p. 18, n. 23; for the lunar world, see Marjorie Hope Nicolson, *A World in the Moon: A Study of the Changing Attitude toward the Moon in the Seventeenth and Eighteenth Centuries*, Smith Studies in Modern Languages, 17.2 (Northampton, MA: Smith College, 1936). Greene rightly criticises their positivist attitudes, arguing instead for a more abstract meaning of these lines ('Worldmaking', p. 15).

34 Spenser's manoeuvre may suggest Lobsien's treatment of imaginative worlds in his monograph on *Imaginationswelten*, where he affirms that '[w]as immer zum Gegenstand einer möglichen Aussage werden kann, dessen Existenz sollte nicht negiert werden' ('Whatever can become the object of a possible statement should not be denied existence'; *Imaginationswelten*, p. 85).

35 The passage runs as follows (II.Pr.4.1–5): 'Of Faerie lond yet if he more inquire, / By certaine signes here set in sundry place / He may it find; ne let him then admire, / But yield his sence to be too blunt and bace, / That no'te without an hound fine footing trace.' David Ian Galbraith maintains that reading allegory is here presented as a 'complex process' for the ordinary reader, whereas Queen Elizabeth I, as the text's ideal reader, can connect much more directly to the poem, because it is conceived as a representation of herself (see *Architectonics of Imitation in Spenser, Daniel, and Drayton* (Toronto, London: University of Toronto Press, 2000), pp. 14–16).

36 See also Woodcock, *Fairy*, pp. 69–70 and pp. 73–4.

that the poem is a well-calculated creation.[37] Its allegorical otherworld presents imaginative spaces, beings and heroic characters as a sequence of correlating verbal and allegorical signs that point to the poetic maker who orchestrates a secondary world through constant communication with the first.[38] Spenser's panegyric therefore offers a strikingly direct 'reader's guide' that marks the poem's main setting, and by extension every other locale, as narrated permutations of his contemporary historical reality.[39] It is the readers' task to engage with the universe of discourse by bringing the primary level of the poem's narrative in line with the secondary meanings of allegory.[40]

Into the Wandering Wood: The heterocosm as labyrinth

In *The Faerie Queene*, the topos of finding orientation and direction through the careful interpretation of signs in Spenser's heterocosm occurs already in the Wandering Wood narrative of Book I, Canto i. In this emblematic representation of the monstrous heterocosm, the forest with a monster at its centre is implemented as the governing metaphor for the poem and its main organisational principle: the labyrinth as *textus*. The canto relates how Redcrosse, Una and her dwarf flee into a wood to seek shelter from an oncoming tempest;[41] enter the Wandering Wood, in the words of Corinne Saunders the 'nucleus of adventure' in the romance;[42] to get lost in the maze of its winding paths; meet the biform monster Errour in her den; and exit the forest again after she is defeated by Redcrosse. As Matthew Fike argues convincingly, this sequence of narrative units suggests the myth of Theseus, who enters King Minos's subterranean labyrinth, confronts and vanquishes the biform Minotaur, and leaves the

37 In his dedicatory sonnet to Lord Burghley, Spenser similarly explains that reading *The Faerie Queene* means lifting the veil of allegory to reach a deeper truth, an exercise that tells the good reader from the common people: 'Yet if their [i.e. the rhymes'] deeper sence be inly wayd, / And the dim vele, with which from comune vew / Their fairer parts are hid, aside be layd, / Perhaps not vaine they may appear to you' (9–12).

38 Cf. Lobsien, *Imaginationswelten*, pp. 85–6, and King, *Middle English Romance*, pp. 161–5.

39 Among others, Geryoneo and Geryono's dragon, who usurp Belge's kingdom, are figurations of the Spanish inquisition, and hence part of Spenser's historical allegory.

40 Both Erickson and Woodcock argue that reading Spenser's long poem entails a difficult process, and interpret Spenser's remarks on 'finding Faeryland' in the Proem to Book II as indicative of such a method (see Erickson, *Mapping*, pp. 11–12 (on 'Letter') and p. 32 (on II.Pr.), as well as Woodcock, *Fairy*, pp. 69–74).

41 The episode takes place after a general exposition in I.i.1–6.4.

42 Corinne J. Saunders, *The Forest of Medieval Romance: Avernus, Brocelainde, Arden* (Cambridge: Brewer, 1993), p. 189.

labyrinth again. Spenser makes this general resemblance more explicit when describing the Wandering Wood as a 'labyrinth' (I.i.11.4).[43]

Spenserian critics have discussed the general relevance of the labyrinth for this part of *The Faerie Queene*.[44] While some of them interpret the labyrinth as a universal principle whose origin cannot be determined exactly,[45] others join the labyrinth with other recurring locations. Angus Fletcher, for instance, sees the labyrinth and the temple as the 'two archetypes' which 'organize the overall shaping of *The Faerie Queene*'.[46] He argues that the labyrinth 'specifies the large and open extensions of faerieland', where Spenser's characters get lost on their wanderings, while the temple is Faeryland's 'perfect enclosure', a sacred locus whose various figurations appear at central moments of the individual books.[47] William

43 See Matthew Fike, '"Not without Theseus"', pp. 231–49 (acknowledged by Hamilton, note to I.i.11.5), and Pugh, *Spenser and Ovid*, p. 66 and p. 133. On Spenser's general allusions to the Theseus myth, see D'Orsay W. Pearson, '"Unkinde" Theseus: A Study in Renaissance Mythography', *English Literary Renaissance* 4 (1974), 276–98, and his entry 'Theseus, Hippolytos' in the *Spenser Encyclopedia*, ed. by Hamilton, p. 668. It is in the context of the Theseus myth that the term labyrinth is first used in English, namely in Trevisa's Middle English rendering of Ranulfus Higden's *Polychronicon*, I.9 ('þis matir, as laborintus, Dedalus hous, haþ many halkes and hurnes … wyndynges and wrynkelynges'; see *OED*, s.v. 'labyrinth, *n.*', 1). D'Orsay W. Pearson cites Thomas Watson's *Hekatompathia*, LV, from 1582 as evidence for the currency of the labyrinth metaphor in Spenser's age (see 'Spenser's Labyrinth – Again', *Studies in Iconography* 3 (1977), 70–88 (p. 74)). Nohrnberg offers a host of useful references on labyrinths in *Analogy*, pp. 137–8 and note 108; among others, he refers to Natale Conti, *Mythologiae*, VII, ix; Guillaume de Deguilleville, *Pilgrimage of the Life of Man, as Englished by John Lydgate*, ed. by . J. Furnivall, EETS, 2 parts in 2 vols (London, 1899–1904), II, 459; and Petrarch on the opening of the *Aeneid*: 'The wood is truly this life, full of shadows and errors, tangled and uncertain paths, and inhabited by beasts' (quoted in Nohrnberg, *Analogy*, pp. 138–9).

44 On the labyrinth, see W. H. Matthews, *Mazes and Labyrinths: Their History and Development* (London: Longmans, Green and Co., 1922; repr. New York: Dover Publications, 1970); Janet Bord, *Mazes and Labyrinths of the World* (New York: E. P. Dutton, 1975); Hermann Kern, *Labyrinthe: Erscheinungsformen und Deutungen. 5000 Jahre Gegenwart eines Urbilds* (Munich: Prestel, 1999). These monographs focus mostly on visual labyrinths. For an indispensable and thought-provoking study that treats the labyrinth as a conceptual metaphor of literary works from the classical and medieval periods, see Penelope Reed Doob, *The Idea of the Labyrinth from Classical Antiquity Through the Middle Ages* (Ithaca: Cornell University Press, 1990), p. 97. On Spenser and the labyrinth, see Blissett, 'Labyrinths, Mazes', pp. 422–3; D'Orsay Pearson, 'Spenser's Labyrinth – Again'; Parker, *Inescapable Romance*; Fletcher, 'The Image of Lost Direction'; Huston Diehl, 'Into the Maze of Self: The Protestant Transformation of the Image of the Labyrinth', *Journal of Medieval and Renaissance Studies* 16 (1986), 281–99. A. C. Hamilton also interprets the labyrinth as a subtext underlying the *Shepheardes Calender*; see '"The Grene Path Way to Lyfe": Spenser's *Shepheardes Calender* as Pastoral', in *The Elizabethan Theatre VIII*, ed. by George R. Hibbard (Port Credit: Meany, 1982), pp. 1–21.

45 See Blissett, 'Caves, Labyrinths', pp. 283–4.

46 Fletcher, *Prophetic Moment*, p. 11, and for the labyrinth, pp. 24–34.

47 Fletcher, *Prophetic Moment*, p. 31.

Blisset, on the other hand, stresses that Spenser creates a unique 'amalgamation of cave and labyrinth and its concentration of evils therein',[48] and follows the permutations of these motifs, with the help of classical *testes* like Virgil, Ovid and Pliny, through the various stages of Spenser's long poem. Although venturing into the right direction, neither of these approaches fully elaborates on the conceptual implications of the Wandering Wood for Spenser's creation of the 'universe of discourse'.[49] What is more, the emphasis on cave or temple as sites related to the labyrinth draws attention away from the key role that the monster Errour plays in the world-making of the poem. From this perspective, the labyrinths Spenser draws on are meaningful locales, exactly because they also house a monster at their centre. If one relates this finding to Cowley's, and Addison's notion of *natura altera* as a place defined by the presence of the monstrous, then both the labyrinth and the heterocosm share the monstrous as their common denominator.

The labyrinth is significant for Spenser's world-making, because it introduces his readers to two essential aspects of *The Faerie Queene*: (1) to astute reading as the prerequisite of finding orientation in a long and demanding poem; and (2) to the heterocosm as the universe of partly monstrous discourse. Both notions inhere in the original cultural image of the labyrinth. The first defining aspect, the obligation of astute reading, relates to the alleged etymology of the term labyrinth. Derived from the Latin *labor intus*, i.e. 'labour within',[50] the labyrinth points to the laborious interpretation of signs in the situation of lost direction.[51] In his seminal study on labyrinths and mazes,[52] W. H. Matthews divides labyrinths into

48 Blissett, 'Caves, Labyrinths', p. 284. Saunders suggests very convincingly that Spenser's forests stage the battle between good and evil in her monograph on the rich tradition of the forest in medieval romance (see Corinne J. Saunders, *The Forest*, p. 195, with reference to III.vi.36).

49 Abrams, *The Mirror and the Lamp*, p. 272, and MacCaffrey, *Spenser's Allegory*, p. 67.

50 Penelope Reed Doob points out that the phrase *labor intus* can have various meanings; (1) for *labor* as a noun: 'an artistic *opus* lies within'; 'hardship, or fatigue, or exertion, or application to work lies inside'; (2) for *labor* as a verb: 'I fall, or perish, or err, or go wrong within (or while going in)' (*Idea of the Labyrinth*, p. 97).

51 Spenser employs a series of periphrases in I.i.10.4–9 to translate Redcrosse's and Una's disorientation into verse. The 'image of lost direction' is a concept first put forward by Northrop Frye in his *Anatomy of Criticism: Four Essays* (Princeton: Princeton University Press, 1957), p. 150: 'we have in this world the labyrinth or maze, the image of lost direction, often with a monster at its heart like the Minotaur'. Fletcher develops Frye's ideas into a sustained psychological argument ('The Image of Lost Direction', pp. 329–46). The classic example of this topos is Dante, *Inferno*, I.1–3: 'Nel mezzo del cammin di nostra vita / mi ritrovai per una selva oscura, / ché la diritta via era smarrita' ('In the middle of the journey of our life, I came to myself in a dark wood, for the straight way was lost').

52 The terms *labyrinth* and *maze* were used synonymously in the Renaissance. See the

unicursal and multicursal ones. While the former consist of a 'single unbranched path', the latter puzzle travellers with cross-connecting paths and force them into choosing new directions.[53] As Doob explains, this type of maze is defined by labyrinthine routes (Latin *ambages*) that make progress a laborious effort (*labores*) and bring travellers to many an error (*errores*).[54] Literary mazes, unlike visual and architectural ones, are primarily multicursal,[55] and so is the Wandering Wood. Spenser expands, or rather unfolds, its topography through developing a web of misdirections and endless paths: as a place of numerous routes and crossings, of '[s]o many pathes, so many turnings' (I.i.10.8), Spenser's heterocosm requires constant orientation and careful reading.[56] The second aspect, i.e. the labyrinth as a form of the monstrous, harks back to the Minotaur in the Theseus myth. The Minotaur, like Spenser's monsters discussed in Part II, is a puzzling and perverse creature, a human–animal composite that is dangerous and threatening, and requires interpretation. It is every hero's ultimate adversary, and as such needs to be vanquished. When Spenser has Redcrosse and Una find the serpent-woman Errour, the

respective entries in the *OED* ('labyrinth, *n.*', and 'maze, *n.*1'). In his entry in the *Spenser Encyclopedia*, William Blissett explains rather vaguely that *labyrinth* is the more literary term, while *maze* is familiar from everyday usage; in 'Caves, Labyrinths', he is even less specific when remarking that 'no distinction has even been made to stick in common usage' (see 'Labyrinths, Mazes', in *Spenser Encyclopedia*, ed. by Hamilton, p. 422; 'Caves, Labyrinths'; and 'Caves, Labyrinths, and *The Faerie Queene*', in *Unfolded Tales: Studies in Renaissance Romance*, ed. by George M. Logan and Gordon Teskey (Ithaca, London: Cornell University Press, 1989), pp. 281–311 (p. 286 and p. 286, n. 7)). But, *pace* Blissett's distinction, I disagree, compare: Crooke calls man's body a '*mazey laberynth* of small veines and arteries' (Helkiah Crooke, *Mikrokosmographia: A Description of the Body of Man* (London: William Iaggard, 1615), p. 465; emphases added); Ben Jonson also uses *maze* and *labyrinth* interchangeably in his masque *Pleasure Reconciled to Virtue* ('all actions of mankind / Are but a laborinth, or maze', *Pleasure*, 261–2; *Ben Jonson*, VII, 488).

53 Matthews, *Mazes*, pp. 184–6. He also warns against a too rigid distinction between these types. Spenserians like Pearson and Blissett have likewise offered typologies of labyrinths. Pearson categorises labyrinths as simple (like the lover's plight), complete (i.e. as a structure with release) and complex (as the labyrinth of life that offers no easy exit for the concupiscent; see Pearson, 'Spenser's Labyrinth – Again', pp. 71–6). Blissett distinguishes between the transit maze, the centre-seeking labyrinth and the there-and-back-labyrinth (see 'Labyrinths, Mazes', pp. 422–3, and 'Caves, Labyrinths', pp. 286–7). Angus Fletcher, following Kern, tells the metaphorical labyrinth from the *intrico de vie* (an intricate system of many paths) and the labyrinth proper (see 'The Image of Lost Direction', in *Centre and Labyrinth: Studies in Honour of Northrop Frye*, ed. by Eleanor Cook (Toronto: Toronto University Press, 1983), pp. 329–46 (pp. 334–5)).

54 See Doob, *Idea of the Labyrinth*, pp. 17–38 and p. 224.

55 See the extended discussion in Doob, *Idea of the Labyrinth*, pp. 39–63.

56 On error and the 'conscientious reader', see Nohrnberg, *Analogy*, pp. 123–4. Galbraith links the image of the labyrinth to the deceptive mode of allegory (see *Architectonics of Imitation*, p. 33).

summa of all that is other and abject,[57] '[a]mid the thickest woods' (11.7), he hence structures the opening narrative like the myth, and establishes the monstrous as a central influence in his heterocosm and as a central theme of his poem.

Both wood and monster are readily identifiable as emblems of Spenser's secondary nature and also represent the defining characteristics of epic romance.[58] They interlink through naming, with Latin *error* relating directly to 'wandering';[59] they evoke the idea of knight errantry, and with it the chivalric romance, as well as the moral, and monstrous aberrations that henceforth appear in the poem.[60] What is especially striking is that Errour's tail, in many ways the quintessential monstrous signifier, is described like a labyrinth.[61] When the narrator explains that her 'huge long tail' is 'in knots and many boughtes vpwound' (15.2–3) he draws on a cluster of terms that also figure in the lexicon of mazes: the *knots*, for instance, are joints in the design of a maze, especially in the interlacing concatenations of three-dimensional knot labyrinths;[62] they shape *boughts* which here refer to the individual coils formed by the monster's long and winding tail.[63] These terms thus anatomise both the cross-sections and the lines that lead to them. The Wandering Wood likewise consists of these two elements, namely the paths and the turn-

57 Steadman discusses the connection between the two mythological elements of the forest-labyrinth, and the serpent-woman (*Nature Into Myth*, pp. 159–60).

58 Cf. also Jack in *Variorum*, I, 175–6.

59 See also the entries on *errare* and *error* in Cooper's *Thesaurus*.

60 On the significance of *errare* for Ariosto and Spenser, see Parker, *Inescapable Romance*, pp. 16–39 and pp. 66–70: '"Error" is not only a romance pun, sign of the interplay between mental and geographical "wandering"; it is also the concept which connects the diverse aspects of a long and complex poem'. Cf. Blissett, 'Labyrinths, Mazes', pp. 422–3; 'Caves, Labyrinths', p. 306; and Maureen Quilligan, *The Language of Allegory: Defining the Genre* (Ithaca and London: Cornell University Press, 1979), pp. 35–7 and pp. 256–8.

61 Diehl argues in favour of an analogy between the serpent and the labyrinth that lies in a set of common denominators characterising the world as an evil, satanic and sinful place. He traces this connection in Milton's *Paradise Lost*, where the image of the serpent is frequently linked to that of the labyrinth ('Maze of Self', p. 293). Spenser also suggests an etymological link, because *errare* is often used to describe Daedalus's labyrinth in classical texts. See Virgil, *Aeneid*, V.591 ('inremeabilis error') and VI.27 ('inextricabilis error'), and Ovid, *Metamorphoses* VIII.160–1 ('lumina … / ducit in errorem' (Daedalus 'led the eyes into error')), and 167–8 ('inplet / innumeras errore vias' ('he filled innumerous ways with "error"')).

62 On knot labyrinths, see Bord, *Mazes*, p. 86, with reference to Dürer's *Sechs Knoten* (*Six Knots*). See also Gervase Markham, *Certaine Excellent and New Inuented Knots and Mazes* (London: John Marriott, 1623). Doob identifies knots as emblems of difficulty (see *Idea of the Labyrinth*, p. 206).

63 *Bought* can refer both to the part between the ends or points of attachment, and thence also specifically to the coils of a serpent (see *OED*, s.v. 'bought, *n.*1', 2a and 2b).

ings which link different alleys with one another.[64] Spenser's repeated use of the adjective *many* in close textual proximity connects, I would argue with Steadman, the 'many boughtes' of the monster's tail (15.3) with the 'many pathes' of the wood (10.8), and marks them both as figurations of multiplicity.[65] As figurations of the maze, monster and wood are coexisting entities, whose interplay symbolises the larger framework of the poem, with the Wandering Wood representing the entire textual world and Errour standing for the monstrous beings appearing in it.[66]

Yet, unlike the wood, Errour is a dynamic entity: as she enfolds and unfolds her tail to entangle and disorient Redcrosse during combat,[67] her body is a living labyrinth that encloses the champion. Errour's constant physical transformation has significant implications, for it marks her ability to dissimulate through reconfiguring the 'boughts' and 'knots' of her tail, which establishes multiple new patterns of intersections, junctions and nodes.[68] On the narrative level, this enhances the monster's multiformity; on a more abstract level, however, the authorial exclamation 'God helpe the man so wrapt in *Errours* endlesse traine' (18.9), which moralises the allegorical aspects of this guileful creature,[69] marks the

64 For the use of *turnings*, see Samuel Daniel, *The Complaint of Rosamund*, 470–6, and Milton, *Comus*, 569; for the texts, see Samuel Daniel, *The Complete Works in Verse and Prose*, ed. by Alexander B. Grosart, 5 vols (New York: Russell and Russell, 1963), I.

65 Cf. Steadman, *Nature into Myth*, p. 164.

66 Turning entities that would not normally be considered labyrinthine into labyrinths was not uncommon practice in the sixteenth century. On man's labyrinthine corporeality, see Crooke, *Mikrokosmographia*, p. 431 (of the brain: 'so many Labyrinthes and Meanders are therein'), and Samuel Purchas, *Microcosmvs, or the Historie of Man* (London: W[illiam] S[tansby], 1619), pp. 82–3 (of the brain) and p. 302 ('this confused Labyrinth of Himself'). The woodcuts in Francesco Segala's sixteenth-century *Libro de laberinti de Franc* may be used as examples to show that anything from ships, human beings and animals could be iconographically transformed into, and hence perceived as labyrinths. For the illustrations from Francesco Segala's *Libro de laberinti de Franc*, see Kern, *Labyrinthe*, pp. 350–1. Placed into the tradition of anthropomorphic and theriomorphic woodcuts, Spenser's Errour becomes a teratomorphic figuration of the labyrinth.

67 The verbs *to display* (I.i.14.7, 16.3), and *to stretch* (16.4) describe the act of unfolding, whereas *to gather round* (18.2), *to wrap around* (18.5) and *to wind about* (18.7) are synonyms for infolding. Fletcher's observation that the 'desert darkness' (I.i.16.8) Errour creates when tying herself into knots is continuous with the darkness of the forest's foliage stresses the monster's relation to the Wandering Wood, and additionally draws attention to the specific movements that turn her into an animated maze. See Fletcher, *Prophetic Moment*, p. 26. On the darkness of mazes, see Doob, *Idea of the Labyrinth*, p. 76.

68 On the use of the term *node* as a juncture of many paths, see Matthews, *Mazes*, p. 190, and *OED*, s.v. 'node, *n.*', 9a and b.

69 Spenser here puns on the two meanings of the word *train*, namely 'the elongated body of a serpent' and 'treachery, guile; trap' (see *OED*, s.v. 'train, *n.*1', I.6, and 'train, *n.*2'). On Spenser's establishing Errour as moral error, see Fletcher, *Prophetic Moment*, pp.

monster as an image of the aberrations and misdirections into which the poem will again lead its characters and its readers. Errour is hence also an allegory representing the difficulty of reading.[70]

Reading the labyrinth

The Wandering Wood episode announces to the reader that reading *The Faerie Queene* is difficult. Patricia Parker and Rufus Wood have independently pointed out that Una and Redcrosse at the beginning of Book I figure as readers that have to bring sense and orientation to the polysemous attributes of the wood, to name the trees and to beware of the threat posed by Errour, a monster that may also be interpreted as the danger of reading, as is suggested by Una's adhortation 'Therefore I read beware' (I.i.13.8).[71] The readers, like Una and Redcrosse 'in diuerse *doubt*' (I.i.10.9; emphasis added) about the path they should choose inside the Wandering Wood, have to engage with an allegorical text, which is '*doubtfully* … construed' ('Letter', 3; emphasis added). Both statements underline the fundamental difficulty of making choices and finding single directions, both for Spenser's characters and for his readers,[72] and are taken up later in Spenser's call for astute reading in the proem to Book II. Yet, if the Wandering Wood episode, by signalling the dangers of reading Spenser's romance, accentuates that the problem, according to Parker, 'from the beginning, is learning how to read',[73] it also offers a model of how the poem has to be read as a gigantic connection exercise, part of which is determined by the monstrous. The labyrinth is therefore the key metaphor of the complex web of interaction Spenser weaves on the various macro- and micro-levels of the poem, which comprises the narrative, thematic, and semantic arrangement of his universe of discourse.

These complexities and ambiguities mark Spenser's poem as a multi-

216–17, and Hamilton, note to I.i.18.9. Steadman amply documents the Renaissance interpretation of Echidna as 'multiform erudition' and the 'association of the serpent's coils with rhetorical persuasion', and applies it to Errour (see *Nature Into Myth*, pp. 160–2 (p. 162)).

70 On the notion that the Errour episode reflects the experience of a reader dealing with allegory, see Nohrnberg, *Analogy*, pp. 149–51, and 'Acidale', *Spenser Encyclopedia*, ed. by Hamilton, pp. 4–6 (p. 6).

71 See Parker, *Inescapable Romance*, pp. 64–6, and Wood, *Metaphor and Belief*, pp. 28–30, as well as Nohrnberg, *Analogy*, p. 146.

72 Spenser refers to the difficulty of reading his poem, which resembles the 'hardy enterprize' (II.Pr.2.3) of discovering new countries (see Woodcock, *Fairy*, p. 70), at various stages of his main work and the back matter (see 'Letter', 3–7 and 21–3, II.Pr.4.1–5, and the 'Dedicatory Sonnet to Lord Burleigh', 9–12).

73 Parker, *Inescapable Romance*, p. 65.

cursal venture in which the reader can get lost if he merely follows the pleasure aspect of the romance.[74] Taking a promising theoretical direction in his *Prophetic Moment*, Angus Fletcher defines a labyrinth as a construction that suspends contrasts and creates a continuum between oppositions.[75] In *The Faerie Queene*, the textual structure of the labyrinth, encompassing the normative and the monstrous, links various parts of the text with one another, thus likewise creating, through the use of interconnected references, a continuum between its different aspects, which often calls for concordantial readings.[76] Such interconnections include, among others, the interlaced plots of the romance and the link between major and minor themes, which in *The Faerie Queene* are represented by the nodes and paths in the labyrinthine wood, and Errour's knots and bouts.[77]

Once the monster is identified as the figuration of specific structural aspects in Spenser's poem, it is possible to follow Rufus Wood's argument that Errour's 'huge long taile' (I.i.15.2) symbolises, *qua* homonym, the huge long *tale* of the poem, and accordingly the infinite and twisting tales of the narrative.[78] Like the Wandering Wood, Errour represents the complex narrative methods of the text,[79] but, unlike the forest, symbolises the influence of the monstrous on *The Faerie Queene*. Together, wood and monster figure forth the dual textual labyrinth in that they represent, in emblematic form, the complexity of the poem and its narrative manoeuvres, as well as the bearing of monstrous aberrations on the poem's narratives.[80]

In this labyrinthine heterocosm, the monstrous is of central impor-

74 Blissett notes that such complexities contradict the centre-seeking orderliness Spenser elaborates on in the 'Letter', which defines Gloriana and Cleopolis as the very core of his poetic world (see 'Caves, Labyrinths', p. 311).

75 See Fletcher, *Prophetic Moment*, pp. 31–2. Doob regards the labyrinth as the 'embodiment of paradox', because it affirms antinomies, such as 'order/chaos, imprisonment/liberation, linearity/circularity, clarity/complexity, stability/instability' (*Idea of the Labyrinth*, p. 9).

76 See Kaske, *Spenser and Biblical Poetics*.

77 See Pugh, *Spenser and Ovid*, p. 51, with reference to the *OED*, s.v. 'knot, *n.*', II.1.b, 'a mediaeval usage'; and 'bout, *n.*', 1, 'a roundabout way'. On the relationship between interlacement and the labyrinth, see Doob, *Idea of the Labyrinth*, p. 203 and pp. 206–11.

78 See Wood, *Metaphor and Belief*, p. 33, and Pugh, *Spenser and Ovid*, p. 51.

79 Gordon Teskey describes how the passage covering II.ii.19–23, in which Sir Hudibras and Sansloy attack Sir Guyon at Medina's Castle, is entangled with other histories, narratives, character biographies and events. The scene, he writes, is 'richly entangled in its widening context and flows into them like the ripples from a stone dropped in a pool' ('Thinking Moments in *The Faerie Queene*', *Spenser Studies* 22 (2007), 103–25 (pp. 109–10)). Teskey, through recourse to Hegelian theory, postulates that thinking in *The Faerie Queene* is 'not an answering but a searching of questions initially asked, leading to the totally unexpected, the new' (p. 103).

80 Cf. also Doob's remarks on interlaced story-telling in *Idea of the Labyrinth*, pp. 206–8.

tance, like Errour '[a]mid the thickest woods', because Spenser sets it up as a counter-discourse that plays off the various affirmative discourses of each book and the more comprehensive themes laid down in the entire poem.[81] Additionally, the monstrous affirms itself as a discourse of its own that can link unconnected sections with one another,[82] and create intertextual references to, among others, scripture and mythology, which establish bonds between different monsters.[83] Such interlacing also figures in recurring monstrous attributes, such as the tails and mouths of various monsters or the frequent occurrences of burning eyes:[84] forming anatomical and verbal clusters that thematically link one part of the poem with another, they create interlocking, interacting nodes that enhance the complexity of Spenser's text. Even on the semantic level, Spenser creates a sustained 'deformed discourse' by employing a lexical set of monstrous epithets that interrelate with one another and form interdependent sections that show the labyrinthine complexity of his allegorical heterocosm.[85]

By establishing connections between different monsters on various inter- and intratextual levels, Spenser conceives his poem as a *textus*, i.e. an interwoven, interlaced structure, which he emblematises in the image of the labyrinth.[86] Thus construed, the emerging poem retains its power

81 An especially clear thematic antinomy is presented in Book V, the Legend of Justice, where the monstrous, in figures like the Egalitarian Giant, or Geryoneo and his monster, features as the representation of injustice and tyranny.

82 One such instance is Geryoneo's female dragon, which appears in Book V, Canto xi, and bears striking similarities with the dragons of Book I. While its maiden face recalls Errour's female torso and face, the fight in which it is slain by Arthur replays a number of incidents from Redcrosse's three-day battle with the Dragon harrowing Eden. Reid explains correctly that Redcrosse's defeat of Errour in Book I, Canto i anticipates his vanquishing the Dragon of Eden in Canto xi (see 'Spenser's Mutability Song', p. 72).

83 Spenser makes Typhon and Echidna, who in classical mythology sired Chimera, Cerberus, the Harpies and the Sphinx, the possible parents of the Blatant Beast (VI.vi and xii; at VI.i.7–8 Calidore explains that the Blatant Beast is the spawn of Cerberus and Chimera). Echidna is also supposedly the mother of Geryoneo's dragon (V.xi.23.4–6), as well as the conceptual mother of Errour (cf. I.i.14–15).

84 For tails, see Errour (I.i.15), Duessa (I.viii.48), Orgoglio's beast (I.vii.18), the Dragon of Eden (I.xi.11) and Geryoneo's dragon (V.xi.24.5–6); and for eyes, Orgoglio's dragon (I.vii.17–19) and the Dragon of Eden (I.xi.14), as well as the 'carles' Despayre, Care, Malengin, Mammon and Malbecco (I.ix.35; IV.v.34; V.ix.10.5; II.vii.3; III.ix.5.5 and 27.6).

85 One such set of loaded terms is the adjective *filthy* and its cognates, which Spenser uses to connect different entities with one another. Errour, for instance, is '[m]ost lothsom, filthie, foule, and full of vile disdaine' (I.i.14.9), while Night, the mother of Duessa, has a face 'so filthy and so fowle' that the night owl continuously howls at it (I.v.30.9); in a different context, Spenser assigns the epithet *filthy* to the various manifestations of beastly lust.

86 On the conceptual link between *textus* and labyrinth, see Doob, *Idea of the Labyrinth*,

to disorient and alienate its characters and readers at all times, because it interlaces, and cross-references each of its parts and plots with possible others, so that the poem's form emerges in the process of reading and finding meaning.[87] One may thus claim that the different aspects of the poem likewise grow different yet intertwining levels of interpretation that encompass the moral, theological and literary aspects of the poem. It is therefore the reader whose orientation and choices make the allegorical poem meaningful, as he has to look behind the veil that the allegorical poet casts about the text's true meaning.[88] Like the characters in the poem, the readers engage with the defining traits of the labyrinth, labouring on a quest for understanding (*labores*), during which they take byways (*ambages*) and are in danger of making mistakes (*errores*).[89] To sum up, in the Wandering Wood canto, Spenser presents a labyrinthine forest in which a labyrinthine monster resides, and develops this labyrinth into the emblematic, condensed representation of his poem as *textus*. It introduces his readers to his romance, announces to them the impact of the monstrous on its plots and themes, and teaches them how to read.

The Wandering Wood and Errour as primordial matter

While the Wood of Errour episode on one level defines the heterocosm as a labyrinthine *textus*, it also taps into another discourse that reflects on crucial aspects of world-making, namely on the source and evolution of the secondary nature Spenser creates for his poem. I would argue that Spenser's descriptions of wood and monster contain 'certaine signes' that point to the philosophico-theological tradition of *prima materia*. In this section I will demonstrate that the Wandering Wood and the monster Errour represent different aspects of first matter, and that Spenser

p. 30 (with reference to Virgil's use of the verb *texere*, 'to weave', in the passage on the Cretan labyrinth), as well as p. 209, p. 228 and p. 259.

87 Wood interprets the Wandering Wood sequence as symbolic of 'the problems of reading properly', also with reference to Una's advice to Redcrosse: 'Therefore I read beware' (I.i.13.8; *Metaphor and Belief*, p. 35).

88 Both Alpers and Quilligan similarly stress the reader's active involvement and frequent frustration when reading and making sense of Spenser's long poem and its allegory (see Alpers, *Poetry*, pp. 137–59, and Quilligan, *Language*, pp. 224–78). While Alpers stresses the calamity of 'ready allegory' that disregards the footfalls and ambiguities of Spenser's text, Quilligan maintains that Spenser's allegory teaches the reader how to read.

89 Nohrnberg similarly argues that in *The Faerie Queene* readers negotiating between the first and second levels of the text experience bewilderment and commit error rather like Redcrosse (see *Analogy*, pp. 101–2, pp. 135–6, and pp. 144–6).

establishes Errour as the material agency from which the monstrosities in Spenser's textual world originate.

The association between romance forests and *prima materia* is traditional, because in Aristotle's *Metaphysics* and especially in Chalcidius's commentary on Plato's *Timaeus* the wood (Greek ὕλη, Latin *silva*)[90] was used as the major metaphor of primordial matter, the chaotic mass from which all things and beings were turned into form (Greek μορφή).[91] In the twelfth century, Bernardus Silvestris, and Alanus ab Insulis further elaborated that this matter was a dark, wild, formless chaos striving for organisation.[92] As critics have variously argued, Spenser's familiarity with this tradition is attested by *The Faerie Queene* and the minor poetry.[93] The Wandering Wood passage in particular reflects Bernardus's rendering of the ὕλη motif.[94] In the *Cosmographia*, Bernardus intro-

90 See Aristotle, *Metaphysics*, VII.iii.3–7 (1029a8–34), and VIII.iv.1–4 (1044a15–36); reference is made to Aristotle, *Metaphysics; Oeconomica; Magna moralia*, ed. and trans. by Hugh Tredennick and G. Cyril Armstrong, 2 vols, Aristotle: Works 17–18, Loeb Classical Library (Cambridge, MA: Harvard University Press; London: Heinemann, 1929; repr. 1960). The complexities of Aristotelian notions of ὕλη are exhaustively dissected and contextualised in Heinz Happ's comprehensive monograph *Hyle: Studien zum aristotelischen Materie-Begriff* (Berlin: Walter de Gruyter, 1971). Aristotle mainly conceived of ὕλη as a single principle; see esp. Happ's discussions in *Hyle*, pp. 260–77 and pp. 302–5. Chalcidius was the first to use *silva* for ὕλη (see Chalcidius, *Platonis Timaeus interprete Chalcidio cum eiusdem commentario*, ed. by Ioh. Wrobel (Leipzig: Teubner, 1876), VII, cxxiii, p. 188, l. 11; cclxviii, p. 299, ll. 15–20; XIII, cclxix, p. 300, ll. 11–12). For commentary, see J. C. M. van Winden, *Calcidius on Matter. His Doctrine and Sources: A Chapter in the History of Platonism* (Leiden: E. J. Brill, 1965), p. 63.

91 See Chalcidius, *Platonis Timaeus*, XIII, cccxxxv, p. 359, ll. 9–10. Servius, commenting on the forests of Virgil's *Aeneid*, called the *silva* the 'elementorum congerie[s]', the 'mass of elements' from which all things are created, and hence described the forest as a place of disorder. See Servius, *Servii grammatici qui feruntur in Vergilii commentarii*, ed. by Georg Thilo and Hermann Hagen, 3 vols (Hildesheim: Georg Olms, 1961), I, 114, note to *Aeneid*, I.314; see also II, 28, note to *Aeneid*, VI.131. These, and other texts cited in this subsection are treated in Saunders, *Forest*, pp. 19–24.

92 See Alanus ab Insulis, *Distinctiones dictionem theologicalium*: 'Dicitur primordialis materia, quae apud Graecos dicitur *yle*, Latine silua, quam etiam Plato silvam vocat; quia, sicut silva materiam praebet aedificiis, sic primordialis materia corporibus universis' ('It is called primordial matter, which among the Greeks is called *yle*, and in Latin *silva*; for as wood renders matter for buildings, so primordial matter for universal bodies'). The Latin quotation is taken from Alanus ab Insulis, *Opera omnia*, ed. by C. de Wisch, Patrologia Latinae, 210, Saeculum XIII (Turnholt: Brepols, 1967), p. 944C.

93 On chaos in *The Faerie Queene*, see Saunders, *Forest*, pp. 189–91, and Hankins, *Source and Meaning*, pp. 65–9. Among others, Nohrnberg explains Florimell's imprisonment in Proteus's submarine cave as the possibility of beauty inherent in chaotic *prima materia*, which is represented by Proteus and his cave (see *Analogy*, pp. 581–4; see also Nohrnberg's interpretation of III.vi.36 on pp. 554–5).

94 George D. Economou argues that Spenser knew Bernardus either directly or indirectly through writers like Alanus ab Insulis or Chaucer (see *The Goddess Natura in Medieval Literature* (Cambridge, MA: Harvard University Press, 1972), p. 59).

duces *silva* as an unformed mass both resisting and craving for order and shape:

> Silva rigens, informe chaos, concretio pugnax,
> Discolor Usie vultus, sibi dissona massa,
> Turbida temperiem, formam rudis, hispida cultum
> Optat, et a veteri cupiens exire tumultu,
> Artifices numeros et musica vincla requirit.
>
> Silva, intractable, a formless chaos, a hostile coalescence, the motley appearance of being, a mass discordant with itself, longs in her tumbulance for a tempering power, in her crudity for form, in her rankness for cultivation. Yearning to emerge from her ancient confusion, she demands the shaping influence of number and the bonds of harmony.[95]

The Wandering Wood and Errour mirror defining characteristics of Bernardus's *silva* in that Spenser projects some of its qualities on to the Wandering Wood and some on to the monster, with the Wandering Wood reflecting the more positive aspects of *silva*, and Errour reflecting its decidedly unwholesome ones. Spenser's Wood of Errour, for instance, is depicted as a place of darkness, abundant vegetation and disorienting paths just like *silva*. Yet since it is also presented as a pleasure grove, it does not suggest full-scale chaos.[96] This is reserved for Errour, who, as a deformity with an overtly chaotic, shifting physique,[97] betrays an unruliness and savagery traditionally associated with ὕλη.[98] Among others, Bernardus assigns *silva* a malignity ('malignitas') that resists form and

95 The Latin original is quoted from Bernardus Silvestris, *Cosmographia*, ed. by Peter Dronke, Textus Minores, 53 (Leiden: E. J. Brill, 1961), I.1 (see also II.3–5); the translation is taken from Bernardus Silvestris, *The Cosmography of Bernardus Silvestris*, trans. by Winthrop Wetherbee (New York and London: Columbia University Press, 1973), p. 69.

96 Saunders links Spenser's wood directly to the larger *silva* tradition (see *Forest*, pp. 189–92).

97 That Spenser places Errour in a cave might not be mere coincidence in this context, as caves were used as ciphers for chaos (see Hankins, *Source and Meaning*, pp. 60–74, and his entry on 'Chaos' in the *Spenser Encyclopedia*, ed. by Hamilton, p. 139).

98 Chalcidius, paragraph 271, refers to a passage from *Timaeus*, 48A, where Plato identifies matter as 'the form of the Errant Cause'. In his commentary on Chalcidius 271, van Winden notes that 'this is the first time the idea of chaos crops up' (*Chalcidius on Matter*, pp. 39–40). This suggests a conceptual link between error and chaos. For *Timaeus*, see Plato, *Timaeus; Critias; Cleitophon; Menexenus; Epistles*, ed. and trans. by R. G. Bury, Plato: Works 9, Loeb Classical Library (Cambridge, MA: Harvard University Press; London: Heinemann, 1929; repr. 1960). Adelman more generally argues that Errour is a grotesque version of the female and maternal 'world of matter into which man is born' ('Revaluing the Body', pp. 17–18 and p. 20).

order: *silva*'s 'restless movement … born of confusion' ('de confusione conceptus, motus … inquietus')[99] also characterises Errour and the motion of her tail. Additionally, the darkness of primordial matter, so central to Bernardus's *Cosmographia*, is figured not only in Errour's wood and den, but also in the coils which she forms with her tail. Even her spawning numerous, variously shaped and deformed serpents offers an important analogy to primordial matter and the genesis of form in the *Cosmographia*. Bernardus maintains that ὕλη is the matter from which all bodies take their shape, a circumstance he stresses by making it the 'generationis uterus indefessus', the 'inexhaustible womb of generation'.[100] Errour herself is just such an 'inexhaustible womb' that generates countless new monsters, and hence represents, in emblematic form, the material agency that conceives novel monstrosities to fill Spenser's textual world.[101]

The relevance of the ὕλη tradition for poetry is attested by sixteenth-century literary criticism, which defined *silva* as the material of poetic making. Cooper's influential *Thesaurus*, for instance, defines 'sylua', among other things, as a 'store of mattier digested together',[102] and Tasso, Spenser's immediate predecessor, explains in his *Discorsi dell' arte poetica e del poema eroico* that the material of poetry 'è simile ad una selva oscura'.[103] Both statements, which interact with the same discourse tradition, characterise *silva* as the source, i.e. as the accumulation of material, from which the poet makes his poem with the power of his imagination, and hence as the 'stuff' from which literature is formed. Spenser's use of the wood as the cipher for poetic making – the source of language and consequently of the text – makes the forest in which Redcrosse and Una experience their first adventure the figuration of the material from which *The Faerie Queene* is created.[104] Yet the wood as the matter of romance poetry is an ambivalent image, because it has the potential to disorientate

99 See Bernardus, *Cosmographia*, II.2.4 and 9–10; and *Cosmography*, p. 70.

100 Bernardus, *Cosmographia*, I.4.1–2; and *Cosmography*, p. 70.

101 See I.i.20.

102 Cooper, *Thesaurus*, s.v. 'sylua', with reference to Cicero, *De oratore*, III, 103: 'Sylua rerum ac sententiarum comparanda est' ('One must accumulate a *silva* of matter and *sententiae*'). Doob also elaborates on *inventio* as a labyrinthine process (see *Idea of the Labyrinth*, pp. 198–201).

103 Tasso, *Discorsi*, in *Prose*, p. 514 ('the material [of poetry] is like a dark forest'; Tasso, *Discourses*, p. 21).

104 Nohrnberg sees a similar link between the variety of trees at the beginning of Spenser's poem and Tasso's notion of poetic diversity: 'niuna selva fu già mai ripiena di tanta varietà d'alberi di quanta diversità di soggetti è la poesia' ('no forest was ever so full of such variety of trees as poetry is of variety of subjects') (see Nohrnberg, *Analogy*, p. 35 and note 85; the quotations are taken from Tasso, *Prose*, pp. 514–15, and *Discourses*, p. 21).

travellers and bring them into danger, and can breed delusion and error.[105] As the 'stuff' of Spenser's poem, the wood of romance has spawned the monster and, on a general level, with her the monsters and monstrous beings that keep appearing in the rest of the poem. Hence, the opening narration allegorises the participation of the monster in the making of every aspect of Spenser's heterocosm.

Concluding remarks

The Faerie Queene illustrates Spenser's self-reflexive engagement with the contemporary discourse on making new worlds and monsters. In the proem to Book II, he pre-empts criticism of the poem as mere fantasy, and instead defines his poem as a secondary nature whose allegorical truths can be traced by careful reading. Spenser engages with the discourse of autonomous creation more extensively in the Wandering Wood episode, which marks the entrance to the text and its world. This complex sequence condenses significant aspects of Spenser's universe of discourse into one multifarious image. On the narrative level, it introduces its heroes to the dangers and challenges of a disorienting world where the monster poses a constant threat to the questers; on a higher plane, it is implemented as a metaliterary emblem that stages the readers' reception of a *textus* of high artistry; and on a distinctly abstract level, the tale of the Wandering Wood and Errour may likewise be interpreted as a meta-poetic allegory illustrating the poet's task in forming his extensive heterocosm. The monster thus plays a decisive role on each level of poetic creation. If Spenser's world-making is hence thematised in the initial episode of his poem, he makes the labyrinth the governing paradigm of his heterocosm, extending far beyond the first canto of the poem and assigning the monstrous a prominent position in it. In *The Faerie Queene*, Spenser hence develops the wood of romance into a complex textual labyrinth. To determine which role the imagination plays in fashioning Spenser's romance heterocosm, we will now enter Phantastes's chamber in the Castle of Alma.

105 Tasso points out that '[l]aonde se l'arte non l'illumina [la selva oscura], altri *errarebbe senza scorta* e *sceglierebbe peraventura il peggio* in cambio del meglio' ('if art does not illuminate [the dark wood], one might *wander without guide* and perhaps *choose the worse* instead of the better'; Tasso, *Discorsi*, p. 514; *Discourses*, p. 21; emphases added). On Tasso's notion of *silva*, see Saunders, *Forest*, pp. 19–24 and p. 190. Cf. also Una's warning: 'the place vnknowne and wilde, / *Breedes* dreadfull doubts' (I.i.12.3–4; emphasis added).

15

In Phantastes's chamber

A discussion of the monstrous and the role the imagination plays in establishing *The Faerie Queene* as a poetic heterocosm leads through Phantastes's chamber, one of the rooms located in the turret of Alma's Castle, a giant architectural allegory of the human body and soul that dominates the narrative of Cantos II.ix–xi.[1] As Spenser also terms this building the House of Temperance (II.ix.arg),[2] he underlines the relevance of this episode for the larger plan of the Legend of Temperance and its eponymous hero Sir Guyon. But apart from its immediate contextual significance, which also rests on Spenser's resorting to the medieval topos of the human body as a castle under siege,[3] the overall depiction of the House of Temperance is so consciously encyclopaedic that it transcends the immediate context in which it appears to include Spenser's entire poem as well as his poetics, specifically his concept of the poetic imagination.

A tour through the castle

The Castle is realised as a gigantic mapping of the human body and soul, through which Alma guides Sir Guyon, Arthur and the Palmer. The amazement that the knights experience at so strange a piece of architecture (II.ix.33.1–4) calls to mind the brilliance of the human body

1 This central sequence has exerted unfaltering fascination on Spenser's readers. Of particular interest are Jonson's marginalia in the 1617 folio of Spenser's works, which illustrate the care with which Jonson studied the Castle of Alma (for the marginalia, see Riddell and Stewart, *Jonson's Spenser*, pp. 175–9).

2 The Castle of Alma therefore relates to the House of Holiness in I.x.

3 See among many others Prudentius's *Psychomachia*, the morality play *The Castle of Perseverance*, and Chaucer's *Tale of Melibee* (*CT*, VII.967–1887). For the *Psychomachia*, see *Prudentius*, ed. and trans. by H. J. Thomson, 2 vols (London: William Heinemann, 1949), I, 274–343; for *The Castle of Perseverance*, consult *The Macro Plays*, ed. Mark Eccles, EETS, OS, 262 (Oxford: Oxford University Press, 1969), pp. 1–111.

expressed at the outset of Canto ix;[4] in metaliterary terms, it reflects the wonder readers experience at Spenser's successful creation of such a gigantic anatomy, enabling them to take a tour through their own bodies to further their self-knowledge.[5]

Alma leads the knights through the bottom and middle sections of the building, which represent the bowels and the heart, to its apex, a 'brain-turret' divided into three compartments, each representing one faculty of the soul.[6] The turret as architectural summit not only corresponds to the peak of human anatomy but also suggests the divine origin of man's rational powers, a circumstance that accentuates the allegorical implication of moving up from the physically base to the height of divine understanding.[7] Every room in the turret is occupied by a sage, and represents a facet of the human brain.[8] Into the first, Spenser places Phantastes, who represents the imagination and fancy (49–52); into the second, an unnamed character who may or may not be Reason (53–4);[9] and into the third, Eumnestes, the personification of Memory, with his young assistant Anamnestes (55–8).[10] Spenser furnishes their chambers with distinctive artefacts that represent the nature of the specific faculty and distinguish them from one another. While Phantastes's room is covered with paintings depicting strange beings and romance characters, the room of the second sage is painted with the deeds of authorities, political institutions and the *artes*. Eumnestes's chamber is devoid of wall-paintings; instead, it is hung with parchment scrolls and books recording past history, among

4 See II.ix.1.

5 On the idea of the wondrous in Spenser, see Biow, *Mirabile Dictu*, pp. 155–71.

6 For erudite discussions of the tour, see Schoenfeldt, *Bodies and Selves*, pp. 50–68, Barkan, *Nature's Work of Art*, pp. 161–73, and Harry Berger, Jr, *The Allegorical Temper: Vision and Reality in Book II of Edmund Spenser's 'Faerie Queene'* (New Haven: Yale University Press, 1957), pp. 64–88.

7 Spenser explains that the turrets are situated 'high aboue this earthly masse' (II.ix.45.3). The architectonic framework is reminiscent of Gothic buildings with peaks reaching upwards to the heavens and God.

8 The turret itself is depicted as a giant head (II.ix.45–6).

9 See Brooks-Davies, *Commentary*, p. 168, with reference to II.ix.54, and King, *Middle English Romance*, p. 165. Miller and Healy identify him as judgement; see David Lee Miller, *The Poem's Two Bodies: The Poetics of the 1590 'Faerie Queene'* (Princeton: Princeton University Press, 1988), pp. 185–6 and pp. 255–6, and Thomas Healy, *New Latitudes: Theory and English Renaissance Literature* (London: Edward Arnold, 1992), p. 100. While James J. Paxson tentatively states that he 'represents all human knowledge that is not fictional' (*The Poetics of Personification* (Cambridge: Cambridge University Press, 1994), p. 143), Hamilton eschews to disclose the sage's identity altogether, but argues that he is 'like the poet … who receives and digests images of sense experience' (note to II.ix.54.2–5).

10 The name Eumnestes, derived from Greek εὐ- + μίμνεμαι, means 'good memory'. Accordingly, the name of his assistant, Anamnestes, from Greek ἀνα- + μίμνεμαι, translates into 'calling to mind'.

them *A Chronicle of Briton Kings* and *The Antiquitee of Faery Lond*, which are presented in Canto x.[11]

Phantastes's chamber

Phantastes, the *spiritus rector* dwelling in the first ventricle of the 'brain-turret', emerges as an allegorical figure under the influence of melancholy: he is a young man of 'swarth complexion' and 'crabbed hew', with 'sharp staring eyes' (representing clarity of vision) under '[b]ent hollow beetle browes' (II.ix.52).[12] As is naturally the case in allegory, his name denotes his fantastic nature,[13] so it does not come as a surprise that the visionary imagination is depicted as an ambivalent faculty which favours the fantastic over a strict *imitatio naturae*.[14] That Phantastes was born under the influence of Saturn emphasises his overriding melancholic qualities, such as profound thought and madness,[15] and testifies to Spenser's involvement in the Renaissance discourse of melancholy.[16] While the genius's youth

11 The Castle of Alma is discussed controversially among critics. Broaddus stresses the 'stability' of the turret, pointing out that such firmness is the result of 'imaginative insight, careful thought, and knowledge and is consequently unrelated to any particular circumstance such as a siege by vices and passions' ('Defense', p. 156). Hadfield, however, casts doubt on the Castle of Alma, arguing that '[t]he mind of the supposedly ideal body is represented as limited and unbalanced', especially because memory and the imagination have become too powerful ('Spenser as Prometheus: A Response to Mark Goth', *Connotations* 20 (2010/11), 189–200 (pp. 194–5)).

12 As has been shown by critics, Phantastes's physiognomy corresponds with melancholy lore; for a representative view, see Brooks-Davies, *Commentary*, pp. 168–9, note to II.ix.55–8. Moreover, Phantastes's complexion evokes that of Maleger and his troops (II.ix.13, and II.xi.22; see Adam H. Kitzes, *The Politics of Melancholy from Spenser to Milton* (New York: Routledge, 2006), pp. 50–2, and Berger, *Allegorical Temper*, pp. 85–7).

13 The name 'Phantastes' derives from the Greek adjective φανταστής, which can also mean 'to be capable of imagining something' (Liddell and Scott, *Greek Lexicon*). Spenser makes this derivation explicit when pointing out that Phantastes has received his name from 'his nature trew' (II.ix.52.2). In a text construed on multi-layered and frequently 'darkened' allegory, such literalism reads like deliberate meta-poetic irony (for similar cases, see Horstmann, *Namen*, p. 131). Paxson erroneously calls Phantastes a 'nonce-word' (*Poetics of Personification*, p. 140). Her reasoning is quite false, as Horstmann's sensible interpretation of the name makes clear (see *Namen*, p. 85 and p. 173).

14 Spenser's use of the term *fantasy* and its variations suggests that its overriding quality lies in its inconstancy. See, among others, Phaedria's 'fantasticke wit' (II.vi.7.2), and Amoret's suffering from 'phantasies / In wavering wemens wit' (III.xii.26.3–4).

15 Elaborating on the positive aspects of Saturn, Stephen H. Rigby explains that the god 'was associated with thoughtfulness, prudence, deep philosophical reflection, with the power of the intellect and ... with reason and understanding' (*Wisdom and Chivalry: Chaucer's 'Knight's Tale' and Medieval Political Theory*, Medieval and Renaissance Authors and Texts 4 (Leiden and Boston: Brill, 2009), pp. 111–12, with reference to Alexander Neckham, William of Auvergne and Christine de Pizan).

16 As Spenser uses the term 'crabbed' also to describe Saturn's 'sterne aspect ... and crabbed

sets him apart from the older sages in the other rooms and relates him to the future, his 'sharpe foresight, and working wit' (II.ix.49.8) clearly mark him as a keen intellect capable of forethought.[17] This puts an important perspective on his melancholic disposition, because it shows that his mental agility has not been lost; on the contrary, Phantastes's wit is 'neuer idle' (49.9). Through such concordantial arrangement, Spenser pits the alert industriousness of the imagination against the idle (i.e. 'vain') fantasies themselves (50.7 and 51.6),[18] thereby consolidating the poet's inclination for quick fantastic thoughts in terms that echo Huarte's call for a 'very *swift* imagination' in the good orator.[19] Additionally, Spenser's polysemic wordplay suggests a positive aspect of *idle* in the sense of 'empty or formless': as Paxson explains, the epithet here can be translated as 'something not fully formed', hence: emergent.[20] As *idle* points to the plenitude of yet undeveloped thoughts and images in Phantastes's chamber, the passage is obliquely linked to the discourse on ὕλη and the emergent cosmos in the Wandering Wood passage. Phantastes is therefore identified as the allegorical representation of human creativity in the making and hence as the source of poetry.

Spenser presents the plenitude of images on Phantastes's tapestries in an ekphrasis that also includes monstrous beings:

---

lookes' in the 'Cantos of Mutabilitie' (VII.vii.52.8), the epithet links Phantastes directly to the mythological source of melancholy. For an extended commentary of the passage, see Brooks-Davies, *Commentary*, pp. 168–9, note to II.I.ix.55–8; for the physiognomic markers, see especially Raymond Klibansky, Erwin Panofsky and Fritz Saxl, *Saturn and Melancholy: Studies in the History of Natural Philosophy, Religion and Art* (London: Thomas Nelson, 1964; repr. Nendeln/Liechtenstein: Kraus Reprint, 1979), p. 290. The term 'crabbed' also opens a channel to the 'cancered crabbed carle' Malbecco (III.ix.3.5), whose vain delusions turn him into personified Gelousie. Phantastes and Malbecco are distinguished by their use of the imagination: the former represents the potentially good creative imagination, the latter stands for the uninhibited, transformative imagination.

17 Hamilton makes a similar observation (see note to II.ix.49.8).

18 Although the ultimate source of the adjective *idle* cannot be determined exactly, the *OED* takes 'empty' as its original meaning (see *OED*, s.v. 'idle, *a.*'). *Idle* and *vain* were frequently used for the products of the imagination; see Sir John Davies, *Nosce Teipsum*, 1649–56, in *The Poems of Sir John Davies*, ed. by Robert Krueger (Oxford: Clarendon Press, 1975); Andreas Laurentius, *A Discourse of the Preservation of the Sight: of Melancholike Diseases; Of Rheumes; and of Old Age*, trans. by Richard Surphlet (London: Felix Kingston, 1599), p. 79; and Bright, *Treatise*, p. 103. For a discussion of the term *idle* in Renaissance literary criticism, see Herman, *Squitter-wits*, pp. 160–2.

19 Huarte, *Examen de ingenios*, p. 131; emphasis added. For a similar contemporary assessment, see John Davies of Hereford's poem *Mirum in Modum*, which explains that the imagination is 'Pow'refull yet … most vnstaid', and 'resteth not' in creating 'visions vaine' (*Complete Works*, I, 7).

20 See Paxson, *Poetics of Personification*, p. 141, with reference to the Old English Genesis, 106.

> ... dispainted all with in,
> With sondry colours, in the which were writt
> Infinite shapes of thinges dispersed thin;
> Some such as in the world were neuer yit,
> Ne can deuized be of mortall wit;
> Some daily seene, and knowen by their names,
> Such as in idle fantasies doe flit:
> Infernall Hags, *Centaurs*, feendes, *Hippodames*,
> Apes, Lyons, Aegles, Owles, fooles, louers, children, Dames.
> (II.ix.50)

Phantastes's frescos immediately suggest the diverse 'rich tapestry' Sidney describes when explaining the poet's creation of a second nature in his *Defence*.[21] Spenser divides the innumerable colourful images (or 'thinges') on Phantastes's walls into two categories: those that do not (yet) exist and cannot be fashioned by a mere mortal, and those that are already known and named. Although the catalogue of known creatures in 50.8–9 baffles through asyndetic enumeration, Spenser takes great pains to place each of the twelve items in a logical sequence.[22] It is noteworthy that more than half of them are potentially monstrous: the 'Infernall hags' relate to hellish sorceresses and monsterised females that try to hinder the paths of romance heroes and heroines;[23] the '*Centaurs*' encode the multitude of possible combinations of man and animal (with particular emphasis on their concupiscence);[24] 'feendes' are non-material agents from hell that are also textually manifested in the many evil sprites conjured to puzzle the poem's protagonists;[25] and the '*Hippodames*' mark the transition towards the wondrous creatures of the sea.[26] Within the cultural norms of the sixteenth century (and of the Middle Ages, for that matter) the ape likewise

21 Tannier ('Bestiere Mannierist', pp. 55–6) recognises the ambivalence of the Spenserian passage, pointing out that the creatures might be the product of 'idle fantasies', but do actually appear prominently in the poem. He claims that Phantastes figures as a melancholic creator of monsters and fantastic animals, and maintains that the plenitude of the monsters and their exuberant descriptions bear witness to Spenser's attempt to constantly seize the readers' attention. Nohrnberg links Phantastes's imaginings directly to the literary theories of Mazzoni and Tasso (see *Analogy*, pp. 760–1).

22 Paxson spots three generic groups: mythology, *Physiologus* and the medieval romance, somewhat disregarding the fact that these sources inevitably inform early modern romances and other contemporary genres (see *Poetics of Personification*, p. 142).

23 See the discussion of the hags in Chapter 10, 'Monstrous humans'.

24 See, e.g., Satyrane and Errour. On Spenser's conceptualisation of centaurs, see Watson, 'Forreine and Monstrous Beasts', pp. 171–2.

25 See for instance Archimago's creation of Una's *doppelgänger* (I.i.45–8), and Malbecco's metamorphosis into Jealousy (III.x.55–60).

26 See the marine creatures in II.xii. The hippodames reappear in another ekphrasis, namely on the tapestries in the House of Busirane (III.xi.40.9).

falls into the category of quasi-human monstrosities.[27] Even when actual animals are mentioned, such as the lion and the eagle, it can be argued that Spenser places them alongside each other not only because they are animal kings ruling over the four-footed beasts of the land and the winged creatures of the air but also because he invites his readers to generate meaning between the two, so as to combine them into the monstrous griffin.[28] In this particular instance, the readers thus re-enact the poet's creating new monstrosities out of known shapes stored in their memories.[29]

At the same time, Spenser's use of the prefix *dis-* to characterise Phantastes's frescos also suggests the faculty's power to bring received data out of shape through disfiguration.[30] Together with similar prefixes like *mal-* and *de-*, *dis-* is frequently used to describe the monsters in the poem. By correlating these prefixes with monstrous descriptions, Spenser comments on the teratological and poetical discourse in which he participates, a connection between the pictorial and the literary that inheres in his use of the word 'writ' (50.2), the generic term for literary production. In this passage, Spenser hence makes explicit the thematic and conceptual importance of the monster for his poem: distorted monstrosities in the literary world of *The Faerie Queene* become bearers of meaning, indeed key elements in the composition of his epic romance.

Each item on Phantastes's frescos has an immediately recognisable referent in *The Faerie Queene*, and in 'fantastic literature' at large, and is carefully chosen by the narrator to draw a comprehensive inventory of literary imaginings and access his readers' literary experiences.[31]

27 See Salisbury, *The Beast Within*, pp. 142–4, and Fudge, *Perceiving Animals*, pp. 29–31.

28 This is also claimed by Hamilton, note to II.ix.51.7–9.

29 Paxson correctly assesses Phantastes as the 'personified, specular image of the process whereby … *The Faerie Queene* … comes into being before our eyes as we read' (*Poetics of Personification*, p. 142; see also Tannier's less elaborated statement in 'Bestiare Manièriste', p. 58). The observation that Spenser's Phantastes triggers the reader's Phantastes calls to mind Plett's explanation of the reciprocity between writing and reading: 'Leistet der Autor die Transformation vom Phantasie- zum Sprachbild, so der Rezipient das Umgekehrte' ('While the author transforms the fantastic image into a verbal one, the reader effects the reverse'; '"… of imagination all compact"', p. 22).

30 Cf. 'dispainted' and 'dispersed' in II.ix.50.1 and 3.

31 Miller critiques Hamilton's advocating a carefully construed catalogue: 'second reading, the mental activity of classifying and deducing relations, is a function of the middle chamber' (*The Poem's Two Bodies*, p. 186). The passage discussed on these pages is not the only monstrous catalogue in the poem. In Book III, Trompart similarly invents a representative list of monsters from the epic and romance traditions to scare Malbecco away from the wilderness. Trompart's catalogue, which includes 'Dragons, and Minotaures, and feendes of hell, / And many wilde woodmen' (III.x.40.5–6), reads like Spenser's meta-poetic nod to the literary background of his own poem, and explains the origin of its monsters in a self-referential statement.

The correlation in density and typology between the monstrous creatures on the walls of Phantastes's chamber and those appearing in *The Faerie Queene* corroborates the conceptual significance of the monstrous for Spenser's poem. Spenser, however, rarely resorts to known creatures, except in similes and metaphors that the reader can decode easily, but rather creates new beings that have no single direct precedent in the world or in earlier poetry. The poet explicitly stresses this penchant for inventing new monstrosities by frequently pointing out that the creatures he describes have never been seen before.[32] Spenser's poetic practice of presenting 'sights never seen' suggests a connection to Phantastes's tapestries and invites a first hypothesis on his idea of the poet:[33] when Spenser claims that the shapes or images that do not yet exist in the world ('in the world were neuer yit'; 50.4) cannot be created by a 'mortall wit' (50.5), he implies, arguably, that it takes a supreme poet, i.e. a creator whose more than mortal wit can take full advantage of his imaginative capabilities. Only a poet who exceeds mediocrity can devise these new creatures from the chaos of '[i]nfinite shapes', and bring them into existence within his own fictional space.[34] This hypothesis brings Spenser's text into close proximity with Sidney's cardinal tenet that the poet making a secondary nature creates 'forms such as never were in nature'.[35] Spenser's Phantastes passage is hence a clear metapoetic nod to the fledgling idea of the poetic heterocosm.

Against the backdrop of the secondary world, the discussion of monstrosities hints at essential aspects of Spenser's art and heightens the readers' awareness of the role the poet takes on when he conceptualises a new poem out of an infinite mass of available and unknown images.[36]

32 See I.viii.48.9 for Duessa's ugly body, and III.vii.22.7 for the hyena's monstrous physique. For the 'sights never seen' topos and its connection to fantasy, see also Spenser's 'An Hymne in Honour of Love', 254–5.

33 Spenser's use of the 'sights never seen' topos suggests not only Sidney's claim that the poet creates 'forms such as never were in nature' (*Defence*, p. 78). It also calls to mind Theseus's speech in Shakespeare's *Midsummer Night's Dream*, which draws attention to the 'forms of things unknown' (V.15) the poet creates. This link is treated in Chapter 16, below.

34 The poet George Chapman similarly marks the '*most geniale, more-then-humane soules*' as the poets' prerequisite for creating living verse and fabulous creatures in his 'Hymnus in Noctem', which forms part of *The Shadow of Night* (London: William Ponsonby, 1594). The poem is discussed in Chapter 17, below.

35 See also Pierre de LaPrimaudaye's verdict that the imagination creates 'those things which neuer haue bin, shalbe, or can be. For it staieth not in that which is shewed vnto it by the senses that serue it' (*The Second Part of the French Academie*, p. 155).

36 Cf. also Heninger's remark that the poet reduces 'the welter of particular events to a unity' ('Aesthetic Experience', p. 92).

Moreover, as representation of plenitude, Phantastes's chamber interacts with the discourse of a fertile nature. In Spenser's poem, the imagination is characterised as a space inviting comparison with the Garden of Adonis, which represents the healthy fecundity of a natural, maternal procreation, where 'Infinite shapes of creatures … are bred, / And vncouth formes, which none yet euer knew' (III.vi.35.1–2).[37] The Garden of Adonis, the expansive *locus amoenus* at the centre of Book III, might oppose the chaos at work within Phantastes's chamber, because it represents Nature in her most positive and divine sense. Nevertheless, Spenser's use of identical phrases in both passages is significant for the discussion of the imagination, and can be explained in a concordantial reading: since the reference to the '[i]nfinite shapes of creatures' derives verbatim from the passage on Phantastes's chamber, where '[i]nfinite shapes of thinges [are] dispersed thin', it becomes apparent that Spenser conceives poetry as analogous to the creation of nature.[38] More precisely, whereas the Garden is the seminary of forms that will progress into the world, Phantastes's chamber is the seminary of internal poetic images that will become part of Spenser's poetic endeavour.

The bee simile

The plenitude of matter and ideas poses a significant problem to the creative imagination, as the next stanza explains:

> And all the chamber filled was with flyes,
> Which buzzed all about, and made such sound,
> That they encombred all mens eares and eyes,
> Like many swarmes of Bees assembled round,
> After their hiues with honny do abound:
> All those were idle thoughtes and fantasies,
> Deuices, dreames, opinions vnsound,
> Shewes, visions, sooth-sayes, and prophesies;
> And all that fained is, as leasings, tales, and lies.
>
> (II.ix.51)

The buzzing flies in Phantastes's chamber, which represent the multitude of unreliable, and fictional images, are a puzzling detail. Commenting on

37 See Helen Andrews Kahin, 'Spenser and the School of Alanus', *English Literary History* 8 (1942), 257–72 (p. 257), Nohrnberg, *Analogy*, pp. 520–3, and Pugh, *Spenser and Ovid*, p. 104 and pp. 135–49. On creation and procreation in the Garden of Adonis, see Broaddus's exhaustive analysis in *Spenser's Allegory of Love*, pp. 70–9.

38 Tannier makes a similar claim (see 'Bestiaire manièriste', pp. 58–9). See also Kaske, *Spenser's Biblical Poetics*, pp. 176–7.

the governing simile that likens the flies to the bees, Tannier takes the easy way out when merely pointing out that bees, after all, bring honey, and therefore carry positive connotations.[39] However, the comparison of flies with bees seems peculiar, for it employs almost identical domains.[40] The rhetorical efficacy of the simile is partly rendered moot by the circumstance that the fly was the generic name for all flying insects.[41] The flies are also dubious in a contextual sense: they hark back to the episode in which Archimago, in a magic ritual in which he creates a second Una, summons a vast number of demons which buzz around his head 'like litle flyes' (I.i.38.2). That Archimago, who is explicitly dubbed a 'maker' by the narrator (45.2), is presented as Beelzebub, the Lord of the Flies, in command of demonic creatures[42] might blemish Phantastes, and hence the imagination.[43] In order to unravel these tangled skeins, the bee simile requires a concordantial reading that works out the significance of flight imagery, as well as the minor and major distinctions between flies and bees, and between Phantastes's flies and Archimago's demons.

One clue to the simile lies in Spenser's serious play with the traditional use of flight imagery to describe the feats of the imagination in the early modern period. A representative example figures in John Davies of Hereford's *Mirum in Modum*, where the imagination 'with hir wings (that can out-fly the wind;) / Through *Heau'n*, *Earth*, *Hell*, and what they hold, doth fly'.[44] Consonant with this tradition, Spenser uses the verb *to flit* in the Phantastes passage to describe the flight of fantasies and to anticipate the buzzing flies.[45] Quite significantly, he resorts to this term again in Book III to characterise the flight of Pegasus, the mythological emblem of poetry.[46] Yet Spenser subverts the image of the high-flying fantasy in the

39 See Tannier, 'Bestiare manièriste', p. 56.

40 Metaphors are not necessarily daring when they yoke together strikingly dissimilar domains as in metaphysical poetry, but also when the target and source domains of the comparison are too close for comfort; see Harald Weinrich, 'Semantik der kühnen Metapher', *Deutsche Vierteljahresschrift für Literaturwissenschaft und Geistesgeschichte 37 (1963)*, 325–44.

41 See *OED*, s.v. 'fly, *n.*1'.

42 See Hadfield, 'Prometheus', p. 196.

43 The link between demons buzzing like flies around Archimago and the flies in Phantastes's chamber is additionally strengthened by the fiends depicted on Phantastes's tapestries (II.ix.50.8).

44 See John Davies of Hereford, *Mirum in Modum*, in *The Complete Works*, ed. by Alexander B. Grosart (1878), Anglistica and Americana, 2 vols (Hildesheim: Georg Olms, 1968; reprint of 1878 edn), I, 9; Sir John Davies, *Nosce Teipsum*, 1093–6; and Spenser, 'October Eclogue', 83–4 (cf. also Plett, '"... of imagination all compact"', pp. 19–20).

45 See II.ix.50.7 ('Such as in idle fantasies do flit').

46 See III.xi.42.9, where Spenser relates the origin of the winged horse ('faire *Pegasus*, that flitteth in the ayre'). Cf. also I.ix.21.9 (a brief simile), V.vi.7.8 (the topos of the winged

Castle of Alma episode by contextualising it into an indoor scene, which restricts any flight of fancy to the confines of the room. This emphasises the centrality of Phantastes's own claustrophobic chamber of the imagination, as well as the ideas and sense impressions buzzing about in it, and thus draws attention to the sage's creative autonomy. The swift flight of the insects figures forth the quick-wittedness of the imagination, and describes it as an internal process.[47] The image also harks back to Sidney's concept of the second nature created by the poet, more specifically to the notion that the poet 'rang[es] only within the zodiac of his own wit'.[48] Although the image of the zodiac is much more expansive than that of the room, Sidney emphasises the relevance of the imagination within the brain chambers just as much as Spenser does.[49] Assessed from this point of view, Sidney's notion of the 'high-flying liberty of conceit', which underscores the potentially unlimited range of an imagination that can access the high heavens, the pit of hell and the realm of the supernatural, is a pronounced interior process.[50] Nature might thus be the poet's guide, but it is his own internal creativity that can transform nature into a secondary poetic world. Both Sidney and Spenser therefore emphasise the potential plenitude of their creations on the grounds of artistic autonomy.

A second clue to the simile lies in the negative connotations of the flies. The comparison jars with known animal lore, for as Batman reports in his translation of Bartholomaeus's *De proprietatibus rerum*, some types of flies were the innate enemies of honey-gathering bees, either killing them or robbing them of their sustenance.[51] Additionally, while the former are animals feeding on and breeding in carrion, the bees actively create a useful (nourishing) and pleasing (tasteful) product by gathering the best raw material from the freshest flowers.[52] In classical and early modern

thoughts), III.iv.54.4–5 ('thousand fancies bett [Arthur's] ydle brayne / With their light wings'), as well as *The Ruines of Tyme*, 426 and 645–58, where Spenser draws a connection between fame and poetry.

47 See also Puttenham's idea of a 'sharpe and quick inuention' (*Arte*, p. 307). On the proverbial swiftness of the imagination, see generally Plett, '"... of imagination all compact"', pp. 18–19.

48 Sidney, *Defence*, p. 78. Nohrnberg points out that the zodiac is the symbol of 'the poet's imaginative population of physical nature with creatures of his own begetting', and may also represent the Comanian notion of *pansophia*, or world-wisdom (*Analogy*, pp. 761–72).

49 Puttenham uses similar terms when remarking that the 'poet makes & contriues out of his owne braine' (*Arte*, p. 3).

50 Cf. also John Davies of Hereford, *Mirum in Modum*, in *Complete Works*, I, p. 9. When Robert Burton relates how some people tell of 'strange things of heaven and hell' (Burton, *Anatomy*, I, 254), he questions the supremacy of the poet's imagination.

51 See *Batman vppon Bartholome*, XVIII.12.

52 *Batman vppon Bartholome*, XVIII.12, also stresses their cleanliness.

literary theory, the bee simile was therefore used in connection with Horace's *utile dulci*, as well as the poet's collecting ideas and selecting from the best materials.[53] In addition to these common notions, flies and gnats are also used as negative images in *The Faerie Queene*, with Spenser employing them as embodiments of annoying and persistent groups of people,[54] which makes the image problematic.

Even more significantly, Spenser sometimes resorts to flies when he describes a multitude of monsters, thereby stressing the disreputable nature of these animals: at the outset of Redcrosse's adventure in Book I, Errour's deformed spawn is compared to gnats, and so are Maleger's monstrous troops right before the Knight of Temperance and his companions enter Alma's Castle.[55] These examples suggest continuity between the monsters the poet creates for the outside world of his poem and the flies buzzing inside Phantastes's chamber. The text of the poem supports such an assessment, for Spenser enhances this thematic interrelation by using the verb *to encumber* both in Phantastes's chamber and in Errour's den: Phantastes is 'encombred' by the flies in his chamber just as Redcrosse is 'encombred sore' by Errour's spawn.[56] The connection between flies and monsters that these examples suggest is strengthened by the various depictions of deformities on Phantastes's walls, and the monsters

53 The bee metaphor has a long history. Brian Vickers discusses Seneca, *Epistulae morales* 84.3–6 as the seminal passage for this development, and refers to Plutarch, *How a Young Person Should Study Poetry*, 28 E–F, 30 C–D and 32 E–F ('Introduction', *English Renaissance Literary Criticism*, ed. by Brian Vickers (Oxford, Clarendon Press, 1999), pp. 24–5). Even the reader became a bee, distinguishing the useful parts of a work from the potentially unhealthy. See generally Jürgen von Stackelberg, 'Das Bienengleichnis: Ein Beitrag zur Geschichte der literarischen *Imitatio*', *Romanische Forschungen* 68 (1956), 271–93. Jonson writes in *Timber* that the writer 'draw[s] forth out of the best, and choicest flowers, with the Bee, and turn[s] all into Honey'. For the texts, see: Lucius Annaeus Seneca, *Ad Lucilium epistulae morales*, trans. by Richard M. Gummere, 3 vols, Loeb Classical Library (Cambridge, MA: Harvard University Press; London: Heinemann, 1917–25), II (1920), 276–81; Plutarch, *Moralia I: The Education of Children. How the Young Man Should Study Poetry. On Listening to Lectures. How to Tell a Flatterer from a Friend. How a Man May Become Aware of His Progress in Virtue*, trans. by Frank Cole Babbitt, Loeb Classical Library (Cambridge, MA: Harvard University Press; London: Heinemann, 1927); and Ben Jonson, *Ben Jonson*, ed. by C. H. Herford, Percy and Evelyn Simpson, 11 vols (Oxford: Clarendon Press, 1954–60), VIII (1954), 639.

54 Cf., among others, the brigands assaulting Calidore at VI.xi.48. The fullest account of Spenser's use of flying insects features in Watson's article 'Emblem and Experience', pp. 117–19, which elaborates on Spenser's indebtedness to the emblematic tradition, as well as his personal observations of these animals. She maintains that this cluster of images is usually deployed for negative comparisons.

55 For Errour's spawn, see I.i.22–3, and for Maleger's troops besieging the Castle of Alma, see II.ix.16. See also I.i.38, where flies are used to illustrate the multitude of sprites assisting Archimago in his magic rituals. Cf. Kitzes, *Politics of Melancholy*, pp. 50–1.

56 Compare I.i.22.9 and 23.5 with II.ix.51.3.

besieging Alma's Castle, which rise from the ground like gnats from the fens of Allan. On a poetic level, these examples establish a connection between the winged insects in Spenser's similes and the discourse of the monstrous, in that they create a close bond between the external threat of the monsters and the internal trouble of the flitting fantasies.[57]

The image of the swarming flies, which as nearly insubstantial, physically delicate creatures of the air also evoke the thinly painted, almost insubstantial frescos on Phantastes's walls, additionally stresses the difficulty of artistic creation in the larger poetical context of the early modern romance. The stanza hence illustrates the problematic process of bringing order among a host of disorienting images (i.e. the flies in the simile) that impair 'inner' vision just as much as Maleger's monstrous rabblement upsets 'external' sight (and other sense perceptions). The simile, however, not only illustrates the difficulty of poetic creation but also specifies the process that informs it. Quite surprisingly, this process inheres in the trope itself. Generally, a poetic simile projects a source domain on a target domain in a one-way transaction that alters the readers' received view of the target domain. In the bee simile, however, source and target domains are so identical that the simile amounts to a transformation of the flies into bees, with the conjunction *like* highlighting this change. The pronounced similarity between flies and bees necessitates a concordantial reading. The useless flies, which otherwise impair sight and hearing, are here turned into honey-bees that can become useful parts in the secondary nature designed by the creative fantasy. In Phantastes's chamber, the proverbial 'bees in the head'[58] are hence an important source for poetic creation, as they can become the useful 'stuff' of (emergent) poetry. As such, the simile, like the notion of *prima materia* discussed in Chapter 14 above, is a figuration of the matter, or storehouse from which poetry and the heterocosm are made. Andrew King comes close to the poetical impact of the Phantastes passage when explaining that 'in [the imagination's] alchemical workings, buzzing flies become honey-laden bees'.[59] Alchemy, however, is not implied in this simile. Rather, what lies at the core of this image is the transformative power of the imagination that can, but does

57 Healy points out emphatically that the similarities between Phantastes's fancies *inside* the Castle and Maleger's troops *outside* illustrate that '[t]he interior, too, contains elements which are potentially destructive'. Such an evaluation brings into relief the ambiguity of the flies. See Healy, *New Latitudes*, pp. 100–1, as well as below.

58 For the proverbial 'head full of bees', see M. P. Tilley, *A Dictionary of the Proverbs in England in the Sixteenth and Seventeenth Centuries* (Ann Arbor: Michigan University Press, 1950), H 255 and P 452.

59 King, *Middle English Romance*, p. 166

not necessarily, turn the mass of empty delusions in Spenser's list (51.6–9) into the living, speaking images of romance poetry. Fantasy, if under the control of the poet, can transform this onslaught of figments into the material necessary for literary production, and from it fashion a poetic heterocosm.[60]

A third clue inheres in the relation between the bee simile that describes Phantastes's flies, and the fly simile that describes the demons in Archimago's magic ritual:

> And forth he cald out of deepe darknes dredd
> Legions of Sprights, the which like litle flyes
> Fluttring about his euerdamned hedd,
> A waite whereto their seruice he applyes,
> To aide his friendes, or fray his enimies[.]
>
> (I.i.38.1–5)

The fly simile here underscores the demonic nature of the sprites and marks Archimago as a type of Beelzebub. As both passages use similar imagery to illustrate a creative process,[61] Spenser's readers are required to read these far-flung passages concordantially, and to establish differences between them. In the Archimago passage, the magician conjures up demons from 'deepe darknes' (38.1), and it is these demons that are likened to flies; in the Castle of Alma episode, Phantastes's chamber is already filled with flies, and the flies are compared to bees. Spenser here effects a *distinctio* between two related, but different modes of making. Archimago uses his power for black magic, and uses the conjured spirits to evil ends, that is to create a false Una who thwarts Redcrosse's quest.[62] Phantastes represents the active, potentially good imagination, which can turn already existing thoughts and fantasies (the flies) into good creations of proper poetry (the bees). The bee simile hence figures as the antitype of the fly simile in the earlier passage. The only demons in Phantastes's chamber are the fiends depicted on Phantastes's tapestries (II.ix.50.8); as part of an ekphrasis, these reprehensible creatures are associated with the works of art in which they appear.

Without pushing analogies too far, one can trace a resemblance between the depiction of poetic creation in the bee simile, which characterises the

60 Grant Williams argues in favour of a connection between the flies, Phantastes, and memory; see 'Phantastes's Flies: The Trauma of Amnesic Enjoyment in Spenser's *Memory Palace*', *Spenser Studies* 18 (2004), 231–52 (pp. 244–5).

61 Cf. II.ix.51.

62 Archimago 'with charmes and hidden artes, / Had made a Lady of that other Spright' (I.i.45.1–2).

poet's task as a deliberate transformative process taking place in the imagination, and Puttenham's distinction between *phantastici* and *euphantasiotae*, which has been outlined in Chapter 13, above. The central simile of the Phantastes sequence characterises the creative imagination as a transformative agency that can turn bewildering sense impressions into choice poetic images, i.e. from something merely fantastic into something that is good and useful.[63] A similar difference inheres in Puttenham's terminology. When Puttenham describes the orderly imagination neutrally as the 'phantasticall part of man' where beautiful and truthful images are created, and only later tells *phantastici* from *euphantasiotae*, he pits the monsters that the imagination creates itself without the control of reason (i.e. *sponte sua*) against images that the poet creates actively for his poem. The addition of the prefix εὐ-, which derives from Old Greek ἀγαθός and means 'good', therefore implies the active literary transformation involved in creating good poetry from what the imagination has to offer. If one applies Puttenham's terminology to Phantastes's work as described in the bee simile, the comparison sketches the change from merely 'fantastic' imaginings into useful 'eu-fantastic' ones that manifest the poet's grasp on form, which stems from his ability to transform images, even those of monsters, into meaningful and usable poetic material. Puttenham's distinction, albeit resorting to monstrous rhetoric to set a negative example, interacts with Spenser's depiction of poetic creation, because it characterises the poet's task as a deliberately transformative process taking place in the imagination.

Summarising statements

The three stanzas depicting Phantastes's chamber testify to Spenser's sustained interest in the imagination and its importance for the creation of the poem. He employs a cluster of terms to describe Phantastes and Eumnestes which he already used in the proem to Book II to describe possible accusations against his poem. Among others, Phantastes's 'idle fantasies' (II.ix.50.7), and his chamber 'filled … with flyes' (51.1) recall the 'th'aboundance of an ydle braine' (II.Pr.1.3); Phantastes's 'dispainted' frescos and Eumnestes's parchments (ix.50.1) call to mind the proem's 'painted forgery rather than matter of iust memory' (II.Pr.1.4); and phrases like 'famous antique history', 'antiquities' and 'this antique ymage' in the proem relate directly to the faerie chronicle stored in Eumnestes's chamber, the '*Antiquitee* of *Faery* lond' (II.ix.60.2).[64] By thus correlating

63 See II.ix.51.
64 Cf. also the 'antique rolls' in I.Pr.2.4.

these passages, Spenser does not only conceptualise his own approach to poetic creativity against the backdrop of the general view of the imagination; as the issues influencing the imagination are equally applicable to describe the poet's process of world-making, he also shows that both discourses are closely linked.[65] It is the reader's task to read both passages carefully to arrive at a proper understanding of the imagination's use for poetic world-making. The frescos covering the chamber's walls, and the multitude of flies buzzing around Phantastes mark the imagination as a bountiful faculty that conceives the poetic images the poet brings alive in his work. Drawing on a large number of topoi, such as melancholy, idleness, the flight of fancy and the insubstantiality of ideas, Spenser explicitly characterises this creation of known and unknown monstrous shapes, and, ultimately, of the heterocosm as possibilities inherent in the imaginative faculty. Implicitly, he also establishes cross-references to monstrous passages in the poem, thus creating a monstrous subtext to the discourse on the imagination and his own poem. It is no coincidence that Sir Guyon and the Palmer fight Alma's monstrous enemies, and, after leaving the Castle of Alma, embark on a voyage over monster-infested waters to the Bower of Bliss, where the victims of concupiscence have been transformed from humans into animals by Acrasia: these tales reflect on the workings of the characters' imaginations, and thus serve as textual manifestations of the poetic subtext established in Phantastes's chamber.[66]

Giamatti's assessment that Phantastes's chamber is 'Spenser's clearest vision of the potential for deformation that is implicit in the process of transformation'[67] is borne out by every detail in Spenser's carefully painted portrait of the fantastic imagination. The unease expressed by critics such as Murrin, who reads into the Phantastes episode Spenser's misgivings about the human imagination,[68] and Felicity A. Hughes, who maintains that Spenser subscribed to a largely negative view of the imagination,[69] is therefore overstated. Yet almost every critic dealing with Phantastes ultimately accentuates his negative qualities. Where MacCaffrey argues

65 Compare also Spenser's reference to 'th'abundance of an idle braine' (II.Pr.1.3) that might have produced the poem to the '[i]nfinite shapes of thinges' (II.ix.50.3) residing in Phantastes's chamber.

66 This is in line with King's argument, who reads the destruction of the Bower of Bliss as the castigation of the imaginative faculty (see *The Middle English Romance*, p. 166). On the hypertrophic imagination of Spenser's characters, see Chapter 16, below.

67 Giamatti, *Play of Double Senses*, p. 109.

68 See Michael Murrin, *The Allegorical Epic: Essays on Its Rise and Decline* (Chicago: University of Chicago Press, 1980), p. 134.

69 See Felicity A. Hughes, 'Imagination', *Spenser Encyclopedia*, ed. by Hamilton, pp. 392–3, and Herman, *Squitter-wits*, pp. 145–72.

that 'imagination's inherent duplicity' turns *The Faerie Queene* into a 'vast Phantastes-chamber',[70] Spenser would acknowledge that the items in his catalogue are vital ingredients in his heroic poem that he can control with his reason. A more productive view is to diagnose Phantastes as the *sine qua non* for poetry, embodying the two main results of the creative imagination, namely disfiguration, which is shown in his own dishevelled appearance and the 'dis-painted' frescos, and artistry, which is contained in the simile transforming the deafening and bamboozling flies into bees. It is this transformation that underscores the literary purpose of the strange beings and fanciful characters depicted on Phantastes's frescos, and their significance for fashioning a secondary world.

70 MacCaffrey, *Spenser's Allegory*, p. 242.

16

Animating the monstrous imagination in *The Faerie Queene*

An educated sixteenth-century reader of Spenser's *The Faerie Queene*, upon entering the turret in which the three faculties of the brain reside, also entered the contemporary discourse of interior physiology. The link between Alma's Castle and the growing Renaissance interest in anatomy has been picked up by Spenserians of almost all generations; in turn, the encyclopaedic quality of the passage has also made it attractive for critics interested in the anatomical concepts of the early modern period. As a consequence, Spenser's Phantastes has become isolated from the poetic context in which he originally appeared.[1] The mutual influence between literary and scientific investigations is not a twentieth-century phenomenon. In fact, Renaissance writers indulged freely in an interactive discourse that turned the imagination into a complex web of interrelating and concurring ideas.

Hence, Spenser's interest in the workings of the imagination was not exceptional in the Renaissance.[2] This circumstance is not surprising, as the imagination was generally regarded as the source of the poet's creative work. In consequence, poets and playwrights alike probed the nature of this faculty,[3] whether in a ludic manner as George Peele in his *Old Wives'*

1 William Rossky, for example, treats Spenser's architectural vision of the body indiscriminately as a source text for his larger argument on the Renaissance imagination, thus somewhat bypassing its fictional nature. See Rossky, 'Imagination', pp. 59–61, and, critically, Kitzes, *Politics of Melancholy*, pp. 28–9.

2 The authoritative implications of II.xi are indeed so prominent that E. Ruth Harvey briefly summarises Guyon's visit to the tower at the beginning of her short monograph *The Inward Wits* to illustrate the anatomical concept that had been internalised by Spenser's early modern readership; see E. Ruth Harvey, *The Inward Wits: Psychological Theory in the Middle Ages and the Renaissance*, Warburg Institute Surveys, 6 (London: The Warburg Institute [at the] University of London, 1975), pp. 1–2, and her entry on 'Psychology', in *Spenser Encyclopedia*, ed. by Hamilton, pp. 565–8.

3 The most valuable and thoroughgoing account of the imagination is still Murray W. Bundy's time-honoured *The Theory of Imagination in Classical and Medieval Thought*. The role and concept of the imagination in the early modern period are treated in:

Tale, which is framed by a sub-plot featuring three comic characters by the name of Antic, Frolic and Fantastic,[4] or in a more serious fashion as Shakespeare in his *Midsummer Night's Dream*, where Theseus voices his contempt for the uninhibited imagination of the poet, the madman and the lover.[5] In '*Mirum in Modum*, A glimpse of Gods Glorie, and *the Soules Shape*' (1603), John Davies of Hereford then uses lyrical poetry for doctrinal *explicatio*, extensively elaborating on the subdivisions of the soul and their operations.[6] More importantly, the late sixteenth and early seventeenth centuries saw the publication of such seminal medical and philosophical works as Timothy Bright's *A Treatise of Melancholie* (1586), Robert Burton's *The Anatomy of Melancholy* (1621) and Francis Bacon's *The Advancement of Learning* (1605).[7] Spenser's *The Faerie Queene* is hence part of a larger discourse. As these texts are indicative of the traditions and developments informing the transitional period between the two centuries, they cast light on Spenser's position in the discourse of the imagination, and bring into relief his notion of poetic transformation and image-making in the context of the monstrous.

In this chapter, I argue that Spenser deliberately animates seminal aspects of the monstrous imagination in his *natura altera* in order to relate literary monsters to contemporaneous cultural ideas, a link that marks the monstrous beings in *The Faerie Queene* as self-reflexive poetic

---

Murray W. Bundy, '"Invention" and "Imagination" in the Renaissance', *Journal of English and Germanic Philology* 29 (1930), 535–45; Rossky, 'Imagination', 49–73; Harry Berger, Jr, 'The Renaissance Imagination: Second World and Green World', *The Centennial Review* 9 (1965), 36–78; and E. Ruth Harvey, *The Inward Wits*. Cf. also Nicholas H. Steneck, 'Albert the Great on the Classification and Localization of the Internal Senses', *Isis* 65 (1974), 193–211, and Edward P. Mahoney, 'Sense, Intellect, and Imagination in Albert, Thomas and Siger', in *The Cambridge History of Later Medieval Philosophy*, ed. by Norman Kretzmann, Anthony Kenny and Jan Pinborg (Cambridge: Cambridge University Press, 1982), pp. 602–22. See also the monograph and two articles by Broaddus, which have already been mentioned: *Spenser and the Allegory of Love: Social Vision in Books III, IV, and V of 'The Faerie Queene'*; 'Renaissance Psychology and Britomart's Adventures in *Faerie Queene* III'; and 'Renaissance Psychology and the Defense of Alma's Castle'.

4 See George Peele, *The Old Wives' Tale*, in *The Minor Elizabethan Drama, Vol. 2: Comedies*, Everyman's Library, 492 (London: J. M. Dent; New York: E. P. Dutton, 1910), pp. 131–5 and p. 160. For a discussion of the passage, see Lengeler, *Tragische Wirklichkeit*, pp. 17–21.

5 See Shakespeare, *A Midsummer Night's Dream*, V.i.4–22.

6 For the entire text, see John Davies of Hereford, *Complete Works*, I, 4–30.

7 All references to Bacon's writings are to: Francis Bacon, *The Works of Francis Bacon*, ed. by James Spedding, Robert Leslie Ellis and Douglas Denon Heath, 7 vols (London: Longman, 1857–59). I use Bacon and Burton in order to give a comprehensive overview of faculty psychology and its development up to the early seventeenth century, to trace the evolution of critical thought on poetry and poetics in that period and to show Spenser's own position in current trends and future developments.

creations. In the context of the imagination, monsters become related to the discourse on melancholy, the heroes' imagination and the topography of the poem. To facilitate the understanding of a 'monstrous' imagination at work in Spenser's epic romance, I will first survey Bright's, Burton's and Bacon's representative works on the imagination.

The anatomy of the brain

The treatises by Bright and Burton, both essentially medical investigations into melancholy, offer seminal accounts of man's inner anatomy. In the system of internal forces they set up, the common sense, the imagination and memory make up the three inward senses,[8] with the imagination at the centre.[9] Reason, which is also situated in the brain,[10] presides over these internal agencies, and guides their functions as long as the humours are kept in balance,[11] but is also dependent on the accuracy of the images transferred to it by the imagination.[12] Anatomising the parts of the sensible soul, Burton explains that the common sense first receives the information transmitted from the outer senses of sight, hearing, smelling, taste and touch;[13] it then performs the function of the 'judge or moderator', i.e. it distinguishes between individual objects, and consecutively sends them to the imagination, which can penetrate the nature of things better than the common sense. Unlike the outer senses and the common sense, but like reason, 'phantasy' does not depend on objects that are actually present, because it can also draw them from memory. The imagination is therefore granted the autonomy to fashion 'new of his own'.[14]

8 Burton, *Anatomy*, I, 159. The passage forms part of a 'Digression of Anatomy', which is inserted into Section 1 of the work ('Of Diseases in General, and of Melancholy'; Burton, *Anatomy*, I, 130–77). The 'trilogy' of chambers is a medieval development of the classical six-part system of classical antiquity (cf. Bundy, *Imagination*, pp. 39–40).

9 'His organ is the middle cell of the brain' (Burton, *Anatomy*, I, 159).

10 Bright calls the brain 'the instrument of reason', 'an instrument of conceite', and 'the chiefe instrument of sense, and motion' (Bright, *Treatise*, 'The Epistle Dedicatorie', p. ij, p. 42 and p. 47).

11 In *Anatomy*, I, 257, Burton likens the human organism to a ship guided by reason, which uses the imagination as its rudder and guiding star. When reason is overruled by the imagination, the ship becomes subject to the whims of fancy.

12 See also Rossky, 'Imagination', p. 52. Katherine Park explains that the imagination is the *sine qua non* for cognition, because it transmits data perceived by the senses to reason (see 'Bacon's "Enchanted Glass"', *Isis* 75 (1984), 290–302 (p. 294)).

13 Burton here follows the medieval hierarchy of the five senses, from the purest to the least pure (see *Anatomy*, I, 157–9). The inner and outer senses form the 'apprehensive faculty' which perceives and stores 'the species of sensible things' (*Anatomy*, I, 157).

14 'Phantasy, or imagination … is an inner sense which doth more fully examine the

In a well-functioning mind reason remains in charge, distinguishing like an arbiter between fake and real objects, lest the sensible soul is deceived by the images created in the imagination.[15] The processes taking place in the sensible soul therefore depend on the command of reason to keep its subordinate forces in balance. However, the faculties residing in the ventricles of the brain also communicate with the rest of the body. Bright describes how body and soul interrelate,[16] paying particular attention to the communication between the brain, which holds reason, and the heart, which houses the passions and affections.[17] In this field of forces, the imagination becomes a precarious faculty, because it can influence the body by directing the images it receives to memory, which stores them, but also to the heart, where they can excite the passions.[18] At the same time, the imagination is not only the agent of such changes; it is itself subject to humoral influences, which can corrupt its proper function.[19] However, the imagination is not only the central faculty influencing the inner world of the human being. As it receives what the five wits perceive through the common sense and transmits it to the inner senses, it performs the fundamental function of connecting humans to their outer reality, and thus is the decisive agent to further their understanding of the material world.

Francis Bacon's *The Advancement of Learning* goes one decisive step further in the evaluation of the imagination, especially with regard to its

species perceived by common sense, of things present or absent, and keeps them longer, recalling them to mind again, or making new of his own' (Burton, *Anatomy*, I, 159; cf. also Andreas Laurentius, *Discourse*, p. 16). Memory records the perceptions of the outer senses 'as a good register' (Burton, *Anatomy*, I, 160), and can be accessed both by the imagination and by reason.

15 Burton, *Anatomy*, I, 160: 'In men [the imagination] is subject and governed by reason, or at least should be'. For similar statements, see *Anatomy*, I, 253.

16 Bright treats the interdependency of body and soul at some length on pp. 39–67 of the *Treatise*.

17 'The hart is the seate of life, and of affections, and perturbations, of loue, or hate, like, or dislike; of such thinges as fall within compasse of sense; either outward, or inward; in effect, or imagination onely' (Bright, *Treatise*, p. 47).

18 See also Wright, *Passions*, p. 45: 'First then, to our imagination commeth by sense or memorie, some obiect to be knowne, conuenient or disconuenient to Nature … presently the purer spirits, flocke from the brayne, by certain secret channels to the heart, where they pitch at the dore, signifying what an obiect was presented, conuenient or disconuenient for it. The heart immediately bendeth, either to prosecute it, or to eschew it: and the better to effect that affection, draweth other humours to help him.'

19 Levinus Lemnius stresses the imagination's susceptibility to humoral changes when stating that 'ill humours' may send 'confused ymaginations and vayne foolish visions vp into the chiefe Castle of the mynde' (Levinus Lemnius, *The Touchstone of Complexions*, trans. by Thomas Newton (London: Thomas Marsh, 1581), fol. 95r). See Rossky, 'Imagination', p. 56.

function as an interface between the inner and the outer worlds, and its significance for human understanding. Following the medieval tradition, Bacon dispenses entirely with the common sense, and places the imagination *vis-à-vis* man's sensory perception, thus assigning it the central role between the outer senses and reason.[20] To be more precise, fantasy, set in 'the very citadel of mind and understanding',[21] serves as a pre-rational '*nuncius*' that mediates between the senses and reason but does not judge incoming data, a circumstance that marks the imagination as an extra-rational faculty.[22] Bacon makes clear that the imagination is not merely instrumental in relating humans to the world around them. On the contrary, the imagination emerges as an agency that furthers insight into notions that transcend the rational.[23] Bacon argues that this is especially so 'in matters of Faith and Religion', where 'we raise our Imagination above our Reason'.[24] In contrast to *ratio*, which remains tied to the nature of things,[25] *imaginatio* can call to mind and make understandable truths that are beyond the physicality of the world, because it can disconnect itself from material reality. Bacon's elevating the concept of the imagination also applies to poetry, which uses the imagination as the creative force behind its representations of universal truths.

Spenser's own framework only superficially concurs with the seminal tripartite anatomies put forward by Bright and Burton.[26] Like Bacon's, Spenser's system disregards the common sense, thereby establishing a more immediate connection between the outer and inner worlds. This proximity casts light on the link between the brain turret of Alma's Castle and its immediate surroundings: the monstrous men swarming like flies outside the Castle are linked to the monstrous creatures on the tapestries and the flies in Phantastes's chamber.[27] On an abstract level, the interac-

20 As Katherine Park points out, Bacon's tendency to reduce the internal senses to three is influenced by contemporary medical discourse (see 'Bacon's "Enchanted Glass"', pp. 293–4).

21 Bacon, *De augmentis*, VI.2, in *Works*, IV, 406.

22 'For Sense sendeth over to Imagination before Reason have judged, and Reason sendeth over to Imagination before the decree can be acted. For Imagination ever precedeth Voluntary Motion' (Bacon, *Advancement*, in *Works*, III, 382). In the later *De augmentis* (V.1), Bacon explains that the imagination is more than just a messenger (see *Works*, IV, 406).

23 See Ahrends, 'Transformationen', pp. 8–9.

24 Bacon, *Works*, III, 382.

25 In contrast to the imagination, reason 'doth buckle and bow the mind unto the nature of things' (Bacon, *Advancement*, in *Works*, III, 344).

26 See the representative commentary provided by Brooks-Davies, *Critical Commentary*, pp. 167–70, notes to II.ix.44–59, and Hamilton, notes to II.ix.47–58.

27 See II.ix.16 and 51; compare with Healy, *New Latitudes*, pp. 100–1.

tion between these textual *loci* suggests that the input of the outer senses, especially of sight, has the force to promulgate new and indistinct images directly in the imaginative faculty, just as much as inner images can be projected on to the outside. The marginal position fantasy occupies in the brain assigns the task of distinguishing between the various perplexing images simultaneously taking shape in the mind to the unnamed sage in the middle chamber,[28] which lies between the imagination and memory. This arrangement of the three chambers reflects the critical interdependence between the story world of the poem and the internal faculties of the mind.

In such a framework, the imagination is essentially ambivalent. Poised between the external and the internal forces, and performing the conflicting roles of agent and receiver, the imagination can be both subject and object of malfunction. This change resulted in a paradigm shift in the late Middle Ages, when the imagination became an active faculty in the work of Fracastoro, while simultaneously the Platonic distinction between eikastic and fantastic imagination became porous.[29] Eventually, the imagination became generally mistrusted. If one follows Rossky's argument, this notion stems from three main reasons, all of which are directly related to the intricate operations of the imagination.[30] The first factor is the uneasy dependence of fantasy on the external senses, and thus its proximity to the flesh rather than to the spirit; the second is the incorrectness of the images transmitted from the senses, because postlapsarian man is only given unreliable 'external' images of the real world;[31] the third reason points directly to the monstrous, for the imagination has the power to distort images internally. John Davies of Hereford emphasises this aspect of the imagination when arguing that 'Fantacie, / … doth so forme reforme, and it deformes, / As pleaseth hir fantasticke faculty'.[32] Davies's witty *figura etymologica*, which yokes the word stem to different prefixes, illustrates the imagination's bent towards making new combinations, and additionally suggests that the imagination's creative compounding has a decisively linguistic quality which relates directly

28 On his possible identities, see Chapter 15.

29 In the Middle Ages, the imagination was seen as the passive receiver of data; answering Plato's verdict in the *Politeia* (605d), Fracastoro redefines the imagination as a higher mental exercise in his *Turrius sive De Intellectione*. This development is fully discussed in Murray W. Bundy, 'Fracastoro and the Imagination', in *Renaissance Studies in Honour of Hardin Craig*, ed. by B. Maxwell and others (Stanford: Folcroft Library, 1941), pp. 44–57.

30 See Rossky, 'Imagination', pp. 54–5; Bundy marks the dubiousness of the imagination as a medieval development (see *Imagination*, pp. 208–24).

31 This circumstance was universally acknowledged; see Bright, *Treatise*, p. 122.

32 See John Davies of Hereford, *Mirum in Modum*, in *Complete Works*, I, 9–10.

to the making of literature.[33] In other words, Davies's rhetorical flourish implies that the fashioning of new 'forms' from old ones is indicative of a creative reorganisation of known linguistic material.[34]

It is hardly coincidental that Rossky's individual arguments can indeed be traced in the Phantastes sequence discussed above: Maleger's dishevelled and multiform monstrous troop represents the 'fallen' signs and sense impressions bewildering Alma's psyche and buzzing around Phantastes's head, whereas the imagination's tendency to distort images in the mind becomes evident in the sage's partly grotesque frescos.[35] This interaction is even more precarious, because in the world of the poem it can simultaneously work vice versa, for instance when a diseased mind projects inner images on to the outside world. Phantastes's chamber is therefore also a concise allegorical representation of the monstrous image and its source.

Hypertrophy: Sleep and melancholy

The deformation of images is the main symptom of the malfunctioning imagination. Such distortions, Bright and Burton aver, occur mainly when the hierarchy between reason and the imagination becomes disrupted, as is the case during sleep, and under the impact of a heightened melancholy. In sleep, for instance, reason lies dormant, so the imagination can take over control, 'conceiv[ing] strange, stupend, absurd shapes'.[36] When Burton adds that this phenomenon is reminiscent of his observation of 'sick men', he establishes a connection between disease and the figuring forth of grotesque, monstrous forms. This link is especially virulent for people suffering from melancholy, the very condition informing Phantastes, because they are most conducive to 'producing many monstrous

33 This tallies well with Du Bellay's precept that 'fantasie' is the origin of language; see Joachim du Bellay, *La defence et illustration de la langue francoyse*, ed. by Henri Chamard (Paris: Albert Fontemoing, 1904), pp. 47–8.

34 The imagination's creating 'things vnlikely' from 'things likely' through deformation (John Davies of Hereford, *Complete Works*, I, 9) recalls Aristotle's notion of the monstrous as dissimilar derivation (see Chapter 3).

35 See Nohrnberg's detailed chart of Spenserian beasts, which establishes connections between Isaiah 13 and 34, Maleger's bands, Phantastes's mind, Guyon's voyage, Alcina's beasts and Malengin (Analogy, p. 330).

36 Burton, *Anatomy*, I, 159; cf. John Davies of Hereford, *Mirum in Modum*, in *Complete Works* I, 9. In *Anatomy*, I, 253, Burton more specifically links the dreamer's visions to the 'humours and concourse of vapours'. Rossky observes correctly that 'in its own right melancholy had a claim on the power to distort images of imagination, a claim easily as great as that of madness, since almost anything from diet to sin could cause melancholy' ('Imagination', p. 55).

and prodigious things' out of objects 'presented to [the imagination] from common sense or memory'.[37] Although melancholy was seen as the main motor behind poetic creativity by writers from Aristotle to Burton,[38] it remained dubious. Bright explains that the prevalence of melancholy upsets the interdependence between body and soul, and hampers the communication between the brain and the heart, which is severed from the inner senses, and produces terrifying illusions that dissemble the mind.[39] In effect, both present and absent objects are deformed and become deceptive through the workings of a hypertrophic imagination that ultimately clouds reason. The danger of the aberrant imagination therefore lies in its power to transform reliable images into monstrous ones. In its wake, the writers that diagnose and analyse these transformative processes also resort to the rhetoric of the deformed.

Bright is a case in point. The language he employs to describe the humoral workings of melancholy mark it as a grisly physical agent that turns the body into a locus of filth, for the melancholy spirits 'darken … and … defile [the spirits] with the fogge of that slime, and fennie substance'.[40] Bright maintains that, in consequence, the overheated imagination 'forge[s] monstrous fictions'[41] without external causes, and transfers them to the heart, where they trigger fear and terror, which counterbalance reason. In the central simile of this passage Bright compares 'the externall sensible darkenes', which impairs the clarity of perception and evokes false illusions through the force of the imagination, to

37 See Burton, *Anatomy*, I, 159: 'In melancholy men this faculty is most powerful and strong, and often hurts, producing many monstrous and prodigious things, especially if it be stirred by some terrible object, presented to it from common sense or memory'. In the chapter about the outward senses, Burton explains that the perception of unpleasant objects has the power to hurt the recipient physically (I, 157–9).

38 The assumption that melancholy is especially conducive to profound thought and poetic creativity rests on Aristotle's verdict in the *Problemata physica*, Problem XXX.I. Aristotle's text is treated in Klibansky, Panofsky and Saxl, *Saturn and Melancholy*, pp. 15–41 (this section also offers the complete original text and an English translation); see also Burton, *Anatomy*, I, 409. For recent scholarship, see Kitzes, *Politics of Melancholy*, pp. 1–23, and Douglas Trevor, *The Poetics of Melancholy in Early Modern England* (Cambridge: Cambridge University Press, 2004).

39 Bright argues that the heart is 'shut vp … as it were in a dungeon of obscurity' (*Treatise*, p. 100).

40 Bright, *Treatise*, p. 100.

41 Bright, *Treatise*, p. 102. Bright frequently uses the term *to forge* to refer to creations of the mind (e.g. on p. 103 and pp. 105–7). In this passage, he draws on the ambivalence of the verb, which can both be synonymous with *to make* and signify deceptive imitation, as in the noun *forgery* (cf. *OED*, s.v. 'forge, *v.*1', and 'forgery, *n.*'). In fact, all the major texts about the imagination use verbs of active making, such as *to frame*, and *to coin* (see Rossky, 'Imagination', p. 57).

melancholy's 'internall darkenes', which also creates terrifying shapes without any outer stimulus. This darkness is a manifest '*presence* of a substantiall obscurity' (emphasis added); it takes control over the brain, and abuses it as the 'habitate of depraued conceite', i.e. as a place where terrifying and corrupt images are created. The pathological result: common sense makes 'phantasticall apparitions', and fantasy creates shapes through reconfiguring known material.[42] The mind becomes fixated on monstrous shapes that do not exist in nature, and therefore have been neither perceived nor imagined by a human *not* afflicted with melancholy. Under these circumstances, the mind visualises 'monsters, which nature neuer bred'.[43] Once reason becomes dysfunctional, it allows the inner senses to produce dissembling images, which finally reach the heart; the individual, falling prey to the symptoms of melancholy, loses hope and joy, and becomes subject to fear and despair. What thus starts as a humoral change effects the transformation of nature, and results in the individual losing his sense of reality. In literary terms, the process of visualising fantastic objects violates the principle of *imitatio naturae*, and is hence reprehensible.

As creator of such delusions, and deformations, the imagination has a distinct monstrous quality that can also be observed in *The Faerie Queene*. If outer and inner darkness create delusions and monsters, it is notable that Spenser's monsters frequently take shape visually in dark places, where the hero cannot perceive clearly. The concept of a dark matter spawning monsters in the mind links fairly well to the topographical details of *The Faerie Queene*'s dark allegory, which become the external textual manifestations of the internal imagination. Redcrosse, after entering the darkness of Errour's den, can see the two-natured monster only by the 'litle glooming light' (I.i.14.5) of his armour, while the rest of her body is shrouded in blackness. Errour, the monstrous female version of abstract error, thus appears in a textual topography, as Cheney astutely points out, that enables Redcrosse 'to see – or imagine' the monster.[44] Similarly, Geryoneo's dragon emerges 'out of an hidden shade' under the idol she protects (V.xi.22.3). When Spenser so specifically stresses that the creature stretches and flexes her body 'as it had long lyen still' (22.6), he additionally marks Geryoneo's dragon as a specimen of the dragons in effigy,[45]

42 'an other parte of internall sense compoundeth, and forges disguised shapes' (Bright, *Treatise*, p. 103). The upsurge of melancholy finally upsets memory (see Bright, *Treatise*, p. 102). See also Andreas Laurentius, *A Discourse*, p. 91.

43 Bright, *Treatise*, p. 106.

44 Cheney, 'Spenser's Parody', p. 5.

45 See the discussion of dragons in Chapter 6, above.

which becomes animated through the activity of Arthur's imagination, and his desire to fight the monstrous.[46] As John C. Ulreich points out elsewhere, 'the desire *makes* the object in which it seeks fulfilment'.[47] Consonant with this finding, the sudden appearances of the monstrous satyr who rapes Thyamis, and Lust, who abducts Amoret, are similarly powerful manifestations of the women's intimate fears and desires projected on to the poem's topography. With such descriptions Spenser hints at the possibility that the monsters in *The Faerie Queene* are directly linked to the characters perceiving them. In the Hugh Mclean Memorial Lecture of 2004, Janet Adelman elaborates on the central query, 'Whose monster is Error?',[48] arguing that the creature figures as Redcrosse's 'troubled sexual imagination'.[49] This verdict again stresses that Spenser's monsters in *The Faerie Queene* are, strictly speaking, not Spenser's own miscarried productions, but represent the *internal* psychic state of his characters, which becomes apparent in Spenser's stressing the gazers' reactions to monsters and monstrous beings. James W. Broaddus similarly argues that Spenser does not only use his own imagination to write the poem but that he also has the imagination operate differently in his characters.[50] Broaddus's notion can be positively applied to the malfunctioning imagination, because Spenser employs a dual strategy in which he imagines the monstrous imaginations of his characters. As the author in charge of making monsters for his poem, he animates, in Bright's words, the 'habitate[s] of deprаued conceite', where the monster comes into being, and projects it on to the topography of his poetic heterocosm.

As the medical writers point out, making monstrous images also blemishes the poet, who in Bright's opinion is largely informed by his melancholy disposition. When stating the case against 'these stormes and tempests of passion, these delusions, feares, false terrours, and poeticall

46 Janet Adelman maintains that Errour 'emerges partly from Red Cross's own eagerness to fight her' ('Revaluing the Body in *The Faerie Queene I*', Hugh Mclean Memorial Lecture, December 2004, *Spenser Review* 36.1 (Winter 2005), 15–25 (p. 19)).

47 John C. Ulreich, 'Making Dreams Truths, and Fables Histories: Spenser and Milton on the Nature of Fiction', *Studies in Philology* 87 (1990), 363–77 (p. 371).

48 Adelman, 'Revaluing the Body', p. 18.

49 Adelman, 'Revaluing the Body', p. 19. She continues to explain that Errour is also 'a wrong version of the body and the material world'.

50 See Broaddus, 'Britomart's Adventures', pp. 190–1. Broaddus, e.g., elaborates on the psycho-physiological processes at work in Britomart's and Malacesta's sexual desire: in Britomart it rises from the vegetable to the higher faculties, where the imagination is controlled by the image of Arthegall; in Malacesta, the process begins in the higher, but corrupted, faculties, and proceeds to sexual appetite (see 'Britomart's Adventures', pp. 193–4).

fictions of the braine',[51] Bright contextualises the poetic into his overarching argument on the pathology of monstrous melancholy, and lists poetry as just another manifestation of an overheated imagination. That the language Bright employs in this poetic context resembles that of his pathological observations renders the connection between the poet and the melancholy madman all the more conclusive.[52] Indeed, Burton's referring to poets when explaining the effects of a melancholic imagination raises further suspicion about the sanity of creative writers, also because he uses similar terms for the distorted images created in the madman's mind: 'In poets and painters', he states, 'imagination forcibly works, as appears by their several fictions, antics, images: as Ovid's house of Sleep, Psyche's palace in Apuleius'.[53] In this passage, Burton considers the imagination the cause of grotesquery, as the word *antic* indicates, which was the standard term for the grotesque until the mid-seventeenth century.[54]

The distorting power of the monstrous imagination is particularly emphasised when Burton mentions the House of Sleep in Ovid's *Metamorphoses*, and Cupid's Palace in Apuleius's work of the same name, as examples of such fictions, for he brings poetry into uneasy proximity with uninhibited dream work.[55] As poetic places replete with phantasms and ekphrases, these settings and textual *loci* figure as 'stage productions' of the poetic imagination both in an objective sense, i.e. as artworks, and in a subjective sense, i.e. as representations of the characters' imaginations. They also bear witness to the fecundity of the poet's imagination, which can vividly create the entirely 'unreal' localities and characters Ovid and Apuleius describe. As the products of a 'dreamy imagination', new 'monsters of the mind' become the outgrowth of unrestrained poetic creativity. The forcible workings of the imagination can be observed in *The Faerie Queene* not only in Spenser's own version of the House of Sleep (I.ii) but also in the potentially deceptive dream visions of the characters, be they Redcrosse's or even Arthur's.[56] The most immediately recognisable

51 Bright, *Treatise*, p. 115.

52 Bright's assessment of the poet and his work is, as Kitzes rightly observes, 'more diagnostic than appreciative in nature' (*Politics of Melancholy*, pp. 29–30).

53 Burton, *Anatomy*, I, 159–60.

54 See Lengeler, *Tragische Wirklichkeit*, pp. 4–23. Ahrends also notes the relevance of the term *antic* in this context (see 'Transformationen', p. 3).

55 Burton refers to the tale of Amor and Psyche, one of the novelistic stories embedded into Apuleius, *Metamorphoses*, IV.28 to VI.24. For the text, see Apuleius, *The Golden Ass: Being the Metamorphoses of Lucius Apuleius*, trans. by William Adlington, Loeb Classical Library (Cambridge, MA: Harvard University Press; London, Heinemann, 1971).

56 Even Arthur's singularly important dream vision of the Faery Queene sports a close resemblance to the imagination's unrestrained activity during sleep (cf. Ulreich, 'Making

indicator of Spenser's animating a distorting, 'monstrous' imagination in *The Faerie Queene* is the shape-shifting sorcerer Archimago, who deceives his victims with lies, false dreams and magic illusions.[57] Not only an 'Arch-magician' by name but also the 'Arch-image' or 'Arch-imagination' in the poem, he figures as the devious, Protean agency that can transform itself into various shapes,[58] and affect humans with deluding, lascivious and unwholesome dreams.[59] By establishing Archimago as the archetypal, uninhibited imagination, Spenser shows that he also seeks to animate imaginative processes that violate the rules of nature in the secondary world he creates.[60] Against this backdrop, Spenser's deliberate use of grotesquery and 'antics' marks the poem as a space where the imagination works forcibly, similar to the 'dreamy' locales in the texts by Ovid and Apuleius. The rhetorical distortions in Phantastes's chamber therefore generally relate to the overtly fantastic products of a hypertrophic imagination in the entire poem. As the romance images in Phantastes's chamber, according to Paxson, also evoke those in well-known dream visions,[61] Spenser inscribes the potentially unrestrained and unlimited force of the dreamy imagination into his poem. *The Faerie Queene* is therefore not designed to be mimetic in the traditional sense, i.e. it does not represent the world in an unadulterated fashion, but brings it to the reader in a strikingly altered form. In order to do so, it requires the inventive imagination of the autonomous poet, who designs a heterocosm in which he can also animate the internal psychological processes of the imagination.

Dreams', p. 372).

57 Broaddus explains how Archimago uses rhetoric in his retelling of Redcrosse's alleged rape of a maiden to manipulate Guyon's imagination in II.i.9–20 (see 'Renaissance Psychology and the Defense of Alma's Castle', p. 141).

58 Judith H. Anderson explains concisely that 'Archimago's name connects him with magic, with images, and with the human imagination' ('Mutability and Mortality: Reading Spenser', in *Celebrating Mutabilitie*, ed. by Grogan, pp. 246–74 (p. 253)). On Archimago's names and natures, see Nohrnberg, *Analogy*, pp. 103–4, 110–15, and 124–6. For Archimago as shape shifter, see I.ii.10, and Chapter 10, 'Monstrous humans'.

59 See, for instance, Archimago's creation of dream phantasms to haunt Redcrosse (I.i.36–55). Anderson argues that Archimago is both an external and an internal force, i.e. both 'diabolical tempter' and Redcrosse's 'sinful nature' ('Mutability and Mortality', pp. 253–4).

60 On Archimago as a poetic maker resorting to demonic means, see Genevieve Guenther, 'Spenser's Magic, or Instrumental Aesthetics in the 1590 *Faerie Queene*', *English Literary Renaissance* 36 (2006), 194–226 (pp. 195–6).

61 See Paxson, *Poetics of Personification*, p. 141.

The poetic transformation of the self

If the instability of images and the impact of melancholy and dreams provoke the Renaissance critique of fantasy, transformation becomes a moot point, because it epitomises the uninhibited force of the imagination.[62] The many temporary transformations and permanent metamorphoses in *The Faerie Queene* discussed in Chapter 10 of this study stress the changeability of poetic material and human bodies, and foreground the force of an imagination that can effect such changes. The medical writers elaborate on the implications of these mutations with particular care, because their concept of transformation as the outcome of an overheated imagination applies not only to objects but also to the subject, or self.[63] These changes, which stress the relation between image and physical form, can exhibit a pathological disposition: among others, a hypertrophic imagination that generates visions, and ecstatic states of mind can have real effects, such as maladies, and even cause changes in the human body.[64] Pregnant women, for instance, can give birth to a deformed offspring if they are startled by a terrifying object, or if they have a sexual, 'depraved phantasy' when they are with child,[65] for they transfer the imprint the imagination leaves in their minds to the shape of their embryos.[66] In other extreme cases, the imagination can even effect the loss of self, as in those instances where the affected are under the impression that they are a different person, or even an animal.[67] The loss of identity can in turn result in a genuine crossing of physical boundaries when the body undergoes a significant transformation.[68]

The early modern concept of the transforming imagination casts light on the transformations in *The Faerie Queene*. Malbecco's flight and metamorphosis into Jealousy underlines the imagination's power to transform

62 See Nohrnberg, *Analogy*, pp. 122–3 and 126–7.

63 For the full account, see Burton, *Anatomy*, I, 253–8.

64 See Burton, *Anatomy*, I, 253–4.

65 See Burton, *Anatomy*, I, 254–5.

66 Hence, a pregnant woman 'imprints that stamp upon her child which she conceives unto herself' (*Anatomy*, I, 255). The same sentiment is expressed in Paré's *Of Monsters*, which notes that 'the force of the imagination hath so much power over the infant, that it sets upon it the notes or characters of the thing conceived' (*Works*, p. 978). On the history and reception of such wonders, see Daston and Park, *Wonders and the Order of Nature*, pp. 39–59. This phenomenon is extensively treated by Marie-Hélène Huet, who breaks down her argument into the various factors of conception in the imagination, such as the mother's fancy, and the monstrous father (see *Monstrous Imagination* (Cambridge, MA, and London: Harvard University Press, 1993)).

67 See Burton, *Anatomy*, I, 255.

68 In *Anatomy*, I, 257, Burton refers to Proteus and the chameleon, the two traditional images of transformation. See also Barkan, *Nature's Work of Art*, pp. 248–9.

the self particularly well, because his disintegration, caused by continuous physical fragmentation, takes place when he abandons himself to his wild fancies and anxieties.[69] Bright explains that the person afflicted with a melancholy disposition becomes prone to excess suspiciousness, jealousy and fear;[70] he flees into the wilderness to exile himself from other humans, his body becomes meagre and lean, he lives on a disorderly diet that adds fuel to the fire of his afflictions.[71] Malbecco is Spenser's animated literary version of these internal changes sketched in the *Treatise of Melancholie*. The transformative processes observable in Malbecco are the outcome of a hypertrophy generated by his jealous disposition, which in turn is strengthened by his bent towards melancholy and madness. By the end of the episode, Malbecco accordingly becomes the very embodiment of the other.

The sequence also manifests the transforming power of Spenser's own poetic fantasy. The forceful imagination of the romance poet transforms the poeticised object in such a way that, through the use of vivid language, he creates the illusion that the subject or character changes himself. Malbecco's metamorphosis into the monstrous other of jealousy therefore ultimately represents the monstrous other called forth deliberately in the poet's creative imagination. As was the case with the monsters rising from the darkness, Spenser sets up a dual discourse: his controlled poetic transformations stage the uncontrolled transformations of the characters. The metamorphoses in *The Faerie Queene*, especially those that involve the properties of monstrous signifiers, thus bear witness to the imagination's power to transform any physical and corporeal shape textually.[72]

Mental propagation as physical procreation

One important aspect of the monstrous imagination is its ability to transform objects, and even the self, a process that can lead to the creation of reprehensible beings. The concept of 'otherness' also influences the

69 See III.x.54–60, and the discussion in Chapter 10, 'Monstrous humans', above.

70 Lovers prone to jealousy devolve 'in bestie naturam' ('into the nature of a beast'), as Marsilius Ficino explains in the *Oratoria septima*, caput XII of *Über die Liebe oder Platons Gastmahl*, trans. by Karl Paul Hasse, ed. by Paul Richard Blum, 2nd edn, Philosophische Bibliothek, 368 (Hamburg: Felix Meiner, 1984), p. 348.

71 See Bright, *Treatise*, p. 102, p. 106, p. 111, p. 124, p. 126, pp. 131–3, as well as Burton, *Anatomy*, I, 288.

72 This is consonant with Lobsien, *Imaginationswelten*, p. 26: 'Die in und als Literatur arbeitende Imagination ist explizierbar in Begriffen wie Alterierung, Transformation, Meta- und Anamorphose, Transition, Rhetorisierung, semiotische und hermeneutische Unruhe' ('The imagination which works in and as literature can be explicated in terms such as alteration, transformation, metamorphosis and anamorphosis, transition, rhetoricising, semiotic und hermeneutic unrest').

creation of images. In the concise entry in his *Thesaurus*, Thomas Cooper defines the imagination as a 'conceiuing in thy minde'.[73] The verb to *conceive*, which describes the origin and genesis of the abstract conceit or idea, opens up semantic possibilities that hint at a crucial subtext of the imagination: as any work of art is the manifest outcome of ideas (also in Sidney's theory of poetic making),[74] Cooper's definition illustrates the making of poetry as a *taking shape* in the mind, a supposition stressed by John Davies of Hereford's verdict that fantasy 'imprintes [images] liuely in the Minde'.[75] Reduced to its literal sense, the bringing forth of *concetti* suggests an overtly biological subtext, since the verb originally denotes sexual conception.[76] This etymological quibble, which appears in a host of early modern texts,[77] brings 'physical procreation' and 'mental propagation' into close conceptual contact.[78] The semantic breadth of the term 'conceiuing' therefore points to the complex relation between the imagination and the fashioning of poetry.[79] In terms of early modern psychology, the fashioning of newly created 'images' out of new 'ideas' is the outcome of a stored sense perception that it develops *qua* imaginative

73 Cooper, *Thesaurus*, s.v. 'imaginatio'.

74 On the supremacy of the idea over the work itself, see Sidney's poetic remarks in *Defence*, p. 79.

75 John Davies of Hereford, *Mirum in Modum*, in *Complete Works*, I, 9.

76 Although the main sense of *conceit* in early modern English is that of 'idea' (see *OED*, s.v. 'conceit, *n.*'), its original meaning 'implies a sexual act between a male form (usually the human soul) and a female mass of matter (usually the human body)' (Heninger, *Sidney and Spenser*, p. 564, n. 138). It is used in this sense in *Batman vppon Bartholome*'s section on child conception (VI.4).

77 While Halio traces the notion of the 'procreative imagination' in Elizabethan writers, Bauer more specifically treats the theological and philosophical aspects of this phenomenon from Plato, St Augustine, Aquinas and Michelangelo to the *cinquecento* and the English Elizabethan writers, arguing that the seventeenth century sees the decline of this concept due to the radical changes instigated by René Descartes and John Locke. See Jay L. Halio, 'The Metaphor of Conception and Elizabethan Theories of the Imagination', *Neophilologus* 50 (1966), 454–61 (among the sources Halio quotes and analyses are: John Davies of Hereford, *Microcosmos*; Spenser, *Daphnaida*; George Chapman, *Byron's Conspiracy*; Ben Jonson, *Discoveries*); and Robert J. Bauer, 'A Phenomenon of Epistemology in the Renaissance', *Journal of the History of Ideas* 31 (1970), 281–8. Paré uses repetition to emphasise the analogy: 'that which is strongly conceived in the mind, imprints the form into the infant conceived in the womb' (*Works*, p. 978).

78 The terms are taken from Bauer, 'A Phenomenon of Epistemology', p. 281. The idea of 'poetic conception' presumably originates from Plato's *Symposium*, more specifically from Diotima's speech on poets (in *Symposion*, 208E–209A). Cf. Bauer, 'A Phenomenon of Epistemology', p. 282, and Halio, 'Metaphor of Conception', p. 455.

79 This reading also inheres in Cooper's explanation of the term *idea*, which he defines as '[t]he figure conceyued in Imagination, as it were a substance perpetuall, being a paterne of al sorts or kind, as of one seal procedeth many printes, so of one *Idea* of man proceede many thousandes of men' (*Thesaurus*). Again, the verb *to conceive* hints at physical procreation.

power, and transforms into the final artistic product.[80] The writer therefore translates these immaterial beings to the material page when writing his poem; from there they 'materialise' in the reader's mind. Hence, the act of artistic fashioning is 'para-creative',[81] i.e. it is not procreative in the strict sense of the word but works along analogous parameters.

In brief, the conception of an image starts with a conscious idea and results in its physical manifestation in a text or artwork, a process similar to the three stages of creation set up in Sidney's poetics, from idea to fore-conceit to conceit. Caution is thus called for when the imagination creates something spontaneously or unconsciously on its own, because this upsets the balance of forces, and can result in uncalled-for, monstrous images. Earlier in this chapter, attention was turned to Bright's explanations of how melancholy affects the imagination and helps bring an infinity of monstrous shapes to the mind. In the *Treatise of Melancholie*, he argues that these melancholy spirits 'darken … and … defile [the spirits] with the fogge of that slime, and fennie substance', making the whole passage replete with monstrous terms. But this choice of language, which resorts to a heavy repetition of words like 'monstrous', and 'phantasticall', does not only complement the contents of the passage, and render Bright's theories more palpable for his readership. More importantly, the choice of register also reveals that Bright draws on the discourse of the monstrous precisely because it provides him with the conceptual basis for the discussion of the hypertrophic imagination. Like the fens, and the foggy and dark habitats of the romance epic, the slimy and 'fennie' black bile serves as the ideal breeding ground of the monstrous.[82] In consequence, the material blackness of melancholy conceives the immaterial monsters of the mind on the inner senses. A passage from Thomas Nashe's *Terrors of the Night* provides a useful gloss for Bright's *Treatise*.[83] In terms strikingly reminiscent of Bright's, Nashe elaborates on melancholy's monstrous implications, and characterises it as a 'foggie-braind' faculty, whose 'thicke steaming vapours' confuse fantasy:

80 Bauer describes the process as a progression from the 'embryo' to the final 'work of art' ('A Phenomenon of Epistemology', p. 281). On monstrous procreation, see Huet's monograph, *Monstrous Imagination*.

81 The happy term is Bauer's ('A Phenomenon of Epistemology', p. 282). In the act of fashioning, the human being then emulates God's creation.

82 For the rearing of Errour, the Blatant Beast and other monsters in amphibious habitats, cf. Part II.

83 As G. R. Hibbard shows, Nashe wrote the text in 1593, and published it a year later; see *Thomas Nashe: A Critical Introduction* (London: Routledge and Kegan Paul, 1972), p. 108.

> And euen as slime and durt in a standing puddle, engender toads and frogs, and many other vnsightly creatures, so this slimie melancholy humor still still [*sic*] thickning as it stands still, engendreth many mishapen obiects in our imaginations.[84]

Like Bright, Nashe uses the mire to illustrate melancholy,[85] but elaborates on it to mark it as an 'amphibious' habitat that spawns toads and frogs through abiogenesis.[86] More precisely, he draws on the notion that amphibians are potentially poisonous and monstrous, i.e. half-formed and physically unspecified creatures.[87] This is a precarious image for the conceits evoked by a melancholy disposition. Under these circumstances, the imagination becomes an agency that can create independently from reality, and will bring to life only unfinished, 'miscarried' permutations of real shapes that border on the abject. Since his argument hinges on the link between engendering creatures and conceiving ideas, Nashe's late sixteenth-century text bears witness to a more thoroughgoing association between the imagination, black bile and the generation of monsters than Bright's treatise at first suggests, and marks the imagination as the site of prodigious fecundity that has the tendency to violate proper conception.[88] Abiogenesis, which rests on the instability and innate fertility of physical forms, is a process caused by a deviant melancholy imagination, just as much as the transformation of the self described above. Both types of malfunction are thus closely linked to the monstrous.

The notion of abiogenesis is significantly taken up in poetical treatises, albeit in subdued form. In his *Arte*, Puttenham explicitly points out that a disordered fantasy 'breede[s] *Chimeres* and monsters in mans imagination'.[89] The subtext of Puttenham's statement is exactly that of abiogenesis. That it is also the subtext of Spenser's poem becomes clear when Una warns Redcrosse in the Wandering Wood that 'the place

84 Nashe, *Terrors of the Night*, pp. 353–4; all references are to R. B. McKerrow's complete edition of Nashe's works: Thomas Nashe, *The Works of Thomas Nashe*, ed. by Ronald B. McKerrow; with corrections and supplementary notes ed. by F. P. Wilson, 2nd edn, 5 vols (Oxford: Basil Blackwell, 1958), I, 353–4. Cf. also Rossky, 'Imagination', pp. 55–6. For a good introduction to Nashe's *Terrors*, cf. Hibbard, *Thomas Nashe*, pp. 107–22.

85 On Nashe's penchant for elaborate formal similes, cf. Hibbard, *Thomas Nashe*, p. 114.

86 For a further example on the interaction between abiogenesis and imagination, see John Marston, *What You Will*, II.i.185–92 (John Marston, *Works*, ed. by Arthur Henry Bullen, 3 vols, Anglistica and Americana, 89 (London: John C. Nimmo, 1887; repr. Hildesheim: Georg Olms, 1970), II). Spenser's use of abiogenesis is also discussed in the analysis of Errour and her spawn in Chapter 8, 'Human–animal composites'.

87 This is especially so when they are created through abiogenesis. See Topsell, *Historie*, III, 718 and 728.

88 Cf. also Rossky, 'Imagination', pp. 55–6.

89 Puttenham, *Arte*, p. 19.

vnknowne and wilde, / *Breedes* dreadfull doubts' (I.i.12.3–4; emphasis added) – just before he sets out to attack Errour in her cave. Una's admonition here harks back to the *silva* tradition and the dubious nature of the wood discussed in Chapter 14. Spenser's predecessor Tasso, for instance, identifies the forest as the origin of delusion and error when he notes that 'the falsitie of the reasons and perswasions … are *ingendred* in the wood' in the *Allegoria del poema*.[90] Spenser, who establishes the Wandering Wood as the source of language and consequently of the text, here suggests that the wood of romance has spawned the monster *sponte sua* and, on a general level, with her the monsters and monstrous beings that keep appearing in the poem.

The monstrous language set up by Bright and Nashe to describe the impact of a melancholy disposition creates a topography of the imagination that is strongly reminiscent of the habitats in which Spenser's monsters are reared. Since notable creatures like Orgoglio's dragon, Errour, the giant Cormorant and the Blatant Beast were nurtured in fens and similar amphibious surroundings, the conditions under which monsters take shape in the poet's textual habitat and in the mind of melancholy men are in fact so similar that a mutual influence between romances and certain aspects of the imagination as a topography made fertile by melancholy can be posited for the late sixteenth century. Spenser highlights his awareness of abiogenesis and its creation of deformities when likening Errour's vomit of filth, toads and books to the muds of the river Nile, which breeds many a monstrous form:[91]

> As when old father *Nilus* gins to swell
> With timely pride aboue the *Aegyptian* vale,
> His fattie waues do fertile slime outwell,
> And ouerflow each plaine and lowly dale:
> But when his later spring gins to auale,
> Huge heapes of mudd he leaues, wherein there breed
> Ten thousand kindes of creatures partly male

90 The text is quoted from Edward Fairfax's translation of Tasso's *Gerusalemme Liberata* in *Godfrey of Bulloigne*, ed. by Kathleen M. Lea and T. M. Lang (Oxford: Clarendon, 1980), p. 90; emphasis added. Nohrnberg likewise cites this passage to elaborate on the programmatic relevance of Spenser's Wandering Wood for *The Faerie Queene* (see *Analogy*, p. 123; cf. also *Analogy*, p. 21: 'A distracting forest comes to Tasso as as an immemorial symbol of romance').

91 See Miller, *The Poem's Two Bodies*, p. 247, for a discussion of the effect of this simile. Pugh identifies Ovid, *Metamorphoses*, I.416–37, as the main source for this passage (see Pugh, *Spenser and Ovid*, pp. 51–2). For the Nile as a breeding-ground of the monstrous, see *Liber monstrorum* II.21 (in Orchard, *Pride and Prodigies*, pp. 298–9), as well as Van Duzer, '*Hic sunt dracones*', pp. 401–2.

And partly femall of his fruitfull seed;
Such vgly monstrous shapes elswher may no man reed.
(I.i.21)

In this passage, Spenser accentuates the link between the monstrous and abiogenesis: the 'fertile slime' from which the infinity of half-formed creatures springs corresponds to the 'fennie slime' in Bright and Nashe, so that this *locus horribilis* becomes the rhetorical and topographical representation of 'internal' monsters in the psyche and 'external' textual ones. This finding connects the general discourse of the imagination with Phantastes in Alma's brain-turret, and casts light on its interaction with its geographical and textual vicinities. Consequentially, Maleger's monstrous troops, 'idle shades' rising like gnats '[o]ut of the fennes of Allan' (II.ix.15.8 and 16.2) and Acrasia's many monsters surfacing from the sea become geographical variations on the theme of the monstrous habitat in the imagination from which monsters take shape (II.xii).[92]

Summarising statements

The various malfunctions of the imagination – melancholy and uninhibited dream-work, the distortion and transformation of beings, as well as the spontaneous birth of monstrous images – impinge upon poetry and all creative art, because they distort the true aspect of nature and reality. Bright and Burton explicate that poetry loses its mimetic quality under such conditions, because common sense and imagination send deformed or monstrous images to the brain. As the work of the poet is therefore closely associated with the strange shapes conjured up by the sick man's mind, their concept of the imagination amounts to a refutation of works that are not strictly mimetic. In consequence, the romance poet, trapped between his power to transform nature and the danger to lose his sanity to melancholy, is little more than a dealer in figments. In contemporary theory, the hypertrophic imagination therefore emerges as the *locus* where the monstrous other comes to life, and is turned into text.

It is significant that the symptoms sketched above can be diagnosed in *The Faerie Queene*, because they underline Spenser's deliberate participation in the larger discourse on the imagination. More specifically, the topography of the imagination, with its amphibious locales and dark caves where the monster runs wild, reappears in the geography of the

92 For Maleger, Maleger's troops, and Acrasia's monsters, see Chapter 10, 'Monstrous humans'.

poem. These habitats obliquely relate to Phantastes's fancy, but they also figure as Spenser's own reconstructions and animated versions of the monstrous imagination. Against this backdrop, *The Faerie Queene* testifies to its maker's acute awareness of the imagination, even of its reprehensible qualities, because Spenser creates his secondary world in such a way that it bodies forth various significant malfunctions of the imagination, among them exactly those that were associated with poetic making. He thus dons the robe of the sophisticated maker-poet whose genres of choice, epic and romance, invite the use of the monstrous. Yet rather than simply copy the monsters inherent in these 'fantastic' genres into his own text, Spenser's animation of the imaginative processes, also in the figure of the magician Archimago,[93] suggests that he deliberately *shows* his readers the origin of the monsters and monstrous beings in the imagination. Accordingly, Phantastes exists on two levels, representing both the characters' imaginative processes and the poet's own creative work.[94] The success of this duality relies heavily on Spenser's manipulative use of a poetic language that transforms the textual habitat of his poem. When deciding to write romance, Spenser consciously enters the realm of the monstrous imagination, but approaches the genre with a degree of self-consciousness that foregrounds the use and the abuse of the poetic imagination through a double strategy. Spenser's presentation of the monstrous imagination illustrates the poet's ability to turn such malfunctions, which represent the imagination *in malo*, into useful assets for his ambitious poem.

Spenser's transformations of individual characters and their selves, as well as his sometimes radical alterations of reality, ultimately foreground the poet's art of creating a heterocosm. In his book on imagination and literature, Eckhard Lobsien offers the tautological witticism that 'die Imagination der Imagination ist Literatur' ('the imagination of the imagination is literature').[95] Spenser's *The Faerie Queene* is no exception, for Lobsien's aphorism also characterises Spenser's calculated imagination of the (uncontrolled) monstrous imagination as an act of making literature, which is ultimately reflected in his fashioning his own *natura altera* through far-reaching transformative processes.[96] An analysis of

93 On Archimago as the figuration of the human imagination, see Nohrnberg, *Analogy*, pp. 102–10, pp. 114–16 and pp. 118–25.

94 Cf. also Plett's remarks on Theseus's speech in *A Midsummer Night's Dream* in '"... of imagination all compact"', p. 33.

95 Lobsien, *Imaginationswelten*, p. 25.

96 These transformative processes are discussed together with Puttenham's four modes of making in Chapter 18, below.

Spenser's actual creation of the monsters and monstrous beings in his poem can demonstrate even more clearly how imagining and making monsters underscores the poet's autonomy, which enables him, in Shakespeare's words, 'to bod[y] forth / The forms of things unknown' (*MND*, V.i.14–15). It is to the process of making monsters, i.e. 'giving shape to them',[97] that the next chapter now turns.

97 See Plett, '"... of imagination all compact"', pp. 22–3.

17

Poetic creation: Spenser as Prometheus

The imagination as the faculty which fashions things anew and relocates sense perceptions to create monsters of the mind and other impossible things; the poet as a 'maker', or second creator who exercises his divine imagination to create a poem depicting new beings in a new poetic heterocosm: these are singularly important prerequisites for fashioning novel poetry. Spenser's insight into these discursive patterns is displayed in *The Faerie Queene* both in explicit and more subdued form, and casts light on his self-awareness as the maker of a romance whose plot, heroes and monsters test the limits of what was deemed possible and acceptable in poetry. Viewed from this perspective, making poetry becomes a quasi-divine act of creation. It is therefore especially telling that Eumnestes's chamber among all the historical documents also stores the record of a divine act of creation: the '*Antiquitee* of *Faery* lond' (II.ix.60.2), which traces the history of the Faeries from their origin to the poem's present. It initially explains that Prometheus created the first Faerie out of the parts of animals, and animated him with fire stolen from heaven, for which he was subsequently punished by Jove (II.x.70). The interpretation of this myth, which Spenser revised to fit the context of Faeryland's past, yields important information about the different aspects involved in 'manufacturing' textual and 'physical' beings, and brings to light crucial similarities between the god and the poet.

Prometheus's creations

As is the case with every other classical myth, literary accounts of the Prometheus myth sometimes differ substantially from one author to another.[1] The standardised version narrates how Prometheus, whose name

1 The literature and criticism on Prometheus is vast, and can be treated only in selection here. The most exhaustive overview of classical sources is given in Wilhelm Hein-

means 'forethought' (from Old Greek προ– + μηθ-, or μαθ-, 'to think', as in προ-μηθής),[2] creates man from clay or animal parts,[3] literally modelling him on the form of the Olympian gods, and animates him either with fire stolen from heaven[4] or with his own divine breath or spirit.[5] As punishment for stealing fire from the gods, Zeus has Prometheus chained to Mount Caucasus,[6] where an eagle eats away his ever regrowing liver. According to this myth, Prometheus's act of creating man is akin to an artisan manufacturing a clay sculpture.[7] Prometheus thus emerges as a *deus artifex*, a role that is also emphasised in the many versions that depict his creation of the beasts.[8]

---

rich Roscher, ed., *Ausführliches Lexikon der griechischen und römischen Mythologie*, 10 vols (Hildesheim: Georg Olms Verlagsbuchhandlung, 1965–77 (reprint of Leipzig 1884–1937), III.2, 3031–110; for a concise version, see *Der Neue Pauly: Enzyklopädie der Antike*, ed. by Hubert Cancik and Helmuth Schneider, 16 vols (Stuttgart: J. B. Metzler, 1996–2003), X, 402–6; on the Prometheus myth from its classical to its Renaissance permutations, see Olga Raggio, 'The Myth of Prometheus: Its Survival and Metamorphoses up to the Eighteenth Century', *Journal of the Warburg and Courtauld Institutes* 21 (1958), 44–62, and for Spenser, Philip J. Gallagher's entry on Prometheus in the *Spenser Encyclopedia*, ed. by Hamilton, pp. 557–8. The fullest philosophical treatment is still Hans Blumenberg's *Arbeit am Mythos* (Frankfurt am Main: Suhrkamp, 1979).

2 For the etymology of the word 'Prometheus', see Hjalmar Frisk's entry on προμηθής in *Griechisches etymologisches Wörterbuch*, 3 vols (Heidelberg: Winter, 1960–70), II, 599, and 'Prometheus', *Der Neue Pauly*, X, 402.

3 See Apollodorus, *Library*, I.vii.1, Ovid, *Metamorphoses*, I.69–88, and Lucian, 'Prometheus', 12 (in Lucian, *Works*, trans. by A. M. Harmon, 8 vols (London: Heinemann; Cambridge, MA: Harvard University Press, 1961), II). In some versions Prometheus also creates humans from animal material; see Aesop, *Fables*, 240 (for the text, see *Aesopica. A Series of Texts Relating to Aesop or Ascribed to Him or closely Connected with the Literary Tradition that Bears His Name*, coll. and crit. ed., in part translated from Oriental languages, with a commentary and historical essay, by Ben Edwin Perry, 3 vols (Urbana: University of Illinois Press, 1952), III, 415). Cf. also Plato, *Protagoras* 320C–322A (for the text, see Plato, *Protagoras*, trans. by C. C. W. Taylor, Clarendon Plato Series; rev. ed. (Oxford: Clarendon Press, 1991)). Philemon relates that Prometheus created all living beings (see Frg 89K in *The Fragments of Attic Comedy*, after Meineke, Bergk, and Kock; augmented, newly ed. with their contexts, annotated, and completely trans. into English verse by John Maxwell Edmonds, 3 vols (Leiden: Brill, 1957–61), III.a, 58–9).

4 See Hesiod, *Works and Days*, 50–2.

5 Boccaccio relates that Prometheus breathed life into man (*Genealogie*, IV.xlii (47C); see Giovanni Boccaccio, *Genealogie deorum gentilium libri*, ed. by Vincenzo Romano, 2 vols (Bari: Gius. Laterza & Figli, 1951), I, 197).

6 Prometheus's other possible transgressions are bringing fire to man, and tricking Jove of sacrificial offerings. See Hesiod, *Theogony*, 507–616, esp. 521–5, *Works*, 42–105, and Apollodorus, *Library*, I.vii.1.

7 Lactantius severely criticises Prometheus, emphasising that the novelty and subtlety of Prometheus's art stirred his witnesses into wonder (*Epitome divinarum institutionum*, 20.12–13; for the text, see Lucius Caecilius Firmianus Lactantius, *Epitome divinarum institutionum*, ed. by Eberhard Heck and Antonie Wlosok, Bibliotheca scriptorvm Graecorvm et Romanorvm Tevbneriana (Stuttgart: Teubner, 1994)).

8 See Aesop, *Fables* 240, which explains the existence of 'beastly' humans.

Spenser's version of the Prometheus myth is recorded in one of the scrolls stored in Eumnestes's chamber. While young Arthur, not yet King of Britain, reads *The Chronicles of Briton Kings* to acquaint himself with the history of his people and his own destiny, Guyon, a knight of Elfin extraction, devotes his attention to a volume called the '*Antiquity* of *Faery* lond', which begins the history of the Faeries with the tale of their origin:

> It told, how first *Prometheus* did create
> A man, of many parts from beasts deryu'd,
> And then stole fire from heuen, to animate
> His worke, for which he was by *Ioue* depryu'd
> Of life him self, and hart-strings of an Aegle ryu'd.
>
> That man so made, he called *Elfe*, to weet
> Quick, the first author of all Elfin kynd:
> Who wandring through the world with wearie feet,
> Did in the gardins of *Adonis* fynd
> A goodly creature, whom he deemd in mynd
> To be no earthly wight, but either Spright,
> Or Angell, th'authour of all woman kynd;
> Therefore a *Fay* he her according hight,
> Of whom all *Faryes* spring, and fetch their lignage right.
> (II.x.70.5–71.9)

Spenser here invents a Promethean myth of his own to explain the creation of the Elves. The narrative of a deity manufacturing a man who finds his mate in a garden, where both become the *authours* of the Faery race,[9] presents a procreational pattern substantially based on the Edenic narrative in the Book of Genesis. In his revision, Spenser replaces God the Maker with the pagan deity Prometheus, who creates the ancestor of all Faeries or Elves in *The Faerie Queene* as '[a] man, of many parts from beasts deryu'd' (70. 6). As Prometheus created '[a] man' and not 'Man' as such, the passage clearly identifies the Greek god as the founding father of the Elves, a particular race in Spenser's literary cosmos that closely resembles humans. Moreover, as neither the characters in Faeryland nor the narrator can distinguish consistently between human beings and Faeries, Spenser implies that there are no physical markers that help tell the Elves from the Britons, despite their different origins.[10] This renders

9 Brooks-Davies identifies the elf as the flesh and the fay as the spirit; in consequence, every Faery is a combination of body and soul (see *Critical Commentary*, p. 172, note to II.x.70).

10 See, e.g., Floris Delattre, *English Fairy Poetry from the Origins to the Seventeenth Century* (quoted in *Variorum*, II, 335). Even the instructive entry in *The Spenser Encyclopedia*

the analogy between humans and Faeries more complete.[11]

Spenser is very specific about the raw material Prometheus uses in the creation of Elfe: as the latter is 'of many parts from beasts deriyu'd', Spenser makes clear that Prometheus patterns Elfe entirely on animal parts.[12] Spenser's omission of any other ingredient creates a version of the Prometheus myth that differs from most traditional ones, in which Prometheus creates man from clay in the likeness of the gods. By emphasising Elfe's animal origin and nature, Spenser elaborates on the concept of the animal human, which is an important strand in the history of early modern ideas.[13] Spenser's use of Prometheus to create what Jürgen R. Meyer terms the 'Renaissance humanimal'[14] is not without precedent. Lotspeich traces the influences for this passage to Horace and to Natale Conti, one of Spenser's chief sources for mythological material.[15] Horace relates that the primal mud from which Prometheus created man was insufficient to complete his creation, so that he had to gather additional material to finish his work. Among other things, he placed the lion's anger into man's stomach.[16] In the early modern period, the Italian

---

(A. C. Hamilton and others, 'Faeries', in *Spenser Encyclopedia*, ed. by Hamilton, pp. 295–6) and C. S. Lewis's tripartite classification (*Discarded Image*, pp. 123–38) raise questions as to the unity underlying Spenser's portrayal of the Fairies. In his admirable full-length study on the notion of *fairy*, Woodcock wisely eschews applying any simplified meaning to these beings. Instead, he underscores that the concept of *fairy* in Spenser's poem rests on polysemy and indeterminateness (*Fairy*, pp. 76–87). For an extended discussion that emphasises the differences between Britons and Elves see Anthea Hume, *Edmund Spenser: Protestant Poet* (Cambridge: Cambridge University Press, 1984), pp. 145–61.

11 The analogy between the scriptural creation of man and the Spenserian creation of the Elves is further underlined by the linguistic coincidence that the name *Adam* translates into 'Man', which makes Elfe a secondary Adam. In Hebrew, Adam (*'ādhām*) means '(hu)man', a name that puns with *'ădhāmā*, 'ground' (see Cassuto, *Commentary*, p. 94 and p. 100).

12 On the use of the verb *to derive* in the context of source and origin, see *OED*, s.v. 'derive, *v.*', 6c.

13 Bacon marks man as the being with the highest degree of composition, because Prometheus created him by mixing clay and animal parts (*Works*, VI, 747).

14 Jürgen R. Meyer, '"Italianate Englishmen" and the Renaissance "Humanimal"', in *Anglistentag 2007 Münster: Proceedings*, ed. by Klaus Stierstorfer (Trier: Wissenschaftlicher Verlag Trier, 2008), pp. 25–37.

15 See William Nelson, *The Poetry of Edmund Spenser: A Study* (New York and London: Columbia University Press, 1963), p. 263.

16 Horace, *Odes*, I.I.16. 13–16, describes how Prometheus added animal parts when creating humans: 'Fertur Prometheus addere principi / limo coactus particulam undique / desectam et insani leonis / uim stomacho apposuisse nostro' ('They say Prometheus had to add to the primeval slime / a particle cut from every animal [MG: *undique* actually means 'from all over the place'] / and grafted the violence of a rabid lion / on to our stomach'). For text and translation, see Horace, *Odes I: Carpe diem*, ed. and trans. by David West (Oxford: Clarendon Press, 1995).

mythographer Natale Conti elaborates on Horace's version, explaining that Prometheus furnished man with the fear of the hare, the astuteness of the wolf, the boastfulness of the peacock, the fierceness of the tiger, the wrath of the lion and the magnitude of the soul.[17] Conti's version is therefore designed to give a mythological explanation for the beastly qualities of human behaviour.[18]

Conti's mythographical entry is significant, because it helps emphasise the chief characteristics of Spenser's version. Like Conti, Spenser accentuates the animal heritage of Prometheus's creation, but applies the aetiology to his fictional invention, and thereby recontextualises it into his own referential system. The most important deviation is Spenser's literalisation of Conti's version: where Conti uses the Prometheus myth to explain the animal characteristics of human behaviour, Spenser emphasises that Elfe was literally manufactured out of the 'parts' of animals, thereby turning Conti's quasi-psychological explications into a narrative about the body and its creation, which foregrounds man's animal heritage.

Matthew Woodcock, who has devoted an entire book to the idea of 'Elf-Fashioning', points out quite rightly that Spenser's brief tale of Prometheus is replete with 'references to artifice and "making"'.[19] But while Woodcock states that the Elves are 'manufactured', he offers no sustained analysis of the creation myth.[20] Yet the myth pertains to the idea of making in *The Faerie Queene* and, against the backdrop of Sidney's definition of the poet's nature, also to the core of poetic creation. The circumstance that Spenser's take on the Prometheus myth leaves out any reference to clay, the raw material in most versions, focusing instead on making Elfe from animal matter and bringing him to life with the fire stolen from Jove, allows for the deduction that the poet deliberately emphasises the transgressive act of animating parts derived from animals to create a new species, a latent composite creature that looks like 'a man'. That transgression is involved becomes all the more plausible as it is not explicitly clear which of Prometheus's acts caused Jove's anger: the creation, the theft of

17 See Conti, *Mythologiae*, IV.6: 'dixerunt timorem leporis, astutiam vulpis, pavonis ambitionem, tigridum feritatem, leonum iracundiam et magnitudinem animi fuisse hominibus ab ipso Prometheo iniunctas' ('they say that men were given the fear of the hare, the astuteness of the wolf, the boastfulness of the peacock, the fierceness of the tiger, the wrath of the lion, and the magnitude of the soul by Prometheus himself'; *Mythologiae*, p. 98a.31–3).

18 The tradition originates from Aesop, *Fables*, 240.

19 Woodcock, *Fairy*, p. 130.

20 Woodcock has recently elaborated on these issues in 'Elf-Fashioning Revisited', pp. 210–20.

the fire or, indeed, both.[21] Hence, it could be argued that Prometheus's transgression is constituted by the pursuit of his own creative designs.

Spenser is not the only early modern writer resorting to the Prometheus myth. In his 'Hymnus in Noctem' from *The Shadow of Night* (1594), George Chapman explicitly identifies poets with Prometheus. Half-way through the poem, Chapman gives an account of human beings with degenerate and hence monstrous souls, an observation that he uses as an introduction to a discussion of more general poetic issues, namely the nature of the poet and the *telos* of poetry. In the following passage, which emphasises the poet's didactic duty, he makes his readers aware of man's possible monstrosity:

> *Therefore Promethean Poets with the coles*
> *Of their most geniale, more-then-humane soules*
> *In liuing verse, created men like these,*
> *With shapes of Centaurs, Harpies, Lapithes,*
> *That they in prime of erudition,*
> *When almost sauage vulgar men were growne,*
> *Seeing them selues in those Pierean founts,*
> *Might mend their mindes, asham'd of such accounts.*[22]

This passage, which calls to mind Sidney's design of 'another nature' inhabited by fantastic beings, characterises poets as Promethean makers, whose quasi-divine souls can create monsters similar to those on Phantastes's frescos, ranging from composite races such as Centaurs to infernal creatures such as Harpies, and animate them with the force of '*liuing verse*'.[23] Chapman conceives of these monstrosities as powerful didactic tools, because they will make readers recognise their own depravity and convert them into morally sound people. The notion that '*verse*' – which refers to the individual members and 'organic units' of poetry, but here metonymically applies to poetry at large – is a '*liuing*' entity that in turn bestows life on the beings created by the poet, opens a channel to Spenser's Promethean myth. To be more precise, the notion of *living* verse recalls the name which Spenser's Prometheus chose for his creation,

21 As the species is the product of composite derivation, one could in fact argue that Spenser permanently violates the dividing line between man and beast by turning hybridity into a ubiquitous phenomenon in *The Faerie Queene*.

22 The marginalia of the poem's first edition (London: William Ponsonby, 1594) explain this passage at some length: 'He [i.e. the poet] cals them Promethean Poets in this high conceipt, by a figuratiue comparison betwixt them, that as Pro[metheus] with fire fetcht from heauen, made men: so Poets with the fire of their soules are sayd to create those Harpies, And Centaures, and thereof he calls their soules Geniale.'

23 Chapman harks back to the concept of monstrous men, i.e. men whose souls have degenerated into the monstrous and bestial.

namely '*Elfe*', which, according to Spenser, means 'quick' or 'living'. Spenser's explanation elevates the Prometheus myth to an important metapoetical level, because poetry emerges as an art form that animates an autonomous idea or fore-conceit. In the allegorical world of the poem, Prometheus could hence be deemed the fictional cipher for the real creator of the Faeries, namely Spenser the poet, who brings to life a new race, as well as a cast of novel characters, deities and monsters. The qualities that define Prometheus are therefore equally applicable to the poet. Spenser describes Prometheus as a godhead that can create a new organic being through the process of physical derivation. This makes Prometheus a 'maker' and, thus, the poet's kin. In his version of the Prometheus myth, Spenser hence elaborates on the notion of the creator-poet, and thereby resorts to and 'images forth' Sidney's idea of the poet as a maker developing a secondary nature, which here is exemplified by Prometheus's creating a secondary man through creative derivation.

Spenser's creations

If one takes Spenser's revision of the Prometheus myth seriously, Faeryland is populated with the descendants of Elfe, a 'humanimal' created as an emulated version of the animals. In addition, Spenser's version of the Prometheus myth may also be read as an allegory of the poet's creative process. The detailed discussion of monsters and monstrous beings offered in Part II reveals that monstrosities are indeed fashioned by means of descriptions that mirror the process of creation, and place the monster into the rhetorical, and conceptual frame of the poem.[24] Viewed in this context, the extended physiological presentations of, among others, Duessa, Geryoneo's dragon or Lust are necessarily based on advanced stylistic and poetic strategies, because they determine the literary feasibility and vividness of these creatures. While Duessa's bodily ugliness is defined by the complete absence of symmetry, Spenser's drawing an extended *descriptio personae* from the upper to the lower half of her face before turning to her breasts and skin, her tail and, finally, her feet betrays the premeditated formalism of a creator fashioning new textual beings by following the precepts laid out in rhetorical handbooks. In this context, the term 'rompe' (I.viii.48.3) becomes a meta-poetic marker that indicates how Spenser manufactures Duessa by attaching

24 Hanafi explains that '[d]escription not only describes, it also creates, orders, sets the object in a context of rhetorical meaning and institutional forces' (*Monster in the Machine*, p. 25).

various disparate animal parts to an unspecified body. Hence, Duessa illustrates Spenser's creating beings from reconfigured and animated body parts. Like Prometheus's Elfe, Duessa is 'of many partes from beasts deryu'd', but in such a way that the process of textual making results in an overtly monstrous human–animal composite. The extended Petrarchan catalogue therefore is the rhetorical means to break down Duessa into her various body parts,[25] but it simultaneously creates the monster in such a way that the reader re-members her in the act of reading.[26] Duessa's unique physique therefore bears witness to Spenser's penchant for new combinations, and points to the method of fashioning grotesque novelties from animal parts by means of distortion.[27]

If human–animal composites bring into palpable relief the combinatory possibilities of the Promethean poet, so do more traditional monstrosities. Whereas terms like 'stump',[28] 'sinke'[29] or 'block',[30] among others, are employed as verbal raw material for the textual creation of monstrous beings, even Spenser's stanzaic arrangement can become essential in constructing the grossest of deformities. Spenser, for example, breaks down the description of the Great Dragon into seven stanzas (I.xi.8–14), a strategy that maps a symmetrical structure on the monster's otherwise indeterminate proportions.[31] Spenser's constructionist agenda is perhaps best illustrated by Geryoneo's dragon. As the following schema shows, Spenser breaks down the stanza into individual segments that correlate to the monster's body parts and their functions (V.xi.24):

lines	*body part*	*animal*	*significance*
1–2	torso	dog	greediness
3–4	claws	lion	power of destruction
5–6	tail and sting	dragon	causes of lethal wounds
7–9	wings	eagle	scope and speed render monster inescapable

Spenser's symmetrical mapping of the creature's body makes the composition of the stanza analogous to the creation of the monster from known

25 Gender criticism usually reads the beauty blazon as a means of fragmenting and objectifying the female body; see among others Vickers, 'Diana Described'.

26 See Plett, '"... of imagination all compact"', p. 22.

27 Cf. also Spenser's use of the verb 'dispaint' for Phantastes's frescos (II.ix.50.1).

28 See I.xi.39.9 (Redcrosse vanquishes the Dragon).

29 The term 'sinke' is used only for female monsters; see I.i.22.5 (Errour) and V.xi.31.6 (Geryoneo's dragon).

30 See I.viii.10.6 (Orgoglio's arm falling to the ground).

31 The individual stanzas describe the Dragon's entire body (8), its scales (9), wings (10), tail and stings (11) and claws (12); then the beast's jaw (12), teeth and the smoke emitted from its mouth (13), as well as its eyes (14).

animal parts. The principle elements that hold the stanza together, such as rhyme, metre and verbal form, also join the various parts of the monster, with the semicolons at the end of lines 2, 4 and 6 as syntactical suture.[32] Hence, physical creation and poetic fashioning work along similar parameters, as putting together '*liuing verse*' results in a living poetic entity. In effect, the Spenserian monster is a paradoxical product, because it is created as a disfigured monster with unsuited body parts through well-wrought poetry. Therefore, these newly invented creatures do not at all lack composition, as a downright monstrous imagination would suggest, but foreground Spenser's deliberation as well as his rhetorical and stylistic proficiency.[33] This skill adds a calculated vividness to the fantastic image, and thus joins the rhetorical precept of *enargeia*, the heightened vividness of description, to its ultimate effect, *energeia*.[34] Spenser hence uses his 'learned discretion'[35] to create speaking images that are not disordered fantasies.

Spenser's Promethean expertise in creating Geryoneo's dragon is therefore heavily dependent on his ability to draw on the physical data stored in his memory, and to use it intentionally for the design of his poem. The imagination of Renaissance authors was, however, equally influenced by the host of textual material they had read and digested. With the dragons, mention has been made of scriptural monsters such as the monsters of the Apocalypse, and classical creatures such as the Hydra. In the case of Geryoneo's dragon, the textual pedigree includes, among other things, the locusts in Revelation, Gerïon from Dante's *Inferno*, the Sphinx from Boiardo's *Orlando Inammorato* and Natale Conti's account of the Sphinx in classical mythology. If the physical features of the Sphinx form the basis of the physique of Geryoneo's monster, Spenser emulates his own creation on a received phenotype. As the horrifying physique of Geryoneo's dragon is also an intertextual creation, the monster, like Spenser's entire heterocosm, is not only 'of many parts from beasts deryu'd' but also 'of many parts from texts deryu'd'. Spenser starts out with a number of descriptive sources (notably the references in Revelation and Conti),

32 By comparison, Gerïon in Dante's *Inferno*, XVII.7–25, and the Sphinx in Boiardo's *Orlando Innamorato*, I.v.70, lack such clear rhetorical organisation.

33 Cf. also the arrangement of the Duessa stanzas in I.viii.47–8.

34 On the concept of *enargeia*, which was frequently confused with *energeia*, see Bundy, *Imagination*, p. 109, Plett, '"... of imagination all compact"', p. 21, and Linda Galyon, 'Puttenham's *Enargeia* and *Energeia*: New Twists for Old Terms', *Philological Quarterly* 60 (1981), 29–40 (pp. 29–32, with reference, among others, to Longinus, Plutarch and Cinthio).

35 Sidney, *Defence*, p. 81.

then by combining them rebuilds his own version of the specimen through rhetorical or stylistic means and finally animates his creation in the context of his – and here I would like to hark back to Chapman's text – '*liuing verse*'.[36] The idea of derivation put forward in the Prometheus passage is thus also applicable to Spenser's textual practices, for even in the sixteenth and seventeenth centuries the verb *to derive* could be applied to the construction of texts and the formation of words.[37]

The poet's creating a textual being that he can disfigure or change at his own design is reminiscent of Bacon's conviction that the imagination has the autonomous ability to join or take apart sense perceptions and received data at will.[38] Spenser's monsters therefore show the poet as a self-governing creator who transforms his received knowledge into new texts. In extreme cases, Spenser even takes the liberty of misplacing correlating body parts. Lust's face, for instance, is an animated version of the male and female genitalia, for which the poet deliberately mars the usual allocation of physical members in normative bodies. The standard verdict was, of course, that such practices be avoided, as Pseudo-Longinus states in *On the Sublime* when expounding the necessity to imitate nature, which hides man's genitals and excretions from view, lest man's beauty be spoiled.[39] The effect of violating this rule is well calculated by Spenser.

The means by which Spenser manufactures Lust and other monsters shows that the creation of textual and physical beings takes place in two decisive steps: in dislocating segments from animals or texts, and in relocating them into a new unit (be it the text or the body) in the process of creative transformation. The poet thus needs the dislocating energy of the poetic imagination to fashion something new. Ultimately, Spenser's monstrous discourse is a *discordia concors* yoking together two disparate voices: while his use of descriptive referents taints monsters as gross and abject deformities, his poetic practice belies such heinousness, because these monsters are realised as perfect rhetorical forms, and therefore show, as Ben Jonson puts it, the poet's 'learned hand, and true *Promethean* art'.[40]

36 Woodcock notes that the Faeries and their history are an amalgamation of textual sources (see *Fairy*, pp. 130–1).

37 See the respective entries in the *OED*, s.v. 'derive, *v.*', 6a, 9b, 10b and 4b.

38 Bacon notes that the imagination 'being not tied to the laws of matter, may at pleasure join that which nature hath severed, and sever that which nature hath joined, and so make unlawful matches and divorces of things' (*Advancement*, in *Works*, III, 343).

39 Longinus, *On the Sublime*, XLIII.4. The text is included in the Loeb edition of Aristotle's *Poetics*, pp. 119–254 (pp. 246–7).

40 See Ben Jonson, *Epigrammes*, CX.17, 'To Clement Edmonds, on his Caesar's *Commentaries obserued, and translated*'. Jonson here praises Edmonds for his achievement,

Returning to Phantastes's chamber

The monstrous beings in *The Faerie Queene* make manifest Spenser's, as it were, 'constructionist' agenda. They also put the spotlight firmly on the human agency that ultimately constructs them: the poet's active and creative imagination. The discussion of Spenser's poetic making as exemplified by his monstrous creatures brings the argument back full circle to the context in which Spenser embeds his tale of Prometheus: the Castle of Alma. Prometheus dwells, as it were, in a scroll stored in Eumnestes's chamber of memories, and is hence the memorial token of a divine and autonomous creative process, which tells of the animation of a new living being from different animal parts. By embedding the version of Prometheus's tale into his allegory of the tripartite brain-turret, Spenser implicitly relates the creational myth to the larger issue of the imagination. Prometheus displays surprising similarities with Phantastes, whose fly-infested chamber is painted with the types of monsters and romance characters that also appear in *The Faerie Queene*. The imagination is usually assigned the capacity to put together disparate material into newly fashioned beings. Huarte, among others, emphasises that the imagination 'hath force not onely to compound a figure *possible* with another, but doth ioyne also (after the order of nature) those which are *vnpossible*' (emphases added).[41] This brings out an important similarity with Prometheus's compounding Elfe. In his anatomy of the brain cells, Spenser emphasises that Phantastes is endowed with 'fore-sight', as well as with 'quick pre[-]iudize', a word, as A. C. Hamilton informs us, that means 'prejudgment', but also 'fore-thought'.[42] Phantastes thus has the ability to look into the future, and to create with premeditation, a quality that is also emphasised by his ponderous melancholy. Phantastes's creative capability connects readily with Prometheus's nature, because his name (Greek Προ-μήθευς) defines him through his ability to 'fore-think'.[43] It is exactly the ability of 'fore-thought' in Phantastes and Prometheus that stresses deliberation as the defining quality of fashioning, and characterises poetic creation, even that

---

linking the idea of Promethean skill to Edmonds's turning the *Commentarii* into a 'new Creation' ('Edmonds', 18). The text is taken from Ben Jonson, *Works*, VIII, 71.

41 Huarte, *Examen de ingenios*, p. 132. See also de LaPrimaudaye, *Second Part of the French Academie*, p. 155. As quoted above, John Davies of Hereford notes that 'Fantacie, / … doth so forme reforme, and it deformes, / As pleaseth hir fantasticke faculty' (*Complete Works*, I, 9). It is through this mechanism that the imagination creates 'things vnlikely' from 'things likely'. For a similar statement, see Bacon, *Advancement*, in *Works*, III, 343. See, above all, Rossky, 'Imagination', pp. 58–9.

42 The explanation is Hamilton's (note to II.ix.49.7).

43 The etymological name gave Bacon the idea to interpret the god as a kind of Providence (see *Works*, VI, 747).

of monstrous or human-animal composites, as intentional. This correlation between the names and natures of Prometheus and Phantastes is hardly coincidental in a work in which names form such complex patterns of meaning, and which draws so heavily on contemporary poetical issues.

As fantasy has access to memory and can create new combinations from what it has stored, Good Memory (Eumnestes) is the decisive tool for the visualisation of new beings, since this faculty provides the matter, or raw material, for creating these new combinations from physical and textual data. Making poetry is an act of creation based on the combination and animation of physical and textual material, which – to use the central term from Spenser's Prometheus myth – is 'deryu'd' from memory, a process which is at work in Spenser's *The Faerie Queene*, and which parallels Prometheus's fashioning Elfe from the parts of animals. In the context of this theory, the poet is not merely the vessel of divine inspiration; rather, he emerges as a maker striving for autonomy, which leads to his hubris and transgression.[44] It thus becomes apparent that Spenser's fashioning, literally com-posing a poem full of extraordinary characters, strange bodies and topographical details, is just as much an act of making as Prometheus's fashioning Elfe: Prometheus, like Spenser, is a poet in the etymological sense of the word. Spenser thus shows that the imagination which fashions monsters does not necessarily 'breed' these '*Chimeres*' like the *phantastici* Puttenham condemns in his *Arte of English Poesie*; on the contrary, Spenser's formalism shows the deliberation that can inform the making of the monstrous, and hence again establishes the poet as a 'eufantastic' maker.[45]

If one extrapolates from these findings, textual embodiment becomes the governing process behind the creation of literary monsters. Spenser's main task as a romance poet therefore strikingly resembles Theseus's famous speech in *A Midsummer Night's Dream* from the mid-1590s:

> And as imagination bodies forth
> The forms of things unknown, the poet's pen
> Turns them to shapes, and gives to airy nothing
> A local habitation and a name.
>
> (Shakespeare, *MND*, V.i.14–17)

44 It is noteworthy that the verb *to derive* can be applied to mental processes, as it means 'to obtain by some process of reasoning, inference or deduction; to gather, deduce' (*OED*, 7, gives evidence from the 1500s and 1600s), which suggests a link between Prometheus's etymological name and the notion of derivation.

45 In the 'Letter to Raleigh', 48, Spenser also points out that the poet is '*recoursing to the thinges forepaste, and diuining of thinges to come*', thus emphasising the joint efforts of memory and the imagination to fashion poetry.

Both Prometheus and Spenser indulge in 'bodying forth' 'unknown things' by giving shape to their 'airy nothing[s]', i.e. their very own ideas and imaginings. This delicate, 'airy' quality recalls the flies but also the frescos in Phantastes's chamber, and even the giant wind-bag Orgoglio, thus marking Spenser's creations as products of the poet's lively and supreme imagination. Additionally, Spenser, like Prometheus, gives these beings names; the poet, however, transcends the god by designing for them a 'local habitation': Faeryland and its adjacent textual realms, which are compounds of topographical referents animated within the confines of his poem.[46] In his treatment of the Promethean myth, Spenser hence reflects on his own critical awareness of the poet as an autonomous maker who brings to life a secondary nature, a heterocosm in which he also places different types of new monsters as defining and consciously fashioned parts of his 'rich tapestry'. Such poetic making is already introduced in the Wandering Wood passage, where Spenser reimagines the wood of romance as a heterocosm harbouring a monster at its centre.

The problem of autonomy

Prometheus's alleged deeds have earned him various epithets. On the one hand, the theft of fire and the creation of man marked him as an antagonist of the gods, and stigmatised him as a lawbreaker driven by excessive vanity and curiosity.[47] The myth also lent itself to positive allegorical readings, which interpreted Prometheus as the bringer of culture, i.e. of philosophy, letters and learning.[48] These characteristics are in no small part influenced by the etymology of his name. In his *Genealogie deorum*,

46 Theseus's speech is thoroughly analysed in Plett's article '"... of imagination all compact"', which deals with the various stages of the poet's composition, and argues that Theseus does not discredit poets; for further poetical criticism, see Rainer Lengeler, *Das Theater der leidenschaftlichen Phantasie: Shakespeares 'Sommernachtstraum' als Spiegel seiner Dichtungstheorie*, Kieler Beiträge zur Anglistik und Amerikanistik, 11 (Neumünster: Wachholtz, 1975), pp. 108–17 and pp. 129–31; Diana Akers Rhoads, *Shakespeare's Defense of Poetry: 'A Midsummer Night's Dream' and 'The Tempest'* (Lanham: University Press of America, 1985), pp. 61–96; and Ekbert Faas, *Shakespeare's Poetics* (Cambridge: Cambridge University Press, 1986), pp. 136–50.

47 Isidore of Seville marked him as the inventor of idolatry, because he first created humans in effigy (see *Etymologiae*, VIII.xi). Cf. also Lactantius, *Epitome*, 20.12–13, and the entry on Prometheus in Cooper's *Thesaurus* (Prometheus 'first inuented makynge of ymages').

48 First put forward by Theophrast, Fragment 50 in *Theophrasti Eresii opera, quae supersunt, omnia*, ed. and trans. by Friedrich Wimmer (Paris: Diderot, 1866). Dieter Bremer discusses Prometheus's role as the bringer of human culture and self-responsibility in the classical age (see 'Prometheus: Die Formation eines Grundmythologems', in *Prometheus: Mythos der Kultur*, ed. by Edgar Pankow and Günter Peters (Munich: Fink, 1999), pp. 35–42 (pp. 35–8)).

Boccaccio stresses the necessity to read myths allegorically, and sets up the concept of the 'duplex Prometheus': while the first is the syncretistic cipher for God, the maker of man, the second is a wise teacher that turns ignorant, and unruly men into a civilised people. As Prometheus's educational programme is basically a second creation that turns human beings from physical into cultural beings, man likewise has a 'double nature'.[49] Accordingly, Susanna Barsella interprets Boccaccio's use of the Prometheus myth as a strategy to reclaim for himself 'the lofty role of "civilizator"'.[50] In a more critical move, Spenser, who acknowledges the tension between the poet's creative autonomy and its dangers throughout his work (in figures like Bonfont/Malfont and Archimago),[51] emphasises that the poet must act transgressively by manufacturing something new and living from disparate parts in order to create a work that likewise helps civilise, i.e. fashion the perfect gentleman.[52] This observation renders more profound the conceptual link between the creator of Elfe and the maker of *The Faerie Queene*, precisely because both employ analogous methods.[53] Since the monsters and monstrous beings in and outside of Faeryland consist of reconfigured and animated body parts, which are also derived from pre-existing textual material, Spenser establishes the Promethean discourse as the pattern of the poet's office. The paradigm of Prometheus thus ultimately accounts for the '*liuing verse*' of *The Faerie Queene*, which is very much a coagulation derived from different texts, and genres amalgamated into a unified whole by Spenser the poet, who cannot create *ex nihilo*,[54] but has to draw on existing

49 See Boccaccio, *Genealogie*, IV.xliv (47C). In the early seventeenth century, Bacon thus assesses Prometheus 'not as the founder only but also as the amplifier and enlarger of the human race', and hence the driving force behind any cultural progress (*De sapientia veterum*, in *Works*, VI, 745). Bacon argues that Prometheus's giving fire to man is the origin of science and craftsmanship. Truly Promethean human beings are characterised by wisdom and thoughtfulness (see *Works*, VI, 751).

50 See Susanna Barsella, 'The Myth of Prometheus in Giovanni Boccaccio's *Decameron*', *Modern Language Notes* 119 (2004), 120–41 (Italian issue).

51 Nohrnberg elaborates on the critical connection between Archimago and the poet (see *Analogy*, p. 105, p. 116 and p. 119).

52 Hadfield raises a similar issue when stating that 'Spenser … was always eager … to demonstrate that poetic creation had to take risks and try out new ideas and new forms of writing' ('Prometheus', p. 197). On the perfect gentleman, see 'Letter to Raleigh', 7–8.

53 Duessa's symmetrical arrangement of asymmetrical body parts, Geryoneo's dragon's multiform physique, as well as its lineage show that the individual segments or facets of their being are also largely created from textual material.

54 Andrew Ford maps the genesis of the term ποιητής in the classical period, arguing that it marks a paradigm shift in the conception of verbal art from performance to composition. The term connotes the 'production of something material', which the writer does not create '*ex nihilo*' (*The Origins of Literary Criticism: Literary Culture and Poetic Theory* (Princeton and Oxford: Princeton University Press, 2002), pp. 131–9, here p. 134).

material, which he recalibrates and animates textually.[55]

As a poet, Spenser prefers inventing new monstrosities to copying familiar ones.[56] If one takes Sidney's verdict seriously that the superior poet forms things 'quite anew', these novelties must be examples of Spenser's poetic achievement. Accordingly, Spenser's harking back to Hesiod's monsters and medieval monstrosities is a means of resorting to the readers' common knowledge to make his new creations feasible. The originality of Spenser's monsters also explains why he anatomises them to such a great extent, for he utilises shapes that both poet and reader have stored in their memories. In consequence, memory offers tools for the visualisation of new beings, since it helps the mind to create new combinations and to communicate them with *enargeia*.[57] Construction and animation hence permeate the different aspects of the poet's work, and constitute the basis of his craft. Only by using his imagination can the writer become a true Prometheus, who bestows unto man the gift of light, knowledge and culture. Spenser, as an early modern Prometheus, seeks to reassess the task of the poet as an act in which the creator becomes a rightful second god if foresight and forethought guide his steps.

55 The same method is used in Spenser's presentation of historical material, as Woodcock points out (see *Fairy*, p. 128). René Girard also notes that new monsters are created 'from various forms' extracted from sources and recombined at the poet's will. Hence, the literary monster does not come into being *ex nihilo* (*The Scapegoat*, trans. by Yvonne Freccero (Baltimore: Johns Hopkins University Press, 1986), p. 33).

56 In I.viii.48.9, and III.vii.22.7, Spenser stresses that the creatures he describes have never been seen before.

57 Cf. Burton, *Anatomy*, I, 166–72.

18

The poet's autonomy and the use of the monstrous imagination

As a maker consciously creating topographical representations of the monstrous imagination, as well as a host of novel characters and monsters, Spenser fashions an extensive heterocosm in which the poem's complex plots can take place. The poem is hence everything but a direct representation of the first world created by God, but transforms the material it offers into a secondary world, where events take place that are only possible within the fictional 'spatio-temporal net' of the poem.[1] Such far-reaching transformative and manipulative processes suggest Spenser's conscious participating in the poetic discourse of the autonomous imagination. While his world-making in *The Faerie Queene* generally implies Scaliger's *alter deus* creating a *natura altera*,[2] it more specifically recalls those precepts in Sidney's *Defence* which appraise the poet's work as the modulation, or enhancement of reality, because it contains 'forms such as never were in nature, as the Heroes, Demigods, Cyclops, Chimeras, Furies'.[3] This secondary world is distinct from the first world, while simultaneously drawing on its material as recognisable references triggering the memory of the reader.[4] In order to reinforce and develop Spenser's interaction with a contemporary poetic discourse that seeks to elevate the status of creative autonomy, I will survey Puttenham's concept

1 The phrase is MacCaffrey's (*Spenser's Allegory*, p. 71). Lobsien describes the second world as a continuing transformation of the first (see *Imaginationswelten*, p. 100). On time in *The Faerie Queene*, see Michael Murrin, *The Veil of Allegory: Some Notes Toward a Theory of Allegorical Rhetoric in the English Renaissance* (Chicago: Chicago University Press, 1969), pp. 109–10. He argues that Spenser uses a four-fold time scheme that comprises biblical times, the fourth century, the sixth century and the Elizabethan age.

2 See Scaliger, *Poetices libri septem*, I, 70–2, and Chapter 13, above.

3 Sidney, *Defence*, p. 78. Tasso also implicitly discusses such a realm in the *Discorsi* (see *Prose*, pp. 588–9, and *Discourses*, pp. 77–8).

4 The relation between first and secondary world inheres in Sidney's tenet that the poet 'goeth hand in hand with nature', but has the sovereignty to roam 'freely … within the zodiac of his own wit' (*Defence*, p. 78). For a theoretical discussion of similar principles, see Lobsien, *Imaginationswelten*, p. 33.

of art adapting itself to different poetic contexts, before I discuss Philip Sidney's tenets on the imagination and allegorical poetry. I will argue that Spenser goes one decisive step further than Sidney when conceiving his heterocosm as a world of monsters and the malfunctioning imagination.

Modes of poetic making

Although Sidney's *Defence* and Scaliger's *Poetices libri* contain the more famous, because more emphatic, Renaissance testimonies on the emergent notion of the heterocosm, it is Puttenham's *Arte* which offers a detailed gloss on how to create such a secondary world. On the final pages of his poetics, Puttenham, like Sidney a spokesman for the idea of the poet's creative autonomy, distinguishes between modes of poetic making that sport a striking resemblance to Spenser's various uses of the imagination. They more specifically illustrate the transformative poetical manoeuvres Spenser undertakes to fashion *The Faerie Queene* as a poetic heterocosm, and thus bring into relief Spenser's own interpretation of his role as the maker of Faeryland.

Puttenham assigns art four roles, which are determined by art's differing relations with nature: art is 'an ayde and coadiutor to nature'; 'a surmounter of [nature's] skill'; 'a bare immitator of natures works'; and 'an encountrer and contrary to nature'.[5] Puttenham's plethora of artistic functions demonstrates that the power of art does not solely lie in imitative representation, but that it significantly entails the transformation of nature through the calculated use of the imagination.[6] Puttenham first maintains that art can be an 'ayde and coadiutor to nature', and is thus endowed with the ability to tend nature like a physician or gardener. He grants art the power to, as it were, upgrade nature and thus to bring it to greater perfection, a tenet that recalls Sidney's idea of the golden world.[7] Puttenham raises art to an even more independent level when claiming that it can also be 'an *alterer* [of nature in all her action], and in some sort a *surmounter* of her skill', because it can make things 'more beautifull or straunge and miraculous'.[8] Puttenham's underscoring the transformative

5 Puttenham, *Arte*, pp. 303–4. See also Rölli-Alkemper, *Höfische Poetik*, pp. 270–1.

6 In fact, three of the four modes involve a transformation of some kind. The only exception is type three, 'a bare immitator of natures works'.

7 See Sidney, *Defence*, p. 78.

8 Puttenham, *Arte*, pp. 303–4; emphases added. Bushnell examines the image of gardening used by Puttenham, Bacon and Sidney to show that horticultural imagery illustrates the concept of a more autonomous poetry (see Rebecca Bushnell, 'Experience, Truth, and Natural History in Early English Gardening Books, 1520–1630', in *The Historical Imagination*, ed. by Kelley and Sacks, pp. 179–209 (pp. 197–8)).

quality of creative fashioning asserts the possibility inherent in any work of art to design the unfamiliar and exceptional, i.e. the not previously perceived or conceived. From this point of view, the wondrous outgrowth of the transformative imagination becomes a crucial ingredient in any literary genre. This is especially so in epic romance, whose success relies heavily on the writer's ability to evoke wonder through the vivid depiction of, among other things, the supernatural or preternatural, in Puttenham's terminology the 'straunge' and 'miraculous'. Such a display of the ideal and marvellous inevitably corroborates poetic independence.[9] The poet's sovereignty over his creation is again strengthened when Puttenham, after profiling type three as 'bare' imitation,[10] professes that art can also be an 'encountrer and contrary to nature'. This supposition expands what is artistically possible and licit, because it leads to 'strange and diuerse' things whose forms are not borne out of the rigid imitation of nature, although they are 'made of' it.[11] This statement leaves an argumentative loophole for literary works foregrounding creative licence, especially as the phrase 'contrary to nature' translates the Latin *in naturam* and Old Greek παρὰ φύσιν, which traditionally define the monstrous.[12]

Since Puttenham sees art as a mixture of these four modes, he leaves it to the poet and his reliance on rational control to decide which of them he needs to deploy for a particular situation in his overall creative design. David Attridge might critique the 'instability and the undecidability' between art and nature evident in these lines,[13] but it is precisely this poetic

9 See Biester, 'Fancy's Images', p. 296.

10 Puttenham, *Arte*, p. 304. He compares these poets to alchemists counterfeiting nature. Cf. also the witch's use of alchemy to create Snowy Florimell in III.viii.5–10.

11 See Puttenham, *Arte*, pp. 304–5, for the entire passage: 'Finally in another respect arte is as it were an encountrer and contrary to nature, producing effects neither like to hers, nor by participation with her operations, nor by imitation of her paternes, but makes things and produceth effects altogether strange and diuerse, & of such forme & qualitie (nature alwaies supplying stuffe) as she neuer would nor could haue done of her selfe, as the carpenter that builds a house, the ioyner that makes a table or a bedstead, the tailor a garment, the Smith a locke or a key, and a number of like, in which case the workman gaineth reputation by his arte, and praise when it is best expressed & most apparāt, & most studiously.'

Although Rölli-Alkemper holds the view that Puttenham severs art from nature, it should not be forgotten that the poet needs data from the external world (read: nature) to create things anew. This becomes especially clear in the recurring carpenter simile, which explains that even objects fashioned contrary to nature are 'made of' nature (see *Höfische Poetik*, pp. 270–1).

12 See Chapter 3, above. Cf. also Sidney's tenet of the poet going 'hand in hand with nature' (*Defence*, p. 78, and Heninger, *Touches of Sweet Harmony*, p. 307).

13 Derek Attridge, 'Puttenham's Perplexity: Nature, Art, and the Supplement in Renaissance Poetic Theory', in *Literary Theory / Renaissance Texts*, ed. by Patricia Parker and David Quint (Baltimore and London: Johns Hopkins University Press, 1986), pp. 257–79 (p. 273).

openness that makes Puttenham's tenets significant. In other words, he offers a way out of the cul-de-sac of strict imitation,[14] but does not quite make the transition to a more developed autonomy like Spenser, because he is not yet aware of the full potential latent in his own precepts.[15] This is especially so since he hints at a close connection between nature and the poet, claiming that the poet who casts aside the shackles of rigorous imitation becomes 'but euen as nature her selfe working by her own peculiar vertue and proper instinct'.[16] Granted autonomy over his work like Nature herself, the poet has the ability to fashion the poetic heterocosm according to his own design. Consequentially, one should reassess Puttenham as an important example in the development of fantasy, for he enriches the concept of *imitatio*, a term he uses in the broadest sense, with that of the creative, combinatory imagination, which has the power to transform objects and perceptions.[17]

Puttenham's taxonomy obliquely helps elaborate on the notion that Spenser is a Promethean maker who brings to life creatures of his own devising in a heterocosm that he creates like a secondary god. In order to exert such autonomy, Spenser depends on the transforming power of the imagination, through which he can manipulate the material stored in his memory to forge new beings, characters and places. These poeticised objects are created by drawing on various modes of making, ranging from the strict imitation to the idealised presentation of nature, and from the depiction of wondrous, miraculous incidents to the fashioning of hideous creatures that inspire horror.[18] Spenser's own interpretation of the poet's office in *The Faerie Queene* hence vacillates between the modes of making postulated by Puttenham, but also transcends them, because Spenser expands the monster, the being that is *in naturam*, into a central poetic concept that becomes the manifestation of his poetic sovereignty.

In the text of *The Faerie Queene*, Spenser foregrounds his deliberate use of the imagination both by realising monsters as rhetorical beings

14 Daston and Park observe, with reference to Puttenham, that 'art might still ape nature, but it also might extend, assist, complete, contravene, or even surpass her' (*Wonders and the Order of Nature*, p. 264 and p. 426, n. 9).

15 This is similarly observed in Ahrends, 'Transformationen', p. 12. Type four of Puttenham's modes of poetic fashioning makes room for more autonomous poetry, but does not quite make the transition to the monstrous, as the various similes in the passage show.

16 Puttenham, *Arte*, p. 307. Attridge renders Puttenham's thesis more philosophical when pointing out that the 'ideal is to *be* natural, by being yourself as nature is' ('Puttenham's Perplexity', p. 274).

17 Heninger maintains that Puttenham joins 'making' to 'imitating' (*Touches of Sweet Harmony*, pp. 303–4).

18 In his essays on the 'fairy way of writing', Addison stresses the horror elicited by Spenser's monsters (see *Spectator*, III, 570, and Chapter 14, above).

significant for his poem and by projecting their origin in the imaginative faculty on to the topography of Faeryland. Through such implicit and explicit self-reflexivity, which he represents emblematically in his version of the Prometheus myth, Spenser demonstrates his command over his material, and simultaneously confronts the ubiquitous accusation that the poet is a mere madman whose mind is troubled by monstrous imaginings he cannot control. In order to consolidate his poetic autonomy, Spenser also introduces into his poem an important *distinctio* between two kinds of imagination: one is uninhibited and morally dubious, the other good because well-calculated and useful. Throughout the poem, he accordingly marks practitioners of black magic like Archimago and the witch as bad makers, while associating himself with Prometheus as a good, albeit controversial, maker.[19] Consequentially, Spenser seeks to transcend the major antipoetic tenets that condemn the poet, his poem and eventually his readers as fantastic monstrosities.[20] Spenser's choice of the epic romance as a proverbially monstrous text additionally testifies to the validity of the monstrous as a key *sujet* in *The Faerie Queene*: for the poet venturing into the realm of romance and epic, the monstrous, contextualised into the larger plan of the poem and encroaching upon its various layers of meaning, is a major criterion determining his literary prowess.

Sidney and the use of poetry

Spenser's maintaining a high level of self-awareness and poetic formalism connects well with his moral aim, and again saves the imagination that creates monsters from blame. The various modes of poetic making serve the goal Spenser expounds in the 'Letter to Raleigh', namely '*to fashion a gentleman or noble person in vertuous and gentle discipline*'.[21] Spenser's grand didactic design to compose a '*continued Allegory*', in which he, as the title page informs his readers, also 'Fashions XII. Morall vertues', hence rests partly on creating monsters as ciphers for the reprehensible.[22] This programmatic statement implies that Spenser uses the transformative imagination to convert his readers into morally sound people through the vivid depiction of monstrous beings and locales.

19 Cf. Hadfield, 'Prometheus', p. 197.

20 See the remarks by Tasso, Pellegrino, Ascham and Gosson surveyed in Chapter 13, above.

21 Spenser, 'Letter', 8.

22 On the poet's creating monsters as ciphers for the reprehensible, see also the discussion of Chapman's *Hymnus* in Chapter 17, above.

From here, one has to hark back towards Sidney's positive evaluation of the imagination in *The Defence of Poesy* to specify where Spenser positions himself as a poet and to explain why the monstrous can be useful. Individual aspects in Sidney's argumentation from his *Defence* invite comparison with Spenser and his own making of poetry. Spenser's poetics bears a particularly striking resemblance to Sidney's postulation that poetry is an art that relies on 'representing, counterfeiting, or figuring forth' images of vices and virtues, which illustrate universal truths in particular examples.[23] For Sidney the power of poetry hence does not lie in writing 'affirmatively' (i.e., literally), but in composing 'allegorically and figuratively'.[24] Such poetry rests on the dynamics of a symbolical, figurative language that fashions 'speaking pictures'[25] to visualise otherwise non-apprehensible truths.[26]

According to Sidney, the imagination is of paramount importance in the creation, communication and reception of these speaking pictures. As explained above, the images or representations are created with the help of the imagination,[27] which endows the poet with the ability to turn ideas into fore-conceits, and finally into proper conceits.[28] The speaking pictures then become active in the reader's mind because they access the imagination, where they can unfold their power:

23 Sidney, *Defence*, pp. 79–80 (see also p. 81: 'it is that feigning notable images of virtues, vices, or what else, with that delightful teaching, which must be the right describing note to know a poet by'). See Rossky, 'Imagination', p. 68.

24 Sidney, *Defence*, p. 103. Sidney's attitude to allegory has been subject to some controversy. While Heninger claims that Sidney disparages allegory and considers it childish (see *Sidney and Spenser*, pp. 247 and 273), critics like Rosamunde Tuve, Mindele Anne Treip, Kenneth Borris and Michael Mack have variously underscored Sidney's indebtedness to and use of allegory. See Kenneth Borris, *Allegory and Epic in English Renaissance Literature: Heroic Form in Sidney, Spenser, and Milton* (Cambridge: Cambridge University Press, 2000), pp. 109–35; Mindele Anne Treip, *Allegorical Poetics and the Epic: The Renaissance Tradition to 'Paradise Lost'* (Lexington: University of Kentucky Press, 1994), pp. 45–7; Michael Mack, *Sidney's Poetics: Imitating Creation* (Washington: Catholic University of America Press, 2005). Mack particularly focuses on Sidney's heavy use of typology (*Sidney's Poetics*, p. 41).

25 Sidney, *Defence*, p. 85. On Sidney's notion of the 'speaking image', see Heninger, 'Speaking Pictures: Sidney's Rapprochement between Poetry and Painting', pp. 3–16. Robinson explains that the poet fuses 'moral abstractions with actual characters' to produce images in the reader's mind (see *Shape of Things*, pp. 100, 103–4, and for the full discussion, pp. 99–108).

26 See also Bacon, *Advancement*, in *Works*, III, 410. On the classical notion of poetry as painting in, among others, Horace and Plutarch, see Heninger, 'Speaking Pictures', pp. 9–10, and *Sidney and Spenser*, pp. 105–8.

27 Cf. Herman, *Squitter-wits*, p. 67.

28 See Sidney, *Defence*, p. 79, and Wood, *Metaphor and Belief*, p. 95.

> [the poet] yieldeth to the powers of the mind an image of that whereof the philosopher bestoweth but a wordish description, which doth neither strike, pierce, nor possess the sight of the soul so much as that other doth. … so no doubt the philosopher with his learned definitions – be it of virtue, vices, matters of public policy or private government – replenisheth the memory with many infallible grounds of wisdom, which, notwithstanding, lie dark before the imaginative and judging power, if they be not illuminated or figured forth by the speaking picture of poesy.[29]

Sidney's argument hinges upon the contrast between the philosopher and the poet: while the philosopher uses words to formulate general precepts, the poet creates speaking pictures to represent these principles. When mentioning the 'imaginative and judging power', Sidney rehearses early modern faculty psychology to explicate the influence the speaking picture has on the reader: the poetic image first impacts forcefully on the reader's senses,[30] then enters the soul through the imagination and is finally assessed by reason.[31] Sidney's use of the word 'illuminated' is significant: as it contrasts the dark (and hence useless) exhortations of the philosopher with the poet's creative and moral supremacy, the imagination emerges as an agency participating in the reader's enlightenment, provided the poet depicts these speaking pictures with the liveliness of *enargeia*, so they can appear to the mind's eye.[32] Sidney's model of communication in poetic texts hence depends on the imagination, and appraises it as a faculty that helps poets and readers alike in comprehending abstract precepts, if they are given proper poetic form.[33]

29 Sidney, *Defence*, pp. 85–6.

30 Maslen explains that the triad of *strike*, *pierce* and *possess* characterises the impact of the speaking image as a 'physical assault' ('Introduction', p. 50). See also Heninger, *Sidney and Spenser*, p. 267.

31 Maslen explains that the term *judgement* in Sidney's *Defence* refers to 'the power of rational assessment' ('Introduction', p. 39). See also Bacon, *Advancement*, in *Works*, III, 382.

32 See Heninger, 'Speaking Pictures', p. 14: 'it is precisely this enargeic power of the poet which bestows superiority to poetry over philosophy'. The notion of the mind's eye stems from Cicero's *oculi mentis* and was later taken up by Quintilian (see Heninger, *Sidney and Spenser*, pp. 268–9). Sidney cites this notion when commenting on 'that unspeakable and everlasting beauty to be seen by the eyes of the mind' evoked in poetry (*Defence*, p. 77; cf. Heninger, *Sidney and Spenser*, pp. 288–9). On the notion of external and internal sight, see also Pico, *A Platonick Discourse Upon Love*, trans. by Thomas Stanley, ed. by E. G. Gardner (Boston: The Merrymount Press, 1914), p. 27: 'sight is twofold, corporeal, and spiritual; the first is that of Sense, the other of the Intellectual faculty, by which we agree with Angels' (quoted in Robinson, p. 55).

33 Bergvall gives a lucid elaboration of the communicative model informing Sidney's poetic theory and practice in *The 'Enabling of Judgement'*, pp. 17–41. He starts out with the semiotic model of communication, and adapts it first to Augustinian epistemology and then to Melanchthon's *Elementorum rhetorices* (1531), which, he claims, informs Sidney's thinking.

Sidney underlines the pivotal role of the imagination in the communication between the poet, the poem and the reader, when introducing Turnus's reflections on his possible death before his battle against Aeneas in an explicatory passage on the power of *movere*:[34] 'Whom doth not these words of Turnus move, the tale of Turnus having planted this image in the imagination[?]'.[35] According to the *Defence*, Virgil fashioned 'the tale of Turnus' as an image that can take effect in the readers' imagination to move their emotions and stir them into righteous behaviour.[36] Sidney illustrates the placement of the image in the mind as planting to accentuate the potential growth contained in the speaking picture. He establishes a further link to the imagination when he uses the planting metaphor to describe the poet's moral *telos*. The poet, he claims, 'take[s] naughtiness away and plant[s] goodness even in the secretest cabinet of our souls'.[37] As the reference to the 'cabinet' implies faculty psychology, Sidney draws, I would argue, an analogy between placing images in the imagination to move readers and placing goodness in the faculties of the soul where they can develop into virtuous actions.[38] By imagining such placing as 'planting', Sidney proposes that the imagination serves the essential function of promulgating images and thereby furthers the reader's ethical, moral and spiritual growth.[39]

Sidney's poetic tenets explain in some detail why the composition of speaking pictures may surpass reality and to what ends this poetic licence can be used. As the Fall reduced phenomenal reality to a diminished state, its 'proportions' are now inferior to the soul.[40] In order to appeal to the reader's heightened mental attention, the poet creates a poem that presents a better nature, a 'rich tapestry' in which he 'make[s] the too much loved earth more lovely', and creates with the help of the imagination a world with 'pleasant rivers, fruitful trees, sweet-smelling flowers'.[41] The notion that the poet fashions a golden world surpassing the squalid 'brazen' world of phenomenal reality[42] is closely linked to the require-

34 See Virgil, *Aeneid*, XII.645–6.

35 See Sidney, *Defence*, p. 92.

36 In the passage on heroical verse, Sidney ranks Turnus among the great heroes Achilles, Cyrus, Tydeus and Rinaldo (see *Defence*, p. 98).

37 Sidney, *Defence*, p. 85.

38 On the importance of *movere*, see Robinson, *Shape of Things*, p. 42.

39 On Sidney's use of gardening metaphors, see Maslen, 'Introduction', pp. 43–4.

40 Rossky argues that man was able to see the true nature of things only in his pre-lapsarian state (see 'Imagination', pp. 53–4, with reference to Bright, *Treatise*, p. 122). On poetry and its link to the Fall, see also Maslen, 'Introduction', pp. 37–44.

41 Sidney, *Defence*, p. 78.

42 In his *Advancement*, Bacon likewise claims that allegorical poetry contains 'a more

ment that the reader should experience the act of reading as a 'journey … through a fair vineyard', whose grapes induce him 'to pass further'.[43] The notion of the golden world enticing its readers establishes delight as the mandatory prerequisite of successful poetry. While underlining the close bond between delighting and teaching, Sidney differentiates between the effects both have on the reader: delight moves men to good action ('to take … goodness in hand'), and teaching imparts understanding of virtue ('to make them know that goodness whereunto they are moved').[44] The genre that excels all other kinds of poetry in these respects is 'heroical verse', because it 'teacheth and moveth to the most high and excellent truth; who maketh magnanimity and justice shine through all misty fearfulness and foggy desires'.[45] In order to elaborate how exactly 'heroical verse' can teach and move its readers into adopting noble conduct and proper rational judgement,[46] Sidney harks back to the notion of the speaking picture: while 'the image of each action stirreth and instructeth the mind', 'the lofty image of such worthies most inflameth the mind with desire to be worthy, and informs with counsel how to be worthy'.[47] Sidney's choice of the verbs *stir* and *inflame* underlines the impact a poem fashioned along these parameters exerts on the readers: it involves them in a prolonged engagement with the text, fills them with the desire for the golden, ideal world of the poet[48] and awakens their wish to imitate such perfection in their intellectual habit and moral conduct.[49] For

ample greatness, a more exact goodness, and a more absolute variety, than can be found in the nature of things' (*Works*, III, 343). This passage compares well with Spenser's tenet of the '*variety of matter*' that has to be presented in a heroic poem ('Letter to Raleigh', 10).

43 Sidney, *Defence*, p. 92. Similarly, Bacon explains that poetry acquires a magnitude and diversity that overcomes the ordinary events in 'real history', because it brings to the page a 'more heroical' history, garnished with rare and unexpected events (Bacon, *Advencement*, in *Works*, III, 343).

44 Sidney, *Defence*, p. 81. Sidney formulates the goals of poetry as teaching 'the knowledge of a man's self', and stirring him into 'virtuous action' (*Defence*, p. 83). Robinson elaborates on the significance of delight in Sidney's poetics (see *Shape of Things*, p. 45).

45 Sidney, *Defence*, p. 98, and cf. *Defence*, p. 90: 'Well may you see Ulysses in a storm, and in other hard plights; but they are but exercises of patience and magnanimity, to make them shine the more in the near-following prosperity'. Cf. also Bacon's notion that allegorical poetry serves a threefold goal, namely 'magnanimity, morality, and … delectation' (Bacon, *Advancement*, in *Works*, III, 343).

46 The idea of magnanimity originates from Aristotle, *Nicomachean Ethics*, IV.iii; for the text, see *Nicomachean Ethics*, trans. by H. Rackham, Aristotle: Works 19, Loeb Classical Library (Cambridge, MA: Harvard University Press; London: Heinemann, 1934).

47 See Sidney, *Defence*, p. 98, and cf. Robinson, *Shape of Things*, p. 103.

48 Cf. also Eugene P. McCreary, 'Bacon's Theory of Imagination Reconsidered', *Huntington Library Quarterly*, 36 (1973), 317–26 (pp. 323–4).

49 See Maslen, 'Introduction', p. 42.

Sidney, the poet is 'the agent of moral regeneration',[50] and heroic poetry the supreme kind of writing, because its ultimate aim is to elevate the human soul, which is confined in 'clayey lodgings', to the highest possible perfection.[51]

Spenser and the use of the monstrous imagination

Sidney's poetic theory links directly to Spenser's poem, because in the 'Letter to Raleigh' the poet of Faeryland characterises his enterprise in terms strikingly similar to Sidney's. Like Sidney's ideal poetry, *The Faerie Queene* is designed to instruct its readers not by doctrine and precepts, but to delight and teach them by allegorical images and devices which create '*a gentleman or noble person in vertuous and gentle discipline*'.[52] By combining the history of Prince Arthur with the speaking pictures of heroic verse into his '*continued Allegory, or darke conceit*',[53] Spenser establishes the preconditions necessary to discuss the abstract universal truths of theology and philosophy, morals and ethics in a textual milieu that gives them apprehensible, or tangible, form and poetic substance, and activates the reader's imagination. In order to do so, Spenser might need Eumnestes for the records of past events; but it is Phantastes who endows him with the ability to feign, or counterfeit a '*historicall fiction*'[54] set in a believable fictional cosmos, and to narrate it with the vividness of *enargeia* or *evidentia* to make it impact on the reader with 'forcibleness or *energeia*'.[55] In the entire poem, then, Spenser uses his imagination

50 Heninger, 'Speaking Pictures', p. 15.

51 See Sidney, *Defence*, p. 82, and cf. p. 78: 'our erected wit maketh us know what perfection is, and yet our infected will keepeth us from reaching unto it'.

52 Spenser explains at some length that the subject matter of *The Faerie Queene* is not '*deliuered plainly in way of precepts, or sermoned at large*', but is '*clowdily enwrapped in Allegoricall deuises*'. Such a method makes the poem's teachings '*delightfull and pleasing*', as well as '*more profitable and gratious*' ('Letter', 21–8). Distinguishing Spenser from Sidney, Hamilton notes that in Spenser, allegory lies behind the fiction (see *Structure*, p. 12), whereas in Sidney, the meaning of the image is found within it. Mack correctly claims that, despite this difference, Sidney's notion of fiction '"includes" the allegorical tradition' (*Sidney's Poetics*, p. 40), and underscores the similarity between Sidney's poetics and Spenser's allegory, especially in their use of typology (see *Sidney's Poetics*, p. 42, with reference to Spenser's Arthur as allegory and model, and Tuve, *Allegorical Imagery*, p. 122).

53 Spenser, 'Letter', 4. Spenser's '*darke conceit*' echoes Sidney's earlier explanation that some poetry is 'written darkly' to conceal transcendent truth from 'profane wits' (see *Defence*, p. 121, and Mack, *Sidney's Poetics*, p. 52).

54 Spenser, 'Letter', 9.

55 Sidney, *Defence*, p. 117. Robinson argues that Sidney's notion of *energeia* is closely tied to the idea: for Sidney, *energeia* signifies 'conceptual clarity … and arises in a poem only

to express special ideas, or 'conceits' along significantly 'formalist' verbal parameters recorded in contemporary poetics like Puttenham's *Arte*, lest he violates the early modern sense of form.[56] This explains Spenser's heavy use of figures of speech, tropes and other rhetorical devices,[57] because they are linguistic 'shapes' which can be created only by an intact and serviceable imagination.[58] If Spenser submits these speaking pictures to the mind desiring these novelties, he does so with the self-conscious use of rhetorical forms and traditions. He thus shows that the supreme poet can unbind, by dint of the imagination, the physical and textual material he has stored in his memory to create a meaningful set of creatures, and to turn them into rhetorically feasible products that give the textual heterocosm in which they appear cohesion and sense.

Spenser interacts with Sidney's and Puttenham's major poetic precepts partly by following them, and partly by transcending them. Sidney's treatment of monsters is a case in point. Spenser's heavy use of monstrosities in his poetic heterocosm echoes Sidney's tenet that monsters can play a significant role in the creation of a second nature. However, Sidney's distinction between *eikastike* and *phantastike* introduced earlier in this chapter seemingly jars with this programmatic passage, especially as Spenser's monsters do not per se figure forth the 'good things' Sidney's definition of *eikastike* suggests, but are portrayed as utterly 'unworthy objects'.[59] In the context of Sidney's famous distinction, the monsters and topographic depictions of the monstrous imagination in *The Faerie Queene* define Spenser as a poet who sees the possibility of the ugly and 'fantastic' for the Renaissance romance he writes, and incorporates both in his poem. But this does not compromise his eikastic programme. Although the

---

when the writer has his moral abstraction ... clearly in view before he begins to write' (*Shape of Things*, p. 135). Bacon calls *enargeia* a 'lively representation' (*Advancement*, in *Works*, III, 410).

56 This link has been established in Chapter 13. Etymologically, idea and form are connected, because the Latin *forma* translates the Greek *idea* (see Heninger, *Touches of Sweet Harmony*, p. 295, and Wels, 'Imaginatio oder Inventio', p. 67, with reference to Ronsard's *Abbrégé*).

57 Contrasting Spenser with Sidney, Heninger criticises Spenser's resorting to 'the generous palette of schemes and tropes', and claims that Spenser's use of speaking pictures is less advanced than Sidney's, because word and meaning are not merged into a unity but kept apart in the first and second meanings of allegory (*Sidney and Spenser*, p. 390). For a critique of such a view on allegory, see Mack, *Sidney's Poetics*, p. 42.

58 When Bacon maintains that religion gains 'access to the mind by similitudes, types, parables, visions, dreams', which are forged by rhetoric (Bacon, *Advancement*, in *Works*, III, 382), he offers a list that can be read as an enumeration of poetic tropes found in *The Faerie Queene*, and hence also in its presentation of monsters. Cf. Parks, 'Bacon's "Enchanted Glass"', p. 292.

59 Sidney, *Defence*, p. 104.

creatures he fashions are, in Bacon's terms, 'unlawful matches and divorces of things',[60] he contextualises them into an overriding moral design with a distinct didactic programme, whose ultimate aim is the representation of Arthur's magnanimity,[61] and the moral education of his readers. While Spenser's monsters are hence fantastic if understood as manifestations of the characters' monstrous imagination, they are certainly eikastic from the point of view of the poet fashioning them as vivid representations of his main ideas.[62] Even on a textual level, Spenser's fantastic creations foreground the poet's deliberate making and excelling invention: no matter how physically distorted he makes them, he always fashions them in such a way that they exhibit rhetorical forms, such as tropes and stylistic devices.[63] It is this formalism and the use of the monstrous in Spenser's overall plan that brings monsters to the level of a grander eikastic scheme furthering truth; this scheme – and here I once more need to hark back to Puttenham's classification of the imagination – makes his monsters and the secondary nature in which they are placed entirely 'eu-fantastic', with Spenser turning the flies buzzing in the imaginative faculty into the bees of his poetry.[64] Spenser, in effect, dissociates the discourse of the monster from the discussion of poetic flaws and errors by claiming the fantastic for the eu-fantastic, truthfully eikastic poet.

Hence, Spenser enhances the concept of the poet laid down by Sidney and Puttenham by claiming the monstrous as the poet's meaningful terrain, as he is able to conjure up fantastic images to show that the morally corrupt is also corrupt in shape.[65] Since he does so in conjunction with nature, the provider of his 'raw material', his use of monsters is endorsed by the poetical precepts he takes.[66] Spenser's use of the

60 The phrase is Bacon's (*Advancement*, in *Works*, III, 343).

61 See Spenser, 'Letter', 39, and Dedicatory Sonnet 5, 'To the right honourable the Earle of Cumberland', 12. Spenser, who uses both magnanimity and magnificence, might have seen 'magnificence as an expansion of Aristotelian magnanimity' and defined it as 'the doing of great deeds for the sake of glory' (Hugh MacLachlan and Philip B. Rollinson, 'Magnanimity, Magnificence', in *Spenser Encyclopedia*, ed. by Hamilton, p. 448). See also Sidney, *Defence*, p. 98 ('Heroical [poetry] maketh magnanimity and justice shine through all misty fearfulness and foggy desires').

62 Spenser hence follows Mazzoni's notion that allegory is 'icastic poetry because below the fanciful surface the allegorical discourse is straight exposition of dogma, a portrait, in other words, of true being' (Hathaway, *Marvels and Commonplaces*, p. 75).

63 On the relation between poetic forms and the eikastic, see Park, 'Bacon's "Enchanted Glass"', p. 297.

64 See the bee simile in *FQ*, II.ix.51, and discussion in Chapter 15, above.

65 In rhetorical terms, Spenser establishes the interdependency between *enargeia* and *energeia*.

66 Cf. also the proem to Book II, in which Spenser takes issue with the accusation that he has created a world that does not exist.

'fantastic' imagination is therefore tantamount to elevating the fantastic faculty to the central tool for understanding higher truths, because the monstrous serves the general purpose of advancing moral learning in order to fashion a gentleman or noble person.[67] Thus employed, the imagination does not create the kind of Siren song that Ascham criticises, but indeed furthers the 'purifying of wit' advocated by Sidney. What makes Spenser special, and even makes him the spearhead in the development of a distinctly fantastic *and* truthful heterocosm, is his deliberate, calculated use of monsters and the monstrous imagination.

If Spenser thus puts into practice Sidney's tenet of creating a second nature inhabited by monstrous beings, he does so by making a greater imaginative leap. This leap is also manifest in the dual perspective he brings to the monstrous in the double imaginative act of the poet, who imagines the various psychological conditions of the human being (e.g. melancholy) and the characters suffering from them. To use a phrase by Puttenham, Spenser's poem 'breeds' Chimeras and other monsters (just like the Wandering Wood '[b]reedes dreadfull doubts'; I.i.12.4), and hence evokes the notion of the hypertrophic imagination; yet it does so because Spenser willingly sets up the text as a topography of the imagination.[68] Spenser sees poetic possibilities of abject objects that Sidney is not aware of, if only because they do not fully fit his predecessor's overall poetical thinking. This hypothesis is borne out by Sidney's poetic practice, because monsters make only rare and fleeting appearances in his *Arcadias*.[69] If writers generally saw poetry as the path to absolute beauty,[70] then Spenser stresses that the path to virtue and beauty requires a detour through absolute ugliness and deformity. Sidney hints at the use of the ugly when discussing the didactic impetus of comedy, which describes the vicious to accentuate the good: 'who seeth not the filthiness of evil wanteth a great foil to perceive the beauty of virtue'.[71] Spenser carries

67 This tallies well with Rossky's assumption that '[t]he feigned image is a calculated and selected agent for achieving the end of virtue' ('Imagination', p. 72).

68 See MacCaffrey, *Spenser's Allegory*, p. 74.

69 See, e.g., the two revengeful giants in the *New Arcadia*, II.9 and 23, as well as the monster set on Pyrocles in II.23: he was 'to be deuoured by a monstrous beast, of most vgly shape, armed like a Rhinoceros, as strong as an Elephant, as fierce as a Lion, as nimble as a Leopard, and as cruell as a Tigre'. Cf. also the riddle of the two monsters in the 'Second Eclogues'. On the close relation between Sidney's *Defence* and the *Arcadias*, see Maslen's introduction to the *Apology*, pp. 37–44, Neil L. Rudenstine's *Sidney's Poetic Development* (Cambridge, MA: Harvard University Press, 1967), and Bergvall's *The 'Enabling of Judgement'* (the *Defence* 'is the theoretical underpinning of the corpus and spells out the strategies exemplified in the fiction'; p. 15).

70 See Fracastoro, *Naugerius*, p. 128 and p. 41.

71 Sidney, *Defence*, p. 95.

this idea further by conceiving *The Faerie Queene* as the site of fantastic creation, a heterocosm in which he can highlight the beautiful and virtuous through the constant juxtaposition with the utterly hideous.[72]

The poem as the result of fantasy therefore becomes the manifestation of the poet, who, in Sidney's words, 'bringeth his own stuff'[73] to create exciting 'speaking pictures' as the product of the wilful transformation of nature. These work on the readers' imagination and move them to lead a life according to the good and the virtuous. Spenser hence uses the monstrous as a 'speaking picture' brought before the readers' imagination and judging power to evoke a calculated response.[74] It is thus possible that the recipient perfects his soul through reading poetry, even if this poem is a romance that in the opening canto has been emblematised as a labyrinthine wood with a monster at its centre. The question is, then, how exactly the monsters and the malfunctioning imagination affect the readers' interpretation of Spenser's '*continued Allegory*'. It is to this problem that the next chapter turns.

72 See Uhlig, 'Sidneys *Defence*', pp. 83–4.
73 Sidney, *Defence*, p. 99. Cf. the view expressed by Leimberg in 'Dichtungstheorie', p. 101.
74 See Heninger, *Touches of Sweet Harmony*, p. 308.

19

Interpreting the monstrous

Interpreting monsters and monstrous beings in an allegorical framework is a complex exercise for Spenser's readers, partly because the text validates an interplay between the four senses of scripture.[1] In his monograph *Metaphor and Belief*, Wood argues that the complexity of allegory stems from implementing a 'double function of the literal'.[2] Explaining that allegory is a literary mode that 'presents a system of signs which map easily onto a literal system of signifieds', he extrapolates that these signifieds 'in turn constitute a secondary system of signs which map onto at least one (and frequently more than one) secondary system of signifieds'.[3] Allegory therefore works on two levels: as the signified in a first narrative and descriptive system, and as the signifier in a second figurative system. In Spenser's poem, it is the reader's task to get beyond the first level and to reach the second through tracing the similarities of possible interpretations with the narrative world. But this second level is not fixed. As the first level's similarities with various figurative meanings and their shifting connections open multiple possibilities, Spenser does not use allegory as a literary strategy to discipline reading and the meaning of his text for his readers. On the contrary, Spenser, despite his didactic programme, realises in his poem the very polysemy that constitutes language.[4]

1 Michael Murrin dissects the various levels of allegorical interpretation in the early modern period (see *Veil of Allegory*, pp. 98–134). Cf. also Harington's 'Preface' to his translation of the *Orlando Furioso*.

2 Wood, *Metaphor*, p. 37.

3 Wood, *Metaphor*, p. 37.

4 Wolfgang Iser advances a similar argument for *The Shepheardes Calender* in *Das Fiktive und das Imaginäre: Perspektiven literarischer Anthropologie*, Suhrkamp Taschenbuch Wissenschaft (Frankfurt am Main: Suhrkamp, 1993), esp. pp. 78–83. Wood likewise relates the difficulty of reading the poem to the openness of the second level of signification as opposed to the first level of literal signification (see *Metaphor and Belief*, p. 37). On the polyvalence of *The Faerie Queene*, cf. Freeman, 'Metamorphosis', p. 308. Cf. also Teskey's explanation that readers are 'to be morally changed not just by seeing examples

Hence, allegory comes with a certain amount of interpretative disorientation, which is generated by the necessity to ascend to one or more secondary levels of signification. This brings the discussion of Spenser's heterocosm and the monstrous imagination back to the idea of the labyrinth elaborated in Chapter 14, for every interpretation discovers a new 'turning' that opens up ever-new directions in the larger maze of the text: the many paths in the Wandering Wood, which forced Redcrosse and Una into a series of choices, hence also open up for the reader.[5] In this context, the monsters increase the reader's uncertainty and need for orientation, because they, as part of Spenser's allegory, build multiple new connections, and create a disorientation in the reader that is additionally stressed through the interplay between multiple inter-, intra- and extratextual references.

In the overarching literary framework of the poem, it is to some extent the polyvalence of the monsters or monstrous signifiers that guarantees an increase in interpretative complexity, because, as a derivative of the Latin *monstrare* ('to point to'),[6] the monsters always *point to* various possible meanings.[7] One such example is the Dragon in Eden, which lends itself to all four senses of scripture.[8] Read historically, the Dragon suggests Pope Gregory XIII;[9] in anagogical terms, the Dragon's corporeal similarities with the red dragon of the Apocalypse relate to the End of Days;[10] tropologically, the Dragon, as the embodiment of evil, elicits Redcrosse's *imitatio Christi*;[11] and typologically, the Dragon refers simultaneously to the serpent in Genesis, Leviathan in the Book of Job and the red dragon in the Book of Revelation. Similarly, Errour sets the reader the task to make sense of her 'serpentine' and 'sexed' body, of her 'religious' and 'biblical' implications, and of the Nile simile, which suggests

of admirable conduct but by becoming engaged, through the play of interpretation, in the theory of virtue. Spenser's allegorical writing, like Dante's, fashions an intellectual habit' ('Allegory', in *Spenser Encyclopedia*, ed. by Hamilton, pp. 17–18).

5 Cf. Nohrnberg, *Analogy*, pp. 148–9.

6 See Chapter 3.

7 The monster can actually be deemed the ultimate allegorical signifier, because allegory is a poetic mode that 'points to' something beyond the literal sense (cf. Puttenham, *Arte*, p. 186).

8 See Chapter 4 for the full discussion of the Dragon's allegorical meanings.

9 See Elizabeth See Watson, 'Spenser's Flying Dragon'. For the Dragon as a figuration of the Spanish Armada, see Rose, *Spenser's Art*, p. 135.

10 See Sandler, '*The Faerie Queene:* An Elizabethan Apocalypse'; Watkins, 'Apocalypse Deferred: Seventeenth-Century Appropriations of Spenser'; and Rose, *Spenser's Art*, p. 134.

11 See Hamilton, 'The *Vision of Piers Plowman* and *The Faerie Queene*', and Kaske's elaborations in 'The Dragon's Spark and Sting'.

that the monster relates to 'the origin of life, … generation and birth'.[12] Another adversary, Maleger in Book II, may signify, among other things, sin, death, evil, disease or the curse of mortality, a confluence of meanings rendered even more puzzling by the sevenfold paradox he poses (II. xi.40.4–9)[13] and by his polyvalent name.[14] The names of other creatures likewise defy attempts at reducing them to a single denotation. The name of the 'Blatant' Beast, for instance, can only be inconclusively approached from various languages.[15] Incoherent spelling further obfuscates clarity, for the monster is both referred to as '*Blatant*' (V.xii.37.7) and 'Blattant' (VI.i.7.1).[16] As no single etymological interpretation explains the exact meaning of the present participle, the name becomes in itself a composite term that creates different interacting interpretations.[17] The clash between the monster and its meaning hence results in interpretative displacement, as the monster always is 'something other than itself'.[18] If one extrapolates from this hypothesis, the monster functions as a phenomenon that forces the reader into ongoing interpretation, while simultaneously withholding finite meaning. As a signifier containing many concurring meanings, the monster epitomises the polyvalence, polysemy and indeterminacy of Spenser's allegorical heterocosm.

Spenser's rhetorical and stylistic presentation of monsters and their anatomy additionally complicates interpretation. This is partly due to his connecting contradictory or incongruent body parts with a host of descriptive tropes, a strategy that allows for no final, but many hypothetical

12 Anderson, 'Mutability and Mortality', pp. 252–3.

13 See Rollinson, 'Arthur, Maleger', pp. 107–8; Rollinson, 'Maleger', p. 450; and Broaddus, 'Renaissance Psychology and the Defense of Alma's Castle', p. 135, and especially endnote 1 (pp. 150–1) for instructive surveys of critical literature on Maleger. Maleger is discussed in Chapter 10, above.

14 Suggested etymologies are *malaugurio*, 'ill omen'; *malus*, 'evil', 'deformed'; or *male*, 'badly', connected to *aeger*, 'sick' (see Brooks-Davies, *Critical Commentary*, pp. 176–7, note to II.xi.20–3); his name has been translated as 'desperately diseased' (Hamilton, note to II.xi.23), and 'to rule badly or wrongly', from Latin *male* and *regere* (Rollinson, 'Maleger', p. 450).

15 Hamilton (note to V.xii.37.7) mentions the following etymologies: Latin *blaterare* ('to prattle', 'to babble') and *blateratus* ('barking'), English *to blatter* ('to speak or prate volubly'), and Greek βλάπτειν ('to hurt'). See also Gross, *Spenserian Poetics*, p. 230, n. 22, and, above all, Chapter 7, 'Four-footed beasts'.

16 See also Wood's note on the 'duplicitous' spelling of Errour's name in *Metaphor and Belief*, p. 32.

17 For a full discussion of the monster and its name, see Chapter 7, 'Four-Footed Beasts'.

18 The phrase is taken from Cohen, *Of Giants*, p. xiv. As Berger explains, Acrasia, the maker of the monsters in Book II, also has a name that shifts between various possible Greek etymologies which logically exclude one another, namely *krasis* ('a compounding'; 'climate'), *kratos* ('strength'; 'force'; 'mastery') and *akratos* ('unmixed, pure'; 'unrestrained'; 'violent'; see *Allegorical Temper*, p. 66).

forms, which may all be valid for a unified interpretation. The Dragon in I.xi, for instance, eludes any specific measurement, and shifts from one explanatory marker or image to the next, thereby creating a continuum of literal and figurative descriptions: this specimen, which has eyes glowing like beacons, becomes just about any thing or creature, from an eagle to a knight in armour, from ship to hell mouth to mountain.[19] None of these markers is self-inclusive; like all other monsters and monstrous beings, the Dragon embodies all statements made about it, thus resisting classification and transcending understanding. Incorporating the beastly, the quasi-human and even the mechanic, the Dragon is realised not as a coherent, unified whole but as a serialisation of differences, with the monster's shape, size and imagery changing under the impact of Spenser's rhetoric.

Similar descriptive inconsistencies abound in the poem. The Blatant Beast is a monster with especially indefinable attributes. The narrator is never clear about the exact number of the Beast's disparate tongues, for his description oscillates between one hundred and one thousand.[20] That the monster is additionally graced with two lineages makes it conceptually even more elusive,[21] and attests the deliberately puzzling nature of Spenser's detailed descriptions. Disdayne is another striking exemplar of such a bewildering strategy, because he is changed from iron to gold in the 1596 edition of *The Faerie Queene*, and receives a series of decentring attributes that set the reader the task to make them cohere with previous descriptions: among other things, Disdayne is realised as an automaton striding like a crane with eyes shining like beacons, and as a racialised giant wearing a turban like the 'Mores of Malaber' (VI.vii.43.6). This incongruence reaches its climax when, despite his golden materiality, he falls down like a lump of dirt when defeated by Arthur.[22] Such examples show that monsters and human beings in *The Faerie Queene* can in general change their bodies momentarily in similes and metaphors, which map differing images on the bodies of the creatures they describe.[23]

19 The Dragon of Eden is analysed in Chapter 6, above.

20 For one hundred, see V.xii.41.7; for one thousand, see VI.i.9.3, and VI.xii.27.1. The combination of human and animal tongues confers well to the Virgilian Fama in *Aeneid*, IV.173–97 (see Nohrnberg, *Analogy*, p. 688).

21 The Blatant Beast's parents may be Cerberus and Chimera (VI.i.7–8), or Echidna and Typhon (VI.vi.9). The giant Lust, on the other hand, has no lineage at all.

22 See VI.vii.42–3, and viii.25–6. For a full discussion of Disdayne, see Chapter 11, 'Automata'. Cf. also Talus, the iron man, who, despite his metal body, moves as lightly and swiftly as a swallow (see V.i.20.2–4).

23 Cf. also the giant Ollyphant, whose name disfeatures his humanoid body by the interplay between the giant, the elephant, and its tusk (IV.vii.48). See also Chapter 9, 'Giants'.

Spenser has the proclivity to change the body of individual monsters with every detail he adds and anatomises in his descriptions. The reader accordingly faces the difficult task of suturing each item of the monster's anatomy and its metaphorical representations into a unified whole. In her book on late classical and medieval image-making, Mary Carruthers maintains that grotesque images 'demonstrate too what the brain must do to start thinking: it must gather, put together, conjoin by likeness and by contrast, the bits from its memory inventory, stored there in images'.[24] Her main idea, which resembles late medieval and early modern conceptions of the tripartite brain chambers, can be applied to the task faced by the readers: they need to recombine stored data through exercising their imagination, in order to bring these monsters and monstrous beings, like the asymmetrical human–animal composite Duessa, the ongoing metamorphosis of Malbecco, or the creation of Snowy Florimell from inchoate ingredients, in front of their eyes, and, on a more advanced level, make intellectual sense of them.

The continuation of descriptive items creates an assembly of details, and ultimately marks these monstrous creatures as the true conceptual offspring of Errour, who constantly reconfigures her tail, and thus becomes emblematic of the dynamic textual process that portrays monsters and disorients readers. Consequently, the monstrous beings challenge the readers' imagination and the ability to, as it were, re-member them: as rhetorically ambivalent creations that 'engage [the reader's] interpretive faculties only to resist them',[25] monsters move and morph over the textual landscape, never assuming any definitive form.

The reader's problem of interpreting the monstrous is additionally enhanced through Spenser's often ambivalent versification. Genevieve Guenther maps the reading process set off by Amoret's appearance at the end of the Masque of Cupid, which Spenser stages in such a way that the reader needs to determine whether the 'dolefull Lady' (III.xii.19. 4) at the end of the pageant is really Amoret, or villainous, monsterised Cruelty. Faced with such uncertainty, readers have to make 'provisional sense'[26] of the stanza. Spenser's descriptions of the monstrous carry the readers' temporary reorientation to further extremes, not only because

24 Mary Carruthers, *The Craft of Thought: Meditation, Rhetoric, and the Making of Images, 400–1200* (Cambridge: Cambridge University Press, 1998), p. 164. Her tenet resembles Plett's explanation of the reciprocity between writing and reading (see '"... of imagination all compact"', p. 22).

25 Adam McKeown, 'Looking at Britomart Looking at Pictures', *Studies in English Literature 1500–1900* 45 (2005), 44–63 (p. 55).

26 Guenther, 'Spenser's Magic', p. 225.

their readings depend on a series of contradictory details. In the case of the Blatant Beast, the relation between the tongues and stings in its mouth is inconclusive due to the ambivalent use of syntax: when Spenser maintains that 'them amongst were mingled here and there, / The tongues of Serpents with three forked stings, / That spat out poyson and gore bloudy gere' (VI.xii.28.1–3), he leaves open whether there are three sets of stings in the entire maw, or whether they are on the tips of each split tongue, which would multiply these venomous organs and enhance the Beast's deformity.

Further instances of difficult versification can be witnessed in Spenser's descriptions of the monstrous hyena and the giant Orgoglio. Spenser depicts the hyena in III.vii.22 in such a way that the beast constantly bypasses any proper *gestal*: he merely explains that it looks horrifying (22.1–3), it is deformed and spotted (22.4–5), flies like the wind (22.6) and has no animal precedent but resembles the hyena most (22.7–9). Withholding any defining epithet until the final couplet, Spenser makes any interpretation provisional – only to frustrate his readership in the couplet when making the beast 'likest to', i.e. not exactly like, a hyena, a four-footed animal with likewise indeterminate distinctive features.[27] The giant Orgoglio, an empty yet terrifyingly massive windbag, is another striking paradox. When introducing him as a 'monstrous masse of earthly slyme, / Puft vp with emptie wynd, and fild with sinfull cryme' (I.vii.9.8–9), Spenser enhances the giant's monstrosity by bringing inchoate epithets and mutually exclusive descriptive markers like 'masse' and 'emptie' into the close proximity of the stanza's final couplet. He raises this method to an even more critical level when using rhyme to translate Orgoglio's grotesque paradoxical nature into grotesque doggerel verse: after the giant's death, his 'monstrous mas' an 'emptie blader was' (I.viii.24.8–9).

It is not only Spenser's manipulation of rhyme that makes monsters difficult to visualise and to interpret but also the overall arrangement of the verse and its contents. A good example of such 'stanzaic labyrinthism' is the depiction of Redcrosse's single combat with Sansjoy. In the epic simile that likens the *monomachia* between the knights to the monster combat between a griffin and a dragon, the reader experiences bewilderment about the exact relation between the human characters and their correlating animal counterparts.[28] The reader's perplexity is enhanced by pronoun confusion and the ambivalent subtext of these creatures, which allow for interpretations *in bono* and *in malo*. On a different level, the

27 For the argument, see the analysis in Chapter 7, 'Four-footed beasts'.
28 See I.v.8; the passage is discussed in detail in Chapter 10, 'Monstrous humans'.

need to make provisional sense may also become virulent in the case of monsters featuring excess body parts, like the giant Geryoneo, who sports a triple body,[29] 'armes and legs of three' (V.x.8.9), and 'three double hands thrise multiplied' (xi.6): versification in these lines renders the giant's physique, already difficult enough to visualise, even more puzzling.

Spenser's complex approach to the monstrous has far-reaching implications for the rhetorical parameters governing the poem and establishing its heterocosm. Spenser realises the presentation of monsters and monstrous beings as a process in which stylistic, metaphorical and anatomical discourses interact to create textually unstable beings. The act of description, although implying stasis, consists in a dynamic transformation largely informed by the poet's awareness that the monstrous elides any specific form. The reader, overwhelmed by a flood of descriptive markers, undergoes a continual process of interpretation, because Spenser's elaborate and richly detailed rhetorical presentation of the monstrous in an allegorical framework suggests that continued analysis will finally yield a truthful, valid interpretation. The monster's changing bodies, the tangled skein of monstrous signifiers, their correlation and differing interpretations evoke the monster Errour, more precisely the disorienting tangles of Errour's tail-labyrinth, and with them the lexical and syntactical ambiguity of the labyrinthine text.[30] Like Errour rearranging her knots and bouts, the monstrous is constantly un-folding and en-folding, i.e. yielding and withholding form and meaning.[31] The many different forms monsters receive in the act of description are just such a succession of yielding and withholding meaning, on which the monster creates its matrix of multiple significance.

Fashioning secondary levels of interpretation in the polysemy and multi-referentiality of Spenser's allegorical heterocosm is a complex task, as it requires his readers to substantiate their interpretations by finding items in the poem which correlate and interact with them.[32] The act of reading and interpreting might hence be less conclusive than

29 Cf. V.x.8, and xi.6.

30 Cf. Doob, *Idea of the Labyrinth*, p. 246.

31 As already stated, 'unfolding' is also used as a conceptual term for allegory yielding meaning (see Heninger, 'Aesthetic Experience', pp. 82–9; see also MacCaffrey, *Spenser's Allegory*, pp. 61–4).

32 The method of intra-textual connection qualifies *The Faerie Queene* as a quasi-biblical text in that Augustine warranted scriptural cross-referencing as a means of making sense of opaque images (see Augustine, *De doctrina christiana*, III.27.38 in *De doctrina christiana*, ed. by Joseph Martin; *De vera religione*, ed. by K.-D. Daur, Opera, Pars IV, 1, Corpus Christianorum, Seria Latina, 32 (Turnhout: Brepols, 1962); the passage is discussed in Wood, *Metaphor and Belief*, p. 128).

expected; however, in Renaissance humanism, such difficult analytical reading was the enactment of man's rational faculties,[33] and as such the chief characteristic that distinguished him from the animals.[34] In this cultural framework, the complex, labyrinthine text of *The Faerie Queene* becomes the touchstone for the reader's moral and intellectual advancement. If the poem and especially its monsters eschew clear-cut solutions, then the entire poem is not about simple equations, but, in the words of Isabel MacCaffrey, 'about processes of coming to know'.[35] This heuristic setup makes the monsters a significant part of the heterocosmic poem as a 'thinking machine' which produces a furtherance of learning by 'fashion[ing] an intellectual habit'.[36]

The problems inherent in interpreting the monsters and monstrous beings in *The Faerie Queene* bring the discussion of the imagination and Spenser's heterocosm full circle with the seventeenth-century criticism of *The Faerie Queene* discussed in Chapter 14: writers like Davenant and Cowley simply missed the point when charging Spenser with driving man rather than the monster away from Faeryland. From Spenser's point of view, it is not the poet's task to create a harmless realm when writing epic or romance. Rather, Spenser deliberately construes his secondary world by animating monsters, and by setting his readers the task to drive away these monstrous beings from themselves. The constant interpretation of the monstrous body eventually constructs the readers' maturity, on which their gentlemanly or noble nature is founded. This method conjures up the association of the medieval *demande d'amour*,[37] which involves lovers in literally endless debates about problems of *amour courtois* in order to further their understanding of love. By analogy, *The Faerie Queene* is to some extent a *demande de monstres*, which triggers a myriad of readings in the interaction between text and reader, which further the reader's

33 See also Spenser's comments on the difficulty of reading his '*continued Allegory*' in the 'Letter', 3–7 and 23. Gay Clifford, when discussing the role of the reader in allegory, remarks that writers like Spenser and Bunyan counted on the reader's desire to decipher the riddles of the text (see *The Transformations of Allegory* (London: Routledge, 1974), p. 42).

34 Fudge elaborates on 'the notion of humanist learning as a labour', an idea that tallies well with my assumption that reading makes the man (*Perceiving Animals*, p. 71).

35 MacCaffrey, *Spenser's Allegory*, p. 8.

36 Teskey, 'Allegory', pp. 17–18. In the light of this interpretation, it is a revealing circumstance that the articles in the 2007 issue of *Spenser Studies* tend to showcase *The Faerie Queene* as a 'thinking machine'. See especially Teskey's article, 'Thinking Moments in *The Faerie Queene*'.

37 For an example and introduction, see *The Demaundes off Love*, ed. by W. L. Braeckmann, SCRIPTA: Medieval and Renaissance Texts and Studies, 7 (Brussels: Research Center of Medieval and Renaissance Studies, 1982).

insight without unlocking all of its mysteries. When Spenser likens the language of Geryoneo's dragon to the riddle uttered by the Sphinx and takes particular care to underline that 'no wight / Could euer loose' it (V.ix.25.5–6), then such a statement becomes equally applicable to the interpretation of Spenserian monsters.

Epilogue: the Blatant Beast escapes

This is the very core of *The Faerie Queene*: as a heterocosmic, textual world, the poem, like a labyrinth, involves its addressees in a prolonged reading process. Although the monstrous hence remains essentially puzzling, it is precisely this process of attempted sense-making that constantly advances the reader's understanding, and will finally '*fashion a gentleman or noble person in vertuous and gentle discipline*'. However, when, at the end of Book VI, the Blatant Beast eventually escapes from Faeryland to harrow Spenser's contemporary world, to assault the poet and to attack his poem, Spenser presses home that such an involvement in the literary otherworld of *The Faerie Queene* ultimately calls for a commitment to trace and face the monstrous forces at work in his historical reality. Such an obligation is rendered all the more emphatic, as Spenser develops the Blatant Beast from an allegorical representation in his literary text to a physical presence in the real world. With no one in the present age to tame the monster, it has become entirely unfettered,[38] so much in fact that it has increased in size and strength, a growth that seems to be facilitated by an age itself out of joint.

Spenser stresses the monster's physical impact on his day and age by maintaining its monstrosity: through coupling the Beast's male personal pronoun with a cluster of its defining actions,[39] he harks back to previous descriptions of the monster and at first perpetuates its existence as creature well into his historical reality. When fearing that even his poem faces the Beast's 'venomous despite' (VI.xii.41.2), Spenser refers to the creature's defining corrosive poison, thus referring back to its 'spitting forth the poyson of his spight' (29.4), in order to actualise the monster's corporeality in the real world. A few lines later, he relates to his readers that 'some wicked tongues did … backbite' (41.5) his poetry, although it lacked the grounds of provoking such accusations. While citing the negative reactions of certain individuals ('some wicked tongues') that have brought

38 See VI.xii.40.3.

39 Cf. 'raungeth', 'rageth', 'Barking and biting', 'Ne spareth', 'rends' (VI.xii.40).

him into the discredit of a mighty peer,[40] Spenser deliberately makes this line consonant with the description of the Blatant Beast in Book VI: the tongues evoke the Beast's monstrous mouth in VI.xii.27–8;[41] the epithet 'wicked' echoes the characterisation of the creature and its poison;[42] and the reference to backbiting (41.5) implies the Beast's favourite mode of attack and injury, as the monster 'bet abacke, threatning in vaine to bite, / And spitting forth the poyson of his spight' under Calidore's attack (29.3–4).[43] Even in the Elizabethan age, the Blatant Beast keeps its characteristic monstrous features, albeit in a toned-down version (41).[44] Spenser's choosing not to reduce the Blatant Beast unambiguously into metaphor has an important consequence: as the monster still appears in rather unadulterated form, the poet brings the heterocosm into such close proximity with Elizabethan England that the monster, as Erickson points out, 'breaches the boundary between fiction and reality'.[45]

The physicalisation of allegory Spenser effects at the end of Book VI has a striking effect: the manoeuvre in which the Blatant Beast is partly reconfigured into the source material that inspired its creation, namely backbiting and slander, explicitly reveals the monsters and monstrous beings in Spenser's secondary nature as representations of first-world matter. Spenser's narrative twist makes explicit that the labyrinthine heterocosm of the poem, which was figured in the Wandering Wood and Errour, is at all times a transformed image of the real world, and as such marks Spenser's historical reality, like the Wandering Wood, as a place of disorientation with monstrous forces at its centre.[46] When the veil is thus lifted off the allegory in the attack of the Blatant Beast, Spenser's readers no longer simply participate in an intellectual *demande de monstres*, but are required to transfer the training of careful reading into

40 The *communis opinio* identifies the 'mighty Pere' as Lord Burghley (see Hamilton, note to VI.xii.41).

41 See also VI.xii.38.4.

42 For *wicked* as a marker of the Blatant Beast, see 'wicked fate' (VI.xii.38.7), 'wicked poyson' (VI.i.9.9), 'wicked monster' (VI.vi.12.3) and 'wicked feend' (VI.ix.6.2). Enuie, one of the two personifications with which the Beast enters the narrative at the end of Book V, is named a 'wicked hag' (V.xii.35.7).

43 See also VI.vi.9 (the Blatant Beast's teeth), as well as Spenser's description of Enuy in the Procession of the Seven Deadly Sins (I.iv.32).

44 This alteration is, arguably, tantamount to the development of the figurative to the literal.

45 Erickson, *Mapping*, p. 128. McCabe poignantly remarks that the monster cracks 'the "mirrour" of art' (*Pillars of Eternity*, p. 79). Most emphatic of all, Maria A. Rohr Philmus alleges that '[b]ursting through the boundaries of the fictional world of the poem, the Beast now roars into the present to make havoc in the poet's historical world' (Maria A. Rohr Philmus, '*The Faerie Queene* and Renaissance Poetics: Another Look at Book VI as "Conclusion" to the Poem', *English Studies* 6 (1995), 497–519 (p. 511)).

46 See Chapter 2, 'Monsters in the early modern period'.

a cultural practice in order to detect and defuse these monstrous forces. The flight of the Beast thus initiates them into their own quest:[47] they are made painfully aware that it is their turn to vanquish the monsters and monstrous beings running rampant in their world, and to continue Spenser's project on their own.[48]

47 If argued from Spenser's 'Letter', the reader therefore has finished his education as a '*gentleman or noble person in vertuous and gentle discipline*' ('Letter', 8). Nohrnberg similarly points out that the end of Book VI 'seems designed to warn us' (*Analogy*, p. 733).

48 The question whether the end of Book VI also marks the end of Spenser's poetic venture has been variously addressed by Spenserians. Susanne Woods explains that '[b]y the end of Book VI, Spenser has done his job, and he has had enough' ('Closure in *The Faerie Queene*', *Journal of English and Germanic Philology* 76 (1977), 195–216 (p. 215); see also Nohrnberg, *Analogy*, p. 657, and Bayley, *Prince of Poets*, p. 152). Similarly, David R. Shore notes that Spenser began to realise the clash between his vision and the quest, which caused 'the end of epic' (*Spenser and the Poetics of Pastoral: A Study of the World of Colin Clout* (Montreal: McGill-Queen's University Press, 1985), p. 159). David Lee Miller diagnoses 'Spenser's dispirited surrender to the Blatant Beast' in the last canto of Book VI ('Spenser's Vocation, Spenser's Career', *English Literary History* 50 (1983), 197–231 (p. 224)). Wayne Erickson contends that Spenser 'writes an ending for Book 6 that serves as a satisfyingly consistent conclusion to the whole poem' (*Mapping*, p. 120). Quite differently, C. S. Lewis states that Spenser was to continue his long poem after Book VI (see *The Allegory of Love: A Study in Medieval Tradition* (Oxford: Oxford University Press, 1936), p. 353).

José Angel García Landa positions himself between these poles, maintaining that the poem 'seems to be unwittingly heading towards incompleteness' ('"Another Game in Vew": The Representation of the Poet in *The Faerie Queene*', *Revista Alicantina de Estudios Ingleses* 2 (1989), 65–81 (p. 77)). Balachandra Rajan, distinguishing between *incomplete* works that are 'possible and proper to complete' and *unfinished* ones that 'have evolved in such a way as to make it improper to finish them', argues that *The Faerie Queene* has started as an incomplete poem in the 1590 edition, and developed into an unfinished poem in the 1596 edition (Rajan, *Form of the Unfinished*, pp. 44–84, esp. p. 44 and p. 77).

Whether the poem offers structural closure or develops towards openness has been discussed controversially by critics. Woods claims that Book VI of *The Faerie Queene* has 'a structure which *may be seen as* closed' (emphasis added; Woods, 'Closure', p. 198). Other critics opting for closure are Jerome S. Dees, 'The Narrator of *The Faerie Queene*: Patterns of Response', *Texas Studies in Literature and Language* 12 (1971), 537–68 (p. 567); Paul A. Marquis, 'Problems of Closure in *The Faerie Queene*', *English Studies in Canada* 16 (1990), 149–63 (Marquis argues that Book VI closes its own narration and the moral education of the reader); Richard Neuse, 'Book VI as Conclusion to *The Faerie Queene*', *English Literary History* 35 (1968), 329–53 (pp. 330–1); and Williams, *World of Glass*, p. 223. Stanley Stewart, on the other hand, maintains that 'of all the "finished" books in *The Faerie Queene* none seems less inclined towards "closure" than Book VI' ('Sir Calidore and "Closure"', *Studies in English Literature* 24 (1984), 69–86 (p. 85)).

Recently, the 'Two Cantos of Mutabilitie' have been cited as evidence of Spenser's continuation of the poem. Julian B. Lethbridge contends that Spenser compiles assorted material from *The Faerie Queene* into the Cantos towards the end of his life (see 'Spenser's Last Days'). Robert Lanier Reid argues that the 'Cantos of Mutabilitie' were conceived as a transition to the second half of *The Faerie Queene*, which is part of the journey to the heavenly city (see 'Spenser's Mutability Song').

PART IV

Conclusions

In a perceptive article on Mandeville, Sarah Salih observes that, in the cultural framework informing the *Travels*, 'all things speak of their Creator, but strange ones do so more emphatically'.[1] The monsters and monstrous beings in *The Faerie Queene* likewise speak emphatically of their maker: Spenser develops the monstrous not only into a characteristic feature of his epic romance but also into a force that influences every aspect of the poem, from the creation of individual monsters, and the poet's reflection on his office as 'maker', to the fashioning of a heterocosmic universe of discourse that will in turn '*fashion a gentleman or noble person in vertuous and gentle discipline*'.

As the taxonomic essays in Part II have illustrated, monsters and monstrous beings in *The Faerie Queene* emerge on every level of animate nature, and may also bring to life inanimate matter. The interpretations of the dragons, four-footed beasts, human–animal composites, giants, monstrous humans and automata have revealed the inventiveness with which Spenser realises the inexhaustible combinatory possibilities of the monstrous. It is these monsters and monstrous forces that the human characters in *The Faerie Queene* must constantly overcome either by battling them (as with the dragons and giants) or by steering clear of their corrupting influences (as with the 'carles' and hags). Against this background, it is especially striking that monstrous humans make up the largest and most diverse taxonomical category in the poem. The monstrous here figures as a destabilising force that can disfeature human beings and even completely annihilate their humanity, either through permanent metamorphosis or through ephemeral transformation. At a time when man's inner monstrosity was made the subject of broadsides and pamphlets, Spenser's creatures are powerful corporeal examples

1 Salih, 'Idols and Simulacra', p. 114.

demonstrating the workings of human viciousness, and warning against its debilitating consequences.

In order to animate his novel monstrosities in the text of *The Faerie Queene*, Spenser draws on a vast number of monster texts and traditions, and sets up a discourse of the deformed that yokes together two mutually exclusive principles into one paradoxical unity: on the one hand, Spenser's extended and detailed descriptions mark monsters as chaotic and disgusting creatures showcasing a plethora of monstrous terms and signifiers, as well as the confused mingling of the four elements; on the other, his protracted use of rhetorical forms and stylistic features marks them as the product of his well-wrought allegory. The feasibility of such a *discordia concors* relies just as much on Spenser's skill in making monstrous bodies as on his accomplished use of formalist literary strategies. Spenser's resorting to disparate imagery and body parts, to inconsistent details and anatomical boundary-crossing additionally establishes his monsters as puzzling creatures which tease the reader into interpretation but which cannot be fully comprehended as unified beings. Hence, Spenser's monsters do not only exist for the sake of simple allegory, since they frequently evade clear-cut interpretations and cannot be approached exclusively as signifiers ready for quick decoding.

Spenser's use of the monstrous as a major, indeed defining property of his long poem engages with a poetic discourse that criticised monsters as illicit products of a hypertrophic fantasy. By surveying the contemporary context exemplified mainly by the writings of Sidney, Puttenham, Bright, Burton and Bacon, Part III has presented the discourse on the imagination and the poet's status as maker as the background of Spenser's theoretical assessment of the poet's office. Spenser counters the antipoetic attacks in the late sixteenth century by fashioning himself as a secondary maker who can purposely create a secondary world harbouring monsters and monstrosities.

The Renaissance notion of the poem as secondary world propagated by Sidney and Scaliger is an early figuration of the heterocosm. Spenser's *The Faerie Queene* figures as a master text interacting with this fledgling poetic discourse: following Sidney's *Defence*, early critical statements identify monsters as the defining ingredient of this *natura altera*. Spenser pre-empts potential contemporaneous criticism in the proem to Book II by stating that his poem is conceived as an allegory that reveals its truth through careful reading. The major site of Spenser's engagement with the notion of the heterocosm is the opening narrative of the poem, in which Redcrosse and Una enter the Wandering Wood and find

Errour in her den. On one level, monster and wood are speaking pictures defining the poetic text as a labyrinth that generates disorientation and alienation. In such a textual world, the readers, like the characters, have to orientate themselves through constant interpretation, and may always be confronted by monsters and monstrous beings. On another level, forest and monster can also be interpreted as representations of ὕλη, or *silva*, the major metaphor of primordial matter from which all things and beings were turned into form. The episode hence allegorises the Wandering Wood and Errour as the material from which the poem and its monstrosities are made.

Spenser's heightened awareness of the discourse of the monstrous imagination and its link to poetic making becomes manifest in the Castle of Alma episode, where he anatomises the internal faculties as a tripartite brain-turret. As Phantastes's chamber, which represents the imagination, displays frescos that depict characters, animals and monsters typical of romance, Spenser directly relates the fictional images residing in the imagination to the defining ingredients of the genre in which he consciously writes. Spenser compares the flies buzzing around Phantastes's head to honey-laden bees in order to illustrate the transformative power of the imagination, which may turn confusing ideas and imaginings into the useful images of poetry.

In all six books of *The Faerie Queene*, Spenser engages with the problem of the monstrous imagination on two levels: on one level, he develops strategies to animate the workings of the monstrous imagination in his poem; on another, he realises monsters as the outcome of the poet's conscious making. Spenser's presentation of the monstrous imagination elaborates on a number of characteristic malfunctions that are well-documented in the medical treatises by Bright and Burton: the hypertrophy caused by melancholy and sleep; the transformation of self under the impact of an unrestrained imagination; and the spontaneous birth of monstrous images. Spenser's animating the monstrous imagination, which bears witness to his participation in the poetico-medical discourse of his age, is a self-reflexive strategy indicative of a double imaginative act. When Spenser, for instance, describes how monsters and monstrous beings emerge from dark locales like caves or temples to attack the poem's characters, he projects the 'dark' imagination of his *personae* on to the topography of his poem. Spenser's dual strategy thus shows the source of the monstrous in the characters' hypertrophic imagination, and additionally bears witness to the poet's deliberate depiction of such monstrous, or pathological situations.

When creating the actual monsters and monstrous beings, Spenser dons the robe of the Promethean maker, who brings to life new textual creations by exercising his autonomy. The link between Spenser and Prometheus is suggested by Spenser's version of the creation of the Elves, which is recounted in one of the scrolls stored in Eumnestes's memory chamber. As the elfin chronicler relates how Prometheus, whose name translates into 'fore-thinking', created the first Elf from the parts of animals, Spenser develops an analogy between the Greek god and himself, the maker of *The Faerie Queene*, Faeryland, its characters and its monsters. Like the god's making of Elfe, Spenser's transgressive creation displays deliberation, because he manufactures monstrous beings from various physical and textual parts, using his poetical expertise to give them rhetorical form and to make them cohere with his entire poem.

In *The Faerie Queene*, Spenser therefore reacts to contemporary trends and ideas about poetry, and transcends them by making the monstrous a significant part of his poem and its meaning. If contextualised in the discourse of poetic fantasy in the early modern period, *The Faerie Queene*, as the manifest outcome of Spenser's deliberate use of the imagination, can be read as its author's engagement with the tenets Sidney voiced in *The Defence of Poesy*. Like Sidney's poet, Spenser brings to life a secondary creation by reifying his abstract ideas, and by placing them in a secondary world. However, Spenser's use of the monstrous as an integral part of his poem goes one decisive step further, because he expands the monstrous into a central poetic concept. As the monsters and monstrous beings in the poem 'image forth' aberrations, corruption and vices within the framework of a '*continued Allegory*', they become the textual manifestation of the *deus alter*'s calculated making. Spenser, as an early modern Prometheus, seeks to reassess the task of the poet as an act in which the creator becomes a rightful secondary god if foresight and forethought guide his steps.

Spenser's strategies of transforming nature into a *natura altera* resemble the four modes of making distinguished by Puttenham. Thus construed, *The Faerie Queene* becomes a useful poem in Sidney's sense: turning monsters into feasible rhetorical creations representing universal truths, the poet uses his imagination to advance his readers' understanding by likewise appealing to their imagination. Such advancement becomes a demanding interpretative process, especially with regard to the monstrous beings, because they force the readers into advanced exercises of interpretation, which the monsters as polysemous entities never fully satisfy. By setting his readers the task of interpreting the monsters in his poem in an elaborate *demande de monstres*, the poet activates the readers' formation of identity, and educates them as gentlemen or noble persons. When the Blatant Beast assaults contemporary England at the end of Book VI, Spenser makes his readers aware that the monstrosities in his poem are representations of the monstrous forces in the real world, which they have to detect and defuse on their own.

If the monsters and monstrous beings in *The Faerie Queene* thus speak emphatically of their maker, they especially emphasise the poet's ability to fashion a plenitude of different monstrous permutations by the protracted manipulative use of a transforming imagination. That *The Faerie Queene* does not turn into a grotesque textual monster is due to Spenser's poetical power to give shape to the body of his text and simultaneously create monstrous deformities, thus fashioning an amalgam of form and formlessness (or, in abstract terms, of order and chaos, like the Wandering Wood and Errour). On another note, such a rich amount of monstrosities is also evidence of an inventiveness that can bring these monstrosities on to the page and into the minds of his readers. The use of monsters and the monstrous in his *The Faerie Queene* hence consistently points to the poet as the secondary maker who controls even the creation of monsters and monstrous beings. His fashioning a fictional heterocosm as an allegorical universe of discourse makes Spenser a poet in the etymological sense of the word: a maker whose imagination grants him access to the four elements, the high heavens and the pit of hell, as well as all physical and textual data stored in his memory.

By assigning monsters a central role in the poem, Spenser emphasises the autonomy of an author whose creatures, such as the Blatant Beast, have become almost as autonomous as the poet himself. With these precepts, Spenser paves the way towards new realms and otherworlds in which the poet's wit roams freely. Joseph Warton, one of Spenser's eighteenth-century critics, praises the 'richness of [Spenser's] fancy', which vividly depicts 'life and motion'. That he makes these remarks when discussing Malbecco's transformation into a disfigured abstraction is clear evidence for the conceptual significance of the monstrous. Warton's ensuing comment on Malbecco's metamorphosis is a eulogy on the poet's power of imagination, and brings into relief the effect the monstrous can have on the reader's experience of the poem: 'here we behold the true Poet or MAKER; this is creation'.[2]

2 Joseph Warton, *An Essay on the Genius and Writings of Pope*, 2 vols (London: J. Dodsley, 1782), II, 36.

Bibliography

Primary sources

Aesopica. A Series of Texts Relating to Aesop or Ascribed to Him or closely Connected with the Literary Tradition that Bears His Name, coll. and crit. ed., in part translated from Oriental languages, with a commentary and historical essay, ed. by Ben Edwin Perry, vol. 1 (Urbana: University of Illinois Press, 1952)

Alanus ab Insulis, *Opera omnia*, ed. by C. de Wisch, Patrologia Latinae 210, Saeculum XIII (Turnholt: Brepols, 1967)

Alciato, Andrea, *Emblematum liber* (Padua: Tozzi, 1621), accessed *via* www.mun.ca/alciato/

Das altfranzösische Rolandslied, ed. by A. Hilka, rev. and emend. by Gerhard Rohlfs, Sammlung romanistischer Übungstexte, 2 vols (Tübingen: Max Niemeyer, 1960)

An Anthology of Elizabethan Prose Fiction, ed. by Paul Salzman, The World's Classics (Oxford: Oxford University Press, 1987)

Apollodorus of Athens, *The Library*, ed. and trans. by J. G. Frazer, 2 vols, Loeb Classical Library (Cambridge, MA: Harvard University Press; London: Heinemann, 1921; repr. 1963)

Apollonius of Rhodes, *Argonautica*, ed. and trans. by William H. Race, Loeb Classical Library (Cambridge, MA: Harvard University Press, 2008)

Apuleius, *The Golden Ass: Being the Metamorphoses of Lucius Apuleius*, ed. and trans. by William Adlington, Loeb Classical Library (Cambridge, MA: Harvard University Press; London, Heinemann, 1915; repr. 1958)

Aquinas, Thomas, *Summa contra gentiles*, German and Latin, ed. and trans. by Karl Allgeier, 2nd edn, 4 vols (Darmstadt: Wissenschaftliche Buchgesellschaft, 2005)

——, *Summa theologiae*, ed. by P. Caramello, 4 vols (Turin and Rome: Marietti, 1952)

Ariosto, Lodovico, *Ludovico Ariosto's Orlando Furioso Translated into English Heroical Verse by Sir John Harington (1591)*, ed. by Robert McNulty (Oxford: Oxford University Press, 1972)

——, *Orlando Furioso*, ed. by Lanfranco Caretti, La Letteratura Italiana: Storia e testi, 19 (Milan: Ricciardi, 1963)

Aristotle, *Generation of Animals*, ed. and trans. by Arthur Lee Peck, Aristotle: Works 13, Loeb Classical Library (Cambridge, MA: Harvard University Press; London: Heinemann, 1943; repr. 1960)

——, *On the Heavens*, ed. and trans. by W. K. C. Guthrie, Loeb Classical Library (London: William Heinemann, 1939; repr. 1962)

——, *Metaphysics; Oeconomica; Magna moralia*, ed. and trans. by Hugh Tredennick, and G. Cyril Armstrong, 2 vols, Aristotle: Works 17–18, Loeb Classical Library (Cambridge, MA: Harvard University Press; London: Heinemann, 1933; repr. 1963)

——, *Nicomachean Ethics*, ed. and trans. by H. Rackham, Aristotle: Works 19, Loeb Classical Library (Cambridge, MA: Harvard University Press; London: Heinemann, 1934)

——, *Physics*, ed. and trans. by P. H. Wicksteed, and F. M. Cornford, 2 vols, Aristotle: Works 4–5, Loeb Classical Library (Cambridge, MA: Harvard University Press; London: Heinemann, 1929; repr. 1960)

——, *The Poetics*, trans. by W. Hamilton Fyfe; 'Longinus', *On the Sublime*, ed. and trans. by W. Hamilton Fyfe; Demetrius, *On Style*, trans. by W. Rhys Roberts, Aristotle: Works 23, Loeb Classical Library, rev. edn (Cambridge, MA: Harvard University Press; London: Heinemann, 1932)

——, *On the Soul; Parva naturalia; On Breath*, trans. by W. S. Hett, Loeb Classical Library (Cambridge, MA: Harvard University Press; London: Heinemann, 1957)

Ascham, Roger, *The English Works of Roger Ascham: Toxophilus, Report of the Affairs and State of Germany, The Schoolmaster*, ed. by William Aldis Wright (Cambridge: Cambridge University Press, 1904)

Augustine, *The City of God against the Pagans*, ed. and trans. by R. W. Dyson, Cambridge Texts in the History of Political Thought (Cambridge: Cambridge University Press, 1998)

——, *De civitate Dei*, ed. by B. Dombart and A. Kalb, Opera, Pars XIV, Corpus Christianorum, Seria Latina, 47–8 (Turnhout: Brepols, 1955)

——, *De doctrina christiana*, ed. by Joseph Martin; *De vera religione*, ed. by K.-D. Daur, Opera, Pars IV, 1, Corpus Christianorum, Seria Latina, 32 (Turnhout: Brepols, 1962)

Bacon, Francis, *The Works of Francis Bacon*, ed. by James Spedding, Robert Leslie Ellis and Douglas Denon Heath, 7 vols (London: Longman, 1857–59)

Barker, John, *The true description of a monsterous Chylde, borne in the Ile of Wight* (London: W. Gryffith, 1564)

Bartholomaeus Anglicus, *Batman vppon Bartholome, his Booke De proprietatibus rerum,* newly corrected, enlarged and amended: with such Additions as are requisite, vnto euery seuerall Booke: Taken foorth of the most approued Authors, the like heretofore not translated in English (London: Thomas East, 1582)

Bernardus Silvestris, *Cosmographia*, ed. by Peter Dronke, Textus Minores, 53 (Leiden: E. J. Brill, 1961)

——, *The Cosmography of Bernardus Silvestris*, trans. by Winthrop Wetherbee (New York and London: Columbia University Press, 1973)

Bestiarium. Die Texte der Handschrift MS. Ashmole 1511 der Bodleian Library Oxford in lateinischer und deutscher Sprache. ed. and trans. by Franz Unterkircher. Codices Selecti, 76 (Graz: Akademische Druck- und Verlags-Anstalt, 1986)

Biblia sacra iuxta vulgatam versionem, ed. by Robert Weber, 4th edition, revised by Roger Gryson (Stuttgart: Deutsche Bibelgesellschaft, 1994; originally published 1969)

Blundeville, Thomas, *The True Order and Methode of Wryting and Reading Hystories*, ed. by Hans Peter Heinrich, Bibliotheca Humanistica, 2 (Frankfurt am Main: Lang, 1986)

Boccaccio, Giovanni, *Genealogie deorum gentilium libri*, ed. by Vincenzo Romano, 2 vols (Bari: G. Laterza, 1951)

Boethius, Anicius Manlius Severinus, *Theological Tractates; The Consolation of Philosophy*, trans. by H. F. Stewart, E. K. Rand and S. J. Tester, Loeb Classical Library (Cambridge, MA: Harvard University Press; London: Heinemann, 1918; repr. 1962)

Boiardo, Matteo Maria, *Opere*, ed. by Ferruccio Olivi, I classici italiani (Milan: Mursia, 1986)

The Book of Beasts, Being a Translation from a Latin Bestiary of the Twelfth Century, ed. and trans. by T. H. White (New York: G. P. Putnam, 1954)

Bright, Timothy, *A Treatise of Melancholie*. Reproduced from the 1586 edition printed by Thomas Vautrollier, with an introduction by Hardin Craig, Publication No. 50 of the Facsimile Text Society (New York: Columbia University Press, 1940)

Browne, Thomas, *Pseudodoxia epidemica: or, Enquiries into Very many received Tenents, and commonly presumed Truths* (London: Edward Dod, 1646)

Burton, Robert, *The Anatomy of Melancholy*, ed. by Holbrook Jackson, 3 vols (London: J. M. Dent, 1932; repr. 1964)

Calvin, John, *Calvin's Bible Commentaries: Genesis, Part I*, trans. by John King (London, 1847)

——, *Institutes of the Christian Religion*, trans. by Henry Beverige (Peabody: Hendrickson, 2008)

Campanella, Tommaso, *De homine: Theologicorum liber IV*, ed. and trans. by Romano Amerio, 2 vols, Edizione nazionale dei classici del Pensiero Italiano, II, 13 and 14 (Rome: Centro Internazionale di Studi Umanistici, 1960)

Carroll, Lewis, *Alice's Adventures in Wonderland and Through the Looking-Glass*, ed. by Roger Lancelyn Green, Oxford World's Classics (Oxford: Oxford University Press, 1998)

Chalcidius, *Platonis Timaeus interprete Chalcidio cum eiusdem commentario*, ed. by Ioh. Wrobel (Leipzig: Teubner, 1876)

Chapman, George, *The Shadow of Night: Containing Two Poeticall Hymnes* (London: William Ponsonby, 1594)

Chaucer, Geoffrey, *The Riverside Chaucer*, gen. ed. by Larry D. Benson, 3rd edn (Oxford: Oxford University Press, 1987)

Chrétien de Troyes, *The Knight with the Lion, or Yvain (Le chevalier au lion)*, ed. and trans. by William W. Kibler, Garland Library of Medieval Literature, Series A, 48 (New York and London: Garland Publishing, 1985)

Cicero, *De officiis*, trans. Walter Miller, Loeb Classical Library (Cambridge, MA: Harvard University Press; London: Heinemann, 1913; repr. 1961)

——, *De senectute, De amicitia, De divinatione*, ed. and trans. by William Armistead Falconer, Loeb Classical Library (Cambridge, MA: Harvard University Press; London: Heinemann, 1923; repr. 1964)

Conti, Natale, *Natale Conti's Mythologiae*, trans. by John Mulryan and Steven Brown, 2 vols, Medieval and Renaissance Texts and Studies, 316 (Tempe: ACMRS, 2006)

——, *Natalis Comitis Mythologiae, sive explicationum fabularum libri decem. In quibus omnia prope naturalis & moralis philosophie dogmata sub antiquorum fabulis contenta suisse demonstratur* (Venice: n. pub., 1568)

Cooper, Thomas, *Thesaurus Linguae Romanae & Britannicae, tam accurate congestus, vt nihil penè in eo desyderari possit, quod vel Latinè complectatur amplissimus Stephani Thesaurus, vel Anglicè, toties aucta Eliotae Bibliotheca: opera & industria Thomae Cooperi Magdalenensis. Accessit dictionarium historicum et poëticum propria vocabula Virorum, Mulierum, Sectarum, Populorum, Vrbium, Montium, & caeterorum locorum complectens, & in his iucundissimas & omnium cognitione dignissimas historias* (London: Henry Wikes, 1565)

Critical Essays of the Seventeenth Century, ed. by J. E. Spingarn, 3 vols (Bloomington: Indiana University Press, 1957)

Crooke, Helkiah, *Mikrokosmographia: A Description of the Body of Man. Together with the Controversies and Figures thereto belonging.* Collected and Translated out of all the Best Authors of Anatomy, Especially out of Gasper Bauhinus, and Andreas Laurentius (London: William Iaggard, 1615)

Daniel, Samuel, *The Complete Works in Verse and Prose*, ed. by Alexander B. Grosart, 5 vols (New York: Russell and Russell, 1963)

Dante Alighieri, *The Divine Comedy of Dante Alighieri. Volume 1: Inferno*, ed. and trans. by Robert M. Durling; introduction and notes by Ronald M. Martinez and Robert M. Durling (New York and Oxford: Oxford University Press, 1996)

——, *The Divine Comedy of Dante Alighieri. Volume 2: Purgatorio*, ed. and trans. by Robert M. Durling; introduction and notes by Ronald M. Martinez and Robert M. Durling (New York and Oxford: Oxford University Press, 2003)

Davenant, William, *Gondibert: An Heroick Poem* (London: J. Holden, 1651)

Davies, John, Sir, *The Poems of Sir John Davies*, ed. by Robert Krueger (Oxford: Clarendon Press, 1975)

Davies of Hereford, John, *The Complete Works*, ed. by Alexander B. Grosart (1878), Anglistica and Americana, 2 vols (Hildesheim: Georg Olms Verlagsbuchhandlung, 1968; reprint of 1878 edition) de LaPrimaudaye, Pierre, *The Second Part of the French Academie. Wherein, as it were by a naturall historie of the bodie and soule of man, the creation, matter, composition, forme, nature, profite and vse of all the partes of the frame of man are handled, with the naturall causes of all affections, vertues and vices, and chiefly the nature, powers, workes and immortalitie of the soule*, trans. by T. B. (London: G.B., R.N., R.B., 1594)

della Mirandola, Giovanni Pico, *Oration on the Dignity of Man: A New Translation and Commentary*, ed. and trans. by Francesco Borghesi, Michael Papio and Massimo Riva (Cambridge: Cambridge University Press, 2012)

——, *A Platonick Discourse Upon Love*, trans. by Thomas Stanley, ed. by E. G. Gardner (Boston: The Merrymount Press, 1914)

The Demaundes off Love, ed. by W. L. Braeckmann, SCRIPTA: Medieval and Renaissance Texts and Studies, 7 (Brussels: Research Center of Medieval and Renaissance Studies, 1982)

Dering, Edward, *A briefe and necessary Instruction, Verye needefull to bee knowen of all Housholders, whereby they maye the better teach and instruct their Families in such pointes of Christian religion as is most meete* (London: John Awdely, 1572)

de Ronsard, Pierre, *Œuvres complètes*, ed. by Jean Céard, Daniel Ménager and Michel Simonin, 2 vols (Paris: Gallimard, 1994)

The description of a monstrous Pig, the which was farrowed at Hamsted besyde London, the. xvi. day of October this present yeare of our Lord God. M.D.LXII. (London: Alexander Lacy, 1562)

A description of a strange (and miraculous) Fish, cast upon the sands in the meads, in the Hundred of Worwell, in the County Palatine of Chester, (or Chesshiere. The certainty whereof is here related concerning the said most monstrous Fish (London: Thomas Lambert, n.d.)

The discription of a rare or rather most monstrous fishe taken on the East cost of Holland the. xvii. of Nouember, Anno 1566 (London: Thomas Purfoote, 1566)

Dryden, John, *The Dramatic Works*, ed. by Montague Summers, 6 vols (London: Nonesuch Press, 1932)

du Bellay, Joachim, *La defence et illustration de la langue francoyse*, ed. by Henri Chamard (Paris: Albert Fontemoing, 1904)

Early Prose Romances, ed. by Henry Morley (London: George Routledge, 1889)

Elizabethan Critical Essays, ed. by Gregory G. Smith, 2 vols (Oxford: Oxford University Press, 1904; repr. London, 1959)

Elyot, Thomas, *Bibliotheca Eliotae: Eliotes Dictionarie*, by Thomas Cooper the third tyme corrected (London: Th. Bertheleti, 1559)

——, *The Book Named the Governor*, ed. by S. E. Lehmberg, new edn, Everyman's Library (London: Dent; New York: Dutton, 1967)

Fasciculus Morum: A Fourteenth-Century Preacher's Handbook, ed. by Siegfried Wenzel (University Park and London: Pennsylvania State University Press, 1989)

Ficino, Marsilius, *Über die Liebe oder Platons Gastmahl*, trans. by Karl Paul Hasse, ed. by P. R. Blum, 2nd edn, Philosophische Bibliothek, 368 (Hamburg: Felix Meiner, 1984)

The Florentine Fior di Virtu of 1491, trans. into English by Nicholas Fersin with facsimiles of all of the original woodcuts, ed. by L. J. Rosenwald (Washington: Library of Congress, 1953)

Florio, John, *A Worlde of Wordes, or Most copious, and exact Dictionarie in Italian and English* (London: Arnold Hatfield, 1598)

Four Romances of England, ed. by Ronald B. Herzman, Graham Drake and Eve Salisbury (Kalamazoo: Medieval Institute Publications, 1999)

Fracastoro, Girolamo, *Naugerius, sive de poetica dialogus*, trans. by Ruth Kelso, with an introduction by Murray W. Bundy, University of Illinois Studies in Language and Literature, Vol. IX, No. 3 (Urbana: University of Illinois, 1924)

The Fragments of Attic Comedy, after Meineke, Bergk, and Kock, augmented, newly ed. with their contexts, annotated, and completely transl. into English verse by John Maxwell Edmonds, 3 vols (Leiden: Brill, 1957–61)

Friar Jordanus, *Mirabilia descripta: The Wonders of the East*, trans. from the Latin original, as published at Paris 1839, in the Recueil de Voyages et Mémoires, of the Society of Geography (London: Printed for the Hakluyt Society, 1863; repr. New York: Burt Franklin, no year)

Fulwood, William, *The Shape of ii. Monsters M.D. Lxii* (London: J. Alde, 1562)

Gascoigne, George, *Certayne Notes of Instruction Concerning the Making of Verse or Ryme in English*, in *Elizabethan Critical Essays*, ed. by Smith, I, 46–57.

The Geneva Bible: A Facsimile of the 1560 Edition (Madison, London: University of Wisconsin Press, 1969)

Geoffrey of Monmouth, *The Historia regum Britannie of Geoffrey of Monmouth. I: Bern, Burgerbibliothek, MS. 568*, ed. by Neil Wright (Cambridge: Brewer, 1985)

Gerarde, John, *The Herball, or Generall Historie of Plantes* (London: John Norton, 1597)

Gesner, Conrad, *Historiae animalium*, 5 vols (Zurich: Jacob Gesner, 1551–87)

Gosson, Stephen, *The School of Abuse and A Short Apologie for the Schoole of Abuse*, ed. by E. Arber, English Reprints (London: Murray, 1868)

Granger, Thomas, *A Moste true and marueilous straunge wonder, the lyke hath seldom ben seene, of. XVII. Monstrous fishes, taken in Suffolke, at Downam brydge, within a myle of Ipswiche. The .XI. daye of October. In the yeare of our Lorde God. M.D.LX.VIII.* (London: Thomas Colwell, 1568)

Herodotus, *The Persian Wars*, trans. by A. D. Godley, 4 vols, Loeb Classical Library (Cambridge, MA: Harvard University Press; London: Heinemann, 1920–25; repr. 1961)

Hesiod, trans. by Glenn W. Most, new and rev. edn, 2 vols, Loeb Classical Library (Cambridge, MA: Harvard University Press; London, Heinemann, 1936; repr. 1964)

Hobbes, Thomas, *Leviathan*, ed. C. B. Macpherson, Penguin Classics (Harmondsworth: Penguin, 1985)

Holinshed, Raphael, *Chronicles: England, Scotland, Ireland*, ed. by Henry Ellis and others, 6 vols (London: J. Johson, 1807–8; repr. New York: AMS Press, 1965)

The Holy Bible – Douay Rheims Version, revised by Richard Challoner (1749–52) (Rockford: Tan Books, 1971)

Homer, *The Iliad*, ed. and trans. by A. T. Murray, 2 vols, Loeb Classical Library (Cambridge, MA: Harvard University Press: London: Heinemann, 1924; repr. 1960)

——, *The Odyssey*, trans. by A. T. Murray, 2 vols, Loeb Classical Library (Cambridge, MA: Harvard University Press: London: Heinemann, 1919; repr. 1960)

Horace, *Odes I: Carpe diem*, ed. and trans. by David West (Oxford: Clarendon Press, 1995)

——, *Satires; Epistles; The Art of Poetry*, ed. and trans. by H. Rushton Fairclough, Loeb Classical Library (Cambridge, MA: Harvard University Press: London: Heinemann, 1929; repr. 1961)

Horapollo, *Des Niloten Horapollon Hieroglyphenbuch*, Vol. 1: Text und Übersetzung, ed. and trans. from the Greek by Heinz Josef Thissen, Archiv für Papyrusforschung und verwandte Gebiete, Beiheft 6 (Munich and Leipzig: K.G. Saur, 2001)

Huarte, Juan, *The Examination of mans Wits* [*Examen de Ingenios*], trans. out of the Spanish tongue by M. Camillo Camili, Englished out of his Italian, by R. C. Esquire (London: Adam Islip, 1594)

Isidore of Seville, *Etymologiarium sive originum libri XX*, ed. by Wallace Martin Lindsay, 2 vols, Oxford Classical Authors (Oxford: Clarendon Press, 1911)

——, *The Etymologies of Isidore of Seville*, trans. by Stephen A. Barney, W. J. Lewis, J. A. Beach and Oliver Berghof (Cambridge: Cambridge University Press, 2006)

Jonson, Ben, *Ben Jonson*, ed. by C. H. Herford, Percy and Evelyn Simpson, 11 vols (Oxford: Clarendon Press, 1954–65)

King Arthur's Death: The Middle English Stanzaic Morte Arthur; Alliterative Morte Arthure, ed. by Larry D. Benson (Kalamazoo: Western Michigan University for TEAMS, 1994)

Klaeber's Beowulf, ed. R. D. Fulk, Robert E. Bjork, John D. Niles, 4th edn, Toronto Old English, 21 (Toronto: University of Toronto Press, 2008)

Knox, John, *First Blast of the Trumpet Against the Monstrous Regiment of Women* (Whitefish: Kessinger Publishing, 2004)

Lactantius, Lucius Caecilius Firmianus, *Epitome divinarum institutionum*, ed. by Eberhard Heck and Antonie Wlosok, Bibliotheca scriptorvm Graecorvm et Romanorvm Tevbneriana (Stuttgart: Teubner, 1994)

Lancelot–Grail: The Old French Arthurian Vulgate and Post-Vulgate in Translation, ed. by Norris J. Lacy, 5 vols, Garland Reference Library to the Humanities (New York and London: Garland, 1993–96)

Laurentius, Andreas (André du Laurens), *A Discourse of the Preservation of the Sight: of Melancholike diseases; Of Rheumes, and of Old age*, translated out of French into English by Richard Surphlet (London: Felix Kingston, 1599)

Leland, C. G., ed., *The Unpublished Legends of Virgil* (London: Elliot Stock, 1899)

Lemnius, Levinus, *The Touchstone of Complexions, Generallye appliable, expedient and profitable for all such, as be desirous and carefull of theyr bodyly health*, trans. by Thomas Newton (London: Thomas Marsh, 1581)

Lucian, *The Downward Journey or The Tyrant. Zeus Catechized. Zeus Rants. The Dream or The Cock. Prometheus. Icaromenippus or The Sky-man. Timon or The Misanthrope. Charon or The Inspectors. Philosophies for Sale*, ed. and trans. by A.M. Harmon, Lucian: Works 2, Loeb Classical Library (London: Heinemann; Cambridge, MA: Harvard University Press, 1915; repr. 1960)

Lucretius, *On the Nature of Things*, trans. by W.H.D. Rouse, rev. by Martin Ferguson Smith, Loeb Classical Library (London: Heinemann, 1975)

Lycosthenes, Conrad, *Prodigiorum ac ostentorum chronicon, quae praeter naturae ordinem, et in superioribus et his inferioribus mundi regionibus, ab exordio mundi usque ad haec nostra tempora acciderunt* (Basle: H. Petri, 1557)

The Macro Plays, ed. by Mark Eccles, EETS, OS, 262 (Oxford: Oxford University Press, 1969)

Malory, Thomas, Sir, *Le Morte Darthur: The Hoole Book of Kyng Arthur and of His Noble Knyghtes of the Rounde Table*, ed. by Stephen H. A. Shepherd, Norton Critical Editions (New York and London: W. W. Norton, 2004)

Mandeville's Travels (Cotton Version), ed. by M. C. Seymour (Oxford: Clarendon Press)

Markham, Gervase, *Certaine excellent and new inuented Knots and Mazes* (London: John Marriott, 1623)

Marston, John, *Works*, ed. by Arthur Henry Bullen, 3 vols, Anglistica and Americana, 89 (London: John C. Nimmo, 1887; repr. Hildesheim: Georg Olms, 1970)

Melanchthon, Philipp, and Martin Luther, *Of Two VVoonderful Popish Monsters, to wyt, Of a Popish Asse which was found at Rome in the riuer of Tyber, and of a Moonkish Calfe, calued at Friberge in Misne*, trans. by John Brooke (London: Thomas East, 1579)

The Middle English Breton Lays, ed. by Anna Laskaya and Eve Salisbury (Kalamazoo: Western Michigan University for TEAMS, 1995)

Milton, John, *A Critical Edition of His Major Works*, ed. by Stephen Orgel and Jonathan Goldberg, The Oxford Authors (Oxford: Oxford University Press, 1991)

The Minor Elizabethan Drama, Vol. 2: Comedies, Everyman's Library, 492 (London: J. M. Dent; New York: E. P. Dutton, 1910)

Munster [Münster], Sebastian, *A Briefe Collection and compendium extract of straunge and memorable thinges, gathered oute of the Cosmographye of Sebastian Munster* (London: Thomas Marshe, 1572)

Nashe, Thomas, *The Works of Thomas Nashe*, ed. by R. B. McKerrow, 2nd edn, rev. by F. P. Wilson, 5 vols (Oxford: Oxford University Press, 1958)

Ovid, *Metamorphoses*, ed. and trans. by Frank Justus Miller, 2nd edn, 2 vols, Loeb Classical Library (Cambridge, MA: Harvard University Press; London: Heinemann, 1921; repr. 1961)

——, *Ovid's Metamorphoses*, trans. by Arthur Golding, ed. by Madeleine Forey (Baltimore: Johns Hopkins University Press, 2002)

Paré, Ambroise, *The Workes of that famous Chirurgion Ambrose Parey*, trans. out of Latin and compared with the French by Thomas Johnson (London: Th. Cotes and R. Young, 1634)

Peacham, Henry, *Henry Peacham's Manuscript Emblem Books*, ed. by Alan R. Young, The English Emblem Tradition, 5 (Toronto: University of Toronto Press, 1998)

Pellegrino, Camillo, *Il carrafa, o vero della epica poesia*, in *Trattati*, ed. by Weinberg, III, 307–44

P[h]illips, J., *A mervaylous straunge deformed Swyne* (London: W. How, 1570)

Plato, *Charmides. Alcibiades I and II. Hipparchus. The Lovers. Theages. Minos. Epinomis*, ed. and trans. by W. R. M. Lamb, Plato: Works 12, Loeb Classical Library (Cambridge, MA: Harvard University Press; London: Heinemann, 1927; repr. 1999)

——, *Euthyphro. Apology. Crito. Phaedo. Phaedrus*, ed. and trans. by H. N. Fowler, Plato: Works 1, Loeb Classical Library (Cambridge, MA: Harvard University Press; London: Heinemann, 1914; repr. 1960)

——, *Lysis; Symposium; Gorgias*, ed. and trans. by W. R. M. Lamb, Plato: Works 3, Loeb Classical Library (Cambridge, MA: Harvard University Press; London: Heinemann, 1925, repr. 1961)

——, *Protagoras*, trans. by C. C. W. Taylor, Clarendon Plato Series; rev. ed. (Oxford: Clarendon Press, 1991)

——, *Republic*, ed. and trans. by Paul Shorey, 2 vols, Plato: Works 5–6, Loeb Classical Library (Cambridge, MA: Harvard University Press; London: Heinemann, 1930 and 1935; repr. 2006)

——, *Theaetetus; Sophist*, ed. and trans. by Harold North Fowler, Plato: Works 7, Loeb Classical Library (Cambridge, MA: Harvard University Press; London: Heinemann, 1921; repr. 1999)

——, *Timaeus; Critias; Cleitophon; Menexenus; Epistles*, ed. and trans. by R. G. Bury, Plato: Works 9, Loeb Classical Library (Cambridge, MA: Harvard University Press; London: Heinemann, 1929; repr. 1960)

Pliny, *Natural History*, ed. and trans. by H. Rackham, 10 vols, Loeb Classical Library (Cambridge, MA: Harvard University Press; London: Heinemann, 1938–1962)

Plutarch, *Lives VII*, trans. Bernadotte Perrin, Loeb Classical Library (Cambridge, MA: Harvard University Press; London: Heinemann, 1919; repr. 1970)

——, *Moralia*, Vol. VII, Fasc. 1, ed. by C. Hubert, Bibliotheca Scriptorum Graecorum et Romanorum Teubneriana (Leipzig: Teubner, 1959)

——, *Moralia I: The Education of Children. How the Young Man Should Study Poetry. On Listening to Lectures. How to Tell a Flatterer from a Friend. How a Man May Become Aware of His Progress in Virtue*, ed. and trans. by Frank Cole Babbitt, Loeb Classical Library (Cambridge, MA: Harvard University Press; London: Heinemann, 1927)

Pomponius Mela, *Kreuzfahrt durch die Alte Welt*, ed. and trans. by Kai Brodersen (Darmstadt: Wissenschaftliche Buchgesellschaft, 1994)

Porta, Giovanni Battista della, *Della fisionomia dell' huomo et la celeste* (Venice: Presso Sebastian Combi and Giovanni La Noù, Alla Minerva, 1652; facsimile Castel Negrino: Gruppo Editoriale, 2006)

Prudentius, ed. and trans. by H. J. Thomson, 2 vols, Loeb Classical Library (Cambridge, MA: Harvard University Press; London: Heinemann, 1949)

Purchas, Samuel, *Purchas his Pilgrim. Microcosmvs, or The Historie of Man. Relating the Wonders of his Generation, Vanities in his Degeneration, Necessity of his Regeneration* (London: W[illiam] S[tansby], 1619)

Puttenham, George, *The Arte of English Poesie*, ed. by Gladys Doidge Willcock and Alice Walker (Cambridge: Cambridge University Press, 1936)

——, *The Art of English Poesy: A Critical Edition*, ed. by Frank Whigham and Wayne A. Rebhorn (Ithaca and London: Cornell University Press, 2007)

Quintilian, *Institutio oratoria*, ed. and trans. by H. E. Butler, 4 vols, Loeb Classical Library (London: Heinemann; Cambridge, MA: Harvard University Press, 1920–21; repr. 1960)

Raleigh, Sir Walter, *The Works of Sir Walter Raleigh, Now First Collected. To which are prefixed the Lives of the Author, by Oldys and Birch*, 8 vols, Burt Franklin Research and Works Series, 73 (Oxford: Oxford University Press, 1829; facsimile New York: Burt Franklin, 1966)

Robert Mannyng of Brunne, *The Chronicle*, ed. by Idelle Sullens, Medieval and Renaissance Texts and Studies 153 (Binghamton: State University of New York at Binghamton University, 1996)

The Romance of Guy of Warwick, ed. from the Paper MS. Ff. 2.38 in University Library, Cambridge by Julius Zupitza, EETS, Extra Series, 25/26 (London: Trübner, 1875)

The Romans of Partenay, or of Lusignen, Otherwise Known as the Tale of Melusine, ed. by W. W. Skeat, EETS, O, 22 (London: K. Paul, Trench, Trübner & Co, 1866)

Scaliger, Julius Caesar, *Poetices libri septem: Sieben Bücher über die Dichtkunst*, ed., trans. and intr. by Luc Deitz, 5 vols (Stuttgart-Bad Cannstadt: Frommann-Holzboog, 1994–2003)

Secretum secretorum: Nine English Versions, ed. by M. A. Manzalaoui, EETS, 276 (Oxford: Oxford University Press, 1977)

Seneca, Lucius Annaeus, *Ad Lucilium epistulae morales*, trans. by Richard M. Gummere, 3 vols, Loeb Classical Library (Cambridge, MA: Harvard University Press; London: Heinemann, 1917–25)

Servius, *Servii grammatici qui feruntur in Vergilii commentarii*, ed. by Georg Thilo and Hermann Hagen, 3 vols (Hildesheim: Georg Olms, 1961)

Shakespeare, William, *Coriolanus*, ed. by Philip Brockbank, The Arden Edition of the Works of William Shakespeare, 2nd series (London: Methuen, 1976)

——, *King Lear*, ed. by R. A. Foakes, The Arden Shakespeare, 3rd Series (Walton-on-Thames: Thomas Nelson. 1997)

——, *A Midsummer Night's Dream*, ed. by Harold F. Brooks, The Arden Edition of the Works of William Shakespeare, 2nd series (London: Methuen, 1979)

——, *Othello*, ed. by E. A. J. Honigmann, The Arden Edition of the Works of William Shakespeare, 3rd series (Walton-on-Thames: Thomas Nelson. 1997)

Sidney, Philip, *An Apology for Poetry, or The Defence of Poesy*, ed. by Geoffrey Shepherd, 2nd edn (Manchester: Manchester University Press, 1965)

——, *An Apology for Poetry or The Defence of Poesy*, ed. by Geoffrey Shepherd, 3rd edn rev. and expanded by R. W. Maslen (Manchester and New York: Manchester University Press, 2002)

——, *The Countess of Pembroke's Arcadia (The Old Arcadia)*, ed. by Jean Robertson (Oxford: Clarendon, 1973)

——, *Miscellaneous Prose of Sir Philip Sidney*, ed. by Katherine Duncan-Jones and Jan van Dorsten (Oxford: Clarendon Press, 1973)

——, *The Poems of Sir Philip Sidney*, ed. by William A. Ringler, Jr (Oxford: Clarendon, 1962)

——, *The Prose Works of Philip Sidney*, ed. by Albert Feuillerat, 4 vols (Cambridge: Cambridge University Press, 1963)

Sir Perceval of Galles and Ywain and Gawain, ed. by Mary Flowers Braswell (Kalamazoo: Medieval Institute Publications, 1995)

Solinus Caius, Julius, *C. J. Solini Collectanea Rerum Memorabilium*, revised by Theodor Mommsen (Berolini: Weidmann, 1864)

The Spectator, ed. by Donald F. Bond, 5 vols (Oxford: Clarendon Press, 1965)

Spenser, Edmund, *The Faerie Queene*, ed. by A. C. Hamilton; text ed. by Hiroshi Yamashita and Toshiyuki Suzuki, Longman Annotated English Poets (London: Longman, 2001)

——, *A View of the Present State of Ireland*, ed. by W. L. Renwick (Oxford: Clarendon, 1970)

——, *The Works of Edmund Spenser: A Variorum Edition*, ed. by Edwin Greenlaw, Charles Grosvenor Osgood and Frederick Morgan Padelford, 11 vols (Baltimore: Johns Hopkins University Press, 1932–45)

Suetonius, *Lives of the Caesars; Lives of Illustrious Men*, trans. by J. C. Rolfe, 2 vols (Cambridge, MA: Harvard University Press; London: Heinemann, 1914; repr. 1964)

Tasso, Torquato, *Discourses on the Heroic Poem* [*Discorsi dell' arte poetica e del poema eroico*], trans. from the Italian by Mariella Cavalchini and Irene Samuel (Oxford: Oxford University Press, 1973)

——, *Godfrey of Bulloigne*, trans. by Edward Fairfax, ed. by Kathleen M. Lea and T. M. Lang (Oxford: Clarendon, 1980)

——, *Poesie*, ed. by Francesco Flora, La Letteratura Italiana: Storia e testi, 21 (Milan: Ricciardi, 1952)

——, *Prose*, ed. by Ettore Mazzali, La Letteratura Italiana: Storia e testi, 22 (Milan: Ricciardi, 1959)

Theophrastus, *Theophrasti Eresii opera, quae supersunt, omnia*, ed. and trans. by Friedrich Wimmer (Paris: Diderot, 1866)

The Thornton Romances, ed. by James Orchard Halliwell (London: Camden Society, 1844)

Topsell, Edward, *The History of Four-footed Beasts and Serpents … Collected out of the Writings of Conradus Gesner and other Authors, by Edward Topsel. Whereunto is now Added, The Theater of Insects … by T. Muffet*, 3 vols (London: E. Cotes, 1658; facsimile New York: Da Capo Press, 1967)

Trattati di poetica e retorica del cinquecento, ed. by Bernard Weinberg, 4 vols (Bari: Laterza, 1983)

Vickers, Brian, ed., *English Renaissance Literary Criticism* (Oxford, Clarendon Press: 1999)

Virgil, *Works*, ed. and trans. by H. Rushton Fairclough, revised by G. P. Goold, new and rev. edn, 2 vols, Loeb Classical Library (Cambridge, MA: Harvard University Press, 2000)

Warton, Joseph, *An Essay on the Genius and Writings of Pope*, 2 vols (London: J. Dodsley, 1782)

Warton, Thomas, *Observations on 'The Faerie Queene' by Spenser*, 2 vols (London: Dodsley, 1762; facsimile Farnborough: Gregg, 1969)

Whitney, Geoffrey, *A Choice of Emblemes, and other Deuises, For the moste parte gathered out of sundrie writers, Englished and Moralized* (Leyden: Christopher Plantyn, 1586)

Wright, Thomas, *The Passions of the minde in generall* (London: Valentine Simmes, 1604)

Ywain and Gawain, ed. by Albert B. Friedman and Norman T. Harrington, EETS, OS, 254 (London: Oxford University Press, 1964)

Secondary sources

Abrams, M. H., *The Mirror and the Lamp: Romantic Theory and the Critical Tradition* (Oxford: Oxford University Press, 1971)

Adelman, Janet, 'Revaluing the Body in *The Faerie Queene I*', Hugh Mclean Memorial Lecture, December 2004, *Spenser Review* 36.1 (Winter 2005), 15–25

Adler, Doris, 'Imaginary Toads in Real Gardens', *English Literary Renaissance* 11 (1981), 235–60

Ahrends, Günter, 'Transformationen des Subjekts und der Realität: Konzepte der Imagination im medizinischen und poetologischen Diskurs der englischen Renaissance', in *Zum Begriff der Imagination*, ed. by Beyer, pp. 1–15

Ahrens, Rüdiger, and Erwin Wolff, eds, *Englische und amerikanische Literaturtheorie. Band I: Renaissance, Klassizismus und Romantik* (Heidelberg: Winter, 1978)

Alexander, R. McN., 'The Evolution of the Basilisk', *Greece and Rome*, 2nd Series, 10 (1963), 170–81

Alpers, Paul J., *The Poetry of 'The Faerie Queene'* (Princeton: Princeton University Press, 1967)

——, ed., *Elizabethan Poetry: Modern Essays in Criticism* (New York: Oxford University Press, 1967)

Anderson, Judith H., 'Arthur, Argante, and the Ideal Vision: An Exercise in Speculation and Parody', in *The Passing of Arthur*, ed. by Baswell and Sharpe, pp. 193–206

——, '"A Gentle Knight was pricking on the plaine": The Chaucerian Connection', *English Language Review* 15 (1985), 166–74

——, 'Mutability and Mortality: Reading Spenser', in *Celebrating Mutabilitie*, ed. by Grogan, pp. 246–74

Andrew, Malcolm, '*Patience*: The *Munster Dor*', *English Language Notes* 14 (1977), 164–7

Aptekar, Jane, *Icons of Justice: Iconography and Thematic Imagery in Book V of 'The Faerie Queene'* (New York: Columbia University Press, 1969)

Attridge, Derek, 'Puttenham's Perplexity: Nature, Art, and the Supplement in Renaissance Poetic Theory', in *Literary Theory*, ed. by Parker and Quint, pp. 257–79

Barkan, Leonard, *Nature's Work of Art: The Human Body as the Image of the World* (New Haven and London: Yale University Press, 1975)

Barsella, Susanna, 'The Myth of Prometheus in Giovanni Boccaccio's *Decameron*', *Modern Language Notes* 119.1 (2004), Italian issue, 120–41

Baswell, Christopher, and William Sharpe, eds, *The Passing of Arthur: New Essays in Arthurian Tradition* (New York: Garland Press, 1988)

Batt, Catherine, 'Malory's Questing Beast and the Implication of Author as Translator', in *The Medieval Translator*, ed. by Ellis, pp. 143–66

Bauer, Robert J., 'A Phenomenon of Epistemology in the Renaissance', *Journal of the History of Ideas* 31 (1970), 281–8

Bayley, P. C., *Edmund Spenser: Prince of Poets*, English Literature (London: Hutchinson, 1971)

Bellamy, Elizabeth Jane, 'The Broken Branch and the "Living Well": Spenser's Fradubio and Romance Error in *The Faerie Queene*', *Renaissance Papers* 32 (1985), 1–12

Berger, Harry, Jr., *The Allegorical Temper: Vision and Reality in Book II of Edmund Spenser's 'Faerie Queene'* (New Haven: Yale University Press, 1957)

——, 'The Renaissance Imagination: Second World and Green World', *The Centennial Review* 9 (1965), 36–78

——, 'A Secret Discipline: *The Faerie Queene*, Book VI', in *Form and Convention*, ed. by Nelson, pp. 35–75

Bergvall, Åke, *The 'Enabling of Judgement': Sir Philip Sidney and the Education of the Reader*, Acta Universitatis Upsaliensis, Studia Anglistica Upsaliensia (Uppsala: Almqvist and Wiksell, 1989)

Berlioz, Jacques, 'Le crapaud, animal diabolique: une exemplaire construction médiévale', in *L'animal exemplaire*, ed. by Berlioz and de Beaulieu, pp. 267–88

——, and Marie Anne Polo de Beaulieu, eds, *L'animal exemplaire au Moyen Âge Ve–XVe siècles* (Rennes: Presses Universitaires de Rennes, 1999)

Beyer, Manfred, ed., *Zum Begriff der Imagination in Dichtung und Dichtungstheorie. Festschrift für Rainer Lengeler zum 65. Geburtstag* (Trier: Wissenschaftlicher Verlag Trier, 1998)

Biester, James, 'Fancy's Images: Wit, the Sublime, and the Rise of Aestheticism', in *Wonders, Marvels, and Monsters*, ed. by Platt, pp. 294–327

Bildhauer, Bettina, 'Bloodsuckers: The Construction of Female Sexuality in Medieval Science and Fiction', in *Consuming Narratives*, ed. by McAvoy and Walters, pp. 104–15

——, and Robert Mills, 'Introduction', in *The Monstrous Middle Ages*, ed. by Bildhauer and Mills, pp. 1–27

——, and Robert Mills, eds, *The Monstrous Middle Ages* (Toronto: University of Toronto Press, 2003)

Biow, Douglas, *Mirabile Dictu: Representations of the Marvelous in Medieval and Renaissance Epic* (Ann Arbor: University of Michigan Press, 1996)

Blissett, William, 'Caves', *Spenser Encyclopedia*, ed. Hamilton, pp. 138–9

——, 'Caves, Labyrinths, and *The Faerie Queene*', in *Unfolded Tales*, ed. by Logan and Teskey, pp. 281–311

——, 'Labyrinths, Mazes', in *Spenser Encyclopedia*, ed. by Hamilton, pp. 422–3

Bloomfield, Morton W., *The Seven Deadly Sins: An Introduction to the History of a Religious Concept with Special Reference to Medieval English Literature* (East Lansing: State University Press, 1952)

Blumenberg, Hans, *Arbeit am Mythos* (Frankfurt am Main: Suhrkamp, 1979)

Boardman, John, '"Very Like a Whale" – Classical Sea Monsters', in *Monsters and Demons*, ed. by Farkas, Harper and Harrison, pp. 73–84

Bond, Ronald B., 'Blatant Beast', in *Spenser Encyclopedia*, ed. by Hamilton, pp. 96–8

Bord, Janet, *Mazes and Labyrinths of the World* (New York: E. P. Dutton, 1975)

Bordman, Gerald Martin, *Motif-Index of the English Metrical Romances*, FF Communications 190, Vol. 79, 2 (Helsinki: Suomalainen Tiedeakatemia, 1963)

Borris, Kenneth, *Allegory and Epic in English Renaissance Literature: Heroic Form in Sidney, Spenser, and Milton* (Cambridge: Cambridge University Press, 2000)

——, 'Fortune, Occasion, and the Allegory of the Quest in Book Six of The Faerie Queene', *Spenser Studies* 7 (1987), 123–45

——, *Spenser's Poetics of Prophecy in 'The Faerie Queene' V* (Victoria: English Literary Studies, 1990)

Bovilsky, Sarah, 'Spenser's Robots', abstract in: *Spenser Review* 37.1 (2006), 29

Brammall, Kathryn M., 'Monstrous Metamorphosis: Nature, Morality, and the Rhetoric of Monstrosity in Tudor England', *Sixteenth Century Journal* 27 (1996), 3–21

Bremer, Dieter, 'Prometheus: Die Formation eines Grundmythologems', in *Prometheus*, ed. by Pankow and Peters, pp. 35–42

Brill, Leslie, 'Paridell', in *Spenser Encyclopedia*, ed. by Hamilton, p. 529

Broaddus, James W., 'Renaissance Psychology and Britomart's Adventures in *Faerie Queene* III', *English Literary Renaissance* 17 (1987), 186–206

——, 'Renaissance Psychology and the Defense of Alma's Castle', *Spenser Studies* 19 (2004), 135–57

——, *Spenser's Allegory of Love: Social Vision in Books III, IV, and V of 'The Faerie Queene'* (London: Associated University Press, 1995)

Broedel, Hans Peter. '"Now I Will Believe That There Are Unicorns": The Existence of Fabulous Beasts in Renaissance *Historiae Naturales*', in *Renaissance Medievalisms*, ed. by Eisenbichler, pp. 287–302

Brooks-Davies, Douglas, *Spenser's 'Faerie Queene': A Critical Commentary on Books I and II* (Manchester: Manchester University Press, 1977)

Brown, Carmen, 'Bestiary Lessons on Pride and Lust', in *The Mark of the Beast*, ed. by Hassig, pp. 53–70

Bruce, J. Douglas, 'Human Automata in Classical Tradition and Mediaeval Romance', *Modern Philology* 4 (1913), 511–26

Bundy, Murray Wright, 'Fracastoro and the Imagination', in *Renaissance Studies*, ed. by Maxwell and others, pp. 44–57

——, '"Invention" and "Imagination" in the Renaissance', *Journal of English and Germanic Philology* 29 (1930), 535–45

——, *The Theory of Imagination in Classical and Mediaeval Thought*, University of Illinois Studies in Language and Literature 12, Nos 2–3 (Urbana: University of Illinois Press, 1927; facsimile Norwood: Norwood Editions, 1978)

Burchmore, David W., 'The Medieval Sources of Spenser's Occasion Episode', *Spenser Studies* 2 (1981), 93–120

Burnett, Mark Thornton, *Constructing 'Monsters' in Shakespearean Drama and Early Modern Culture*, Early Modern Literature in History (London: Palgrave Macmillan, 2002)

Burrow, Colin, 'Original Fictions: Metamorphoses in *The Faerie Queene*', in *Ovid Renewed*, ed. by Martindale, pp. 99–119

Bushnell, Rebecca, 'Experience, Truth, and Natural History in Early English Gardening Books, 1520–1630', in *The Historical Imagination*, ed. by Kelley and Sacks, pp. 179–209

Bynum, Caroline Walker, *Metamorphosis and Identity* (New York: Zone Books, 2001)

Camille, Michael, *The Margins of Medieval Art* (London: Reaktion, 1992)

Campbell, Mary, 'The Nude Cyclops in the Custome Book', in *Marvels, Monsters, and Miracles*, ed. by Jones and Sprunger, pp. 285–301

——, *The Witness and the Other World: Exotic Travel Writing 400–1600* (Ithaca and London: Cornell University Press, 1988)

Canby, Sheila R., 'Dragons', in *Mythical Beasts*, ed. by Cherry, pp. 14–43

Cancik, Hubert, and Helmuth Schneider, eds, *Der Neue Pauly: Enzyklopädie der Antike*, 16 vols (Stuttgart: J. B. Metzler, 1996–2003)

Cargo, R. T., and E. J. Mickel, Jr, eds, *Studies in Honor of Alfred G. Engstrom* (Chapel Hill: North Carolina University Press, 1972)

Carruthers, Mary, *The Craft of Thought: Meditation, Rhetoric, and the Making of Images, 400–1200* (Cambridge: Cambridge University Press, 1998)

Cassuto, U., *A Commentary on the Book of Genesis, I: From Adam to Noah*, trans. by I. Abraham (Jerusalem: Magnes Press, 1961)

Cavanagh, Sheila T., 'Nightmares of Desire: Evil Women in *The Faerie Queene*', *Studies in Philology* 91 (1994), 313–38

——, *Wanton Eyes and Chaste Desires: Female Sexuality in 'The Faerie Queene'* (Bloomington: Indiana University Press, 1994)

Ceard, Jean, *La Nature et les prodiges*, Travaux d'Humanisme et Renaissance, 158 (Geneva: Droz, 1977)

Chaudhuri, Supriya, 'Grill', in *Spenser Encyclopedia*, ed. by Hamilton, p. 342

Cheney, Donald, *Spenser's Image of Nature: Wild Man and Shepherd in 'The Faerie Queene'* (New Haven and London: Yale University Press, 1967)

——, 'Spenser's Parody', *Connotations* 12 (2003), 1–13

Cheney, Patrick, and Lauren Silberman, eds, *Worldmaking Spenser: Explorations in the Early Modern Age* (Lexington: The University of Kentucky Press, 2000)

Cherry, John, ed., *Mythical Beasts* (London: British Museum, 1995)

Christianson, Paul, *Reformers and Babylon: English Apocalyptic Visions from the Reformation to the Eve of the Civil War* (Toronto: University of Toronto Press, 1978)

Clifford, Gay, *The Transformations of Allegory* (London: Routledge, 1974)

Cohen, J. J., *Of Giants: Sex, Monsters, and the Middle Ages*, Medieval Cultures, 17 (Minneapolis and London: University of Minnesota Press, 1999)

——, 'The Limits of Knowing: Monsters and the Regulation of Popular Culture', *Medieval Folklore* 3 (1994), 1–37

——, 'Monster Culture (Seven Theses)', in *Monster Theory*, ed. by Cohen, pp. 3–25

——, ed., *Monster Theory: Reading Culture* (Minneapolis: University of Minnesota Press, 1996)

Cook, Eleanor, ed., *Centre and Labyrinth: Studies in Honour of Northrop Frye* (Toronto: Toronto University Press, 1983)

Cook, Patrick J., *Milton, Spenser, and the Epic Tradition* (Aldershot and Brookfield: Scolar, 1996)

Cooper, Helen, *The English Romance in Time: Transforming Motifs from Geoffrey of Monmouth to the Death of Shakespeare* (Oxford: Oxford University Press, 2004)

Cosman, Madeleine Pelner, 'Spenser's Ark of Animals: Animal Imagery in *The Faery Queene*', *Studies in English Literature 1500–1900* 3 (1963), 85–107

Craig, Martha, 'The Secret of Wit of Spenser's Language', in *Elizabethan Poetry*, ed. by Alpers, pp. 447–72

Cummings, R. M., *Spenser: The Critical Heritage* (London: Routledge and Keegan Paul, 1971)

Daston, Lorraine, and Katharine Park, *Wonders and the Order of Nature 1150–1750* (New York: Zone Books, 1998)

Davidson, Clifford, and Thomas H. Seiler, eds, *The Iconography of Hell*, Early Drama, Art, and Music Monograph Series, 17 (Kalamazoo: Medieval Institute Publications, Western Michigan University, 1992)

Davies, Surekha, 'The Unlucky, the Bad and the Ugly: Categories of Monstrosity from the Renaissance to the Enlightenment', in *The Ashgate Research Companion to Monsters and the Monstrous*, ed. by Mittman and Dendle, pp. 49–75

Dees, Jerome S., 'The Narrator of *The Faerie Queene*: Patterns of Response', *Texas Studies in Literature and Language* 12 (1971), 537–68

Diehl, Huston, 'Into the Maze of Self: The Protestant Transformation of the Image of the Labyrinth', *Journal of Medieval and Renaissance Studies* 16 (1986), 281–99

Doob, Penelope Reed, *The Idea of the Labyrinth from Classical Antiquity Through the Middle Ages* (Ithaca: Cornell University Press, 1990)

Douglas, Mary, *Purity and Danger: An Analysis of the Concepts of Pollution and Taboo* (London: Routledge and Kegan Paul, 1966)

Eco, Umberto, *The Search for the Perfect Language* [*La Ricerca della Lingua Perfetta nella Cultura Europea*], trans. by James Fentress, The Making of Europe (Oxford: Blackwell, 1995)

Edson, Evelyn, 'Mapping the Middle Ages: The Imaginary and the Real Universe of the *Mappaemundi*', in *Monsters, Marvels, and Miracles*, ed. by Søndergaard and Hansen, pp. 11–25

Eisenbichler, Konrad, ed., *Renaissance Medievalisms*, Publications of the Centre for Reformation and Renaissance Studies, Essays and Studies, 18 (Toronto: Centre for Reformation and Renaissance Studies, 2009)

Ellis, Roger, ed., *The Medieval Translator: Theory and Practice in the Middle Ages* (Cambridge: Cambridge University Press, 1989)

Erickson, Wayne, *Mapping 'The Faerie Queene': Quest Structures and the World of the Poem*, Garland Studies in the Renaissance, 3 (New York and London: Garland Publishing, 1996)

Ernout, A., and A. Meillet, *Dictionnaire etymologique de la langue Latine: histoire de mots*, 4th edn (Paris: Librairie C. Klincksieck, 1967)

Evans, Jonathan D., 'The Dragon', in *Mythical and Fabulous Creatures*, ed. by South, pp. 27–59

Evans, Maurice, 'Guyon', in *Spenser Encyclopedia*, ed. by Hamilton, pp. 343–4

Faas, Ekbert, *Shakespeare's Poetics* (Cambridge: Cambridge University Press, 1986)

Farkas, A. E., P. O. Harper and E. B. Harrison, eds, *Monsters and Demons in the Ancient and Medieval Worlds: Papers Presented in Honour of Edith Porada* (Mainz: von Zabern, 1987)

Felton, Debbie, 'Rejecting and Embracing the Monstrous in Ancient Greece and Rome', in *The Ashgate Research Companion to Monsters and the Monstrous*, ed. by Mittman and Dendle, pp. 103–31

Ferry, Anne, *The Art of Naming* (Chicago: University of Chicago Press, 1988)

Fike, Matthew, '"Not without Theseus": The Mythic Weave of *The Faerie Queene*, Book 1', *Classical and Modern Literature* 17 (1997), 231–49

Fletcher, Angus, 'The Image of Lost Direction', in *Centre and Labyrinth*, ed. by Cook, pp. 329–46

——, *The Prophetic Moment: An Essay on Spenser* (Chicago and London: University of Chicago Press, 1971)

Flood, John L., 'Sankt Georg', in *Herrscher, Helden, Heilige*, ed. by Müller and Wunderlich, pp. 589–606

Flores, N. C., '"Effigies amicitiae ...veritas inimicitiae": Antifeminism in the Iconography of the Woman-Headed Serpent in Medieval and Renaissance Art and Literature', in *Animals in the Middle Ages*, ed. by Flores, pp. 167–95

——, ed., *Animals in the Middle Ages. A Book of Essays* (New York: Garland, 1996)

Ford, Andrew, *The Origins of Literary Criticism: Literary Culture and Poetic Theory* (Princeton and Oxford: Princeton University Press, 2002)

Forste-Grupp, Sheryl L., 'A Possible Irish Source for the Giant Coulin in Spenser's *Faerie Queene*', *Studies in Philology* 96 (1999), 42–50

Freedman, Paul, 'The Medieval Other: The Middle Ages as Other', in *Marvels, Monsters, and Miracles*, ed. by Jones and Sprunger, pp. 1–24

Freeman, Louise Gilbert, 'The Metamorphosis of Malbecco: Allegorical Violence and Ovidian Change', *Studies in Philology* 97 (2002), 308–30

Freeman, Rosemarie, '*The Faerie Queene*': *A Companion for Readers* (London: Chatto and Windus, 1970)

Friedman, John Block, 'Monsters at the Earth's Imagined Corners: Wonders and Discovery in the Late Middle Ages', in *Monsters, Marvels, and Miracles*, ed. by Søndergaard and Hansen, pp. 41–64

——, *The Monstrous Races in Medieval Art and Thought* (Cambridge, MA: Harvard University Press, 1981)

Frisk, Hjalmar, *Griechisches etymologisches Wörterbuch*, 3 vols (Heidelberg: Winter, 1960–70)

Frushell, Richard C., and Bernard J. Vondersmith, eds, *Contemporary Thought on Edmund Spenser* (Carbondale: Southern Illinois University Press, 1975)

Frye, Northrop, *Anatomy of Criticism: Four Essays* (Princeton: Princeton University Press, 1957)

Fudge, Erica, *Perceiving Animals: Humans and Beasts in Early Modern English Culture* (Urbana and Chicago: University of Illinois Press, 2002)

Galbraith, David Ian, *Architectonics of Imitation in Spenser, Daniel, and Drayton* (Toronto, London: University of Toronto Press, 2000)

Gallagher, Philip J., 'Prometheus', in *Spenser Encyclopedia*, ed. by Hamilton, pp. 557–8

Galyon, Linda, 'Puttenham's *Enargeia* and *Energeia*: New Twists for Old Terms', *Philological Quarterly* 60 (1981), 29–40

Garber, Marjorie, *Shakespeare's Ghost Writers: Literature as Uncanny Causality* (New York: Routledge, Chapman & Hall, 1988)

Giamatti, A. Bartlett, *Play of Double Senses: Spenser's 'Faerie Queene'* (Englewood Cliffs and London: Prentice-Hall, 1975)

Gilbert, Ruth, Erica Fudge and Susan Wiseman, eds, *At the Borders of the Human: Beasts, Bodies and Natural Philosophy in the Early Modern Period* (Basingstoke: Palgrave, 1999)

Girard, René, *The Scapegoat*, trans. by Yvonne Freccero (Baltimore: Johns Hopkins University Press, 1986)

Gless, Darryl J., *Interpretation and Theology in Spenser* (Cambridge: Cambridge University Press, 1994)

Goth, Maik, *From Chaucer's Pardoner to Shakespeare's Iago: Aspects of Intermediality in the History of the Vice*, Studien zur englischen und amerikanischen Literatur, 22 (Frankfurt am Main: Lang, 2009)

Grabes, Herbert, *Speculum, mirror und looking-glass: Kontinuität und Originalität der Spiegelmetapher in den Buchtiteln des Mittelalters und der englischen Literatur des 13. bis 17. Jahrhunderts*, Buchreihe der Anglia, 16 (Tübingen: Niemeyer, 1973)

Grant, Edward, *Planets, Stars, and Orbs: The Medieval Cosmos, 1200–1687* (Cambridge: Cambridge University Press, 1996)

Gray, M. M., 'The Influence of Spenser's Irish Experiences on *The Faerie Queene*', *Review of English Studies* 6 (1930), 413–28

Greenblatt, Stephen, 'Murdering Peasants: Status, Genre, and the Representation of Rebellion', *Representations* 1 (1983), 1–29

Greene, Roland, 'A Primer of Spenser's Worldmaking: Alterity in the Bower of Bliss', in *Worldmaking Spenser*, ed. by Cheney and Silberman, pp. 9–31

Grogan, Jane, ed., *Celebrating Mutabilitie: Essays on Edmund Spenser's Mutabilitie Cantos*, ed. by Jane Grogan, The Manchester Spenser (Manchester: Manchester University Press, 2010)

Grootkerk, Paul, 'The Satyr', in *Mythical and Fabulous Creatures*, ed. by South, pp. 207–24

Gross, Kenneth, 'Reflections on the Blatant Beast', *Spenser Studies* 13 (1999), 101–23

——, *Spenserian Poetics: Idolatry, Iconoclasm, and Magic* (Ithaca: Cornell University Press, 1985)

Guenther, Genevieve, 'Spenser's Magic, or Instrumental Aesthetics in the 1590 *Faerie Queene*', *English Literary Renaissance* 36 (2006), 194–226

Guldon, Ernst, 'Das Monster-Portal am Palazzo Zuccari in Rom', *Zeitschrift für Kunstgeschichte* 32 (1969), 229–61

Hadfield, Andrew, '*The Faerie Queene* IV–VI', in *The Cambridge Companion to Spenser*, ed. by Hadfield, pp. 124–42

——, 'Spenser as Prometheus: A Response to Maik Goth', *Connotations* 20 (2010/2011), 189–200

——, ed., *The Cambridge Companion to Spenser*, Cambridge Companions to Literature (Cambridge: Cambridge University Press, 2001)

Halio, Jay L., 'The Metaphor of Conception and Elizabethan Theories of the Imagination', *Neophilologus* 50 (1966), 454–61

Hamilton, Albert Charles, '"The Grene Path Way to Lyfe": Spenser's *Shepheardes Calender* as Pastoral', in *The Elizabethan Theatre VIII*, ed. by Hibbard, pp. 1–21

——, 'The Visions of *Piers Plowman* and *The Faerie Queene*', in *Form and Convention*, ed. by Nelson, pp. 1–34

——, and others, 'Faeries', in *Spenser Encyclopedia*, ed. by Hamilton, pp. 295–6

——, ed., *Essential Articles for the Study of Edmund Spenser* (Hamdon: Archon Books, 1972)

——, gen. ed., *The Spenser Encyclopedia* (Toronto: University of Toronto Press; London: Routledge, 1990)

Hamlin, William M., *The Image of America in Montaigne, Spenser and Shakespeare: Renaissance Ethnography and Literary Reflection* (New York: St Martin's Press, 1995)

Hanafi, Zakiya, *The Monster in the Machine: Magic, Medicine, and the Marvelous in the Time of the Scientific Revolution* (Durham, NC, and London: Duke University Press, 2000)

Hankins, John E., *Source and Meaning in Spenser's Allegory: A Study of 'The Faerie Queene'* (Oxford: Oxford University Press, 1971)

Happ, Heinz, *Hyle: Studien zum aristotelischen Materie-Begriff* (Berlin: Walter de Gruyter, 1971)

Hardin, Richard F., *Civil Idolatry: Desacralizing and Monarchy in Spenser, Sidney, and Milton* (Newark: University of Delaware Press, 1992)

Harvey, E. Ruth, *The Inward Wits: Psychological Theory in the Middle Ages and the Renaissance*, Warburg Institute Surveys, 6 (London: The Warburg Institute [at the] University of London, 1975)

——, 'Psychology', in *Spenser Encyclopedia*, ed. by Hamilton, pp. 565–68

Hassig, Debra, ed., *The Mark of the Beast: The Medieval Bestiary in Art, Life, and Literature*, Garland Medieval Casebooks (New York: Garland Publishing, 1999)

Hathaway, Baxter, *Marvels and Commonplaces: Renaissance Literary Criticism*, Studies in Language and Literature, 23 (New York: Random House, 1968)

Healy, Thomas, *New Latitudes: Theory and English Renaissance Literature* (London: Edward Arnold, 1992)

Heninger, S. K., Jr, 'The Aesthetic Experience of Reading Spenser', in *Contemporary Thought*, ed. by Frushell and Vondersmith, pp. 79–98

——, *A Handbook of Renaissance Meteorology* (Durham, NC: Duke University Press, 1960)

——, 'The Orgoglio Episode in *The Faerie Queene*', *English Literary History* 26 (1959), 171–87

——, 'Sidney and Serranus' *Plato*', in *Sidney in Retrospect*, ed. by Kinney, pp. 27–44

——, *Sidney and Spenser: The Poet as Maker* (University Park, and London: Pennsylvania State University Press, 1989)

——, 'Speaking Pictures: Sidney's Rapprochement between Poetry and Painting', *Sir Philip Sidney and the Interpretation of Renaissance Culture*, ed. by Waller and Moore, pp. 3–16

——, *Touches of Sweet Harmony: Pythagorean Cosmology and Renaissance Poetics* (San Marino: The Huntington Library, 1974)

Henley, Pauline, *Spenser in Ireland* (Dublin: Cork University Press, 1928)

Herman, Peter C., *Squitter-wits and Muse-haters: Sidney, Spenser, Milton and Renaissance Antipoetic Sentiment* (Detroit: Wayne State University Press, 1996)

Hibbard, George R., *Thomas Nashe: A Critical Introduction* (London: Routledge and Kegan Paul, 1972)

——, ed., *The Elizabethan Theatre VIII* (Port Credit: Meany, 1982)

Höfele, Andreas, *Zoologie der Tragödie: Von Menschen und Tieren bei Shakespeare. Vorgetragen am 26. Oktober 2002*, Schriften der Philosophisch-historischen Klasse der Heidelberger Akademie der Wissenschaften, 30 (Heidelberg: Winter, 2003)

Hollings, Marion D., 'Fountains and Strange Women in the Bower of Bliss: Eastern Contexts for Acrasia and Her Community', in *Consuming Narratives*, ed. by McAvoy and Walters, pp. 140–56

Holmes, Urban Tigner, 'The Monster in Mediaeval Literature', in *Studies in Honor of Alfred G. Engstrom*, ed. by Cargo and Mickel, Jr, pp. 53–62

Horstmann, Ulrike, *Die Namen in Edmund Spensers Versepos 'The Faerie Queene': Immortal Name, Memorable Name, Well-becoming Name*, Studien zur englischen Literatur, 10 (Berlin, Hamburg: LIT Verlag, 2001)

Hough, Graham, *A Preface to 'The Faerie Queene'* (New York: Norton, 1963)

Houwen, L. A. J. R., 'Bestiarien', in *Dämonen, Monster, Fabelwesen*, ed. by Müller and Wunderlich, pp. 59–75

——, 'Flattery and the Mermaid', in *Animals and the Symbolic*, ed. by Houwen, pp. 77–92

——, 'Sex, Songs and Sirens: A New Score for an Old Song', *The Profane Arts / les arts profanes* 6 (1996), 103–21

——, ed., *Animals and the Symbolic in Medieval Art and Literature*, Mediaevalia Groningana, 20 (Groningen: Egbert Forsten 1997)

Huet, Marie-Hélène, *Monstrous Imagination* (Cambridge, MA, and London: Harvard University Press, 1993)

Hughes, Felicity A., 'Imagination', in *Spenser Encyclopedia*, ed. by Hamilton, pp. 392–3

Hughes, Merrit Y., 'Spenser's Blatant Beast', *Modern Language Review* 13 (1918), 266–75

Hulse, Clarke, '"Painted Forgery": Visual Approaches to *The Faerie Queene*', in *Approaches to Teaching Spenser's 'Faerie Queene'*, ed. by Miller and Dunlop, pp. 93–105

Hume, Anthea, *Edmund Spenser: Protestant Poet* (Cambridge: Cambridge University Press, 1984)

Humfrey, Belinda, 'Dragons', in *Spenser Encyclopedia*, ed. by Hamilton, pp. 223–4

Iser, Wolfgang, *Das Fiktive und das Imaginäre: Perspektiven literarischer Anthropologie*, Suhrkamp Taschenbuch Wissenschaft (Frankfurt am Main: Suhrkamp, 1993)

Javitch, Daniel, *Proclaiming a Classic: The Canonisation of 'Orlando Furioso'* (Princeton: Princeton University Press, 1991)

Jewell, Keala, ed., *Monsters in the Italian Literary Imagination* (Detroit: Wayne State University Press, 2001)

Jewiss, Virginia, 'Monstrous Movement and Metaphors in Dante's *Divine Comedy*', in *Monsters in the Italian Literary Imagination*, ed. by Jewell, pp. 179–90

Jones, Malcolm, 'Monsters of Misogyny: Bigorne and Chicheface – Suite et Fin?', in *Marvels, Monsters, and Miracles*, ed. by Jones and Sprunger, pp. 203–21

Jones, Timothy, and David A. Sprunger, 'Introduction: The Marvelous Imagination', in *Marvels, Monsters, and Miracles*, ed. by Jones and Sprunger, pp. XI–XXV

——, eds, *Marvels, Monsters, and Miracles: Studies in the Medieval and Early Modern Imaginations*, Medieval Institute Publications: Studies in Medieval Culture, 42 (Kalamazoo: Western Michigan University, 2002)

Jones-Davies, Marie-Thérèse, ed., *Monstres et prodiges au temps de la Renaissance*, Université de Paris-Sorbonne IV, Institut de Recherches sur les Civilisations de l'occident Moderne, Centre de Recherches sur la Renaissance, 5 (Paris: Touzot, 1980)

Jordan, Richard D., 'Satyrs', in *Spenser Encyclopedia*, ed. by Hamilton, p. 628

Judson, Alexander, *The Life of Edmund Spenser* (as: *Variorum*, XI) (Baltimore: Johns Hopkins University Press, 1945)

Kahin, Helen Andrews, 'Spenser and the School of Alanus', *English Literary History* 8 (1942), 257–72

Kang, Minsoo, *Sublime Dreams of Living Machines: The Automaton in the European Imagination* (Cambridge, MA: Harvard University Press, 2011)

Kaplan, M. Lindsay, *The Culture of Slander in Early Modern England* (Cambridge: Cambridge University Press, 1997)

Kappler, Claude, *Monstres, démons et merveilles à la fin du Moyen Age* (Paris: Payot, 1980)

Kaske, Carol V., 'Bible', in *Spenser Encyclopedia*, ed. by Hamilton, pp. 87–90

——, 'The Dragon's Spark and Sting and the Structure of Red Cross's Dragon-Fight: The Faerie Queene, I.xi–xii', *Studies in Philology* 66 (1969), 609–38

——, 'Hair', in *Spenser Encyclopedia*, ed. by Hamilton, pp. 344–5

——, *Spenser and Biblical Poetics* (Ithaca: Cornell University Press, 1999)

Kawanishi, Susumu, 'Lust', in *Spenser Encyclopedia*, ed. by Hamilton, pp. 442–3

Kelley, Donald R., and David Harris Sacks, eds, *The Historical Imagination in Early Modern Britain: History, Rhetoric, and Fiction, 1500–1800* (Cambridge: Cambridge University Press, 1997)

Ker, William Paton, *The Dark Ages* (London: Nelson, 1904)

Kern, Hermann, *Labyrinthe: Erscheinungsformen und Deutungen. 5000 Jahre Gegenwart eines Urbilds* (Munich: Prestel, 1999)

King, Andrew, *'The Faerie Queene' and Middle English Romance: The Matter of Just Memory*, Oxford English Monographs (Oxford: Clarendon Press, 2000)

——, 'Sidney and Spenser', in *A Companion to Romance*, ed. by Saunders, pp. 140–59

King, John N., *Spenser's Poetry and the Reformation Tradition* (Princeton: Princeton University Press, 1990)

Kinney, Arthur F., ed., *Sidney in Retrospect: Selections from 'English Literary Renaissance'* (Amherst: University of Massachusetts Press, 1988)

Kisacky, Julia M., *Magic in Boiardo and Ariosto*, Studies in Italian Culture: Literature in History, 25 (New York: Lang, 2000)

Kitzes, Adam H., *The Politics of Melancholy from Spenser to Milton* (New York: Routledge, 2006)

Klein, H. Arthur, *The Graphic Worlds of Pieter Bruegel the Elder* (Toronto: Dover, 1963)

Klein, Wolf Peter, *Am Anfang war das Wort: Theorie- und wissenschaftsgeschichtliche Elemente frühneuzeitlichen Sprachbewußtseins* (Berlin: Akademie-Verlag, 1992)

Klibansky, Raymond, Erwin Panofsky and Fritz Saxl, *Saturn and Melancholy: Studies in the History of Natural Philosophy, Religion and Art* (London: Thomas Nelson, 1964; repr. Nendeln: Kraus Reprint, 1979)

Kline, Naomi Reed, 'The World of Strange Races', in *Monsters, Marvels, and Miracles*, ed. by Søndergaard and Hansen, pp. 27–40

Knapp, Jeffrey, *An Empire Nowhere: England, America, and Literature from 'Utopia' to 'The Tempest'*, New Historicism: Studies in Cultural Poetics Series, 16 (Berkeley and Los Angeles: University of California Press, 1991)

Kocher, Paul H., *Science and Religion in Elizabethan England* (San Marino: Huntington Library, 1956)

Kollmann, Judith J., 'The Centaur', in *Mythical and Fabulous Creatures*, ed. by South, pp. 225–39

Kretzmann, Norman, Anthony Kenny and Jan Pinborg, eds, *The Cambridge History of Later Medieval Philosophy* (Cambridge: Cambridge University Press, 1982)

Krier, Theresa M., *Gazing on Secret Sights: Spenser, Classical Imitation, and the Decorums of Vision* (Ithaca: Cornell University Press, 1990)

Krueger, Roberta L., ed., *The Cambridge Companion to Medieval Romance*, Cambridge Companions to Literature (Cambridge: Cambridge University Press, 2000)

Landa, José Angel García, '"Another Game in Vew": The Representation of the Poet in *The Faerie Queene*', *Revista Alicantina de Estudios Ingleses* 2 (1989), 65–81

Laurence, Elizabeth Atwood, 'The Centaur: Its History and Meaning in Human Culture', *The Journal of Popular Culture* 27 (1994), 57–68

Lecouteux, Claude, *Les monstres dans la littérature allemande du moyen âge: Contribution à l'étude du merveilleux médiéval*, 3 vols (Göppingen: Kummerle, 1982)

——, *Les monstres dans la pensée médiévale européenne essai de presentation*, Cultures et civilisations médiévales, 10 (Paris: Presses Universitaires de Paris-Sorbonne, 1993)

Leimberg, Inge, 'Die Dichtungstheorie der englischen Renaissance unter dem Gesichtspunkt von Kunst und Natur', in *Englische und amerikanische Literaturtheorie*, ed. by Ahrens and Wolff, pp. 94–120

Lengeler, Rainer, *Das Theater der leidenschaftlichen Phantasie: Shakespeares 'Sommernachtstraum' als Spiegel seiner Dichtungstheorie*, Kieler Beiträge zur Anglistik und Amerikanistik, 11 (Neumünster: Wachholtz, 1975)

——, *Tragische Wirklichkeit als groteske Verfremdung bei Shakespeare*, Anglistische Studien, 2 (Cologne: Bohlau, 1964)

Leslie, Michael, *Spenser's 'Fierce Warres and Faithfull Loves': Martial and Chivalric Symbolism in 'The Faerie Queene'* (Woodbridge: Brewer, 1983)

Lethbridge, Julian B., 'Spenser's Last Days: Ireland, Career, Mutability, Allegory', *Edmund Spenser: New and Renewed Directions*, ed. Lethbridge, pp. 302–36

——, ed., *Edmund Spenser: New and Renewed Directions* (Madison and Teaneck: Fairleigh Dickinson University Press, 2006)

Lewis, Clive Staples, *The Allegory of Love: A Study in Medieval Tradition* (Oxford: Oxford University Press, 1936)

——, *The Discarded Image: An Introduction to Medieval and Renaissance Literature* (Cambridge: Cambridge University Press, 1964)

——, *Spenser's Images of Life*, ed. by Alastair Fowler (Cambridge: Cambridge University Press, 1967)

Lewis, L. T., and L. Short, *A Latin Dictionary* (Oxford: Oxford University Press, 1962)

Lexikon des frühgriechischen Epos, ed. by Thesaurus Linguae Graecae, 4 vols (Göttingen: Vandenhoeck & Ruprecht, 1979–2010)

Liddell, Henry George, and Robert Scott, *A Greek–English Lexicon*, revised and augmented throughout by Sir Henry Stuart Jones, 9th edn (Oxford: Clarendon, 1940)

Lobsien, Eckhard, *Imaginationswelten: Modellierungen der Imagination und Textualisierungen der Welt in der englischen Literatur, 1580–1750*, Neues Forum für allgemeine und vergleichende Literaturwissenschaft, 15 (Heidelberg: Winter, 2003)

Logan, George M., and Gordon Teskey, eds, *Unfolded Tales: Studies in Renaissance Romance* (Ithaca and London: Cornell University Press, 1989)

Lotspeich, Henry Gibbons, *Classical Mythology in the Poetry of Edmund Spenser* (Princeton: Princeton University Press, 1932; repr. New York: Gordian Press, 1965)

Lovejoy, Arthur O., *The Great Chain of Being: A Study of the History of an Idea. The William James Lectures Delivered at Harvard University, 1933* (Cambridge, MA, and London: Harvard University Press, 1936)

MacCaffrey, Isabel G., *Spenser's Allegory: The Anatomy of Imagination* (Princeton: Princeton University Press, 1976)

Mack, Michael, *Sidney's Poetics: Imitating Creation* (Washington: Catholic University of America Press, 2005)

MacLachlan, Hugh, 'Britains, Britons', in *Spenser Encyclopedia*, ed. by Hamilton, p. 113

——, and Philip B. Rollinson, 'Magnanimity, Magnificence', in *Spenser Encyclopedia*, ed. by Hamilton, p. 448

Mahoney, Edward P., 'Sense, Intellect, and Imagination in Albert, Thomas and Siger', in *The Cambridge History of Later Medieval Philosophy*, ed. by Kretzmann, Kenny and Pinborg, pp. 602–22

Mallette, Richard, 'Book V of *The Faerie Queene*: An Elizabethan Apocalypse', *Spenser Studies* 11 (1994), 136–49

Manning, John, and Alastair Fowler, 'The Iconography of Spenser's Occasion', *Journal of the Warburg and Courtauld Institutes* 39 (1976), 263–6

Marotti, Arthur F., 'Animal Symbolism in *The Faerie Queene*: Tradition and the Poetic Context', *Studies in English Literature, 1500–1900* 5 (1965), 69–86

Marquis, Paul A., 'Problems of Closure in *The Faerie Queene*', *English Studies in Canada* 16 (1990), 149–63

Marre, Louis A., *Ironic Historian: The Narrator of Books III and IV of 'The Faerie Queene'*, Salzburg Studies in English Literature: Elizabethan and Renaissance Studies, 98 (Salzburg: Institut für Anglistik und Amerikanistik, Universität Salzburg, 1980)

Martindale, Charles, ed., *Ovid Renewed: Ovidian Influences on Literature and Art from the Middle Ages to the Twentieth Century* (Cambridge: Cambridge University Press, 1988)

Matthews, William Henry, *Mazes and Labyrinths: Their History and Development* (London: Longmans, Green and Co., 1922; repr. New York: Dover Publications, 1970)

Maurice, Klaus, and Otto Mayr, eds, *The Clockwork Universe: German Clocks and Automata* (Washington: Smithsonian Institution; New York: Neale Watson Academic Publications, 1980)

Maxwell, Baldwin, William Dinsmore Briggs, Francis Rarick Johnson, and Elbert Nevius Sebring Thompson, eds, *Renaissance Studies in Honour of Hardin Craig* (Stanford: Folcroft Library, 1941)

McAvoy, Liz Herbert, 'Monstrous Masculinities in Julian of Norwich's *A Revelation of Love* and *The Book of Margery Kempe*', in *The Monstrous Middle Ages*, ed. by Bildhauer and Mills, pp. 55–74

——, and Teresa Walters, eds, *Consuming Narratives: Gender and Monstrous Appetite in the Middle Ages and the Renaissance* (Cardiff: University of Wales Press, 2002)

McCabe, Richard A., *The Pillars of Eternity: Time and Providence in 'The Faerie Queene'*, Dublin Studies in Medieval and Renaissance Literature (Dublin: Irish Academic Press, 1989)

McConnell, Winder, 'Mythos Drache', in *Dämonen, Monster, Fabelwesen*, ed. by Müller and Wunderlich, pp. 171–83

McKeown, Adam, 'Looking at Britomart Looking at Pictures', *Studies in English Literature 1500–1900* 45 (2005), 44–63

McManus, Caroline, 'The "carefull Nurse": Female Piety in Spenser's Legend of Holiness', *Huntington Library Quarterly* 60 (1997), 381–407

Meis, Morgan, 'Science as a Cure for Fear: The Status of Monsters in Lucretius', in *Monsters and Philosophy*, ed. by Wolfe, pp. 21–35

Mellinkoff, Ruth, 'Cain's Monstrous Progeny in Beowulf: Part II, Post-diluvian Survival', *Anglo Saxon England* 9 (1981), 183–197

Meyer, Jürgen R., '"Italianate Englishmen" and the Renaissance "Humanimal"', in *Anglistentag 2007*, ed. by Stierstorfer, pp. 25–37

Miller, David Lee, *The Poem's Two Bodies: The Poetics of the 1590 'Faerie Queene'* (Princeton: Princeton University Press, 1988)

——, 'Spenser's Vocation, Spenser's Career', *English Literary History* 50 (1983), 197–231

——, and Alexander Dunlop, eds, *Approaches to Teaching Spenser's 'Faerie Queene'*, Approaches to Teaching World Literature, 50 (New York: Modern Language Association of America, 1994)

Mittman, Asa Simon, 'Introduction: The Impact of Monsters and Monster Studies', in *The Ashgate Research Companion to Monsters and the Monstrous*, ed. by Mittman and Dendle, pp. 1–14

——, with Peter J. Dendle, eds, *The Ashgate Research Companion to Monsters and the Monstrous* (Farnham: Ashgate, 2012)

Müller, Ulrich and Werner Wunderlich, eds, *Dämonen, Monster, Fabelwesen*, Mittelalter Mythen, 2 (St Gallen: UVK, 1999)

——, *Herrscher, Helden, Heilige*, Mittelalter Mythen, 1 (St Gallen: UVK, 1996)

Murrin, Michael, *The Allegorical Epic: Essays in Its Rise and Decline* (Chicago: University of Chicago Press, 1980)

——, 'The Audience of *The Faerie Queene*', *Explorations in Renaissance Culture* 23 (1997), 1–21

——, 'The Varieties of Criticism', *Modern Philology* 70 (1973), 342–56

——, *The Veil of Allegory: Some Notes Toward a Theory of Allegorical Rhetoric in the English Renaissance* (Chicago: Chicago University Press, 1969)

Nelson, William, 'The Boundaries of Fiction in the Renaissance: A Treaty Between Truth and Falsehood', *English Literary History* 36 (1969), 30–58

——, *The Poetry of Edmund Spenser: A Study* (New York: Columbia University Press, 1965)

——, 'A Source for Spenser's Malbecco', *Modern Language Notes* 68 (1953), 226–9

——, ed., *Form and Convention in the Poetry of Edmund Spenser: Selected Papers from the English Institute*, English Institute Essays, 35 (New York: Columbia University Press, 1961)

Neuse, Richard, 'Book VI as Conclusion to *The Faerie Queene*', *English Literary History* 35 (1968), 329–53

Nicholson, Lewis E., ed., *An Anthology of 'Beowulf' Criticism* (Notre Dame: University of Notre Dame Press, 1963)

Nicolson, Marjorie Hope, *A World in the Moon: A Study of the Changing Attitude toward the Moon in the Seventeenth and Eighteenth Centuries*, Smith Studies in Modern Languages, 17.2 (Northampton, MA: Smith College, 1936)

Nitze, William A., 'The Beste Glatissant in Arthurian Romance', *Zeitschrift für Romanische Philologie* 56 (1936), 409–18

Nohrnberg, James, 'Acidale', *Spenser Encyclopedia*, ed. by Hamilton, pp. 4–6

——, *The Analogy of 'The Faerie Queene'* (Princeton: Princeton University Press, 1977)

——, '*The Faerie Queene*, Book IV', *Spenser Encyclopedia*, ed. by Hamilton, pp. 273–80

Ochsner, Beate, 'Monster: More than a Word. From Portent to Anomaly, the Extraordinary Career of Monsters', in *Monsters and Philosophy*, ed. by Wolfe, pp. 231–79

O'Connell, Michael, '*The Faerie Queene* Book V', in *Spenser Encyclopaedia*, ed. by Hamilton, pp. 280–3

Ohly, Friedrich, 'Vom geistigen Sinn des Wortes im Mittelalter', *Zeitschrift für deutsches Mittelalter und deutsche Literatur* 89 (1958/1959), 1–23

Olsen, Karin, and L. A. J. R. Houwen, eds, *Monsters and the Monstrous in Medieval Northwest Europe*, Mediaevalia Groningana, New Series, 3 (Leuven: Peeters, 2001)

Olsen, Robert, and Karin Olsen, 'Introduction: On the Embodiment of Monstrosity in Northwest Medieval Europe', in *Monsters and the Monstrous*, ed. by Olsen and Houwen, pp. 1–22

Oram, William A., 'Elizabethan Fact and Spenserian Fiction', *Spenser Studies* 4 (1983), 33–47

Orchard, Andy, *Pride and Prodigies: Studies in the Monsters of the 'Beowulf'-Manuscript* (Cambridge: Brewer, 1995)

Osborne, Marijane, 'Die Monster in *Beowulf*', in *Dämonen, Monster, Fabelwesen*, ed. by Müller and Wunderlich, pp. 161–9

Osgood, Charles G., 'Comments on the Moral Allegory of *The Faerie Queene*', *Modern Language Notes* 46 (1931), 502–7

——, *A Concordance to the Poems of Edmund Spenser* (Gloucester, MA: Peter Smith, 1963)

Oswald, Dana, 'Monstrous Gender: Geographies of Ambiguity', *The Ashgate Research Companion to Monsters and the Monstrous*, ed. by Mittman and Dendle, pp. 343–63

Oxford English Dictionary at www.oed.com

Pankow, Edgar, and Günter Peters, eds, *Prometheus: Mythos der Kultur* (Munich: Fink, 1999)

Park, Katherine, 'Bacon's "Enchanted Glass"', *Isis* 75 (1984), 290–302

Parker, Patricia A., *Inescapable Romance: Studies in the Poetics of a Mode* (Princeton: Princeton University Press, 1979)

——, and David Quint, eds, *Literary Theory / Renaissance Texts* (Baltimore and London: Johns Hopkins University Press, 1986)

Paster, Gail Kern, *The Body Embarrassed: Drama and Disciplines of Shame in Early Modern England* (Ithaca: Cornell University Press, 1993)

Patterson, Annabel, and Ann Coiro, 'Fables', in *Spenser Encyclopedia*, ed. by Hamilton, pp. 257–8

Patrides, C. A., and Joseph Wittreich, eds, *The Apocalypse in English Renaissance Thought and Literature: Patterns, Antecedents, and Repercussions* (Ithaca: Cornell University Press, 1984)

Paxson, James J., *The Poetics of Personification* (Cambridge: Cambridge University Press, 1994)

Pearson, D'Orsay W., 'Spenser's Labyrinth – Again', *Studies in Iconography* 3 (1977), 70–88

——, 'Theseus, Hippolytos', in *Spenser Encyclopedia*, ed. by Hamilton, p. 668

——, '"Unkinde" Theseus: A Study in Renaissance Mythography', *English Literary Renaissance* 4 (1974), 276–98

——, 'Witches', in *Spenser Encyclopedia*, ed. by Hamilton, pp. 729–30

Perkins, Patrick, 'Spenser's Dragon and the Law', *Spenser Studies* 21 (2006), 51–81

Pheifer, J. D., 'Errour and Echidna in *The Faerie Queene*: A Study in Literary Tradition', in *Literature and Learning*, ed. by Scattergood, pp. 127–74

Philmus, Maria A. Rohr, '*The Faerie Queene* and Renaissance Poetics: Another Look at Book VI as "Conclusion" to the Poem', *English Studies* 6 (1995), 497–519

Platt, Peter G., ed., *Wonders, Marvels, and Monsters in Early Modern Culture* (Newark: University of Delaware Press)

Plett, Heinrich F., '"… of imagination all compact": Ein metapoetischer Kommentar zu Shakespeares *Sommernachtstraum* V.i.4–22', in *Zum Begriff der Imagination*, ed. by Beyer, pp. 16–33

——, *Rhetorik der Affekte: Englische Wirkungsästhetik im Zeitalter der Renaissance*, Studien zur Englischen Philologie, New Series, 18 (Tübingen: Niemeyer, 1975)

Pluskowski, Aleks, 'Apocalyptic Monsters: Animal Inspirations for the Iconography of Medieval North European Devourers', in *The Monstrous Middle Ages*, ed. by Bildhauer and Mills, pp. 155–76

Prescott, Anne Lake, 'Giants', in *Spenser Encyclopedia*, ed. by Hamilton, pp. 332–33

Pugh, Syrithe, *Spenser and Ovid* (Aldershot: Ashgate, 2005)

Quilligan, Maureen, *The Language of Allegory: Defining the Genre* (Ithaca and London: Cornell University Press, 1979)

——, 'Reader in *The Faerie Queene*', in *Spenser Encyclopedia*, ed. by Hamilton, pp. 585–6

Raggio, Olga, 'The Myth of Prometheus: Its Survival and Metamorphoses up to the Eighteenth Century', *Journal of the Warburg and Courtauld Institutes* 21 (1958), 44–62

Rajan, Balachandra, *The Form of the Unfinished: English Poetics from Spenser to Pound* (Princeton: Princeton University Press, 1985)

Read, David, *Temperate Conquests: Spenser and the Spanish New World* (Detroit: Wayne State University Press, 2000)

Reid, Robert Lanier, 'Spenser's Mutability Song: Conclusion or Transition?', in *Celebrating Mutabilitie*, ed. by Grogan, pp. 61–84

Rhoads, Diana Akers, *Shakespeare's Defense of Poetry: 'A Midsummer Night's Dream' and 'The Tempest'* (Lanham: University Press of America, 1985)

Rhu, Lawrence F., 'Romancing the Word: Pre-Texts and Contexts for the Errour Episode', *Spenser Studies* 11 (1994), 101–9

Riches, Samantha J. E., 'Encountering the Monstrous: Saints and Dragons in Medieval Thought', in *The Monstrous Middle Ages*, ed. by Bildhauer and Mills, pp. 196–218

——, *St George: Hero, Martyr and Myth* (Stroud: Sutton, 2005)

Riddell, James A. and Stanley Stewart, *Jonson's Spenser: Evidence and Historical Criticism*, Duquesne Studies, Language and Literature Series, 18 (Pittsburgh: Duquesne University Press, 1995)

Rider, Jeff, 'The Other Worlds of Romance', in *The Cambridge Companion to Medieval Romance*, ed. by Krueger, pp. 115–32

Rigby, Stephen H., *Wisdom and Chivalry: Chaucer's 'Knight's Tale' and Medieval Political Theory*, Medieval and Renaissance Authors and Texts, 4 (Leiden and Boston: Brill, 2009)

Roberts, Gareth, 'Women and Magic in English Renaissance Love Poetry', in *Representing Women*, ed. by Summers and Pebworth, pp. 59–75

Robinson, Forrest G., *The Shape of Things Known: Sidney's 'Apology' in Its Philosophical Tradition* (Cambridge, MA: Harvard University Press, 1972)

Robinson, Lillian S., *Monstrous Regiment: The Lady Knight in Sixteenth-Century Epic*, Garland Publications in Comparative Literature (New York: Garland, 1985)

Rölli-Alkemper, Dorothee, *Höfische Poetik in der englischen Renaissance: George Puttenhams 'The Arte of English Poesie' (1589)*, Figuren, 4 (Munich: Fink, 1996)

Rollinson, Philip, 'Arthur, Maleger, and the Interpretation of *The Faerie Queene*', *Spenser Studies* 7 (1986), 103–21

——, *Classical Theories of Allegory and Christian Culture* (Oxford: Oxford University Press, 1989)

Roscher, Wilhelm Heinrich, ed., *Ausführliches Lexikon der griechischen und römischen Mythologie*, 10 vols (Leipzig: Teubner, 1884–1937; repr. Hildesheim: Georg Olms Verlagsbuchhandlung, 1965–77)

Rose, Mark, *Spenser's Art: A Companion to Book One of 'The Faerie Queene'* (Cambridge, MA: Harvard University Press, 1975)

Rossky, William, 'Imagination in the English Renaissance: Psychology and Poetic', *Studies in the Renaissance* 5 (1958), 49–73

Rudenstine, Neil L., *Sidney's Poetic Development* (Cambridge, MA: Harvard University Press, 1967)

Rupprecht, Carol Schreier, 'Radigund', in *Spenser Encyclopedia*, ed. by Hamilton, pp. 580–81

Said, Edward, *Orientalism: Western Conceptions of the Orient* (New York: Random House, 1978)

Salih, Sarah, 'Idols and Simulacra: Paganity, Hybridity and Representation in *Mandeville's Travels*', in *The Monstrous Middle Ages*, ed. by Bildhauer and Mills, pp. 113–33

Salisbury, Joyce E., *The Beast Within: Animals in the Middle Ages* (New York; London: Routledge, 1994)

Sammer, Marianne, 'Basilisk – regulus', in *Dämonen, Monster, Fabelwesen*, ed. by Müller and Wunderlich, pp. 135–60

Sandler, Florence, '*The Faerie Queene* : An Elizabethan Apocalypse', in *The Apocalypse*, ed. by Patrides and Wittreich, pp. 148–74

Saunders, Corinne J., *The Forest of Medieval Romance: Avernus, Broceliande, Arden* (Cambridge: Brewer, 1993)

——, 'Malory's *Book of Hunting*: The Tristram Section of the *Morte Darthur*', *Medium Aevum* 62 (1993), 270–84

——, ed., *A Companion to Romance from Classical to Contemporary*, Blackwell Companions to Literature and Culture, 27 (Oxford: Blackwell, 2004)

Sawday, Jonathan, '"Forms Such as Never Were in Nature": The Renaissance

Cyborg', in *At the Borders of the Human*, ed. by Gilbert, Fudge and Wiseman, pp. 171–95

Scafella, Frank A., 'The Sphinx', in *Mythical and Fabulous Creatures*, ed. by South, pp. 179–91

Scattergood, John, ed., *Literature and Learning in Medieval and Renaissance England: Essays Presented to Fitzroy Pyle* (Dublin: Irish Academy Press, 1984)

Schäfer, Jürgen, '"Twins by Birth": Literaturtheoretische Aspekte elisabethanischer Rhetorik', in *Englische und amerikanische Literaturtheorie*, ed. by Ahrens and Wolff, pp. 45–72

Schmidt, Gary D., *The Iconography of the Mouth of Hell: Eighth Century Britain to the Fifteenth Century* (London: Associated University Presses, 1995)

Schmidtke, Dietrich, *Geistliche Tierinterpretation in der deutschsprachigen Literatur des Mittelalters (1100–1500)* (Berlin: Ernst-Reuter-Gesellschaft, 1968)

Schoenfeldt, Michael, *Bodies and Selves in Early Modern England: Physiology and Inwardness in Spenser, Shakespeare, Herbert, and Milton*, Cambridge Studies in Renaissance Literature and Culture, 34 (Cambridge: Cambridge University Press, 1999)

Schroeder, John W., 'Spenser's Erotic Drama: The Orgoglio Episode', *English Literary History* 29 (1962), 140–59

Schuler, Robert M., 'Alchemy', in *Spenser Encyclopedia*, ed. by Hamilton, pp. 12–14

Scott, Shirley Clay, 'From Polydorus to Fradubio: The History of a Topos', *Spenser Studies* 7 (1986), 27–57

Seiler, Thomas H., 'Filth and Stench as Aspects of the Iconography of Hell', in *The Iconography of Hell*, ed. by Davidson and Seiler, pp. 132–40

Seznec, Jean, *The Survival of the Pagan Gods: The Mythological Tradition and Its Place in Renaissance Humanism and Art*, trans. from the French by Barbara F. Sessions, Bollingen Series, 38 (Princeton: Princeton University Press, 1972)

Shore, David A., *Spenser and the Poetics of Pastoral: A Study of the World of Colin Clout* (Montreal: McGill-Queen's University Press, 1985)

Shuger, Debora, *Censorship and Cultural Sensibility: The Regulation of Language in Tudor–Stuart England* (Philadelphia: University of Pennsylvania Press, 2006)

Silberman, Lauren, *Transforming Desire: Erotic Knowledge in Books III and IV of 'The Faerie Queene'* (Berkeley and Los Angeles: University of California Press, 1995)

Skulsky, Harold, 'Malbecco', in *Spenser Encyclopedia*, ed. by Hamilton, pp. 448–9

——, 'Malengin', in *Spenser Encyclopedia*, ed. by Hamilton, p. 450

——, *Metamorphosis: The Mind in Exile* (Cambridge, MA: Harvard University Press, 1981)

Smith, Norman R., 'Portentous Births and the Monstrous Imagination in Renaissance Culture', in *Marvels, Monsters, and Miracles*, ed. by Jones and Sprunger, pp. 267–83

Søndergaard, Leif, 'Far West of Spain – The Land of Cockaigne', in *Monsters, Marvels, and Miracles*, ed. by Søndergaard and Hansen, pp. 173–208

——, and Rasmus Thorning Hansen, eds, *Monsters, Marvels, and Miracles: Imaginary Journeys and Landscapes in the Middle Ages* (Odense: University of South Denmark Press, 2005)

South, Malcolm, ed., *Mythic and Fabulous Creatures: A Source Book and Reference Guide* (Westport: Greenwood Press, 1987)

Springborg, Patricia, 'Leviathan, Mythic History, and National Historiography', in *The Historical Imagination*, ed. by Kelley and Sacks, pp. 267–97

Steadman, John M., *Nature Into Myth: Medieval and Renaissance Moral Symbols* (Pittsburgh: Duquesne University Press, 1979)

——, 'Spenser and the *Virgilius* Legend: Another Talus Parallel', *Modern Language Notes* 73 (1958), 412–13

Steel, Karl, 'Centaurs, Satyrs, and Cynocephali: Scholarly Teratology and the Question of the Human', in *The Ashgate Research Companion to Monsters and the Monstrous*, ed. by Mittman and Dendle, pp. 257–74

Steneck, Nicholas H., 'Albert the Great on the Classification and Localization of the Internal Senses', *Isis* 65 (1974), 193–211

Stewart, Stanley, 'Sir Calidore and "Closure"', *Studies in English Literature* 24 (1984), 69–86

Stierstorfer, Klaus, ed., *Anglistentag 2007 Münster: Proceedings* (Trier: Wissenschaftlicher Verlag Trier, 2008)

Strickland, Debra Higgs, 'Monstrosity and Race in the Late Middle Ages', in *The Ashgate Research Companion to Monsters and the Monstrous*, ed. by Mittman and Dendle, pp. 365–86

Strong, Roy, *The Renaissance Garden in England* (London: Thames and Hudson, 1979)

Sullivan, Penny, 'Medieval Automata: The "Chambre de Beautés" in Benoît's *Roman de Troie*', *Romance Studies* 6 (1985), 1–20

Summers, Claude J., and Ted-Larry Pebworth, eds, *Representing Women in Renaissance England* (Columbia: University of Missouri Press, 1997)

Summers, David, 'Pandora's Crown: On Wonder, Imitation, and Mechanism in Western Art', in *Wonders, Marvels, and Monsters*, ed. by Platt, pp. 45–75

Suzuki, Mihoko, *Metamorphoses of Helen: Authority, Difference, and the Epic* (Ithaca: Cornell University Press, 1989)

Tannier, Bernard, 'Animals, fabulous', in *Spenser Encyclopedia*, ed. by Hamilton, pp. 41–2

——, 'Un bestiaire maniériste: monstres et animaux fantastiques dans *La Reine des Fées* d'Edmund Spenser', in *Monstres et prodiges*, ed. by Jones-Davies, pp. 55–65

Teskey, Gordon, 'Allegory', in *Spenser Encyclopedia*, ed. by Hamilton, pp. 16–22

——, *Allegory and Violence* (Ithaca and London: Cornell University Press, 1996)

——, *Delirious Milton: The Fate of the Poet in Modernity* (Cambridge, MA: Harvard University Press, 2006)

——, 'Thinking Moments in *The Faerie Queene*', *Spenser Studies* 22 (2007), 103–25

Thompson, Stith, *Motif-Index of Folk-Literature. A Classification of Narrative*

Elements in Folktales, Ballads, Myths, Fables, Mediaeval Romances, Exempla, Fabliaux, Jest-Books, and Local Legends, 6 vols, FF Communications, 106 (Helsinki: Suomalainen Tiedeakatemia, 1932)

Tilley, M. P., *A Dictionary of the Proverbs in England in the Sixteenth and Seventeenth Centuries* (Ann Arbor: Michigan University Press, 1950)

Tillyard, Eustace Mandeville Wetenhall, *The Elizabethan World Picture* (Harmondsworth: Penguin, 1943; repr. 1973)

Tolkien, John Ronald Reuel, '*Beowulf*: The Monsters and the Critics', in '*Beowulf*' *Criticism*, ed. by Nicholson, pp. 51–103

Tonkin, Humphrey, *Spenser's Courteous Pastoral: Book Six of 'The Faerie Queene'* (Oxford: Clarendon Press, 1972)

Treip, Mindele Anne, *Allegorical Poetics and the Epic: The Renaissance Tradition to 'Paradise Lost'* (Lexington: University of Kentucky Press 1994)

Trevor, Douglas, *The Poetics of Melancholy in Early Modern England* (Cambridge: Cambridge University Press, 2004)

Tuve, Rosamund, *Allegorical Imagery: Some Mediaeval Books and Their Posterity* (Princeton: Princeton University Press, 1966)

Twomey, Michael W., 'Falling Giants and Floating Lead: Scholastic History in the Middle English *Cleanness*', in *Marvels, Monsters, and Miracles*, ed. by Jones and Sprunger, pp. 141–65

Uhlig, Claus, 'Sidneys *Defence of Poesie* und die Poetik der Renaissance', in *Englische und amerikanische Literaturtheorie*, ed. by Ahrens and Wolff, pp. 73–93

Ulreich, John C., 'Making Dreams Truths, and Fables Histories: Spenser and Milton on the Nature of Fiction', *Studies in Philology* 87 (1990), 363–77

van der Toorn, Karel, Bob Becking and Pieter W. van der Horst, eds, *Dictionary of Deities and Demons in the Bible*, 2nd revised edn (Leiden: Brill, 1998)

Van Duzer, Chat, '*Hic sunt dracones*: The Geography and Cartography of Monsters', in *The Ashgate Research Companion to Monsters and the Monstrous*, ed. by Mittman and Dendle, pp. 387–435

van Winden, Jacobus Cornelis Maria, *Calcidius on Matter. His Doctrine and Sources: A Chapter in the History of Platonism* (Leiden: E. J. Brill, 1965)

Vickers, Nancy J., 'Diana Described: Scattered Woman and Scattered Rhyme', *Critical Inquiry* 8 (1981), 265–79

von Blanckenhagen, Peter H., 'Easy Monsters', in *Monsters and Demons*, ed. by Farkas, Harper and Harrison, pp. 85–94

von Stackelberg, Jürgen, 'Das Bienengleichnis: Ein Beitrag zur Geschichte der literarischen *Imitatio*', *Romanische Forschungen* 68 (1956), 271–93

Voss, Paul J., '*The Faerie Queene* 1590–1596: The Case of Saint George', *Ben Jonson Journal* 3 (1996), 59–73

Walde, A., *Lateinisches etymologisches Wörterbuch*, 3rd edn revised by J. B. Hofmann, 3 vols (Heidelberg: Winter, 1954)

Wallace, Howard, 'Leviathan and the Beast in the Revelation', *Biblical Archaeologist* 11 (1948), 61–8

Wallace, Nathaniel, 'Talus: Spenser's Iron Man', *Spenser Studies* 10 (1992), 277–9

Waller, Gary F., and Michael D. Moore, eds, *Sir Philip Sidney and the Interpretation of Renaissance Culture: The Poet in His Time and in Ours: A Collection of Critical and Scholarly Essays* (London and Totawa: Croom Helm, 1984)

Waswo, Richard, 'The History That Literature Makes', *New Literary History* 19 (1987/1988), 541–64

Waters, D. Douglas, *Duessa as Theological Satire* (St Louis: University of Missouri Press, 1970)

Watkins, John, 'Apocalypse Deferred: Seventeenth-Century Appropriations of Spenser', in *Worldmaking Spenser*, ed. by Cheney and Silberman, pp. 156–73

——, 'Spenser's Monsters: A Response to Maik Goth', *Connotations* 20 (2010/11), 201–9

Watson, Elizabeth Porges, 'Emblem and Experience: Spenser's Use of Insect Imagery', *Reinardus* 1 (1988), 113–20

——, '*The Faerie Queene*: Spenser's Chivalric Bestiary', *Reinardus* 11 (1998), 161–74

——, 'Forreine and Monstrous Beasts: Spenser's Anti-Bestiary', *Reinardus* 13 (2000), 169–80

——, 'Shepherds, Wolves, Foxes and Others in Spenser's *Shepheardes Calender*', *Reinardus* 7 (1994), 113–26

——, 'Spenser's Submarine Creation', *Reinardus* 9 (1996), 121–34

Watson, Elizabeth See, 'Spenser's Flying Dragon and Pope Gregory XIII', *Spenser Studies* 14 (1994), 293–301

Weatherby, 'Two Images of Mortalitie: Spenser and Original Sin', *Studies in Philology* 85 (1988), 321–52

Webster, John, and Richard Isomaki, 'Pyrocles, Chymocles', in *Spenser Encyclopedia*, ed. by Hamilton, p. 574

Weinrich, Harald, 'Semantik der kühnen Metapher', *Deutsche Vierteljahresschrift für Literaturwissenschaft und Geistesgeschichte* 37 (1963), 325–44

Wells, Whitney, 'Spenser's Dragon', *Modern Language Notes* 41 (1926), 143–57

Wels, Volkhard, 'Imaginatio oder Inventio: Das dichterische Schaffen und sein Gegenstand in Puttenham, Sidney und Temple', *Poetica* 37 (2005), 65–91

Williams, David, *Deformed Discourse: The Function of the Monster in Mediaeval Thought and Literature* (Montreal and Kingston: McGill-Queen's University Press, 1996)

Williams, Grant, 'Phantastes's Flies: The Trauma of Amnesic Enjoyment in Spenser's Memory Palace', *Spenser Studies* 18 (2004), 231–52

Williams, Kathleen, *Spenser's 'Faerie Queene': The World of Glass* (London: Routledge, 1966)

Wofford, Susanne Lindgren, *The Choice of Achilles: The Ideology of Figure in Epic* (Stanford: Stanford University Press, 1992)

Wolfe, Charles T., ed., *Monsters and Philosophy*, Texts in Philosphy, 3 (London: College Publications, 2005)

Wood, Rufus, *Metaphor and Belief in 'The Faerie Queene'* (London: Macmillan; New York: St Martin's, 1997)

Woodcock, Matthew, 'Elf-Fashioning Revisited: A Response to Maik Goth',

Connotations 20 (2010/11), 210–20
——, *Fairy in 'The Faerie Queene': Renaissance Elf-Fashioning and Elizabethan Myth-Making* (Aldershot and Burlington: Ashgate, 2004)
Woodhouse, Arthur Sutherland Pigott, 'Nature and Grace in *The Faerie Queene*', *English Literary History* 16 (1949), 194–228
Woods, Susanne, 'Closure in *The Faerie Queene*', *Journal of English and Germanic Philology* 76 (1977), 195–216
Wunderlich, Werner, 'Dämonen, Monster, Fabelwesen', in *Dämonen, Monster, Fabelwesen*, ed. by Müller and Wunderlich, pp. 11–38
Ziolkowski, Jan M., 'Literary Genre and Animal Symbolism', in *Animals and the Symbolic*, ed. by Houwen, pp. 1–23
Zumthor, Paul, *Essai de poétique médiévale*, Collection Poétique (Paris: Seuil, 1972)

Index

Notes: (1) 'n.' after a page reference indicates the number of a note on that page. References to notes are only given if the key word does not occur in the main text; (2) literary works can usually be found under authors' names.

CPSIA information can be obtained
at www.ICGtesting.com
Printed in the USA
JSHW031934100720
6553JS00013B/51

9 781526 139498